ANTHONY HUXLEY, M.A., V.M.H.

HUXLEY'S ENCYCLOPEDIA OF GARDENING

FOR GREAT BRITAIN AND AMERICA

ILLUSTRATIONS BY VANA HAGGERTY

UNIVERSE BOOKS
NEW YORK

Published in the United States of America in 1982
by Universe Books
381 Park Avenue South, New York, N.Y. 10016

Library of Congress Catalog Number: 81–40852
ISBN 0–87663–377– 7

Printed in the United Kingdom

FOREWORD

The aim of this encyclopedia is to explain words used in any technical sense that may be found in gardening writing in Britain and the United States. It is primarily a reference to aspects of the craft of gardening, and hence to the cultural practices, techniques, tools and other equipment involved, and both the specialist's terminology and gardener's jargon applied to them. Beyond the basic definition, where a gardening operation is involved, say digging, drainage or the many methods of propagation, there is a full description of *how* to carry it out. Additionally, the main groups of diseases and pests are described and present-day control measures against diseases, pests and weeds are set out.

The main historical styles of gardening, and design features associated with them, are also defined and described. The reader will find botanical terms used in describing plants and explanations both of botanical and horticultural classification and the various groupings into which plants fall for gardening purposes. Some terms may of course have currency outside botany or gardening, but they are defined in their relative sense here. The work does not deal with individual plants; many excellent encyclopedias are available for these.

However, words used in a general sense for certain plant families, e.g. aroid, bromeliad, cycad, orchid, are defined, and likewise the classificatory terms defining sections of popular exhibition flowers including carnations, chrysanthemums and dahlias.

Some entries have been put into historical perspective because it seemed of interest to do so, tracing for example the evolution of certain tools and operations. A few obsolete terms and expressions have been included because of the possibility that readers may encounter them in old books and will find it impossible to obtain definitions. Conversely, every effort has been made, by recourse to new technical works and the most recent catalogues, to bring all other entries fully up to date, especially in the field of the chemical control of diseases, pests and weeds.

In this field we are faced with continual research, new materials and the gradual elimination of out-dated or toxic ones. In Britain and Europe, garden chemicals are subject to E.E.C. regulations. In the U.S. regulations vary from state to state, and many chemicals are kept from amateur use only by their non-availability in small packs. In any case, there is a considerable difference in controls and remedies, as of course in the diseases, pests and weeds concerned, on each side of the Atlantic.

In this connection, the user of this encyclopedia should note that while inorganic chemicals, like many fertilizers, and organic materials of plant origin, e.g. derris, have individual entries, modern complex organic chemicals (e.g. malathion, 2,4-D, benlate) are not listed alphabetically. They will be found in the appropriate entries for fungicides, pesticides and weedkillers.

Those who prefer to avoid the use of chemicals will find that the entries 'Biological Control' and 'Organic Gardening' present the other side of the picture.

The few measurements in the text are given in feet and inches. A table to convert weights and measures into metric units, noting the difference between British Imperial and American fluid measures, follows this Foreword, together with details of British weights and measures.

Most entries are self-contained but definitions may be repeated in general contexts, as in the case of terms relating to flowers and leaves. Extensive cross-referencing leads both to other, directly relevant terms or their opposites, and to related information.

Cross-references are made in SMALL CAPITALS which always indicate the headword of another main alphabetical entry. This applies also in the lists of garden chemicals. The symbol ⬦ means either 'see' or 'see also' and sometimes refers to other entries with relevant illustrations.

As far as I know, this work is unique in its coverage and in its purpose of providing a rapid reference to terms, especially in specialist areas, which may be encountered by the gardener. At the same time it provides practical help on a wide range of gardening operations. The armchair gardener may also find much of interest in browsing, aided by the extensive cross-referencing.

A number of people and organizations have assisted me with some detailed problems. I would like in particular to acknowledge the help of the following: Mr C. D. Brickell, Director, Royal Horticultural Society's Garden, Surrey; Mr Larry Burrill and colleagues at the International Plant Protection Center, Oregon State University; Mr D. G. Gooding, Synchemicals Ltd, London; Mr J. E. Y. Hardcastle and Mrs N. Riley, Weed Control Organization, Oxfordshire; Mr Arthur Hellyer; Dr V. Kendall, British Agrochemicals Association.

Not least, I thank Michael Dover, my editor at Penguin Books, for much general help and consideration; the artist Vana Haggerty, who worked closely with me in preparing the line drawings; and my secretary, Mrs Anne Torrens, who uncomplainingly deciphered my manuscript and typed nearly a quarter of a million words.

Anthony Huxley, February 1981

CONVERSION TABLE

Metric/U.S./Imperial

To convert	*into*	*multiply by*
acres	hectares	0.4
centimetres	inches	0.394
cubic centimetres	cubic inches	0.061
cubic feet	cubic metres	0.0283
cubic feet	gallons (U.S.)	7.51
cubic feet	gallons (Imperial)	6.23
cubic inches	cubic centimetres	16.387
cubic inches	litres	0.0164
cubic metres	cubic feet	35.314
cubic metres	cubic yards	1.308
cubic yards	cubic metres	0.765
feet	metres	0.3048
gallons (Imperial)	gallons (U.S.)	1.205
gallons (U.S.)	gallons (Imperial)	0.833
gallons (Imperial)	cubic feet	0.161
gallons (U.S.)	cubic feet	0.134
gallons (Imperial)	litres	4.543
gallons (U.S.)	litres	3.785
grams	ounces	0.0352
hectares	acres	2.471
inches	centimetres	2.54
inches	metres	0.0254
kilograms	ounces	35.274
kilograms	pounds	2.205
kilometres	miles	0.621
litres	cubic inches	61.025
litres	gallons (Imperial)	0.22
litres	gallons (U.S.)	0.264
litres	pints (Imperial)	1.76
litres	pints (U.S.)	2.113
metres	feet	3.281
metres	inches	39.37
metres	yards	1.094
miles	kilometres	1.609

CONVERSION TABLE

To convert	into	multiply by
ounces	grams	28.349
ounces	kilograms	0.0283
pints (Imperial)	litres	0.568
pints (U.S.)	litres	0.473
pounds	kilograms	0.454
square centimetres	square inches	0.155
square feet	square metres	0.0929
square inches	square centimetres	6.452
square kilometres	square miles	0.386
square metres	square feet	10.764
square metres	square yards	1.196
square miles	square kilometres	2.59
square yards	square metres	0.836
yards	metres	0.914

Weights and Measures (Imperial)

Linear Measure

12 inches (″)	= 1 foot (′)
3 feet	= 1 yard
16½ feet	= 1 rod
22 yards	= 1 chain
10 chains/40 rods	= 1 furlong
8 furlongs	= 1 mile
1,760 yards/5,280 feet	= 1 mile

Surveyor's Measure

7.92 inches	= 1 link
100 links	= 1 chain
80 chains	= 1 mile
100,000 square links/10 square chains	= 1 acre

Square Measure

144 square inches	= 1 square foot
9 square feet	= 1 square yard
30¼ square yards	= 1 square rod, pole or perch
40 square rods, poles or perches	= 1 rood
4 roods/4,840 square yards	= 1 acre
640 acres	= 1 square mile

Cubic Measure

1,728 cubic inches	= 1 cubic foot
27 cubic feet	= 1 cubic yard

Weight (avoirdupois)

16 drams	= 1 ounce (oz.)
16 ounces	= 1 pound (lb.)
14 pounds	= 1 stone
2 stones/28 pounds	= 1 quarter (qtr)
4 quarters/112 pounds	= 1 hundredweight (cwt)
20 hundredweight/2,240 pounds	= 1 ton (long ton)
2,000 pounds	= 1 tonne (short ton)

Capacity

5 fluid ounces	= 1 gill
4 gills/20 fluid ounces	= 1 pint
2 pints	= 1 quart
4 quarts/8 pints	= 1 gallon
2 gallons	= 1 peck
4 pecks	= 1 bushel
8 bushels	= 1 quarter
5 quarters	= 1 load
2 loads	= 1 last

Temperature Conversion

To convert °C into °F, multiply by 9, divide by 5, and add 32.

To convert °F into °C, subtract 32, multiply by 5, divide by 9.

THIS BOOK IS DEDICATED TO ARTHUR HELLYER,

MY MENTOR FOR MANY YEARS

A

Abscission The separation of a leaf from its stem, notably occuring in deciduous trees in autumn as they enter their resting period; also the separation of fruits from their stems. To allow this to occur, a layer of thin-walled cells (the abscission layer) is formed, as well as a layer of corky tissue, which cuts off the food supply to the leaf or fruit and also protects the wound formed when either has dropped. ⟡ DECIDUOUS; REST PERIOD.

Acaricide Any chemical material used to kill parasitic mites such as red spider mites. ⟡ PESTICIDE.

Acaulescent A botanical term meaning 'without a stem', applied to stemless or nearly stemless flowers; usually rendered as *acaulis* or *acaule* in specific names.

Accelerator A chemical whose purpose is to speed up the decay of matter placed on a COMPOST HEAP.

Acclimatization Plants need acclimatization to cooler conditions in various circumstances. Bedding plants, half-hardy annuals and other tender plants, including some crops like tomatoes, destined to be put outside during summer, need 'hardening off' from the warm greenhouse in which they have been raised or overwintered. Young plants, even if basically hardy, often need acclimatizing to the open garden or they may be damaged by frost or wind. ⟡ FRAME; HALF-HARDY; HARDENING OFF; HARDY; LATH HOUSE; LATH LIGHT; TENDER.

Achene A dry, one-seeded fruit, not splitting open along a well-defined line; many achenes are usually found in one fruiting head, as in buttercups (*Ranunculus*).

Acicular A botanical term meaning needle-shaped; usually applied to leaves. ⟡ LEAF.

Acid Soil, potting mixtures, water and other materials can be either acid, alkaline or neutral. Acid materials turn the blue litmus dye pink; alkaline ones turn the pink litmus dye blue. The degree of acidity or alkalinity is measured on what is known as the pH scale. For further information, ⟡ pH.

Acorn The fruit of oak trees (*Quercus*): botanically a nut, it is a single, hard-coated seed carried in a stalked cup or cupule attached to the twig, and when ripe falls out of the cup. ⟡ CUPULE; NUT.

Acre ⟡ WEIGHTS AND MEASURES (p. viii).

Actinomorphic A botanical term meaning radially symmetrical, mainly applied to flowers; for instance, a single rose is actinomorphic.

Activator An accelerator, a chemical substance used to speed up decay in a COMPOST HEAP.

Active Growth Period That period within a 12-month season, not necessarily a calendar year, when a plant produces leaves, new shoots and often (though not always) flowers, in contrast to its resting period or dormancy. During the active growth period plants typically need more water, feeding, and often a higher temperature than when RESTING.

Acuminate A botanical term meaning tapering to a long point with sides curving inwards, usually applied to leaves. ⟡ LEAF.

Acute A botanical term meaning ending in a sharp point with straight or outward-curving sides; usually applied to leaves. ⟡ LEAF.

Adelgids ⟡ APHIDS.

1

Adpressed A botanical term meaning pressed flat to another surface, as with leaves close-pressed to a stem, or pressed together; it can also refer to hairs on leaves, stems, etc. Also spelt appressed.

Adult Used of mature foliage in trees which have distinctly different leaf shapes when juvenile, as in eucalyptus and conifers. ◊ JUVENILITY.

Adventitious A growth or organ produced by a plant at a point where such growths or organs do not normally occur is termed adventitious. Examples are: viviparous plantlets produced on leaves; shoots that appear on pollarded or cut trees, often from the trunk, despite the absence of buds there previously; roots made at the tips of blackberry canes on contact with the soil; roots on leaf or stem cuttings. Many succulents produce roots on above-ground stems, and it is sometimes possible to cause such roots to grow on other plants by applying root-forming hormones to their shoots. ◊ AERIAL ROOT; HORMONES; NODE; POLLARD; RUNNER; STOLON; SUCKER (1); VIVIPAROUS; WATER SHOOTS.

Aeration In gardening this refers to the soil particles having adequate air spaces between them, which allows healthy root growth. Soils which are inadequately aerated, either by their nature (like heavy clays) or because they have become unnaturally compacted by continuous walking or rolling or excessive use of heavy machinery, allow harmful anaerobic micro-organisms to build up. This, together with stagnant water in the soil, will rot roots or prevent them penetrating, and can kill trees over a period. Much-used lawns often become compacted in this way, and gardeners spike or slit them with special devices or a garden fork, to admit air again. Heavy garden soils are aerated by digging and forking and by incorporating coarse sand or other gritty materials, or other soil conditioners, and such materials are used in many potting mixtures to ensure adequate aeration. ◊ AEROBIC; ANAEROBIC; SOIL CONDITIONER; SLITTING; SPIKING.

Aerial Root Any root produced above ground level is known as aerial. Such roots are of two main kinds. Many climbing plants, such as *Ficus pumila*, ivies and trumpet vine (*Campsis*), cling to trees, walls, etc., with them. Plants like monstera do this too, but also send out thick aerial roots which can in nature descend from tree-top height to ground level, forming water-absorbing systems additional to the original stem. Plants which naturally live on trees (epiphytes), like many orchids and bromeliads, without contact with the ground, also cling with aerial roots, but in these cases the roots are specially adapted to absorb atmospheric moisture as well.

Aerial roots can be difficult to cope with on pot-grown plants. They can either be encouraged to root into a moss pole or, if long enough, directed into the potting compost in the pot. It is best to avoid cutting them off.
◊ EPIPHYTE; MOSS POLE.

Aerobic Applied to bacteria which need air to live and multiply, as against anaerobic ones which do not. Most aerobic bacteria in garden soils are beneficial, for example in breaking down decaying materials to release plant foods. Soil cultivation and aeration naturally favour aerobic bacteria and discourage the anaerobic ones, which are mostly harmful to plants. ◊ COMPOST HEAP.

Aeroplane House A very large greenhouse for commercial purposes. ◊ GREENHOUSE.

Aerosol Many substances are marketed as aerosols, in which they are formulated as a colloidal suspension in a gas under pressure. A push-button on top liberates the substances as an extremely fine mist. Several fungicides and pesticides are available in aerosol form, which is especially convenient for use on indoor plants, but this is a relatively expensive way of applying them. Check the instructions carefully: they will warn of a minimum distance for application, since if used too close to plants, the force of the mist-spray can damage plant tissue.

Aggregate Any material used with cement to bulk out concrete, like ballast, sand or gravel; also similar materials forming any rooting medium in soilless cultivation, or the basal rooting layer in ring culture of tomatoes. ◊ CONCRETE; GRAVEL; RING CULTURE; SOILLESS CULTIVATION.

Air Drainage Like water, cold air will flow or drain downhill; if it ends up in a depression where it can be trapped, a frost pocket is created. Although this may be impossible to avoid in certain terrains, air drainage can often be improved – for instance an open fence instead of a wall, or even a barred gate within a wall which runs across a slope, will release air on a sloping site so that it can drain further down and not create a frost pocket on the upper side of the wall. Air drainage is affected not only by solid barriers like walls or buildings, but by hedges and other close-packed plants. Successful air drainage can also be achieved by directing cold air coming down a slope above a garden, by building a wall or planting a hedge on the upper side in such a way that the air will travel round the garden and not into it. ◊ FROST POCKET.

making new plants from the upper growth of specimens which have become too tall, as often happens on house plants. The method involves wounding the stem and keeping the area moist. It is sometimes called Chinese layering after its inventors; the ancient Greeks and Romans also practised it. Originally it involved cutting a clay pot in half, tying the two halves around the wounded stem, and filling this receptacle with soil or moss which had to be kept moist; alternatively, a piece of cloth or sacking was tied around the moss. Nowadays plastic sheeting has eliminated the need for repeated watering.

To make an air layer, either cut and remove a ring of bark about $\frac{1}{2}"$ wide (A) or make a slit about 1" long into the stem from below upwards (B), then push a sliver of wood into it to keep it open (C), in each case at the point where roots are wanted. Dust the cut with a hormone root-forming powder if available. Next, bind a handful of moist sphagnum moss in and around the cut (D) with a few turns of thread; surround this with a piece of polythene sheet (or a polythene bag cut open) (D), overlapping it well and tying firmly top and bottom. (F, G). Alternatively pack moss into the polythene as illustrated (E).

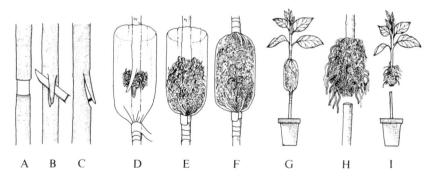

A　B　C　　D　　E　　F　　G　　H　　I

AIR LAYERING. See text for explanation

Air Layering A method of propagation in which roots are induced to form on stems or branches. It is used on woody plants, difficult to layer normally or to grow from cuttings, and is valuable in

A few weeks after roots show through the moss, cut the stem below the moss ball (H, I) and carefully pot up the new plant. The old stem can be cut back nearly to soil level to encourage new growth from

the base. Air layering is also known as marcottage and pot layering.
◊ LAYER.

Air Pine, Air Plant ◊ BROMELIAD.

Alate Literally, having wings; usually applied botanically to a flat appendage to some part of a plant. ◊ WING (1).

Albino Usually applied to animals, including humans, whose hair or skin lacks the normal colouring matter and is therefore white, it is sometimes, though seldom, used of white forms of flowers normally of other colouring, which may be given the varietal name *alba* or *album*.

Algae Primitive plants including seaweeds, pond plants, and others that form a slippery green film on damp surfaces like clay pots and even soil. Some pond algae, notably that called blanket-weed or flannel-weed, can become a considerable nuisance to gardeners and must be picked or raked out or destroyed with an algicidal compound. The film-forming algae can be a hazard on paving surfaces, especially brick, and can be scrubbed off or killed with a suitable algicide. ◊ ALGICIDE; NITROGEN FIXATION; POOL.

Algicide A chemical substance used to destroy algae. In ponds, it is usual to use copper sulphate at the rate of 23 grains to 1000 gallons of water, bearing in mind that any excess will kill both ornamental plants and fish. Potassium permanganate is somewhat safer, used at ½ oz. to 1000 gallons. There are also more powerful chemical algicides mainly designed for use in swimming pools. The film-forming algae can be cleaned with tar oil, sodium bisulphite solution, or benzalkonium chloride, obtainable as a wettable powder.
◊ ALGAE; TAR OIL WASH.

Alginate Colloidal materials obtained from seaweeds which have proved valuable as soil conditioners since they cause fine clay particles to coagulate into bigger units, forming a more granular tex-

ture with many more and larger air spaces.
◊ AERATION; COLLOID; SOIL CONDITIONER.

Alkaline The opposite of acid. ◊ ACID; pH.

Allée, Alley In garden design, an alley is a walk or ride cut through dense woodland (boskage) or made by close planting of shrubs and trees. Derived from the French word *allée*, the French originated its garden use in the sixteenth century. The trees edging the alleys would be trimmed, giving them a formal quality, and they were often laid out to meet at foci called *ronds-points*. Many formal French gardens have alleys, but in Britain few examples exist, though one is at Bramham Park, Yorkshire. Alley also refers to a type of bowling green. ◊ AVENUE; BOSKAGE; BOWLING GREEN; ROND-POINT; WALK.

Allotment A word first used (in Britain) in 1629 as denoting a portion of land assigned to a particular person or a special purpose. An Act of Parliament permitting parishes to acquire land to provide plots for poor people to grow vegetables was passed in 1819. This was followed at intervals by further Acts, notably the Enclosure Act of 1845 under which provision was made for the allotment of a part of the land to be enclosed 'for field gardens for the labouring poor', and for recreation; hence the word allotment. This was reinforced by the Commons Act of 1876.

Strictly speaking, an allotment is an area of up to two or, rarely, five acres provided by a local authority for use as a farm, smallholding or garden by a tenant under a landlord; but the word is commonly used for what are technically allotment gardens, which do not exceed a quarter-acre and are provided for the occupier to raise crops for home consumption, not for sale. The 1908 Allotment Act made it obligatory for borough, urban and parish councils to provide both allotments and allotment gardens if six ratepayers or registered parliamentary electors applied to them, and this still stands – provided the council is able to find suitable land – under the 1950 Allotments Act which governs matters such as tenure and compensation. There is a National Allotment and Gardens Society which offers advice for ratepayers seeking to obtain allotments, and on many other related matters.

Nowadays allotment gardens are usually rectangular 90′ × 30′ plots.

Allotment gardens exist in many European countries where they often provide a weekend retreat some distance from the occupier's home. In the United States a more recent equivalent has come into existence under the name Community Gardens, using otherwise waste spaces belonging to public authorities, such as those under electric power lines. ◊ COMMUNITY PLOTS.

Alluvial Used of soils which have been deposited by rivers or floods, and which consist of very fine silt, easily worked and usually fertile, as in the fenlands of southeastern Britain, but which at the same time need careful management, especially under agricultural conditions when erosion in dry weather too readily occurs. Alluvial soils especially suit root crops and bulbs, since they do not contain any stones which can cause these to become misshapen. ◊ SOIL.

Alpine Though an alpine is strictly a plant naturally growing high up on mountains, the word has come to be used of any plant suitable for a rock garden. Even in nature it is a relative term: plants from high altitudes in the European Alps can be found at sea level in Scandinavia, and some in Western Ireland.

True high alpines, as understood by specialist growers, tend to be low growing and compact, and need very well-drained soil or potting mixtures, and full light. This applies to northern-hemisphere plants; species from similar altitudes in South America or the Far East may be much taller and less hardy, since minimum temperatures may be much higher than in Europe or North America.

◊ ALPINE HOUSE; ROCK GARDEN; ROCK PLANTS; SCREE.

Alpine House A glasshouse used for the cultivation of alpines and other perennial plants, including bulbs, which can be grown in pots, or sometimes in scree-like beds, with no heat or only just enough to keep out severe frost (which can kill roots in pots). The alpine house usually has a low-pitched roof and more ventilators, both in the roof and at staging level, than a conventional greenhouse. To maintain a continuous display of flowers, plants are often brought to the flowering stage in plunge beds in cold frames. ◊ FRAME; GREENHOUSE; PLUNGE.

Alpine Meadow The true, natural high-alpine meadow in which alpine plants grow among fine grasses is extremely difficult to simulate artificially. However, 'meadows' in which the grass is replaced with low growing plants like thyme have been fairly successful. The term alpine meadow is, however, often used to denote an ordinary piece of grassland in which bulbs especially, and perhaps a few vigorous flowering herbaceous plants, are naturalized. In this they resemble the lower meadows of alpine regions in which vigorous grasses and flowering plants grow and are cut for hay. Such meadows must at all costs be left uncut until the bulb foliage has gone yellow and withered, or the bulbs will not survive for long, nor will they have the opportunity to set seed. Some gardeners leave them uncut most of the summer, allowing native plants like cow parsley to come to flower. This form of wild gardening is sometimes called meadow gardening. ◊ WILD GARDEN.

Alternate Applied to leaves occurring singly on a stem at different heights, alternating – more or less – from one side to the other. This term is often used in keys to aid identification, in contrast to leaves in opposite-facing pairs, or in whorls. ◊ LEAF; OPPOSITE; WHORL.

American Blight ◊ WOOLLY APHID.

American Garden A collection of trees and shrubs native to North America; a term occasionally used in the early nineteenth century when such plants were beginning to be imported. Also sometimes used of PEAT BEDS.

Ammonia This pungent gas (chemically NH_4) contains nitrogen, one of the essential plant foods, but in its normal domestic form of a solution in water it is too likely to scorch plants to be used directly in the garden. However, various ammonium salts can be applied as a fertilizer, the most popular being sulphate of ammonia. Since domestic ammonia is used as a cleaner it can be added to water when cleaning greenhouses and similar structures. ◊ SULPHATE OF AMMONIA.

Ammonium sulphamate (AMS) A weed-killer, not to be confused with sulphate of ammonia. ◊ FRILL-GIRDLING; TREE STUMPS; WEEDKILLER.

Amplexicaul A botanical term rendered in English as CLASPING.

Anaerobic Applied to bacteria which live in stagnant soils without air, as opposed to aerobic ones. ◊ AEROBIC; COMPOST HEAP; PEAT.

Androecium The male parts of a flower collectively. ◊ FLOWER.

Anemone-centred A term applied to composite flowers, especially chrysanthemums and dahlias, in which the tubular florets of the central disk are enlarged so that they

ANEMONE-CENTRED (dahlia)

form a kind of cushion, sometimes of a contrasting colour, among the flat ray florets. Certain peonies and camellias are sometimes also called anemone-flowered, but in these the cushion-like centre is composed of stamens modified into small petals (petalody). ◊ COMPOSITE; PETAL; PETALODY.

Angiosperm One of the major classes of the vegetable kingdom, the flowering plants. The word means, literally, having 'ovules enclosed' in an ovary, as opposed to Gymnosperms, which do not have enclosed ovules. Angiosperms not only have such ovules and resulting seeds, but have true flowers. ◊ CLASSIFICATION; FLOWER.

For other classes of interest to gardeners, ◊ GYMNOSPERM; PTERIDOPHYTE.

Animal Repellents ◊ REPELLENTS.

Annual A plant which grows from seed to maturity within one year (not necessarily a calendar year), flowering and setting seed, then dying. Annuals for cultivation in Britain and Northern Europe are usually classified as hardy annuals (abbreviated H.A.) which can be sown in the open garden where they are to flower, and half-hardy annuals (H.H.A.), the seeds of which are raised either in a greenhouse in some warmth or in the open when danger of frost is past. This need is not found in warmer climates. There are also tender annuals of tropical or sub-tropical origin which always need to be germinated in fairly high temperatures. A few perennials (e.g. antirrhinums) are normally treated as annuals since their survival rate is low and newly raised plants perform much better than old ones. ◊ BIENNIAL; OVERWINTER-ING; PERENNIAL.

Annulation The reabsorption or disappearance of latent buds after a period of years. In fruit trees this, with the corresponding bare stem incapable of producing flower buds or leaf growth, is avoided by judicious pruning which stimulates the latent buds. ◊ BUD; LATENT.

Anterior A botanical term meaning the front, or on the front.

Anther The part of the flower which produces pollen, from which the male sex cells develop. It usually consists of two lobes, each of which contains two sacs of pollen. Anthers, which are often large and decorative as in lilies, are usually carried on slender stems called filaments, the whole being known as a stamen; but in some flowers the anthers are smaller and may even be carried directly on the petals, without filaments. In a few special groups, including the orchids and conifers, the pollen is carried in different ways. ◊ COLUMN (1); EMASCULATION; FLOWER; GYMNOSPERM; POLLEN; STAMEN.

Anthracnose A term for several fungus diseases which cause dark spots or lesions on leaves, stems, pods and other fruits. ◊ LEAF SPOT.

Antibiotics Substances produced by certain fungi which kill or control infections by some other fungi or bacteria. They are mainly used to treat such infections in man and animals: penicillin is an antibiotic. Cyclohexamide and streptomycin have been developed for use against plant diseases, such as fire blight, and some lawn infections. The use of these is apparently restricted to the U.S. at present. ◊ FUNGICIDES.

Anti-transpirant A substance designed to be sprayed onto leaves – usually by an aerosol – which checks their transpiration and hence water loss from the plant. This is particularly valuable when plants, especially evergreens, are being transplanted in full leaf, and may be in a condition when the roots are unable to take up adequate moisture. Without an anti-transpirant, severe wilting and possibly death may occur. Anti-transpirants, sometimes called transplanting sprays, are also sold to stop the premature dropping of needles by Christmas trees, once indoors. ◊ TRANSPIRATION.

Ants These common garden insects can be harmful for various reasons. Their nests in open ground can loosen and dry out the soil abnormally around plants; they are a nuisance on lawns and, in pots under glass, can be disastrous. They sometimes attack ripening fruit and occasionally remove newly sown seeds from seed pans or boxes. They are also harmful because of their predilection for the 'honeydew' that aphids excrete, which induces the ants actually to transport the aphids (sometimes also young scale insects) to new 'pastures' on tender plant shoots.

Ants can be destroyed by a number of contact insecticides, which are best applied around their nests; there are also baits containing borax which the ants will take back to their nests, with lethal results to themselves. Where ants infest a pot they can usually be evicted by plunging the pot up to its rim in water for some time. ◊ APHIDS; BORAX; PESTICIDE.

Anvil The flat-surfaced blade of one type of SECATEURS.

Apetalous Applied to flowers which have no petals.

Apex, Apical The apex is the tip of a branch, seed, etc.; apical means at the tip or summit. For apical cuttings, ◊ MERISTEM.

Aphids A general term for a large number of closely related sap-sucking insects, sometimes known as plant lice. Popular names include greenfly, blackfly (also known as dolphin fly), blue fly, and woolly

APHID. *Left*, wingless aphid; *right*, winged female (much magnified)

aphid or American blight. Older gardeners sometimes refer to them simply as 'blight' (a misleading word since this properly applies to some fungus diseases). *Aphis* is the scientific name of one important genus of these insects.

Aphids (the plural is sometimes rendered as aphides) may attack the upper part of a plant including flowers and fruits, or the roots. By sucking the plant sap they weaken it and cause parts to become distorted, yellowed and sometimes to collapse, especially when they attack the newest growth, which they favour. Certain aphids cause galls on conifers (in U.S.). When root aphids are present the first signs of attack are usually flagging, and in dry weather plants may die if not treated.

Apart from this weakening effect aphids are particularly dangerous since they can carry virus diseases from infected plants to healthy ones which they may then inoculate. Their excretions, in the form of a sweet substance called honeydew, are attractive to ants, which will actually transport aphids to unattacked plants in order to 'pasture' them and so obtain honeydew. Furthermore, a fungus will readily grow upon these excretions when they drop onto other foliage and, although basically harmless, this 'sooty mould' reduces the leaf's photosynthetic capacity and is very unsightly.

In general, aphids start their life-cycle in the form of overwintering eggs. When these hatch in favourable spring weather they give rise to wingless but otherwise adult aphids which in the right conditions may rapidly multiply by giving birth to living young without fertilization by males (parthenogenesis). After several such generations, winged aphids are produced which can migrate. Though some aphids will feed on a wide range of plants, quite a number are specific to one host and very often migrate in summer to an alternative host, where they continue to multiply. In autumn, another winged migration returns them to the first host where they lay eggs which are necessary to them, since adult aphids may be killed by hard weather. Under glass or in the home, however, aphids can go on multiplying without an egg stage if unchecked.

Aphids are normally destroyed by spraying, or sometimes dusting, with a suitable insecticide, of which there are many. Root aphids are much harder to kill; a systemic insecticide can be used or the soil be soaked with a normal type; with pot plants it may be necessary to shake off all soil and wash the roots in an insecticide solution. Overwintering eggs, which are usually of aphids attacking trees and shrubs, are destroyed by winter washes on deciduous trees; or it may be necessary to spray in order to kill the newly emerging first generation in spring. Fruit growers especially learn to spot the small dark eggs usually laid at the ends of shoots. Hot-water treatment is occasionally used against aphids, as with strawberry plants.

There are a number of natural enemies (predators) of aphids, which include ladybirds (lady bugs) and their larvae, the larvae of lacewing and syrphid flies, and braconids.

Many aphids are fragile and soft-skinned but some, like the cabbage aphid, have a waxy coating which makes them harder to destroy. The above-ground woolly aphid, and the minute Adelges which attack conifers and may cause galls on them, are enclosed in a kind of wool which liquids penetrate with difficulty; many of the root aphids have a mealy covering which has the same effect.

Aphids are usually referred to under the names of their host plants. Some of the commonest are as follows: Apple aphids (including apple/grass; green; rosy; rosy leaf-curling); auricula root aphid; beech aphid; black bean aphid; cabbage aphid; cherry blackfly; chrysanthemum aphid; currant and gooseberry or currant root aphid; currant/sowthistle aphid; gooseberry aphid; lettuce aphid; lettuce root aphid; mealy plum aphid; peach-potato aphid; pear/bedstraw aphid; plum aphid; potato aphid; raspberry aphid; red currant blister aphid; rose aphid; shallot aphid; spruce aphid; strawberry aphid; tulip bulb aphid; waterlily aphid.

◊   ANTS;   HONEYDEW;   HOT-WATER

TREATMENT; INSECTICIDE; PARTHENO-GENESIS; PREDATORS; PESTICIDE; SOOTY MOULD; VIRUS; WINTER WASH.

Apiculate A botanical term, usually applied to leaves, meaning terminating in a small, broad but sharp point. ◊ LEAF.

Apomixis The formation of seed and, where applicable, fruit from female flowers which have not been pollinated or fertilized. Also known as apogamy, fruit so formed (as in certain pears) is termed apomictic or parthenocarpic. A number of plants reproduce normally or frequently in this way, notably blackberries and their relations (*Rubus*), hawkweeds (*Hieracium*) and dandelions (*Taraxacum*). The occasional mutation gives rise to numbers of distinct races, descended from the female parent of course, which many modern authorities recognize as species. ◊ CLASSIFICATION; PARTHENOCARPIC.

Appressed ◊ ADPRESSED.

Approach Graft ◊ INARCHING.

Aquatic Any plant living in water. Aquatics are typically subdivided by nurserymen into waterlilies, floating plants (i.e. without roots lodged in soil), submerged or oxygenating plants, and marginals which – with roots often partly above the water level – might better be termed subaquatic. ◊ MARGINAL; OXYGENATORS; POOL.

Arachnoid In botany, meaning like a spider's web, referring to fine web-like

ARACHNOID (*Sempervivum arachnoideum*)

hairs over a plant; sometimes giving rise to a specific name as in the Cobweb House-leek, *Sempervivum arachnoideum*.

Arboretum Literally, a tree-garden: a garden or park devoted chiefly to a collection of different trees and shrubs. The word was first used in 1838, though arboreta have been planted since ancient times, as by the Persians. ◊ PARADISE GARDEN.

Arbour In principle, 'a bower or shady retreat', to quote the *Oxford Dictionary*; arbours were made in the Middle Ages, either of trellis on which climbing plants including vines were trained, or in the form of tent-like canopies. It was then spelt *herber*, as found in Chaucer's writings. Many arbours of the period extended into long tunnels or galleries, although by 1727 the author Richard Bradley was reserving the word *bower* for such tunnels – 'always built long and arch'd' – in contrast to the arbour which 'is either round or square at Bottom, and has a sort of Dome or Ceiling at the top'. As such, arbours could include garden houses of brick or timber. By 1712 the word seems to have been used also of covered alleys and walks.

The word has also meant 'a garden of herbs or flowers' (*Oxford Dictionary*), a grassy sward, and an orchard, all sixteenth-century usages.

◊ ALLEY; WALK.

Arcade A series of arches forming a decorative garden feature, often as part of a loggia. Ruined arcades are sometimes treated as colonnades. ◊ COLONNADE; LOGGIA.

Arching ◊ ARCURE; BENDING.

Arcure A system of training fruit trees, primarily apples and pears, popular in France. The branches are curved into horizontal arches, first one way and then the other, until the required height is reached, by allowing the latent topmost bud of each arch to develop into a 'gourmand' shoot. The subsequent arching checks the upward flow of sap and so increases fruitfulness in

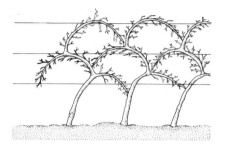

ARCURE

the other buds which are pruned to form fruiting spurs. A very decorative method. ◊ BENDING; GOURMAND; LATENT; SPUR.

Areole An organ unique to cacti (family *Cactaceae*): a modified side-shoot, usually cushion-like, from which arise spines, wool, leaves if present, side branches and flowers. Sometimes called the spine-cushion. ◊ CACTUS.

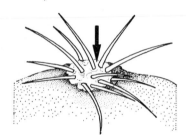

AREOLE

Aristate Having AWNS.

Armed In botany, any plant bearing spines, thorns or prickles. ◊ SPINE.

Aroid Any plant belonging to the family *Araceae*, which includes wild lords-and-ladies and jack-in-the-pulpit, the arum or calla lily (zantedeschia), anthurium, philodendron and monstera. These are characterized by an inflorescence consisting of a cylindrical spadix, densely packed with tiny flowers, the male towards the top and the female below, and having a single bract known as a spathe at the base. This is almost always the showy part of the plant, and may

be flattish, as in the anthurium, or more or less rolled around the spadix, as in the arum lily and lords-and-ladies. ◊ BRACT; IN-FLORESCENCE; SPADIX; SPATHE.

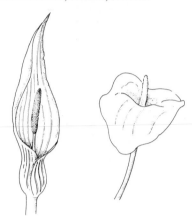

AROID. *Left, Arum maculatum; right,* anthurium

Arris Rail The horizontal member of a section of close-boarded or lapped wooden fence. When arris rails perish or loosen where they enter the upright posts, arris-rail repair clamps of metal can be obtained to secure them. ◊ FENCES.

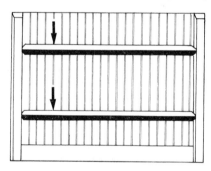

ARRIS RAIL

Articulate Jointed. ◊ NODE.

Artificial Key A method of establishing the identity of plants by means of a series of paired statements of relevant contrasting characters, each of which leads to a further pair or to the identification. In systematically arranged botanical works, it is customary to have keys to the families, under families keys to the genera, and under genera keys to species. A number of horticultural works employ keys mainly to species. ◊ CLASSIFICATION.

Ascending Stems which curve upwards or obliquely, rather than being prostrate or erect.

Asexual Literally, sexless. In botany this can refer to methods of increase like division in bacteria, but in gardening it applies to methods of propagation other than seed-raising, such as division, grafting, or taking cuttings. ◊ APOMIXIS; PROPAGATION.

Ashes The gardener can use dry wood ashes as a useful fertilizer since they contain carbonate of potash. Ashes from coke or hard coal, such as is used in hot-water boilers, can be used to lighten heavy soils, as a hard, free-draining standing ground for pots, or in plunge beds. Nowadays, when boilers using such fuels are seldom seen, such ashes are much less used than they were. Ordinary coal ash from domestic fires is not useful, since it is not coarse and gritty. ◊ POTASH.

Asparagus Knife A tool with a short saw-edged blade on a long metal shank fixed into a wooden handle, used around 1900 for cutting asparagus spears, but apparently no longer made.

Aspect Meaning facing in a particular direction, the word is often used in describing the most suitable position for plants. Thus peaches prefer a south aspect, with maximum sun; morello cherries are perfectly at home with a sunless northern aspect.

Asphalt ◊ PATHS.

Attenuate In botany, tapering naturally; also used of plants which have grown taller but thinner than normal owing to unnatural circumstances.

Auricle, Auriculate An auricle is a small ear; auriculate is a botanical term meaning 'having ears' and referring to ear-like projections or organs such as are found at leaf-bases in grasses.

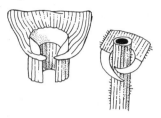

AURICLE

Autospade ◊ SPADE.

Auxin A plant hormone which promotes new growth in stems and roots, while preventing unwanted growth of side buds below the growth bud at the shoot tip.

A number of auxins, including synthesized ones, are used by gardeners to stimulate root production on cuttings, set fruit, prevent fruit drop, retard plant growth and kill weeds. ◊ HORMONES.
◊ CUTTING; NICKING AND NOTCHING; VASCULAR SYSTEM.

Avenue Though now in general use to mean a tree-lined road or path, until the seventeenth century this word was used solely to mean an approach. Avenues were widely used in garden design in that century, until the new fashion for landscaping was responsible for many being destroyed; they returned, in a limited way, in the early nineteenth century.

Averruncator A word in use from 1842 till the last years of the nineteenth century for long-handled pruners working on the principle of secateurs or shears, operated by a string or wire. ◊ SECATEURS; SHEARS; TREE PRUNERS.

Awl-shaped A term usually applied to leaves, indicating resemblance to a cobbler's awl with its sharp, up-turned point. Certain conifers have awl-shaped leaves. ◊ LEAF.

11

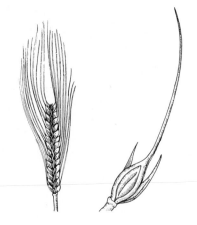

AWN. *Left*, head of barley; *right*, single seed with awn

Awn A thread-like termination to a fruit, seed or leaf; the word is most commonly applied to the 'beard' on the seeds of many grasses and cereals, as in barley. The 'beak' on cranesbill fruits is another type of awn. The awn is, probably, basically a dispersal mechanism, attaching itself to the coats of animals, or in some cases light enough to enable the seed to be carried in the wind. A plant with awns may be described as awned or aristate, the latter sometimes Latinized as a specific name. ◊ BEARD.

Axil, Axillary The angle between a leaf-stalk and the stem from which it is growing. Any bud in this position is known as an axillary bud. Buds of this type are used in the grafting operation known as BUD-DING.

A.Y.R. An abbreviation for 'all the year round', applied especially to chrysanthemum culture, aimed at production of either cut sprays or dwarfed pot plants throughout the year by manipulation of day-length. ◊ DAY-LENGTH; DWARFING.

B

Back-bulb An orchid-grower's term referring to the rearmost, and hence oldest, pseudobulb on certain orchids, which can be separated from the parent plant and induced to produce new shoots. ◊ PSEUDOBULB.

Bacteria Microscopic, single-celled, very primitive organisms which exist everywhere in vast quantities, reproducing by division. Most soil bacteria are beneficial to plants: they are mostly those needing air (the aerobic type) which are largely responsible for the final stages of breaking down organic matter into plant foods. The anaerobic bacteria, which need no air, are associated with ill-drained or stagnant soils and may be harmful to plants.

Beneficial bacteria include those which 'fix' atmospheric nitrogen, some of which live free in the soil while others inhabit root nodules in certain plants. Harmful bacteria include a number which cause plant diseases such as bacterial canker and crown gall, and certain soft rots. There are few chemical remedies; antibiotics are of value against certain diseases.

◊ ANTIBIOTICS; CANKER; GALL; HOST PLANT; NITROGEN FIXATION; NODULE; WILT.

Bag Fertilizer Sometimes used of concentrated fertilizers which are necessarily obtained in a bag. ◊ FERTILIZER.

Bagging Hook A kind of garden sickle. ◊ SICKLE.

Bait A material which lures unwanted animals to a trap or to eat a poison with which it is mixed. The gardener may use baits to trap small mammals like mice and moles, and against various lesser creatures including ants, crickets, cockroaches, leatherjackets and woodlice. One of the most familiar baits is bran mixed with metaldehyde used against slugs and snails.

Balcony Garden ◊ ROOF GARDEN.

Ball (1) The mass of soil or potting mixture plus roots (sometimes called a root ball) of a pot-grown plant when removed from its container; also the similar ball made by certain very fibrous-rooted plants such as rhododendrons and some conifers in the open soil. In repotting, the root ball should come out intact; to ensure clean separation from the container and minimum damage to roots, it is important that the container should be quite clean initially: roots stick very readily to encrusted soil in old clay pots. When lifting plants from open-soil nursery beds it is important, especially with evergreens (including conifers), to keep their root balls intact while they are being handled or transplanted; where not container-grown, these root balls are wrapped in hessian, polythene sheet or sacking which is not removed until the plant is actually in its final new planting hole. ◊ BALLED-AND-WRAPPED; CONTAINER-GROWN; PLANTING; REPOTTING.

(2) A condition of rose blooms, especially those of very double varieties, when the blooms refuse to open properly and decay in the bud stage. This trouble is called 'balling' and usually follows very wet weather, especially if the plants have been over-fed or too much thinning has been carried out.

(3) A class of dahlias with spherical flowers and short tight-packed florets, larger than the similar POMPONS.

Ballast A general term covering gravel, broken stone, rubble, etc. ◊ AGGREGATE; CONCRETE; GRAVEL.

Ballbarrow An ingenious modern form of wheelbarrow in which the normal wheel is replaced by a large plastic ball, which spreads the weight more widely and makes the loaded barrow easier to push. ◊ WHEELBARROW.

13

Balled-and-wrapped Trees and shrubs lifted with a good ball of soil around the roots, which is wrapped and tied in burlap or sacking before being offered for sale. Such plants transplant much better than bare-rooted ones. ◊ BALL (1); BARE-ROOT; CONTAINER-GROWN.

Banding A method of applying fertilizers to certain vegetables that are sown in widely spaced rows. A narrow trench is hoed or dug out to a depth 1″–2″ below that at which the seed is to be sown. Fertilizer is placed (at the rate recommended for surface application before digging in) in a narrow band a little to the side of the seed-sowing line in the trench, or more lightly over the bottom of the trench, which is then partly refilled and the seed sown at the appropriate depth. Soon after the seedlings germinate their roots reach this extra food supply. The method is particularly suitable for peas and beans.

Bare-root The state of trees, shrubs, etc., lifted from the nursery and dispatched to customers without soil around the roots. Nowadays container-growing is replacing this old practice which, naturally, gives the plants a big shock to get over, but the majority of roses are still sent out in this way. Roots of such plants should be well soaked in water before planting. ◊ CONTAINER-GROWN.

Bark The outermost layer on the trunk and branches of woody plants, a protective layer outside the phloem and cambium, typically composed of dead, corky cells and continuously added to from within. This allows for the expansion of the trunk or branch, though the exterior of the bark is likely to split, or break into scales or plates as in plane and pine trees. However, some barks are fibrous or membranous, and can often be peeled off in strips. Bark can be anything from a millimetre or two thick, as in cherries, to the thick spongy layer of the cork oak or giant redwood; in the latter, bark can become 12″ or more thick. Many barks contain tannins and other substances

(quinine is one), which are probably waste products, but being bitter frequently act as a deterrent to animals which would otherwise attack tree trunks. Trees with thin bark may get gnawed by such animals in bad weather conditions anyway, but if the tree is not killed by such attack the bark usually regenerates, though this is a slow process.

In the garden some plants are grown partly or even mainly for the attractiveness of their barks. This includes colour, as in some birches, dogwoods and willows, sometimes allied to a glossy shine as in *Prunus serrula*; pattern, as in the 'snake-bark' maples; and peeling to reveal a different colour, as in the paperbark maple and some birches.

Shredded bark has recently become popular for use as a mulch, as an alternative for peat, and as an ingredient in potting composts for orchids.

◊ BARK-BOUND; CAMBIUM; COMPOSTS, SEED AND POTTING; MULCH; PHLOEM; RAFT; RINGING.

Bark-bound Soil dryness, lack of plant food, and damage to roots sometimes cause trees and, to a lesser extent, shrubs to grow so slowly that the bark becomes extra hard, cannot expand as it normally does, and literally 'strangles' the plant, preventing further development. Even if the causes of this condition are removed, trees may continue bark-bound for years. Occasionally they 'cure' themselves by bursting the bark in a long vertical split. The gardener can effect this remedy himself by making a similar split in the bark with a sharp pointed knife, avoiding penetrating the wood of the tree as much as possible, in spring just as growth is starting. It is advisable to apply a proprietary wound dressing to such slits, and to feed and water the tree generously in the forthcoming one or two seasons.

Bark-ringing ◊ RINGING.

Barrier Banding The U.S. term for GREASE BANDING or TREE BANDING.

Basal Often used, especially in botanical works, to refer to the lower leaves of a plant, which may differ considerably from those on the stem. Plants forming basal leaf rosettes, for instance, often have isolated alternate leaves on the flower stems.

Basal Cluster The group of leaves at the base of a fruit shoot, which grow close together with very short INTERNODES.

Basal Stem Rot ♢ COLLAR ROT.

Base Dressing ♢ DRESSING.

Basic Slag The waste product from the lining of blast furnaces, which when crushed forms a valuable fertilizer. It contains phosphoric acid and also calcium in the form of free lime. The proportions vary: the phosphoric acid content lies between 8 and 18.5 per cent, and the lime is around 3 per cent. As important as these levels in assessing a sample is its solubility, which can range from below 40 to over 80 per cent – the higher the better.

While the rate of liberation of phosphoric acid will depend on the fineness of the grinding, it is always relatively slow, so that this material is valuable as a long-term fertilizer.

Basic slag is best applied in autumn and winter, and is specially useful on acid soils because of its lime content. However, it should not be mixed with organic manures or mixtures containing ammonium salts or superphosphate of lime.
 ♢ FERTILIZER.

Basket Large open-work baskets, usually of cast iron, sometimes including thin flat metal strips, were popular as plant containers in Victorian days, though now seldom seen. ♢ HANGING BASKET; TRUG.

Basketweave ♢ FENCES.

Bass ♢ RAFFIA.

Bastard Trenching Another term for double digging. ♢ DIGGING.

Bastion A garden feature occasionally created in the early eighteenth century, in which arrow-shaped bastions, in plan like those used in military fortifications but constructed of low walls, projected outwards at the boundaries of a garden or wood to provide viewing places into the surrounding countryside.

Bat Guano Bat droppings may be used as a plant food if they occur locally in sufficient quantity in a bat-filled cave; they are occasionally imported for the purpose. The chemical analysis varies considerably and is often low in nitrogen and phosphoric acid, but can be equivalent to medium-quality bird guano. Bat guano, which is a dry, powdery material, can be used at 2–4 oz. per square yard. ♢ GUANO.

Batter The slope from the vertical of an upright surface such as a wall or bank; mainly applied to the slope created on a hedge by clipping. Tall narrow hedges in particular are best clipped to provide a slight batter or inward slope from base to top on both sides. This gives a neater appearance, prevents the hedge from becoming top-heavy and its upper growths spreading out, and helps to avoid damage from snow. ♢ HEDGE; WALLS.

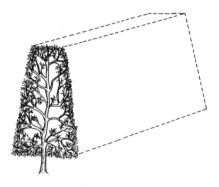

BATTER (of a hedge)

Beard A growth of hairs, in particular that occuring on the lower petals (falls) of some irises; there is a whole class of irises known

15

as bearded. The long awns on some cereals and ornamental grasses are also known as beards. ♢ AWN.

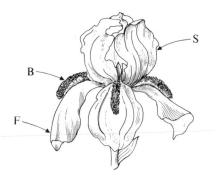

BEARD. B, beard of iris flower; F, fall; S, standard

Bed A rather loose term, usually taken to mean an area of open soil cut from a grassed area, enclosed in very low hedges, or set into paving, used for plantings aimed at providing maximum display. ♢ BEDDING PLANT; SEED BED.

Bedding Plant, Bedding Scheme A bedding plant is one used for temporary display which is planted or 'bedded out' in quantities, often after being grown almost to flowering stage elsewhere. Bedding plants may be hardy or tender, and can be annuals, biennials or perennials. Their common denominator is their ability to provide a display for long periods (most are used for summer display) and their ease of multiplication.

It is usual to have more than one kind of plant in a display, and this entails working out *bedding schemes* in which plants are contrasted as to colour and form. Thus spring displays often feature tulips among plants of very different habit, and summer ones may have foliage plants combined with flowering ones, some of the former growing much taller than the overall flowering display, when they are called dot plants.

♢ CARPET BEDDING; DOT PLANT; SUB-TROPICAL.

Bee (1) The well-known honey-making insect; also the bumble bee and solitary bee, which are equally useful in pollinating fruit trees, etc.; and the leaf-cutting bee, which can be a tiresome pest. Some of the solitary bees can also become pests if quantities of them make burrows in lawns or paths, though it is usually easy to remove the mounds of soil they make by rolling or sweeping. These are called mining bees.

It is always important to avoid spraying open flowers, especially those of fruit trees, with insecticides which will kill the useful honey-bees visiting them.

(2) The word bee also denotes the petaloid centre of a delphinium floret, which is often black. ♢ FLORET; PETALOID.

Bee Bole An occasional feature of older gardens from Tudor times to the mid-nineteenth century, bee boles are wall niches around 2′ wide and 3′ high, often with arched tops, which served to protect, in winter, the fragile straw bee-skeps which were universally used until modern wooden 'lift' hives were invented. In some gardens, as at Packwood, Warwickshire, there were large arrays of bee boles.

Beet Fork ♢ FORKS.

Beetle (1) Beetles are insects of the class *Coleoptera*, with six legs, biting mouthparts, and forewings modified into the form of hard wing-cases under which the hindwings used for flying are folded when not in use. Beetles may live above or below ground, and there are a great many species. Many are beneficial, both in the larval and adult stages, like the carabids, devil's coach-horse and ladybirds (U.S. lady bugs); others are pests in both adult and larval stages. Thus cockchafer grubs can severely damage roots and the adults eat flowerbuds; leatherjackets, the larvae of craneflies, feed on many kinds of plant roots; in the U.S. Japanese beetles attack grass roots; cockroaches can severely damage greenhouse and indoor plants; and bark beetles are frequently injurious to trees, and include those which carry the dreaded dutch elm disease. Some beetles live in water; the giant water beetle (*Dytiscus*) can attack fish, and the waterlily beetle feeds on waterlily leaves and spoils their appearance. Beetles are closely related to weevils. ♢ JAPANESE BEETLE; WEEVIL.

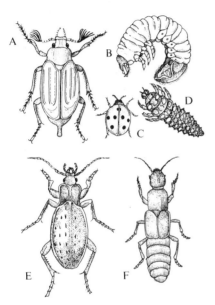

BEETLE. A. cockchafer; B, cockchafer grub; C, ladybird; D, ladybird larva; E, common garden beetle; F, devil's coach-horse

(2) The word beetle also refers to a tool usually shaped like a huge mallet, with a heavy head and stout handle, used to drive in fence-posts or wedges, to settle paving slabs, and to ram turf into place. The head of this ancient tool, which is still used by some gardeners today, is typically a short wide cylinder of wood bound with iron hoops. Another kind of beetle was formed from a rectangular slab of wood with a long handle fixed obliquely to its centre. A book of 1706 explains: 'This serves to smooth the walks; and hinders most effectively the growing of weeds upon them'. Turf beetles or beaters are still desirable when making lawns from turf today. One type resembles the last described, using a piece of wood around 15″ × 12″ and 2″ thick. Another is of a wood block 10″–12″ long and 4″–6″ wide and deep, with a shaped handle projecting at one end, and is used with a beating action.
 ♢ LAWN; TURF.

Bell Glass A large glass jar shaped like a bell, around 15″ tall and 17″ wide, often with a knob for handling at the top, which was developed in France by market gardeners during the seventeenth century. They used it for intensive cultivation of early crops, placing it over individual plants or groups of small plants. The French word for bell glass is *cloche*, a word which in Britain came to be applied to the continuous structures constructed of glass panes and wire, and more modern protective devices. Bell glasses are now practically unobtainable in this country, the lantern cloche being the nearest approach where it is wanted to maintain a very close, humid atmosphere over cuttings. A large jam jar makes a good substitute. ♢ CLOCHE.

Bellows Among the earliest methods (around the beginning of the nineteenth century) of dispensing pesticides – which were then usually in the form of powders like sulphur dust – were bellows like those used for fires but fitted with a reservoir in which the powder was placed. Powder insecticides are still available in packs with a kind of bellows built in, although most 'puffer packs' are now of pliable plastic which can be squeezed in the hand. ♢ PUFFER.

Belvedere A look-out; usually in the form of a turret or 'lantern' on a tower or roof, but also used of a garden house or temple built on a high point to command a view. An occasional architectural feature in older gardens. ♢ GAZEBO.

Bench Grafting Applied to any grafting method performed with neither stock nor scion planted, so called because it is normally carried out on a potting bench. Bench grafting typically involves as stock either a smallish root or a stem cutting which has produced roots. In other cases bench grafting is carried out on full-size stocks which have been lifted for transplanting, giving the opportunity for grafting under cover. ◊ GRAFTING.

Bending In general, woody plants produce more flower buds, more evenly spaced, if branches are bent or arched over near or below the horizontal. This encourages the sprouting of latent or dormant buds. This principle is used by fruit growers: arcure training is a method which uses the principle in an ornamental manner. Bending works well on the growths of vigorous climbing roses and can be applied to many other shrubs. Apart from careful training, or tying to a trellis, wall wires, etc., bending can be carried out on free-standing bushes by tying growths to lower branches, the trunk, or pegs in the ground; or weights can be attached to branches. Bending is also important in shaping bonsai specimens. ◊ ARCURE; BONSAI; GOURMAND; LATENT.

Berry Botanically, a berry is a succulent fruit in which the usually hard seeds (or single seed) are embedded in pulp and protected only by an outer fleshy wall formed from the ovary, as opposed to the drupe or stone fruit in which the seed is enclosed in a distinct hard coat, or a 'stone', as well as outer pulp. In common parlance the word is very loosely applied: thus raspberries and blackberries are botanically compound drupes, and the fruits of cotoneasters and hawthorns are botanically pomes. Many true berries are never commonly recognized as such, e.g. the cucumber, grape, melon, orange, pomegranate and tomato. The date is a berry – its hard 'stone' is all seed, not forming a coat around the seed; so is the banana, though the edible kinds seldom produce seed. ◊ DRUPE; FRUIT; POME.

Besom A long narrow broom made of a bunch of twigs fastened to a handle. Birch is usually employed though heather is sometimes seen. The besom has been in use for centuries and, though seldom used by gardeners today, is still an ideal tool for removing dead leaves and other debris, and wormcasts, from lawns. ◊ LAWN.

Bicolor Two-coloured: usually used of flowers in which two colours contrast sharply.

Biennial A plant which flowers and seeds in the second season from seed germination, in contrast to the annual which completes its growth cycle within a single season, and the monocarpic plant which also dies after producing seed but takes an indefinite number of years to reach maturity. Many important vegetables are biennial, including cabbages, beetroots, turnips and other members of the crucifer family. A feature of many biennials is that they form a rosette, or sometimes a fleshy root, during the first year, from the centre or top of which the single flowering stem arises in the second year. Canterbury bells and foxgloves are true biennials; quite a number of other plants which are technically perennials are typically treated as biennials, including double daisies, sweet williams and wallflowers. ◊ ANNUAL; MONOCARPIC; OVERWINTERING; PERENNIAL.

Biennial Bearing The habit of certain top fruit trees of producing a crop one year and little or none the next. Some varieties have a marked natural tendency to this habit; others can fall into it if the crop is very light in one year, usually as the result of frost at blossom time, unpruned and starved trees being most liable. Biennial bearing can normally be altered to more regular cropping in various ways. On small trees, removal of many of the flowers in the prolific or 'on' year will help. Spur-pruned trees are more liable to this effect than more lightly pruned ones, so an alteration of pruning may be advisable. Finally, ample feeding will help the tree both to carry a crop and to make fruit buds for

the following year. ◊ DEBLOSSOMING;
SPUR (1) (2).

Big Bud A gall of currants caused by a
mite, which can entirely curtail cropping.
◊ GALL; MITE.

Bigeneric A hybrid plant resulting from
the breeding ('crossing') of parents from
two distinct genera. Most though certainly
not all bigeneric hybrids occur in the orchid
and bromeliad families. ◊ PLANT BREED-
ING.

Bilabiate Having two lips. ◊ FLOWER;
LIP.

Billhook A heavy knife-like instrument
with a wide blade more or less curved into
a hook shape near the tip, used for clearing woody undergrowth and cutting
hedges.

BILLHOOK

The billhook was invented by the
Romans; in its simplest form (*falx
arboraria*) it had a single cutting edge,
curving inwards towards the tip to form a
'beak'. From it they developed the vine-
dresser's tool (*falx vinitoria*) which additionally had a fine edge for paring, a
pointed projection for gouging or hollowing, and a miniature axe-blade on the back.
This tool was developed during the sixteenth century for fruit-tree work in
general, the axe-blade being replaced by a
'chisel' which was sometimes quite long
and narrow. The Roman vine-grower's
billhook design was still in use, virtually
unchanged, in the early part of this century;
it only went out of manufacture when the
secateur was introduced.

Apart from simple versions with one cutting edge, it is possible nowadays to obtain
a type with a sharp cutting edge on one
side and a stouter axe-like blade of some

length on the other; another combines a
curved cutting edge on one side with a
long straight one on the other. The hedge
or pruning bill, used for 'dressing' or tidy-
ing up the sides of hedges, had a slightly
curved blade attached to a handle up to
4′ long, angled slightly from the blade so
that the operator could stand clear of the
hedge; some versions had an axe-like blade
or miniature saw on the side opposite the
knife blade. Such tools are now known as
slashers or brushing hooks.
◊ SECATEURS; SICKLE; SLASHER.

Billiard Table A name used among gardeners for raised beds made for alpines,
etc., especially those of rectangular outline.
◊ RAISED BED.

Binomial Modern botanical classification
is based on the binomial system, the first
name being that of the genus and the
second that of the species. ◊
CLASSIFICATION.

Biodynamic Method ◊ DEEP BED METHOD.

Biological Control This encompasses ways
of destroying pests and weeds by basically
natural methods, rather than by using
chemicals. In its simplest form, biological
control uses a naturally occurring enemy
of the pest. To be really effective it is
necessary to breed the predator in quantity
and to release it in the pest-infected area.
In Britain a certain amount of success has
been achieved with the white fly parasite,
a kind of wasp, liberated in greenhouses. A
predatory mite has also been used against
the glasshouse red spider mite. The method
has been used with considerable success on
many tropical crop plants. Weed control
by this method has also been successful,
notably in the virtual elimination of the
prickly pear (opuntia) introduced into
Australia, by bringing in the cochineal
insect which feeds upon it.

Another large-scale method is to breed
large numbers of male insects which are
sterilized by irradiation before being released in areas where the insect is a pest.
These sterile males breed with the wild

19

females and can greatly reduce the numbers of fertile eggs laid.

Yet other methods involve the culturing of bacterial, fungus or virus diseases to which the pests in question are prone, and spraying or dusting crops with materials prepared from the diseased insects. Of these *Bacillus thuringiensis* and *B. popilliae* (milky spore disease), prepared from spores of insect-infecting bacteria, which control caterpillars and Japanese beetle grubs respectively, are now available to amateurs (the latter in U.S. only).

All these methods have the enormous advantage of being specific to the pest concerned, though there are cases where artificially bred predators have turned to attack other beneficial insects, or those aimed at weed plants have likewise attacked useful ones.

In the garden, apart from the very few specially bred pests, like the white fly parasite, which can be obtained, the only method of biological control really possible is to avoid pesticide spraying of any kind and thus to encourage the natural predators; but this can be a somewhat hit-or-miss method if only because neighbours are likely to spray and thus destroy many predators.

In the U.S. biological control is sometimes referred to as integrated pest management.

◊ ORGANIC; PEST; PREDATORS.

Biotic Literally, pertaining to life. Sometimes used to describe environmental factors with their origin in living organisms; thus a pest or fungus disease is a biotic factor in the environment of the host plant.

Bipinnate ◊ LEAF; PINNATE.

Birds, Bird-scarers Although birds eat a very large quantity of garden pests, ranging from greenfly, caterpillars, larger insects, slugs and snails to mice, they also attack flowers, fruit and flower buds on shrubs and trees, fruits and vegetable crops; they can also cause damage to seed beds and newly sown lawns by dusting themselves and by scratching for the seeds, and to small plants which they root up in their search for food. Blackbirds are particularly tiresome in this respect among alpines. In Britain the bullfinch, which attacks buds, and pigeons and stock doves are the worst enemies, doing far more harm than good. The gardener cannot normally use either a shotgun against these or the noise-makers used by commercial fruit-growers, and has to rely on defensive measures.

Bird-scarers (such as rags tied to string, strips of shiny metal or kitchen-foil, or propellers turning in the wind) should be frequently changed, or birds soon lose their fear of them. Those which combine movement, glitter and some noise seem most effective, though noise may be offensive to neighbours.

Other bird scarers which have been claimed to work include lengths of hose-pipe supposed to resemble snakes, stuffed or imitation cats and owls, and hawk-shaped kites or hawk outlines kept in the air by a balloon (note that the head of the hawk must point into the wind for birds to consider it dangerous!).

Seed rows and bright low-growing spring flowers are best protected by arched guards of wire netting (pea guards), or by making a network of dark-coloured thread strung over short sticks. Whenever thread is used it should be thin cotton, not nylon; the latter will not break and can maim birds severely in their struggles to escape. Fruit bushes and medium-sized fruit trees can be covered with fine netting, and there is a proprietary deterrent made from rayon fibre which decays in a few months. It is also possible to erect cages of netting on a rigid frame-work: these are usually called fruit cages but lower ones are equally advisable over vegetable plots in pigeon-infested areas. Netting should be regularly inspected because birds may become entangled in it and need liberating.

Newly sown lawns may be protected with a network of black cotton or by fine plastic netting stretched on upright canes. Strips of rag or tinfoil tied to lengths of string between canes act as scares. It is also possible to treat the seed before sowing by moistening it with paraffin and shaking it up with red lead dust: this makes it distasteful to the birds, and has no effect on the seeds.

Established lawns are sometimes visited by large birds like rooks and starlings, which tear up chunks of turf. These birds are searching for leatherjackets and other grubs, and their attacks will demonstrate the presence of these pests. The best counter-measure is to deal with the grubs – an action necessary for the well-being of the lawn in any case.

Finally there are a number of proprietary bird repellents, based on substances like anthraquinone, quassia and thiram; these are mainly for spraying on trees and shrubs since they give buds and berries a bitter taste. Although said to remain effective for long periods, they may need renewing after heavy rain.

Despite the gardening problems created by birds listed above, very many gardeners will doubtless wish to attract some birds at least to the garden both for the pleasure and interest they provide, as well as for the benefits in pest elimination. Briefly, the enticements include the feeding of birds, especially in winter; the provision of nesting boxes, together with a supply of water in shallow containers; where space permits, the creation of secluded shrub and tree groupings with special emphasis on evergreens for winter shelter and on species producing plenty of palatable berries. In a bird sanctuary like this, many plants which the gardener normally considers weeds should be encouraged, since their seeds are attractive to birds. ◊ FRUIT CAGE.

Bisexual Equivalent to HERMAPHRODITE.

Biternate Of leaves with three divisions each subdivided into leaflets. ◊ LEAF.

Bitumen, Bituminous Bitumen is a natural tar-like hydrocarbon of varying consistency. Bituminous paint can be used to seal wood which is to be immersed in water, and to protect metal against rust; it is also used as a wound dressing. ◊ WHALE-HIDE; WOUND DRESSINGS.

Bizarre A type of carnation, mainly grown for exhibition, with patches ('flakes') of two or more colours on a differently coloured ground. ◊ BROKEN.

Blackleg ◊ COLLAR ROT.

Black Spot A number of fungus diseases produce black spots on plant leaves, the most notorious of which is that attacking roses. These diseases can be checked by regular spraying with suitable fungicides, including spraying the soil in winter to destroy resting spores, and by collecting and burning affected leaves from the ground. Rose black spot, which is often very hard to control in areas unaffected by industrial pollution (which has a fungicidal effect), is probably encouraged by too much nitrogenous fertilizer. ◊ FUNGICIDES; FUNGUS.

Blade The flat portion of a leaf, as distinct from its stalk; also known as the lamina or limb. ◊ LEAF.

Blanching Literally, making white. The gardener blanches certain vegetables by depriving them of light, a practice begun in the mid-seventeenth century. These include leeks and celery, where as much as possible of the stem is blanched; chicory and seakale, where the entire growing shoot arising from a forced root is blanched; and the lettuce-like endive and dandelion, where the centre of the leaf rosette at least is blanched. The latter can be done by placing a saucer, tile, etc., over the plant. Leeks and celery are 'earthed up' by gradually drawing soil around the stems, which are sometimes protected by tubular cardboard or paper 'collars' especially for exhibition use. With chicory and seakale, roots are packed tight in containers, covered with soil and forced in a dark place. Blanching makes the vegetables more tender and in some cases removes natural bitterness. ◊ EARTHING UP; ETIOLATED; FORCING.

21

Blanket-weed Filamentous algae which form large interlocking masses in pools and ponds, choking ornamental plants and making life difficult for fish; also called flannel-weed or silkweed. On a small scale this should be removed by hand or with a rake or a special water-rake, although it is difficult to clear it around ornamentals without damaging them. On a larger scale it is possible to use chemical treatment. ◊ ALGAE; ALGICIDE; POOL.

Bleeding If there is an overflow of sap when a plant is cut, this is called bleeding. It is most often seen on shrubs and trees pruned over-late in spring, when the sap is rising; early pruning prevents this, since wounds will have healed over. One of the most spectacular examples is that of a late-pruned grapevine. Greenhouse plants often bleed, especially if the pot soil is rather moist. Rubber plants, spurges and other latex-producing plants bleed a white sap, and some red. Bleeding looks alarming and is usually thought to be harmful, though scientific research has shown that this is not usually the case. To stop bleeding, gardeners apply powdered charcoal or sulphur dust, or seal the cut with a red-hot iron, but it usually stops of its own accord within hours, or a few days at most. One instance of harmful bleeding occurs in beetroots which lose much colour if leaf stems are cut off; twisting the tops off at lifting is recommended.

Blight A word used for several centuries to describe any kind of plant pest or disease; gardeners today often describe severe attacks of greenfly or black fly as 'blight'. Strictly speaking, it should be applied only to potato blight, a disease caused by a fungus.

Blind Applied to plants when loss of the growing point has stopped growth, as often occurs in seedlings of cabbages and other brassicas, especially after attack by the cabbage root fly maggot. Plants thus damaged will make neither a new growing point nor further growth, and should be discarded.

Gardeners sometimes use the word of plants, especially bulbs, which fail to produce flowers, which can be due to immaturity or overcrowding.

Blinds Glass structures, mostly greenhouses but also sometimes frames, are sometimes protected from too-strong sunshine by using blinds. Such blinds used to be of paper or oiled silk; today they may be of wooden slats, split bamboo, hessian or burlap, fine plastic mesh or opaque PVC sheeting. They may be fitted inside or outside a greenhouse and should be arranged so that they can readily be rolled up when not needed. It is sometimes believed that blinds will prevent heat loss at night but in fact they are not efficient in trapping heat. However, a blind over a cold frame will reduce the effects of severe frost. ◊ SHADING.

Blocking The technique of compressing seed and potting composts into square, cylindrical or hexagonal blocks, using a special machine; seed is sown direct into the blocks and the young plants grown on in them. This method does away with any form of pot and allows the young plants to be potted on or planted out with the minimum check.

When first developed some decades ago, blocking was carried out entirely with soil-based composts, hence the phrase 'soil blocks' was used for the result. Blocks were also made from sifted soil mixed in equal parts with sifted garden compost. Recently the technique has been resuscitated, after a period of limited use, for soilless composts; devices for making blocks and special formulations known as blocking composts are available. Block-making devices usually produce one block at a time, but some will make four or five blocks simultaneously.

The mixture for blocking should be quite moist but not too wet. When made, the blocks should be handled near the base only, and as little as possible. They are placed in seed trays, nearly touching, and should be used as soon as possible after being made: seed is sown, or seedlings or cuttings planted, in the shallow central depression left by the blocking machine. Blocks should be watered with a fine-rosed can and never allowed to dry out. When roots begin to show on the outside of the blocks they are ready for planting out.

and all the stone-fruits like plums – to wilt suddenly; it is likely to infect and kill the blossom-bearing spurs and may even penetrate the branch. Although sulphur-containing sprays can help, the only sure

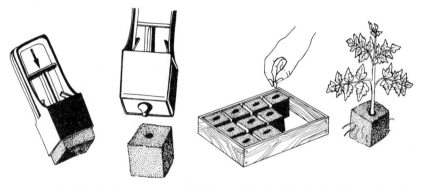

BLOCKING. *Left*, blocks of compost are made by filling a block-making device: *right*, seeds are then sown in the blocks placed in a box, and when roots appear are planted out

Blood Dried blood is a quick-acting plant food, containing 10–12% nitrogen, either to be applied to the soil and dug in, or to be used as a liquid manure mixed with water. Either way, it can be used on growing plants at around 1 oz. per gallon. Fresh blood is unpleasant to deal with but if a supply is available it can be applied to vacant ground and be well dug in. ⋄ FERTILIZER.

Bloom Apart from its frequent use as an equivalent of flower or blossom, bloom refers to the whitish or bluish powdery or waxy coating on certain leaves and fruits, easily removed by handling. Its purpose is probably as an insulator against strong sunlight, and to reduce water loss. ⋄ CUTICLE; WAX.

Blossom Fall ⋄ BUD STAGES.

Blossom Wilt A condition, caused by the attack of some closely related fungi, which causes flowers of top fruits – apples, pears

remedy is to cut out all affected spurs and shoots, and to spray with tar oil the following winter.

Blueing The process of making red or pink hydrangea flowers turn blue. Hydrangeas are very sensitive to the pH of the soil, and will only produce blue flowers on acid soil; on alkaline ones the flowers will be red, pink or mauve. It is sometimes possible to 'blue' them by applying certain chemicals. The best is aluminium sulphate used at around ¼ lb. per stem. Alum or sulphate of iron can also be tried, and some people use iron filings or masses of small iron nails; sequestered or chelated iron can also be used. ⋄ ACID; SEQUESTROL.

Board Fence ⋄ FENCES.

Boardwalk ⋄ PATHS.

Bog Garden Bog or marsh plants like water continually near their roots, but these should neither be continuously submerged nor be allowed to dry out. Artificial

23

bog gardens are not very easy to maintain since they usually need to be topped up with water in summer and partly drained in winter. Also, the plants will not thrive in stagnant water. Bog gardens can be created in a basin made of cement or plastic sheeting, but these must have outlets of some kind, preferably controllable. The basin is then filled with suitable soil, e.g. a mixture of good but rather heavy loam and peat, which is then kept moist. There are many very attractive plants suitable for bog gardens, so the trouble is well worth while.

Bole The main trunk of a tree below its point of branching.

Bolting The premature production of flowers in a vegetable. In hot, dry weather, if checked by lack of food or, in some cases, if sown at the wrong time, leafy vegetables – lettuces and Chinese cabbage are the usual culprits – may form no hearts at all or run up to flower soon after hearting, instead of remaining in a kitchen-worthy condition for several weeks as they should.

Bone Manures Animal bones contain phosphorus and nitrogen; a typical analysis is 20–25 per cent phosphorus acid and 1–5 per cent nitrogen. Calcium is also present. Whole bones decompose extremely slowly, but powdered bones provide a valuable source of these plant foods. Finely ground bonemeal or flour is quick-acting; coarser grades will be correspondingly slower to deliver their plant food content, and can be used as long-term feeds. A useful mixture for this purpose contains bonemeal and HOOF-AND-HORN meal in the proportion of roughly 2:1. Fine bonemeal can be used at 3–4 oz. per square yard, coarser grades at up to 8 oz. Bonemeal is sometimes used, at around 4 oz. per bushel, to replace superphosphate of lime in potting mixtures. Bones which have just been crushed rather than ground can be worked into planting sites for trees, vines and other long-term plants. Crushed bones are sometimes added to meat meal. ◊ FERTILIZER; MEAT GUANO.

Bonfire Originally a fire in which bones were burnt (a bone-fire), funeral pyre, or a fire in which witches or heretics were burned, this now refers to a fire made in the open air for any purpose. The gardener usually makes bonfires to burn garden rubbish, and fire has an important use in the destruction of woody prunings, weed seed-heads, and diseased plant material which might continue to spread the disease if placed on the compost heap. However, those who burn *all* their garden rubbish rather than composting it are to be pitied, if not censured, for they deprive themselves of an invaluable, free source of humus-rich material.

Bonfires can be made on the ground or in an incinerator; the latter are certainly easier to light and keep going unless large pieces of wood are being burned. Bonfires should always be made well away from wooden fences, sheds and greenhouses, and from valued plants which can be badly scorched by a fire even some distance away.

Although there may be local by-laws to prevent bonfires being lit before 6 p.m. (and in some British council estates fires may be entirely forbidden), there is in Britain no general rule of law controlling or forbidding bonfires, nor is a bonfire normally subject to the Clean Air Act unless it is exceptionally smoky. A normal, well-managed bonfire is very seldom considered a 'nuisance' in the legal sense, though a very smoky one may be, or one lit every day. Sensible gardeners will not light bonfires on windy days when smoke is likely to annoy neighbours, or if washing is hanging out in a neighbouring garden.

Boning Rod ◊ LEVELLING.

Bonsai A method of dwarfing trees or shrubs by special techniques. It was originally invented by the Chinese, who call it Penjing, perhaps as long as 2000 years ago, and is still practised and enjoyed by them today; later it was taken up by the Japanese who train enormous numbers of bonsai trees, so that we now tend to regard it as primarily a Japanese art. The first pictorial representations of Japanese bonsai appear in a scroll on the life of St Honen (A.D. 1133–1212), but there are references to the art in the records of the Kasuga Shrine which, though they date to 1309, mainly illustrate life in the Heian period (A.D. 794–1191), so bonsai may have existed in Japan in the ninth century.

Bonsai means literally 'planted in a small pot', and the Chinese and Japanese did and occasionally still do grow other plants in root-restricting pots; but today the art is almost entirely concerned with trees and shrubs, though bonsai chrysanthemums are sometimes seen.

The best bonsai are wild trees very carefully extracted from rock fissures or similar root-constricting habitats; however, most bonsai today are grown from seed or from seedlings dug up from nurseries or the wild, especially those which have already become distorted in some way.

Although bonsai *can* be grown in ordinary flower pots, the recognized type of container, better both for cultivation and appearance, is a wide, relatively shallow one, round, oval or oblong, glazed on the exterior, and slightly raised on little plinths at the corners (to discourage plants rooting through the drainage holes). Either a single plant or a group may be planted, and further effects are obtained from planting on top of small rocks and training the roots into the soil in the container. The Japanese recognize fifteen or more styles of bonsai based upon their growth patterns.

Basic growth restriction, and hence stunting of growth, is carried out by trimming the roots annually at first, later every three or four years, removing in particular strong-growing ones. Early each spring all unwanted growth buds are rubbed out, and during the growing season unwanted leaves and shoots are pinched or cut out. Training into the shape required is done either by pulling a growth into position with twine tied to the trunk, to other branches or to the container, or by twisting soft copper wire around the growths and bending them, by degrees, into the desired shapes. Ties or wire must be removed when growths have taken on the form desired.

Many bonsai trees look contorted, and indeed one of their fourteenth-century critics wrote, 'to find pleasure in curiously curved potted trees is to love deformity'. The Chinese seem always to have preferred the most contorted specimens. A good 'classical' bonsai should in fact be a miniature image of the species as a full-size, mature plant; however, modern nurserymen often choose the short cut of digging up a plant several years old, cramming it into a container and cutting it back to a low stump from which ugly new shoots arise. Such plants have no resemblance to properly grown bonsai.

Borax, Boron Borax is a salt combining sodium and boron; the latter is one of the essential plant foods, though required in very small quantities, and hence regarded as one of the trace elements. If a boron deficiency is suspected the rate of application is 2 oz. per 30 square yards. The deficiency causes a condition known as brown heart in beetroots, mangolds, swedes and turnips. In excess, boron is poisonous to plants. Borax is also used as an ant and cockroach killer, in the form of sodium or disodium tetraborate or in combination with equal parts of caster sugar; and as a long-persisting weedkiller. ◊ ANTS; COCKROACHES; TRACE ELEMENTS; WEED-KILLER.

Bordeaux Mixture A fungicidal mixture of copper sulphate and lime. ◊ COPPER; FUNGICIDES.

Border Originally, a border was simply a long oblong strip of cultivated ground alongside a wall or path. Today the word is much more loosely applied to any more or less oblong strip of ground, whether backed by a wall or hedge or cut in grass, which may be used for perennials (herbaceous borders), annuals, shrubs, bedding plants, or sometimes for utilitarian plants like vines in a greenhouse. In principle a border is differentiated from a bed, which is defined as a display feature cut into grass, or enclosed in very low hedges; however, confusion is caused by the so-called 'island border' in which herbaceous plants are grown in large irregular beds cut in grass. The main meaning of 'border' is still a long oblong strip, backed in some way, in which herbaceous plants are grown. A shrub border is any area in which shrubs are concentrated. ◊ COLOUR BORDER; HERBACEOUS BORDER; SHRUBBERY.

Border Fork ◊ FORKS.

Border Shears ◊ SHEARS.

Borers The U.S. term for larvae of moths, beetles, sawflies and sometimes bees which tunnel into plant stems. ◊ CATERPILLARS.

Borning Rod Also boning rod. ◊ LEVELLING.

Boron ◊ BORAX.

Boskage A mass of trees or shrubs; a grove or thicket. A generalized form of BOSKET.

Bosket A plantation or thicket of trees in a park or garden; the word derives from French *bosquet* and, presumably, Italian *bosco*. In the large formal garden a bosket might form an immediate background to a parterre, or be placed at the end of an alley. Within a bosket there might be walks and enclosures in which statuary, waterworks and the like are placed. Boskets exist in French gardens like Versailles, but all British examples seem to have been destroyed. In Malta there is a valley called Buskett which holds the only large concentration of trees on the island. Bosket is derived from the same root as the now obsolete 'bosk', meaning a bush or thicket, and the occasionally used, poetic 'bosky'. ◊ ALLEY; PARTERRE.

Botanic Garden A garden designed to aid in the study of plants, often attached to a university, or laid out by a specialist plant society. Apart from often containing collections of specific groups of plants, including trees, they usually include 'order beds' in which a selection of plants is set out in their natural orders or families. Botanic gardens are frequently associated with a herbarium where pressed plant specimens can be studied. ◊ HERBARIUM; PHYSIC GARDEN.

Botany Derived from the Greek word meaning a herb, this is the branch of science dealing with plant life. The scientific study of plants falls into several sections: morphology considers their external form; physiology is concerned with the ways in which plants live and function; histology deals with internal tissues; teratology is the study of growth abnormalities; and taxonomy is concerned with the identification and classification of plants. The related science of ecology considers plants in their natural surroundings including the animal life naturally associated with them.

Botrytis ◊ GREY MOULD.

Bottle Garden A modern version of the Wardian Case, in which small, slow-growing plants, usually those classed as house plants, are grown in bottles, carboys or other glass containers. Ideally, these have a relatively small opening so that a humid atmosphere is readily maintained within. If the opening is too small to admit the hand, as in a standard carboy, tools such as a spoon tied to a cane for planting, and a cotton-reel pushed onto a cane to firm down soil, are used. Because the atmosphere stays humid even if the bottle remains unstopped, the soil needs very little watering. ◊ HOUSE PLANT; WARDIAN CASE.

Bottle Graft A form of inarching, or grafting by approach, in which the scion is cut from its parent and placed in a bottle of water until union is complete with the stock, grown in soil or a pot, to which it is grafted. ◊ INARCHING; SCION.

Bottom Heat Warmth applied from below, especially for a frame or propagator. The oldest method is to rest a frame on a bed of fermenting manure and/or tan bark; modern methods use either electric heating cables laid under the soil in a frame, or a flat metal or plastic plate in which a heating element is embedded. It is possible to provide bottom heat in a greenhouse warmed by hot water pipes by making a bed of soil enclosing a section of pipe. ◊ FRAME; HOTBED; PIT.

Bottoming Another word for crocking of pots. ◊ CROCKS.

Bottom Worked ◊ WORKED.

Boulingrin ◊ BOWLING GREEN.

Bourse ◊ KNOB.

Bower Originally meaning nothing more than a dwelling, bower in gardening refers to any shady recess and is often considered the same as an arbour; but older writers reserved the term for long arched galleries of climbing plants grown on a wooden framework. The word has also referred to 'fancy rustic cottages' (*Oxford Dictionary*). ◊ ARBOUR.

Bowl Garden A miniature garden made in a shallow bowl for indoor decoration. Various plants can be used, including alpines; but cacti and other succulents are most favoured since they mostly grow very slowly and many of them are not affected too quickly by lack of adequate light. However, it must be emphasized that, except in particularly well-lit positions, bowl gardens need renewing periodically as the plants grow spindly and out of character. Because bowls are usually glazed and have no drainage holes, it is essential to place a layer of drainage material up to half the depth of the bowl, and to water sparingly – another reason why succulents are the most satisfactory plants. Bowl gardens are sometimes equipped with miniature Japanese buildings, bridges, etc., of painted clay and a small piece of mirror to represent water. ◊ MINIATURE GARDENS.

Bowling Green A lawn created specially for the game of bowls, which was first recorded in the early Middle Ages. There were originally three types of bowling green. Of these the alley, a narrow, level green, is not apparently used today, though some ancient examples are still to be seen in Britain. In the crown green or 'open ground of advantage' there is an 8″–10″ fall from centre to boundaries; such greens are supposed to be 45 yards square but are more usually 40 × 45 yards, and are today restricted to Yorkshire and Lancashire. The standard 'Rink Game' is played on a flat green which should by regulation be not more than 44 yards square.

Bowling greens today are made of the finest turf on very well-drained plots, and need high standards of maintenance. They are mostly a feature of public rather than private gardens.

The French word *boulingrin*, adapted from 'bowling green', refers to a sunken grass area in the centre of a bosket or woody dell, itself often centred with a fountain, and has nothing to do with a game. The French game of *boules* is not played on grass but on any piece of more or less flat ground.

Bract A modified leaf at the base of a flower stalk or the stem of a flower cluster, or forming part of the flower head itself, as in composite plants. Bracts often resemble ordinary leaves but may be large and brightly coloured on the one hand, or reduced to small scales on the other. When brightly coloured, they tend to be grouped

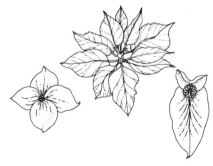

BRACT. *Left*, cornus; *centre*, poinsettia; *right*, davidia

27

around clusters of tiny flowers lacking petals as in the poinsettia (*Euphorbia pulcherrima*), many dogwoods (*Cornus*) and the pocket-handkerchief tree (*Davidia*). The showy part of an arum lily is technically a bract, while in the globe artichoke the edible parts are the fleshy bases of the involucral bracts. ◊ AROID; COMPOSITE; INVOLUCRE; NUT.

Braird First used in 1450, meaning the first shoots of grass, corn, etc., to appear; and as a verb, to sprout. Sometimes used today by turf specialists.

Bramble Scythe ◊ SCYTHE.

Brand First used in 1639, and sometimes seen in old gardening books, to refer to certain fungus diseases which gave affected plants a burnt or scorched appearance, notably some rust diseases. Even today, one specific disease of rose stems is known as brand canker. ◊ RUST.

Brassica The botanical genus which includes the cruciferous vegetables: cabbages, cauliflowers, broccoli, brussels sprouts, kales, turnips and swedes, often spoken of in gardening books as brassicas, and needing similar soil conditions. ◊ ACID; CRUCIFER; ROTATION.

Break (1) A gardener's word for growth made from an axillary bud – a branch or fork. The term is especially used by chrysanthemum and carnation growers, who pinch out the tips of their plants at an early stage in order to induce them to 'break', i.e. to produce side-shoots which they might otherwise not do. If a rooted chrysanthemum cutting is left to its own devices it will usually, after a time, produce an abortive bud at the top of the stem. This prevents further lengthening of the stem and forces it to produce side-shoots. Hence this abortive bud is often known as the break bud. When a variety produces side growths without pinching out the growing tip, these are called natural breaks. ◊ AXIL; BUD; PINCHING.

(2) In a more general sense 'breaking' is

commonly used to describe opening buds. ◊ BUD STAGES.

(3) The word break is also sometimes used to denote a MUTATION, or 'sport'.

For 'broken' tulips, ◊ BROKEN.

Breaking ◊ BUD STAGES.

Breast Plough An ancient type of light plough mounted at the end of a long pole or squared length of wood, with a crosspiece at the other end. The latter was held by the operator at hip height so that he could drive the blade through the soil. In some primitive examples the pole was held by the operator at arm's length while he pushed his hips against its end which was heavily padded into a roll shape; in other versions the wife pushed at the same time onto a short vertical rod near the plough blade so as to keep it firmly in the soil. Such ploughs with a cross-piece were in use in Britain for paring turf and for cultivating allotments and gardens into the 1930s. ◊ CULTIVATOR.

Breastwood Shoots which grow forwards from vertically trained fruit trees like espaliers or wall shrubs, and are thus difficult to train. Breastwood must normally be removed from fruit trees when summer pruning, and from ornamentals whenever convenient. ◊ ESPALIER; SUMMER PRUNING.

Breeder Apart from its basic meaning of a person who hybridizes plants or animals, a breeder is a type of tulip. ◊ BROKEN.

Breeding ◊ PLANT BREEDING.

Bridge A structure carrying a path or road over a water-course, a gorge or gully, or a road. Apart from their functional uses, bridges are important aesthetic features of many gardens, from landscapes to Japanese. Bridges can be of stone, timber, or reinforced concrete; in most small gardens central supports may not be needed as the bridge rests on the two banks.

Bridge Grafting A form of grafting designed to overcome the total girdling of a tree, by animals eating the bark, by canker disease or by the careless use of implements, which will almost always kill the tree in time, if not dealt with. It is also used to bridge incompatible graft unions which are liable to break cleanly a few years after being made. The method involves the use of relatively thin 'bridges' prepared as if they were scions but at both ends, making comparable cuts on the damaged tree to which the bridges are fixed with small nails. The commonest method used is similar to rind grafting. The bridges or scions are best obtained as fairly thin dormant shoots

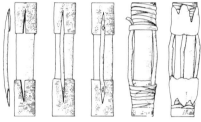

BRIDGE GRAFTING

from the upper part of the damaged tree. If the work needs to be done in summer, shoots of the previous season's growth can be used; their leaves should be removed and the operation carried out as soon as possible after cutting them.

Where the damaged trunk is around 1″ in diameter a single bridge will suffice, but larger trunks need more, roughly one bridge for every inch of diameter. Rough edges of bark should be trimmed before the bridging operation and, if girdling is due to canker, all infected tissue, which will be discoloured, must be pared away first. All cut surfaces should be well sealed with grafting wax so that no water can enter; the repaired tree should be protected against further animal damage and against rubbing or bumping by hoses and tools.

◊ GRAFTING; GRAFTING WAX; IN-COMPATIBLE (2); RIND GRAFTING; TREE GUARDS.

Brindille A specialist fruit-grower's term of French origin for a thin shoot intermediate between the short dard and a fully-developed shoot which will not produce flower buds in its first year. ◊ DARD.

Bristly Covered with stiff, dense hairs; equivalent to hispid, sometimes found as a specific name, e.g. *hispidus*. ◊ HAIRY.

Broadcasting Scattering seeds all over the soil rather than sowing in the usual straight rows or drills. It is mainly used when sowing lawns, sometimes for annual flowers, and occasionally when sowing plants such as brassicas for later transplanting. To sow evenly by this method needs practice. After broadcasting seed it should be covered either by raking it into the surface or by covering it with a thin layer of fine soil. ◊ DRILL; SEED SOWING.

Broad-leaved Applied to trees and shrubs with broad, flat leaves as opposed to the needle-like ones of conifers; usually to imply that such plants are deciduous with a winter resting season. However, there are evergreen broad-leaved trees and shrubs such as camellias, laurels and evergreen oaks. ◊ CONIFER; DECIDUOUS; EVER-GREEN.

Broken Applied by gardeners primarily to kinds of tulip in which an overall flower colour is broken into elaborate patterns or 'feathering' in a different shade. It was a

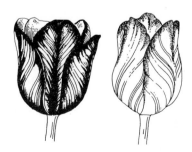

BROKEN. *Left*, a 'flamed' and, *right*, a 'feathered' tulip

29

word first used by tulip fanciers in the seventeenth century who only prized the broken varieties, retaining plain-coloured varieties as potential 'breeders'. Fanciers' tulips might be feathered, in which the marking was essentially fine and symmetrical on each petal; flaked in streaks or bands of different colour; or flamed when, in addition to feathering, there was a band of solid colour up the centre of the petal. Today, these tulips are grouped together as Rembrandt varieties, and there is still a class called Breeders, of the same external outline. In tulips, breaking is caused by a virus disease which does not, however, weaken the plants.

Feathering is sometimes entirely natural, as in certain crocus species. The word 'flaked' is mostly applied to carnations, where show classes used to exist for flakes, though few now exist. A true flake had streaks or bands of colour on a white ground. Incidentally, the word 'feather' in horticulture refers to a lateral growth on a one-year (maiden) tree.

◇ BIZARRE; MAIDEN; VIRUS DISEASES.

Bromeliad A term for any member of the large family *Bromeliaceae*, many of which are popular houseplants. Bromeliads are almost always rosette plants, usually with long, narrow, stiff leaves which overlap at the base to form a tube or cup. Many grow naturally as epiphytes, and those cultivated often have showy flower-heads of numerous small, 6-parted blooms. ◇ EPIPHYTE.

Brown Rot A fungus disease of many fruits (mainly apples, cherries, pears and plums), in which the fruit, almost always infected via damage caused by insect attack or bruising, rapidly becomes brown and decayed, later showing concentric rings of white to buff-coloured pustules, and finally becoming dry and mummified. The fruit-bearing spurs may also be affected. Decaying and especially mummified fruits should be destroyed since the disease spreads from these, and dead or dying spurs should also be cut off and burned.

Various fungicidal sprays can lessen the risk of infection. ◇ FUNGICIDES.

Brush Cutter An American tool with a short, stout, narrow-oblong blade at a slight angle to a long handle, used with a swinging movement to sever brushwood and weeds at ground level.

Brushing Hook, Brushing Slasher ◇ BILL-HOOK; SLASHER.

Brushwood Killer ◇ WEEDKILLER.

Brutting The fracturing of one-year fruit-tree shoots at about half their length, so that the ends remain still attached to the tree. This is sometimes done to prevent late summer growth after summer pruning in a wet season, and is a typical feature of hazel-

BRUTTING

nut cultivation, but is also a suitable method for wall-trained apples and pears, and ornamental flowering shrubs like chaenomeles. Brutted shoots are cut back to a few buds below the fracture in the autumn.

Bryophytes Primitive plants including LIVERWORTS and MOSSES.

Bubbler A device of fairly recent invention in which water is forced up through a hole in a millstone, a shaped concrete slab or a large boulder to run down over its surface; or a very small water jet emerging between cobblestones. Bubblers are normally created as self-contained devices with a submerged pump in a waterproof base, so that the water is recycled. ▷ FOUNTAIN.

Bud A condensed shoot containing embryo leaves, flowers or flower clusters, typically protected by overlapping scales. A study of buds is often very useful to the gardener, who can judge from them the progress of growth, whether any pruning is necessary and, if so, how and when to do it. The fruit grower in particular must learn the difference between growth or wood buds and so-called fruit buds which are first of all flower buds. Growth buds can sometimes develop into fruit buds. The peach sometimes has triple buds, consisting of two fruit buds and one growth bud.

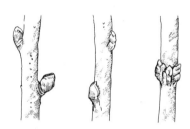

BUD. *Left*, fruit buds; *centre*, growth buds; *right*, a triple bud

A terminal bud is one at the tip of a shoot, and an axillary bud one found in the axil of a leaf. A break bud is the first, normally abortive bud on a chrysanthemum, around which new shoots arise; crown buds are viable buds also surrounded by growth points capable of growing into branches.

In the normal course of events, many buds do not develop, but if the upper part of a trunk or stem is destroyed these latent or dormant buds will become active and produce growth.
▷ AXIL; BREAK; BUD STAGES; EYE; LATENT; NICKING; PRUNING; TURION.

Bud Burst ▷ BUD STAGES.

Bud Cutting ▷ LEAF BUD CUTTING.

Budding A type of grafting widely used to propagate all kinds of fruit trees and roses. The commonest kind is shield budding,

BUDDING. Shield-budding a rose

usually done in summer when the plant is in full growth: plump axillary buds are cut from the middle portion of firm young shoots of the scion variety in the centre of a long narrow 'shield' of bark; a T-shaped cut is made in the bark of the stock, and into this the bud is pushed; the graft is then bound with raffia and may be coated with grafting wax. In patch budding, usually reserved for walnuts, a patch of bark about $\frac{1}{2}''$ square containing the bud is cut from the scion variety and an identically sized patch is cut in the bark of the stock. The bud is pushed into place and tied securely.
▷ AXIL; GRAFTING; SCION; STOCK; SUCKER.

Budding Knife A knife designed for the operation of budding. The blade usually

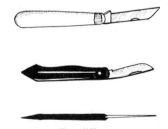

BUDDING KNIFE. Two different types

curves back at its end so that the tip meets the upper edge, but some users prefer a knife with a sharply angled point at the end of the cutting edge. The handle is flat in section and is further flattened at its rounded end so that it can be used to lift up the bark when the necessary incisions have been made. One version has a thin rounded protuberance on the upper edge near the point for the same purpose. One very modern version has a wedge-shaped blade sharpened at its wider end; it is used by pushing into the bark like a chisel rather than with a slicing action. Budding knives usually have a blade under 2″ long and a handle of up to 4″. ♢ BUDDING.

Bud Disease Applied to a condition in which the flower stem just behind the bud shrivels and collapses. Though occasionally caused by chewing insects like weevils or caterpillars, or by a fungus attack, it seems to be usually the result of weak growth or inadequate water at the root. Sun scorch on dew-wetted stems is also sometimes blamed. Peonies and roses are the usual sufferers but many other kinds of plant may be affected in this way.

Bud Dropping Some plants are particularly prone to dropping flower buds before they develop, among them tuberous begonias, lupins and sweet peas and, among vegetables, runner beans and tomatoes. This is due entirely to external conditions, mainly to abnormally low night temperatures, and there is little to be done for outdoor plants except to wait for better conditions; however, sodden soil may contribute, while under glass extra heat at night can be given and draughts must be avoided.

Bud Stages With all kinds of fruit the exact stage that the flower buds have reached is important in timing insecticidal and fungicidal sprays. These timings cannot depend on the calendar since seasons vary so much. Manufacturers give recommendations for applying sprays according to these stages.

Bud stages vary according to the fruit concerned. The more important ones are as follows:

TOP FRUITS

Apple and Pear

Dormant Buds not visibly growing in any way.

Swelling Bud enlarges, bud scales begin to separate.

Breaking or Green tip Bud scales open enough to show the tips of the green leaves.

Bud burst The green leaf tips start to open out.

Mouse ear Leaves fully defined and the green blossom buds within can just be seen.

Green bud or green cluster The clustered blossom buds are clearly seen; outer scales fall.

Pink bud (in apples), *White bud* (in pears) Blossom buds are expanded but not open, and the petal colour can be seen.

Full blossom 80–90 per cent of the flowers are fully open.

Blossom or petal fall 80–90 per cent of the petals have fallen.

Fruitlet The small fruits are clearly visible as they start to swell.

BUD STAGES. Bud stages of apples *from left to right*: dormant; bud burst; green bud; pink bud; petal fall; fruitlet

Cherry As for apple and pear except for:

White bud The unopened blossom buds are by now at the end of long stalks.

Plum As for apple and pear except for:

Cot split After blossom fall, the yellow calyx segments split off the tiny green fruitlets and fall.

BUSH AND CANE FRUITS

Black Currant

Dormant Buds appear inactive.
Breaking Green tips show on opening buds.
Burst Leaves start to unfold.
Grape Leaves now about 1″ across; unopened green flower buds appear like miniature bunches of grapes.

Gooseberry

Dormant Buds appear inactive.
Breaking Green tips show on opening buds.
Early flower Flower buds are just visible.
Fruit set The fruitlets below the open flowers are clearly visible.
Fruit swelling Fruitlets enlarging rapidly. Three weeks after fruit set.

Raspberry

Dormant Buds appear inactive.
Burst Leaves start to unfold.
Green bud Leaves open and green flower buds can be seen.
Fruitlet The green fruits are clearly starting to swell.

Bug Used loosely to refer to any kind of insect. Specifically, a bug belongs to the order Heteroptera in which the overlapping wings are folded over the back when the insect is at rest, alongside a characteristic three-cornered 'shield' which gives larger examples the name shieldbugs. Bugs vary greatly in size and, like their relatives the aphids or plant lice, and scale insects, are all equipped with piercing and sucking mouthparts. Many are serious plant pests, including capsid bugs, chinch bug, lacebug and tarnished plant bug. Some, however, like the black-kneed capsid, are predators on other insects. ⬦ PEST; PREDATORS.

Bulb A storage organ, usually but not always growing underground, resembling a bud structure, with fleshy scales, which are swollen, modified leaf bases, in which food materials are stored during a resting period. In the centre of the bulb there is an embryo shoot, and in mature specimens a complete embryo flower. In many bulbs, e.g. narcissus, tulip and onion, the leaf bases are tightly packed and not readily separated, and the bulb is typically enclosed in a papery tunic which may be green in above-ground bulbs but is otherwise brown, black or translucent. In those bulbs where the leaf bases are scale-like, e.g. lilies, the scales can be detached readily, and the bulb has no tunic.

BULB. *Left*, tulip bulb in section with embryo flower in centre; *right*, lily

Tunic-covered bulbs often increase themselves by offsets or bulblets which begin life within the leaf bases and finally emerge on their own; others split up into separate bulbs. Scale-forming bulbs may produce offsets or will grow from separated scales if these are pressed into moist peat, sand or a similar medium. A few bulbs grow new individuals at the ends of stolons. Others can reproduce from bulbils, miniature bulbs formed on the flower stems.

The word 'bulb', and its adjective 'bulbous', are often loosely applied for convenience as a portmanteau term to any kind of plant with a specialized fleshy stem or rootstock, including CORMS, RHIZOMES and TUBERS.

⬦ BULBIL; STOLON; TUNIC.

Bulb Fibre A growing medium for bulbs grown for indoor decoration in ornamental containers without drainage holes. In such conditions ordinary soil, or soil-based potting mixtures, would become water-logged and 'sour', so a special peat-based mixture is used instead. The original formula contains 6 parts peat, 2 parts crushed oyster shell, and 1 part crushed charcoal. If oyster shell is not available it can be replaced with vermiculite or perlite. In modern practice peat-based potting composts work equally well, especially if mixed with about one-eighth crushed charcoal, and have the advantage of giving some nourishment to the bulbs which bulb fibre does not. In principle, bulbs grown for indoor decoration in this way should never be grown for the same purpose a second year; if planted in the garden in spring they will usually flower again after a year or two. ◊ CHARCOAL; COMPOSTS, SEED AND POTTING; PERLITE; VERMICULITE.

Bulb Flies Various kinds of fly lay their eggs in or near narcissus and onion bulbs, the resultant grub-like larvae feeding in the centre of the bulbs and causing them to collapse and decay. The initial egg-laying can be prevented by dusting around the bulbs with a suitable insecticide at regular intervals; with narcissi, regular hoeing or raking to fill soil crevices attractive to the flies may prevent attack. Affected bulbs are usually best burned, but in the early stages narcissus bulbs can be saved by hot water treatment, or by soaking for three hours in an insecticidal solution. ◊ HOT-WATER TREATMENT; ROOT FLIES; STERILIZATION.

Bulb Frame Many bulbs from climates in which there is a long dry season need to be kept entirely dry during their resting period. To ensure this, specialist growers grow these bulbs under tall all-glass, metal-edged frames which are kept entirely closed and unwatered during the summer. ◊ FRAME.

Bulbil, Bulblet A miniature bulb produced by certain bulbous plants for reproductive

purposes, often on the stems, as in lilies, and sometimes in the flower head, where – as in certain alliums – the bulbils can replace flowers. The word bulbil is applied

BULBIL (on lily stem)

loosely to miniature tubers found on the stem of some begonias, or leafy plantlets with swollen bases as in some ferns, both being capable of developing into mature plants as with genuine bulbils. The specific name *bulbiferum* is sometimes found referring to such plants. A number of plants, e.g. oxalis, produce bulbils in association with a fleshy root. Small bulbs appearing round a parent bulb are usually referred to as bulblets. ◊ BULB.

Bulb Mite ◊ MITES.

Bulb Planter A tool whose business end consists of an open cylinder, sometimes very slightly tapered, which, when forced into the soil then withdrawn, removes a plug of soil. The bulb is then placed in the hole and the soil plug replaced above it. Bulb planters may have a short handle immediately above the cylinder, or a long vertical one equipped with a cross-piece near the base so that foot-power can be applied to speed work when many bulbs are involved. Some versions are also equipped with a lever to eject the soil plug without difficulty.

The present-day bulb planter (sometimes called a turf plugger in the U.S.) is a direct descendant of the sixteenth-century transplanter, and tools similar to the modern ones were widely used in the nineteenth century for transplanting growing plants, a task now usually fulfilled by the trowel. ⟡ POTATO PLANTER; TRANS-PLANTER; TROWEL.

Bulb-scale Mite ⟡ MITES.

Bulk Measures ⟡ WEIGHTS AND MEAS-URES (p. viii).

Bulky Applied to organic manures which occupy a large amount of space relative to the food materials they contain, and used not only to provide plant food but to increase the humus content of the soil and thus improve its texture. Farmyard manure is the typical example, containing around 75 per cent water. ⟡ MANURE.

Bullate A botanical term applied to leaves in which the main surface rises above the leaves, giving a blistered, puckered or inflated appearance. ⟡ LEAF.

Bunch Generally refers to a collection of flowers as bought from the florist, or fruits in a natural cluster. The term sometimes appears in flower show schedules, where it should be qualified (when referring to flowers) to stipulate the number of stems to be staged in a vase, or the number of small vegetables, e.g. spring onions, which are tied together round their stem or leaves.

Burgundy Mixture ⟡ WASHING SODA.

Burlap ⟡ HESSIAN.

Burst ⟡ BUD STAGES.

Bush An old word meaning a single shrub, a thicket, low undergrowth not necessarily of a woody nature, or low woodland generally. One of its roots etymologically is the same as that from which bosket is derived. Gardeners usually restrict their use of this word to small shrubs, including soft fruits like gooseberries and currants which are often called 'bush fruits'. However, confusingly enough, to the fruit grower a bush tree is one allowed to branch from the base from a very short trunk, and usually pruned on the delayed open-centre method, in contrast to half- or full-standards with distinct trunks. A bush tomato grows numerous branches ending

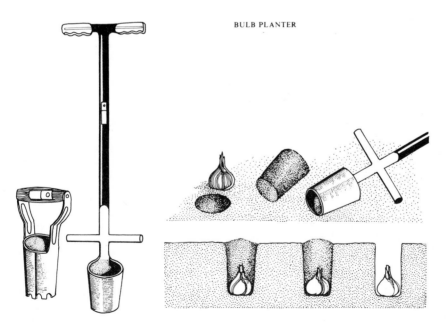

BULB PLANTER

35

in flower trusses rather than a single main stem. ◊ BOSKET; DELAYED OPEN-CENTRE; DETERMINATE; SHRUB; STANDARD.

Bushel ◊ WEIGHTS AND MEASURES (p. x).

BUTTERFLY (Painted Lady)

Butterflies Insects closely related to moths, usually distinguishable because when at rest the wings are folded together vertically, not held horizontally, and the antennae are clubbed at the end; this does not occur in most moths, the antennae of which are feathery. Butterflies generally fly by day. Adult butterflies are harmless, apart from laying eggs, but all have a caterpillar stage before pupating and final metamorphosis into adult insect, and some of these caterpillars are harmful pests. ◊ CATERPILLARS.

Buttoning Applied to cauliflowers when the white 'curd' begins to open into flowers while still quite small; a condition usually due to some check to growth, e.g. dryness.

Butyl-rubber A strong flexible sheeting used to line pools. ◊ POOL LINER.

C

Cactus (1) Any member of the family *Cactaceae*. The word is very often wrongly used to mean any plant with fleshy leaves or stems (correctly referred to as succulents). All cacti (plural) except a few shrubby kinds are succulents, but not all succulents are cacti. The shrubby cacti, which are primitive members of the family, have orthodox leaves. Leaves also appear in a few other species, but in general cacti are leafless, the stem having taken on the functions of leaves. In two groups, of which the Christmas cactus and prickly pears are examples, the stems appear leaf-like, but most cacti are globular or cylindrical. Most bear spines which, like the flowers, and leaves if produced, spring from cushion-like growths called areoles, characteristic of the family. ♢ AREOLE; SPINE; SUCCULENT.

(2) The word cactus is also applied to a group of dahlias having long rolled-up petals so that the whole flower has a spiky appearance.

Caducous A botanical term referring to an organ which falls off at an early stage.

Calcareous Applied to alkaline soils containing chalk or limestone, and to rocks mainly composed of these materials.

Calcicole A plant which enjoys an alkaline or limy soil. Also rendered calciphile (i.e. chalk-loving); the adjectives calcicolous or calciphilous are sometimes used. ♢ ALKALINE; pH.

Calcifuge The opposite of calcicole, and therefore a plant which will not tolerate alkaline soils, lime or chalk, or even water containing these substances; these are often called lime-haters. ♢ ACID; pH.

Calcium A chemical element which is, in small quantities, an essential plant food, except for lime-hating plants. Usually provided by adding lime to the soil. ♢ LIME.

Calcium cyanamide A chemical with both fertilizing and weedkilling properties, often mentioned in older books but now apparently unobtainable.

Calcium sulphate ♢ GYPSUM.

Callus A growth of corky tissue which forms naturally over any wound made in a plant, emanating from the layer of tissue immediately under the bark (the cambium). If a tree branch is cut off, the callus will gradually cover the wound and new bark eventually forms over it, or at least round the margins of the cut. A wound healed in this way is sometimes said to be occluded.

In a similar way a callus is formed at the base of cuttings, and it is partly from the callus that new roots are produced; they may also be formed from the cells immediately above the callus. Paradoxically, the callus can sometimes prevent root

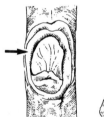

CALLUS. *Left*, around tree wound; *right*, at base of cutting

formation; camellia cuttings are an example: they can remain healthy but without making any growth for years. In such cases, the callus has to be scraped off, after which the cutting should be dipped in hormone rooting powder and repotted. In grafts the cut surfaces of stock and scion both produce callus tissues which eventually join and seal the union. Callus will form more quickly and evenly on a clean, tidy wound, and this should be borne in mind when pruning and taking cuttings.

◊ CAMBIUM; CUTTING; GRAFTING; HORMONES; SCION; SUCKER.

Calomel The common name for mercurous chloride, a poisonous chemical used for preventing club root disease of brassicas, white rot of onions, and several fungus diseases of turf. As from 1981, EEC regulations forbid its recommendation against cabbage and other root flies in the UK. It is usually obtained and applied as a 4 per cent dust, but it is also effective if made into a paste with water into which the roots of seedlings are dipped before they are planted. ◊ GARDEN CHEMICALS.

Calyx A flower is composed of much-modified leaves, and the outer series of these is known as the calyx (plural: calyces), each separate lobe or segment being called a sepal. Sometimes the sepals and petals are very similar, as in cacti, water lilies, true lilies and tulips, but usually they are different, the sepals often having, in the bud stage, a protective function to the inner parts of the flower. The sepals may be joined into a tube or cup, or may be separate. Commonly the calyx is small and green, but in some cases, e.g. anemones and clematis where there are often no petals at all, the calyx may be coloured and decorative. Other examples of decorative calyx include the winter aconite (eranthis) and the shell flower (molucella). ◊ FLOWER; PAPPUS; PERIANTH; SEPAL.

Cambium A continuous cylindrical sheet of cells within the stems and roots of dicotyledonous plants and conifers, which is responsible for increase in girth, constantly producing new cells outside and inside. In woody plants the cambium is a layer one cell thick near the outside of the stem; it is sandwiched between the thin

outer ring of phloem and the central xylem. In herbaceous plants it is the layer below the outer skin of the stem, which is usually readily peeled off. The existence of the cambium is important to gardeners. With cuttings, it is the cambium that produces the protective callus from which roots are formed; or, with root cuttings, new shoots. In grafting and budding, the cambium is the only point at which new cell growth to unite stock and scion can take place, and thus the cambial layers of each should touch at as many points as possible. If the cambium is severed all round, the tree so treated will die. ◊ BARK; CALLUS; CUTTING; GRAFTING; PHLOEM; RING-BARKING; RINGING; VASCULAR SYSTEM; XYLEM.

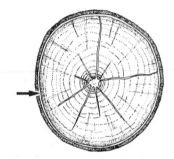

CAMBIUM. Layer (exaggerated) in tree trunk section

Camellia House When camellias were first introduced to Britain early in the nineteenth century they were considered tender, and special greenhouses were often erected to house collections. These camellia houses differed from other greenhouses only in shape: they were often much wider, being square or broadly rectangular.

Campanulate A botanical term meaning 'bell-shaped', and so applied to flowers of this form. The harebell or bellflower family, *Campanulaceae*, is so called because many of the species have flowers of this form, especially in the genus *Campanula*.

Canal In gardening design a canal is a long, narrow, straight stretch of water.

Canals were a feature of formal gardens, both western and Mughal, and are often associated with fountains. ◊ WATER GAR-DEN.

Cane Fruits The group of fruiting plants which make long, cane-like, usually prickly stems, including blackberry, loganberry, raspberry and the less well known boysenberry and Japanese wineberry, all of which belong to the genus *Rubus*. In general terms, it is best with these plants each year to cut out old canes (stems) which have fruited, and allow new young canes to replace them.

Canescent A botanical term meaning covered with dense, short, whitish hairs. ◊ HAIRY.

Canker An overall term, sometimes also called necrosis, for a number of distinct diseases, caused by both fungi and bacteria, which make the bark or skin of plants split, resulting in decay; the wound usually becomes sunken but may be surrounded by unnatural growth of the plant tissue. If a canker wound spreads right round a shoot or branch, this will cause the upper parts to die. Cankers on fruit trees can often be eradicated by cutting them out cleanly if they are caught early enough, and there are proprietary canker remedies available for these, e.g. cresylic acid. On roses the affected shoots are best cut off below the point of attack. There is also a canker disease which attacks tomatoes near the base of the stem; in this case the affected plants must be removed and burnt. Canker of parsnips is apparently not an infectious disease but often occurs on heavily manured ground. ◊ CRESYLIC ACID.

Canterbury Hoe ◊ HOE.

Capillary Attraction Describes the force that makes a liquid rise in any very fine tube or up a wick as in an oil lamp. Moisture will also rise by capillary attraction in the small spaces between close-packed particles, as in soil. ◊ CAPILLARY WATER-ING.

Capillary Bench ◊ CAPILLARY WATER-ING.

Capillary Watering It is possible to water plants by placing a wick well into the drainage hole of a pot, spreading its strands so they are in contact with the potting mixture, and letting the other end hang in water below; or by using a wick to convey water from a reservoir to the soil at the top of the pot. The water movement in these occurs by CAPILLARY ATTRACTION. A modern method using this force is to stand pots on a bed of sand or peat kept constantly moist (a capillary bench) or on a kind of felt matting specially formulated for the purpose, one end of which dips into a water reservoir (this last is specially useful for indoor plants). The potting mixture in the pots must be in the closest possible contact with the moist layer below, which means not using drainage crocks, and that thin plastic pots work much better than thick clay pots – though with the latter the method can be guaranteed by using a wick in the pot drainage holes. This method suits a wide range of plants, which draw up only the amount of moisture they need, but is progressively less effective with pots of over 6″ diameter. Various devices can be obtained to keep a peat or sand bed constantly moist, the simplest being to invert a narrow-necked jar of water in a shallow trough connected to the layer, or placing trickle irrigation tubes connected to the water mains directly onto the layer. ◊ POT; SELF-WATERING; TRICKLE IRRIGATION.

Capitate Literally, having a head; botanically this refers to inflorescences of many florets in a head or capitulum, as in composites. ◊ COMPOSITE; INFLORESCENCE.

Capitulum A little head: in botany, a tight inflorescence of sessile (stalkless) flowers. ◊ INFLORESCENCE.

Capping (1) The hard crust which may form on a soil surface in dry conditions.
(2) A layer of soil, or of plastic sheeting, placed over a COMPOST HEAP.

Capsid Bugs Close relations of the aphids, these include many harmful sap-sucking insects, though a few are useful predators on other pests. Their feeding deforms young shoots, leaves, fruits and flower buds; when the latter are attacked they may not open, or the flowers may fail to develop properly, as often happens on chrysanthemums. Capsid attack on fruits like apples results in corky scab-like patches. Such damage can be a considerable puzzle to gardeners because they can find no insects associated with it, and the reason for this is that the capsids are active insects which leap away or drop to the ground when disturbed. While contact insecticides can be used, best control will follow the use of systemics, or of fumigation under glass. ◊ FUMIGATION; PREDATORS; SYSTEMIC.

Capsule A dry (as against a pulpy) fruit which splits or opens up to discharge its seeds, and consists of several carpels joined together. Foxglove and iris have capsules which split open; in poppies a row of apertures is formed to disperse the seed. Special kinds of capsule include the follicle, found in peonies and monkshoods (aconitum), and the pod, as in peas. ◊ CARPEL; FOLLICLE; POD.

CAPSULE. *Left*, poppy; *right, Iris foetidissima*

Carbon Dioxide A gas, abbreviated as CO_2, occurring in the atmosphere at 3 parts in 10,000 of air, vital to plants in photosynthesis and providing their only source of carbon, an element essential in all the chemical processes in a plant which result in products including sugars, starches, cellulose and proteins. Despite its low natural concentration, the amount available to plants is normally adequate. However, for intensive cultivation and for extra speed of growth, as in greenhouse growing of lettuces, an extra supply of carbon dioxide is sometimes supplied, either by releasing the compressed gas or by burning propane gas which releases it. ◊ PHOTOSYNTHESIS.

Carnivorous Plants Several plants from different families have developed the ability to trap insects. All grow in nitrogen-deficient habitats, usually bogs, or actually in water, and insects help them to balance their diets. They include the passive traps of pitcher plants in which insects fall into a digestive liquid; the 'lobster-pot' mechanism of the water-living bladderworts; the sticky enfolding tentacles of sundews; the sticky 'fly-paper' leaves of butterworts; and the amazing quick-shutting trap of the Venus fly-trap, composed of two leaf lobes with interlocking bristles and set off by trigger hairs.

Carnivorous plants usually need specialized growing conditions including wet, acid soil or moss to grow in, high humidity and good light.

Carpel One female unit in a flower, consisting of ovary, style and stigma. Carpels can be numerous in one flower, either distinct as in buttercups or united as in irises; or there may be only one to a flower, as in the genus *Prunus* (cherries, etc.). ◊ FLOWER; OVARY; PISTIL; STIGMA; STYLE.

Carpet Bedding A specialized form of bedding out, in which the dwarfest plants are used, including flat-growing succulents like echeverias, houseleeks and sedums, and others with colourful foliage which is regularly pinched back when they exceed $1''–2''$ high, so as to maintain the carpet-like effect. Often a carpet bed will depict a town's name or coat of arms, while floral clocks include low plants growing on the hands. ◊ BEDDING PLANT; PARTERRE.

Cascade (1) A relatively small waterfall,

especially one of a series. Artificial cascades were important in formal gardens as at Chatsworth, Derbyshire, usually in combination with fountains and other waterworks. ⟡ WATERWORKS.

(2) Cascade is also applied to a form of chrysanthemum with small single flowers. The cascade varieties are vigorous and naturally capable of making much-branched plants with long wiry stems; the lateral growths are regularly stopped to ensure the maximum number of side growths. Although the cascade is naturally more or less upright-growing, it is trained downwards by tying the leading growth to a nearly vertical support, so that eventually the plant produces a waterfall effect. Cascade chrysanthemums, long grown in China and Japan, have been popular for centuries (especially in Japan), though hardly known to the West before 1930. The biggest specimens at Japanese exhibitions have exceeded 14′ in length.

Castor Meal Though seldom seen in Britain nowadays, castor meal, a by-product in the making of castor oil, is a useful organic fertilizer with an analysis of 5–6 per cent nitrogen, 1–2 per cent phosphoric acid and around 1 per cent potash, which can be used at up to 8 oz. per square yard. Gardeners in countries where castor oil is made may find it useful.

Catch Crop The growing of a rapidly maturing vegetable crop in the interval between harvesting one main crop and planting or sowing another on a given piece of ground. This is normally a summer operation and the obvious catch crops are radishes, lettuces and spring onions. Catch-cropping is often confused with the closely related technique of INTERCROPPING.

Caterpillars The larval stage of butterflies and moths; the word is often applied also to the similar larvae of beetles and sawflies. They are grub-shaped, segmented creatures, mostly having three pairs of legs near the head, four pairs of feet equipped with suckers around the middle, and another pair of sucker feet on the last segment.

Caterpillars vary enormously in size and colouring; some are smooth and others more or less hairy. They are voracious feeders and can cause a great deal of damage in the garden. Fortunately, relatively few of those producing attractive adults feed on ornamental garden plants.

Caterpillars fall into several groups needing different treatment.

Leaf and stem eaters Use a suitable insecticide which will poison the caterpillars as they feed.

Stem and fruit borers Stem borers are difficult to detect except by noting sawdust-like frass (excreta) on the exterior, and it is often only possible to destroy them by pruning and burning affected shoots, though sometimes they can be hooked out or killed by a piece of softish wire pushed into their tunnels; where borers are common preventive sprays of insecticide can prevent egg-laying. Fruit borers, of which the codling moth is the most common, must be dealt with by using an appropriate insecticide before the caterpillars enter the fruits.

Cutworms or soil caterpillars These fat, greasy-looking larvae feed on roots and rootstocks and can easily kill plants before being detected; control is by dusting the soil with an appropriate insecticide, or watering it with a solution.

Leaf-rollers The small caterpillars of tortrix moths which feed on leaves, shoot tips, flower buds and on opening flowers. From an early age they spin silk shelters, and as they mature these hold together the edges of leaves which tend to retain a rolled-up form, as well as binding together flower petals, shoots to leaves, etc. Those attacking fruit trees also spoil the developing fruitlets. Control is by spraying with an appropriate insecticide when the moths are seen and before rolling starts, because it is very difficult to get at the caterpillars once within rolled-up leaves; otherwise hand-picking affected leaves, or crushing them to kill the caterpillars, must be undertaken.

Tent or web caterpillars Various kinds which live communally, spinning a web around themselves and a shoot of the plant on which they feed. In the garden most such colonies and their 'tents' are relatively small, but some which attack trees, like the Mediterranean processing caterpillars on conifers, make tents many inches wide and deep. As with leaf-rollers, it may be very difficult to reach the caterpillars with the appropriate insecticide, and the tents may need removal by hand, by burning them off with a blow-lamp, or by cutting off affected shoots and burning these.

In the U.S. the word 'worm' is often applied to caterpillars as in bagworm, cankerworm, hornworm, inchworm and webworm.

Catkin A particular kind of flower spike, usually pendulous, of stalkless flowers which often have no petals and are surrounded with small scale-like bracts; the flowers are almost always of one sex only, and the male and female catkins may be of quite different shapes, as in the hazel, one of the most familiar catkin-bearing trees. The male form has long catkins, while the female has very small isolated flowers. The willow is a tree with erect catkins; here the catkins are of similar sizes, the male being the familiar 'pussy' willow. ◊ FLOWER.

CATKIN. *Left*, male and, *right*, female willow

Cats These domestic pets can be very tiresome in the garden, especially if they belong to other people, in scratching up soil for use as a lavatory. They are particularly fond of freshly stirred earth, which frequently means seed beds and, if they have access to greenhouse or conservatory, they will also go for newly filled seedpans, bulb pots, etc. In play and in jumping down from walls or fences they can damage plants, and if they can leap onto greenhouse roofs they may break the glass. They will sharpen their claws on tree trunks, which can cause serious damage to newly planted specimens.

In Victorian times spiky devices called cat-teasers were sold to discourage cats from crossing garden boundaries. Apart from erecting such unsightly and often ineffective barricades, there are various chemical deterrents available, as well as old-fashioned pepper-dust, but they are by no means infallible and need renewing after rain. Young trees should have their trunks protected with a piece of fine wire netting formed into a tubular guard; trunks already attacked should be treated with a wound dressing. Stray cats can usually be put off visiting one's garden by making menacing noises, or by a well-aimed water jet, but against one's own the only real precaution is protection of areas likely to be favoured with their visits by wire or plastic netting until plants have grown. This applies especially to newly made seed beds. It is not possible to train them not to use the garden!

Cats will eat certain plants for therapeutic reasons; apart from catmint and one or two similarly pungent plants, they will chew up chlorophytum and cyperus leaves indoors. If they show a predilection for a particular plant, spraying with quassia will probably stop them.

In British law it is accepted that cats, like dogs, have a natural propensity to wander and that their owners cannot be held responsible for their visits. Even apparent strays are deemed to have an owner and there is no right to kill or injure one; such action can result in prosecution and an owner can sue for damages. Gardeners can expel cats by reasonable means, using no more force than necessary.

Finally, remember that slug pellets,

especially those based on bran, closely resemble dried cat food and are sometimes eaten by cats with dire results, since the metaldehyde they contain is poisonous.

Cell All plant tissues of whatever kind are built up of individual cells, units within a thin wall which retains sap, protoplasm and a nucleus. Besides forming distinct organs, sequences of cells may conduct water and food-bearing fluid. In trees the water-conducting cells are often woody and without living content. Cells at the tips of shoots and roots (in the meristems) and in the cambium layer multiply by continuous division to extend growth lengthwise and in girth respectively. Sizes of plant cells vary enormously: usually they are microscopic, as small as one-thousandth part of a millimetre, but some can be a few centimetres long. ⟡ CAMBIUM; MERISTEM; VASCULAR SYSTEM.

Centipede Long, narrow, wingless animals with numerous legs, each pair arising from a body segment. Centipedes are beneficial creatures which eat only tiny soil animals, not plant tissue like their relatives, the millepedes. Centipedes are typically brown or golden in colour with slightly flattened bodies and relatively long, quick-moving legs numbered in tens rather than the hundred suggested by their name; they are more likely to move fast when disturbed than to curl up. ⟡ MILLEPEDES; PREDATORS.

CENTIPEDE

Chalk A soft, white form of limestone consisting of calcium carbonate, or carbonate of lime ($CaCO_3$). This earth, a widespread formation in Britain, is the source of quicklime – to which it is converted by burning in kilns – which itself becomes hydrated lime after exposure to water or a damp atmosphere. Like lime, it is valuable to offset acidity in a garden soil; some gardeners prefer ground chalk for this purpose as more pleasant to handle, of longer-lasting efficacy and because it absorbs water, which is beneficial on light soils. It can also be incorporated in soil-based potting mixtures since it does not scorch roots and is so used – instead of ground limestone – in the John Innes seed and potting composts.

A naturally chalky soil, or a thin soil overlying pure chalk, can make for difficult gardening; lime-hating plants may grow poorly and become chlorotic because chalk 'locks up' other essential plant foods. Chalky soils usually benefit from heavy dressings of animal manure, peat or leafmould. Some plants are happy naturally on chalky soil, including most members of the wallflower family, *Cruciferae*, most of the pink family, *Caryophyllaceae*, clematis, helianthemums, irises and scabious.

⟡ CHLOROSIS; CRUCIFER; LIME; COMPOSTS, SEED AND POTTING; SEQUESTROL.

Channelled In botany, refers to organs hollowed like a gutter, especially to long narrow leaves with upturned edges, and also to stems hollowed on one side to form an elongated depression.

Charcoal The black, porous residue produced by burning wood slowly with a limited air supply, in a covered fire or a metal cylinder. Consisting entirely of carbon, it is used by the gardener in crushed or powdered form, especially in potting mixtures, to absorb surplus moisture and harmful substances, as in bulb fibre used in undrained containers – what the gardener calls 'keeping the mixture sweet'. It does not nourish the plant in any way. Powdered charcoal is sometimes used to reduce 'bleeding' as when taking cuttings of latex-bearing plants like ficus. ⟡ BLEEDING; BULB FIBRE.

Charm A kind of chrysanthemum which,

43

without being stopped, produces a rounded plant covered with masses of small single flowers, throwing out secondary shoots from the base, each of which terminates in clusters of bloom. The charm chrysanthemum first arose as a more compact sport of a cascade variety. ◊ CASCADE (2).

Chelate ◊ SEQUESTROL.

Chemicals ◊ GARDEN CHEMICALS.

Cheshunt Compound A mixture of copper sulphate and ammonium carbonate used, apparently only in the UK, in solution against damping-off disease of seedlings and similar diseases attacking lower stems of plants, especially cuttings. ◊ DAMPING OFF; FUNGICIDES.

Chilean Potash Nitrate ◊ NITRATE OF POTASH.

Chimaera A mythological monster with head, body and tail of different animals. Botanically, a plant in which two separate kinds of tissue exist, usually as a result of a mutation or 'sport'. There are several types of chimaera. In one the skin layer has one character and the inner tissue another, as in the potato Golden Wonder, the tubers of which have a russet skin. If propagated from buds induced to form in the flesh, the resulting tubers are the smooth-skinned variety Langworthy. Some variegated plants are chimaeras with one layer of tissue colourless, which looks white or yellowish in the absence of the other (green) layer, as at the edges of certain pelargonium varieties. In some cases the green layer overlies a colourless one. The latter may take over some leaves entirely, as sometimes happens on variegated ivies. If used as cuttings, shoots bearing such leaves only will die, since they have no green colouring matter (chlorophyll). In the Sword Plant, *Sansevieria trifasciata*, the popular yellow-edged form known as *laurentii* is a chimaera and will not reproduce from cuttings; these revert to the plain form. Sometimes apples and chrysanthemums have sectors of a different colour, in which one kind of tissue lies alongside the other and not over or under it; these again are chimaeras.

Some chimaeras are produced by grafting; the most notable example of this is *Laburnocytisus adamii*, created by grafting laburnum on the broom *Cytisus purpureus*. The stock tissue becomes mingled with that of the scion, so that the tree produces, at random, laburnum growth and flowers, broom growth and flowers, and intermediate growth with laburnum-like flowers which, however, purplish like those of the broom. ◊ CHLOROPHYLL; CUTTING; GRAFTING; MUTATION; VARIEGATED.

Chinese Layering ◊ AIR LAYERING.

CHIMAERA. *Left*, pelargonium; *centre*, sansevieria (with normal leaf); *right*, apple

Chinese Method ◊ DEEP BED METHOD.

Chinoiserie A style, the western interpretation of what was believed to be Chinese taste, which influenced many facets of decoration, including gardening, from the late seventeenth century. The first descriptions of Chinese gardens in English were those by Sir William Temple in an essay on gardens published in 1685. Apart from the fashion which arose for Chinese-style garden buildings, bridges and ornaments, the main feature of this influence was the belief that Chinese gardens were deliberately irregular and asymmetrical – which Sir William Temple called 'artificial rudeness'. This has been claimed as the main origin of the English landscape garden, though in fact the latter developed under a variety of influences of which the so-called Chinese style was a minor one. However, for a time there was much interest in what was generally known as *le jardin anglo-chinois* in Europe; though this started in Britain it was rapidly eclipsed here by the true landscape garden. Very few Chinoiserie gardens still exist in Europe, but plenty of examples of Chinese-style buildings do, the most familiar in Britain probably being the Pagoda at Kew Gardens, built in 1761. The grotto also owes much to the Chinese love of grotesque stones or tufa formations. ◊ GROTTO; LANDSCAPE GARDENING; SHARA-WADGI.

Chipmunk These attractive American rodents can be garden pests owing to their tunnelling activities, eating bulbs and so on. Bulbs can be protected by dusting with insecticides such as chlordane, or trapping can be resorted to.

Chipping The puncturing of a hard seed coat, by filing or nicking with a knife, in order to hasten germination; often carried out with sweet peas for example.

Chippings Small stone chippings or grit – as opposed to rounded water-worn particles – are sometimes used in potting composts to keep them 'open', especially by growers of alpines. With these plants chippings of $\frac{1}{8}''-\frac{1}{4}''$ can be mixed with the soil used for making a rock garden with the same intention, while a layer of chippings on top is valuable in preventing rotting at the crowns and attack by slugs, especially in scree gardens where much of the mixture may be of quite coarse chips. Chips both in the soil and on the surface are even more important in small areas like raised beds and sink gardens and for pot-grown specimens. A thick layer of chippings regularly worked into heavy and waterlogged soils improves their texture over the years. Chippings from various stones can be obtained, but limestone and granite are the most common. Limestone should not, however, be used with lime-hating plants. ◊ RAISED BED; ROCK GARDEN; SINK GARDENS.

Chisel Ordinary carpenters' chisels are sometimes used in pruning where a saw cannot be handled, for smoothing pruning cuts, and in tree surgery. Chisels of various forms are used for specialized grafting methods. Such 'graffing chesills' were more important in the seventeenth century – when there was enormous interest in different grafting techniques – than they are today. Apart from instruments with a single chisel blade, there were many composite tools with a chisel blade protruding from one side, which might be called pruning knives or billhooks. ◊ BILL-HOOK; GRAFTING.

Chitting Chit is a word dating back to 1601 and means to sprout; though the *Oxford Dictionary* suggests it is now only in dialect use, chitting is frequently used by gardeners to refer to the pre-planting sprouting of potatoes, which are placed in boxes with the 'rose-end', containing most 'eyes' or latent buds, uppermost. The word is also used when seeds are germinated on damp flannel or absorbent paper or by other means before sowing, as by the method called fluid sowing. The noun 'chit', meaning a sprout or shoot, is now seldom used. ◊ EYE; FLUID SOWING; SPROUT.

Chlorophyll The green pigment found in virtually every plant (except some parasites and saprophytes) which differentiates the plant kingdom from the animals. This pigment absorbs the red, orange and blue parts of sunlight and uses this radiant energy to combine water with carbon dioxide and produce sugar, the initial material from which the complex substances used by plants for growth are synthesized. In the course of this process, known as photosynthesis, oxygen is given off. Plants vary enormously in the level of light needed for photosynthesis which can, of course, occur only in daylight or under suitable artificial lighting. Chlorophyll is normally found in leaves but may also exist in stems, e.g. in plants like cacti and many brooms which have dispensed with leaves. Leaves which for any reason are white or yellow, because of chimaeras, viruses, or chlorosis, cannot carry out photosynthesis.
◊ CHIMAERA; CHLOROSIS; LIGHT; PARASITE; PHOTOSYNTHESIS; SAPROPHYTE; VIRUS DISEASES.

Chlorosis A condition which makes leaves lose or become deficient in chlorophyll, resulting in starvation and possibly eventual death. Though chlorosis in the broad sense may be due to virus diseases, the word is mainly reserved for leaf-yellowing of physiological cause, almost always lack of certain minerals, notably iron and magnesium. Lack of iron is usually due to excessive alkalinity which 'locks up' the metal in the soil. Chelated or sequestrated compounds may be used to counter this condition. ◊ ALKALINE; CHLOROPHYLL; SEQUESTROL.

Chromosome The chromosomes are microscopic rod-like bodies found in the nucleus of all living cells. They contain the numerous genes which are the units of inheritance and control the development and appearance of the plant. In ordinary cells the chromosomes divide when the cells do so, so that the number in each cell remains the same. However, the divisions by which male and female sex cells are formed result in each cell having only half

the basic chromosome complement: this is called the haploid number. Thus, when two sex cells fuse at fertilization, each contributes its half share so that the original chromosome number is restored and each parent contributes half its characteristics to the offspring.

Each species of plant (and animal) has a characteristic basic number of chromosomes, which may, however, be altered either accidentally in nature or by artificial means such as the application of colchicine or atomic irradiation. Plants with the normal chromosome count are called diploids (abbreviated: 2x), whereas abnormal ones are called polyploids. The latter usually look different, and may be bigger and more valuable for garden purposes. Those with twice the normal chromosome complement are known as tetraploids (4x). Some fruit trees have one and a half times the normal number; these triploids (3x) produce very little fertile pollen and must have a pollinator.
◊ FERTILITY RULES; HYBRID; MUTATION; TETRAPLOID; TRIPLOID.

Chrysalis ◊ PUPA.

Ciliate A botanical term meaning fringed with hairs, usually applied to leaves. The word is derived from Latin *cilium*, an eyelash. ◊ HAIRY.

Circle A term sometimes used for a WHORL.

Circumpose A word dating from 1578, now obsolete, meaning literally to place around; used in gardening to mean the potting of a plant. ◊ POTTING.

Circumposition A word used in the late fifteenth and sixteenth centuries – rarely today – for the operation of AIR LAYERING.

Cladode A stem which has taken on the function and often the appearance of a leaf. That they are in fact stems is demonstrated by their carrying the flowers, which leaves almost never do. The most familiar example is the Butcher's Broom, *Ruscus acu-*

leatus. In *Colletia cruciata* the true leaves are almost microscopic, while the thorny stem ends carry out the leaf functions. Cladodes (or phylloclades, as they are sometimes known) are usually tough and

CLADODE. *Left, Ruscus aculeatus; right, Colletia cruciata*

hard, and are usually adaptations to dry conditions. Sometimes, as in some brooms, there are neither leaves nor leaf-like structures; here the whole stem is green and carries out the leaf functions. These are known as switch plants.

Clair-voyée Literally, a 'clear-view'. As it became less vital, after the lawless Middle Ages in Europe, to enclose one's property in a solid wall, apertures were cut in them to allow the countryside outside to be viewed from within. Small apertures would be protected by a grill set into the wall, while the older Dutch version was a wrought-iron screen, often of great size and magnificence, set between brick, stone or metal piers. Nowadays, we would refer to such structures as open fences. Either type of *clair-voyée* was typically placed at the end of a walk or alley, which might be continued in a vista in the countryside beyond, though those in fence style might actually replace a solid wall entirely. *Clair-voyées* in Britain, several of which still exist, date from the early eighteenth century. ◊ ALLEY; WALK.

Clamp Derived from an old Dutch word meaning a heap, in gardening this refers to a method of storing fairly large quantities

of tender vegetable roots in the open, while protecting them from frost and rain. To clamp roots properly, they are arranged on a flat piece of well-drained ground, in a conical or ridge-shaped pile. This is covered with a layer of straw at least 1′ thick; this in turn is covered with relatively fine soil which, when beaten smooth with the back of a spade, should form a layer at least 9″ thick. The sides of the clamp should be as steep as possible.

Clamps are typically 3′–4′ high and 4′–5′ wide at the base, though they can be smaller. A good clamp will have ventilation shafts at intervals along the ridge, or one at the top of a cone-shaped clamp; they are made by pulling a handful of straw out through the soil covering, and are desirable to let warm, moist air, which the roots may generate, escape from the interior and so avoid rotting. (It is of course essential to store only unblemished roots to start with.)

Clamps are generally used for potatoes, but other roots, including dahlia tubers, can be stored in this way. With hardy roots like turnips or carrots, a less elaborate

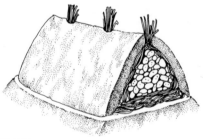

CLAMP

method can be used: the roots are stacked in circles with their top ends outwards, then are lightly covered with sand or sifted boiler ash.

When only some of the roots are removed from a clamp it must be very carefully re-sealed to avoid frost getting in.

Clasping A term applied almost always to stemless leaves which partly or entirely surround the stem from which they grow.

The Latin derivation equivalent to this, sometimes used in specific names, is amplexicaul. ◇ LEAF.

Classification The purpose of plant classification is to provide every plant with a name which is understood and accepted throughout the world. To do this botanical classification is in Latin, an internationally recognized scientific language. Colloquial names may seem preferable to ordinary gardeners, but these are hopelessly imprecise. The name 'lily' for example has been applied to hundreds of plants, many of which are not related at all to true lilies. But there are at least 80 wild species and hundreds of man-made varieties of *Lilium*, so even restricting 'lily' to where it really belongs does not help identification. In any case, a colloquial name in one language is not understood in others. Latin names are thus essential for precise identification of plants.

The Binomial Every wild plant is normally given a name consisting of two words. The first, which we can compare with a person's surname, is the *genus*; the second – resembling a Christian name – the *species*. The genus (plural: genera) defines a group of plants (or animals, since all biologists use this terminology) which are similar in structure and may be supposed to have evolved from a common recent ancestor. The members of a genus are called species (the same word is used for singular or plural, abbreviated sp. and spp. respectively). Though these may vary slightly from individual to individual, they will normally breed true in the wild as to their main characters. This pair of words, the binomial, provides the name for the basic unit of modern taxonomy or classification, known as the *taxon* (plural: *taxa*).

It is an unfortunate fact that botanists do not always agree, and at the same time continuing research may suggest new name combinations. In some confusing genera, botanists may not agree on the characters of species and may even use the term in different senses. Botanists are often jokingly referred to as 'splitters' and 'lumpers' –

those who tend to give specific rank to every minor variation and those who prefer to lump together plants which, though varying considerably, appear to be similar in overall characters. Sometimes also, what was thought of as a species in its own right is a natural hybrid. It is useful to remember that the species concept is man-made: plants at different stages of evolutionary development, especially those which seem not to have settled down to a consistent uniformity, will therefore inevitably produce problems in any classification system. Nature is not necessarily tidy.

All these botanical problems give rise to a further complication – species may be named in ignorance of their earlier naming by other botanists, in which case the rule of priority is normally invoked. This gives rise to equivalent names or synonyms, which most gardeners and nurserymen find very irksome and confusing. Horticulturists tend to adopt new names slowly, but scientifically minded writers and nurserymen try to include the most modern names as well as the best-known synonyms. In some cases a name which has been suppressed botanically continues to be used as a popular name by gardeners. Examples are azalea, botanically one group of *Rhododendron*, and pyrethrum, botanically reclassified under *Chrysanthemum*.

Variation: Subspecies, Varieties and Cultivars In the wild, species can vary from the norm owing to geographical and ecological factors, to mutations, or to accidental cross-breeding, and this gives us a set of taxa in a third rank. Once a plant is in use by gardeners, such variations may be seized upon and further developed by selection or breeding.

The first possible sub-division of a species is the subspecies, abbreviated ssp. Subspecies are recognized when an important character, for instance overall size or leaf shape, is habitually different from that in the species proper. Lesser natural variations are called varieties, abbreviated var. It is possible for either species or subspecies to have such varieties. Variations which have, or are believed to have, arisen in cultivation, whether through breeding or selection, are also given a third name. This may in the past have been in Latin, but the modern rule lays down that such variations must have names in a modern language, which may commemorate people if desired. These cultivated variations are called cultivars (abbreviated cv.).

Botanists world-wide have agreed to an 'International Code of Botanical Nomenclature', and horticultural names are governed by the 'International Code of Nomenclature for Cultivated Plants'. In publications set out according to the rules in these Codes, Latin binomials are written in italics. Varieties arising in the wild are also written in italics, and may or may not be qualified by the abbreviation var. Thus a very bristly version of *Rosa pimpinellifolia*, the Scotch or Burnet Rose, is called *Rosa pimpinellifolia* (var.) *hispida*, which may for convenience be abbreviated as *R.p. hispida*. Names of cultivars, however, are not rendered in italics, even if they are Latin words; they should have capital letters and be printed within single quotation marks. A good yellow variant of the Scotch Rose which has arisen in cultivation is thus known as *R.p.* 'Lutea', and another with semi-double magenta flowers is *R.p.* 'William III'.

Minor variations subsidiary to the variety or cultivar are sometimes labelled as forms (of wild plants) and selections or stocks (of cultivated ones). (The word strain is commonly used for the latter although not acceptable under the horticultural Code.)

In some groups of plants variations of variations may occur, and where these have proved worthwhile to gardeners very cumbersome names may be used. These are particularly prevalent among dwarf conifers where five-stage names are not uncommon, for example *Chamaecyparis pisifera* 'Plumosa Compressa Aurea'. However, such lengthy names are no longer permitted for newly introduced cultivars.

One important rule of horticultural naming is that no two plants within the same genus should be given the same variety or cultivar name.

Hybrids Hybrids arose by accidental or deliberate cross-breeding ('crossing') of two species (very occasionally genera), or of varieties or cultivars. In botanical nomenclature hybrids between two species of the same genus (interspecific) should have the sign 'x' before the specific name, as in *Rosa* x *reversa*, a hybrid between *R. pendulina* and *R. pimpinellifolia*. With intergeneric hybrids the x precedes the name, as in x *Cupressocyparis*, a hybrid between species of *Cupressus* and *Chamaecyparis*.

The Group In certain plants, seedlings raised from a given hybrid can vary sufficiently for these third-rank derivations to deserve names themselves. In such cases the original hybrid is known as a group: it is rendered in Roman letters *without* quotation marks, while its cultivar derivations are given quotation marks. Thus *Lilium* Bellingham Hybrids, derived from a complicated cross, form a group, varying in characters to a limited extent but defined within certain limits by the nature of the original parent species. Cultivars may be selected from a group, propagated vegetatively, and named. An example is *Lilium* (Bellingham Hybrids) 'Shuksan'.

The word 'grex', meaning a flock or swarm, is retained for groups of seedlings raised from a given cross among orchids.

The Clone A clone (sometimes abbreviated cl.) is a collective term for all individual plants vegetatively produced (i.e. not from seed) from one original parent or from its vegetative offspring.

Families Genera themselves are grouped in families in which certain overall characters are constant or are at least readily differentiated from those of other families. The characters used for defining plant families and genera are almost exclusively those of the flower, fruit and seed; leaves and overall habit may vary widely within a single genus, let alone a family. Often genera of one family look superficially very different, as for instance in the rose family, *Rosaceae*, but close examination of the floral characters reveals the relationship.

Botanists may also divide families into sub-families and within the latter into tribes and even sub-tribes, but these are only confusing to the gardener. The term NATURAL ORDER refers to an order (see below), but older authorities sometimes treat this term as designating a single family, which is an erroneous use today.

Major Divisions Above the family level there are further major divisions. Botanists may group families into orders, and orders into superorders. The most basic major division is between plants which flower (phanerogams) and those which do not (cryptogams), of which ferns and fungi are familiar examples, though there are many further kinds of cryptogam. The phanerogams are then divided into two classes: angiosperms (the word referring to the ovule – which when fertilized develops into a seed – being protected within an ovary), and gymnosperms (in which the ovule is not so protected). The latter include the cone-bearing pines, cedars and other conifers, and the angiosperms plants which we usually consider as 'flowers', e.g. roses, sweet peas and daisies.

Finally, the angiosperms are subdivided into two sub-classes, monocotyledons, in which the seedlings typically only have one seed-leaf or cotyledon, and dicotyledons, in which there are typically two seed-leaves.

It is not vital for the gardener to know much about classification above genus level, though some knowledge of plant families can be both useful and, on occasion, surprising. The gardener is clearly most interested in genera, species, varieties or cultivars, and sometimes groups, and an understanding of this classification system is really essential if full value is to be obtained from horticultural books and catalogues.

To summarize this system we can write down two examples as follows:

FAMILY:	*Ericaceae*
GENUS:	*Rhododendron*
SPECIES:	*fortunei*
CULTIVAR:	'Mrs Charles Butler'
FAMILY:	*Liliaceae*
GENUS:	*Lilium*
SPECIES CROSS:	*pardalinum* x *humboldtii*
GROUP:	Bellingham Hybrids
CULTIVAR:	'Shuksan'

The selection of names for genera and species, and the rules laid down for cultivar names by the International Code, are discussed in the entry NAMING OF PLANTS.

◊ ANGIOSPERM; APOMIXIS; CLONE; CROSS-FERTILIZATION; CULTIVAR; DICOTYLEDON; HYBRID; GYMNOSPERM; INTERGENERIC; INTERSPECIFIC; MONOCOTYLEDON; MUTATION; NAMING OF PLANTS; PLANT BREEDING; RACE; SELECTION.

Claw Hoe ◊ CULTIVATOR; HOE.

Clay A stiff sticky substance, technically an earth, largely composed of aluminium silicate, the basis of which is very fine particles of sand. It is found in impervious beds or deposits at varying depths below the soil surface, and in its pure form is used for making pottery and bricks, and waterproofing pond linings.

It is impossible to garden directly in pure clay. A 'clay soil' is one in which there is a preponderance of clay in relation to the other constituents, namely humus and coarser sand: in 'heavy' clay soil there is a large proportion of clay, and in a 'medium' clay soil rather less. The more clay there is, the more difficult the soil is to cultivate: it does not break up into small particles when dry, retains water in wet weather and may bake hard on the surface in hot dry conditions. However, clay soils are usually quite fertile; they retain fertilizers and, of course, water far more than do really sandy soils. It is therefore worth improving their texture and ease of cultivation.

This can be done chemically and mechanically. Exposure of dug soil to severe frost helps to break it up, though the effect is temporary, so that frequent digging in moderately dry weather is necessary. Lime has a marked effect on the texture of clay, and regular dressings can be given where this will not make the soil too alkaline for the plants being grown. The best way to improve the texture of a clay soil, however, is to work in over the years as much humus-forming material as possible – leafmould, peat, straw or manure, and gritty materials such as coarse sand and ashes from which the dust has been sifted out. Working in quantities of stone chippings is also effective. There are also a number of proprietary conditioners designed to improve clay soils.

Clay soil alone is a problem that can be overcome in time. A layer of impervious clay near the soil surface presents a different problem and one which cannot be solved by cultural means. Some trees and larger shrubs detest the layer of permanently wet soil that often forms above a clay deposit; only trial and error can determine which plants will tolerate this and which will succumb in the shallow soil above it.

⟡ FLOCCULATION; HUMUS; LIME; SOIL; SOIL CONDITIONER.

Claye An old word, now seldom used, meaning a HURDLE.

Clay Granules ⟡ HYDROLECA.

Cleft Used of leaf margins indented at least halfway to the middle of the blade. ⟡ LEAF.

Cleft Chestnut ⟡ FENCES.

Cleft Graft ⟡ GRAFTING.

Climate For relevant entres ⟡ ACCLIMATIZATION; FROST; HALF-HARDY; HARDY; SUB-TROPICAL; TEMPERATE; TEMPERATURE; TENDER; TROPICAL; ZONING.

Climber Any plant that actually climbs, or has a tendency to do so; known as vines in the U.S. True climbing plants have special methods or devices for the purpose, such as twining stems or leaf-stems, ten-

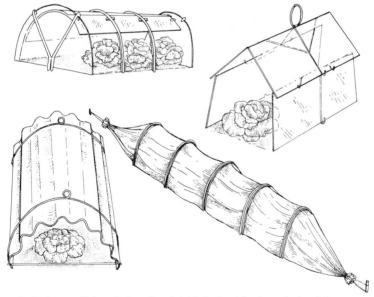

CLOCHE. *Left, above and below*: cloches of semi-rigid plastic; *right above*: cloche of glass panes on wire structure; *right below*: tunnel cloche

drils, suckers on the end of tendrils, or aerial roots. Many have down-pointing thorns which help them to become wedged into surrounding bushes and trees, e.g. roses and brambles, but these may more accurately be called scramblers. A number of plants often advertised as climbers are in fact nothing more than stiff-growing, more or less erect plants which can readily be trained against walls and fences with the aid of a little support and judicious pruning, like some ceanothus and pyracanthas. Most climbers need some kind of support to which they can fix themselves or be tied. ◊ AERIAL ROOT; SCRAMBLER; SELF-CLINGING; SUPPORT; TENDRIL.

Cloche A French word meaning bell, originally applied in gardening to the bell glass and handlight, and now referring to their derivation, the continuous cloche. This was originally composed of glass panes held together with clips or wires to make a rigid structure, which could be easily dismantled. These cloches are made in different sizes and patterns among which are the tent, low barn, large barn and tomato cloche. Such glass cloches can still be obtained but most modern cloches are now based on plastic materials. These include many unit cloches, usually 2′–3′ long, which use different kinds of rigid or semi-rigid plastic sheeting, and often a wire frame; and tunnel cloches, in which a length of thin plastic sheet is stretched over wire hoops.

A recent development akin to the cloche is the use of flexible slitted plastic film placed over growing plants such as lettuces and tomatoes, which expands as they grow and results in faster growth and earlier maturity.
◊ BELL GLASS; HANDLIGHT.

Clod In gardening, a solid lump or mass of soil; roughly a spadeful.

Clone A collective term for all the plants vegetatively produced at any time from one original parent or from the vegetative offspring of that parent. Thus all cuttings, layers or runners from, say, one carnation or one strawberry plant form a clone, but not plants raised from seed from one parent. Plants from one clone are the same in all botanical respects, with certain exceptions where juvenile growth is used for propagation. When a clone is used for extensive propagation it sometimes loses vigour, becomes prone to disease and may die out altogether. ◊ CLASSIFICATION; MERISTEM; VEGETATIVE PROPAGATION.

Close In gardening, this refers to atmospheric conditions in which the air is charged with humidity, as in a hot greenhouse, in a propagator or under a bell glass or similar device. Such close atmosphere is conducive to the rooting of cuttings. A close cold atmosphere, however, is often harmful to plants in general and may result in fungal infections.

Close-boarded ◊ FENCES.

Clove (1) Generally used to describe the young bulbs produced by shallots or garlic; in the latter case they are gathered under the outer skin.

(2) An aromatic spice in the form of the flower buds of a tree, *Eugenia aromatica*.

(3) Kinds of carnation with strong fragrance which are known as clove-scented and sometimes (especially in older literature) just as cloves.

CLOVE. *Above left*, cloves of shallot and, *right*, garlic. *Below*, spice cloves

Club Root An aptly named, widespread fungus disease affecting cruciferous plants including stocks and wallflowers, though normally troublesome on cabbages and other brassicas. The fungus lives in the soil: when a plant is attacked, its fibrous roots are destroyed and the larger roots become gnarled and swollen, eventually decaying with a disgusting odour. Superficially, club root may resemble the damage caused by the gall weevil, but the latter can readily be diagnosed by cutting into the swollen root when the weevil grubs will be seen within. The club root fungus thrives in poorly drained acid soils – not alkaline ones – so the best way of preventing it is to make sure that the soil in which brassicas are to be grown is made alkaline by adequate liming.

CLUB ROOT

Plants attacked by club root are best lifted and burned. Attack can be prevented by sprinkling calomel dust into planting holes and along the rows, or more effectively by making a suspension of calomel (1lb. of 4 per cent calomel dust in about ¼ pint water) or a paste of thiophanate-methyl and dipping the roots of seedlings into this just before planting. Brassicas should not be planted in soil which has carried an infected crop for at least 3 years.
    ◊ ALKALINE; BRASSICA; CALOMEL; GALL WEEVIL; LIME.

Cluster Cups A popular name to describe the minute structures formed by rust fungi

in one of their life stages. These are spore-producing bodies which break through the plant's epidermis in a group and, when they split to release spores, resemble tiny cups. Typically yellow or orange, they are likely to be found on gooseberries and currants. ◊ RUST.

Coal Tar A thick black viscous liquid, largely composed of hydrocarbons, a product of the destructive distillation of bituminous coal. From it are derived many familiar products such as carbolic acid, paraffin and aniline dyes, as well as other 'tar acids' of importance in gardening. Coal and wood tar both give rise to the interrelated cresols and phenols which have fungicidal and pesticidal properties and form part of proprietary disinfectants and sterilants, as well as the related naphthalene. ◊ CREOSOTE; CRESYLIC ACID; NAPHTHALENE; STERILIZATION; TAR.

Cobble A rounded, water-worn stone. Cobbles are sometimes used for paving or to make attractive patterns among paving stones, and in bubblers. When used for paving very even cobbles should be selected, these being laid in a 2″ layer of concrete over a 2″ layer of sand, all having a solidly packed hardcore base. ◊ BUBBLER; PAVING.

Cockroaches Large beetle-like insects (order *Dictyoptera*) which may feed on seeds, seedlings, young shoots and leaves, and aerial roots of orchids. All too common in older dwellings, where they may damage houseplants, they sometimes become tiresome pests in greenhouses. Cockroaches can be caught in proprietary traps, or in jamjars sunk into the soil to the rim level and partly filled with beer, treacle or sugar diluted with water; suitable insecticidal dusts may be used or a borax-based bait as used against ants. ◊ BORAX.

Coconut Fibre The outer husk of the coconut provides this fibre, also known as coir, which was at one time widely used in gardens, both as a material for plunge beds and, chopped finely, as a rooting medium. It holds a great deal of moisture while remaining well aerated. Today it has largely been replaced for these purposes by peat. Matting of coconut fibre is still made and will provide a valuable insulator against frost if placed over garden frames at night. ◊ COIR; FROST PROTECTION; PLUNGE.

Codling Moth A pest of apples, the caterpillars of which eat the developing fruits. Apart from this direct damage, brown rot disease often infects the affected fruits, which remain on the tree until mature with the eight-legged caterpillars still within. This is in contrast to the otherwise similar damage caused by apple sawfly, larvae of which have ten legs and attack very immature fruit which falls before ripening. Codling moth attack can be prevented by carefully timed sprays of suitable insecticide. ◊ BROWN ROT; SAWFLIES.

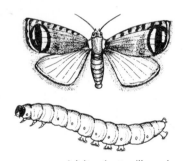

CODLING MOTH. Adult and caterpillar, enlarged

Coir The prepared fibre from coconut husks. Coir screening woven from the fibre was at one time much used to shelter crops and tender plants from wind and also as a frost protector; being very light, rotproof (if stored dry) and non-stretching, it remains valuable for these purposes when obtainable. For screening purposes it should be fixed firmly to wooden stakes which are driven into the ground; for storage such screens can be rolled up without removing the poles. Nowadays

coir has largely been replaced by synthetic materials. ◊ COCONUT FIBRE; FROST PROTECTION.

Colchicine The very poisonous alkaloid derived from the colchicum or 'autumn crocus', which had been used, in minute doses, to produce mutations and, in particular, tetraploids in plant-breeding experiments. ◊ MUTATION; TETRAPLOID.

Cold Frame Any type of unheated FRAME.

Cold House A greenhouse without any form of artificial heating. ◊ GREENHOUSE.

Cold Pit ◊ PIT.

Colonnade A feature in formal gardens consisting of a row of columns, or sometimes trees, either forming part of a loggia or leading from one part of a group of buildings to another. ◊ ARCADE; LOGGIA.

Collar (1) A rather loose term sometimes applied to that part of a plant where the roots join the stem, or stems. Some plants, e.g. strawberries, resent having this area buried on planting, so the collar must be kept at or above soil level.

(2) Also used of a strip of zinc formed into a collar around a plant to protect it against slugs. This should be about 2″ wide and of the length necessary to circle the base of the plant, and is pushed firmly into the soil.

Collar Rot A general name for a number of diseases which attack plants in the 'collar' zone. These are many and various, and themselves have imprecise names, e.g. basal stem rot, blackleg, foot rot, and include damping-off disease of seedlings. Common to all is that they are caused by soil-borne fungi. With seedlings and usually cuttings, the first line of protection is to use sterilized soil or seed/potting mixture. There is no cure for an attack of collar rot. Adjacent seedlings can often be saved by applying a suitable fungicide, and cuttings can sometimes be saved by cutting away the rotted portion and using the remainder as a new cutting. ◊ COLLAR; DAMPING-OFF.

Colloid Derived from the Greek word for glue. A substance in the colloidal state is intermediate between a solution – in which the substance is entirely dissolved – and a suspension – in which the suspended particles eventually settle. Particles in a colloid are extremely small and do not settle. Familiar colloids include glues and

Colour Break ◊ MUTATION.

Column (1) A botanical term. In orchids, the female pistils and male stamens are almost always united into the column, a more or less cylindrical organ in the centre of the flower. The pollen is not carried in anthers (as in most other flowers) but in pollinia or pollen-masses. The presence of a column is a diagnostic feature of orchids. Botanists sometimes also apply this term to the elongated tube, consisting of united

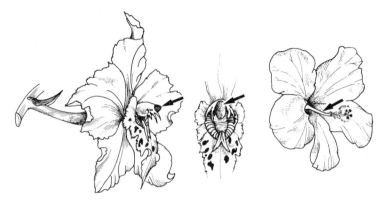

COLUMN. *Left and centre*, orchid (odontoglossum): *right*, hibiscus

jellies, but they can also exist in other forms, including emulsions (one liquid in another), aerosols (a liquid in a gas) and 'smokes' (a solid in a gas).

Copper, sulphur and some other pest-control materials have been prepared as colloidal materials but, although these should have the advantage of very even and continuous distribution, they have mostly been superseded.

Humus in soil is usually in a colloidal state, which is best for the growth of the bacteria which break down organic materials.

◊AEROSOL; EMULSION; HUMUS; SMOKE GENERATOR.

Colour Border A herbaceous border including plants with flowers of only one or sometimes two colours; all-white borders have been specially popular. ◊HERBACEOUS BORDER.

stamens, that surrounds the style in the mallow family, as is especially noticeable in hibiscus. ◊ FLOWER; ORCHID.

(2) In fruit growing, a term applied to a rare upright form of fruit tree with a strong trunk from which radiate many short fruit-bearing shoots. It is suitable only for weak-growing pear varieties which must be pruned by the Lorette method, and is difficult to achieve success with. ◊ LORETTE PRUNING; PILLAR.

(3) Architecturally, a solid ornamental upright or pillar, as used in a colonnade or the pediment to an ornamental temple in gardens; also in the construction of mock ruins.

Combination Hoe ◊ HOE; MATTOCK.

Community Plots Also known as community gardens, these are the equivalent of the British allotment in the U.S. and Canada, where they date from the First World War. Community plots may be cultivated by individuals and families; however, in some places they are cultivated communally by groups of apartment dwellers. They are sometimes associated with schools, colleges and corporations for staff, while others are on public land; they have opened up previously unused areas such as ground below power transmission lines. ◊ ALLOTMENT.

Companionate Planting Certain plants interact with their neighbours. At one level this is merely physical: tall-growing plants can suppress lower ones by making too much shade, or plants will compete for water and nutrients. However, it has been proved that some plants release substances from their roots which are toxic to other plants and may inhibit their growth or even kill them. In companionate plantings, one plant is reputed to have a beneficial effect on its neighbours, sometimes in enhancing their growth but more often in helping them to combat pests. The best-known example is probably that of species of tagetes, which are reputed to prevent white fly infestation on neighbouring plants and are known to have the capacity to repel nematodes in the soil.

Although there is a lot of literature on the subject, few if any controlled experiments have been carried out and in principle the beneficial effects of companionate or companion planting must be regarded as not proven.

◊ EELWORMS.

Compatibility In fruit growing, the capacity of different varieties to pollinate each other, a vital consideration with top fruits, many of which are not compatible. Tables of the compatibility of different varieties of apple, pear, plum and cherry are found in good books on fruit growing.

Grafting also depends upon compatibility between the stock and scion varieties, and this normally occurs only between members of one genus or of closely related genera.

◊ FERTILITY RULES; GENUS; GRAFTING; INCOMPATIBLE; SCION; STOCK.

Composite Any member of the daisy family, *Compositae* – the largest family of flowering plants with around 1100 genera and 25,000 species – in which many small individual flowers, or florets, are united in one head or capitulum. The florets are fixed onto the fleshy termination of the flower stem, which is called the receptacle, and this compound flower has a common calyx-like involucre surrounding the whole. The calyx of each floret is combined with the ovary, often in the form of a pappus consisting of feathery hairs, as in dandelion seeds, or of chaffy scales.

COMPOSITE. *Left, Chrysanthemum leucanthemum* with strap-shaped ray and tubular disk florets drawn separately; *centre, Centaurea cyanus,* where all florets are tubular; *right,* a hieraceum, where all florets are strap-shaped

The florets of composites are of two different kinds. Both may be found together, the tubular ones massed in the centre to form the disk, and the ligulate or strap-shaped ones around these forming the ray, as in the moon daisy, *Chrysanthemum leucanthemum*. For this reason, the two kinds of floret are often called disk and ray florets respectively. Sometimes the flower is entirely composed of tubular florets, as in the cornflower, *Centaurea cyanus*, and sometimes entirely strap-shaped, as in the hawkweeds, *Hieracium* spp.

◊ FLOWER; INFLORESCENCE.

Compost (1) A word describing organic material, usually garden refuse, which can be rotted down and added to soil with beneficial results. ◊ COMPOST HEAP.

(2) The word compost is also used for all kinds of mixtures in which seed can be germinated or plants reared and grown in pots and other containers. These latter are often called seed and potting composts; they include some mixtures based on soil and others, the soilless composts, based on peat. In order to reduce confusion, it might be clearer if these were known as seed or potting mixtures, but the word compost is so generally used in this way in Britain that it is retained here. In the U.S. the words 'medium' or 'mixture' are more likely to be met. ◊ COMPOSTS, SEED AND POTTING.

Compost Heap or Pile, Composting In principle, a heap built up from organic waste material which is allowed to decay out of doors, to produce a spongy, humus-rich end-product which is used to improve soil texture and, up to a point, its quota of plant foods, when dug in; or it can be used as a mulch.

Compost making or composting has been the subject of many theories which need not concern us here. However, it is essential to realize that there are two distinct procedures possible: aerobic, i.e. needing oxygen, and anaerobic, which needs no oxygen. Of these the aerobic method needs much more attention but produces a better end-product in much less time. It should destroy harmful micro-organisms, weed seeds and roots, and should neither smell unpleasant during decay nor encourage flies, mice and rats.

Aerobic composting involves the use of 'bins' or compartments of a minimum size, below which the material does not heat up sufficiently to destroy weed seeds, etc. – what one might call pasteurization. This minimum size is about 3′ in each direction, which can be increased with advantage if space – and the likely amount of compostable material available – permit. There should be at least two compartments, which can with advantage be adjoining,

each having three strong walls of materials providing good heat insulation. Permanent walls can be of breeze blocks, bricks, wooden planks or old railway sleepers. The most effective bins are built of straw bales if these are readily available, though this involves periodic renovation as the bales themselves disintegrate. The compartment's front wall must be removable for access. On a permanent structure it can consist of a wooden door or individual boards made to fit into slots at each side, or a panel with a wooden frame to which wire netting is fixed.

The necessary aeration can be provided on a permanent basis with bricks or small land drains set out with gaps between them, if possible covered with a sheet of strong metal mesh; or it can be provided by making an initial layer at least 3″ deep of woody material such as thick hedge prunings or twiggy brushwood.

After this preparation the compartment can be filled with vegetable wastes. Almost any vegetable matter can be used, including all soft trimmings and unwanted plants from the garden, except of woody stems (which will not rot quickly enough) and material known to be affected by serious diseases. Thick, part-woody material like old cabbage stumps needs to be broken up by chopping with a spade or preferably shredding finely in a mechanical shredder. Perennial weeds need to be dried out in the sun first, or they may continue growing.

Materials like straw and dry bracken, preferably chopped, make excellent compost, but must be soaked with water before being added to the heap. Fallen leaves can also be used, but very durable ones like plane and sycamore are best avoided, and if there is a large supply of finer leaves it is better to rot these down separately to produce leaf mould. Paper can also be placed in the compost heap and will rot down satisfactorily if too much is not used at one time. Kitchen refuse, pet litter, refuse from the bottom of bird-cages, chickens' and pigeons' droppings are all useful additions to a compost heap.

If grass cuttings are included, they should be used in thin layers between other material; a thick layer tends to overheat and produce an evil-smelling, soggy end-product.

Grass cuttings on their own can be rotted satisfactorily with the aid of proprietary 'recyclers' specially devised for this purpose. Grass-only heaps, bins or pits should have a 1″ layer of soil applied to every 6″–9″ layer of grass. No turning is desirable, and it is advisable to cover the heap with a plastic sheet, and bins or pits with a rigid lid, to keep air out and heat in.

Refuse materials of animal origin and even small dead animals (e.g. rats, birds) *can* go into a compost heap, but there are drawbacks. They take much longer to rot down, they are highly offensive if turned up before they have rotted, and they may attract scavenging animals. Only when composting is being carried out on a large scale should such animal ingredients be considered. Where they are readily available, as from nearby farms, animal dung and urine, especially if mingled with strawy litter, can be mixed with garden refuse with advantage.

The larger the quantity of waste added at one time the better, to avoid drying out. If the weather is hot and dry, compost layers 6″–9″ deep should be made and each well watered (although the heap overall should never become saturated, and in high rainfall areas the heap is best made under a roof).

Decay within a compost heap is caused be the activity of microscopic fungi and bacteria which need warmth, humidity and an adequate supply of nitrogen. The last is more likely to be needed in autumn and winter, and to supply it each 9″ layer of refuse can be sprinkled with a nitrogen-rich fertilizer such as sulphate of ammonia at $\frac{1}{2}$ oz. per square yard, dried blood or other organics at 2 lb. per square yard, or covered with a thin layer of fresh bird or animal manure. Proprietary 'accelerators' or 'activators' can also be obtained for this purpose.

To avoid a build-up of acid substances which slow down the rotting process, sprinklings of lime, powdered chalk or similar substances at 4 oz. per square yard

can also be given but, as it is essential that these be kept away from the nitrogen-producing materials, they should be added to alternate layers of refuse. As an alternative, calcium cyanamide can be used, if obtainable, a particularly valuable material in this case since it combines nitrogen and free lime. In the absence of such materials it can be helpful to add a thin layer of garden soil over 9″ refuse layers. A finished heap should be capped with a 1″ layer of soil, and on top of this some heat-retaining material such as sacking, matting, straw, or plastic sheeting with small holes made in it.

About a week after the heap has reached its final height it should if possible be rebuilt by turning it over with a spade or fork so that the outside layers are brought into the centre; this turning can be repeated every 7–10 days if the gardener has enough time and strength. One turning is essential except when straw bales form the compartment walls, since these generate enough heat to make turning unnecessary.

Aerobic composting should result in usable compost in 4–5 weeks in summer and 8–10 weeks in winter.

Anaerobic composting at its simplest involves making a heap of vegetable waste, which is added to as more becomes available; the larger the heap the better. For tidiness, such heaps can be enclosed in solid walls as before or in a simpler enclosure of wire netting firmly fixed to stout corner posts, again with some arrangement for opening up the front. Proprietary compost-making bins are particularly suitable in small gardens to avoid the unsightliness of an open heap. No turning is needed and the addition of extra nitrogen and lime is not essential; however without these decomposition can take up to a year.

Compost is ready to use when it has decayed so far that the original materials can no longer be recognized. It should be moist, crumbly, dark brown, uniform in texture and have no offensive smell. If the fully decayed heap cannot be used for a time, it should be covered with plastic sheeting or similar waterproof material, or the compost stored in an airy shed, to avoid loss of plant foods through leaching.

◊ FEEDING PLANTS; HUMUS; LEAF MOULD; MULCH.

Composts, Seed and Potting In the past, all media used for germinating seed, potting on, and growing plants permanently in containers – known as composts or in the U.S. as mixes or mixtures – were based on soil. Garden soil is very often of unsuitable texture for these purposes, and is also likely to contain disease-producing and other harmful organisms; even the generally useful earthworm is not desirable in the confines of a pot. For success with garden soils, these must first be sterilized.

Soil-based Composts Between 1934 and 1939 the John Innes Horticultural Institute in Britain carried out experiments to determine ideal soil-based mixtures. They ended up with three basic formulae, all based on properly sterilized soil of a specific quality (loam), which are as follows. All parts are by loose bulk.

Seed Mixture 2 parts medium loam; 1 part peat; 1 part coarse sand. To each bushel of this mixture is added $1\frac{1}{2}$ oz. superphosphate of lime and $\frac{3}{4}$ oz. finely ground chalk *or* powdered limestone.

Cuttings Mixture 1 part medium loam; 2 parts peat; 1 part coarse sand.

Potting Mixture 7 parts loam; 3 parts peat; 2 parts coarse sand. To each bushel of this mixture is added $\frac{3}{4}$ oz. ground chalk or limestone and 4 oz. of a mixture of 2 parts (by weight) hoof and horn meal, 2 parts superphosphate of lime, 1 part sulphate of potash (J.I.P. 1).

For potting beyond 4″ pots the chalk/fertilizer mixture is doubled in quantity (J.I.P. 2), and for vigorous plants in 8″ pots and over it is trebled (J.I.P. 3).

For lime-hating plants flowers of sulphur replaces the ground chalk or limestone.

John Innes composts are still available, but it must always be realized that they represent formulas: they are not made under the control of the John Innes Institute. Since soil is such a variable item, and so (to a lesser degree) is peat, some formulations of J.I. composts now available are positively harmful to plants, though good ones can be found. These soil-based composts enriched with fertilizer are also relatively unstable and should ideally be used within 3–4 weeks of being mixed. John Innes composts are not known in the U.S.

Soilless Composts It was mainly because of the variability of soil that soilless composts were devised. All are based on peat, some with the addition of sand, vermiculite, perlite and/or polystyrene chips, and of fertilizers. Ground limestone is often added to bring the pH level near neutral. Because much of the early work was carried out at Cornell University, U.S.A., these are sometimes referred to in the U.S. as Cornell mixes. The plant food content is limited, and most soilless composts only provide enough for 6–8 weeks of growth, after which plants in them *must* be regularly fed with a balanced fertilizer. A few composts contain slow-release fertilizers and are specifically made for relatively long life, usually those recommended for tomato culture. Specialist compost makers may produce a number of different formulations for various purposes. Soilless composts are always used in growing bags. Some makers produce different soilless composts for potting and for growing seeds or cuttings; others recommend one compost for all purposes.

In general, soilless composts differ from soil-based ones as follows: they are much lighter (which is an advantage when transporting them, but can be a disadvantage with large top-heavy plants); because of their texture they need to be made less firm when potting; and the danger of drying out is much greater. There is also the feeding problem already mentioned. In soil-based composts, not only does the fertilizer content last much longer, but the soil acts as a 'buffer' against total infertility.

Specialized materials are used to grow plants which need unusually free drainage. Thus composts containing pine needles may be used for bromeliads, and orchid growers use osmunda fibre and shredded bark.

◊ BARK; GROWING BAG; LOAM; OSMUNDA FIBRE; PERLITE; SAND; SLOW-RELEASE; VERMICULITE.

Compound (1) Used botanically with reference to leaves, flowers or fruits composed of at least two similar parts. Compound leaves are formed of similar leaflets, and a compound flower consists of florets or small flowers united into one 'head' as in the family *Compositae*, and also in most of the family *Dipsacaceae* which includes scabious and teasel. ◊ COMPOSITE; LEAF.

(2) Applied to fertilizers containing several different mineral salts.

Conceit In gardening design a conceit is any fanciful, grotesque or exaggerated feature. The term, which seems to have arisen in the late eighteenth century, did not refer to the temples and other buildings which were habitually used in a landscape design, but to follies, grottoes, mock ruins and the like, or – in baroque terms – to elaborate waterworks. Sometimes an excessive conglomeration of features including buildings might lead to the whole garden or landscape being considered a conceit as was Alton Towers, Staffordshire. Modern examples of conceits might include the life-size models of dinosaurs around the lower lake in the grounds of the Crystal Palace, London, and the Valhalla at Tresco, Isles of Scilly, a courtyard lined with old ships' figureheads. For a summary of such features ◊ GARDEN DESIGN.

Concrete This hard, durable material is the result of mixing lime cement, sand and shingle or stone particles (aggregate) in various proportions according to the desired end-product, with water. It is a valuable material in the garden, both in the form of pre-cast items which include paving slabs of varied form and colour, perforated walling blocks, fence-posts, fence slats and plant containers, and as a material the gardener can use directly to create paths, steps and pools, and to make foundations for walls, greenhouses, etc. On a small scale, concrete is easy enough to mix; however, where large quantities are needed, ready-mixed concrete can be delivered in semi-liquid forms, so needing immediate attention, with all shuttering and reinforcement ready, since it hardens within 2 hours.

Conditioner ◊ SOIL CONDITIONER.

Cone The clustered flowers or fruits of some conifers such as cedar, larch, pine and spruce. The male and female cones are separate. Male cones consist of large pollen-sacs separated by scales, which arise from a central axis. The females develop into the familiar, usually hard, persistent cones, the scales of which usually open to release the seeds. These may have a papery, one-sided wing, and are dispersed by wind, but others, as in the Stone Pine, resemble

CONE. *Left and centre*, female (seed-bearing) cones of Norway spruce and cedar; *right*, male (pollen-bearing) cone of pine

a small nut, and may in fact be eaten. In some cases the cones remain closed and only release the seeds through rotting, animals eating them, or even fire. Some cones point downwards when mature but others remain upright. The yew, maidenhair tree and some other conifers do not have cones. Other groups of plants which have cone-like structures are the seed-bearing cycads and the spore-producing horsetails. ◊ CYCAD.

Conifer A general term for cone-bearing trees such as pine and spruce, but sometimes loosely used as an equivalent to *Coniferae*, the original botanical name for a group now considered to consist of eight families, of which some (including maidenhair tree and yew) do not have cones. Most conifers have linear leaves known as needles. ◊ GYMNOSPERM.

Connate A botanical term used of organs of the same kind which, though distinct in origin, become joined in growth. This often occurs, for instance, with the keel petals of leguminous flowers. Opposite leaves sometimes do this by growing together at the base around the stem, though this might more accurately, if pedantically, be called connate-perfoliate. ◊ LEAF; LEGUMINOUS; OPPOSITE; PERFOLIATE.

Conservatory A word first used (by John Evelyn in 1664) synonymously with greenhouse, meaning a place in which tender plants were 'conserved' in cold weather. By the late eighteenth century the words had diverged. Whereas the greenhouse was a place for growing plants, the conservatory was one in which to enjoy them. Some plants in a conservatory might be permanent, like palms and other trees and climbers, but most flowering plants would be moved in from greenhouses when they were at their best, and returned there when over. Conservatories are almost always attached directly to the dwelling house, sharing the house wall, so that one can enter their green luxuriance just by opening a door from the house – in grander days usually from the ballroom or drawing room. Ideally, the conservatory is large enough to hold a table and chairs. Today, the word has been partly replaced by the 'house extension', although this covers any structure from one in greenhouse style to what is effectively simply another living room. ◊ GREENHOUSE; WINTER GARDEN.

Contact A word applied to pesticides which kill the pests on contact without necessarily being persistent. ◊ PESTICIDES; SYSTEMIC.

Container Plants not grown directly in the soil are grown in containers which may be pots, boxes, tubs, or ornamental containers of virtually any shape. The average plant container should provide roughly the same proportions as a pot for each plant it houses; those which are relatively broad and shallow will need a lot of watering, and those which are extra deep will need extra drainage material or the potting mixture at the bottom may become airless and 'sour'. In principle, any plant container should have one or more drainage holes. The word is most often applied nowadays to the temporary receptacles in which 'container-grown' plants are sold. ◊ CONTAINER-GROWN; WINDOW BOX.

Container-grown It is now commonplace to buy plants, including quite large trees, in containers, from which they can be planted in the garden with virtually no disturbance to the roots. Although this practice is quite ancient in origin, its widespread use is modern, and is due to the increased use of cars, enabling private gardeners to visit 'garden centres' and take away container-grown plants of their choice, rather than having to order plants from nurseries which are then sent by post or carrier, often with little or no soil round the roots. Garden centre container-grown plants may be in orthodox pots but other containers are more common: in U.S. they are often sold in tin cans with holes punched in the bottom, from which extraction is sometimes difficult. More usual materials are waterproofed paper compositions such as 'whalehide', or thin black bags of polythene film with small holes for drainage.

Container-grown plants sold in this way should have been grown in the container for sufficient time to ensure that they have a good root system. A simple way to test this is to lift the plant by its stem. If the container and soil fall away, the plant is almost certainly inadequately established.

The container must be removed before planting, taking care that the soil and roots are not disturbed. Improvement of the soil, and the planting hole, are prepared in the normal way, and any staking necessary is carried out. Container-grown plants can be planted at any time of year unless the soil is frozen or waterlogged, but in hot weather it is imperative to fill the planting hole with water first and to continue watering until you are sure the soil is altogether moist again.

Small plants for growing on may be sold in temporary containers such as compressed peat, sawdust or paper compounds which need not be removed before planting, since roots grow through them; but they should be well moistened first. ◊ PLANTING.

Container Plants Usually refers to plants which have been container-grown for ease of transplanting, but also sometimes to plants for display, notably bedding subjects, which can be readily grown in ornamental containers like tubs or window boxes. ◊ BEDDING PLANT; CONTAINER-GROWN.

Continuous Layering ◊ LAYERING.

Contractile Applied to roots which can contract in length and pull parts of a plant lower into the ground. This occurs for instance in crocuses, where a corm planted too shallowly will have its level rectified by the contractile roots in the growing season.

Controlled Release Of fertilizers, the same as SLOW-RELEASE.

Copper, Copper Compounds The value of copper compounds as fungicides was first discovered around 1878 when it was found that a mixture of copper sulphate and lime – used on grapes as a poisonous deterrent to roadside thefts – was preventing vine mildew disease. This became known as Bordeaux mixture, and is still valuable against some diseases. A strong solution of copper sulphate can be used as a general weedkiller (4 oz. in a gallon of water to 4–5 square yards), and it is also used to clear ponds of blanket-weed and other algae. Other formulations of copper including its oxide and oxychloride are sold as fungicides. Copper naphthenate is widely sold as a wood preservative. ◊ ALGICIDE; FUNGICIDES; WOOD PRESERVATIVES.

Coppicing The practice of regularly cutting down new growth arising from the base of a tree. This creates more and more numerous vertical branches arising from what becomes termed a stool. This is primarily a forestry practice to obtain commercially useful growths, and is carried out every few years. The gardener may cut down growths every year, e.g. to obtain the brightly coloured young growth of certain willows and dogwoods, to maintain the juvenile foliage of eucalyptus, or to ensure very large leaves on trees such as catalpa and paulownia, a practice also known as stooling. ◊ JUVENILITY; STOOLING.

Cordate Heart-shaped: a term usually applied to leaves with a pair of rounded lobes at the base. When the word is part of a longer description, as cordate-ovate, it is to these lobes only that the term applies. ◊ LEAF.

Cordon A normally branching plant, almost always a fruit tree, which is restricted by pruning to one or occasionally more stems. The word was first used in this sense in 1878.

Fruit tree cordon training allows several different varieties to be grown in very limited space, for they are best arranged 2′ apart in a straight line along training wires. Apples and pears are the fruits usually grown as cordons since dwarfing root-stocks, essential to restrict excessive growth, are available for these. Dwarfing rootstocks are not available for other kinds of top fruit so it is not recommended to attempt growing them as cordons. However, gooseberries and red and white currants have proved amenable to training in this way.

Apple and pear cordons are normally trained obliquely since this allows a better length of stem per tree than does vertical training. The gap left above the first oblique cordon in the row can be filled by training one vertical shoot from this tree. Some growers lower their cordons each year as they increase in length till they are only about 40° above the horizontal, and up to 12′ long. The topmost training wire should be 7′ above the ground.

Cordons can be pruned in various ways, but the end result is to produce spurs. One general-purpose method is to reduce all side growths by summer pruning, around the end of July, to five leaves. In November these shortened laterals are further reduced to 2–3 buds. Once spurs have formed, shoots emerging from them are summer-pruned to two leaves and reduced to one bud in winter.

Top fruit cordons are not restricted to upright growth; they are occasionally grown horizontally. Nor are they restricted to single oblique stems, although the possible variations are seldom seen. Vertical cordons can be grown as singles, U cordons of two uprights, double-U cordons and in other attractive upright formations called palmette verriers. The single-U is sometimes grown with a set of horizontal side branches trained from each upright. Oblique cordons can be grown as 45° pairs which when overlapped create 'cross-bars'. The palmette legendre or horizontal cordon is what is normally called an espalier. Finally, there is the oblique palmette which resembles an elaborately trained fan.

Gooseberries and red and white currants are normally trained vertically, the latter restricted to single cordons but gooseberries being grown as double, triple, or double-U cordons with four growths.

Cordon training, or a derivation from it involving hard pruning and restriction to one or more straight growths, can also be applied to woody ornamental plants like ivy and pyracantha.

The word cordon is also applied to the method of growing sweet peas when large, long-stemmed flowers are needed, as for exhibition. Only one shoot per plant is allowed to grow and this is trained up a vertical support 7′–8′ tall; supports should be 9″ inches apart. When the peas have reached the top of their support, each is untied in turn, laid along the ground for 3′–4′ and then tied up again to the appropriate support. This operation is called layering.

◊ ESPALIER; FAN; PALMETTE; SPUR; TRAINING.

Corm, Cormel, Cormlet The corm is a storage organ formed from the thickened base of the stem, usually within some papery protective scales called the tunic. Corms may produce miniatures around their base, called cormels or cormlets, which will grow into mature corms over 2–4 years. A distinctive feature of the corm is that the original corm dries up during the plant's growth period and a new one is formed above it. Typical garden examples are crocuses and gladioli. ◊ BULB; RHIZOME; TUBER; TUNIC.

CORDON

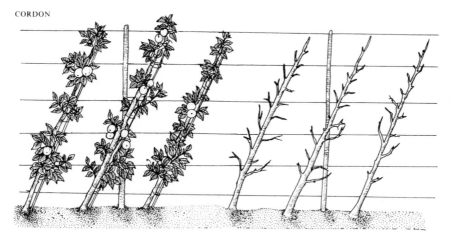

CORM with CORMLETS (gladiolus)

Corolla A general term applied to the petals of a flower or at least to the inner whorl of floral leaves (as opposed to the calyx). The corolla, which is usually – but not always – the most showy part of the bloom, may be of very variable form, and may either consist of distinct segments (petals) or be of one piece. ⟡ CALYX; FLOWER; PERIANTH; PETAL.

Corona Any outgrowth developed on the corolla or perianth of a flower, and often called the crown. It separates the corolla proper from its anthers in the daffodil family, where it forms the cup or trumpet. In the milkweed family (asclepiads) it is actually an outgrowth from the staminal area, as in *Stapelia variegata*. The radiating filaments of a passion flower are also called the corona or crown. ⟡ COROLLA; CUP; FLOWER; PERIANTH; TRUMPET.

Corticium Disease ⟡ RED THREAD.

Corymb ⟡ INFLORESCENCE.

Cot Split ⟡ BUD STAGES.

Cottage Gardens This phrase has come to mean small country gardens planted with 'homely' flowers such as sweet williams, hollyhocks, pinks and pansies, growing in a colourful jumble, without an overall colour scheme and perhaps with vegetables in among them; with fences, walls and porches clothed in honeysuckle and rambler roses. They are gardens that seem just to have happened, full of brightness and scents. In fact, this idiom was partly the creation of the famous Gertrude Jekyll, and she fostered the idea that it sprang from the gardens of country labourers, without reckoning that the killing hours they worked must have left very little time or energy for gardening and that their plots were most often occupied with rabbit hutches, chicken runs, a few vegetables and an earth closet. There is little documentation about real cottage gardens, but it seems probable that they were often planted with medicinal plants and herbs which, of course, did provide some flowers, while no doubt snippets of purely ornamental plants from neighbours would be planted.

Cottage gardens of the sixteenth and seventeenth centuries seem often to have been very formal in layout, with neat beds and a central path leading to the gate in the outer fence. Some cottagers undoubtedly grew flowers for pleasure, and among them were the early working-class 'florists' who specialized in certain kinds of flower and held competitions among their fellows, and the old gardens of such people

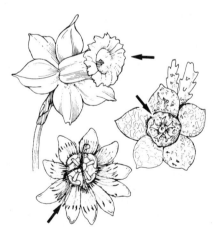

CORONA. *Above left,* daffodil: *above right,* stapelia: *bottom left,* passion flower

sometimes yield up plants believed lost to cultivation. But until working conditions improved during this century, the cottage garden written about by Gertrude Jekyll existed mainly where the cottagers were in fact middle class with less exacting jobs and romantic ideas. However, the idiom is very popular today when close, artless planting fits in with modern ideas about reducing labour.

Cotyledon A seed leaf. The cotyledons are normally the first leaves to appear when a seed germinates, though in some plants, e.g. the pea, they remain below ground. Cotyledons are often quite different in appearance from adult leaves, especially in the class of flowering plants called dicotyledons which normally have two seed leaves as the name suggests, in contrast to monocotyledons which normally have one. Conifers may have from

box or bed; and seedlings are best if actually picked up by a cotyledon, not the brittle stem. At this stage there is the least danger of damaging the root system, though in cases where the plants are too small at this stage they may have to be left till adult leaves appear. The gardener learns to distinguish between seedlings of weeds and cultivated plants in the open ground, so that he can destroy the former and preserve or transplant the latter.

⟡ CLASSIFICATION; PRICKING OUT; ROUGH LEAVES.

Cover Cropping ⟡ GREEN MANURING.

Cow Manure ⟡ MANURE.

Craneflies ⟡ LEATHERJACKETS.

Crazy Paving A term applied to paths or terraces made of broken paving slabs fitted

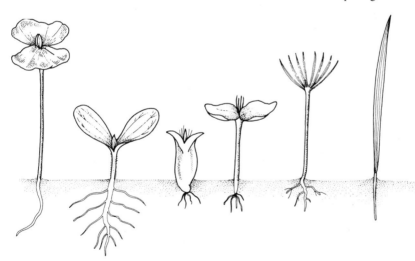

COTYLEDON. *From left to right*, cotyledons or seed leaves of beech, cucumber, cereus cactus, prickly pear, a conifer, date palm

two to seven or more cotyledons, which are needle-like or linear.

It is when the cotyledons are fully developed, but before the first adult leaves have appeared, that seedlings are best pricked out, i.e. moved on from their seed

closely together like a jigsaw. In Britain this seems to have become popular only in Edwardian times: the *Oxford Dictionary* suggests that the first use of the expression was in 1923, but it is certainly to be found in books around 1912. One author of this date (Thomas H. Mawson) wrote that 'in most instances, this form of garden pavement results in one of the worst forms of affectation', which implies that it was a well established practice. However, the same idea was in use by the Chinese many centuries ago, although their version was really a path mosaic of fragments of brick, stone chips and rounded pebbles with which elaborate patterns were created. ◊ PAVING.

Creeper Although strictly referring to plants which spread over the soil surface, rooting as they do so, this word is often loosely applied to climbing and other WALL PLANTS.

Crenate A botanical term, usually applied to leaves, referring to margins having shallow rounded teeth or notches, which might loosely be called scalloped. ◊ LEAF.

Crenulate A diminutive of crenate, referring to margins with small rounded teeth. ◊ LEAF.

Creosote An oily liquid, varying from colourless to blackish brown, obtained by distilling wood- or coal-tar, used by gardeners as a wood preservative. For this purpose it can be brushed or sprayed on, though best results come from soaking the wood in a bath of creosote. It is not as effective as copper naphthenate, and plants can be badly scorched if splashed with creosote, while treated wood can give off fumes harmful to plants for months or even years. A special formulation of creosote has recently proved effective in protecting plants against attack by honey fungus. ◊ COAL TAR; WOOD PRESERVATIVES.

Cresol A constituent of coal-tar and creosote which is used as a disinfectant and is sometimes recommended for sterilizing utensils and soil in gardens, in non-corrosive formulations.

Crested ◊ CRISTATE.

Cresylic Acid Once widely recommended, in the form called 'pale straw-coloured carbolic acid', for disinfection of frames, greenhouses, utensils, etc., and for soil sterilization. It is poisonous and does not appear to be available for garden use today, except as a liquid tree wound dressing and canker cure. ◊ CANKER; COAL TAR; STERILIZATION; WOUND DRESSING.

Crickets Large insects, related to grasshoppers and cockroaches, which are sometimes abundant, especially near refuse tips where they may increase rapidly. They like the shelter of frames or greenhouses where they may destroy seedlings and cause damage to leaves, flowers, and aerial roots of orchids, by feeding on them. Crickets can be killed with borax-based ant-killers, or a mixture of equal parts powdered borax and caster sugar. Because of their love of nooks and crannies they can be trapped in inverted flowerpots raised on sticks an inch or so above the level of soil or staging.

Crinkle A term covering a number of virus diseases, which cause leaves to become crinkled or puckered. The most serious of these attacks strawberries, when it is accompanied by yellow spotting, as also in potato crinkle. ◊ VIRUS DISEASES.

Crinkle-crankle Describes walls built to a serpentine plan, primarily to provide sheltered enclosures for fruit trees. Such walls, which need no buttresses, were in use during the seventeenth century, and some still exist in Britain and the U.S.

Crisped A botanical term referring to a closely curled or finely waved margin to a leaf or other organ; sometimes found in species names as *crispata* or *crispatus*.

Cristate Literally, crested or cockscomb-shaped; applied to certain plants showing this type of fasciation, or abnormal growth in one plane. In most plants any kind of fasciation is more curious than beautiful, and is rarely possible to propagate, though in the celosias the crested forms of *C. argentea* are reproducible from seed and designated by the cultivar name 'Cristata'. In the ferns and the cacti such variations are prized by collectors, and there are many cristate varieties in these two classes of plant, which can be reproduced by division or, with cacti, by cuttings or grafting.

textured potting mixtures do not need this, nor do plastic pots which have a number of small drainage holes; however, large drainage holes may need covering, simply to prevent potting mixture from falling out, and wooden seed boxes may for the same reason need a row of small crocks over the central slit. A deep layer of crocks or similar drainage material may, however, be

CRISTATE. *Left*, of celosia; *centre*, of a fern; *right*, of a cactus

The typical crested fern has a spreading tassel-shaped end to the frond, while cristate cacti exhibit a wide variety of shapes, basically fan-like, often convoluted when growth in one plane at the top of the plant greatly exceeds growth at the base, or producing a large number of tiny heads. This latter type of growth is often technically referred to as monstrous. ◊ FASCIATION; MONSTROUS.

Crocks, Crocking Crocks are pieces of broken flower pot, used to provide drainage in flower pots, pans and seed boxes; the operation is known as crocking. Adequate crocking was thought in the past to be absolutely vital to plants in such containers, but its need sprang largely from the close-textured potting mixtures then in use, and the considerable firming (compression) given to them. Older books will thus recommend that each drainage hole in a pot or similar container should be covered with a large crock placed convex side down, this to be covered with a layer of smaller, thinner crocks, the whole finally to be covered with coarse grit, pebbles or a layer of sphagnum moss. Modern open-

needed for many orchids and other epiphytic plants like some bromeliads, and also in decorative containers which are over-deep in proportion to width, and in undrained containers occasionally used for decorative plants indoors.

In U.S. the word shard or pot-shard may be used for a crock.
◊ CONTAINER; POTTING; POT.

Crocus Pot A small decorative container with 4–9 apertures in the sides in which crocuses are planted. Other plants can of course be used, including small rock plants. There is a range of comparable pots 6″–18″ tall, the larger ones being known as STRAWBERRY POTS.

Crome An old name for a broad, square-tined fork, the tines bent part-way at right angles to the long shaft, which has no hand-grip; particularly useful for earthing up potatoes. This tool – also spelt 'cromb' – is now sold in Britain under the name refuse drag; it is more commonly available as a cultivating tool on the continent. ◊ DRAG; FORKS; TINE.

Crop Rotation ◊ ROTATION.

Croquet Lawn The game of croquet, first devised around 1858 and now much less popular than it was, is played on a dead-flat lawn 35 × 28 yards. In it wooden balls are driven through metal hoops fixed into the ground in a traditional pattern, using a wooden mallet.

Cross A hybrid. The word was first used as a noun in 1760 with reference to an intermixture of breeds or races, mainly in cattle-breeding (*Oxford Dictionary*), and at about the same time as a verb meaning to interbreed or cause to interbreed.
◊ BREEDING; CROSS-FERTILIZATION; HYBRIDIZATION.

Cross-fertilization, Cross-pollination The transfer of pollen from a flower on one plant to one on another plant with the aim of making a cross or hybrid; the terms effectively mean the same, though in fact fertilization cannot be said to occur until the male gametes produced by the pollen have actually reached the female ovule. These terms are opposite to self-fertilization and self-pollination, when the pollen and ovule concerned are on the same plant, and a hybrid cannot be conceived.

It is often important to achieve cross-fertilization between fruit trees because some varieties cannot produce fruit if their flowers are self-pollinated; these are called self-sterile. Successful fertilization of fruit trees is achieved by planting compatible varieties reasonably close together, when bees will normally carry out the operation.

Cross-fertilization is also carried out by plant breeders to produce seed and thence new cultivars from existing plants. Where hybrid progeny are sought it is almost always necessary to emasculate the seed-bearing flower by removing its pollen-bearing anthers before they mature. Pollen from the male parent, which should be dry and powdery, is normally transferred to the stigma of the female on a fine soft brush, after which the female flower should be enclosed in a bag to prevent any accidental pollination from other blooms whether by insects or wind.

Cross-fertilization can normally only be carried out between very closely related plants; success usually follows the crossing of varieties of the same species, sometimes the crossing of species, and very rarely the crossing of genera, though this occurs in the orchid family. It is impossible to cross unrelated plants.
◊ ANTHER; EMASCULATION; FERTILIZATION; HYBRIDIZATION; OVARY.

Crotch The point where tree branches fork from the trunk or each other. Because of the structure of the living wood, branches with a narrow angle from the trunk are far more susceptible to breakage than wide-angled ones if they become too long or overloaded with fruit, so this point should be watched, especially with fruit trees; the branch may need shortening, support or to be fixed to the trunk in some way. Trees whose main stem has divided into two equal forks are particularly liable to breakage, sometimes of both branches. ◊ FORK.

Crown (1) Usually refers to the upper part of a rootstock from which shoots grow, and to which they die back in autumn, as in plants with a fleshy or woody rootstock, e.g. dahlias, delphiniums, lupins, peonies and rhubarb. The word is sometimes used rather loosely to mean the whole of the rootstock, especially when this is lifted for forcing, as in rhubarb and seakale. ◊ ROOTSTOCK.

(2) Synonymous with corona when referring to flowers in which this tubular or cup-shaped outgrowth from the petals occurs, notably daffodils. ◊ CORONA.

(3) Also used of the upper, branching part of a tree.

Crown Bud A term used by chrysanthemum and carnation growers to denote a particular kind of bud. In chrysanthemums the crown bud is one which is surrounded by shoots which can grow on around it, as opposed to the terminal bud which is surrounded by other flower buds. The first crown buds on a chrysanthemum are the first flower buds to appear after one stopping. The second crown buds are those that result from a second stopping, carried out by removal of the first crown buds or shoots which would produce them. With carnations, the crown or terminal bud is surrounded by the flower buds, and all these subsidiary buds are removed to ensure the development of the crown bud to perfection. ◊ BREAK; BUD; STOPPING.

Crown Gall ◊ GALL.

Crown Graft ◊ GRAFTING.

Crown Lifting The removal of lower branches of a tree, usually carried out on ornamental trees to reveal an attractive trunk, remove branches in the way of people or other plants, and to cut out dead or dying branches. This operation is best carried out in autumn or winter.

Crown Thinning The selective removal of tree branches in order to avoid crowding and to let more light and air into the crown.

Crucifer Any member of the mustard family, *Cruciferae*, which includes wallflowers, stocks, aubrieta, arabis, alyssum, sweet rocket, water cress and brassicas. The name refers to the cross-like arrangement of the four petals, which are usually equal in size, though sometimes there are two large and two small petals. There are other plants with four petals, but the com-

CRUCIFER (wild wallflower)

bination of these with four sepals and six (rarely four) stamens makes crucifers readily distinguishable from other plants. Identification of individual crucifers often depends largely on the form of the seed capsule. ◊ BRASSICA.

Crumb In gardening one refers to soil having a good 'crumb structure' when it has a satisfactory texture – neither too sandy nor with too much clay in it, and the soil particles are aggregated into crumblike units of reasonable size for good aeration and root penetration, not into large sticky lumps. In soils which are naturally of unsatisfactory texture, lime or other soil conditioners can be used to improve structure. ◊ HUMUS; LIME; SOIL CONDITIONER; TILTH.

Cuckoo-spit The popular and apt name for a sap-sucking insect pest which in the larval state surrounds itself with a frothy mass providing excellent camouflage. This is the 'spit'; the 'cuckoo' derives from the season in which the insect usually appears, at about the same time as the cuckoo, which in older times was supposed to create the spit. In the U.S. the pest is called spittlebug. Control is by hand picking, a forceful water jet, or a systemic insecticide. The adult, technically a bug, is like a tiny, fat green grasshopper and has similar mobility, hence its further name, froghopper.

Cultifork ◊ FORKS.

Cultivar A term for a plant variation that has originated in cultivation rather than in the wild (when it would be termed a 'variety'), and is sufficiently distinct to warrant propagation and a name of its own. Cultivar names, which should be placed within single quotation marks and have an initial capital letter, are now supposed to be in a modern language, but older ones in Latin exist. Examples are two cultivars of *Geranium sanguineum*, 'Album' and 'Glenluce'.

Cultivars can arise in one of four different ways. One class is of plants all propagated vegetatively from an original parent, i.e. a clone. Another is by propagating from seed and rigorously selecting the offspring so that they are uniform in appearance, i.e. a selection. Another way of creating uniform offspring is by crossing distinct, separately maintained breeding stocks. Fourthly, a cultivar name may be given to an assemblage of plants which are distinct in at least one character from other cultivars, e.g. in the matter of size.

▷ BREEDING; CLASSIFICATION; CLONE; SELECTION; VARIETY.

Cultivation Often used to cover every aspect of growing plants, though originally it referred only to the preparation or tillage of soil so that a crop could be successfully raised. Even in this sense the word has only been in use since about the mid-seventeenth century. Cultivation in this sense covers ploughing, digging, forking, and the use of heavy hoes and mechanical cultivators.

Cultivation of any kind has quite short-term effects on the soil; where a succession of crops is to be raised, as in agriculture or in vegetable gardens, it has to be carried out regularly on a continuous basis. It is important to realize that uncultivated soil usually maintains its physical and chemical status, being enriched by decaying vegetation and the activity, death and decay of soil animals. As soon as cultivation is carried out, this natural balance is destroyed.

The first step must always be to clear the land of weeds and any debris. If the soil is obviously holding water excessively, the improvement of its texture while cultivating will have to be carried out or, in bad cases, drains may have to be put in beforehand. Cultivation operations of any extent are normally carried out in autumn and early winter when soils tend to be relatively dry and the action of frost is helpful in breaking them up. It can be positively harmful to work soils in wet conditions, especially the heavier ones containing much clay, since the mere action of treading, and – even more – the use of a machine, can compact the soil excessively

and affect its structure adversely. Only very open and sandy soils can be cultivated soon after wet weather.

▷ CLAY; CULTIVATOR; DIGGING; DRAINAGE; FORKING; HOE; MANURE; NO-DIGGING; PAN; PLOUGH; WEEDKILLER.

Cultivator Apart from digging sticks and primitive hoes, the oldest implement for cultivating the soil is the plough, which has been in use for at least 4000 years. This is of course primarily an agricultural implement and only concerns us here in small, modified forms, either hand- or power-operated. Most garden cultivators operate by rotating a pair of cultivating rotors equipped with tines of various shapes, and hence are known as rotary cultivators, but many can be adapted to pull a small plough blade or a series of hoe blades through the soil. Some cultivators are fully self-propelled, i.e. the motor drives both wheels and cultivating rotor; in others it is only the motion of the rotor that provides forward (and also backward) motion. Initial breaking up of the hard soil is carried out by pointed pick-tines, while final cultivation is usually done with wide, right-angled blades.

Such cultivators cannot readily be used in ornamentally planted areas, only in vegetable or fruit plots where everything is grown in relatively long rows. This is especially important with larger models which need quite an area of 'headland' to be turned round. Almost all are powered by 2- or 4-stroke petrol engines. Small cultivators with tines rotating at the end of a long handle have been devised for use in confined areas, either operating through a flexible drive from a larger cultivator engine, or directly by electricity, though in the latter the power is often insufficient for anything more than surface stirring and weeding.

The word is also applied to a number of hand-operated tools, primarily to those with three or five recurved prongs, either sharp-pointed or with slightly flattened, arrow-shaped ends, which have also been called claw hoes.

Other forms of hand cultivator have a

wheel mounted in front of long handles, with small plough or hoe blades fixed underneath, or rotating, star-shaped 'millers' fixed behind the wheel. These have quite a long ancestry, but remain more popular in the U.S. and Europe than in Britain.
◊ HOE; TINE.

Cup (1) The name given to the central corona of narcissi when it is shorter than the length of the outer or perianth segments. In large-cupped narcissi, the cup is more than one-third the length of the perianth segments; in small-cupped, less than one-third. Some large-cups look almost like trumpet narcissi, but this term should be reserved for those in which the corona is as long as or longer than the perianth segments.
(2) The fruit of the oak, or acorn, is carried in a cup-shaped receptacle technically known as a CUPULE.
(3) Certain fungi are known as cup fungi because of their form.

CUP. *Left*, small-cupped and, *right*, large-cupped narcissi

Cupule A botanical term meaning a little cup, like that in which an acorn is carried. This is composed of bracts or bract-like scales, external to the flowers, which have become adapted and merged for the purpose. The hazel cupule is basically cup-shaped also, but other cupules differ in shape, like those of the beech and chestnut which envelop the seeds, and burst into divisions (valves) when the latter are ripe; in the hornbeam the cupule forms a three-lobed scale carrying the seed at its base, and in the hop-hornbeam it forms a loose papery envelope to the seed. The specific name *cupularis* refers to a plant with cupules. ◊ ACORN.

Curd The 'head' or flowering portion of cauliflowers and broccoli.

Cushion-forming, Cushion Plant Applied to mainly small plants with dense, close-packed branching which forms flattish to hemispherical cushion-like shapes. This form is characteristic of many alpines and other plants living in arid and windswept places.

Cut Flowers Flowers which are cut for indoor decoration. Commercial growers plant suitable kinds in long rows for ease of cultivation and picking; if space permits in the private garden, rows of suitable perennials, annuals and biennials are best grown in this way: a separate area for cut flowers is better than robbing the ornamental garden.

When cutting flowers in any quantity it is desirable to put them straight into a bucket of water carried with one. Many flowers, e.g. roses, peonies and most annuals, are best cut in bud; if many flowers are carried in a spike, e.g. antirrhinums or lupins, pick these when the lowest flowers are just starting to open. Cutting is best done early or late in the day rather than in midday heat. Evening cutting allows the flowers to have a deep cool drink in a cool place before arranging them the following day. Some cutting material needs special treatment, such as dipping the stems into boiling water, to prevent it from flagging quickly, and specialist literature should be consulted by the regular flower arranger.

Cuticle The outermost layer or skin of a plant organ. It is composed of cutin, a waxy substance more or less impervious to water, and hence protecting the plant cells within from loss of water by evaporation.

71

There is often an additional layer of true wax on top of the cuticle; it is sometimes quite thick and it is this which often gives certain leaves and fruits their whitish or bluish 'bloom'. The cuticle and additional waxy layers are most in evidence on plants which grow in open, sunny and dry conditions, and are less pronounced on shade- and moisture-loving kinds. ◊ WAX.

Cut-leaved Applied to certain aberrant forms of tree and shrub in which the leaves are divided into narrow segments.

Cutting A cutting is a portion of leaf, stem or root separated from a plant and treated in such a way that it produces roots and eventually grows into a new plant. It differs from a division in that the latter will already have some roots, though the phrase 'Irishman's cutting' is sometimes used to denote shoots, pulled from the crown or rootstock of a plant, which have already made roots.

Many plants may be increased by various different types of cutting, especially where stem cuttings are used, when the degree of maturity of the shoot determines the kind of cutting and the time to take it. These are referred to as follows:

soft or softwood cuttings made from immature tip growth on shrubs, including cuttings from herbaceous plants;

half-ripe or semi-hardwood cuttings, taken from shoots just starting to harden or mature at the base;

ripe or hardwood cuttings, made from mature shoots of woody plants.

The last are the easiest, especially as they can usually be rooted in the open without artificial aids such as frames or propagators. With the latter also, a 'heel' of older wood, torn off the main branch by pulling the chosen shoot downwards, is often helpful in getting roots to form. In general, cuttings are trimmed just below a node (a stem joint where leaves appear) but in some cases they need trimming between nodes (internodal).

Cuttings are also sometimes referred to according to the part of the parent plant they are taken from, e.g. axillary and basal cuttings from axillary and basal shoots.

Rooting of many cuttings is hastened by the use of root-forming hormones, but some plants will only root satisfactorily under mist propagation. Cuttings can also be made from roots.

◊ CROWN; DIVISION; EYE CUTTING; HEEL; HORMONES; LEAF BUD CUTTING;

CUTTING. *From left to right,* shrubby stem cutting, heel cutting, nodal and internodal cuttings

LEAF CUTTING; MERISTEM; MIST PROPAGATION; PIPING; PROPAGATION; ROOT CUTTINGS; STRIKE.

Cuttings Compost ◊ COMPOSTS, SEED AND POTTING. (Also a trade name in the U.K. for a kind of treated animal manure.)

Cutworms A term of American origin for caterpillars which live in the soil and attack plants just below ground level, often with fatal results. They are typically fat and sluggish, of greenish or brownish colouring, and are the larvae of moths. They can be destroyed by working suitable insecticidal dusts into the soil or applying them to the surface, or watering with insecticide solution. ◊ CATERPILLARS.

Cycad Any member of the family *Cycadaceae*, a primitive group allied to the conifers, usually with stiff palm-like leaves on short stout trunks.

Cyclic Bearing The production of fruit or seed crops at intervals of more than the normal year, from two to five or six years. The commonest example, found in certain fruit trees, is BIENNIAL BEARING.

Cyclopean Walling ◊ DRY WALL.

Cylinder Mower ◊ MOWERS.

Cyme ◊ INFLORESCENCE.

Cynarrodion ◊ HIP.

❈ D ❈

Daisy Grubber A small handtool with a long narrow blade cut into a V-shaped notch at the business end, and either cranked in the middle or with a metal 'bow' on the underside. Crank and bow are both to provide a leverage point when the notch is pushed into the soil or lawns, centred on a weed's roots, so that the weed may be pulled out by downward pressure on the handle.

Daisy Knife A tool used in the nineteenth century, though no longer available, consisting of a two-edged blade fixed obliquely to a long handle, and used to trim off flowers from daisies and other weeds which might escape the scythe, by sweeping the blade to and fro along the surface of the grass.

Damping Down The operation of wetting greenhouse floors and solid, gravel- or ash-covered stagings in order to provide the humid atmosphere essential in a warm greenhouse. Damping down can be carried out with a hose or a watering can with or without a spray head or rose, depending on the area to be covered and the degree of humidity needed. In hot weather it may have to be done three or four times daily, especially among tropical plants needing high temperatures. In damping down, the plant pots can be wetted but the plants themselves and the potting mixture should normally not be, since this can result in leaf scorch and overwatering. Apart from providing essential growing conditions for many plants, this operation will reduce the spread of the greenhouse red spider mite. ◊ DAMPING OVERHEAD; TRANSPIRATION.

Damping-off A name covering various fungus diseases which attack seedlings in the early stages of germination. Pre-emergence damping-off rots the seed before the first growth has broken through the soil; post-emergence damping-off attacks the seed-lings at soil level when they have produced their first leaves, causing them to topple over. The disease can be largely prevented by using sterilized seed-raising compost and avoiding overcrowding and overwatering. If it starts in a box or pan of germinating seed, there are various fungicides such as Cheshunt Compound which should stop it spreading. The compost can also be watered with a suitable fungicide before sowing, as a precaution.

Both pre- and post-emergence damping-off can affect newly sown grass seed. This is usually caused by sowing too late in autumn and too early in spring, when conditions are likely to be both humid and chilly. Pre-emergence damping-off, in which the seed rots, can be discouraged by treating the seeds with a fungicidal seed dressing before sowing. Should post-emergence damping occur, the spread of the attack is usually preventable by use of an appropriate fungicide.

◊ COLLAR ROT; FUNGICIDES; SEED DRESSING.

Damping Overhead Syringeing plants in a greenhouse with water so that they (as well as their pots and the staging) are left with a film of moisture; this is usually only done in very warm ('stove') greenhouses which are shaded from direct sun, otherwise leaf scorch can readily occur. Overhead damping is best done in the morning, allowing plants to dry out before night when lower temperatures could encourage disease on wet foliage. ◊ DAMPING DOWN.

Dard A fruit-grower's term for a lateral shoot not more than 3″ long, on an apple or pear tree, with a fruit bud at the tip. Should a dard carry only a growth or wood bud it will grow by imperceptible stages into a BRINDILLE.

Day-length The growth and flowering of many plants is controlled by the ratio between the length of day and night. Those which flower when days are long and nights short, as in the British summer, are known as long-day plants; those which do the reverse, only growing in long days and flowering when days are short and nights long, are called short-day plants. Those plants which are not affected by this phenomenon – which is called photoperiodism – may be classed as day-neutral.

In both cases many of the subjects can be induced to flower out of their normal season by artificial means. Long-day plants, if illuminated at night (and this normally means only a brief period of quite low lighting roughly in the middle of the night) can be made to flower in the short days of winter, examples being fuchsias and kalanchoes. Conversely, short-day plants, of which the chrysanthemum is the prime example, can be flowered in the long days of summer by covering them with blackout material at certain times to extend their 'night'. The manipulation of chrysanthemums has made it possible to grow them throughout the year by a combination of blacking-out in long days and extra, bright illumination in long nights. The poinsettia is a familiar example of a short-day plant which will continue to grow well indoors but will seldom flower again in the home because artificial lighting continues to keep the days effectively long. It can be induced to flower again if placed in a completely darkened cupboard every night for at least 13 hours, over a period of about eight weeks in autumn.

Day-neutral Plants unaffected by photoperiodism or DAY-LENGTH.

Dead-heading The removal of faded flowers, carried out partly to keep plants looking attractive but primarily to stop the formation of seed which is liable to discourage more flowers being formed, since a plant's main purpose in life is usually to produce seed. Dead-heading is essential with annuals and bedding plants which will usually die once seed has been formed, but is also desirable on many shrubs, notably roses, to maintain a succession of bloom all summer, and lilacs and rhododendrons to encourage better flowering the following year.

Deblossoming The removal of flowers on fruit trees, either singly or as entire flower clusters. Total deblossoming is advisable on top fruits in the first season after planting, so that the trees can establish themselves without the strain of producing fruit. This is also sometimes carried out on first-year strawberries.

Partial deblossoming is carried out on more established trees if the quantity of blossom suggests an exceptional set of fruit later, especially if the tree bore a very light crop the previous year. If heavy cropping is allowed, the tree may develop the habit of BIENNIAL BEARING.

Deciduous Losing leaves annually, usually in the winter, mainly referring to trees; the opposite of evergreen. When deciduous trees lose their foliage they become dormant, and their growth processes are almost entirely inactive, so that this is the ideal time to transplant them. Some deciduous trees, however, e.g. beech, do not drop their leaves when they are still in a juvenile state, so that a beech hedge retains its dried foliage all winter, a state known as narcescence.
◊ BROAD-LEAVED; EVERGREEN; JUVENILITY.

Deck A kind of terrace, with its origins in the balcony and verandah, made of wood boarding, largely restricted to the U.S. Sometimes decking is simply used as an alternative to more conventional stone or concrete paving; sometimes a deck is made as a slightly raised feature to provide contrast of form as well as finish. Decks supported on stilts are used to provide airy view-commanding platforms leading from houses on steep sites, particularly spectacular when the deck is embowered among the tops of trees; sometimes it is built around tree trunks growing from the ground below. Such decks are perhaps the modern equivalent of the tree house. As the U.S. designer Thomas D. Church has observed, the deck-platform solves the problem of projecting oneself into a natural landscape without destroying it. ◊ TERRACE; TREE HOUSE.

Decorative A classification term for a group of dahlias having broad, more or less flat petals, and for groups of chrysanthemum known as reflexed decorative and intermediate decorative. ◊ INTERMEDIATE; REFLEXED.

Decumbent A botanical term referring to plant stems which sprawl or lie on the ground, turning upwards near their ends.

Decurrent Running down, as when a leaf base is prolonged down the stem. ◊ LEAF.

Decussate A botanical term referring to paired, opposite leaves which grow first in one plane and then at 90° to the first. ◊ LEAF; OPPOSITE.

Deep Bed Method An ancient method of cultivation in which the bed in question is first covered with a generous layer of rotted manure. Following this the area is double dug. After this cultivation the bed must not be trodden on during the coming year; the following winter more manure is applied and the ground is forked over. The aim is to produce a deep bed, which becomes raised above the general level of the soil, of very good texture and high organic content. Because the bed is not to be trodden on, its dimensions must be such that all necessary work can be carried out from outside it. It is suggested that yields four times higher than those from conventional methods can be produced by the deep bed method, which has also been called the Chinese Method, the French Intensive Method and the Biodynamic/French Intensive Method. ◊ DIGGING.

Deep Trenching ◊ DIGGING.

Deer Now fully naturalized in many parts of Britain, and indigenous in North America, deer can cause serious damage in gardens, where they will totally eat up herbaceous plants, the top growth of roses and shrubs, the lower foliage on trees and, in severe weather, will eat the bark round tree trunks, which is likely to kill the trees. The only fully effective deterrent is a fence 7'–8' high (many deer can jump over 6'). Otherwise animal repellents should be used. Tree trunks can be protected with wire or plastic tree protectors. ◊ REPELLENTS; TREE GUARDS.

Deficiency When a soil is lacking in any of the minerals essential to plant growth, plants appear unhealthy and may show specific symptoms of the mineral deficiency concerned. Such deficiencies may be of either the major or minor growth minerals. One frequent cause of mineral deficiency is too much lime in the soil, which 'locks up' necessary minerals such as iron and causes yellowing or chlorosis of the leaves. ◊ CHLOROSIS; FEEDING PLANTS; MINERAL.

Defoliation The practice of removing leaves from tomato plants. This is often done as the fruit begins to ripen in the belief that direct sun will accelerate this process. However, ripening is largely the result of adequate temperature; the prime reason for defoliation is to remove yellowing leaves which are no longer useful and may become disease-infected. Such removal also helps to prevent the build-up of disease by improving air circulation at the base of the plants. Some commercial growers defoliate their tomatoes ruthlessly, leaving only the upper 3' of stem to carry leaves.

Defruiting The removal of immature fruit from a fruit tree, usually carried out if de-blossoming was intended but not done in time, in order to control biennial bearing or to allow a starved tree to build up its strength. Defruiting implies the removal of virtually all immature fruit, not just some as in thinning. ◊ BIENNIAL BEARING; DE-BLOSSOMING; THINNING.

Dehiscent A botanical term referring to fruits and to anthers which split open to release their seeds and pollen respectively. Such fruits – usually dry seed capsules or pods – do not split until ripe, and may do so in various ways, including the splitting accompanied by twisting of the pod walls which causes gorse seeds to be scattered explosively. Anthers likewise dehisce only when the pollen is ripe. ◊ ANTHER; CAPSULE; POD.

Dehorning A rather severe method of pruning old fruit trees which involves the total removal of some of the larger branches. These are cut off flush where they join other branches left in place; cuts should be carefully pared and covered with a wound dressing. The aim of dehorning is to remove dead, decaying or unfruitful wood and to reduce overcrowding; it may also reduce the overall size of the tree. Dehorning of elderly branches, usually the lowest outside ones, is a regular feature of the informal 'American' system of pruning fruit trees. Dehorning is slightly less drastic than HEADING BACK. ◊ WOUND DRESSING.

Delayed Open-centre A form of fruit tree aimed at by one of the informal pruning systems, and really identical to the 'bush'. Selective removal of branches from a central point results in a goblet-shaped outline but with the open centre of the true 'vase' or 'goblet' tree partly filled up by more or less upright branches grown from buds on the suppressed leading growth of the maiden tree. It is an easy system to carry out and suitable for all kinds of top fruit. ◊ BUSH; GOBLET; LEADER; MAIDEN; OPEN-CENTRE.

Delayed Pruning A detail of pruning vital to many of the complex French methods of training fruit trees in which the leader or leading shoot is cut back 2″ above the point at which it was previously pruned, and is subsequently pinched whenever fresh growth is made, so that it does not grow quickly. This method stimulates the buds destined to form main branches in future while preventing the leader from dominating its lower offshoots, and allowing those buds which exist already to grow without too much competition. ◊ LEADER.

Delayed Pyramid A method of pruning fruit trees, similar to that for the orthodox pyramid, which produces a shorter trunk and a thicker but less extensive framework. Such trees are not so neat as pyramids since the branches are likely to arch naturally. This method is favoured in the U.S. ◊ PYRAMID.

Denatured Alcohol or **Spirit** ◊ METHYLATED SPIRIT.

Dendrology The study of trees in all their aspects.

Denitrification Sometimes used to describe a severe reduction of nitrogen in the soil owing to unbalanced bacterial activity.

Dentate Literally, toothed; in botany this refers to leaves with relatively strongly toothed margins. ◊ LEAF; TOOTHED.

Derris An insecticide derived from the roots of a leguminous genus of that name, the active component of which is called rotenone. It is commonly used in dust form but is also formulated as a liquid or a wettable powder, and is effective against many large pests including beetles, weevils and caterpillars, as well as sap-suckers like aphids and red spider mites. It has the great merit of being harmless to warm-blooded animals, but is deadly to fish, so that spray should not get anywhere near garden pools. (Derris root pounded in rivers is used by many primitive people to kill fish.) ◊ PESTICIDE.

Deshooting The removal of very young shoots on trained trees, especially wall-trained fruit trees where shoots growing towards or away from the wall must be removed. Deshooting is best carried out when the shoots are soft enough to be removed by pinching them between the nails of thumb and forefinger. The word disbudding has been used for this operation, but should really be employed only with reference to the removal of blossom buds. ◊ DISBUDDING.

Design ◊ GARDEN DESIGN.

Determinate Describes plants, the stems of which end in a flower bud or truss, as in bush tomatoes; as opposed to standard or indeterminate tomatoes in which the stem can continue growing indefinitely.

Deterrent ◊ REPELLENTS.

Dew, Dewpoint Condensation of water vapour in the open air on cool surfaces results in the deposition of water in the form of small drops: this is dew. The occurrence of dew usually takes place as the temperature falls in the evening after a warm day, because the amount of water vapour a given volume of air can hold becomes reduced as temperature decreases. Thus at a certain low temperature the air becomes effectively saturated: this temperature is the 'dewpoint'. By calculating the dewpoint with a wet-and-dry-bulb thermometer, or using a patent device, the possibility of frost in the coming night can be forecast.

Plant leaves are usually among the first things to be covered with dew since they tend to be cooler than the surrounding air because they are constantly evaporating moisture themselves.

◊ FROST; HUMIDITY; THERMOMETER.

Dibber, Dibble A tool used for making holes in soil into which seeds, seedlings or cuttings may be inserted. The size of the tool varies according to the size of the seed or plant, from something resembling an ordinary pencil, or pieces of dowel with a rounded end, to those the size of a spade-

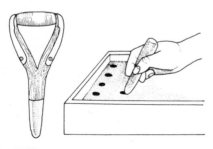

DIBBER

handle. An old spade handle can be converted, or dibbers with steel tips can be bought. It is better to have a rounded end rather than a pointed one. Dibble is an alternative spelling, and is also the verb describing the use of the tool. It is often quicker to dibble in seedlings than to use a trowel, but it is essential to fill in around the roots firmly, which is done by inserting the dibber alongside 1"–2" away. It is not advisable to plant bulbs with a dibber since they often lodge part-way down the hole and fail to form roots because of the airspace below. ◊ MULTI-DIBBER; PRICKING OUT; TROWEL.

Dicotyledon A plant whose seedlings produce a pair of cotyledons or seed leaves in contrast with the single one of monocotyledons; the dicotyledons (often abbreviated dicots) are one of the two great classes of flowering plants. Other distinguishing features include leaves with netted as opposed to parallel veins, flowers with parts in fours or fives as against threes, and a distinctive stem anatomy – though there are exceptions to these characters. ◊ CLASSIFICATION; FLOWER; MONOCOTYLEDON; VEIN.

Die-back A general term covering several fungus diseases that attack many kinds of different plant; they have the common effect of causing shoots or branches to die back from their tips. This dying back is relatively slow in comparison with the condition called wilt, in which the whole shoot collapses more or less at once. Many shrubs, including roses, soft and top fruits, can be affected by die-back, especially as they get old, and also carnations. Affected growths should be cut back well below the point where they are affected and woody branches should be treated with a tree-wound dressing. The phrase 'die-back' is also applied to the death of some shrubs which occurs for no apparent reason, as with *Daphne mezereum*; there is no cure for this. ◊ WILT.

Digging The standard method of cultivation for ordinary gardens, involving the turning over of the soil with a spade (or sometimes, if the soil is particularly stiff, with a fork). The purpose of this operation is to break up compacted soil, improve its crumb structure and aeration, incorporate manure or compost, and bury weeds unlikely to regenerate from their roots. Ground should always be dug over initially before planting up a garden, but regular digging is normally confined to the vegetable plot, which is most likely to become compacted in view of its succession of crops and the gardener's activity. Digging is best carried

DIGGING. See text for explanation

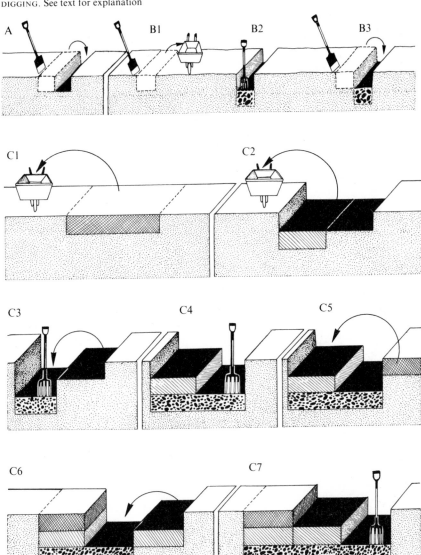

out in autumn or winter when the soil is not sodden or frozen, since there will be a minimum of standing crops at that time and soil can be left rough to benefit from the action of frost and weathering.

Digging can be carried out to varying depths, the operations being known as plain, single or single-spit digging; double digging, double spading or bastard trenching to two spits' depth; and trenching to three spits' depth (spit being the full 10″ depth of the spade).

Single-spit digging This involves forcing the spade (or fork) into the soil vertically to its full working depth, bearing back on the handle so that the soil can be lifted, and turning the tool over so that the soil falls back upside-down into the hole. In this way any surface weeds are fully buried. The clods or spadefuls of soil are not usually broken. In plots of any size a more efficient way of carrying out digging is to make an open trench at the start. This is dug across one end of the plot, removing soil to leave a trench roughly 10″ wide, and a spit's depth; the soil is moved by barrow to the further end of the plot. Digging then proceeds in such a way that the turned-over soil is thrown into this trench, then into the new trench thus formed, and so on, as the digger works to and fro along the width of the area. When he reaches the end of the plot he turns the soil brought from the first trench into the most recently made trench.

Double digging or **spading** (bastard trenching) The method involves removal of soil to a spit's depth and then breaking up the soil in the trench itself with a fork. It can only be done by taking out a trench to begin with in the same way as for single digging, but much wider – 2′. The soil removed is barrowed to the far end of the plot involved as before. The forking is carried on to the full depth of the fork's tines, so that a total depth of 20″ is broken up. After forking the bottom of the first trench, another strip of ground 2′ wide is marked out and the soil from this is thrown forward – and turned over – into the first trench. The bottom of this new trench is

then forked over, and so the work proceeds until the last trench is filled in by the originally barrowed soil from the first.

Trenching By this method soil is cultivated to a depth of three spits, i.e. 30″. To begin, a trench one spit deep is made 3′ wide and the soil is barrowed to the far end of the plot. Next, this trench is marked (by line) to divide it lengthwise. The soil from one half is dug out another spit deep; this is also removed to the far end of the plot, but must be kept separate from the original heap of soil. This 18″-wide trench, 20″ deep, is now broken up with a fork to the fork's depth. Following this, the undug part of the original trench is turned over onto the forked subsoil, and the exposed subsoil forked in its turn.

The digger can now return to surface level, and has to mark out a new 18″ strip; the top-spit soil is then thrown forward to fill the far side of the original trench. The second spit of the new strip is then turned over to fill the corresponding level of the first wide trench, and the subsoil is then forked over. Then the sequence is repeated on a new 18″ strip.

The heaps of top- and second-spit soil originally removed are replaced at the appropriate levels at the end of the operation.

Where very large plots are involved, the labour of transporting soil from one end to the other after digging out the first trench, in any of the methods of digging, can be reduced by dividing the area lengthwise so that in effect there are two plots. Digging proceeds down one plot and up the other; this means that the soil removed from the initial trench has only to be moved across the width of the entire plot, to be in place for refilling the final trench.

It will be noted that in both double digging and trenching, the top, second and third spits of soil are kept in the same relative positions. It is usually important to do this, since subsoil usually lacks the organic matter, bacteria and overall good growing qualities of the topsoil, and often also contains clay or stones. In ground where the soil is of good quality for a considerable depth the mixing of subsoil with topsoil may be carried out to increase the depth of fertile, well-worked soil, but this is rarely to be recommended. This practice is sometimes called deep trenching.

Although full trenching is seldom carried out nowadays, it can be very valuable to break up a hard soil layer or pan which impedes drainage and deep roots.

◊ AERATION; CRUMB; CULTIVATION; FORKING; FORKS; PAN; RIDGING; SPADE; SPIT; SUBSOIL; TOPSOIL; TRENCH.

Digging Stick A primitive tool to break up the soil. Originating perhaps with a deer antler, the digging stick is basically a long straight pole sharpened or flattened at one end, sunk vertically into the ground and pulled back to lift clods of soil, or used to break up the soil surface by repeated vertical movements. Some South American digging sticks, as used by the Incas, might have a foot bar and a curved handle to increase leverage. Digging sticks are more effective in soft, light soils than in heavy ones, and have in most parts of the world been replaced by spade, fork or digging hoe, although they are still in use in some places, e.g. Peru, where an implement very like the ancient Inca digging stick, but now carrying a long narrow metal blade at the end, is a standard implement in upland peasant communities. ◊ FORKS; HOE; SPADE.

Digitate A botanical term meaning 'fingered' and usually referring to leaves having several separate, radiating leaflets arising from one point on a common stalk, as in the horse chestnuts (*Aesculus*). ◊ LEAF; PALMATE.

Dilutor A device which automatically dilutes a concentrated solution of fertilizer or, more rarely, an insecticide or fungicide, when attached to a water pipeline. Dilutors are standard equipment in many commercial glasshouses so that plants can be fed while being watered, either in conjunction with pipelines to hoses or with permanent irrigation systems. Small dilutors can be obtained for use in conjunction with garden hoses. ◊ IRRIGATION.

Dimple A word, now seldom used, describing a disease of pears in which their surface is pitted or dimpled, with small gritty nodules in the flesh beneath each pit. This disease, caused by a virus, is now called STONY PIT.

Dinitro Compounds ◊ DNC; WINTER WASH.

Dioecious In a species described as dioecious the male and female flowers are carried on separate plants. This creates problems for the gardener who hopes for fruits on decorative plants such as hollies, pernettyas and skimmias; in such cases the problem must be solved by planting one male plant among several females to ensure fertilization. ◊ HERMAPHRODITE; MONOECIOUS.

Diploid A plant having the normal number of chromosomes of its species. ◊ CHROMOSOME; POLYPLOID; TRIPLOID.

Diplostemenous Applied to flowers having stamens in two alternating whorls, those in the outer whorl alternating with the petals.

Disbudding The removal of surplus buds or very young shoots, carried out in order to concentrate the efforts of the relevant stem into the one or few buds allowed to remain, so that these develop to the fullest possible extent and produce top-quality flowers or fruits. Disbudding is standard practice in producing exhibition carnations, chrysanthemums (◊ TAKE (2)), dahlias and roses. It is also carried out to restrict the number of side growths allowed to develop on trained grape-vines and fan-trained peach trees, nectarines and apricots (though in the latter case the operation is more accurately referred to as deshooting). With exhibition flowers the bud allowed to remain is normally the terminal one, but there are occasions, notably with roses which produce over-large blooms, when side-buds are selected for development.

Disbudding is usually done at a very early stage by rubbing the unwanted bud off with the thumb or pinching it between

thumb and first finger; occasionally the point of a penknife may be needed.
◊ TERMINAL.

Disc ◊ DISK.

Disease Used by gardeners to denote virtually any ailment of plants not caused by pests. Such ailments include attack by organisms such as bacteria, fungi and viruses, as well as malfunctions caused by faulty cultivation or unsatisfactory growing conditions, often referred to as disorders.

Many diseases have generalized names which refer to symptoms rather than the specific organism responsible, and may often include infections caused by a group of organisms, often quite unrelated. Some plant disorder names are similarly general.

For separate entries on plant diseases ◊ BLACK SPOT; BLOSSOM WILT; BRAND; BROWN ROT; CANKER; CLUB ROOT; COLLAR ROT (BASAL STEM ROT, BLACKLEG); DAMPING-OFF; DIE-BACK; DIMPLE; DOLLAR SPOT; DRY ROT; FIRE; FIRE BLIGHT; FOOT ROT; FUSARIUM PATCH; GALL; GREY MOULD (BOTRYTIS); GUMMOSIS; HONEY FUNGUS; LEAF CURL; LEAF SPOT; MILDEW; MOSAIC; MOULD; NECK ROT; NECROSIS; PHYTOPHTHORA; RED THREAD (CORTICIUM); ROOT ROT; RUBBERY WOOD; RUST; SCAB; SHOT-HOLE DISEASE; SILVER LEAF; SLEEPY DISEASE; SMUT DISEASES; SOFT ROT; SOOTY MOULD; STEM ROT; STONY PIT; STREAK; WART DISEASE; WILT.

For entries on plant disorders ◊ CHLOROSIS; DEFICIENCY; DRY SET; FASCIATION; HEART ROT; LEAF SCORCH; OEDEMA; PEDICEL NECROSIS; ROOT ROT; RUSSETING; SCALDING; SCORCHING; STORAGE ROTS; WILT; WIND.

◊ BACTERIA; FUNGICIDES; FUNGUS; PEST; VIRUS DISEASES.

Disinfection ◊ STERILIZATION.

Disk, Disc The flat compact centre of many composites (members of the daisy family); it is made up of disk florets which are short and tubular. A few composite flowers, like those in thistles, are made up entirely of disk florets, but most composites have a ring of showy ray florets around the disk. Also used of any flat, circular part of a single flower. ◊ COMPOSITE; RAY.

Disorder A word sometimes used to denote virtually any ailment of plants not caused by pests, in the same way as disease, though inclining more towards ailments caused by unsatisfactory soil and mineral deficiencies. ◊ DEFICIENCY; DISEASE.

Displanter An eighteenth-century word for a TRANSPLANTER.

Distichous Of organs set in two vertical rows, like the florets of many grasses, and certain leaves. ◊ LEAF.

Distributor A mechanical device used for spreading various materials, primarily fertilizers, onto lawns, and also on an agricultural scale onto fields. There are several kinds of distributor. The spinner type distributes by centrifugal action. The meter roller has a grooved or dimpled roller, driven from the wheels, and allows material from a hopper to fall through the grooves or pits onto the grass. The variable slit distributor has a slide at the base which is moved to open slits or holes to the size required, the material being worked through these by a rotating brush. The conveyor-belt type has under the feeding hopper an endless belt onto which the material is fed through a variable aperture on the hopper, so as to fall onto the lawn or, in larger models, to be pushed off by a rotating brush.

Only the last type provides really constant and even distribution, though for small lawns the meter roller type is perfectly adequate, provided the fertilizer is absolutely dry.

All distributors should be cleaned at once after use and stored dry: it is essential that no fertilizer remains anywhere in the machine since it will corrode metal parts, can damage plastic and will be a problem if it becomes damp and sets hard.

Distributors are also used for SEED SOW-
ING.

Divided Used of leaves composed of a number of individual leaflets on a common midrib, as when pinnate, trifoliate, etc. The
leaflets may be confused with individual
small leaves on a common stem, but there
will be no buds present in a divided leaf.
◊ LEAF.

Division The easiest way of increasing
clump-forming plants is to cut, pull or tease
the roots apart. With vigorous herbaceous
plants it is often best to retain only the outer
sections of a clump and discard the old,
worn-out centre. Very tough clumps can be
chopped up with a spade, or cut with a
knife, but this will inevitably leave many
roots severed and should be used only on
plants with very hard crowns, e.g. delphiniums, peonies and rhubarb. Fibrous clumps
are better pulled apart by the leverage of
two forks, large or small, placed back to
back, after which the pieces can if desired
be further broken up by hand. With fragile
pot plants, like African violets (*Saintpaulia*)
which make several crowns, hand pulling
aided by the use of a sharp knife is usually
necessary. ◊ CROWN; PROPAGATION.

DIVISION. Using two hand forks back to back.

DNA An abbreviation for desoxyribonu-
cleic acid, a complex molecule found in
chromosomes and generally believed to be
the chemical basis of the genes which contain the genetic information for the development of the organism concerned.
◊ CHROMOSOME; GENE.

DNC, DNOC Abbreviations for the chemical dinitro-ortho-cresol, once used as an ingredient of winter washes, especially in combination with petroleum oil, and referred
to in quite recent reference works. It is now
no longer available for amateur use, despite
its effectiveness against hibernating insects,
eggs and fungus spores, being toxic to human
beings and necessitating the wearing of protective clothing and goggles. It has now
been replaced by winter washes based on
phenols. ◊ WINTER WASH.

Dogs An ill-controlled dog can do much
damage in a garden, but this is a matter
of training and restraint. The commonest
problem with dogs occurs when they urinate on the lawn: the urine of bitches in
particular will scorch the grass, causing
brown patches edged with deep green grass.
The grass in the patches is likely to die,
allowing weeds and coarse grasses to colonize. There is no real cure but, if a dog is
seen to urinate on the lawn, immediate
flooding of the spot with plenty of water
will often lessen the damage.

Dollar Spot A fungal disease of turf which
initially causes round, whitish to golden or
brown spots on turf about 2″ across, though
these may enlarge and form bigger irregular
areas. Though controllable by applying
calomel or more modern lawn fungicides, it
is most likely to occur on under-nourished
lawns, so an application of a fertilizer with
high nitrogen content will help the grass
recover; the disease is usually avoided if the
turf is fed regularly. ◊ CALOMEL.

Dolomite, Dolomitic Limestone ◊ LIME-
STONE.

Dormant, Dormancy Plants are said to be
in a state of dormancy, dormant, or resting,
when visible activity ceases. Thus deciduous trees shed their leaves and herbaceous
perennials die down in winter, when their
internal activity is much reduced though by

no means actually at a standstill: because of this, the dormant period is the best time to move such plants.

Plants with storage roots, including bulbs, corms and tubers, become dormant to such an extent that their roots die away and the roots can often be dug up and stored dry, while some such plants can have their dormancy prolonged by cold storage.

Many seeds undergo a period of dormancy after ripening and it is often impossible to induce them to germinate, though various methods of 'breaking' dormancy or reducing the period involved are used in some cases. Exposure to cold, as by sowing seeds and leaving them outside in winter, or by keeping them refrigerated for a time, will often induce seeds from temperate climates to sprout when warmer conditions are supplied. Buds may be termed dormant or latent when they remain inactive unless stimulated into growth by the renewal of previously active shoots.

⟡ BUD STAGES; BULB; CORM; DECIDU-OUS; LATENT; RESTING; SEED SOWING; TRANSPLANTING; TUBER; VERNALIZA-TION.

Dormant Oil The U.S. name for a winter wash of petroleum oil. ⟡ WINTER WASH.

Dorsal Pertaining to the back; in gardening, largely restricted to describing the middle sepal of orchid flowers, the organ which stands upright at the back of the flower and is very often its most notable part. ⟡ ORCHID.

Dot Plant A tall plant used, especially in bedding schemes, in a groundwork of lower plants, to give contrast and height. Any plant can be so used: among those favoured in formal bedding are variegated abutilons, *Eucalyptus globulus*, cannas, kochias, and standard fuchsias and pelargoniums.

Double, Semi-double Flowers so described have many more than the number of petals normal to the wild species. In fully double flowers, the whole centre is filled with petals, which may sometimes replace stamens and carpels, with the result that no seeds can

be formed and the plant is sterile. Where a flower has more than the usual number of petals but is not fully double it is called semi-double; such flowers usually have a full complement of stamens and carpels, but there is no exact dividing line. However, there is no mistaking the perfect fully double flower such as hybrid tea roses, many camellias, double hollyhocks and most dahlias and chrysanthemums. In members of the composite family, e.g. the last two, doubling is caused by the replacement of all the disk florets by ray florets.

A double flower may be designated botanically by the words *flore pleno*, or the abbreviation *fl. pl.* or the single word *plena* or *pleniflora*.

⟡ ANEMONE-CENTRED; CARPEL; COMPO-SITE; DISK; FLOWER; RAY; SINGLE; STAMEN.

DOUBLE (camellia)

Double Digging ⟡ DIGGING.

Double-leader Applied to trees which have produced twin vertical shoots rather than one at the top.

Double Spading A U.S. term for double digging. ⟡ DIGGING.

Double-working A method of grafting used, mainly on fruit trees, when stock and scion varieties are incompatible, with consequent danger of a break later on at the point of grafting. It involves the use of a short section of an 'intermediate' variety which is compatible with both stock and scion.
⟡ COMPATIBILITY; GRAFTING; INCOM-PATIBLE; SCION; STOCK.

Downy Having very short, fine hairs. ◇ HAIRY.

Downy Mildew ◇ MILDEW.

Drag A tool based on a fork with the tines at right angles. A small version is now known as a fork hoe, and a larger one, like a garden fork with tines bent back almost or completely at right angles, is called a refuse drag in the U.K., though in France and the U.S. it is used as a cultivating tool. The manure drag has its tines bent over right at the base, and has a long handle.

Drag Brush A brush-like device designed to be pulled across turf in order to work in TOP DRESSINGS.

Drainage (1) Very few plants survive in waterlogged soil: most demand well-aerated soil in which, while necessary moisture is retained, any surplus drains away rapidly. Only in these conditions will the roots of the average plant develop properly. Poorly drained soils are inimical to beneficial soil organisms, and take much longer to warm up in spring than open soils, and this will also retard growth.

Most soils can be made reasonably well drained by thorough cultivation, during which heavier, water-retentive soils can be improved by working in bulky organic materials like peat or rotted garden compost or, for a more permanent effect, gritty material like coarse sand or road grit. In some cases trenching or deep ploughing

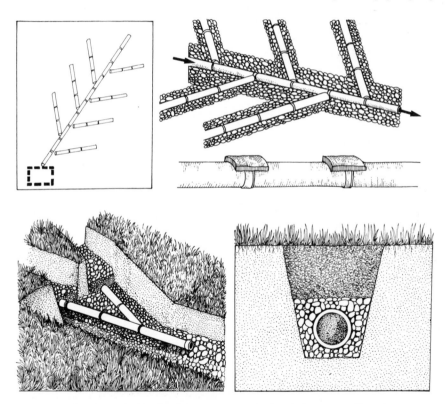

DRAINAGE. *Above left*, typical herring-bone system emptying in a drain or sump. *Above right*, details of junctions. *Below left*, pipes are laid on gravel or cinders and covered with more before trenches are refilled with soil, as in section, *right*

85

may be needed to break up a hard pan (a layer of consolidated soil) below the surface.

If ordinary cultivation is not sufficient to deal with the situation, as when the local water table is near the surface, excess moisture can only be removed by installing a system of land drains. These must normally be arranged in a herringbone pattern, although this can be varied according to the area involved. They should follow any natural slope or, in a flat site, be made with a slight slope towards the lowest point – 1 in 40 is adequate. At the lowest point there should be an outlet into a ditch, stream or an existing drainage system; if there is no suitable outlet it will be necessary to dig a soakaway – a large, deep pit filled with rubble, stones, clinker, etc. Drainage water should not be allowed to end up in neighbouring property and the local official surveyor's office should be consulted for clearance to allow water into existing drainage systems or ditches.

The first step is to dig out trenches for the drainage system. They should ideally be 12″–15″ deep, with side trenches meeting the main trench at an angle of about 45°. The best drains are constructed from earthenware field or pipe drains 2″–3″ in diameter, if possible laid on a 2″ layer of coarse gravel or cinders, well firmed down. Each pipe section should be about $\frac{1}{2}$″ from the next to allow water to seep in, the junction being covered with a piece of slate, tile or similar material to prevent subsequent clogging. The pipes should be surrounded and covered with further gravel or cinders as work proceeds.

An alternative to the rather expensive pipe drains is to fill the trenches with a 4″–6″ layer of fairly small rubble covered with a similar depth of gravel or coarse cinders, and finally with soil and if necessary grass: this is sometimes called a turf drain. Yet another method is to place tight-bound bundles of brushwood in the trenches, although in time these will rot and the trenches will tend to cave in, calling for renewal every few years.

When installing a drainage system in a new plot, the position of any buildings to be erected should be worked out, e.g. greenhouses, sheds and house extensions, since these will all shed water during rain.

Drainage is also important when growing plants in pots and other containers. ◊ POTTING.

◊ AERATION; COMPOST HEAP; CULTIVATION; PAN; PEAT; TOP DRAINING.

(2) The word is also applied to the movement of air down a slope, though this is usually qualified as AIR DRAINAGE.

Draining Tool A spade-like tool, also called a drain spade, with a relatively long, narrow blade, tapering slightly to the usually rounded end, used for digging drainage trenches. ◊ GRAFTING TOOL; SPADE.

Draw Hoe ◊ HOE.

Drawing Making seed drills with a hoe. ◊ DRILL.

Drawn Plants grown in poor light or too crowded become abnormally tall and thin; this is described as being drawn. It is a typical condition of seedlings when seed has been sown too thickly; it can be avoided by careful sowing, early thinning and pricking out, and ensuring that seedlings grown in greenhouses are placed in good all-round light at an early stage. Plants sown on windowsills indoors tend to become drawn by the one-sided light. Any drawn seedling is inevitably weak, and may never get over this check. ◊ ETIOLATED; PRICKING OUT; THINNING.

Drench, Drenching The application of a pest control liquid to the roots of a plant, either to deal with pests in the soil or, with systemic materials, to be absorbed by the roots and taken into the plant's sap above ground; sometimes referred to as soil drenching. ◊ PESTICIDES; SYSTEMIC.

Dressing (1) Any plant food, from bulky organic manure to dry fertilizer, applied in a solid state as opposed to a liquid one. Such dressings are of two types.

Base dressings are applied before planting or sowing crops and are well dug into the topsoil at that time: they are usually of bulky manures, garden compost or slow-acting granular materials such as bone-meal.

Top or side dressings are applied around growing plants on the soil surface. Where top dressings are of bulky manures or compost they are more usually called mulches, and the word 'dressing' is usually restricted to the application of quick-acting fertil-izers, e.g. dried blood, nitrate of soda or lime. With such materials it is important not to touch the leaves of plants, which can be scorched, and equally not to exceed the recommended quantity, which can other-wise result in severe damage to roots. It is seldom necessary to dig or fork in a top dressing, and indeed this could readily damage plant roots.

A top dressing for a lawn involves bulky materials chosen for their physical attributes to encourage root growth and drought re-sistance and to level out any irregularities. Such a dressing should combine sharp sand and organic matter, and might consist of equal parts medium sand and finely sieved, fully decayed garden compost, or of 2 parts sand, 1 part sieved medium loam, and 1–2 parts other organic matter, such as peat or spent hops. Sharp sand can be used alone and is valuable as an autumn dressing, especially over heavy soil. Such dressings need to be evenly spread and worked in with a stiff brush, a drag mat or a lute.

◊ LUTE; MAT; MULCH.

(2) Dressings of fungicides and pesticides may be applied to seeds to prevent disease and pest attack at and after germination. Similar dressings may be applied to bulbs, corms, tubers and similar fleshy roots, both before planting and before storing.
◊ FUNGICIDES; PESTICIDES.

Dribble Bar The same as a SPRINKLE-BAR.

Dried Blood ◊ BLOOD.

Drill A narrow furrow or groove, made in soil, usually with the corner of some kind of hoe, for the sowing of seeds or occasion-ally the reception of seedlings. Seeds sown in this way naturally germinate in straight

lines, as opposed to the scatter from broad-cast sowing. The draw hoe is most often used to make drills, but some gardeners use a dutch hoe held near-vertically; a special drill hoe is also available. Where small drills are needed, as in frames or small beds, a small sowing hoe, strong pointed stick or sharp narrow trowel can be used. Devices with several pointed prongs are available to make multiple furrows in seed beds. Drills in seed boxes are perhaps best made by pressing down with a cane or a piece of wood slat of the right length.

Mechanical implements called seed drills are also available which both make the drill and drop the seeds into it at regular spacings.

DRILL

It is best to use the hoe along a well-stretched garden line but, even so, firmness and control are needed to obtain a drill which is both straight and of the correct depth. In open ground it is essential that the soil is well broken and free of stones, after digging, settling and fine raking. Most seeds need drills of depths only $\frac{1}{4}''-\frac{1}{2}''$; it is very easy to make too-deep drills and thus bury seeds too far. Peas, beans and other large seeds must be buried more deeply.

87

After sowing, the seeds are covered by drawing the displaced soil back into the drill.

◊ GARDEN LINE; HOE.

Drill Hoe ◊ HOE.

Drip Line The position or imaginary line on the soil below a tree where its leaves shed rain drips; this is the area to which feeding roots normally extend and around which fertilizer should be applied.

Drip Watering Another term for trickle irrigation. ◊ IRRIGATION.

Dropsy ◊ OEDEMA.

Drought A period of 14 consecutive days without measurable rainfall is officially termed a drought in Britain. Many plants will flag in such conditions, especially if the lack of rain is accompanied by very hot weather which causes plants to transpire greatly. The normal remedy is to apply extra water, as long as watering restrictions have not been applied. If this is carried out, it must be done daily and an adequate quantity given, the equivalent of $\frac{1}{4}''$ of rain, preferably in a fine spray as provided by a sprinkler rather than a flood from an open hose (which, apart from other problems, can cause an impermeable pan to form on the soil surface). Regular watering causes roots to grow near the surface and irregular application can result in their being scorched on hot days.

Moisture can also be retained in the soil, once it is there, by applying a mulch of bulky organic matter or using plastic sheeting or even a layer of stones for the same purpose.

There are, of course, many plants adapted to living in drought conditions, e.g. succulents, most fleshy-rooted species and certain shrubs, notably those with green stems and small or no leaves, like brooms. Such plants should be selected if a garden is to be made in an abnormally dry area; it is not a frequent problem in Britain but occurs in the Mediterranean, California and desert areas elsewhere.

◊ FLAGGING; MULCH; RAIN; SPRINKLER; TRANSPIRATION.

Drupe A fruit comprising an outer skin, a fleshy layer, and a hard 'stone' protecting the seed proper. Cherries and plums are simple drupes. Compound drupes include those of raspberry and blackberry, in which the flesh-coated seeds are grouped together, and those of holly and elder, in which each 'berry' contains several seeds or nuts. ◊ BERRY; STONE.

Drying Flowers ◊ EVERLASTING.

Dry Rot Apart from the definition of a deadly fungus infection of wood in buildings, dry rot covers several diseases which cause a dry decay in various parts of plants including fleshy roots (bulbs, corms, tubers and rhizomes) and fruit. Typical symptoms are a brown discoloration and shrivelling in patches, sometimes followed by whitish pustules, and eventual shrivelling up and 'mummification' of the organ. Badly stored potatoes and growing gladiolus corms are commonly attacked. Infected organs should be destroyed and any remaining treated with an appropriate fungicide.

Dry Set The condition in which tomato fruits which have apparently set fail to swell from pinhead size, usually occurring in glasshouses with too hot and dry an atmosphere. It can be avoided by spraying the flowering tops of the plants with water or a fruit-setting spray. ◊ HORMONES.

Dry Wall A stone wall built without using mortar. In many parts of Britain such walls are a familiar part of the landscape, especially on high sheep moors. In gardens their attractive appearance and relative ease of construction can be adapted to housing plants. Dry walls can be double-sided but their more frequent use in gardens is as a covering and stabilizer for vertical banks and terrace edges.

Stones used for construction should all be roughly the same thickness (2″–3″ is ideal). Broken York stone paving slabs or more regular reconstituted stone slabs can be used; indeed almost any kind of stone is suitable.

To make a dry wall a trench about 6″ deep should be excavated the length of the wall to a width a little greater than that desired for the base: if the wall is to be of any appreciable height a base not less than 2′ wide is essential. Use the larger pieces at the bottom and build up courses horizontally, checking regularly with a spirit level to make sure that the level is reasonably steady. 'Bond' the wall by ensuring that a joint in one course is covered by a stone in the next. If the wall is to contain plants, place a ½″ layer of soil between each course, filling all the gaps: this soil should be of good quality and contain moisture-holding organic material. The outer face of the dry wall should slope backwards slightly from base to top, at an angle of 15–20°.

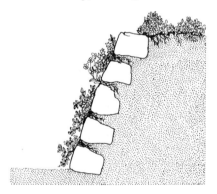

DRY WALL. Section of a retaining wall to hold plants, at the edge of a bank of soil

An alternative method of making a dry wall on a more gently sloping site is to make the courses of flattish pieces of stone, e.g. broken paving slabs, set into the ground vertically, with planting slots between. Sometimes called cyclopean walling, this is effective on slopes of around 45°.

Double-sided free-standing dry walls are usually kept fairly low or they become unstable. A wall 3′ high should be around 18″ across at the base; the outer faces should each slope back at 15–20° as for the single-

faced dry wall. If soil is scarce, the centre, between the two ranks of horizontally placed courses, can be filled with small rubble tightly rammed.

Planting can be done when the wall is completed, but it is much easier to carry out while it is being built, since the roots of each plant can be spread out as required and fully surrounded with soil above and below. Many plants are suitable for walls, especially relatively vigorous alpines, including trailers. Specialist alpine nurseries will make up suitable selections.

Dunse A type of SLASHER.

Duster A device for applying pesticidal or fungicidal dusts. ◇ DUSTING.

Dusting The application of pest and disease control materials in the form of a fine dust rather than a spray. Dusts are sometimes more effective than sprays, e.g. on the cabbage family where liquids are repelled by the waxy coating of the leaves, although they are unsightly in the flower garden. Dusts are most suitable for application onto earth against soil pests. Dusts should be applied in still weather conditions and when the plants are slightly moist, e.g. in the morning before dew evaporates. Dusts can be puffed onto plants or soil from plastic puffer-packs, hand-worked bellows devices or, for large areas, from motor-driven rotary fan applicators. ◇ BELLOWS; PUFFER.

Dutch Garden A style of gardening in Britain, broadly dating to 1688 (when the reign of William and Mary began), although certain published books had encouraged such designs perhaps a century earlier. It is characterized by a great deal of small detail in both layout and ancillary features such as statuary, trees in tubs, topiary and low clipped box hedges, orangeries, and the use of bulbs throughout the season. The Dutch garden reflects the desire of the Dutch, in their relatively small, shut-in gardens, to encompass as much of the large-scale Renaissance garden as possible; it is really a combination of French and con-

89

temporary Dutch influences. A few Dutch gardens still exist in Britain and there are also some renovations and examples of gardening in the Dutch manner.

Dutch Hoe ◊ HOE.

Dutch Light A type of frame light made of a simple wooden frame, usually 59″ × 30¾″ or close to that size, containing a single piece of glass, fitted into slots without the use of putty. The glass is usually the relatively lightweight 21 oz. horticultural type, so that the whole light can be lifted easily by one person. The lights are widely used in commercial horticulture, usually on simple wooden frameworks, though sometimes temporary frames are made by using straw bales for the walls. Dutch light greenhouses are simple structures designed so that the slightly sloping sides and pitched roofs are both formed of as many Dutch lights as desired; sometimes these structures are erected on rails so that the whole can be moved along over a series of crops. The main disadvantage of the Dutch light is the vulnerability of the single large glass sheet.
◊ FRAME; GLASS; LIGHT.

Dwarf, Dwarfing Apart from many naturally very small plants to which the word 'dwarf' might be applied, there are numerous varieties of normally large plants, mostly trees and shrubs, which are naturally dwarfer than the species concerned. These arise by mutation or, in the case of many dwarf conifers, from freaks caused by witches' brooms, and can be increased indefinitely from cuttings. Although it is true that some so-called dwarf trees can grow quite large over a long period, they are certainly much slower-growing than the species concerned.

Besides such naturally occurring dwarfs, plant breeders have succeeded in raising dwarf forms of many popular plants: here the emphasis has been on herbaceous subjects, including delphiniums and sweet peas, where dwarf varieties reduce or eliminate the need for support.

The hereditary nature of such dwarfs is in contrast to artificial dwarfing by cultural methods, notably trees by bonsai. In modern times a range of plants, particularly chrysanthemums, are dwarfed by the use of chemicals to produce very compact pot plants; the effect, however, only lasts for one season and, if grown another year, the plants revert to their natural stature.

Dwarfing of trees, primarily fruits, is also accomplished by grafting them onto 'dwarfing rootstocks' which ensures that even vigorous varieties can be grown in limited space and as trained trees, impossible if they are grown on their own roots or an unselected stock.

◊ BONSAI; GRAFTING; MUTATION; STOCK; WITCHES' BROOMS.

❧ E ❧

Early Flower ◊ BUD STAGES.

Earthing Up To earth up ('hill up' in U.S.) is to draw soil up around plants. This is done for several reasons: with leeks and celery, earthing up over their growing period is done to blanch the stems and make them more palatable; potatoes are habitually earthed up to avoid greening of the tubers and to protect early growth from frost. Leeks and potatoes are earthed up at intervals as they grow, but with celery it is best to wait till the heads are well developed, since the plants make little further growth after being earthed up.

The operation is normally carried out with a draw hoe or a drag fork (a broad-tined fork with tines bent at right angles). With celery and leeks a spade may be more useful since the soil can be piled up quite high and the back of the spade used to firm and smooth the near-vertical ridge produced. In the case of celery, the stems should be tied together to avoid earth getting between them; some growers use a wrapping of strong paper as added protection. Growers of exhibition leeks may employ wooden planks fixed vertically about 5″ from the plants to make a trough which can be filled with soil. Earthing up may also be carried out to prevent wind-rocking of tall brassicas like broccoli, brussels sprouts, cauliflowers and kales; and in layering and

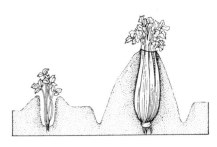

EARTHING UP. *Left*, first stage with celery; *right*, final stage

stooling of fruit rootstocks. ◊ BLANCHING; ETIOLATION; LAYERING; STOOLING.

Earthworms These familiar soil creatures are largely beneficial in the garden, since they tunnel through the soil, mostly by eating their way through it, and also pull debris down into it. The result is improved aeration, texture and organic content. Other species live in compost heaps and help to speed up the process of decay. In the U.S. the breeding and selling of earthworms to gardeners is quite an extensive trade. Worms prefer damp soils rich in organic matter to dry, sandy ones.

However, earthworms can be a nuisance in some areas of the garden, mainly when they create casts (heaps of digested earth) on the surface of fine lawns, which – especially if trodden flat – are likely to smother the grass and cause dead patches. To prevent this, various proprietary worm-killing materials can be obtained to spread on the lawn and water in. The more modern ones kill the worms in the soil, but the older remedy, mowrah meal, causes them to come to the surface where they have to be swept up. Permanganate of potash is another expellent.

Worms are also harmful if they get into plant pots and boxes, either in unsterilized soil or by entering the drainage holes if the pots are stood on soil. Their tunnelling here can interfere with roots and cause them to dry out, and their sticky casts can block the drainage. To prevent worms entering plant pots and containers perforated zinc disks can be placed over the drainage holes at the base of the pots, and pots should be stood on tiles, paving or similar material uncongenial to worms.

Earwigs Insects related to grasshoppers, crickets and cockroaches, with long narrow bodies, short wingcases, and a pair of pincers or prongs at the rear. The derivation of the name is problematical. Earwigs are interesting as being among the few insects where the female tends both eggs and young. This endearing fact is offset by the damage they can cause to plants, making neat holes in petals and leaves and sometimes skeletonizing the latter, although they are basically scavengers that

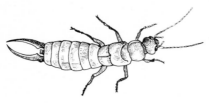

EARWIG

will eat anything organic. They are particularly fond of many-petalled flowers, e.g. chrysanthemums and dahlias, which also provide them with the snug, dark shelter they like in the daytime, since they are mainly active at night. This habit allows the gardener to trap them easily in small rolls of corrugated cardboard, barely open matchboxes placed on the ground, or small flower-pots stuffed with hay or straw placed upside-down on the ground or on canes. Otherwise they can be destroyed by several insecticides, best applied as dusts. Under glass, insecticidal 'smokes' will kill them.

Ecology The study of the relationship of living organisms with their total environment. Factors affecting plants are the climatic; those of physical and topographical features; the soil; and other living organisms (including other plants). Ecology can be applied both in the wild and in the artificial environment of a garden: a good gardener understands these influences – even if instinctively – and a study of them is desirable, especially when plants are grown in natural surroundings among existing trees, etc. ✧ ALPINE MEADOW; NATURALISTIC; WILD GARDEN.

Edging (1) The act of trimming the edges of lawns. ✧ EDGING TOOLS.

(2) The use of solid materials to keep lawn edges tidy and prevent grass growing into beds and borders. These are normally in the form of a long narrow strip of plastic or thin metal which is sunk vertically into the soil with its upper edge just below the grass surface, so that the mower can pass over it. Strips of vinyl floor covering can be used in the same way. These strip materials have replaced once-popular edging tiles. Lawns may also be edged with paving slabs, laid horizontally just below the level of the turf but, though this prevents grass growing beyond the lawn, it will not stop it spreading untidily over the surface of the slabs.

(3) The use of small plants to form an outline to beds or borders, not in any way to control grass. A favourite of past centuries was to use dwarf hedges, of shrubs or sub-shrubs, notably of the dwarf form of box which is sometimes called edging box; other plants used were lavender and cotton lavender. Nowadays it is more common to use low-growing flowering plants.

Edging Iron ✧ EDGING TOOLS.

Edging Tools During the eighteenth century it was considered desirable for lawns to have neat edges where they met beds, borders or paths. This was doubtless carried out originally with a flat-bladed spade, from which a special tool, the edging iron, was derived, with a straight handle fixed in line with a half-moon-shaped blade. This is today usually catalogued as a lawn edging knife. Since the early nineteenth century this has been improved in two ways, one version having the fixed blade replaced by a sharp-edged wheel, the other having a fixed knife-like blade, adjustable for depth, fitted close to a toothed wheel which is pushed along the grass just inside its margin. These were known also as turf-razers (from the French *raser*, to shave) and hence – phonetically – as turf-racers or races, and as verge-cutters. Turf-racers, based on a knife blade drawn towards the operator, rather than pushed away from him, were later primarily used for cutting turf before it was lifted for making lawns. The wheeled type has been improved by replacing the wheel by a small roller, and the knife by a number of small radiating blades. There are several modern variations of these tools, including powered versions. Long-handled shears with the blades in the same plane as the handles are also available,

tating feeding process, which sometimes causes distortion and discoloration of leaves and stems and often severe stunting. Infested bulbs show brown rings if cut across; some species are known as root-

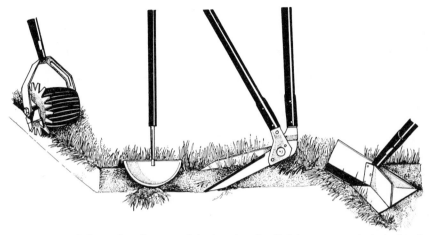

EDGING TOOLS. *Left to right*, roller type; edging iron; long-handled shears; patent dual-edged tool

and one modern hand-pushed edging tool combines vertical and horizontal cutting edges so that the unwanted grass is severed at the roots as well as vertically.

Eelworms Thin worm- or eel-shaped organisms, often placed in a distinct class in the animal kingdom (i.e. comparable with insects or mammals), technically known as nematodes or nematode worms. Though a few may be as long as $\frac{1}{4}''-\frac{1}{2}''$ the majority of species are $\frac{1}{32}''$ long or even less. Many species are quite harmless and feed on decaying matter, but some are extremely serious pests of both garden plants and agricultural crops, since they are virtually impossible to destroy in open soil. Further, they may produce young in egg-like cysts which can remain viable for many years, or may exist as adults in a state of suspended animation during unfavourable conditions. Damage to plants is caused by the eelworms piercing the cells, usually of the roots, sucking up the contents, and entering the plant tissue to continue this debili-

knot eelworms because they produce small swellings on the roots (which should not be confused with the beneficial nodules of nitrogen-fixing bacteria on leguminous plants).

In glasshouses the soil can be sterilized to kill eelworms either chemically or by steam, but the use of chemicals on open ground has been restricted to agricultural land, since they have to be injected deep into the soil and special precautions are needed with the materials used. Hot-water treatment, again only really feasible on a commercial scale with specialized equipment, has been used on bulbs, chrysanthemums and strawberries.

A wide range of plants can be attacked, including potatoes, tomatoes and many ornamentals and pot plants. Most eelworms attack only one kind of plant, so it is essential not to replant an attacked species in the same ground for at least four years. Unfortunately, even this precaution may not serve since it has been shown that the cysts of many eelworms respond to exu-

93

dations made by the roots of the host plant even after a decade or more.
    ◊ HOT-WATER TREATMENT; NODULE; STERILIZATION.

Egg-killing Chemicals ◊ OVICIDE.

Electricity Widely used as a power source for a number of gardening operations. Many mowers and hedge-trimmers, and some smaller devices, for lawn edging, weed cutting and light soil tilling, are powered by electricity. These are usually connected direct to the mains by cable, although a few mowers have rechargeable batteries.
    Electricity also holds an important place in heating greenhouses and propagators: although (at the time of writing) more expensive than other heat sources, it has the great merits of being clean, neat, virtually no trouble after installation, and very accurately controllable by thermostat. It is particularly useful when concentrated in small areas, e.g. in propagators and soil-warmed frames. Electricity also provides one of the quickest and cleanest methods of sterilizing soil for the amateur gardener.
    Electricity is of course used for lighting both gardens and greenhouses decoratively, and for light sources for control of day-length and for out-of-season plant raising.
    ◊ CULTIVATOR; DAY-LENGTH; HEDGE TRIMMING; LIGHT; MOWERS; PROPAGATOR; SOIL WARMING; STERILIZATION; THERMOSTAT.

Electronic Leaf ◊ MIST PROPAGATION.

Elliptic Of leaves shaped like a geometrical ellipse, though often used of those which are oblong with regularly rounded ends. ◊ LEAF.

Emarginate ◊ NOTCHED.

Emasculation The removal of anthers from a flower before the pollen is ripe, carried out to prevent self-fertilization. This is done by plant breeders making deliberate crosses between selected parent plants. Emasculated flowers must be protected from pollination by insects by covering them in muslin or plastic bags. ◊ BREEDING; CROSS-FERTILIZATION.

Embryo In botany, the rudimentary plant contained in the seed, either occupying the whole seed or embedded in food-reserve tissue. ◊ SEED.

Emulsion A preparation in which tiny particles of one liquid are held in suspension in another. Certain insecticides and ovicides can be emulsions, like TAR OIL and WHITE OIL.

Enchytraeid ◊ POTWORMS.

Endemic In botany, a plant species occurring naturally, not introduced; usually used of species unique to a particular country or region.

English Espalier ◊ ESPALIER.

English Garden ◊ JARDIN ANGLAIS.

Entire A botanical term applied to leaves with smooth, unindented margins, whatever their overall shape. Sometimes rendered as plain. ◊ LEAF.

Entomology The study of insects. A person practising this study is an entomologist.

Ephemeral Refers to flowers which last less than a day, e.g. cistuses and morning glory; and to short-lived, fast-seeding plants which in the gardener's experience are mostly weeds, e.g. chickweed and groundsel, which can produce several generations a year.

Epidermis The outermost layer of cells on plant organs, including the upper surface of leaves; this layer may be under a non-cellular layer of cuticle. In woody plants the epidermal layer of the stem and branches is later replaced by bark. ◊ BARK; CUTICLE.

Epiphyte A plant which grows upon another without being in any way a parasite; it obtains lodging but not food from its 'host'. Many orchids and bromeliads are epiphytic, obtaining their nourishment partly from the moist air and partly from decaying leaves, etc., which collect among the roots. Many such plants have aerial roots specially adapted to obtain atmospheric moisture under such conditions, and in cultivation it is beneficial, though by no means essential, to try to imitate natural growth habits. It is not usual to include under this definition plants such as ivies and philodendrons which climb up trees, clinging with aerial roots, but with their main feeding roots in the ground.

When epiphytes have to be started off in cultivation they have to be pressed against the chosen support – cork bark, pieces of tree branch, fern slabs, etc. – until new roots have formed which fix the plant permanently in place. The epiphyte's existing roots are normally first surrounded with moss, bound to the support with fine wire which can be cut away later, or small plants can be fixed with glue. Regular spraying with water is essential to stimulate new root growth.

◊ AERIAL ROOT; BROMELIAD; ORCHID; TERRESTRIAL.

Epsom Salt ◊ MAGNESIUM.

Ericaceous Any plant belonging to the *Ericaceae*, or heather family, which includes arbutus, calluna, erica, kalmia, pieris and rhododendron, to name but a few of the 70 or so genera, mostly (but not all) from temperate climates. Though rhododendrons, including their subdivision the azaleas, usually have open, trumpet-shaped blooms, many ericaceous plants have small bell-shaped or tubular flowers. Almost all the *Ericaceae* are calcifuge plants, unable to grow on limy soils and insisting on acid ones with a pH of 6.5 or less, and thus typical of peaty soils and heaths. Many gardeners with suitable soil conditions concentrate on these plants, especially rhododendrons, to the exclusion of nearly everything else. ◊ ACID; CALCICOLE; HEATH or HEATHER GARDEN; pH.

Espalier (1) A system of horticultural supports for training trees, first used in the eighteenth century. The method is primarily used for apples and pears, less often for other fruits such as apricots, and sometimes for ornamentals like pyracantha and ivies (the latter especially popular in the U.S.). In the original method, the supports were wires stretched horizontally along walls at 16″–20″ vertical intervals, fixed to vertical laths attached to the wall. Nowadays the supports almost always consist of horizontal wires strained at 15″ intervals between stout upright posts standing 5′ or more above ground level at 7′–10′ intervals: this is technically a contre-espalier.

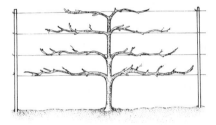

ESPALIER

(2) The word has also come to mean the trees so trained themselves, which might more accurately be termed espalier- or horizontal-trained trees: these have a vertical main trunk from which side branches are trained horizontally along the wires on each side. In effect each branch is a spur-pruned cordon, and is treated as such. In more spacious days, espaliers with 10 or 20 tiers might be trained on walls; nowadays, most gardeners content themselves with a maximum of five. Such a form has been termed an English espalier or palmette legendre. Trees in this form are sometimes used ornamentally instead of hedges, as between the ornamental and vegetable garden, and may be seen planted on each side of paths in older vegetable gardens. Aldous Huxley once referred to espalier-trained trees as 'crucified fruits'.

◊ CORDON; PALMETTE; SPUR; TRAINING.

Established-spur System A method of pruning fruit trees, sometimes used with weak-growing apple varieties. Such trees fruit on short spurs and this system resembles basic spur-pruning, but is not so severe. To this end side growths are left untouched until after fruiting. In winter they are cut back to the fruit bud nearest to their base. Established spurs so produced are cut back in future years according to their vigour: the weakest to one bud, the strongest to four or five. ◊ BUD; SPUR.

Etiolated, Etiolation The result of being blanched (grown without light): a term sometimes used of plants which after growing in the dark or very poor light become almost white, with spindly elongated growth. Although originally used to refer to deliberate blanching of vegetables, it now refers primarily to the results of the accidental exclusion of light.

Etiolation is also used of a process employed in the production of plum and cherry rootstocks by layering. In this method the upright part of a young rootstock plant is bent flat onto the ground and held in place by pegs and hooks. It is then covered with 1″ of soil. When growth from the buds emerges above this layer, a similar new layer is added. This process etiolates the base of each shoot and from the soft, white area so created roots are produced. After this, the new vertical shoots need regular earthing up.

◊ BLANCHING; LAYERING; STOCK; STOOLING.

Evergreen Largely restricted to trees or shrubs which keep their leaves all the year round, in contrast to deciduous kinds which drop their leaves in autumn and put out fresh ones in spring. Of course, there are also evergreen herbaceous plants and most houseplants are evergreen. Evergreens do in fact lose individual leaves through ageing, but do so continuously.

If an evergreen loses a lot of leaves, especially young ones, at once, some problem should be suspected and action taken accordingly. There are in fact some plants which will lose all or most of their leaves in severe winter weather, though they re-

tain them in mild winters and localities. These are described as semi-evergreen: common privet is an example.

Because they retain their leaves permanently, evergreens do not have a dormant or resting period, unlike deciduous plants. The latter may be transplanted with relative impunity when their leaves have fallen, but evergreens resent this and in fact transplanting from open ground should for most be restricted to early autumn or mid spring. The exceptions to this rule are the evergreen conifers which can be moved in winter like deciduous trees and shrubs, since their internal activity is greatly slowed down at that time. Evergreens grown in containers, however, can be planted from these during winter. To reduce harmful checks to growth on evergreens including conifers, their foliage can be sprayed with an anti-transpirant when they are moved.

Evergreens are valuable in gardens to provide a more or less unvarying background and to give a sense of 'furnishing' all winter. Some of the varieties with coloured or variegated leaves are especially valuable in this way, and others, e.g. many conifers, have outlines not to be found in deciduous shrubs and trees.

Many evergreens are valued as hedging plants since they create a permanently clothed barrier or pattern-maker (as in edgings and parterres).

Of course, many evergreens flower in season, some spectacularly like camellias and rhododendrons; and many also carry attractive fruits. Even so, a garden planted exclusively with evergreens is likely to be somewhat oppressive, lacking the interest of changing leaf colour and the contrast between summer and winter appearance.

◊ ANTI-TRANSPIRANT; CONTAINER-GROWN; DECIDUOUS; HEDGE.

Everlasting Though slightly misleading, this word is applied to certain flowers with papery or chaffy petals or bracts which last a very long time, especially if carefully dried. The French word '*immortelle*' is also sometimes used for such flowers. Many are composites (daisy family), including those most commonly called 'everlasting': ammobium, anaphalis, helichrysum, helipterum and xeranthemum. The sea lavenders – several species of statice or, more properly, limonium – the globe amaranth, gomphrena, and the shell flower, molucella, are others. To dry these, they are best cut before fully open, then hung in small bunches in a cool, airy, shaded place. Some garden and wild flowers which may be dried in a similar way include teasels, globe thistles, love-lies-bleeding, *Achillea filipendulina*, grasses, and the seed pods of honesty and physalis or Chinese lantern.

Occasionally dried flowers, like grasses, are artificially dyed; florists use special flower dyes into which the material is dipped. Because many dried flowers have very thin weak stems, it may be necessary to strengthen these, when it comes to arranging them, with florist's wire, wire pipe-cleaners or straw.

Beech leaves are dried by putting branches between sheets of newspaper and laying them below a carpet. Such leaves can also be preserved by placing the cut branches in a half-and-half mixture of glycerine and water, and leaving them there till they become slightly oily or silky to the touch.

Exhibiting The staging of flowers, fruit and/or vegetables in competition. In Britain this practice goes back to the artisan 'florists' of the eighteenth century. However, it seems likely that competitive exhibitions, or shows, were held in Europe before this time, especially in Holland at the time of 'tulipomania' (1634–7); and it is possible that competitive showing occurred in Turkey somewhat earlier, and in China and Japan much earlier.

Apart from major country shows, there are large numbers of local gardening or horticultural societies in Britain and the U.S. which hold at least one show a year. Flower arrangers have a national society in Britain, as in many other countries, and besides exhibiting at their own shows will almost always find classes for flower arrangements in other flower shows. Growing for exhibition involves careful choice of varieties, detailed attention to cultivation, careful packing for transit and special

forms of staging (setting up exhibits), which should be studied in specialist literature. The show schedule and its rules must be scrupulously followed.

◊ EXHIBITION; EXHIBITION BOARD; FLORIST; STAGING.

Exhibition Certain criteria usually exist for judging flowers, fruit and vegetables at flower shows, and varieties more suitable than others for the purpose are sometimes referred to as exhibition varieties. Among vegetables, for instance, certain onions and leeks are prized over others, for both potential size and character. Among flowers, those of a more showy nature with good substance and most regularity are typically selected. Among chrysanthemums one group is actually designated as Large Exhibition.

Exhibition Board In the past the commonest way of staging individual blooms or flower-heads at shows was on a board containing holes through which the flower stems were pushed, the flowers being inserted right up to the board's surface. These exhibition or show boards were usually placed at a slight angle to the horizontal and had water containers below the apertures so that the flowers kept fresh. Often exhibitors combined the board and its water containers with a lid so that the resulting box could be transported from garden to show bench without any further handling except for the final touches. Nowadays most show flowers are staged in vases, but boards are still used in some classes for begonias, camellias, chrysanthemums, dahlias, roses, show pinks and violas. ◊ SHOWS; STAGING.

Exotic Although often used of showy tropical plants, in horticultural terms this word actually denotes any plant not native to the country concerned, regardless of whether it is hardy or tender. ◊ HARDY; TENDER.

Exserted Literally, thrust out from; in botany refers to projecting organs, usually to stamens or pistils which extend beyond the rest of the flower.

Extension Shoot A shoot, especially on a fruit tree, which has been selected to extend the branch framework; more often called a LEADER.

Eye (1) A growth bud, especially that on a tuber, as on a potato where the minute bud lies in a small depression. From these eyes grow the new shoots, seen when potatoes are sprouted. Dormant buds on stems may also be referred to as eyes. ◊ EYE CUTTING; SPROUT; TUBER.

EYE. *Left*, a potato with growth buds; *right*, a pink with different-coloured centre

(2) The centre of a flower when it is coloured differently from the rest, as in many pinks, pansies, auriculas and delphiniums.

(3) Primroses and cowslips are described as pin-eyed or thrum-eyed according to whether the stigma (pin-eyed) or stamens (thrum-eyed) are visible at the top of the corolla tube. This is a botanical device to prevent self-pollination. The word thrum, meaning a tassel or piece of loose yarn on cloth, refers to the anthers bunched together. ◊ ANTHER; FLOWER; STAMEN; STIGMA.

Eye-catcher A feature in a landscape garden which acts as focal point, used especially in the eighteenth century. This could be a garden house, temple, mock ruin, piece of statuary, or a folly, and would normally be placed at the end of a vista or on a piece of rising ground, usually at some distance from the main house of the estate. Larger eye-catchers at the end of vistas were sometimes known as vista-closers.

Eye Cutting A short length of ripened stem containing a single fat growth bud, used to increase plants such as camellias, grape

EYE CUTTING (grape-vine)

vines and wisterias when they are dormant in winter. Similar cuttings can also be used with tender plants like dieffenbachias, where the buds may be quite invisible but exist at every stem joint. ◊ CUTTING; JOINT; RIPE.

❊ F ❊

F.1 Technically, the first filial generation: the first generation arising from a cross between two plants. F.1 plants are usually specially designated as such since they often have hybrid vigour. Seed from F.1 hybrids will not breed true. ◊ CROSS; HYBRID; HYBRID VIGOUR.

F.2 The second filial generation: the offspring arising from seed produced by an F.1. Such offspring is likely to be very varied and will not have hybrid vigour, nor often be particularly noteworthy, though it may be valuable for future breeding.

Fairy Ring Most fungi of toadstool shape tend to grow in rings as the mycelium, or 'spawn', grows outwards from its point of origin. One, *Marasmius oreades*, is so often found in rings that it is called the Fairy Ring Mushroom, and is frequently troublesome on lawns and sports greens – more so than other kinds. The fungus absorbs all the food within the soil it occupies, so that it can only grow outwards; in extreme cases the dead mycelium so fills up the soil that no moisture can be absorbed and the grass above dies, leaving the bare ring, which was attributed to dancing fairies. Often the grass on either side of the ring is more vigorous and of a deeper green and the ring is often visible for this reason – even when no fungi can be seen above ground. On the outside of the ring this is due to the release of ammonia by the living fungus, and within it is due to the release of nitrogenous matter as the dead mycelium decays. Some fungi do not send up the toadstools, which are technically fruit-bodies and shed the reproductive spores, for many years. Huge rings can be found, e.g. on the South Downs in England, which are several centuries old.

On lawns, it is sometimes possible to eradicate fairy rings by pricking or spiking the affected area with a garden fork or lawn spiker and watering it thoroughly every day for at least a month. The addition of fungicides, which has been recommended in the past, is now deemed to have no appreciable effect. The visual effect of most fairy rings can be suppressed by making sure the lawn is fed regularly with nitrogenous fertilizer during the growing season, while the actual mushrooms (which include the edible field variety) or 'toadstools' can be removed for eating or destroyed by wire-raking.

The only type of ring which severely disfigures turf, and will be resented on bowling greens and well-kept lawns, is that caused by *Marasmius*, and the only way of dealing with it is to dig out and remove the soil for 1′ either side, to the depth of about a spit (a spade's length). The trench thus formed is sterilized with 40 per cent formalin and covered with an impermeable material like plastic sheeting for 10 days, after which the trench is refilled with fresh uninfected soil and returfed or reseeded. An alternative method is to remove only the turf from the 2′ circle, fork over the soil below as finely as possible, and treat this with formalin. ◊ FUNGUS.

Falcate Sickle-shaped; in botany usually refers to leaves of this form. ◊ LEAF.

Fall The outer ring of petal-like perianth segments in some irises where these segments tend to hang down or at least project away from the inner upright segments or standards. A feature of the bearded irises, which are the most popular and easily grown. ◊ BEARD.

Fallow The practice of leaving an area of ground empty of any crop for a period so that the weather can improve the soil texture and the soil organisms build up its fertility. This is usually a feature of agricultural practice and is seldom used in horticultural crop rotation, though it may on occasion be desirable to give soil-borne disease or pest organisms a chance to disappear. However, gardeners usually achieve this by next growing a crop which is not susceptible to a disease like club root which has affected a previous crop. In fact, vegetable plots are often largely empty in winter and this gives a sufficient fallow period for soil bacteria to improve fertility quite considerably. ◊ CLUB ROOT; ROTATION.

Family ◊ CLASSIFICATION.

Family Tree A tree in which several different varieties are grafted onto a common rootstock. The term is normally only applied to fruit trees, though ornamentals can be grafted in this way. Commercially available family trees are usually restricted to three varieties, occasionally to five, but there is no limit to the number of varieties one *could* graft onto a large fruit tree: there is one apple tree in the U.S. with, reputedly, over 60 varieties on it.

kept in balance, so that none grows over-vigorously at the expense of the others. In principle, weak leading shoots should be pruned severely and strong ones just tipped, but to avoid imbalance very strong vertical shoots on one variety should be entirely cut out.

The growing of several plants on one stem like this was probably practised in ancient Rome, also many centuries ago in China.

◊ GRAFTING; STOCK.

Fan A self-explanatory word referring to a shape of trained tree on walls, mainly used with peaches, apricots and nectarines, though equally applicable to plums and cherries. Apples and pears lend themselves more to training as cordons and espaliers, but could be trained as fans. In a fan the branches are trained straight, radiating if possible from the top of a central leg, which can be 6″–12″ tall in a dwarf fan, or as long

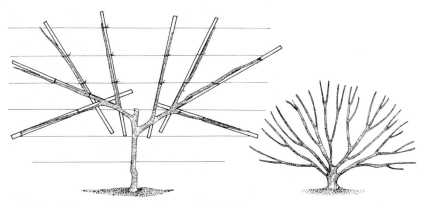

FAN. *Left,* early stages of training: *right,* an established fan

In practice having too many different varieties leads to unbalanced growth, especially on young trees. The great merits of family trees are space saving plus, if the varieties have been carefully chosen, adequate pollination of the flowers of each.

Family trees resemble normal bush trees on dwarfing rootstocks, and pruning follows orthodox lines except that the branches carrying the different varieties must be

as 6′ with a standard fan, now seldom grown. This leg is not allowed to grow on vertically as a central component of the fan, since such a growth would be likely to develop at the expense of the side growths.

The oblique palmette, in which the vertical axis is maintained, looks superficially similar but takes much longer to create.

◊ PALMETTE.

Fancy (1) A nineteenth-century word, now seldom used, to denote all who follow a particular pursuit or hobby, especially the art of breeding plants and animals so as to develop them in specific directions. Thus one might speak of the rose or pelargonium fancy; and the specialists concerned are called fanciers. These fancies are invariably associated with competitive exhibitions in which the flowers concerned had, and in a few cases still have, to comply with very definite standards, even if these made them depart widely from the appearance of the wild species. ◊ FLORIST.

(2) Flowers, especially those favoured for exhibiting, with variegated markings, in contrast to one-coloured varieties (known as selfs). Fancy carnations now include those which used to be known as bizarres and flakes. ◊ BIZARRE; FLAKED.

Farina Literally, farina means flour or meal; it is applied botanically to the powdery coating on the stems, leaves and, occasionally, flowers of certain plants, notably primulas, and is a form of protection similar to the waxy 'bloom' on plums, the leaves of some succulents, etc. This meal is usually white, sometimes bluish or yellowish, and can add to the beauty of the plant. The specific name of *Primula farinosa*, the bird's-eye primrose, describes its dusty appearance. Pulverulent, which literally means dusty, is also used in specific names to describe mealy plants, such as *Primula pulverulenta*. Some garden auriculas are called Dusty Millers for the same reason. The appearance of farina reaches the height of oddity in the show auricula, in some varieties of which the petals have a central zone of mealy 'paste' and an outer zone of lighter meal; the leaves are usually mealy too. ◊ SCURF; WAX.

Farmyard Manure ◊ MANURE.

Fasciation A freak condition in which, typically, the stem of a plant becomes flat and strap-shaped, giving the impression of several stems fused together; the flower at its end may also develop abnormally in one plane, or a great number of flowers be produced. It is common in cacti and ferns, where fasciated plants are called cristates and are prized by collectors. Many garden plants can be affected, including lupins, lilies, delphiniums, primulas, chrysanthemums, gaillardias, etc., and among shrubs forsythia is often fasciated. Sometimes only one stem of a plant is affected and the

FASCIATION

plant will seldom be fasciated the following year. There is nothing to be done about it: the cause is obscure, but seems to be initially due to damage to the microscopic growing tip of the shoot; and the occurrence of fasciation varies from year to year, sometimes being very frequent. It has been suggested that mild, warm weather or other reasons for unusually rapid growth may encourage it. Records show, incidentally, that fasciation was frequent long before atomic radiation was thought of. ◊ CRISTATE; TERATOLOGY.

Fascicle A close cluster, tuft or bundle; botanically this can refer to flowers (as in the flowerhead of sweet william), leaves, stems or roots.

Fastigiate Although this term derives from a Latin word meaning the top of a gable, and in botany means having either flowers or branches making a cone-like outline, it is now used to refer generally to trees of erect habit, and is usually applied to special forms of species which normally have

101

spreading branches. The Lombardy poplar, an erect form of *Populus nigra*, and the cherry Amanogawa, a form of *Prunus serrulata*, are familiar examples, and there are in addition a considerable number of often rather poorly known fastigiate forms, including those of beech, hawthorn, oak and tulip tree, as well as numerous narrowly erect conifers. These trees are valuable as contrasting features in garden design, and also where space is limited.

FASTIGIATE. *Left*, Lombardy poplar, *right*, with normal form of *Populus nigra*

Confusingly, the word originally meant an organ with a flat upper surface, hence old botanical works may use it of flat-topped flowerheads like an umbel ⋄ IN-FLORESCENCE.

Feathered (1) Sometimes used of one-year-old trees (maidens) having an upright trunk and a number of side-growths or feathers. ⋄ MAIDEN.

(2) Used of flowers with feather-like markings of one colour upon a different ground colour, as in some 'broken' tulips. In the strict terminology of flower fanciers, in such markings there is no definite demarcation line between the two colours. ⋄ BROKEN.

Feather-veined Refers to leaves in which veins all spring from the mid-rib, giving the same effect as a feather.

Feathery Of an organ resembling a feather. ⋄ PLUMOSE.

Fedge A composite word of quite recent invention, derived from fence and hedge, and denoting a climbing plant grown up a fence, or a wire or plastic netting screen erected for the purpose. Such a screen can be vertical, or arranged over a framework of steel rods bent into interesting shapes. The ideal plants to grow on a fedge are undoubtedly the numerous varieties of ivy.

Feeding Plants In order to grow, plants require certain foods, of which the most important are nitrogen, phosphorus and potassium (abbreviated N, P and K), the basic ingredients of fertilizers. There are also about 13 other elements essential for plant growth, including carbon, hydrogen and oxygen which are obtained from the air, and which in combination make up at least 90 per cent of the plant's tissues. Of the others, calcium and magnesium may need adding in some quantity if it is proved that they are lacking. The remainder – boron, chlorine, copper, iron, manganese, molybdenum, sulphur and zinc – are required in very tiny amounts and are therefore known as trace elements. An excess of any of these can be positively harmful to a plant, but their absence can also cause severe problems, termed mineral deficiencies. A few other trace elements

FEATHER-VEINED (*Maranta leuconeura* var. *erythroneura*)

are sometimes valuable to certain plants. Sometimes an excess of one element creates a deficiency of another (e.g., in tomatoes an excess of potash may readily bring about magnesium deficiency). In other situations one element may prevent a plant taking up others by 'locking them up', and again causing deficiencies. Thus excess calcium can 'lock up' essential iron and magnesium, resulting in chlorosis. (Such problems can often be cured by the application of sequestered chemicals or sequestrols.)

Plants take up food primarily through the microscopic root-hairs near the extreme tips of the fine roots. It has also been shown that nutrients can be absorbed through the foliage. Actual absorption depends on the food minerals being present in the soil in a solution with water, and it cannot be emphasized too strongly that the minerals are in almost their simplest form, known as salts. The origin of the mineral elements, whether from animal manures or synthetically produced fertilizers, is immaterial to the plant. What is important is a good soil texture in which a thin film of mineral salts in solution can be tapped by the root-hairs while at the same time plenty of air is also available among the soil particles: this is achieved by adequate cultivation and the use of bulky organic materials.

Plants vary a good deal in their needs for extra food. A bromeliad growing epiphytically on a tree branch needs virtually none; but a vegetable grown for a rapidly formed bulk of green matter needs a lot. Most soils contain good quantities of plant foods, but these are released too slowly by the processes of decay for the numerous plants we crowd into a garden, especially in the vegetable plot where there is a constant succession of crops which require quantities of extra food if they are to grow to the required size.

It is very difficult to know exactly how much plant food to provide and when to do it. It is not just a question of what crops are being grown and how intensively the ground is being used. A few soils are so rich that no additional feeding is needed. Then, some fertilizers remain in the ground longer than others, and some – especially nitrogenous materials – can be leached or washed out very quickly by prolonged rain; the quality of the soil itself and whether or not it has received much organic matter have an effect on the rates of disappearance of minerals.

Ideally, soil tests are carried out to determine the existing levels of at least the major food elements. Although soil-test kits for amateur use exist, their results are not always reliable. As a rule of thumb, vegetables can be fed with a mixed fertilizer, applied according to instructions, which provides a steady amount of phosphate and potash; the nitrogen content is adjusted according to the crop. The National Vegetable Research Station in Britain has established the desirable rates of application of nitrogen for a range of 'standard' crops.

It should always be realized that the returns, in terms of extra production or yield, become progressively less as more food than an optimum amount is given, and too much food can actually ,depress yield or even damage crops by scorching roots.

In the flower garden, it is much easier to forget that plants need food. Autumn feeding with materials that release food slowly (like organic manures), and spring feeding with quicker-release materials, are desirable every year, but interim feeding is seldom necessary, except for very quick-growing plants like dahlias.

Plants in containers will need extra food quite often, those in peat-based potting mixtures much more frequently than those in soil-based mixtures.

In very general terms, nitrogen is needed to stimulate growth and the production of leafy matter; phosphorus for the development of healthy roots; and potassium for the production of flowers, the ripening of fruit, and also the hardening up of woody growth so that it is more likely to produce flower and fruit in the future.

Forms of Food Plant foods can be pro-

103

vided from organic materials like animal manures, bones, rotted garden compost, spent hops and so on, or from inorganic ones which can be of natural or synthetic origin. They are often referred to as 'manures and fertilizers', the first to be thoroughly incorporated into soil and the second to be applied in various forms. The latter, which may be quick- or slow-acting depending upon their origin, include granules and powders, and liquids to be further diluted in water. A special form is the frit in which elements, especially trace elements, are produced in tiny glassy fragments; these are insoluble and give up their elements only when root hairs come into contact with them. Thus they are valuable for long-term effect and may be known as slow-release fertilizers.

For the different methods of applying food materials, ⟡ BANDING; BROADCASTING; COMPOSTS, SEED AND POTTING; DILUTOR; DRESSING; FOLIAR FEEDING; LIQUID FEEDING; RING CULTURE.

⟡ CHLOROSIS; CULTIVATION; DEFICIENCY; FERTILIZER; FRIT; LEACH; MANURE; NO-DIGGING; ORGANIC; PHOTOSYNTHESIS; SEQUESTROL; SOIL CONDITIONER; SOILLESS CULTIVATION; TRACE ELEMENTS; URINE.

Felt (1) Plant surfaces are said to be felted when covered with a dense growth of short hairs. Many rhododendrons have felty leaf undersides and some succulents are densely felted. ⟡ HAIRY; INDUMENTUM.

(2) Felt fabric in special formulation is used for some kinds of CAPILLARY WATERING.

Female Flower Although technically the parts of flowers have no sex (⟡ FLOWER for fuller explanation), they are commonly described as having either or both sexes present. In plants which carry flowers of one sex only (known as monoecious) it is important to be able to recognize the male and female blooms when the formation of fruit is the desired result. This occurs primarily with members of the cucumber family, including marrows and melons. In these, the female flower can always be

recognized by having a distinct swelling behind the flower itself, which is an embryo fruit; the male flower has no such swelling. Marrows, melons and outdoor cucumbers may need hand pollination – by applying the anthers of a male flower to the stigma of a female; but with greenhouse cucumbers the male flowers should be nipped off whenever produced, since in these plants pollination produces bitter fruits.

Recognition of male and female flowers is also essential for the plant breeder among other kinds of plant.

Botanists distinguish female forms of plants by the symbol ♀, and call the female part of the flower the gynoecium.

⟡ ANTHER; BREEDING; CROSS-FERTILIZATION; FLOWER; POLLINATION; STIGMA.

Fences, Fencing Boundaries formed of many pieces of wood, wattle, palings or plastic in contrast to solid ones of brick or stone. Barriers formed of horizontal concrete slabs are usually considered to be fences rather than walls, because of their construction from many units not bonded together, by contrast with walls of perforated concrete blocks cemented together. Fences also depend on regular spaced upright supports or posts, whereas these are not found in walls (though walls may have strengthening buttresses). Many fences can be obtained as ready-made units or panels which are often simply fitted into slots on the uprights. These fence posts must be carefully spaced and fixed strongly in the ground.

Types of Fence

Basketweave ⟡ INTERWOVEN (below).

Board fences have vertical posts, three or four horizontal rails, and vertical boards – spaced according to preference – nailed to the rails. The posts can be prolonged upwards to support a further horizontal rail or a lattice section above the boards.

Cleft chestnut fencing consists of individual uprights of chestnut wood, which are basically irregular, fixed at top and bottom onto horizontal lengths of strong wire at short intervals. This is obtained in rolls, and is normally attached to its upright supports with wire.

Close-boarded fences consist of panels of upright or horizontal wooden strips butted together, nailed onto supporting rails on one face.

Hurdles ⟡ Wattle (below).

Interwoven or *basketweave* fences are made of thin, wide strips of wood woven together horizontally and vertically, and made into panels.

Lattice ⟡ Trellis (below).

Louvre fences are a variation on vertical weatherboarding, popular in the U.S., with the overlapping uprights fixed so that air can pass between them. They are sometimes built on the venetian blind principle so that the vertical boards can actually be adjusted to control wind flow.

Netting of wire, plastic or plastic-covered wire, forming diamonds or sometimes squares, is mostly used in utilitarian situations. One form of wire netting, chain-link, has 2″ squares and is particularly strong. This can be obtained plastic-coated.

Paling, Palisade or *Picket* fences consist of well-spaced wooden uprights of some

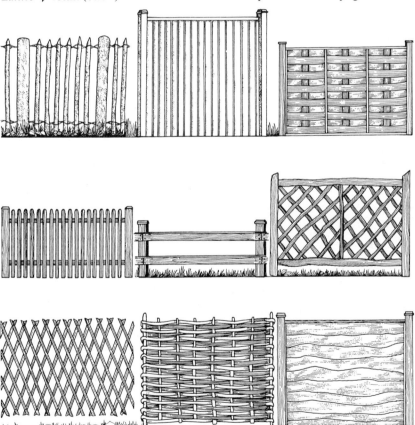

FENCING. *Top row, left to right*: cleft chestnut; close-boarded; interwoven. *Centre row*: paling; ranch; rustic. *Bottom row*: trellis; wattle; weather-board

thickness nailed securely to horizontal rails (arris rails) which are wedged into slots in the upright posts. The uprights can be cut horizontally at the tops or be formed into triangular points or other forms.

Post and board fencing is made by nailing thick, wide wooden boards horizontally to stout well-spaced posts with fairly wide spaces between them. Vertical boards conceal the ends of the horizontal ones and the posts are capped with square pieces of timber.

Ranch fencing is the name given to boundaries of broad, well-spaced continuous horizontal strips, which can be of wood, plastic or, rarely, concrete, fixed to uprights.

Rustic fences are made of young larch or pine poles, sometimes with the bark left on; the uprights are usually 3″–4″ in diameter, the subsidiary poles $1\frac{1}{2}$″–2″. The latter can be formed into various designs but the most usual is a diamond pattern. Rustic fences are usually available in panels.

Spindle fences, used mainly in the U.S., resemble picket fences but consist of rods about $1\frac{1}{4}$″ across, fitted into holes every 5″–7″ in horizontal rails between supporting posts.

Trellis is constructed from light wood slats, square or flat, formed into squares or diamonds, and nailed onto square uprights. This is mainly used for ornament within gardens, and as a support for climbing plants on walls, rather than for boundaries, and is much less substantial than other types. Fences of trellis may be called lattice fences.

Wattle is the name for flexible strips of willow woven horizontally over upright poles, like basketwork. The units are nailed onto strong upright posts or stakes. They provide an informal effect but are apt to disintegrate after a few years. When the strips and uprights are widely spaced, wattle is formed into *hurdles*, which are usually oblong in outline.

Weather-board (or *lapped*) fencing consists of upright or horizontal strips of wood or, rarely, concrete, which are overlapped. The wood strips may be regular along both edges, when they are tapered slightly across the width, or are sometimes uniform in thickness and left irregular on one edge to give an informal appearance.
⟡ TRELLIS; WALLS; WINDBREAK.

Fern A member of the plant group known as *Filices*: non-flowering, rather primitive perennial plants whose green parts are often referred to as fronds and which multiply by spores, not seeds. In this they differ entirely from the so-called asparagus ferns which, though 'ferny' in general appearance (hence their name) are in fact true flowering plants. The spores are carried in sporecases called *sori*, often on the leaf undersides – brown or blackish outgrowths which should not be confused with disease symptoms. Ferns, which are often epiphytic, always have fibrous roots and many kinds have rhizomes or creeping stems; the leaves arise directly from these or from a clump of roots, usually in shuttlecock formation. Many ferns like moist, shady conditions, whether outdoors or in greenhouses or rooms. ⟡ FROND; SORI; SPORE; RHIZOME.

Fern-case A glass-covered structure, often of simple bell-glass form, designed to protect ferns grown indoors from dry air, draughts, etc. A form of WARDIAN CASE.

Fernery A word sometimes used for a FERN-CASE, for a greenhouse devoted to ferns and specially devised for them, or for outdoor areas for their culture, where the plants would be grown among rockwork, old tree stumps and roots. The fernery was devised in Victorian times when so many exotic ferns were introduced, and declined after the Edwardian period.

Fertile Fruitful, prolific, or producing in abundance. Gardeners use 'fertile' to describe rich soils, also varieties of plant, usually vegetables, which produce good crops. A narrower definition concerns the ability to produce seed. ⟡ FERTILIZATION; INFERTILE; SELF-FERTILE.

Fertility Rules Some fruit trees will not set fruit with their own pollen and are known as self-incompatible; others may be only partially self-compatible. Because of this problem, good works of reference on fruit culture include tables showing which other varieties should be planted with those specially desired, to ensure fruiting; these tables also take into account average flowering times. Anyone wishing to grow fruit should consult such 'fertility rules' before planting, to avoid disappointment.

Fertilization The conjunction of a male and female sex cell, giving rise to a new individual. In the case of flowering plants, the male component is produced by the pollen grain, produced in the anther (or corresponding organ, as in orchids), which on contact with the stigma of the female flower extends a tubular growth down the

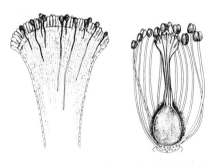

FERTILIZATION. *Left*, pollen grains 'germinating' on stigma of helianthemum flower (section, much enlarged); *right*, the pollen-tubes pass down the style and into the ovary below

style to the ovary where it unites with an ovule, from which the seed develops. This fusion is the actual fertilization. Flowers are self-fertile if they will accept their own pollen, but this is often prevented by devices which are designed to ensure cross-pollination from another flower. Pollen is transferred from one flower to another by insects or wind; plant-breeders do this deliberately, usually first removing the anthers of the female parent (emasculation)

to preclude any risk of self-fertilization. In the case of squashes, marrows and melons it is often desirable to fertilize female flowers deliberately to encourage fruit formation.

It should be noted that the word fertilizing in the U.K. means the act of fertilization, but is often used in the U.S. to mean the feeding of plants with fertilizer. ⟡ CROSS-FERTILIZATION; EMASCULATION; FEMALE FLOWER; POLLINATION.

Fertilizer Any material which provides plant food in relatively concentrated form, as opposed to bulky organic manures. Fertilizers can be of organic or inorganic origin, be produced either naturally or synthetically and be supplied in granular, powder or liquid form. Some organic materials, e.g. bones, are ground down to 'meal'. They may provide one food element only and are then called straight fertilizers, or several – normally the three major foods, nitrogen, phosphorus and potassium – and are known as compound. The concentration of food materials is stated on containers as a percentage; if a fertilizer contains the three primary foods this will be expressed in code form, e.g. 7–7–10, which indicates 7 per cent nitrogen, 7 per cent phosphorus and 10 per cent potash. The higher the percentage, the greater the concentration of plant food per unit of weight, and thus the lower the necessary rate of application. An excess can readily scorch roots: recommended rates of application should never be exceeded.

Except on soils already in very good condition, concentrated fertilizers should always be used in conjunction with bulky organic materials to ensure that satisfactory soil texture is maintained.

For fertilizer materials described in separate entries ⟡ BASIC SLAG; BLOOD; BONE MANURES; CALCIUM CYANAMIDE; FISH MANURES; FLUE DUST; HOOF AND HORN; KAINIT; MAGNESIUM SULPHATE; MEAT GUANO OR MEAL; NATIONAL GROWMORE; NITRATE OF POTASH; NITRATE OF SODA; NITRO-CHALK; PHOSPHATE OF POTASH; SOOT; SULPHATE OF AMMONIA; SULPHATE OF IRON; SULPHATE OF MAGNESIUM;

SULPHATE OF POTASH; SUPERPHOSPHATE OF LIME; UREA; WOOD ASH.

For other plant food materials ◇ MANURE.

◇ FEEDING PLANTS; FRIT; GARDEN CHEMICALS, ORGANIC; TRACE ELEMENTS.

Fertilizer Distributors ◇ DISTRIBUTOR.

Fibre ◇ FIBROUS (2); SHREDS.

Fibrous (1) Applied to plants with a mass of fine roots in contrast to those with fewer coarse roots or fleshy ones.

(2) Refers to loam containing plenty of fibrous roots. Such loam is usually composed of rotted grass and grass roots, often referred to as fibre, and is ideal for soil-based potting composts. ◇ TURF.

Field Capacity Often used in agriculture, sometimes by gardeners, to denote the state of well-cultivated, free-draining soil when it is holding the maximum amount of water against the force of gravity.

Filament The stalk which bears the pollen-bearing anther in many flowers. The filament is usually slender and with the anther comprises the stamen; however, in some flowers there is no filament. ◇ FLOWER.

Fillis A soft string specially made for tying plants to supports, normally coloured green or brown.

Fimbriate A botanical term meaning fringed, most often applied to petals or corollas as in *Dianthus fimbriatus*, the fringed pink.

Finger and Toe Another name for CLUB ROOT.

Fire Loosely used of any disease or cultural problem which makes plant foliage look scorched, specifically in tulip fire, a serious fungus disease of tulips calling for the removal of affected plants and spraying the whole affected area with a suitable fungicide.

Fire Blight A bacterial disease which can attack most woody members of the rose family (*Rosaceae*). It is particularly feared by fruit growers since pears and, to a lesser extent, apples are liable to attack, which can spread rapidly in orchards. Originating in the U.S., it also occurs on the continent and in south-eastern England. Symptoms are a blackened, scorched appearance to the foliage which hangs down, the disease moving steadily down the branches. In Britain this is a notifiable disease and affected plants should be burnt. ◇ FUNGICIDES; FUNGUS.

Firmer A device for making firm the compost in seed boxes, pans and pots, and at the same time making the surface smooth and level. This is usually a flat piece of wood with some kind of handle; firmers are often home-made to fit the various containers used.

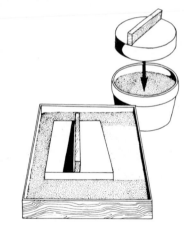

FIRMER

Firming The act of pressing down soil or potting mixtures around plants. Older books often recommend firming pot-grown plants with a rounded wooden stick, but the degree of compression thus achieved was related to the close-textured, soil-based potting mixtures then in vogue for subjects like chrysanthemums. With present-day potting mixtures firming with the thumb while the fingers grasp the pot rim is usually quite sufficient, and peat-based mixtures need much less firming than soil-based ones. However, it is always essential to ensure that the potting mixture has filled all the space between the pot and the original root ball. Before sowing, or transplanting seedlings, compost in seedboxes or pots can be made firm and level by tamping with a firmer. In the open ground newly planted plants of all kinds need firming if they are not to topple over and if the roots are to get into good contact with the surrounding soil. This is most important with shrubs and trees, for which firming with the feet is often desirable. Soil in which seeds are to be planted can be firmed by treading. ◊ COMPOSTS, SEED AND POTTING; CROCKS; TREADING.

Fish ◊ POOL.

Fish Manures North American Indians near the New England coast, and the European settlers who followed their example, used to place a small fish in planting holes before putting seed in place. Fish scraps, if available in quantity from a fishmonger, can be treated in the same way, the best procedure being to bury them at the bottom of a trench a spit deep some time before sowing or planting is carried out. A less offensive material is the mealy substance variously called fish manure, fish meal or fish guano, made by drying and pulverizing fish wastes, which makes a useful substitute for animal manure used at 3–4 oz. per square yard: it is, of course, organic. Application is best made in late winter or early spring; the material should be well forked in to prevent birds eating it, and it should not get into contact with germinating seeds or the roots of small seedlings which it can scorch. Content varies considerably, ranging from 7–10 per cent nitrogen, 5–10 or rarely 15 per cent phosphoric acid, and 2–3 per cent potash. The nitrogen is released slowly so that fish manure has a long-lasting effect. ◊ MANURE.

Flagging ◊ HUMIDITY; TRANSPIRATION; WILTING.

Flaked Describes certain bicoloured flowers in which one colour overlies a ground colour in large splashes. Applied especially to tulips and carnations, this term is seldom used today except by fanciers. ◊ BROKEN.

Flamed Describes flowers in which there is a combination of fine 'feathering' with a band of solid colour up the centre of each petal; applied mainly to tulips by fanciers. ◊ BROKEN; FEATHERED.

Flame Gun A device like an outsize blowtorch in which paraffin is vaporized and passed to a burner under pressure, producing a long flame with intensive local heat. Some flame guns are in the form of long tubes to be held in the hand; others are designed to fit onto a wheeled trolley and have a hood over the down-pointing flame to concentrate it where required and avoid damage to plants or wooden structures. Flame guns can be used to destroy the surface growth of weeds, to ignite damp refuse, and as a rough-and-ready method of sterilizing small areas of soil. ◊ WEED; WEED CONTROL.

Flannel-weed Another name for the blanket-weed alga of POOLS.

Flea-beetles Small beetles which can jump considerable distances when disturbed; tiresome pests of cabbages and other brassicas, in the leaves of which they eat numerous small holes – young seedlings can be rapidly destroyed by their attacks. In some cases the beetle grubs also feed on roots. Control is by insecticidal seed dressings, and by dusting seedling rows and adult plants with a suitable insecticide.

Fleshy-rooted Applied to any plant with thick fleshy roots and also to those with fleshy storage organs such as BULBS, CORMS, RHIZOMES and TUBERS.

Flocculation The joining of small particles to create larger ones with air spaces. In horticulture this is used of methods of improving the crumb or soil texture, especially of heavy clay-based soils. This can be done by liming and the use of other soil conditioners such as alginates. ◊ ALGINATE; CRUMB; CULTIVATION; LIME; SOIL CONDITIONER.

Flora The whole range of plants growing in a particular area or climatic zone; also, a book describing these plants.

Floral Anything which pertains to a flower, e.g. petals, sepals, anthers, etc. Floral arrangement, however, is the art of arranging plant materials which often includes leaves, seed heads and even artificial objects. ◊ FLOWER; SHOWS.

Flore Pleno A botanical expression for a plant having double flowers, added to the basic binomial (as in *Ranunculus acris flore pleno*), or abbreviated as *fl.pl.* The words *plena* or *plenum* are more often used, or a cultivar name. ◊ DOUBLE.

Floret A small flower; mainly used in referring to one component in a many-flowered inflorescence or head, particularly that of a composite. ◊ COMPOSITE; INFLORESCENCE.

Floriculture A word originating in 1822, now seldom used, to denote the cultivation of flowering plants.

Florilegium A collection or selection of flowers; a word originating in 1647, now occasionally used for an anthology about plants, or a selected list.

Florist, Florist Flower One who cultivates, deals in or otherwise specializes in flowers. In horticulture, the term usually refers to specialist growers of highly bred flowers often grown for exhibition; hence also the term 'florist flowers'. This is a meaning of the word which arose in the seventeenth century and was used in relation to the numerous Florists' Societies which flourished up to the end of the nineteenth century. ◊ COTTAGE GARDENS; EXHIBITING; EXHIBITION.

Flower A structure composed of modified leaves – the perianth – which enclose the sexual organs of the flowering plants (angiosperms). The perianth has the dual function of protection and of attracting animal pollinators.

Flowers may be carried singly or in varying numbers forming one unit. The flowering part of a plant is termed the inflorescence, and many different arrangements are recognized. The stem of a single flower within an inflorescence is the pedicel, while the main stem supporting the inflorescence is the peduncle. When a flower stem arises from the base of the plant separate from the leaves, this is called a scape. Flowers without stems may be termed acaulescent.

Although technically the parts of flowers have no sex, since they belong to the asexual phase of plants, flowers *are* responsible for the eventual production of the male and female sex cells or nuclei which fuse together on fertilization to produce the seeds from which further individuals can grow: *this* is the sexual phase. Flowers are therefore commonly described as having a particular sex or carrying both sexes, and the organs involved as male or female.

In these terms, both sexes may be present in one flower (bisexual or hermaphrodite), or the male and female sexes may be carried in separate flowers. When this occurs on the same plant it is termed monoecious, when on separate plants dioecious. In some inflorescences some of the flowers may be sterile: this is usually to provide an insect-attracting display around insignificant fertile flowers.

Pollen grains, which eventually produce the male cells, are typically carried in anthers, though sometimes in other organs such as pollinia. When the anther has a stalk, or filament, the whole is called a stamen, while the male organ overall is the androecium. Flowers with male organs only are known as staminate.

The female or egg cells are carried in structures called ovules within the chamber of an ovary. The ovary is composed of one or more carpels, either separate or fused together. The ovary may be above the

Parts of the flower

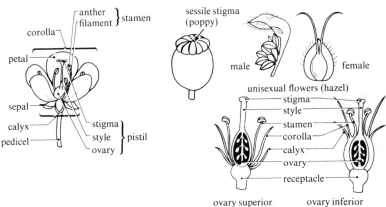

sessile stigma
(poppy)

male

female

unisexual flowers (hazel)

ovary superior   ovary inferior

Monocotyledon flowers

Gamopetalous flower

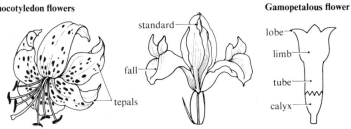

similar perianth segments   *dissimilar perianth segments*

Forms of flower

campanulate   funnelform   rotate   salverform   tubular   trumpet-shaped   urceolate

regular flowers   *irregular flowers*

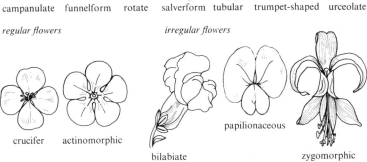

cruardifer   actinomorphic

bilabiate

papilionaceous

zygomorphic

perianth segments (superior) or below them (inferior). Outside the ovary is a surface receptive to the pollen grains, the stigma, often carried on a stalk called a style. The entire female unit is known as the pistil or gynoecium, and flowers with female organs only are known as pistillate.

When pollen grains reach a stigma, this is termed pollination. The grains then develop long tubes which grow through the tissue of the pistil to reach the ovules; they produce the male cells or nuclei, and the final union of male and female sex cells is fertilization. After this, the ovule develops into the seed.

The perianth surrounding the sex organs is typically divided into two series of modified leaves. The outer, usually green and protective, is the calyx; it sometimes replaces the corolla and may then resemble it. Separate segments of a divided calyx are called sepals.

The corolla forms the inner series and is normally showy and coloured. Separate segments of a divided corolla are termed petals; a corolla of one piece is called gamopetalous or sympetalous, and one with separate petals polypetalous. A flower without any petals is termed apetalous.

In monocotyledons there is usually no clear distinction between sepals and petals. When they are similar in form and colouring, as in lilies and tulips, they may be called tepals; otherwise they are known as perianth segments. In some monocotyledons the segments may be of very different form, as in irises with their falls and standards. In some circular flowers the corolla may carry an outgrowth known as the corona, which can be cup- or trumpet-shaped or consist of radiating filaments (this is not unique to monocotyledons).

A special arrangement exists in the daisy family, *Compositae*, where a quantity of small flowers (florets) are assembled in a capitulum (or head). They have no individual calyx as such, but the fleshy termination of the flower stem, the receptacle, on which they are fixed is surrounded by the equivalent of a calyx called the involucre.

Various terms are used to describe the shape of the whole or part of the corolla and, to a lesser extent, the calyx. These include campanulate, or bell-shaped; funnel-form; rotate or wheel-shaped, with spreading lobes; salverform, when the corolla spreads at right angles to a tube and may be termed the limb; tubular; trumpet-shaped; urceolate or urn-shaped. Funnel-form, trumpet-shaped and tubular flowers are sometimes described as having a 'mouth' and a 'throat', and salverform flowers may have an 'eye' when the aperture to the tube, or mouth, is picked out in a different colour.

If one perianth segment becomes much larger and more dominant than the others it is termed a lip; such flowers are labiate. The lip is a feature of most orchids. In some cases lips are formed by the fusion of two or three perianth lobes, and some flowers may have an upper and a lower lobe, to be termed bilabiate. This is typical of the family *Labiatae*.

In another distinct arrangement, found in the pea family, *Leguminosae*, the flower is papilionaceous or butterfly-shaped, with a large back petal or standard, two side petals or wings, and a keel formed by two lower petals which are usually joined together.

Flowers may be classified as regular or irregular. Regular flowers have more than one plane of symmetry: examples are equally four-petalled flowers, e.g. crucifers, and actinomorphic or radially symmetrical ones with three, five or six petals or tepals. Irregular flowers may have a spiral arrangement of parts, or be divisible only in one plane, when they can also be called zygomorphic.

A flower with the normal number of parts for the species is termed single. Abnormal flowers created by mutations may have a few more than, or over twice, the normal number of petals (semi-double or double). Small petals or petaloids may replace stamens and pistils; such forms may be called anemone-centred. In relatively primitive flowers like waterlilies, in which sepals, petals and stamens are numerous, there may be a gradation from one set of organs to the next.

The components of flowers discussed

here may be arranged in many permutations of relative number. Although differing form and size of the parts may make flowers look superficially dissimilar within one family, the classification of flowering plant families is based upon their arrangement.

Most of the technical terms in this account have separate, more detailed alphabetical entries. ◊ BRACT; CARPEL; CLASSIFICATION; DICOTYLEDON; INFLORESCENCE; MONOCOTYLEDON; SEED; SEX.

Flower Box ◊ WINDOW BOX.

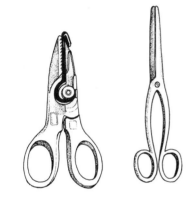

FLOWER GATHERER

Flower Gatherer A special type of secateur, designed to hold a flower stem after cutting it; it is of the anvil type and resembles a pair of scissors. ◊ SECATEURS.

Flower Pot ◊ POT.

Flowers of Sulphur ◊ SULPHUR.

Flue Dust The sweepings from chimneys through which smoke from forced-draught boilers has passed. Because of the intense heat from such boilers, this dust seldom has any fertilizing value, unlike ordinary soot; but if an analysis shows a reasonable proportion of potash, the material can be useful. ◊ POTASH; SOOT.

Fluid Sowing A method of sowing in which seeds are chitted or pre-sprouted, and then mixed into a gel which can either be a proprietary compound or be made from wallpaper paste (of a kind which does not contain a fungicide). The gel/seeds mixture is then placed in a dispenser for sowing which, on an ordinary garden scale, can be a plastic bag which is sealed and has one small corner cut off; from this the gel is sqeezed by hand into the prepared seed drill, using about $\frac{1}{4}$ pint to 30' of row. The method is claimed to speed germination, but it is essential to keep the seed drills thoroughly moistened until the seedlings are well up. The method is also sometimes called liquid sowing, but should not be confused with HYDRO SEEDING.

Flush A burst of production of flowers or a crop; usually describes such bursts by roses and mushrooms, which do not produce continuously.

Fly A two-winged insect with sucking mouthparts. Many true flies are horticultural pests in the larval stage, notably the numerous root flies and bulb flies, and the leaf miners. Various similar insects often called flies are not in fact closely related, e.g. the sawflies, while greenfly, black fly and white fly are not even similar in appearance. ◊ APHIDS; BULB FLIES; ROOT FLIES; SAWFLIES; WHITE FLY.

Foliage Plants Plants grown more for the colour, pattern and texture of their leaves than for their flowers.

Foliar Feeding Though plants basically absorb nutrients through their roots, they can also take in suitably formulated materials through the foliage. This is normally carried out with a liquid fertilizer applied by spray or rosed can. Foliar feeding is especially valuable to correct trace element deficiencies, to provide nutrients when roots are not working properly for some reason (e.g. dryness, cold or damage), and to help plants at their peak of production, especially in summer when it may be impossible to get at the soil to apply nutrients in the

113

normal way. Application should not be carried out in bright sun, or foliage may be scorched, nor if rain is likely, as this will wash off the feed. Ideally, the underside of the leaves should be sprayed as much as the top surface, since the underside appears to absorb moisture better. ◊ FEEDING PLANTS.

Follicle A dry, often pod-shaped fruit which is in fact made of one carpel only, opening by a slit on one side, the seeds being attached to the seam or junction point. Delphiniums and larkspurs have follicles. ◊ CARPEL.

Folly A structure in a garden layout, usually designed only to catch the eye, but having no functional purpose. Follies tend by their nature to be bizarre, and can be in the form of pyramids, pinnacles, towers, mock ruins, or Stonehenge-like stone circles. A few cave follies exist in the form of labyrinths or tunnels decorated with bones. ◊ CONCEIT.

Foot Rot A specific term for a fungal disease which attacks cucumbers, melons and tomatoes; in tomatoes this may affect the stem well above soil level, and also attack the fruits. Also loosely used of damage caused to plants and cuttings by diseases attacking them at or near soil level; the same as COLLAR ROT.

Forcing When plants are hurried into growth at an unnatural time by artificial means this is described as forcing. Gentle heat is the usual accelerator, and is applied in particular to spring bulbs (after a period in cool conditions – ◊ PLUNGE) and to early-flowering shrubs, kept most of the year in cool conditions in pots. Lilies-of-the-valley retarded in cold conditions will then respond rapidly to heat. Some vegetables force better in darkness, notably seakale and chicory, which in any case need blanching, and rhubarb; these can be forced under the greenhouse staging or in a warm shed.

Greenhouses specially designed for the purpose of forcing may be called forcing houses, and pit frames for the purpose forcing pits. In the nineteenth and early twentieth centuries, seakale and rhubarb were often forced outside in earthenware forcing pots, which gave an early, well-blanched crop. These handsome devices are no longer made but are sometimes to be seen in older gardens. ◊ GREENHOUSE; PIT; VERNALIZATION.

Fork On a tree, the point where two branches of similar size and age join, as opposed to the crotch which is the junction of main branches and trunk. ◊ CROTCH.

Fork Hoe ◊ HOE.

Forking Digging into and breaking up ground with a fork. This is basically the same as ordinary digging; on heavy soils a fork may be easier to use than a spade for this job; however, it may be impossible to turn light soils over with a fork. Nor is a fork suitable when cultivating ground covered with weeds or grass, where a spade is essential to cut through such cover cleanly. ◊ DIGGING.

Forks Gardening implements normally with three or four prongs or tines (exceptionally two to ten), which are usually more or less in the same plane as the handle. The latter can be long, without a handgrip, or short with a grip, according to local custom. Although now regarded as one of the vital gardening tools, the fork was developed much later than the spade, originating only in the seventeenth century. Until the beginning of this century, the three-pronged fork was the most common type.

Modern manufacturers call the larger, longer-tined versions digging or garden forks and the lighter, shorter ones border or ladies' forks. The former are best for work in open ground, and the latter, as their name suggests, for more detailed work especially among plants. A normal digging fork has tines abound 12″ long, a border fork as little as 5″ long. Some forks are made with 15″ tines; these are mainly for heavy work like digging up potatoes and beetroots, and are marketed as such. Tines are normally narrow, round or square in section, but the flat-tined fork has broad ones; it is also called a spading fork since it can in certain circumstances replace a spade, e.g. digging heavy soils where a spade would call for more effort. Handgrips may be of D, T or Y pattern as with spades.

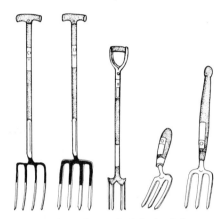

FORKS. *Left to right*, standard digging fork; flat-tined or spading fork; Cultifork; two hand forks (not to scale)

The hollow-tine fork has tubular tines and is used for spiking lawns needing aeration, especially those receiving heavy wear; soil is forced into the tines to leave a pronounced hole in the soil which can be filled with top-dressing material: ◊ SPIKING.

The fork has retained its basic character with little change; the only new type is the Cultifork, a relatively small implement with its four tines arranged in the pattern of a sugar scoop, designed for work in small spaces and for lifting plants.

Small versions of the fork for lifting small plants are called hand, weeding or weed forks, and have a short handle. Sometimes these are mounted on full-length handles and can then be used for weeding and pricking soil in borders, etc. These small forks usually have three broad prongs, sometimes two or four, which may be arranged in either plane.

Tools related to the fork include the manure fork, with distinctly curved tines, and the drags or drag forks in which the tines are bent sharply around the centre. There are also various forked hoes. ◊ DRAG; FORKING; HOE; SPADE.

Form A botanical classification category, of less importance than a variety, when a plant differs from the norm in some quite minor character. The Latin *forma* or the abbreviation *f.* should precede the epithet given to such a plant, as in *Rhododendron carolinianum* forma *luteum*, a yellow-flowered form of a purple-flowered species. The term is also used loosely by gardeners to denote a specially good variation within a species or a cultivar, but it is not now permissible under the 'International Code of Nomenclature for Cultivated Plants' to actually name a plant as 'So-and so's Form'. In horticulture the equivalent word is a selection. ◊ CLASSIFICATION; SELECTION.

Formal Garden A garden with a geometric, usually symmetrical design; usually composed partly of architectural features, often including clipped trees. Although many very early European gardens were of this type, the expression was not widely used until Reginald Blomfield published *The Formal Garden in England* in 1892. This was a counterblast to the wild or naturalistic gardening advocated by William Robinson. ◊ WILD GARDEN.

Formaldehyde, Formalin Formaldehyde is formic aldehyde, a gas used in solution as a disinfectant; formalin is its commercial formulation, a 40 per cent solution in water. This is used for sterilizing soils, and cleaning greenhouses, pots, boxes and tools at a dilution of 1 pint in 6 gallons of water (1 part in 48). A much more dilute solution is sometimes used to sterilize seeds suspected of carrying disease. ◊ STERILIZATION.

Formation Pruning Pruning of trees – usually fruit – to establish a desired shape, whether a 'natural' one like a bush or a strictly trained one like an espalier or fan. It must include adequate spacing of main branches, avoid the development of bare branches devoid of buds, maintain a satisfactory balance between root and branch systems, and prevent the production of fruit if this is likely to affect the building up of the tree's framework.

Fountain A jet or spouting stream of water, produced artificially; nowadays normally operated by easily installed electric pumps. ◊ WATERWORKS.

Frame A garden frame is a structure, usually quite low and seldom exceeding 30″ tall, which can be covered with transparent material: glass, glass substitute, plastic film or sheet. Most frames have solid walls

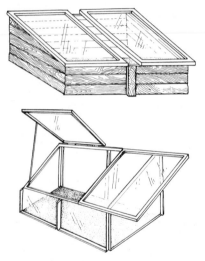

FRAME. *Above*, dutch-light; *below*, modern metal-framed design

but some admit light throughout. The glazing material is normally in the form of a 'light', a framework onto which the glazing material is fixed. The standard old-fashioned garden frames had sliding lights of 6′ × 4′ or 3′ × 4′ with several sash bars like a large window. These have been largely superseded by metal-framed structures and by the dutch-light frame with a light holding a single glass pane roughtly 5′ × 2½′ – the latter is especially suitable for temporary installations. Frames can have permanent walls of brick, concrete or wood, or movable frameworks of wood or metal; temporary frames can be placed on walls made of turves or straw bales.

Frames are used to hasten seed germination, for the rooting of cuttings, to obtain certain crops, e.g. early salads, which could not be grown outside, to harden off tender plants raised in a greenhouse which are to be planted outside, and to protect slightly tender plants in winter. Most frames are unheated, and are often called cold frames, but it is possible to heat a garden frame, the most convenient method being by soil-warming cables – the hotbed of fermenting manure is seldom used today.

Air is admitted to frames when needed by sliding the light along its walls or framework where applicable, or by propping it open with a brick, notched stick or other device.

A propagating frame is usually small and must be tight-fitting to ensure the close atmosphere needed for the rooting of cuttings; it can be placed inside a greenhouse over a source of heat or have its own heating element built in.

◊ BOTTOM HEAT; DUTCH LIGHT; FROST PROTECTION; HARDENING OFF; HOTBED; PROPAGATOR; SAND FRAME.

Frameworking ◊ REWORKING.

French Garden Perhaps better classified as 'French-style garden', this refers to the style of grand garden developed by Le Nôtre in France in the reign of Louis XIV. This style meant that the garden, designed with a series of axes, should be centred upon the house, and should also include a good deal of water, which was often combined in the axes in the form of canals. Other important features of French gardens were elaborate parterres, formal lakes, clipped trees and hedges along straight walks, geometric woods (*bosquets*), *pattes d'oies* and *rond-points* from which a series of avenues could radiate in a fan pattern. The most famous such garden is Versailles. The ideal of the French garden influenced design all over Europe, including Britain; it has its origins in Roman times and, more especially, as a direct influence upon the French, in the Italian Renaissance gardens made in the early sixteenth century. ◊ BOSKET; CANAL; LANDSCAPE GARDENING; PARTERRE; PATTE D'OIE; ROND-POINT.

French Gardening The French system of growing vegetables intensively throughout the year by using frames, cloches and hotbeds, together with the maximum possible catch-cropping and intercropping, often in combination with trained fruit trees. ◊ CATCH CROP; CLOCHE; FRAME; HOTBED; INTERCROP.

French Intensive Method ◊ DEEP BED METHOD.

Friable Crumbly, or capable of becoming so; applied to soil in a condition to be easily worked and broken down into a good crumbly state or tilth. ◊ CULTIVATION.

Frill-girdling A method of killing standing trees. A light axe or a billhook is used to make down-sloping, overlapping cuts all round the trunk as near soil level as possible. Then either a solution of brushwood killer or crystals of ammonium sulphamate is applied over the whole of the 'girdle', so that solution runs down into, or crystals lodge in, each cut. ◊ RING-BARKING; WEEDKILLER.

Frit Fertilizer material created by melting the appropriate chemicals together with a glassy matrix at high temperatures and pouring the molten mass into cold water. This causes it to shatter into minute fragments: these are actually the frits, but they are usually dried and ground into powder. These fertilizers are insoluble, so that they are neither leached away nor 'locked up' by other minerals, and the food materials are only released when roots hairs come into contact with them, presumably because the hairs release ascorbic acid which dis-solves the frit. Frits are often used to supply trace elements and can contain one or several of these. ◊ FEEDING PLANTS; FERTILIZER; TRACE ELEMENTS.

Frog Hopper The insect which produces CUCKOO-SPIT.

Frond Strictly, the leaf-like organ of ferns and some other flowerless plants, in which the stem is an integral part. Also applied, more loosely but initially by no less an authority than Linnaeus, to the often compound leaves of palms, bananas and the like. ◊ FERN; PALM.

Frost When temperature falls below 0°C (32°F), frost occurs, sometimes with the visible effect of hoarfrost, sometimes without. Frost is capable of damaging or killing many garden plants, depending on their degree of hardiness (or of tenderness, according to one's viewpoint). Frost damages plants by freezing their cell sap, which expands and ruptures the cell walls. The actual damage occurs when thawing takes place as in domestic water pipes. In this respect a quick thaw in sunshine is often more harmful than a slow one. Soft plants simply collapse in these conditions; but it may be more difficult to know if woody ones have been killed, and it is much better to leave such plants for as long as possible to see if regrowth occurs. If bark on the trunks or lower stem of woody plants is seen to have split vertically this is usually a sign of death. Frost can also prevent water reaching roots, leading to death by desiccation; evergreens are particularly susceptible, while plants in containers do not usually take kindly to their potting mixture becoming totally frozen. Another cause of damage is by frost-lifting when ice forms in soil and pushes both it and the plants in it upwards, breaking roots and allowing freezing air to get at them. Frost-lifted plants should be well firmed back as soon as possible. For methods of reducing frost damage. ◊ FROST PROTECTION.
  ◊ HARDY; TENDER.

Frost Pocket Cold air will run down slopes

117

like water; this is sometimes referred to as air drainage. If it runs into an obstacle or ends up in a depression, it will remain in this position and thereby create frost hollows or frost pockets as they are commonly called, where tender or early-flowering plants run extra risk of damage. The terrain may prevent any possibility of avoiding this, but if the obstacle is a wall, bank or close-packed hedge it is usually possible to let the cold air proceed downhill away from this by making gaps to improve the AIR DRAINAGE.

Frost Protection Plants can be protected against frost by taking them into the shelter of a greenhouse or frame which, even if unheated, can markedly reduce the likelihood of damage. In severe weather unheated frames can be protected with sacking, old blankets, mats, etc., while extra protection in unheated greenhouses can be given by insulating them. A frame or cloche can be placed over tender plants. Another method is to cover crowns of susceptible plants with a good layer of weathered ashes, sand, peat, straw or chopped bracken. Plants which retain their top growth can be protected by packing straw or bracken around them and holding this in place with twine, netting or split canes. With some plants, it is enough to erect a screen of sacking, hessian or plastic sheeting around canes, held in place by twine; large specimens or groups can be protected with wattle hurdles. Temporary protection for small plants, e.g. early-sown beans or the first shoots of potatoes, can be given with sheets of newspaper held in place with sticks or stones.

Small and trained fruit trees and soft fruit bushes can often be protected from frost killing the flowerbuds or flowers, and hence preventing fruit set, by covering them with muslin, net curtains or very fine mesh plastic netting. Orchard growers may protect their fruit by 'smoke pots' or paraffin burners, or sometimes by the surprising method of providing a continuous fine spray of water from permanently installed sprinklers – the latent heat of freezing keeps the buds above the temperature at which frost can damage them.
◊ FROST; INSULATION.

Frost Resistance Related plants can vary somewhat in their degree of resistance to frost damage, and breeders have tried to improve frost resistance by breeding. These attempts have largely focused on fruit trees where the resistance of blossom to frost damage is the crucial point. Among ornamental plants experience may pin down cultivars which are more frost-resistant than others.

Fruit Botanically, a fruit is the seed-bearing organ of a plant, whether it is a dry capsule, a nut, or a fleshy pear or peach. To gardeners, fruit is restricted to the latter. Top fruits are those produced on trees, e.g. apples and pears; stone fruits are those, also produced on trees, which have a stone rather than pips, e.g. apricots, cherries, peaches and plums; soft fruits are those on low bushes or herbaceous plants, including currants, gooseberries and strawberries; and cane fruits those like raspberries. Nuts are regarded as fruit by the greengrocer, and in show schedules, but cucumbers, marrows, tomatoes, peas and beans, though they are undoubtedly fleshy fruits, are usually classed as vegetables.

Many ornamental shrubs and trees also carry fruits which are an important part of their decorative value. With these the definition is looser, but in general applies to fleshy fruits ranging in size from those of sorbus or cotoneaster to the large ones of crab apples.
◊ ACHENE; BERRY; CANE FRUITS; CAPSULE; CARPEL; CONE; DRUPE; FOLLICLE; HIP; NUT; POD; POME; SAMARA; SOFT FRUIT; STONE; STONE FRUIT; TOP FRUIT.

Fruit Bud A bud which will develop into a flower and finally produce fruit, as opposed to a growth bud which can only develop into a leaf or shoot. ◊ BUD.

Fruit Cage A structure designed to keep birds off soft and cane fruits, usually constructed with a metal or wood framework over which netting is stretched. The latter, which can be of cord, nylon, plastic or wire, should have a mesh not exceeding ¾″ and must be firmly fixed at soil level, or birds will get past it. ◊ BIRDS; NETTING.

Fruit Culture, Pruning and Training Entries relevant to these topics will be found as follows:

Fruit culture ◊ DEBLOSSOMING; DEFRUIT-ING; DESHOOTING; DISBUDDING; FEATHER-ED (1); FERTILITY RULES; GARROTTING; GIRDLING; GRASSING DOWN; MAIDEN; RINGING; ROOT PRUNING; TRUNK SLIT-TING.

Fruit pruning and training ◊ ARCURE; BRINDILLE; BRUTTING; CORDON; CROWN THINNING; DEHORNING; DELAYED OPEN-CENTRE; DELAYED PRUNING; DELAYED PYRAMID; ESPALIER; EXTENSION SHOOT; FORMATION PRUNING; GOURMAND; GUYOT; HEADING BACK; KNOB; LAMBOURDE; LATENT; LATERAL; LEADER; LORETTE PRUNING; MAINTENANCE PRUNING; OPEN-CENTRE; PALMETTE; PYRAMID; REGULATED PRUNING; REJUVENATION PRUNING; RE-NEWAL PRUNING; SAP-DRAWER; SECOND-ARY GROWTH; SPINDLEBUSH; SPUR; SUM-MER PRUNING; SUMMER WOOD; TIP-BEARER; TIPPING; TOP; U-CORDON; VASE; WATER SHOOTS; WHIP; WINGED PYRAMID.

For entries relevant to propagation ◊ BUDDING; GRAFTING; PROPAGATION.

Fruit Garden A garden devoted to fruit growing. Such gardens, usually walled, were often important in the days of land-scape gardens, being tucked out of sight as separate entities. The combination of growing fruit and vegetables, which was more common than growing fruit alone, was carried out in the KITCHEN GARDEN.

Fruit Gatherers Devices for picking fruit off tall trees were first invented early in the nineteenth century, and many exist today, although they are less popular in Britain than in France and elsewhere on the Continent. Many are simply small cups or bags, fixed onto long poles, which are pushed under the fruit so that the pressure causes

FRUIT GATHERERS. *Top row*, devices for picking single fruits from trees; *below*, two soft-fruit picking bags

it to break off and lodge in the container. Some are based on remotely controlled forceps or other devices to ensure more positively that the fruit is readily detached. One device, apparently no longer available, consisted of a metal ring attached to a long plastic tube so that a detached fruit travelled down to the operator, avoiding the need for lowering the pole each time. For picking soft fruit like raspberries, devices have been invented which consist of a collecting bag fixed underneath the hand, avoiding the need to keep transferring picked fruit to a basket.

Fruit House A greenhouse designed for growing fruit, typically a tall, narrow lean-to structure in which the fruit trees are trained on the back wall. ◊ GREENHOUSE.

Fruiting Body The spore-bearing organs of larger fungi, which are usually called mushrooms or toadstools. ◊ FUNGUS.

Fruitlet An immature fruit. ◊ BUD STAGES.

Fruit Set ◊ BUD STAGES.

Fruit Setting When fruit is seen to be developing after pollination, it is said to have set. If conditions are unsuitable for natural fertilization, it is possible to induce fruit to set by spraying the flowers with certain plant hormones or auxins sold for the purpose. This method is primarily used on tomatoes grown under glass, where conditions are often unsatisfactory for natural setting; but successful experiments with various hormone materials have been carried out on strawberries, apples, pears, figs, beans, blackberries and grapes. ◊ SET.

Fruit Swelling Equivalent to fruit set when detailing BUD STAGES.

Fruit Thinning The removal of fruitlets on various kinds of top and stone fruits to ensure that the remaining fruitlets develop satisfactorily and that the tree is not overloaded, which can sometimes cause branch damage, as well as overtaxing the food resources; the latter can sometimes result in biennial bearing. ◊ BIENNIAL BEARING; DEFRUITING.

Fruticose A botanical term meaning shrubby, with woody stems, sometimes Latinized as a specific name. ◊ SHRUB.

Full Blossom ◊ BUD STAGES.

Fumigant A material used for greenhouse FUMIGATION.

Fumigation In gardening, the method of destroying pests or diseases by the use of insecticides or fungicides in gas or smoke form, primarily carried out within greenhouses or other structures which can be reasonably well sealed. Nowadays this is usually accomplished by lighting pellets or firework-like cones or canisters containing the relevant materials. The sulphur candle gives off sulphur when ignited. Other methods include certain chemicals which can simply be placed on the floor to give off fumes, the ignition of nicotine shreds piled on the floor, and the vaporization of nicotine compound in special lamps. The pellets, cones or canisters – which can combine insecticide and fungicide – are now made in various sizes according to the volume of the structure to be fumigated. Doors and ventilators must of course be closed first, and any gaps around these, or elsewhere, may need plugging or covering, wet cloths or sacking being suitable for this.

Special devices are available which give off fumigating materials continuously, either in electrically heated containers or by volatilization from a bar of resinous matter containing the material in suitable form. These methods allow normal work to go on in the structure.

Soil fumigation, used against pests, diseases and sometimes perennial weeds, involves making deep holes at intervals in soil, placing in them a pesticidal substance which gives off fumes naturally, and then sealing the holes with soil; in some cases a special gun is used to inject the material into the soil. These practices are primarily used on a commercial rather than a garden scale.

◊ FUNGICIDES; PEST CONTROL; SMOKE GENERATORS; STERILIZATION; VAPORIZER.

Fungicides Substances used to kill or control fungi and prevent fungus diseases of plants: also substances to kill larger types of fungi like those responsible for fairy rings in lawns. Some are used preventatively as seed dressings and as dips for bulbs, corms, etc. Most fungicides are not only harmless to plants but are almost harmless to human beings and other animals. As with pesticides, most operate as contact materials, but a few enter the plant sap and work systemically, when their effect lasts for a period. Fungicides can be obtained in liquid or powder form, and as 'smokes' for fumigation; one of the earliest fungicides to be used was flowers of sulphur, always applied as a dust.

Fungicides can be inorganic or organic in origin and include a few antibiotic substances (mainly effective against bacterial diseases). Fungicides are sometimes mixed with pesticides to provide general pest and disease control.

The list below summarizes the main uses of widely available fungicides, excluding soil fumigants (for which ◊ STERILIZATION). The names of the fungicides listed are their chemical ones or names coined to avoid complex chemical ones – they are not trade names. Users of fungicides should check the names of their constituent chemicals which, in the U.K. at least, must always be printed on the label. U.K. and U.S. after the name refer to availability for amateur use in either country; many materials are available only in bulk for commercial users.

Fungicides and the diseases they control

Benomyl (U.K., U.S.) Systemic; a wide range of diseases in garden and greenhouse including club root, also storage rots, and as preventive treatment for bulbs, corms, etc.

Bordeaux Mixture (U.K., U.S.) (Copper sulphate and lime) An old remedy against a wide range of diseases, especially potato blight and fruit tree scab. Harmful to fish. ◊ COPPER.

Bupirimate (U.K.) Systemic; mildew and black spot on roses, other ornamental plants, and some fruits; only available combined with triforine.

Calomel ◊ Mercurous chloride (below).

Captan (U.S.) Wide range of diseases, especially scab of fruit trees, rose black spot, and botrytis and mildew under glass. Also for preventive treatment of seed, corms, etc.

Carbendazim (U.K.) Wide range of diseases, including mildews, grey mould, black spot, lawn diseases and storage rots.

Cheshunt Compound (U.K.) (Copper sulphate and ammonium carbonate) Damping-off of seedings; collar rot of cuttings, etc.

Chloraniformethan (U.K.) Systemic; powdery mildew.

Copper Compounds (U.K., U.S.) Inorganic; wide range of diseases. ◊ Bordeaux Mixture, Cheshunt Compound (above); COPPER.

Cyclohexamide (U.S.) Antibiotic; powdery mildew, lawn diseases, cedar-apple rust, damping off. ◊ ANTIBIOTICS.

Dichlofluanid (U.K., U.S.) Wide range of diseases, especially strawberry botrytis, rose black spot and tulip fire. Harmful to fish.

Dichlorophen (U.K.) Lawn diseases; also a moss-killer and bactericide.

Dicloran (*Dichloran*) (U.K.) Botrytis; tulip fire; storage diseases. Treated crops should not be used for three weeks.

Difolatan (U.S.) Fruit and leaf diseases: used when trees are dormant.

Dinocap (U.K., U.S.) (Karathane in U.S.) Powdery mildews. Should not be inhaled and can affect skin; harmful to fish. (Also controls some mites.)

Dinitro Compounds (U.S.) (DNC, DNOC, Dinoseb, etc.) Used as dormant sprays against disease spores; also pesticidal.

121

Dodine (U.S.) Fruit and leaf diseases.

Ferbam (U.S.) Anthracnose and rust diseases, also rose black spot.

Folpet (U.K., U.S.) Many diseases including rose black spot and mildew.

Glyodin (U.S.) Apple scab and leaf diseases. (Also kills mites.)

Karathane ◊ Dinocap.

Lime Sulphur (U.S.) An old combination of lime and sulphur against many diseases, also mites; now generally superseded. ◊ LIME SULPHUR.

Mancozeb (U.K., U.S.) Wide range, including rust and lawn diseases.

Maneb (U.K., U.S.) Wide range, especially downy mildews and rose black spot. Should not be inhaled.

Mercurous Chloride (Calomel) (U.K., U.S.) Club root; onion white rot; lawn diseases. ◊ CALOMEL.

Oxycarboxin (U.K.) Rust diseases.

PCNB ◊ Quintozene.

Quintozene (PCNB) (U.K., U.S.) Lawn diseases; root rots; bulb and corm diseases.

Streptomycin (U.S.) Antibiotic; mostly against bacterial diseases. ◊ ANTIBIOTICS.

Sulphur (U.K. U.S.) Powdery mildews; storage rots. ◊ SULPHUR.

TCNB ◊ Tecnazene.

Tecnazene (TCNB) (U.K., U.S.) As greenhouse fumigant against botrytis and grey mould; also potato dry rot.

Thiobenzadole (U.S.) Turf diseases.

Thiophanate-methyl (U.K.) Systemic; many diseases including mildews, mould, scab, canker, lawn diseases and club root. Also used in some tree wound dressings against fungus infection.

Thiram (U.K., U.S.) Wide range, including mildews, rusts, damping off and lawn diseases; also an animal repellent. May taint fruits and can cause skin irritation.

Triforine (U.K.) Rose black spot and rust. Only available combined with bupirimate.

Zineb (U.K., U.S.) Wide range. Should not be inhaled and may irritate skin.

Ziram (U.S.) Wide range; has largely replaced Zineb.

◊ ANTIBIOTICS; FUMIGATION; FUNGUS; GARDEN CHEMICALS; PESTICIDES; REPELLENTS; STERILIZATION; SYSTEMIC.

Fungus The fungi (plural of fungus) are one of the most important divisions of the vegetable kingdom. Though differing greatly in size, appearance and habits, they all lack chlorophyll, the green colouring matter of ordinary plants; being thus unable to produce their food from simple chemicals via the sun's energy, they must obtain food supplies either from living plants or animals, when they are parasites, or from decaying matter, when they are saprophytes, e.g. most mushrooms and toadstools.

The mushroom or comparable aboveground organ is only the reproductive organ or 'fruit-body' of the fungus, producing the microscopic spores which are the equivalent of seeds. The fungus proper, the mycelium, is a tangle of thread-like growth, as anyone who has grown mushrooms will know; the 'spawn' used to start a mushroom bed is a compact piece of this mycelium.

Fungi which produce large 'fruit-bodies', like mushrooms, toadstools and bracket fungi, are sometimes called macro-fungi.

Many fungi are parasites which cause a variety of plant diseases, such as scab, mildew, black spot, etc. Some of these fungi are microscopic, but others produce large fruit-bodies, e.g. the silver leaf fungus after it has killed its host. However, many fungi are beneficial, for they help to break down dead plant and animal matter and release the valuable chemical plant foods which they contain.

◊ FAIRY RING; HOST PLANT; PARASITE; SAPROPHYTE; SPORE; SYMBIOSIS; WITCHES' BROOMS.

Fungus Diseases Numerous fungi live parasitically on plants and cause fungus diseases. A few, e.g. mildews, live primarily on the exterior of the plants, where they have a smothering effect, impeding photosynthesis and transpiration; but most live within the host's tissues, their microscopic strands or hyphae penetrating and killing the cells as the fungus absorbs nourishment from them. Fungicides are used to combat such diseases. ◊ FUNGICIDES; FUNGUS; PHOTOSYNTHESIS; TRANSPIRATION; WILT.

Fungus Gnats Tiny midge-like flies, also called sciarids, associated with pot plants. Although a few are direct pests of mushrooms and some other plants, notably cucumbers, most are harmless, feeding on decaying organic matter in the potting compost; if the tiny white, black-headed larvae are seen on plant roots, they are usually eating tissues which have died for other reasons. However, the flies may be dealt with by watering the pots with a suitable insecticide.

Funnelform A self-explanatory term used in describing certain flowers or other structures. The Latin equivalent *infundibuliformis* is sometimes seen as a descriptive specific name. ◊ FLOWER.

Fusarium Patch A fungus disease of grass, which after infection dies out in round, brown to yellow patches. In damp weather the fungal mycelium can be seen like whitish or pinkish threads. The disease is encouraged by feeding with high-nitrogen fertilizers in late summer; it can be treated with calomel or certain organic fungicides. Reseeding of badly damaged patches may be needed later.

Fuse, Fusée Applied to a smoke and chemical generator like a small firework used to destroy or drive out moles when placed and ignited in their runs.

Fuseau A fruit-tree form. ◊ PYRAMID.

Fusiform A botanical term meaning spindle-shaped, i.e. thick in the centre and tapering to each end of an elongated growth.

FYM A popular abbreviation for farmyard manure. ◊ MANURE.

ꙮ G ꙮ

Gall Galls are abnormal outgrowths on plants, caused most frequently by insects which lay eggs in the leaf, stem, flower or roots, and also by eelworms, bacteria, mites and fungi. Exactly how they arise is uncertain; the organism responsible irritates the plant tissue (in the case of the insects, probably by a liquid secretion), and the plant reacts by abnormal growth. It is rather mysterious how different insects can affect the same plant in entirely distinct ways, each kind of gall being clearly recognizable.

Most of the insect galls – e.g. oak apples, the hairy 'robin's pincushion' on roses, and the little red knobs on willow leaves, to mention some familiar ones – are virtually harmless, but the gall weevil of cabbage roots sometimes plagues the gardener. Azalea gall is one caused by a fungus; big bud of currants by a mite.

Crown and leafy galls are caused by bacteria, and are apparently wound infections. On fruit trees crown galls form round, hard, woody swellings which are seldom harmful, but on plants like dahlias, chrysanthemums, gladioli, etc., the large, soft swelling weakens the host, and gall, plant and all are best consigned to the fire. Despite their name, crown galls can be formed on the upper parts of a plant, as they often are on raspberries.

Leafy galls are similar but consist of a great number of short, distorted shoots arising from a swollen, distorted stem. Again, affected plants are best destroyed and should certainly not be used for propagation.

Soil in pots which have held plants affected by crown or leafy gall should also be destroyed; greenhouses may need sterilizing and, in the open garden, plants of the kind affected should not be grown in the same site for several years.

Gall Weevil Although galls can be caused by several insects, the cabbage gall weevil is probably most frequently encountered by gardeners. The small whitish grubs of the beetle-like adult attack cabbages and other brassicas near the base of the stem and cause pea-sized galls both above and below ground. In fact they cause little harm, but can be prevented by using a suitable insecticidal powder round the plants. This should not be confused with the much more serious CLUB ROOT disease of BRASSICAS.

Gamopetalous Of flowers with their petals united into a single organ; the same as sympetalous. ◊ FLOWER.

Garden Centre A modern development combining the garden shop and retail nursery in which plants and seeds are available as well as tools, pesticides, fertilizers, potting composts, paving, garden ornaments and other horticultural sundries. The most important difference between a garden centre and a nursery is that the plants offered are container-grown so that they can be examined and bought for instant planting at any time of year (bedding plants, of course, only during a limited season). This development depends largely, of course, on the customer having a car in which to take away whatever he buys. In this way packing and carriage charges are avoided. ◊ CONTAINER-GROWN; NURSERY GARDEN.

Garden Chemicals Many kinds of chemical are used by gardeners, as also in agriculture. These include fertilizers, fungicides, pesticides of all kinds, weedkillers and animal repellents. These may be inorganic elements and salts (mainly fertilizers), or complex organic compounds. By definition, chemicals are not of natural origin from plants but a number of plant extracts *are* used for pest and disease control and, since some are poisonous, the comments below are equally applicable to them.

In principle, fertilizers are not toxic to humans and other mammals in the way that fungicides, pesticides and weedkillers may be, so the comments below generally refer not to fertilizers but to the other materials which control gardeners' enemies – though it is always best to handle fertilizers carefully, not to inhale them when dusting, and to wash well after handling. Although fungicides, pesticides, repellents and weedkillers all have separate alphabetical entries, there are certain overriding considerations in their handling which apply to most of the different materials, in whatever form they may be available to the gardener. With few exceptions, these forms are concentrated and as such present much greater hazards to health than when diluted.

In Britain the availability of garden chemicals to amateur gardeners is governed by the Pesticides Safety Precaution Scheme, which covers the safety of products to man and the environment, and implements an E.E.C. directive effective from 1981 in regard to stringent labelling requirements. In the U.S., each State has its own, sometimes widely differing, safety regulations, and it has sometimes been difficult to distinguish between materials available there which are suitable for gardeners as opposed to those in agricultural use, with which special precautions may have to be taken. However, in general only chemicals suitable for amateur use are mentioned in the separate entries.

The P.S.P.S./E.E.C. labelling requirements for fungicides and pesticides include declaration of the concentration of active ingredients, naming of any toxic or harmful solvents, and the use of hazard symbols. A skull-and-crossbones denotes a toxic or very toxic chemical, and a black cross one classified as harmful. Few garden chemicals come into even the second category. Certain classes of chemical which may be mentioned in older books were prohibited as pesticides in the E.E.C. from January 1981, namely mercury compounds and organochlorines; the only garden chemical involved is calomel (mercurous chloride).

The container label naturally goes on to give instructions as to preparation and application and should be exactly followed if the material is to be effective. It will also warn of the time that must elapse before fruit or vegetables can safely be eaten, give warnings with regard to household pets and fish in pools, and offer information on plants that may be damaged by the chemical concerned.

Apart from following label instructions, gardeners should keep chemicals out of the reach of children, should never transfer concentrates to unmarked receptacles such as drinks bottles, and should keep the materials away from food, drink and animal foodstuffs. When using chemicals, one should not eat, drink or smoke, and ensure that children and pets are well out of range of sprays and dusts and do not go into newly treated areas. Hands and face should be washed after using garden chemicals.

Most solutions of garden chemicals, including weedkillers, are usable only for up to four hours unless the active ingredient is entirely soluble in water. As a rule, surpluses of made-up solutions should be put down a drain after their immediate purpose has been fulfilled.

As already mentioned in the Preface, complex organic chemicals are not cross-referenced in the alphabetical text, but are summarized under the relevant headings. Inorganic materials and those of plant origin have individual entries as well as inclusion in the summaries.

◊ FERTILIZER; FUNGICIDES; PESTICIDE; WEEDKILLER.

Garden Design Many aspects of garden design are dealt with in separate entries, as follows:

For individual garden features ◊ ALLEY; ARBOUR; AVENUE; BEE BOLE; BELVEDERE; BORDER; BOSKET; CLAIR-VOYÉE; COLONNADE; COLOUR BORDER; CONCEIT; DECK; EYE-CATCHER; FOLLY; GARDEN HOUSE; GAZEBO; GROTTO; HA-HA; HERBACEOUS BORDER; ISLAND BED; KNOT; LABYRINTH; LOGGIA; MAZE; MOAT; MOSS HOUSE; MOUNT; NICHE; PARTERRE; PATIO; PATTE D'OIE; PAVILION; PEAT BEDS; PERGOLA; POOL; POTAGER; RAISED BED; ROCK GARDEN; ROND-POINT; ROOF GARDEN; ROOT HOUSE; RUINS; SHELL HOUSE; SHRUBBERY; SHRUB BORDER; SUMMERHOUSE; SUNKEN GAR-

DEN; TAPIS-VERT; TEMPLES; TERRACE; TOPIARY; TREE HOUSE; TREILLAGE; TROMPE L'OEIL; TURF SEAT; TURKISH TENT; URN; VINEYARD; VISTA; WALK; WALLS; WATER GARDEN; WATERWORKS; WELL-HEAD.

For styles and types of garden ⟡ AR-BORETUM; BOTANIC GARDEN; CHINOISERIE; COTTAGE GARDENS; FORMAL GARDEN; FRENCH GARDEN; GARDENESQUE; GOTHIC; INDIANESQUE; INFORMAL; ITALIANATE, ITALIAN GARDEN; JAPANESE GARDEN; JARDIN ANGLAIS; LANDSCAPE GARDEN-ING; MARY GARDEN; NATURALISTIC; OR-NAMENTAL GARDEN; PARADISE GARDEN; PEAT GARDENS; PHYSIC GARDEN; PICTUR-ESQUE; PINETUM; SHARAWADGI; SPANISH GARDEN; SURREY SCHOOL; TUDOR GAR-DEN; WILD GARDEN.

Gardenesque A form of gardening which began in the early nineteenth century as landscape gardening declined, in which both the setting and the plants in it are regarded as being of equal importance. J. C. Loudon, writing in 1843, recognized both 'geometric' and 'pictorial' garden-esque, the one based on regularity and symmetry, and the second informal.

Garden House A phrase which can be ap-plied to any structure in a garden, used either for leisure or as an ornament. Such buildings were certainly made by the Romans, the Chinese and the Persians, and have been a feature of gardens – small as well as large – ever since. The medieval herber or arbour can be included under this umbrella as well as more conventional structures. ⟡ ARBOUR; BELVEDERE; BOWER; CONCEIT; GAZEBO; GROTTO; MOSS HOUSE; ROOT HOUSE; SHELL HOUSE; SUMMER HOUSE; TEMPLES; TURKISH TENT.

Garden Line In its simplest form, a cord tied and wound onto one stick with another at its free end, for laying out straight lines in a garden, especially when making drills or planting rows in a vegetable plot. Ideally, the garden line consists of a small reel above a spike onto which the cord can be wound by turning a handle, attached at the other end to another spike and made taut as required. In some designs the cord can be wound onto a spool rather like a mea-suring tape. ⟡ DRILL.

Garden Styles ⟡ GARDEN DESIGN.

Garrotting A method of restricting growth and encouraging fruiting on fruit trees. Basically, it is carried out by tying a metal wire around a branch, or even the main trunk, and twisting it like a tourniquet so that it bites into the bark. This creates a barrier to the movement of sap and re-distributes the natural hormones made in various parts of the tree. The effect is similar to ringing but is less drastic and shorter-lived. ⟡ HORMONES; RINGING.

Gas ⟡ HEATING.

Gazebo A structure designed as a vantage or lookout point, either a turret or 'lantern' on a house-top, or a separate garden house, usually of two storeys, in either case com-manding a view. The word, first recorded in 1752, later (1843) came also to mean a projecting window or balcony. Its origin is dubious; the word is almost certainly in-vented, either a corruption of 'gaze about' or a mock-Latin word also based on 'gaze' in the manner of *videbo*, to look around. ⟡ BELVEDERE.

Gene The unit of inheritance, found in the chromosomes in the cell nucleus. The very numerous genes control the appear-ance and the development of the plant. ⟡ CHROMOSOME.

Genetics The science of heredity and natural variation, a knowledge of which is essential to the serious plant breeder.

Genus (plural: genera) The basic name unit in the modern classification of living organisms: a family is composed of one or more genera, the similar members of a genus being the species. ⟡ CLASSIFICATION (The Binomial).

Geotropic ⟡ TROPISM.

Germination The moment at which a seed starts into growth. The seed has often been dormant for a period awaiting the most satisfactory conditions. These normally include air, warmth, moisture and sometimes darkness, and it is these which the gardener has to provide for seeds sown artificially. Initially the seed, which contains varying amounts of food reserve, produces a radicle, the equivalent of a root, which grows downwards, and a plumule or shoot growing upwards. When the radicle has found suitable conditions to grow into, and the plumule develops leaves, the seedling may be said to be self-supporting and germination complete. Though a few seeds germinate very quickly after maturing, and may indeed lose their viability (capacity to germinate) soon, others may take a long time to do so, even if suitable conditions appear to exist. For this reason it is wise to leave containers, especially of hard and large seeds, for two years or more before discarding them. In some such cases artificial means like chipping or stratifying will hasten germination. ◊ CHIPPING; CHITTING; DORMANT, DORMANCY; SEED; SEED SOWING; STRATIFICATION; VIABILITY.

Girdling (1) If bark is removed all round a tree's trunk the downward passage of food to the roots is stopped and the tree will eventually die. This can occur when rabbits or deer eat the bark in winter, or sometimes from mechanical damage, e.g. by careless use of cultivating machinery. The fatal result of girdling can be prevented by bridge grafting. Partial girdling, carried out deliberately, can improve fruit bearing: this is usually termed ringing. ◊ BRIDGE GRAFTING; GARROTTING; RINGING.
(2) In the U.S. the word is also used of tree roots which have grown in such a way as to encircle the trunk and prevent its expansion; such roots are most often formed when trees are planted close to masonry, etc., as with street trees. If girdling is suspected, the roots near the trunk must be exposed and the offending root severed and if possible removed.

Glabrous A botanical term meaning 'not hairy'. Sometimes used loosely, and wrongly, in the more positive sense of 'smooth'. However, a glabrous leaf can be rough or irregular, while a technically smooth one cannot.

Gland Plant glands are organs which are presumed to secrete unwanted substances such as resins and ethereal oils. They consist of small vesicles which may be embedded in, on or slightly protruding from, the surface of any part of a plant: stem, leaf, bract, flower parts or fruit. The sugar-secreting nectaries of flowers are a kind of gland, and nectaries are sometimes found outside the flowers, e.g. on the leaves of cherries and of laurel. When the glands are carried on a thin stalk they are known as glandular hairs; sometimes they are carried on relatively very thick stalks, as in *Impatiens glandulifera*. Some of the most interesting and highly developed glandular hairs are those which sting, like those of the nettle, and those of insectivorous plants, e.g. the sundew, which are not only sticky in order to hold, and later digest, insects, but are sensitive to touch and bend over to trap the prey. ◊ NECTARY.

Glass To the gardener glass is important as the main material for glazing greenhouses and frames. Although plastic materials have largely replaced glass in cloches, it is still much more widely used than plastics for larger structures. Glass for such glazing must be of good quality, without bubbles or distortions which can act as lenses and thus, by focusing sunlight onto plants, scorch their foliage. Such damage sometimes occurs in glazed porches and indoors, and often takes the form of a straight band of dry, yellow tissue on a leaf, because of the movement of the sun. Also, both for strength and reasonable heat insulation, glass should not be too thin. It is usual to use '21-oz.' glass: this indicates the weight of a pane one square foot in area. Sometimes 24-oz. glass is used to provide extra strength.

It is not essential that glass should be fully clear for garden purposes, but it must not be too opaque. If cost is a problem,

127

the slightly opaque type known as rolled glass is perfectly satisfactory. Ordinary glass prevents the passage of ultra-violet light, though all visible light passes through; however, this is almost certainly an advantage to most plants. ◊ CLOCHE; FRAME; GLASS SUBSTITUTES; GREENHOUSE.

Glasshouse ◊ GREENHOUSE.

Glass Substitutes A number of plastic materials are increasingly used as substitutes for glass, especially in commercial practice. These range from thin polythene sheet, which is really only suitable for insulation or emergency repairs, to heavy-gauge polythene or PVC sheet. The latter can be obtained in both flexible and rigid form. These firm PVC sheets, acrylic sheets and similar materials can be obtained flat or with wavy or rectangular corrugations which provide extra rigidity. Another rigid kind is formed of two skins with internal bracers at small intervals, producing a honeycomb-like, heat-insulating effect; it is, however, rather opaque. It is also possible to obtain wire-reinforced plastic materials.

Polythene sheet suffers from the drawback that sunlight causes deterioration and a relatively short life, although its lightness means that light, simple metal or wood structures can be used to support it. To ensure maximum life, supports should be no more than 30″ apart and fixing must be done carefully, since it is very easy to tear the sheeting. PVC, especially in its rigid forms, and acrylic sheet, have a longer life, and the wire-reinforced materials have the advantage that they are very easily patched.

Most plastic materials available for garden glazing are reasonably clear and transmit adequate light; the clearer kinds are more expensive. However, a single sheet of plastic does not have the insulating qualities of glass and also tends to produce considerable condensation during cold weather unless the structure is well heated and ventilated.

◊ GREENHOUSE; INSULATION.

Glaucous Bluish green or bluish grey, or covered with a bluish 'bloom' like a plum. ◊ WAX.

Globose Nearly spherical; applied to plant organs such as fruits and also to shrubs of rounded outline and trees with a crown of such form.

Glochid A minute, barbed bristle or spine, occurring in tufts on the woolly areoles of some cacti, especially prickly pears (opuntias). Glochids penetrate the skin at the slightest touch and set up irritation. The easiest way to remove them is by laying surgical plaster over the affected area and peeling it off again, or with forceps. ◊ AREOLE; CACTUS.

Goblet A form of fruit tree. ◊ VASE.

Gootee Another name, Indian in origin, for AIR LAYERING.

Gophers These rodents and other ground squirrels are sometimes garden pests in western North America, burrowing into garden areas with resultant damage to plants. The usual control is to place poisoned pieces of vegetable in the burrows, but this causes painful death and is not permitted in some States. Advice from local pest control officials should be sought.

Gothic, Gothick Gothic refers to a style of architecture of which the pointed arch is an important character, used in western Europe from the twelfth to the fifteenth century. It was revived in the eighteenth century, not only for mansions but for mock castles and ruins erected in gardens, and the spelling 'Gothick' is often used to distinguish work in this mock medieval manner, which can be traced forward right into the 1930s.

Gourmand A French word meaning 'glutton', used by fruit growers to denote extra-vigorous wood shoots which grow on the upper surfaces of the strongest branches, especially at bends. Gourmands (also called gourmand shoots) are sometimes made use of, as when bending (arching) is carried out, and are the shoots retained in many American pruning systems for eventual rejuvenation of the tree's framework. ⟡ ARCURE; BENDING.

Grading The U.S. term for LEVELLING.

Graft (1) The artificial union of plant parts. ⟡ GRAFTING.
(2) A plant shoot suitable for grafting and, loosely, a scion, sucker or branch.
(3) An old word (originating in 1624) for a 'spit' of soil, i.e. a spade's depth. ⟡ DIGGING.
(4) A kind of spade used for digging drains; now known as a GRAFTING TOOL.

Grafter (1) One who grafts.
(2) A kind of hand-saw used in grafting in the early nineteenth century.
(3) A kind of spade, in use during the last century, having a tapering blade with a half-moon section, used for taking out plugs of soil as with transplanters.

Graft Hybrid A hybrid resulting from tissues of the stock and scion mingling together after grafting. ⟡ CHIMAERA.

Grafting A graft is a union between two plants, which can occur in natural conditions (as when two branches rub into each other and finally, as they expand, grow together), but is normally an artificial procedure. It depends for its success on the ability of wounded plant tissue, under the right circumstances, to produce a callus; when wounded tissues are placed together, it is the calluses that unite and eventually enable the two plants to grow as one. Only plants which are quite closely related can be grafted. The principle is widely used to propagate plants which are either difficult or relatively slow to raise from cuttings, which are unsatisfactory on their own roots, or which cannot be raised true from seed – notably fruit trees. Many different methods have been developed according to the plants involved and the parts of the plant used; but in all cases the part of the plant which provides the roots is known as the stock, or rootstock, while the top part, selected for its fruit or flower, is called the scion. The scions are normally bound into position on the stock with raffia, plastic tape or similar flexible material, and the area of graft and binding is entirely covered with grafting wax. This keeps the wounded tissues from possible infection and drying out.

Grafting was known to the Romans and the Chinese, and was very highly developed in Europe by the eighteenth century, when a large range of methods was in vogue. Special grafting benches might be used and

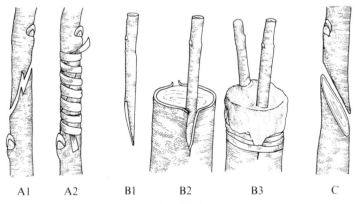

A1   A2   B1   B2   B3   C

GRAFTING. A, whip and tongue; B, rind grafting (B1 single scion); C, splice graft the propagator had a range of tools including chisels of different sizes.

One of the oldest methods is *cleft grafting*, often used for reworking old fruit trees. In this the beheaded stock is simply split with an axe or billhook, and scions of year-old shoots, trimmed on each side at the base to form a long wedge shape, are inserted on each side of the stock. An actual wedge is usually needed to keep the cleft open during insertion of the scions, which become clamped in place when the wedge is removed.

Crown or *rind grafting* is a more sophisticated version of cleft grafting used on old, thick stocks. The stock is beheaded and a pair of vertical cuts 2″ long are made in the bark downwards from the point of beheading for each intended scion. One or more scions are inserted depending on the size of the stock. The scions are made into a wedge shape by trimming one side near the base, and are forced under the narrow piece of bark left between the cuts on the scion.

Perhaps the most commonly used method today is the *whip and tongue*, used with young fruit and ornamental trees. Here stock and scion, if possible of similar size, are cut so as to interlock (as shown in the illustrations). The binding must be quite extensive to ensure rigidity. *Whip* or *splice grafting* is similar, but the cuts on stock and scion are simple oblique ones, so that there is no interlocking and hence more difficulty in positioning the scion.

Perhaps the simplest plants to graft are cacti: with them it is only necessary to cut the two plants concerned so as to provide corresponding flat surfaces, then to fix these in place with ties or by pinning with a cactus spine.

Besides the methods of grafting described above, ◊ BOTTLE GRAFT; BRIDGE GRAFTING; BUDDING; INARCHING; ROOT GRAFTING; SADDLE GRAFT; SIDE GRAFT; STUB GRAFT; TONGUE GRAFT.

◊ BENCH GRAFTING; CALLUS; CHIMAERA; DOUBLE-WORKING; FAMILY TREE; GRAFTING BENCH; GRAFTING KNIFE; GRAFTING WAX; INCOMPATIBLE; REWORKING; SCION; STANDARD; STOCK; SUCKER; UNION.

Grafting Bench In the eighteenth century the skilled propagator would have a complex bench, rather like a cabinet-maker's, on which to use a wide range of tools in making grafts of many different kinds.

Grafting by Approach ◊ INARCHING.

Grafting Clay ◊ GRAFTING WAX.

Grafting Knife A general-purpose knife for grafting, with a blade about 3″ long and handle of 4″–5″. It has an angled point at the end of the cutting edge like some types of BUDDING KNIFE.

Grafting Tool Originally, any tool used in grafting; today restricted to a kind of spade with a relatively long, slightly concave, rectangular blade, used for digging drainage trenches. ◊ SPADE.

Grafting Wax Many substances have been used since ancient times to coat and protect the wounded tissue of grafts. Until the early nineteenth century, 'grafting clay' or 'pug', made of natural clay, horse dung and chopped hay, was often used; the French and Dutch preferred a 'clay' composed of equal parts of fresh loam and cow dung, which was known as Onguent de Saint Fiacre (the patron saint of gardening). However, it became more common to use materials based on wax, pitch, resin, tallow, turpentine, etc., or sometimes petroleum jelly. Early authors sometimes referred to such waxes as 'noble Mummy', presumably in reference to similar coatings used in Egyptian burials. Today, proprietary grafting waxes may be readily bought. ◊ GRAFTING.

Graft-work An old term for spade-work, often used of grave-digging.

Grape (1) The fruit of the grape-vine. (2) ◊ BUD STAGES.

Grass ◊ LAWN.

Grass Cutting ◊ COMPOST; EDGING TOOLS; MOWERS; MOWING.

Grass Hook ◇ SICKLE; SCYTHE.

Grasshoppers These large jumping insects with powerful jaws, which feed on plant material, can be a serious pest of grass, cereal crops and sometimes garden plants in the U.S. if they swarm like locusts. Pesticides will destroy them, though large swarms are difficult to control.

Grassing Down A practice carried out by fruit growers in which the ground around trees is sown with grass and not clean-cultivated. This is done to slow down the rate of growth of the trees and encourage fruiting, following the taking up of water and nutrients by the grass. It should not be done with young trees which might otherwise become stunted; even with mature trees the grass must be kept cut since its over-vigorous growth may cause starvation and loss of fruit production in the trees.

Gravel Smallish, rounded, water-worn stones widely used in gardens, and sometimes referred to as aggregate, ballast or hoggin. A grading from $\frac{3}{16}''$ to $\frac{3}{4}''$ across is used for paths and drives, best mixed with sand to avoid looseness. The same grading is used to cover solid greenhouse staging and to fill gravel trays below pot plants; in both cases water is poured into the gravel layer and evaporates steadily around the plants to their benefit. A slightly coarser grade is used in tomato ring culture and for stabilizing plants in some soilless cultivation methods, including that of growing certain bulbs in water alone. Small, regular gravel, appropriately called pea gravel, is sometimes used by alpine gardeners to surface pots, sink gardens, etc., like stone chippings. Gravel is also often a constituent of the aggregate used in making concrete. ◇ AGGREGATE; CHIPPINGS; CONCRETE; RING CULTURE; SOILLESS CULTIVATION.

Gravel Tray ◇ GRAVEL.

Grease Banding The application of a band of sticky material around the trunks of fruit trees to trap the wingless females of various moths which climb the trees to lay their eggs on the shoots and can cause much trouble later. It is usually done by tying a band of greaseproof paper about 4″ wide around the trunk about 3′ above the ground, and smearing this with specially formulated fruit-tree grease, which is particularly sticky. It is possible simply to apply this grease to the trunk direct, but this precludes the tidy removal of the band after its period of value. This period extends from mid-September to mid-March. ◇ TREE BANDING; WINTER MOTHS.

Grecian Saw A small, narrow-bladed, curved saw (as opposed to a straight one), useful for cutting out small tree branches. The teeth are set so that cutting only occurs when the operator pulls the saw towards him. ◇ SAW.

Green Bud ◇ BUD STAGES.

Green Cluster ◇ BUD STAGES.

Greenfly ◇ APHIDS.

Greenhouse A structure for the cultivation of plants, mainly glazed with glass or glass substitutes, and large enough to be entered by the gardener (as opposed to a frame); also known as a glasshouse. Although the Romans had various kinds of glazed shelter it seems likely they were little more than frames, and the first positive record of a large glazed structure dates from 1619. This was a huge barn-like building erected over citrus trees in winter, in Heidelberg, Germany; there were windows in the walls and it had a solid roof. Such structures became known as orangeries.

Greenhouses of very many shapes were built in the succeeding centuries. Today, the habitual shape is the span-roof, shaped like an orthodox dwelling house with the two sides of the roof sloping equally in each direction. The lean-to has a roof sloping in one direction only and is fixed with the highest point of the roof against a wall. In the three-quarter span or hip-span house the roof is not symmetrical, the longer slope

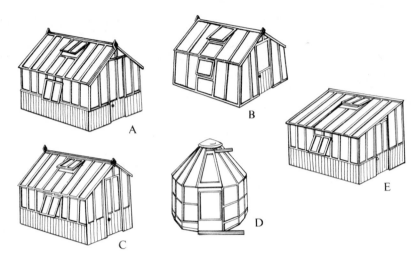

GREENHOUSE. A, span-roof; B, dutch-light; C, three-quarter span; D, multi-sided; E, lean-to

ending much nearer ground level than the shorter. Recent innovations include more or less circular houses with many narrow side and roof panels; there are also dome-shaped greenhouses of geodesic construction.

Besides being described by form, greenhouses are sometimes classified according to their function:

Alpine house – used for the cultivation of alpine plants.

Forcing house – usually low and narrow, so that a high temperature can be maintained economically.

Pit house – nowadays seldom seen, in which the lower half of the structure is below ground level, which economizes in heating.

Plant house – a vague term usually covering tall, airy structures admitting as much light as possible.

Propagating house – which usually has built-in propagating frames and is reserved for increasing plants.

Vinery – often a tall, wide lean-to against a wall, for the cultivation of vines.

Older literature may mention houses for other kinds of fruit tree separately, e.g. peach house and pinery (for pineapples);

the *fruit* or *orchard house* generically was often a tall, narrow lean-to with fruit trees trained against the back wall.

The *conservatory*, *sunroom* or *house extension* is a greenhouse almost always attached to the dwelling house and entered from one of its rooms, primarily used for the display of plants and often designed to be used as an extra living room. It can be of various forms, though usually is rectangular.

Commercial growers may have *aeroplane houses* – in which numbers of wide spans are carried on strong but unobtrusive uprights, so that maximum light reaches a large area of ground which can be cultivated with minimum interference; *dutch* or *dutch-light houses* – made of large single glass panes in wooden frames roughly $5' \times 2'\ 6''$; and *tunnel houses* – in which plastic sheeting is stretched over large metal hoops or an arched framework.

Another form of classification is according to the temperature maintained:

Cold house – has no permanent heating, though some simple heater may be used to try and avoid really low temperatures in severe winter weather.

Cool house – has a minimum winter temperature of 7°C (45°F) and a summer range of 12–18°C (54–64°F). In much of Britain this means that no artificial heat is needed for about two-thirds of the year.

Intermediate house – has a winter minimum of 13°C (55°F) and a summer range of 16–21°C (61–70°F).

Warm house – kept to a winter minimum of 18°C (64°F) and a summer range of 21–27°C (70–81°F). These temperatures are needed for tropical plants only. Such structures used to be called 'stove houses' or 'hot houses'.

Greenhouses can be built of many materials, but the commonest remain wood and metal, usually aluminium. The sides can be glazed with glass or glass substitutes to ground level or only half-way; the latter is perfectly adequate when plants are grown on a waist-high staging, and blocking in the lower part with a solid material, or using a brick wall for it, improves heat insulation and reduces costs.
◊ CONSERVATORY; DUTCH LIGHT; GLASS; GLASS SUBSTITUTES; HEATING; INSULATION; PLASTICS; PROPAGATION; STOVE HOUSE; VENTILATION; WINTER GARDEN.

Greenhouse Heating ◊ HEATING.

Green Manuring The practice of growing certain quick-maturing plants and digging them into the soil to decay and so act as plant food. The method, occasionally known as cover cropping or sheet composting, improves the humus content of the soil, rather than its food potential for later crops, but it can give a fairly high return in nitrogen, especially if the soil has recently had a fertilizer dressing which has not been used up. This is because nitrogen is often readily leached out of soil; however, it will be taken up by a green manure crop and 'locked up' in it until decay liberates it again. Surplus nitrogen will also result if the green manure crop is a leguminous one which has root nodules containing nitrogen-fixing bacteria. Such crops include annual lupins and vetches. Other green manure crops commonly used in gardens are mustard, rape and rye grass; in the U.S., also alfalfa, sweet clover and

soya beans. All these plants are sown from March on, rye grass being useful up to a July sowing and mustard into mid-August. Digging in is usually done just before the plants flower. ◊ NITROGEN; NODULE; SMOTHER CROP.

Green Tip ◊ BUD STAGES.

Grex ◊ CLASSIFICATION (Hybrids).

Grey Mould The descriptive name given to some of the manifestations of the fungus disease *Botrytis cinerea* (others have quite different symptoms). Grey mould is seen primarily on lettuces, pelargoniums and strawberries in the form of a thick, fluffy, greyish mould on leaves, flowers and fruit as applicable. It is a disease of close, cool atmosphere and occurs mostly in dull wet weather. Under glass, raising the temperature, increasing ventilation and care in watering are effective, and fungicidal sprays and 'smokes' can be used. ◊ FUNGICIDES; FUNGUS DISEASES.

Grit ◊ CHIPPINGS.

Groove An early eighteenth-century word for a TRANSPLANTER.

Grotto A natural grotto is a small cave; the word is mainly used of those which are picturesque and of caves which, to quote the *Oxford Dictionary*, make 'an agreeable retreat'. In gardening, artificial grottoes were made over the centuries since Roman times, either by excavating actual underground caves or building a structure which would imitate one internally. Such grottoes were often made of tufa rock. Many were lined with shells, crystals and other geological specimens, bones, pebbles, glass, pieces of coal – anything fanciful. Some grottoes extended into positive labyrinths; others incorporated streams or springs and sometimes artificial waterworks.

Ground Cover Applied to plants which cover the soil surface so fully as to smother weeds and make for minimal cultivation and attention. As such, these plants cover a wide range, including herbaceous peren-

133

nials (especially those which are evergreen), shrubs, and even trees with branches coming down to ground level. Some of the perennials, especially those which creep with runners rooting at intervals and those with spreading underground suckers, are very rampant and should only be introduced into large areas where they will not encroach on more desirable plants.

Many ground-cover plants have attractive flowers in season, notably heaths, but since their efficacy comes from permanent leaf cover they are best considered primarily as plants grown for foliage effect.

Although well established ground cover will largely prevent weed growth, it is essential to remove all perennial weeds before planting, and to keep the areas weeded until the plants knit together.
    ◊ WEED.

Ground Hog ◊ WOODCHUCK.

Ground Squirrel ◊ GOPHER.

Groundwork When a bedding scheme is composed of plants at different levels, the lower one, which forms a kind of carpet to the taller, is called the groundwork. An example is of forget-me-nots used as groundwork to tulips. ◊ BEDDING PLANT.

Group A classification term. ◊ CLASSIFICATION (Hybrids).

Growing Bag A fairly recent invention in which peat-based potting compost is placed inside a large plastic bag. The bag is put where it is desired to grow plants, and cuts are made along marked lines on the bag to expose the compost and allow the grower to plant a number of specimens. Growing bags were originally devised for the culture of tomatoes, but it has been found that a large range of vegetables, herbs and flowering plants can be grown in them. With regular watering and possibly some extra feeding later on, the growing bag provides all the root run and nourishment required for the crop. It is valuable for use in solid-floored greenhouses or where the soil is unsuitable or likely to be disease-contaminated, and for terrace and balcony gardens.

A very recent development is the 'growing board' in which the bag surrounds a light board of dehydrated compost. After soaking in water, this expands into a full-sized growing bag. Its great advantage is its weight of around 7 lb., as against the 40–50 lb. of the growing bag.
    ◊ COMPOSTS, SEED AND POTTING.

Growing Board ◊ GROWING BAG.

Growing Point The tip of a stem, where extension growth will occur. If this is removed by pinching or cutting, growth from lateral buds lower down the stem is normally stimulated and branching thus encouraged. The extremity of a growing point, almost microscopic in size, has the potential of growth in the right conditions, and is used for certain specialized methods of propagation. ◊ MERISTEM.

Growing Room The same as GROWTH CHAMBER.

Growth Chamber A totally enclosed room for growing plants, in which light, humidity and temperature are all controllable, usually automatically. Growth chambers are used for scientific research and by some growers of specialized plants.

Growth Cycle Many plants have well-defined growth cycles in which active growth alternates with more or less dormant periods. The most familiar in the Temperate Zone is that of deciduous trees and shrubs which begin active growth with the putting out of new leaves every spring and lose the leaves the following autumn, when they enter a period of dormancy.

Temperate evergreen trees and shrubs, which do not lose their leaves in winter, do in fact become partly dormant as their activity slows down considerably in cold and poor light.

Many fleshy-rooted plants, e.g. bulbs, are accustomed to long dry summers in which, after flowering, the top growth withers away entirely, and the roots may also wither. In this dormant stage the roots can often be dug up and stored dry.

Plants with this dual cycle can be said to have an active growth period and a resting period. However, many plants from tropical rain forests, which include a large proportion of our house plants, have no resting period in nature, although in some tropical and sub-tropical areas there are marked seasons of low rainfall in which the plants will perforce rest. When grown as house plants, it is as well not to force these to grow as actively during winter as in summer, since low light levels will become a limiting factor and excessive growth then is likely to be etiolated and weak. If adequate artificial light is provided, such plants can be grown without a rest all year.

Growth Regulators Chemical substances which can dwarf normally tall plants, cause low plants to grow tall, or curtail their rate of growth. At present their major commercial use is in growing dwarfed chrysanthemums and poinsettias in pots, and in enhancing compactness and floriferousness in other pot plants, such as azaleas and cyclamens.

Maleic hydrazide, by preventing cell division, inhibits terminal growth of grasses, hedge shrubs and trees (but encourages side growth), and sprouting of onions and potatoes in store. It thus resembles certain hormone compounds used for similar purposes.

The chemical dikegulac has recently been introduced to stop regrowth of hedge plants so that only one trim a year is needed. Materials of similar action are sometimes used on verges and other areas of roughish grass, but are not suitable for lawns.

Research in hand may in the future lead to various developments, which include the possibilities of germinating seeds at lower temperatures than normal, bringing certain fruits to maturity very rapidly, dwarfing fruit trees to reduce the need for pruning, and many more.
⟡ HORMONES; RETARDANT.

Growth Rings If a tree trunk is cut across, clearly defined concentric rings will be seen. These are caused by the growth of cells at different rates during each season and, if counted from the centre, provide an accurate age of the tree in years. ⟡ VASCULAR SYSTEM.

Growth Substances These include GROWTH REGULATORS and HORMONES.

Grub (1) The larva of an insect, especially of a beetle; used generally of maggots, caterpillars and other similar larvae.
(2) To dig, especially to dig out stumps; also to uproot. Now mainly restricted to the removal of tree and shrub stumps or roots. To grub-fell is to cut a tree at the roots. From this usage are devised the names of various tools, some no longer in general use, such as the grub-axe (colloquially 'grubbage') or grubbing mattock, the grub-hoe and the grub-hook. ⟡ INTERCROP; MATTOCK.

Grubber ⟡ DAISY GRUBBER.

Grubbing Mattock ⟡ MATTOCK.

Guano Originally referred specifically to the droppings of sea-birds found on the arid Chincha Islands off Peru. It was first coined by the invading Spaniards in 1604; they based it on the name for dung, *huano*, used by the local inhabitants, the Quichna. Since virtually no rain falls in this locality, the bird droppings accumulated in huge deposits and none of the valuable plant foods in them was washed out. These deposits were commercialized early in the nineteenth century. Peruvian guano, as it was often called, was first imported into North America in 1824 and into Britain in 1840. Although the Chincha Island deposits are now worked out, genuine bird guano, if available, is one of the richest natural plant foods available, containing 10–14 per cent nitrogen, 9–11 per cent phosphoric acid and 2–4 per cent potash, and is used in the garden as a top-dressing at 2–3 oz. per square yard, or in making up potting composts. The term is now, however, loosely used of other concentrated fertilizers, especially those made

135

from fish, sometimes called fish guano. ⟡ FEEDING PLANTS; FERTILIZER.

Gumming The exudation of gum-like resins by various plants especially if wounded, mainly restricted to stone fruits and their ornamental relations (cherries, peaches, etc., of the genus *Prunus*), but also occurring in conifers. The gum itself is harmless, and probably serves to cover up wounds; however, if gumming occurs and no wound is apparent, ill health must be suspected. This may occur on trees growing in poorly drained soil, or after attack by sap-sucking insects, caterpillars or bacterial canker, and remedial action should be taken. Gumming can also occur on the stones of stone fruits. ⟡ CANKER; GUMMOSIS; STONE (2).

Gummosis Sometimes used as an equivalent term to gumming but usually restricted to an ailment of cucumbers, initially caused by fungus diseases, in which gum exudes from small spots on the fruit. A similar condition sometimes occurs on rhubarb stalks, where malnutrition should be suspected.

Guttation The exudation of drops of water, usually on the margins or at the tips of leaves. It can sometimes be seen on garden plants like *Alchemilla mollis* and is a characteristic of many plants from humid habitats. Guttation on house or greenhouse plants can be a sign that the potting compost is too wet.

Guying New-planted trees of any size may need more support than can be given by a stake, and this can be supplied by fixing three wires fairly high up and fastening them to three equally spaced pegs driven into the ground around the tree. It is necessary to prevent the wires chafing the trunk, and this can be done by binding the trunk at the fixing point with cloth or, more easily, by using a small length of hose pipe through which the wire passes while encircling the trunk. Guying can be carried out with trees up to about 15′ tall, which

need to be restored to an upright position after being blown down. ⟡ SUPPORT.

Guyot One of the most widely used methods of growing grapes. In it the lateral growths which bear fruit are cut out after cropping. During the year, two replacement growths are allowed to develop for each fruiting lateral, and in winter, when the cropped cane is removed, the better of these two growths is selected to replace it, the other being removed except for two or three basal buds which will produce new canes in the year ahead. Guyot training is widely used for grapes grown in the open and is easily adapted to grapes grown on walls. ⟡ LATERAL.

Gymnosperm One of the major classes of the vegetable kingdom, including the conifers and their relations. The word means, literally, 'naked-seeded', and refers to the ovules not being enclosed as they are in angiosperms or flowering plants.

For other classes of interest to gardeners, ⟡ ANGIOSPERM; PTERIDOPHYTE.

Gynoecium The female part of a flower as a whole; the pistil. ⟡ FLOWER.

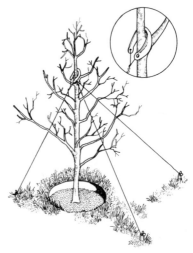

GUYING

Gypsum Sulphate of lime, a chemical having similar properties to lime in improving the texture of clay soils, but it does this without increasing the alkalinity or pH. It is also valuable for restoring the texture and fertility of soil after flooding by sea water. ◊ ACID; ALKALINE; pH; SUPERPHOSPHATE OF LIME.

❧ H ❧

Habit A word often used to describe the characteristic form of growth of a plant: e.g. plants may be described as of creeping or weeping habit.

Ha-ha A boundary in the form of a deep, wide ditch, designed so as to separate a garden or park from the surrounding countryside without creating a visual barrier. Such a 'sunken fence' allows farm animals into the view while keeping them in the pastures. Charles Bridgeman (d. 1738) is generally credited with the invention of the ha-ha, but it is clear from a book published in 1712, itself a translation from an earlier French work by d'Argenville, that the device was in use very early in the eighteenth century. According to this translation, the ha-ha got its name from the exclamation of surprise 'Ah, ah!' reputed to have been uttered by those coming upon it for the first time. In France it was sometimes called a *saut-de-loup* (wolf's leap). At any rate, the use of the ha-ha became standard practice with the landscaper 'Capability' Brown and his followers, and continued well into the nineteenth century. Normally, a ha-ha has the edge on the garden side near-vertical and dressed in stone or brick; but it can be sloped on either side, and in such cases may have an actual fence fixed within it, below surface level.

Hair (1) Animal or human hair dug into the ground both improves soil texture and humus content, and provides nitrogen over a long period. It is sometimes available in quantity from tanneries in the form of scrapings from hides.
(2) Plants may have various kinds of hairs. ◊ HAIRY.

Hairy Many plants have hairs on leaves, stems and also sometimes flowers and fruits, forming a covering or indumentum.

These consist of special cells or series of cells, the sap in which disappears and is replaced with air; they are technically known as trichomes. Some of the longest are found in cacti, notably those covering the stems of *Cephalocereus senilis*, appropriately known as the Old-man Cactus, in which the hairs can be $2\frac{1}{2}''$ long. However, most plant hairs are much shorter and are not always like animal hairs, but can be flat and ribbon-like, spiral, feathery, star-shaped, mushroom-shaped, etc.

The function of hairs appears to be primarily for insulation against heat or cold and to slow down evaporation from the stomata; sometimes they reflect light and heat. Hairs are often found for these reasons on alpine plants, cacti and other succulents, though these certainly do not have a monopoly on hairiness. It is clear also that many hairs are deterrents to grazing animals either because of sharpness or grittiness or because of irritating effects on mucous membranes; many cause irritation to human skin. Some hairs contain irritant substances and others poisons, e.g. nettles: the hairs have brittle ends designed to be broken at a touch and the jagged end left acts like a hypodermic needle to puncture skin and release the poison, often formic acid.

The degree of hairiness on a plant can be denoted by various words, though these are sometimes used rather loosely. One general term is hirsute, which simply means hairy, but refers botanically to coarse, dense hairs, and is sometimes found in specific names as *hirsutus*. Other botanical words which are also sometimes latinized for names include the following:
canescent or hoary indicates dense, short, whitish hairs, too small to be seen individually but making the plant look frosted;
hispid means bristly, with stiff, dense hairs;
pilose means having long, sparse hairs;
puberulent means slightly downy with very short hairs;

138

pubescent means generally downy, with short, fine hairs sometimes barely visible; *setose* indicates bristliness or very stiff, erect, straight hairs;

tomentose is translated variously as woolly, cottony or felted, which are basically self-explanatory; such hairs may be tangled; *villous* denotes a covering of long, weak hairs.

Half-hardy A term applied to plants which, in a given climatic zone, will not stand frost. Usually reserved for annuals which

long narrow handlight was sometimes used in the early nineteenth century. The old bell glass was another type of individual cloche. ◊ BELL GLASS; CLOCHE.

Hanging Basket A container designed to be hung up, in a greenhouse, porch, under eaves, or in similar places, in which to grow plants normally selected for pendulous habit. The typical basket is more or less hemispherical, made either of wire or, nowadays, of plastic, usually 9″–18″ across and 6″–9″ deep; but square baskets of

HANGING BASKET. *Left*, wire construction; *centre*, plastic with built-on drip saucer; *right*, of wood slats for orchids

cannot be sown outside before the danger of frost is past; these are sometimes abbreviated in catalogues as H.H.A. ◊ ANNUAL; HARDY.

Half-ripe Applied to certain kinds of CUTTINGS.

Half-standard ◊ STANDARD.

Hand Fork A small short-handled fork. ◊ FORKS.

Handlight A small cloche designed to be used over individual plants or to protect small batches of cuttings or seedlings; now seldom seen. When handlights were popular they were usually square with a pyramidal top, the latter often being removable; a

wooden slats are also used, and some plastic models are shaped like an orthodox pot. Wire baskets need lining with sphagnum moss, or plastic sheeting in which some small holes are made at the lowest point for drainage, and plants can be inserted in these below the rim, pushed between the wirework through the moss or a slit in the plastic. Many modern plastic baskets have a built-on saucer at the base which facilitates watering and water retention, but plants cannot be planted below their rims. Even plastic baskets with saucers need frequent watering in warm weather.

Baskets made of wooden slats arranged with gaps between them are used for orchids and other epiphytic plants not needing to retain much moisture in the potting material, which is often sphagnum moss.

Haploid Having one (unpaired) set of chromosomes, found in the sex cells of any organism. ◊ CHROMOSOME; DIPLOID.

Hardening Off The process of acclimatizing plants grown in warm, equable conditions to more rigorous ones; usually applied to tender or half-hardy plants germinated under glass in warmth and destined for planting outside during the summer when there is no danger of frost. If hardening off is carried out too quickly, a severe or even fatal check may be given. The first stage of the process may be to remove newly germinated seedlings from a propagator to the main greenhouse; then the plants may be moved to a cool part of the greenhouse and later to a cold frame. Here exposure to the outside air is steadily increased, though air is not admitted, and extra protection may be provided, in cold weather and when frost threatens. Sacking, hessian, burlap or similar materials can be placed over the frame. The plants may have a short period with no top protection before finally being planted out. Any stoppage of growth, or blueing or yellowing of foliage, is likely to indicate that the plants have been subjected to cold too quickly. ◊ ACCLIMATIZATION; FRAME.

Harding A colloquial word for a plant which refuses to thrive, whatever one does to it.

Hard Pruning ◊ PRUNING.

Hardwood (1) Timber from broad-leaved trees as opposed to conifers, which are softwoods.

(2) Applied to certain kinds of CUTTING.

Hardy A relative (and hence rather vague) term which indicates that a plant so described will be capable of growing outside without protection all the year round, in a given area. Clearly, varying climatic conditions, as e.g. between south-west and north-east Britain, will have a great effect on the way in which the term can be applied to a given plant, and in the U.S. no less than ten climatic zones are recognized when specifying hardiness. Local climates, the degree of immediate local shelter, the kind of soil and some physiological factors also affect hardiness. Some woody plants improve their hardiness as they mature. Plants which are perfectly hardy in respect to prolonged cold in their natural habitat may perish in climates in which mild spells alternate with cold ones; and winter rain can also kill such plants which are naturally protected by snow, or by growing in vertical crevices, in winter, like many alpines. The opposite to hardy is tender. ◊ ALPINE; HALF-HARDY; TEMPERATURE; TENDER.

Hare ◊ RABBIT.

Harvesting Gathering any crop or fruit when it is mature. ◊ SEED HARVESTING.

Hastate A botanical term applied mainly to leaves which are pointed with two basal lobes pointing outwards, like a halberd or, less exactly, a spear-head. ◊ LEAF.

Haulm Plant stems, especially those of peas, beans and potatoes, also grasses and cereals. The verb 'haulm' means to lay straw or reeds straight when thatching. Originally spelt 'haum', from which came the word 'haum-barrow', a wheelbarrow with open sides of wood or wicker designed to carry discarded haulm, prunings, leaves and litter, used in Victorian times.

Hay Band An old device for trapping caterpillars of the codling moth on fruit trees, comprising a band of hay tied round the trunk and main branches; a similar effect is obtained from a piece of sacking or corrugated cardboard so fixed. This should be done in early summer, and the bands removed and burned in autumn, by which time the caterpillars will have left the fruits they may have attacked and descended the branches to find shelter in which to pupate, which the bands provide. ◊ GREASE BANDING.

Head (1) Botanically, a dense cluster, or

a short, dense spike, of flowers. ◊ IN-FLORESCENCE.

(2) That part of a tree growing above the clear trunk.

(3) Gardeners use this term loosely for well-developed specimens of vegetables, e.g. 'a head' of lettuce or of celery.

Heading The stage at which a cabbage, lettuce or similar leaf vegetable begins to produce its tight infolded head of growth; also described as hearting.

Heading Back, Heading Down Drastic cutting back of shrubs or, more usually, trees, by shortening all or most of the main branches. The term is most often applied to cutting back of fruit trees, to be followed by top grafting of some kind; with ornamental trees it is more likely to be called lopping or pollarding, and will result in strong new growth. Pleaching involves the same process; dehorning is a less drastic version of it. ◊ DEHORNING; GRAFTING; PLEACH; POLLARD.

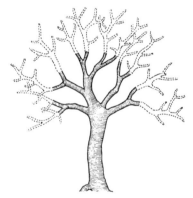

HEADING BACK

Hearting The same as HEADING.

Heart Rot A general term for decay in the internal tissues of a plant. Such decay attacks various vegetables, and is often begun by slug damage which becomes infected by bacteria; in trees, heart rot is the result of fungus infection. ◊ BACTERIA; FUNGUS.

Heart-shaped A description of organs, usually leaves, which are pointed at one end and have a pair of rounded lobes at the other, as in a formalized depiction of a heart. The botanical equivalent is cordate. ◊ LEAF.

Heart-wood The central wood in the branch or trunk of a tree, which consists of dead, non-functioning cells and is harder and usually distinctly darker than the outer wood. ◊ VASCULAR SYSTEM.

Heath or **Heather Garden** An area planted mainly with heathers (*Calluna*) and heaths (*Erica*) species and varieties, usually associated with conifers, other trees such as birches, or other ericaceous plants. Excellent for sandy, acid soils, such gardens can provide colour all the year round from both flowers and foliage, and the heathers themselves are, once established, excellent weed suppressors. ◊ ERICACEOUS; GROUND COVER.

Heating Various methods of heating are used by the gardener to raise the temperature in greenhouses and conservatories, locally in propagators, and occasionally in frames. The general use of greenhouse heating is to enable one to grow various ranges of plants which are not hardy in the particular climate, or need dry atmosphere since they resent winter damp; and to grow certain plants out of season or extend their normal season of growth. Local heating as in propagators is used to germinate many seeds successfully and to encourage formation of roots on cuttings.

Heating methods can be applied to the air and to the soil, the latter often being specially desirable for propagation and for growing plants out of season; soil and air heating are often combined in frames and propagators.

Fuel for heating can be solid (e.g. coal or coke), gas, oil, paraffin (kerosene) and electricity. Solid fuels, oil and, to a lesser extent, gas are used to heat boilers with external flues circulating hot water in pipes fixed in a greenhouse. Oil and gas boilers can be thermostatically controlled within reasonable limits. Gas, both natural and propane, is used in flueless heaters, but has detrimental effects on plants which can only be avoided if a flue to the open air is provided. Paraffin is normally burnt in small flueless heaters within greenhouses; with these it is essential that no fumes should be emitted, since they are very harmful to plants: this means regular attention to the wick and to cleaning the stove, and using best-quality paraffin. Electricity can power tubular, convector or fan heaters, or be connected to cables for heating soil or air in frames and propagators; also to solid panels in which heating elements are embedded. Electricity has the great advantage of requiring no regular attention, producing no fumes and being very accurately controllable by thermostat. ⬦ BOTTOM HEAT; CUTTING; FRAME; GREENHOUSE; HARDY; HOTBED; PROPAGATOR; SEED SOWING.

Heaving (Soil-heaving) ⬦ FROST.

Hectare ⬦ WEIGHTS AND MEASURES (p. viii).

Hedge A boundary or garden division composed of shrubs or trees planted in a continuous line. Boundary hedges can be informal, i.e. allowed to grow naturally or with minimal clipping, or be formally clipped. Such boundaries have several, often overlapping functions: they can be decorative, intruder-proof, act as visual and aural screens, and act as shelterbelts or windbreaks, though plants in the latter two categories are likely to be more widely spaced. Within a garden, hedges are usually for decoration and division of sections. Hedges can vary from very tall (20′ is not uncommon) to very low, though at heights of a few inches the hedge might perhaps better be called an edging, and is generally used as such or to lay out decorative patterns as in knots and parterres.

A vast range of both evergreen and deciduous shrubs and trees is available for hedging, and includes plants grown purely as foliage hedges (e.g. beech, cypress, hornbeam, privet, yew) and some which flower and possibly fruit in season (e.g. berberis, forsythia, rose). The latter must often be grown informally if they are to flower freely.

Since hedges remain in position indefinitely, it is wise to prepare the planting site very thoroughly indeed, digging widely and deeply and improving soil texture and nutrient level as necessary.

Formal hedges need trimming to shape at regular intervals, the frequency depending on the type of plant. In general terms, evergreen hedges are trimmed from early to late summer, while deciduous ones are dealt with in autumn and winter. Any cutting back of informal hedges to keep them within bounds takes place at the same periods.

Trimming of formal hedges is normally carried out with hand shears or mechanical trimmers operated by electricity or via a flexible drive from a separate power unit or garden cultivator. Hedges of large-leaved plants like aucuba and cherry laurel are best pruned with secateurs to avoid unsightly cutting of individual leaves. Informal hedges may need the use of a saw, lopping shears or, on very rough hedges, a billhook or slasher. Certain hedges can be treated with a growth regulator to reduce the frequency of trimming.

⬦ BILLHOOK; EDGING; GROWTH REGULATORS; KNOT; LAYING; PARTERRE; SCREEN; SECATEURS; SHEARS; SHELTERBELT; SLASHER; WINDBREAK.

Hedge Bill ⬦ BILLHOOK; SLASHER.

Hedge Maze ⬦ LABYRINTH; MAZE.

Hedge Trimming ⬦ HEDGE.

Heel If a cutting is prepared by pulling a side-shoot away from the main shoot, rather than cutting it, a small strip of bark and wood from the main shoot is dragged away with it. This is called a heel, and any cutting so prepared is a heel cutting. It is best to trim the ragged edges back neatly, but not to remove the heel because in some cases (though not all) cuttings with a heel strike more readily. ◊ CUTTING.

Heeling In A term used for temporary planting, usually before putting plants in their permanent positions. Shrubs, trees and herbaceous plants may arrive from the

like saxifrages and sempervivums which produce numerous offsets on thin stems radiating from the parent. ◊ PROLIFERA-TION.

Hep An alternative spelling of HIP.

Herb (1) Plants grown for medicinal qualities and for seasoning foods. ◊ POT HERB.
(2) Botanically, any HERBACEOUS plant.

HEELING IN

nursery, or be in process of transfer from another garden, before their permanent site is ready, or when the weather is too wet or cold to allow planting them in their final places. In such cases a trench is dug in any convenient place – avoiding a position likely to become waterlogged – and the plant roots are placed in this close together, covered with soil and made firm with the foot. Plants can remain heeled in like this for several weeks, especially in winter months when they are more or less dormant.

Heeling in is also often used for spring bulbs which must be moved to make room for bedding plants but which have not finished their growth. If heeled in close together the bulbs will have a chance of ripening fully.

Hen-and-chickens A term used when plants proliferate to produce a ring of small florets or flower-heads around the central normal one, as occurs sometimes in daisies. It is also applied to some rosette-forming plants

Herbaceous Any plant with soft upper growth rather than woody growth. Such plants can be annual, biennial or perennial. Herbaceous is the opposite of shrubby. ◊ SHRUB; SUB-SHRUB; WOODY.

Herbaceous Border A garden planting primarily devoted to the cultivation of herbaceous perennials. When first introduced around the end of the nineteenth century under the influence of Gertrude Jekyll and William Robinson, herbaceous borders were wholly devoted to such plants; nowadays, more flexible ideas permit the inclusion of annuals and bedding plants, bulbous and tuberous subjects, roses and other shrubs (these are sometimes known as mixed borders). Although perennials can be planted in quite narrow areas, for a long season of display, a bed less than 5' wide is unlikely to be very effective. Tall plants are in general placed at the back of a border, grading down to low ones at the front, but some medium to tall ones can be planted near the front, forming bays for lower plants in between, to provide informality and irregularity: a herbaceous border should never be planted in regular patterns or ordered lines.

The actual border can be varied in shape but, as the word implies, it is usually a more or less oblong area which can be backed by a wall or hedge or be capable of being viewed from both sides. A modern variation is the ISLAND BED.

◊ COLOUR BORDER; ISLAND BED; MIXED BORDER; SHRUBBERY.

Herbal A book describing herbs used for medicinal and culinary purposes. In past centuries the word could mean a book describing plants in general, those known being then relatively few in number.

Herbarium A collection of preserved plant specimens, mostly in the form of dried and pressed ones, but also including bulky material kept in jars of preserving fluid. Such collections form the basis of botanical identification, classification and taxonomy, and are typically a part of a large BOTANIC GARDEN.

Herber An old word, equivalent to ARBOUR.

Herb Garden Gardens in which culinary and medicinal plants are grown, and which are typically formally laid out following a very long historical tradition. ◊ PHYSIC GARDEN.

Herbicide Any chemical material that will destroy plants, though primarily used for weedkilling. ◊ WEEDKILLER.

Hermaphrodite Having both sexes: botanically, applied to flowers with both male organs (anthers or pollinia) and female organs (pistils), which may also be termed bisexual. ◊ FLOWER.

Hessian Known also as burlap, this is strong, coarse cloth useful for various purposes in the garden. One of the most important of these is to protect frames, cloches, etc., against severe frost; the hes-

sian is put in place in the evening and removed the next morning. Another use is to form windbreaks: individual plants can be protected by tacking hessian to three or four posts knocked in around each, or a strip of hessian can be fixed to posts driven in along a bed or border.

Heterozygous Plants which do not breed true. ◊ HYBRID.

Hilling Up ◊ EARTHING UP.

Hip The fruit of a rose, which is fleshy, hollow and encloses achenes; its technical name (seldom used) is a cynarrhodion. Also spelt hep. ◊ ACHENE.

Hirsute Literally, hairy: in botany, having coarse, dense hairs. The botanical equivalent is *hirsutus*. ◊ HAIRY.

Hispid Bristly; having short, dense hair. Sometimes Latinized as a specific name. ◊ HAIRY.

Hoary Having short, dense, whitish hairs; equivalent to canescent. ◊ HAIRY.

DIGGING HOE

Hoe A long-handled tool, until the eighteenth century often spelt 'how', used to loosen or break up the soil surface, remove weeds, make seed drills, earth up plants and similar tasks. This is one of the portmanteau terms for garden tools and a great many otherwise unclassifiable tools of early agriculture and horticulture are referred to as hoes, starting with the deer antlers, sharp rib bones and tusks used from Palaeolithic times. Early on in history more leverage was given to such implements by binding the 'business end', whether bone, tusk, flint, sharpened branch or eventually shaped metal, onto a longer handle. In these terms the digging stick is basically a type of hoe.

wards the operator who, by exerting some downward pressure, can scrape away small weeds on the surface. The right-angled corner can be used to draw out seed drills (furrows). The operator normally moves forward, and thus walks over ground which has been hoed, which is a slight disadvan-

HOES. *From left to right,* draw hoe; dutch hoe; two types of scuffle hoe; drill hoe; Swoe; Lapthorn hoe

The heavy or digging hoe, marketed in Britain today as the Chillington hoe, is one of the earliest tools, known to the Greeks and Romans, and it continues after over 2000 years to be the basic cultivating tool in many parts of the world. As J. C. Loudon remarked in his *Encyclopaedia of Gardening* of 1834, such tools 'are better adapted for hilly, stony surfaces, and for women and men who do not wear shoes, than spades'. The heavy hoe is used from a stooping position like a mattock or pick-axe, with a chopping motion, the tool being raised in both hands well above shoulder level.

One early version had two pick-like prongs instead of a blade; later, a combination of blade on one side of the handle and a pair of prongs on the other was common. This version survives in shrunken form as a pickfork or combination hoe, while the present-day Canterbury hoe or fork-hoe has three stout prongs; in the U.S., where this tool may have three or four prongs, it is sometimes called a 'speedy cultivator'.

Apart from this heavy version, modern hoes are light tools which fall into two main groups. The draw hoe has a flat blade at right angles to its handle and is used with a chopping motion, or can be drawn to-

tage. The swan-necked hoe works on exactly the same principle but has a curved shaft between blade and handle. A small version of this, with a short handle, is called the hand, onion or rockery hoe, designed to be used at close quarters with one hand only.

It is possible to obtain 'hoe-rakes' with a draw hoe blade on one side and a rake on the other.

In dutch hoes the thin oblong blade is set in the same plane as the handle or at a slight angle to it. The operator pushes the handle forward so that the blade works at or just below the soil surface, and then walks backwards to repeat the stroke.

A considerable number of variations on this exist, sometimes known as push-pull or scuffle hoes. They vary in the shape of the blade and method of attachment between blade and handle. In all cases the blade operates in the same plane as the soil surface.

The longhorn hoe is a large variation with separate hand grips like bicycle handle-bars, which can be fitted with a single wide blade or two separate blades to operate on each side of a crop.

The Lapthorn hoe (a trade name) is a modern invention with a narrow rounded blade having a notch in front and two

145

prongs behind. It is recommended for both breaking up the soil and weeding.

Another modern 'hybrid', the Swoe (a trade name), rather resembles a golf club with an angled blade sharpened on three edges; it can be used with both forward and backward motion.

The drill hoe, known as Warren hoe in the U.S., has a large, slightly rounded, triangular blade at right angles to the handle, the point of which is used for making drills, the back being shaped to enable the operator to fill them in. A heavy-duty version is sometimes called a vine hoe.

Short-handled tools originating in the U.S. include the weeding hoe, with a small blade in shape like a draw hoe at an angle to the handle and, when reversed, three short prongs like those of a hand fork at right angles. The sowing hoe has a flat rounded blade in one position and, when reversed, two fairly broad, flat prongs, in both cases roughly at right angles to the handle.

Hand tools with narrow, much recurved prongs are usually referred to as cultivators rather than hoes.
  ◊ CULTIVATOR; DIGGING STICK; DRAG; MATTOCK.

Hoggin ◊ GRAVEL.

Hollow-tine Fork ◊ FORK; TINE.

Homozygous ◊ TRUE-BREEDING.

Honeydew The name given to the excretions of the sap-sucking aphids and scale insects which create a sticky coating on leaves and stems. It is most markedly seen under lime trees, under which paving is often covered with the thick, sticky residue. The honeydew, which is sweet, is eagerly sought and imbibed by ants, who 'pasture' aphids to ensure a supply; it is often colonized by the sooty mould fungus, which then covers leaves with black patches and reduces their capacity for photosynthesis. Any sign of stickiness on a plant should alert the gardener to the possibility of attack by aphid or scale insect. ◊ ANTS; APHIDS; SCALE INSECTS; SOOTY MOULD.

Honey Fungus Although many fungi attack trees, the honey fungus *Armillaria mellea* (it gets its English name from the colour and scent of the fruiting bodies or toadstools) is one particularly feared by gardeners. It attacks a wide variety of trees and shrubs and has the unique capacity of being able to travel underground from the roots of one infected tree to others. It does this by a unique organ known as a rhizomorph which resembles a black bootlace and can travel for many yards below ground, even travelling through brickwork. When the tree is fatally infected the toadstools appear in clumps close to the stump. Affected plants should be burnt with as much as possible of the root system. Some protection has been achieved in recent years with a special formulation of creosote (*not* ordinary creosote). ◊ FUNGUS.

Hoof and Horn If ground to a powder, the hooves and horns of animals from the slaughter-house produce a valuable organic fertilizer containing 7–15 per cent nitrogen and 1–10 per cent phosphoric acid, and including some calcium phosphate. Coarse grades release these plant foods very slowly, fine ones rather faster. Hoof and horn meal, as it is usually called, can be worked into the ground at around 2 oz. per square yard, and is also valuable as an ingredient in potting composts. ◊ FEEDING PLANTS; FERTILIZER.

Hook A sickle. Some tool manufacturers use the term in preference to SICKLE.

Hops, Hop Manure Used or 'spent' hops from breweries form a very useful material to improve soil texture because of its high humus content, but it has little value as plant food. It should stand outside for a few months before being dug in. Hop manure is made by maturing the material outside and then adding various chemicals to give it more value as plant food, though the food level, and hence the rate of application, varies considerably according to the maker. Since the additions are usually soluble fertilizers, hop manures are best applied in spring, but spent hops can be used at any time of year. ◊ FEEDING PLANTS; MULCH.

Hormones Certain organic chemicals in plants, also known as auxins, control various aspects of growth. In some cases the gardener can turn this to direct advantage, as in nicking, notching and ringing of fruit trees, where the interruption of normal hormone movement results in growth being promoted where it would not naturally have occurred, or being prevented. Some hormones can cause alterations in plant behaviour in unnatural locations and without actually taking part in the changes; thus a root-forming hormone applied to the stem of a susceptible plant like a tomato will cause roots to form at that point.

Root formation on cuttings is one of the most valued uses of hormones which, as sold to the gardener, are often synthetic relations of the natural hormones. Other uses for distinct hormones include fruit formation (setting), delaying or preventing fruit dropping, retarding growth, e.g. potato sprouts and grass, and killing broad-leaved weeds, especially in lawns. The latter are sometimes called hormone weedkillers. They act by disturbing the processes controlled by plant hormones and can cause severe distortion in plants which receive small unintended doses of the material. Tomatoes are especially susceptible; distortion of these can follow the use of selective weedkillers nearby if spray has drifted in the wind.

Growth regulators, e.g. dwarfing compounds, are not hormones although their results may seem similar.
◊ CUTTING; FRUIT SETTING; GROWTH REGULATORS; NICKING AND NOTCHING; RINGING; SELECTIVE; WEEDKILLERS.

Horsehair Worms ◊ NEMATODE WORMS.

Horse Manure ◊ MANURE.

Hortus Siccus Literally 'dried garden'; refers to a collection of pressed, dried plant specimens as found in a HERBARIUM.

Hose Garden hose is used for the vital operation of watering gardens and greenhouse plants. First made of leather, hose is nowadays of plastic or rubber, plastic being on the whole more durable. Both round and flat hose can be obtained, the latter being economical of storage space. It pays to buy really good-quality hose, otherwise kinking and eventual cracking will follow in a season or two; good quality means thickness and sometimes reinforcement of the material. When intended for use under high pressure, hose for the purpose, reinforced with canvas, should be obtained. Hose is available in various internal diameters; $\frac{1}{2}''$ is adequate for average-sized gardens and the normal domestic fittings. Lengths of hose can be joined together with special connectors, and other fittings are available to build up watering systems as required, as well as tap connectors, adjustable spray nozzles and sprinklers.

Correct handling and storage of hose will prolong its life. It is best kept on a hose reel and should not be subjected to large changes of temperature or to frost. Ideally, hose out of use should be rolled into a reel and put into a cool, dark place.
◊ HOSE REELS; IRRIGATION; SPRINKLER; WATERING.

HOSE-IN-HOSE (primula)

Hose-in-hose A floral abnormality akin to doubling, in which one perfect corolla is carried within another, sometimes sufficiently separate to look as if it has grown

147

from the lower one. It particularly affects the primula family, while such duplex mimulus, rhododendrons and azaleas are also found. Many of these mutations are very attractive; the Elizabethans used to prize such flowers and today a considerable number of named varieties of hose-in-hose primroses and polyanthus, in particular, are cultivated.

Hose Reels Reels for rolling up hose are readily obtained, for wall fixing, on a tripod stand or on wheeled trolleys. The most convenient are undoubtedly the through-feed types in which the water supply from the tap feeds into a centrally mounted intake. The use of a special valve enables the hose to be wound or unwound with the water supply permanently connected. ◊ HOSE.

Host Plant Any plant which provides food for a parasite, be this another plant, a bacterium, fungus or virus, or a predator, e.g. an insect. Plant parasites are rare in gardens, though some are serious pests of agricultural crops and forests, especially in warm climates. Apart from mistletoe (*Viscum*) and toothwort (*Lathraea*), they are usually difficult to cultivate deliberately. When plants are attacked by parasites other than insects, these are often called diseases, though this term should be reserved for fungus parasites. Some fungi and insects have two or more hosts in the course of what is often a complicated life cycle, and it is sometimes possible to control the disease by eradicating one of its hosts. ◊ BACTERIA; FUNGUS; INSECT; PARASITE; VIRUS DISEASES.

Hotbed An old method, used since Roman times, for warming soil and thus aiding the production of out-of-season crops. Hotbeds are based largely on the fermentation of horse manure; however, the use of bark used in tanning (tanbark), sometimes in combination with animal manure, led early in the eighteenth century to a revolution in heating both frames and more elaborate structures. It was possible to obtain temperatures of up to 32°C (90°F) from March

till October by preparing a single hotbed, and it was in this way that pineapples were widely grown in Britain for a period. Animal manure does not retain heat for so long. Hotbeds were usually prepared so that frames could be placed upon them when ready, after several turnings-over of the manure.

Tanbark is no longer available today and, with animal manure in short supply, other methods of providing bottom heat are usually employed. However, if manure is plentiful, the old hotbed is still a viable method, and modern rotting agents also permit the use of straw or chaff to build hotbeds.

◊ BOTTOM HEAT.

Hothouse ◊ GREENHOUSE.

Hot-water Treatment A method of controlling certain pests which are difficult or impossible to destroy by chemicals, since they inhabit the actual tissues of the plants or live between scales of bulbs. In principle, the plant material is immersed for a specific time in a bath of water kept controlled to a very precise temperature: if too low, the pests are not destroyed; if too hot, the plant material can be damaged or killed. Because of the precision required it is normally very difficult for an amateur without specialized equipment to carry out hot-water treatment successfully.

The treatment is primarily valuable against eelworms which are otherwise almost impossible to destroy, and is carried out commercially against attack by these pests in chrysanthemum and phlox stools, narcissus bulbs and strawberry runners. Aphids and mites on strawberries and bulbs, rust on mint and bulb flies on narcissus bulbs are also dealt with by hot-water treatment.

◊ APHIDS; BULB FLIES; EELWORMS; MITES; RUST.

House Extension As the term suggests, this is an extra room designed to be built onto an existing dwelling house at ground level; many manufacturers now offer prefabricated extensions. Some of these include transparent roofs or very extensive windows and can thus be used for growing plants. In this respect they are modern equivalents to the CONSERVATORY.

House Plant A rather vague term, but in principle it means any plant that will live more or less indefinitely in a dwelling house rather than in a greenhouse. Obviously what can be grown in an individual house depends on many factors including minimum winter temperature, degree of temperature fluctuation, amount of light and liability to draughts; and also what may be classed as a house plant in northern Europe may be an orthodox garden plant in the Mediterranean or in Florida. As with any kind of gardening, suitable subjects can in fact be found for most positions, as the range of plants sold for the purpose is very large.

One vital factor in growing house plants – adequate air humidity – is likely to be lacking in the average house, but this can be improved locally by plunging house plants in containers filled with peat kept moist, or growing them on gravel trays from which water in the tray base can evaporate; regular mist-spraying is also valuable. Where space and money permit, a plant window can solve this problem.

In general, house plants are evergreen and are grown for foliage rather than flower, although there are notable exceptions, e.g. the bromeliads. There are also many flowering pot plants, which are either short-lived or cannot readily be brought to flower again indoors, available to liven up foliage displays, although the palette of leaf colours and patterns in the foliage plants is in fact remarkable.

◊ BOWL GARDEN; GRAVEL; HUMIDITY; MIST-SPRAYER; PLANT WINDOW; WARDIAN CASE.

Hover Flies ◊ PREDATORS.

Hover Mowers ◊ MOWERS.

Humidity The amount of moisture in the atmosphere. It is measured on a scale of 'relative humidity' (r.h.) in which zero per cent represents totally dry air and 100 per cent air which is saturated, i.e. can absorb no more moisture. It must be emphasized that the term has nothing to do with the degree of dampness of potting mixture or soil. All plants need some air humidity, even cacti which can grow at less than 40 per cent r.h.; for house plants a level of at least 60 per cent is desirable, and tropical plants in a hot greenhouse may require air approaching saturation point. This humidity is needed to counteract the plants' natural loss of water by transpiration, and many thin leaves become limp or wither readily if humidity is too low. Thick, leathery leaves and succulent leaves and stems usually indicate some ability to withstand dry air.

A high humidity is demanded by most cuttings for successful rooting, since the cutting can take up little or no moisture directly until roots are formed.

The problem is complicated by the relation of relative humidity and temperature. At low temperatures air becomes saturated quite readily, but its capacity for absorbing moisture increases with temperature. For example, the water content of a given volume of air needs to be roughly doubled to reach the same r.h. at 21°C (70°F) as there was at 10°C (50°F).

Gardeners can manipulate the level of humidity only within closed structures: frames, greenhouses, propagators and in rooms indoors for house plants. Any enclosed space will retain humidity if water is spread around as by damping down greenhouse floors or staging, or providing devices or material which will evaporate water in the vicinity. Open bowls of water will do this, but for house plants it is best to plunge or set pots in or on containers containing peat kept moist, or on a deep layer of gravel or pebbles which is kept topped up with water to well below the base of the pots concerned. Mist-spraying is also helpful. In greenhouses extra heat can dispel excess humidity which can be harmful at low temperatures, and control of humidity can usually also be achieved by opening or closing ventilators and doors.

Humidity can be measured with a wet

and dry bulb thermometer or more simply by a dial hygrometer.

▷ DAMPING DOWN; HOUSE PLANT; HYGROMETER; MIST-SPRAYER; PROPAGATOR; THERMOMETER; TRANSPIRATION; WARDIAN CASE.

Humus One of the most important factors in gardening and agriculture, humus is, to quote the *Oxford Dictionary*, 'the dark brown or black substance resulting from the slow decomposition of organic matter'; and the scientist would agree with this, though the chemical structure of humus has defied research. The gardener uses the word more loosely to include organic matter which may not be completely decayed. Completely decayed humus is colloidal, i.e. it is a jelly-like substance which coats the soil particles, swelling when wet and shrinking when dry. This is one of its important properties, improving the texture of the soil by making it spongy and water-retaining without spoiling its crumb structure or letting it become waterlogged. In the humus multiply the bacteria which break down the complex materials of dead plant and animal tissue into the simpler chemicals which plants absorb as food.

Humus disappears steadily in any given soil as the bacteria work in it, and any kind of cultivation greatly hastens its destruction. For this reason, humus-providing materials must constantly be added to soil in proportion to the intensity of cultivation. Humus may be supplied by animal manures, vegetable refuse, leaf-mould, sea-weed, peat, spent hops and straw, and also by animal residues such as shoddy, offal and fish waste. Most of these substances, except peat, hops and shoddy, should be rotted down before working them into the soil, and the compost heap is the best place for this. Organic fertilizers such as bone-meal and hoof and horn meal also supply humus in a small degree, unlike inorganic materials. The provision of humus and the consequent improvement of soil texture must not be confused with the food value of any organic material: thus animal manure is nutritious to plants, and peat practically not at all – but both are soil im-

provers. Soil without adequate humus is virtually useless for plant growth, however freely fertilizers are added.

▷ COLLOID; COMPOST HEAP; CRUMB; CULTIVATION; FEEDING PLANTS; ORGANIC GARDENING.

Hurdle ▷ FENCES.

Hybrid To the biologist a hybrid is the result of cross-fertilization between two species of plant or animal; to the gardener the term is also more loosely applied to the results of crossing between varieties. A very few hybrids are true-breeding, but in most cases they are not, and a few are sterile. A primary hybrid – the result of a cross between two species – will usually show some of the characteristics of both parents, and a batch of primary hybrids will usually be similar, if not identical. Once one starts to use plants of hybrid origin as parents, however, the offspring usually become more and more variable, due to the innumerable recombinations of character-carrying genes which can occur. Hybrid plants are technically known as heterozygous.

The botanist indicates a hybrid by the sign × (e.g. *Erica × veitchii* is a cross between *E. arborea* and *E. lusitanica*). A number of intergeneric hybrids are known, i.e. the results of crossing plants of two distinct genera. One of these is the foliage plant *Fatshedera lizei*, the result of crossing the large-leaved, erect *Fatsia japonica* with the climbing *Hedera hibernica*, the Irish ivy. The offspring is an upright plant with ivy-like leaves.

Intergeneric hybrids are common among orchids, where three or even four genera may have been used as grandparents and parents. Such hybrids are commonly given composite names like *Brassolaeliocattleya* – hybrids between *Brassavola*, *Laelia* and *Cattleya*.

Breeders describe the hybrid between two parents as the F.1 generation; if not self-sterile the progeny of the F.1 are called the F.2. Plants of special known character can be produced by annual cross-breeding of specific parents to give an F.1; despite the cost and time, this is done especially with annuals and vegetables grown from seed, and such plants as lilies where new bulbs grown from seed are desirable because old ones so readily become infected with disease. The F.2 generation will in most cases show great variation, and it is not normally any use saving seeds from an F.1 because of this. The F.1 is likely to show great uniformity in the individual plants and is also likely to have hybrid vigour.

◊ CHROMOSOME; CLASSIFICATION; FERTILIZATION; HYBRIDIZATION; HYBRID VIGOUR; TRUE-BREEDING.

Hybridization The deliberate act of making a hybrid or cross between two parent plants. This involves taking pollen from the plant selected as male parent and transferring it to the stigma of the female parent. It is often essential to remove the pollen-bearing anthers from the female parent to prevent self-pollination (this is called emasculation), and to protect the female flower against casual pollination by insects or wind, by surrounding it with a plastic or muslin bag. ◊ EMASCULATION; HYBRID; PLANT BREEDING.

Hybrid Vigour If two distinct, selected forms of a plant are crossed, the offspring will often (but by no means always), have what is called hybrid vigour, shown in larger size or improved cropping or flowering capacity. This principle has been applied, for instance, to sweet corn and tomatoes, and to certain flowers, e.g. petunias, on a commercial scale. Hybrid vigour declines in subsequent generations. This means that the original cross has to be made each year to produce a new batch of hybrids, known as F.1. It is therefore usually pointless to save seeds from an F.1 showing hybrid vigour, or indeed grown for other characteristics, especially since the offspring are likely to show great variation. ◊ HYBRID; HYBRIDIZATION.

Hydraulics ◊ WATERWORKS.

Hydroculture Growing plants in food-enriched water. Really, the same as hydro-

ponics but also used to cover the growing of plants in sterile aggregates. ◊ HYDROPONICS; SOILLESS CULTIVATION.

Hydroleca 'Leca' is the abbreviation for Lightweight Expanded Clay Aggregate. Clay is 'bloated' into very light granules which have a hard skin and a honeycombed interior. Leca granules are used in the construction industry as an aggregate for making concrete which is much lighter than gravel ballast and has high insulating capacity. Leca granules are sometimes used as an aggregate on greenhouse staging.

Hydroleca is a selected grade of leca with rounded granules of a consistent size around $\frac{1}{2}''$ diameter. They are used in a specialized form of soilless cultivation, since they allow adequate aeration and the upward movement of moisture above water level by capillary attraction. Furthermore, they absorb moisture slowly when soaked and release it gradually.

◊ SOILLESS CULTIVATION; STAGE.

Hydrophyte A technical term for plants living in water or very wet places.

Hydroponics Growing plants in water containing plant foods in dilute solution. In this early form of soilless cultivation plants were supported above the fertilizer solution by fine wire netting fixed on top of the container, above which a layer of peat, glass or wood wool, or similar material was sometimes placed for added support. Though occasionally used for growing house plants, this method has now been largely superseded by methods of soilless cultivation, sometimes called aggregate culture, in which the plant roots are supported by an inert substance such as gravel, baked clay granules (hydroleca) or sand irrigated with the fertilizer solution. However, 'hydroponics' is sometimes loosely and inaccurately used to describe the whole range of SOILLESS CULTIVATION.

Hydro Seeding A method in which grass seeds are sown in a stream of water directed at the area to be seeded. It is usually confined to large-scale works, but can sometimes be used in gardens, e.g. on steep banks, where normal sowing methods cannot be used.

Hygrometer An instrument which measures air humidity. This can take the form of a wet and dry bulb thermometer, which is rather tedious to use, or an electrolytic instrument which gives a very accurate reading but is only used for specialist applications. For normal use in greenhouses, dwellings and other places where plants may be grown, a dial hygrometer gives an accurate enough reading on a clock-like dial. These hygrometers are based on a coil of hair or specially treated paper which expands as it takes up moisture and is linked to the needle on the dial. ◊ HUMIDITY; THERMOMETER.

Hypertufa An invented name for an artificial medium with very absorbent properties similar to tufa rock. It is made by mixing 1 part cement, 1 or 2 parts sand, and 2 parts finely granulated peat which has been previously moistened; enough water is added to make a workable mix.

Hypertufa can be used to simulate lumps of tufa by digging a hole of the required size in vacant ground, embedding stones in the sides and base of the hole to form the number of planting cavities required, then filling the hole with the hypertufa mix. After about six days the hypertufa lump can be dug out and the stones removed. Before use, the lump should be soaked in water for a couple of days.

The material can also be used to form planting troughs for alpines in a mould. Drainage holes must be provided for while the process is carried out.

Finally, ordinary glazed sinks can be coated with hypertufa to improve their appearance. In this case a strong adhesive is painted onto the sides and the moist hypertufa mix is applied with the fingers to make a layer $\frac{1}{4}''-\frac{1}{2}''$ thick on the exterior and, if desired, the interior.

◊ ROCK POT; TROUGH GARDENS; TUFA.

Hypha The microscopic thread-like growth of a fungus, a large mass of hyphae (plural) making up the mycelium. ◊ FUNGUS; MYCELIUM.

<table>
<tr><td colspan="2" align="center">❁ **I** ❁</td></tr>
</table>

Ichneumon ◇ PREDATORS.

Imbricate This term is directly derived from a Latin word which simply means overlapping, and usually refers to leaves, scales or bracts laid closely one on the other. Tree buds are often covered with imbricated scales. The word is sometimes used as a specific name: thus the monkey-puzzle was originally called *Araucaria imbricata* (now it is *A. araucana*), because of the closely overlapping leaves.

IMBRICATE. *Left*, buds with imbricated scales; *right*, imbricated leaves of monkey-puzzle

Immortelle A French word meaning immortal, sometimes applied to EVERLASTING flowers.

Immune Plants are described as immune to disease or, less frequently, to pests when unaffected by these organisms. Such immunity may be due to poisons or antidotes within the tissue or to superficial processes such as specialized hairs on the exterior. Immunity to one disease does not mean immunity to all. Breeding for immunity to specific diseases is often an important aim of plant breeders: the results are called immune varieties.

The word is sometimes used of plants which show no disease symptoms, nor are adversely affected, even though they may

in fact be infected. This occurs among e.g. dahlias and strawberries. Such varieties do, of course, have the value of what would better be termed tolerance, and is sometimes called resistance, to the disease concerned. However, they can form a source of infection to other plants, especially of virus diseases.

Pests can also develop immunity to pesticides.

◇ PESTICIDES; VIRUS.

Imparipinnate ◇ PINNA.

Inarching A method of grafting sometimes more descriptively known as grafting by approach. In this technique the scion continues to grow on its own roots until the union with the stock is made. This means that the plant providing the scion is grown in a pot, and sometimes the stock plant is too. Where the scion plant cannot conveniently be brought to the stock, even in a pot, the bottle graft may be used, in which the base of the scion is kept in water until union is made.

The plants are arranged so that the stems are alongside, and in the simplest method a sliver of bark and wood about 2″ long is taken off each, on the facing sides. Other methods include the use of 'tongues' and 'inlays'. The two cut surfaces are then bound together with raffia and the whole area covered with grafting wax, as in other methods of grafting. When the two cut surfaces have made a good union the scion is cut just below the point of union and the upper part of the stock is likewise removed. (See illustration overleaf.)

◇ BOTTLE GRAFT; GRAFTING.

Inbred If a hermaphrodite (bisexual) flower pollinates itself, seed produced as a result is said to be inbred, and plants arising from it may be called an inbred line.

Incinerator Equipment for the burning of

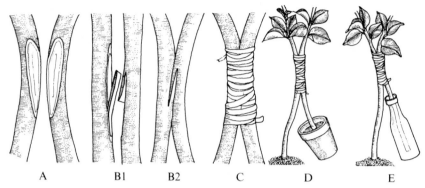

INARCHING. A, standard method of preparing stock and scion; B, tongue method; C, graft bound before covering with grafting wax; D, scion in pot; E, bottle graft

rubbish. Many ready-made incinerators can be bought, usually consisting of metal bars or mesh on a round or square framework, the base kept off the ground by legs. Home-made incinerators can be made from an old oil-drum with the top removed or from a metal dustbin, with holes punched in the base and sides, placed on three or four bricks. Alternatively, bricks can be formed into a round or square box, leaving a small gap between each and placing a metal grid inside, a little above ground level. An incinerator for garden rubbish should generally be at least 15″ across.

The purpose of the incinerator should be to destroy woody prunings and other pieces and diseased plant material. Soft material should normally be placed on a compost heap for, if burnt, all its organic and food value is lost. The ash left after incineration is, however, a useful source of potash.

  ♢ COMPOST HEAP; POTASH.

Incised A botanical term applied mainly to leaves with deep indentations in the margin, looking as if cut or slashed. ♢ LEAF.

Incision ♢ BARK RINGING; GARROTTING; NICKING AND NOTCHING; RINGING.

Incompatible (1) When pollen of one variety of a plant will not fertilize another, the varieties are termed incompatible. This occurs primarily among sweet cherries, which fall into several incompatible groups. ♢ FERTILITY RULES.

(2) In grafting, a given stock can be incompatible with a scion, resulting after some years' growth in a break at the grafting point (union). Thus some pears are incompatible with the quince rootstock widely used, and certain plum rootstocks are incompatible with some varieties. In pears double-working (double-grafting) is used to overcome this problem; this involves the use of a short 'bridging' section of an 'intermediate' variety which is compatible with both stock and scion. In plums, careful choice of suitable rootstocks is the normal method of avoiding a problem. ♢ GRAFTING.

Incurved, Incurving Literally meaning curving inwards, incurving is applied mainly to a group of chrysanthemums in which the florets turn loosely upwards and inwards. Incurved refers to the group in which the florets curve very closely and tightly together, the result being a compact globular flower. The opposite of RECURVED and REFLEXED.

Indeterminate Applied to plants, the stems of which can continue growing indefinitely, as opposed to determinate kinds where shoots terminate in a flower bud or truss. The most common example is the tomato.

Indianesque A garden style into which enter supposed elements of Indian gardening, especially ornaments and architectural detail. This was occasionally practised by Humphry Repton and his followers around the end of the eighteenth and early nineteenth centuries; the best remaining example is the water garden at Sezincote, Gloucestershire.

Indore Process A method of making compost in which both vegetable refuse and animal remains can be combined in specific proportions with dung and urine. The mixed materials are placed in a pit about 1 yard deep, with chalk or slaked lime to counteract acidity. The name comes from the Indore Research Station in India where the late Sir Albert Howard carried out so much research into making COMPOST HEAPS.

Indumentum Any covering; in plants, any growth of hairs. Sometimes used in the restrictive sense of a dense, felt-like covering of short hairs, especially when referring to rhododendron leaves which may have such 'felt' on their undersides. ◊ HAIRY.

INCURVED

Inferior A term found in botanical de-

scriptions indicating that one organ is inferior to, i.e. below, another. The typical reference, as in artificial keys to identification, is to the relative position of the ovary and floral envelopes (corolla and/or calyx); when the latter are inserted above the ovary, this organ is inferior. ◊ ARTIFICIAL KEY; FLOWER; SUPERIOR.

Infertile Lacking in fertility: often used of poor soils but also in reference to fruit trees and bushes which refuse to crop for whatever reason.

Inflorescence A portmanteau term which covers the flowering part of a plant, however great the number of individual flowers grouped together or their size. Inflorescences fall into three categories. In cymose inflorescences a flower is produced at each terminal growing point, and later flowers from lateral growing points. These are usually called cymes, although botanists have other terms for some unusual cymose arrangements.

Racemose inflorescences have an active growing point and can in theory develop indefinitely, with the youngest flowers at the tip or apex.

Thirdly, there are 'mixed' inflorescences which fall into neither category.

When an inflorescence has a central axis this may be called the rhachis.

The most frequent kinds of inflorescence are listed below; racemose ones are indicated by (r).

Capitulum (r) Literally, a 'little head' – a tight inflorescence of stalkless flowers, as in composites.

Catkin A mixed inflorescence of stalkless flowers, often of one sex only.

Corymb A more or less flat-topped flower cluster, in which the usually small flowers or flower-heads are all carried at about the same height, but the flower stalks spring from the main stem at different points, as opposed to an umbel in which they radiate from one point.

Cyme A word covering a variety of inflorescences, in all of which the growing

INFLORESCENCE. The larger the dot, the older the flower

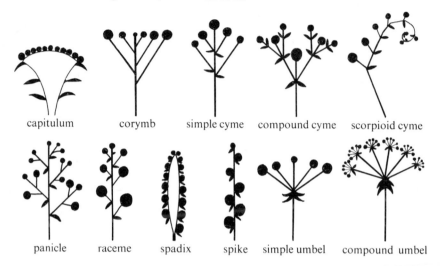

capitulum   corymb   simple cyme   compound cyme   scorpioid cyme

panicle   raceme   spadix   spike   simple umbel   compound umbel

points end in a flower, successive flowers being carried on a succession of side stems, usually in opposite pairs. Such inflorescences are often dome-shaped or more or less flat, with the oldest flower in the centre; in the scorpioid or helicoid cyme the inflorescence is one-sided, and unrolls from a spiralled centre.

Panicle (r) Though often used to describe any inflorescence with complex branching, this term is strictly applied to a branching raceme in which each branch resembles an individual raceme, the youngest flowers appearing at the apex of each branch. Branches may alternate or be opposite each other.

Raceme (r) An elongated, unbranched inflorescence in which each flower has a short individual stalk (in contrast to the spike). The youngest flowers are near the apex.

Spadix (r) A spike with a fleshy, usually swollen, central axis.

Spike (r) An inflorescence with a vertical axis and numerous stalkless or nearly stalkless flowers, the youngest near the apex.

Thyrse A mixed inflorescence which is densely branched as in a raceme, but each branch is a scorpioid cyme; the clusters are usually broadest in the middle.

Umbel (r) An inflorescence in which the individual flower stalks (sometimes called rays) arise from a central point at the top of the main stem, as in an umbrella. Umbels may be simple, with one set of rays, or compound, when each main ray branches into a secondary set which supports the flowers. The umbel is the characteristic inflorescence of the cow parsley family, *Umbelliferae*, though it is also found in other families.

Verticillaster A false whorl, composed of a pair of opposite simple cymes; characteristic of labiates in which verticillasters are carried at intervals on a main stem. Some botanical books refer to these as superimposed whorls.

The words 'head' and 'truss' are loosely used to denote tight-packed inflorescences, and 'spike' is often loosely used for any inflorescence which is long and narrow, even if it is technically a raceme with stalked flowers.

◊ CATKIN; COMPOSITE; FLOWER; HEAD; TRUSS; WHORL.

Informal (1) The opposite of formal in garden design, applied to gardens not laid out in geometrical designs or in patterns of repeated beds, paths and so on. Examples are landscape, rock, wild and woodland gardens. ◊ NATURALISTIC.

(2) Also sometimes used for varieties of a flower, the form of which is irregular as opposed to the majority of varieties in which symmetry is prized, e.g. camellias, chrysanthemums and dahlias.

Injection Sterilizing materials are sometimes placed in the soil by an injection process involving hollow spikes forced into the ground, through which the chemicals are pumped. This method combines efficiency with safety as regards the usually poisonous materials; but the equipment is mainly confined to commercial use.

Injection of chemicals into tree trunks or branches, by types of syringe, has been used in attempts to combat mineral deficiencies, but the development of sequestrols has largely superseded this method. It has also been used in attempts to combat tree diseases like dutch elm disease.

◊ SEQUESTROL; STERILIZATION.

Inorganic Refers to substances which, being neither animal nor vegetable in origin, do not contain carbon. Soils contain many inorganic substances in the form of grit, sand and stones, while many plant nutrients either derive from minerals or are synthetically produced. Nutrients can be either inorganic or organic in origin; there is a school of thought that condemns the inorganics because they cannot improve soil texture by adding essential humus, whereas organic ones usually do. It is true that, used in an unbalanced manner on a large scale, inorganic fertilizers have ruined large areas, helping to create 'dust-bowls' and erosion; but this is the fault of the farmers, not the materials. If used sensibly, in conjunction with organic materials that may sometimes have no food value at all (e.g. peat), inorganics are very valuable, being compact, convenient to use and often cheaper than their organic equivalents; they also often produce the desired results faster. The 'organics-only' school sometimes contends that inorganics are 'unnatural', but since many are still made from naturally occurring minerals, this is absurd. ◊ FERTILIZER; HUMUS; ORGANIC; SOIL.

Insect A huge group of animals sharing certain overall characteristics: they have a body divided into three distinct segments (the head, thorax and abdomen), the head carrying a pair of antennae or 'feelers', and the thorax the six legs. Many but not all insects have wings, also carried on the thorax, often protected by horny wing-covers. They typically have a life-cycle of four separate stages: egg giving rise to larva (which may be called a caterpillar, grub or maggot) which when ready becomes an immobile pupa or chrysalis, from which the adult insect emerges. These insects include beetles, bugs, butterflies and flies, some of which are harmful to garden plants and are thus classed as pests; others are harmless; and yet others are helpful, in that they feed on other pests – these are known as predators. The word 'insect' is sometimes loosely and wrongly used to cover the eight-legged mites and also all smaller creatures found in gardens, such as centipedes, spiders and woodlice.

◊ PEST; PEST CONTROL; PREDATORS.

Insecticide Any substance which kills insects. The term is often loosely used to cover materials which kill different classes of pest, especially small ones like MITES which are technically acaricides, often including MOLLUSCICIDES against SLUGS and snails, and NEMATICIDES against EELWORMS. These have individual entries, while the principles of their application and action are dealt with under PESTICIDES.

Insectivorous Insect-eating. Though sometimes applied to animals which eat insects, the gardener normally considers only insectivorous plants which are adapted to trap insects, digest their tissues and obtain useful nutrients from them. Most insectivorous plants live naturally in bogs, marshes and other watery habitats where nitrogen is not readily available, and their insect-eating habits have evolved to deal with this situation.

Insects, Friendly Although many insects are harmless to plant life, the expression 'friendly insects' is normally reserved for those predators which feed on pests. ⬦ BIOLOGICAL CONTROL; PREDATORS.

Instant Gardening A phrase of recent origin arising from the modern tendency to sell mature plants in containers, which can make an instant effect when planted. ⬦ CONTAINER-GROWN; GARDEN CENTRE.

Insulation The principle of double glazing is used to insulate greenhouses and conserve heat by fixing inside, a short distance from the glass, a second layer of transparent or translucent material. Insulation with a second pane of glass is usually impracticable owing to weight problems, though greenhouses first available in 1980 offered this facility, so plastic of various kinds is normally used for insulation. Ordinary polythene sheet suffers from the disadvantage that it creates a lot of condensation which can drip onto plants with harmful effects, but specially treated polythene is available which reduces this problem. Various more elaborate kinds of sheeting provide better heat retention, such as one enclosing air bubbles between two layers, and one of three separate layers. Another type of insulating sheet has minute slits in it. Yet another plastic is rigid with two outer layers and transverse strengthening layers in between, giving a honeycomb effect; this is rather opaque. Finally, one can use rigid transparent plastics such as acrylic sheet, but this is much more expensive than the others mentioned.

Fixing the material depends upon the greenhouse construction. With wooden framework, drawing pins can be used; on metal framework double-sided adhesive tape, 'sticky pads', or various proprietary clips, are available.
⬦ CLOCHE; GREENHOUSE.

Integrated Pest Management A U.S. term for BIOLOGICAL CONTROL.

Intercrop The growing of one rapid-maturing crop between rows of other, slower-developing ones in order to make the maximum use of available ground. As with the related practice of catchcropping, the usual intercrops are radishes and lettuces. Apart from providing an extra crop, the quick-germinating seeds can be helpful in indicating the position of rows before the main crop germinates.

Intercropping can also take place on a longer time-scale: fruit growers sometimes plant bush fruits (e.g. gooseberries or currants) between the rows of a newly planted top-fruit orchard, the bush fruits being grubbed out when the apples, pears, etc., have grown sufficiently and begin to crop. ⬦ CATCH CROP.

Intergeneric Refers to hybrids made between species or varieties belonging to distinct genera. ⬦ CLASSIFICATION; BREEDING; HYBRID.

Intermediate Applied to a group of chrysanthemums with flowers intermediate in form between the tight globular shape of the incurved group and the drooping florets of the reflexed group.

Internode The length of stem between nodes or leaf-joints on any plant having the latter; hence, an internodal cutting which is trimmed halfway between nodes, not close below one. ⬦ CUTTING; NODE.

Intersowing The same as sowing an INTERCROP.

Interspecific Refers to hybrids made between species of one genus. ⬦ BREEDING; CLASSIFICATION.

Interwoven Fence ⬦ FENCES.

INVOLUCRE. *Left to right*, on dipsacus (teasel), astrantia, and anthyllis (kidney vetch)

Involucre A collection of bracts, often leaf-like and usually in a whorl, at or just below the base of an inflorescence (flower-cluster), the latter typically being a condensed or compound head of small flowers so that the involucre forms a structure more or less resembling a calyx but enclosing several flowers. The latter may or may not have individual calyxes. The involucre is a characteristic structure in the daisy family (*Compositae*), where it is often composed of several rows of bracts, but also occurs in many others. ◊ BRACT; COMPOSITE; INFLORESCENCE.

IRISHMAN'S CUTTING

Irishman's Cutting A piece of a plant used for propagation which already has some ready-formed roots on it; most often used in connection with chrysanthemum propagation. Such a piece is really a small division. ◊ CUTTING; DIVISION.

Irregular Flowers are said to be irregular when they cannot be made into equal halves in any plane, or when they can only be halved in the vertical plane; the latter state is also called zygomorphic. Flowers which radiate regularly from a central point are called actinomorphic. ◊ FLOWER.

Irrigation In a broad sense, irrigation simply means the delivery of water for ensuring or improving plant growth. More precisely, it refers to water delivery through channels or devices other than a hand-held hose, though often fixed to the end of a hose. These include both fixed and moving sprinklers which deliver a fine rain-like spray; on a commercial scale, metal spray lines fixed to an oscillating device throw jets of water out through small holes. Individual crop rows can be irrigated via canvas tubing through which water slowly seeps. Another method which delivers water to individual plants is by trickle irrigation, in which flexible tube is fitted with nozzles at intervals. A variation on this, most often used on pot plants in greenhouses, has an individual small tube to each plant, fed from a larger one, sometimes known as spaghetti watering. Such methods are especially valuable for crops in frames or cloches; some of these devices may have built-in irrigation. ◊ CAPILLARY WATERING; SOILLESS CULTIVATION; SPRINKLER; TOP DRAINING; WATERING.

159

Island Bed A modern term used for relatively large beds devoted to herbaceous perennials, in which the display can be seen from all sides, unlike most HERBACEOUS BORDERS.

Italianate, Italian Garden The first Western gardens of note were made by the Romans, and from them descended the great gardens of medieval and Renaissance Italy normally thought of as Italian gardens. In very general terms, these are formal gardens where stonework, statuary and waterworks play a far more important part than do plants, which are normally treated as formal objects such as hedges, topiary, trimmed shrubs in containers, knot gardens and parterres. Because of their dependence on stone, a great many Italian gardens survive virtually unchanged (as do their contemporaries, the Mughal gardens of India, which exhibit an extraordinary parallelism).

The Italian Renaissance gardens were the first outstanding gardens of post-medieval Europe; the reasons for this, to quote Derek Clifford (*A History of Garden Design*) were first 'the great commercial wealth of Italy which gave men a taste for display; and second was the relative tranquillity of that country (compared with the rest of Europe) which gave men leisure'. Further, 'in one respect Italy excelled all other lands – the physical remnants of the great past were thicker on the ground there than anywhere else'.

The formality of the Italian garden was developed in various directions elsewhere in Europe, and was actively copied in what may be called the Italianate or Neo-Italian style in Britain between 1830 and 1860, of which Wilton House, Wiltshire, is the first and most remarkable example. In most cases the Italianate garden was filled with Roman statues, urns and sarcophagi brought back from Italy.

✿ KNOT GARDEN; MUGHAL GARDENS; PARTERRE; WATERWORKS.

J

Japanese Beetle This large, handsome beetle, introduced to the U.S. by accident in 1916, has become one of North America's most serious insect pests, particularly in the eastern half of the continent. The adult beetles feed voraciously on leaves, buds and flowers of a wide range of both ornamental and edible plants, while the large grubs feed on roots, especially of grass, and cause much damage to turf.

Adult beetles can be killed by applying suitable pesticides to plants or, where infestations are small, by handpicking, disposing of the beetles in a mixture of kerosene and water. Traps baited with a mixture of Eugenol and Geraniol are sometimes used. A number of pesticides can be applied to grass to kill the grubs, including the biological control milky spore disease. Though giving long-term protection this acts rather slowly and is better suited to use in parks and sports grounds than on good-quality lawns.
◊ BEETLE (1); BIOLOGICAL CONTROL.

Japanese Dwarf Trees ◊ BONSAI.

Japanese Garden Gardens in Japan date from around the third century A.D. Originally they were landscape gardens which tried to out-do reality, what one might call 'picture gardening' similar in principle to early British landscape gardening. After about the twelfth century, a combination of tradition, symbolism and Zen Buddhism controlled Japanese garden design, in which quiet meditation was the primary aim, with flowers reduced to a minimum and planting sometimes reduced to a handful of trees (often regularly clipped according to strict rules so that they retained their shape for scores of years), cultivated moss, rocks, water (or raked sand to symbolize water in 'dry landscapes'), stepping-stones and certain architectural features. The smallest area is regarded as of garden potential.

The Japanese style became popular in Britain and elsewhere in Europe only in Victorian and Edwardian times. With one or two notable exceptions which were laid out by Japanese designers, the Japanese garden in Britain seized on only the superficialities of the style, without realizing that, however stylized it might appear, it was based upon an innate love of nature and intimacy with it. The results in Britain and the U.S. are thus normally lakes with stepping-stones, islands, arched bridges, a few stone lanterns and bronze cranes.

Though the Japanese cult was strong while it lasted, it was decidedly impermanent in Britain, running as it does so strongly against the British instinct of plantsmanship. ◊ PLANTSMAN.

Jardin Anglais, le Literally, 'the English garden': a phrase which came to be accepted in Europe to mean the landscape garden. Among other places, the craze for *le jardin anglais* resulted in the destruction of a number of formal Italian gardens around Florence in the late eighteenth and nineteenth centuries, Florence being 'the cultivated Englishman's spiritual home' (Derek Clifford). ◊ LANDSCAPE GARDENING.

Jardinière A French word meaning an ornamental stand or receptacle for plants, normally used indoors.

Jiffy Pot ◊ PEAT POTS.

John Innes Composts ◊ COMPOSTS, SEED AND POTTING.

Joint ◊ NODE.

Jokes, Water ◊ WATERWORKS.

June Drop A phrase to describe the frequent dropping of many of the immature fruits on apples and other top fruits. This is basically a natural balancing act by the tree, which reduces the crop to manageable proportions; but it may also be caused by external factors, e.g. lack of pollination at flowering time, inadequate moisture and lack of vigour. Thus June drop can be partly offset by adequate feeding and correct pruning of fruit trees; in any case it is wise to defer thinning an apparently large fruit crop till the natural fall in June (and often into July) is complete. ⟡ THIN-NING.

Juvenility A number of trees start with one type of growth and foliage which alters as the plant becomes more mature. Juvenile growth is a feature of conifers and some other trees, notably eucalyptus. Some conifers never grow beyond this stage and can grow into full-sized trees with juvenile foliage, though most juvenile forms are of limited vigour and remain dwarf. With eucalyptus, regular cutting back or stooling can keep the often attractive juvenile foliage going permanently. Curiously enough, conifers can occasionally set seed, and eucalyptus flower and seed, in a juvenile state. Young beech trees produce normal foliage but retain the leaves in winter, unlike adult trees; in this case, clipping trees as hedge plants causes them to retain this juvenile character, which is technically known as marcescence.

JUVENILITY. *Above*, juvenile and, *below*, adult foliage of *Eucalyptus globulus*

K

Kainit A natural mineral containing sulphate of potash as well as sodium chloride (common salt), sulphate of magnesium and sometimes other impurities. Because of this variability, and the damage the impurities can cause to plants, kainit is now seldom used, although it has its value, especially in fruit orchards as an autumn or winter dressing, when it is applied at 2–4 oz. per square yard.

Keel The boat-shaped organ, composed of two joined petals, in the centre of the flowers of leguminous plants such as sweet peas. Some seeds also have a ridge or projection which is called a keel. ♢ LEGUMINOUS.

Kelp Specifically, certain very large kinds of seaweed; sometimes used generally for all seaweeds, which are often collected for use as fertilizer in seaside locations. Also, the ashes resulting from the burning of seaweed, a useful source of potash. ♢ SEAWEED.

Key (1) (also key-fruit) A winged seed as in sycamores and maples, technically called a samara.

(2) A method of identifying plants. ♢ ARTIFICIAL KEY.

Kitchen Garden A plot of ground devoted entirely to edible produce – vegetables, herbs and fruit – and often including greenhouses for growing crops out of season. In older times, kitchen gardens were usually entirely walled in, the walls being used for trained fruit trees. Cut flowers and pot plants for the house might also be grown in kitchen gardens, which are functional rather than ornamental.

Knife ♢ BUDDING KNIFE; GRAFTING KNIFE; PRUNING KNIFE.

Knife Ringing ♢ RINGING.

Knob A fruit grower's term for the swollen point at which the previous year's fruit stalk was joined to the branch. The knob is a source of future fruit buds and should not be cut away. The equivalent French word *bourse* is sometimes used.

Knock-down A term used of quick-acting, non-persistent pesticides. ♢ PESTICIDES.

KNOT. Sixteenth-century designs for knot gardens

Knot, Knot Garden This word originated in the garden sense in 1494 and refers to a bed laid out in an intricate pattern, sometimes resembling a maze, made from low-growing or clipped plants such as dwarf box, cotton lavender, thrift, etc. The area around and between these outlining plants might be filled with flowering plants replaced in season, but, especially in Tudor times when bedding plants as such were unknown, these areas were often left bare or covered with inert materials such as coloured sands, chalk or coal, to make colourful patterns. In any case the edging remained a permanent decorative feature which, of course, compensated for lack of colour.

Knots, or knot gardens, which were specially popular in the sixteenth and seventeenth century, were originally designed mainly to be seen from above, from raised terraces or upstairs windows. The name came about from the resemblance of the permanent pattern to a huge knot of rope arranged on the ground. Some knots were very elaborate and designed to resemble embroidery with its over-and-under stitching. Knots are still occasionally contrived today. (See illustration on p. 163.)

◊ MAZE; PARTERRE.

L

Label, Labelling The accurate naming of plants is important to most gardeners. Records of plant names seem to have begun in early herbal and botanical gardens, although this was usually done by keeping a written record. Later, the plant would be identified by a tally, a stick or stone on which reference numbers were notched or painted. The present-day idea of attaching the plant's name directly to it, or inserting its name beside it, dates only from the early nineteenth century.

The simplest label is a flat, pointed wooden one, usually coated with white paint. Metal and plastic labels of many shapes, upon which names can be written in pencil or ink, can be found; special inks have been devised to eat into metal or plastic. Another near-permanent method is to stamp the name, letter by letter, into a narrow metal strip. It is also possible, if expensive, to obtain cast metal labels, and to have names printed on plastic. One popular modern method is to stick names, printed onto plastic tape by a patent 'tapewriter', onto metal labels. Many patent labelling methods have been used in the past, including labels placed in glass containers, for instance sealed into glass tubes.

When using a specific type of label, the gardener should consider how permanent it needs to be. The name on a painted wooden label is unlikely to last a year but this may be perfectly satisfactory for seeds and annuals. Apparently very long-lived labels sometimes fail for unexpected reasons, e.g. lead strips are enjoyed by squirrels and other rodents. Labels which clip or fold around plant stems are likely to last longer than those tied on, even with metal wire which eventually corrodes. Labels pushed into soil are easily dislodged and birds often remove them. In gardens open to the public, labels tend to disappear, whatever their permanence and fixing, because visitors find it easier to pocket a label than to write down the name of a plant they are interested in.

Labellum The Latin for LIP.

Labiate Having a LIP.

Labyrinth In garden layout, effectively the same as a maze but, in older literature at least, referring to cavernous passages and hedge-mazes. ◊ MAZE.

Laced Applied to cultivars of border pinks which have an edging to the petals of a colour contrasting with the ground colour, laid down in a narrow scalloped band and looking like lacework. Usually, the ground colour reappears as a very thin border on the actual petal margin.

Lacewing Fly ◊ PREDATORS.

Laciniate A botanical term meaning cut into narrow segments; applied mainly to leaves, but also to petals in which the narrow segments look like a fringe. ◊ LEAF.

Ladybird, Lady Bug ◊ PREDATORS.

Lambourde A French word sometimes used by fruit growers for a fruit spur. ◊ SPUR.

Lamina A word synonymous with blade or limb, meaning the expanded part of a leaf. ◊ LEAF.

Lanceolate A botanical term literally meaning lance-shaped, applied to leaves and sometimes other organs which are a good deal longer than wide and taper to a point; often seen as a specific name. ◊ LEAF.

Land Measures ◊ WEIGHTS AND MEASURES (p. viii).

Landscape Gardening, Landscaping To garden historians these terms are relevant primarily to the art of laying out an estate so that it blended with the surrounding natural countryside, which began in the early eighteenth century when there was a revolt against formality and enclosure in gardening. The 'landscape era' and the activities of the 'landscape school' are sometimes restricted to that century, for by the early nineteenth century the era of the vast landowner was rapidly passing as the Industrial Revolution reduced most properties to an acre or two; but the principle of landscaping has continued into the present time, even if the common use of the terms 'landscape gardening' and 'landscape architect', applied as they are to the pettiest forms of garden design and construction, is nowadays so often absurd. ⟡ JARDIN ANGLAIS.

Landskip A poetic word for a landscape garden.

Lantern Cloche ⟡ CLOCHE.

Lapthorn Hoe ⟡ HOE.

Larva The second stage in the usual life-cycle of an insect, when the egg hatches to produce a usually many-legged, mobile, wingless grub, caterpillar or maggot. After a period, the larva becomes an immobile pupa or chrysalis, from which the winged adult emerges. ⟡ INSECT.

Latent Literally, hidden: used by gardeners mainly of buds which remain immature, and sometimes even unperceived, until stimulated into growth as by the removal of hitherto active shoots by accident or pruning. In fact, the presence of latent buds is the basis of almost every form of pruning and of the success of such forms of training as arching or bending. The word 'dormant' is equivalent when referring to buds. ⟡ ANNULATION; ARCURE; BENDING; BUD; DORMANT; NICKING AND NOTCHING; PRUNING.

Lateral A side-growth of any kind on a shrub or tree. The treatment of laterals, and their relation to the leaders or terminal shoots, is vital in most methods of pruning and training of fruit trees. The laterals are usually the fruit-producers, and if left uncut they produce fruit buds relatively quickly. Fruit tree laterals are sometimes described as maiden or one-year, two-year, and three-year laterals, according to their age, such definition being necessary in understanding tree pruning.

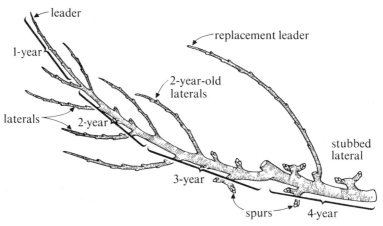

LATERAL

These terms can, of course, also be applied to shrubs and trees of all kinds, but detailed study of lateral growth is seldom required on ornamental kinds.
◇ LEADER; PRUNING.

Latex Milky or yellowish sap which occurs in a number of plants, often hardening on contact with the air. As such, it may be partly a healing agent, but its function is still obscure; it is sometimes considered a waste product, but may possibly be reserve food material. Rubber is obtained from the latex of numerous plants as different as the commercial tropical rubber-tree (*Hevea*) and the dandelion. Latex is often acrid, as in the spurges (euphorbias), and should not be allowed to get into cuts or eyes. ◇ SAP.

Lath House A structure covered with spaced wooden laths or trelliswork which allows air to enter, but is sufficient to break the full force of the sun and also to provide some protection against wind and light frost. The lath house seems to have originated in the southern U.S. for growing shade-loving plants in very sunny areas, but is now widely used by nurserymen in temperate climates for acclimatizing newly propagated stock, by bonsai growers to give adequate protection to their plants, and by orchid growers in the Far East to give partial shade. ◇ PROTECTION.

Lath Light A frame light of builders' wooden laths fixed to a framework at intervals, providing on a smaller scale the advantages of a LATH HOUSE.

Lattice Another word for trelliswork, especially when made of metal. ◇ FENCES; TRELLIS.

Lawn An area covered with grass or other plants designed to produce a low dense cover or sward, and a feature of the majority of British and American gardens today. The actual word is not recorded before 1674, and its modern meaning of a closely mown cover not till 1733; but turf has been treated as a garden feature since the fourteenth century. It was then used both as a decorative feature and for tournaments and games such as bowls. Most early lawns were made by laying turf cut from wild grassland and then beating it down with a wooden mallet or 'beetle'; growing lawns from seed did not start till around 1700. Medieval lawns were only cut two or three times a year, but by the seventeenth century regular cutting was practised. This cutting was of course done with a scythe; the lawn mower, which revolutionized cutting, was not invented till 1830.

Today lawns can be grown from seed, which is available in many different mixtures according to the quality of lawn required, the amount of wear it is likely to have, and the soil of the site. Turfing produces a usable lawn much faster, but is much more expensive. The difficulty of obtaining suitable wild turf, free from weeds, is being overcome by the commercial growing of turf of guaranteed quality. Another method of making lawns is by the use of tufts of creeping grass, planted at intervals, which rapidly knit together.

This method of planting pieces is also used with various plants sometimes used instead of grass, such as fragrant chamomile, and with some of the substitutes for grass, such as dichondra, used in hot climates where grass will not survive.

It must never be forgotten that grass is the most ill-used plant in the average garden, being regularly cut down and constantly trampled. Thorough preparation of the soil before starting a lawn is therefore essential, to level the ground, create the best texture and nutrition level, remove stones, and also to get rid of weeds, especially perennial kinds. Regular feeding is desirable, and most people prefer to keep their lawns free of weeds or any other plant growth (although there is sometimes a case for combining grass with clover, for instance). Lawns also often need watering in dry weather; aeration with a fork or special tool if the sward gets very compacted; and raking to remove matted dead grass, moss, debris and leaves.
◇ AERATION; BOWLING GREEN; CRO-

QUET LAWN; DRESSING; EDGING; LAWN RAKE; LAWN SAND; LEAF SWEEPER; LUTE; MAT; MOWERS; ROLLER; SCYTHE; SPIKING; TOP DRESSING; TURF; TURF PERFORATOR; TURF SEAT; WEEDKILLERS.

Lawn Clippings or **Mowings** ◊ COMPOST HEAP; MOWING.

Lawn Edging ◊ EDGING; EDGING TOOLS.

Lawn Edging Knife ◊ EDGING TOOLS.

Lawn Mowing ◊ MOWERS; MOWING.

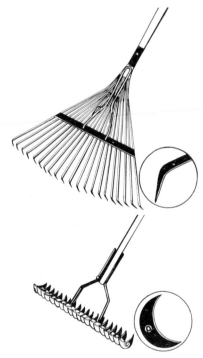

LAWN RAKE. *Above*, wire type; *below*, scarifying rake

Lawn Rake Special kinds of rake are used on lawns for the removal of matted grass, moss, debris and leaves. These are normally composed of long thin wire, or sometimes plastic, prongs bent over at their extremities; such tools may be called wire rakes. Other patent types of scarifying rake, sometimes called lawn combs, have short crescent-shaped blade-like teeth, and bamboo lawn rakes shaped like an orthodox rake, but with bamboo prongs, are sometimes seen. ◊ LAWN; RAKE.

Lawn Sand A combination of sand and various chemicals for killing weeds and moss on lawns. The standard formula is a mixture of 3 parts sulphate of ammonia, 1 part sulphate of iron and 20 parts fine silver sand (all parts by weight), which is applied at 4 oz. per square yard. Modern lawn sands may contain mercuric compounds such as calomel against moss. Lawn sand can be used in spring or summer, but hot dry spells are best avoided as grass can be scorched. After acting as a weedkiller lawn sand stimulates grass growth.

Lawn Shears ◊ SHEARS.

Lawn Sweeper ◊ LEAF SWEEPER.

Layer, Layerage (U.S.), **Layering** (1) Layering is a method of propagation in which a shoot is made to form roots while still attached to the parent plant. Many plants do this naturally, and artificial layering can be carried out only with plants which produce suitable growths which can be pulled down to soil level where the operation takes place. The shoot being rooted, and the same shoot when it has formed roots and been severed from the parent to be planted elsewhere, is referred to as a layer.

When making a layer it is advisable to wound the stem, or to twist it or bend it unnaturally in order to check the flow of sap at the point of contact between stem and soil. Wounding can be done by making a slit to form a 'tongue' of tissue (A.1), by making a notch in the shoot or by removing a ring of bark. The wounded or bent portion is buried in the soil, which can with advantage contain gritty material; it may be necessary to hold down the layer either with a large stone or, more usually, with a peg of wood or wire (A.2).

Layering is the usual method of in-

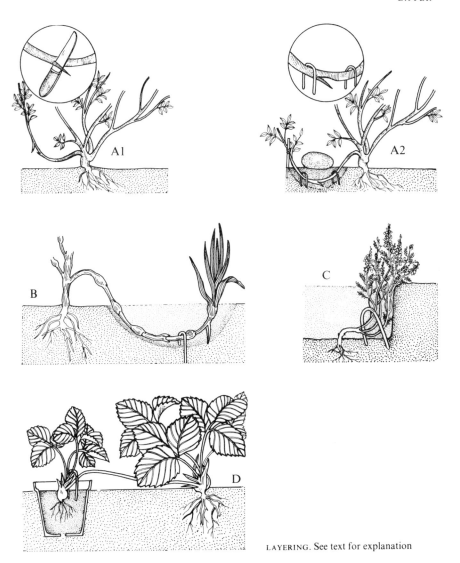

LAYERING. See text for explanation

creasing border carnations (B) but is mainly used with woody plants, especially those difficult to root from cuttings.

Various forms of layering exist, including tip layering which takes advantage of the natural propensity of plants like blackberries to form roots at the tip of shoots; suitable shoots are bent down and their tips buried in the soil. Plants with long flexible stems, e.g. honeysuckles and jasmines, will readily form roots along their stems; in the method called serpentine layering a stem is brought down to the ground and pressed into a succession of hollows so that it alter-

169

nately curves down into these and up into the air. The hollows are filled in with soil and in some cases, as with clematis, slanting cuts are made into the stem at joints where roots are to be formed.

When layering fruit rootstocks, the pegged-down branch is entirely covered with soil, and another layer of soil is placed over the shoots when they grow up from the branch. This is called continuous layering or etiolation.

Mound layering is similar. Appropriate plants, e.g. soft fruit bushes and many ornamental shrubs, are cut down to ground level, and as new young shoots appear they are covered with soil, when they will form roots. Heathers are layered in a similar way by lifting plants and planting them in a trench so that only the tips of the shoots protrude when it is filled with soil (C).

Rooting strawberries from plantlets on the runners (D), and bramble fruits by burying the shoot ends in the soil, is also sometimes called layering.

If it is impossible to bring a branch into contact with the soil it is usually possible to increase the plant by air layering.

◊ AIR LAYERING; RUNNER.

(2) The term layering is also applied to the process, when growing sweet peas with very long single stems on the cordon system, of detaching the growth from its initial vertical support when it has reached the top, laying it down on the ground, then fixing it to another support further along the row.

Laying Describes the old and efficient way of forming farm or rough hedges. In this, unwanted growths are first removed, and those retained are partly cut through near their base. These cut growths are then bent over at an angle of not less than 45° to the ground, and woven in and out of vertical wooden stakes driven into the centre of the hedge. ◊ HEDGE.

Leach Literally, the percolation of liquid through a material, but it is usually used to refer to plant foods being washed down through the soil out of reach of plant roots by rain or excessive watering. The more

soluble a fertilizer, the more likely it is to be leached: this is particularly the case with nitrogenous materials. Leaching occurs also in winter when fertilizers applied in summer but not fully used tend to disappear in the absence of crops to take them up. Waste of fertilizers by leaching can be reduced by ensuring that an excess is not applied at any time and that the materials are applied when the plants are growing actively and can make full use of them. ◊ FEEDING PLANTS; GREEN MANURING.

Leader The shoot at the end of a branch, which if left to its own devices will extend it in the same overall direction. The central leader is the vertical continuation of the main trunk. Leaders are usually pruned lightly, if at all, in contrast to lateral growths which are usually cut back. ◊ LATERAL.

Lead-headed Nail ◊ WALL NAIL.

Leaf, Leaflet In most plants the leaves are the 'food factories' where the pigment chlorophyll is concentrated, whereby the process of photosynthesis is carried out. In this, the action of light combines water and carbon dioxide to produce glucose; from that base are produced the more complex carbohydrates, which the plant needs for its growth processes, in combination with minerals brought up from the soil in solution via the roots.

Leaves may be deciduous, i.e. they fall before winter and new ones appear in spring, or evergreen, when they last indefinitely and are not subject to seasonal change.

In the great majority of plants leaves are flat and the plant is often able to turn them to the most effective position for receiving the amount of light required.

Leaves may have a stalk or petiole, when they are termed petiolate, or have no stalk, i.e. are sessile; or may be attached to the stem in other ways. These include: amplexicaul, clasping the stem; decurrent, having the leaf base prolonged down the stem; peltate, with the stem terminating in the centre of the leaf; perfoliate, with the stem

Whole leaves

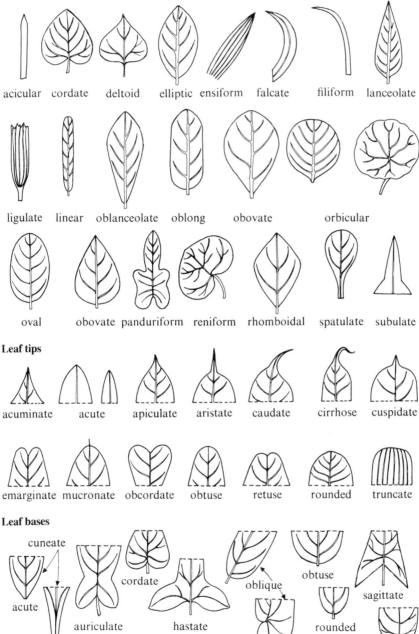

acicular · cordate · deltoid · elliptic · ensiform · falcate · filiform · lanceolate

ligulate · linear · oblanceolate · oblong · obovate · orbicular

oval · obovate · panduriform · reniform · rhomboidal · spatulate · subulate

Leaf tips

acuminate · acute · apiculate · aristate · caudate · cirrhose · cuspidate

emarginate · mucronate · obcordate · obtuse · retuse · rounded · truncate

Leaf bases

cuneate

acute

attenuate

auriculate · cordate · hastate · oblique · obtuse · rounded · sagittate · truncate

Compound leaves

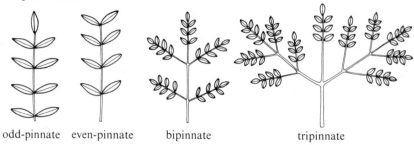

odd-pinnate   even-pinnate   bipinnate   tripinnate

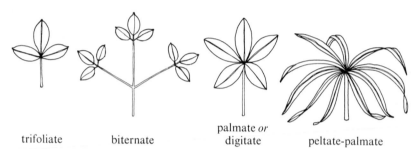

trifoliate   biternate   palmate *or* digitate   peltate-palmate

Leaf arrangements

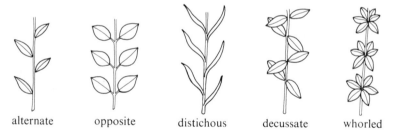

alternate   opposite   distichous   decussate   whorled

Connection with stem

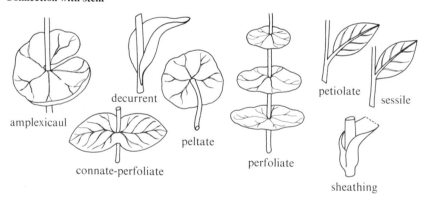

amplexicaul   decurrent   connate-perfoliate   peltate   perfoliate   petiolate   sessile   sheathing

172

Leaf margins

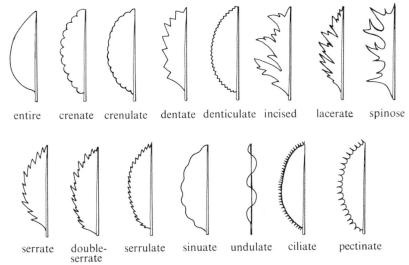

entire   crenate   crenulate   dentate   denticulate   incised   lacerate   spinose

serrate   double-   serrulate   sinuate   undulate   ciliate   pectinate
           serrate

Leaf lobing

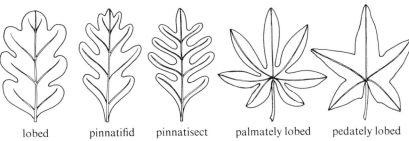

lobed   pinnatifid   pinnatisect   palmately lobed   pedately lobed

Venation

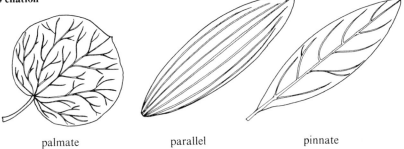

palmate   parallel   pinnate

continuing through the leaf; or sheathing, with the leaf base forming a tubular structure where it meets the stem.

The flat part of the leaf may be called its blade, lamina or limb. The vascular bundles which conduct water and nutrients in and out of the leaf diverge into its tissues as ever-decreasing veins or nerves. Main veins may project from the leaf underside, when they are termed ribs, and in symmetrical leaves, especially those with a stalk, there is often a pronounced midrib along the centre of the underside. It is usually on the underside that the microscopic stomata or breathing pores are found, through which air and water vapour diffuse. The rest of the leaf has a water-resistant skin or cuticle, the effect of which may be augmented by a thick layer of wax or by hairs of various kinds. The leaf surface can also be blistered or puckered (bullate) or wrinkled (rugose).

Leaves may be of one piece only, in which case they may be called simple or unifoliolate, or of several leaflets, when they are called compound.

Simple leaves have an enormous variety of shapes (as demonstrated in the accompanying drawings) which include references to shapes at the tip and base of leaves where appropriate: it is often necessary to describe these separately for accuracy.

Various terms are used to describe compound leaves. Those of three leaflets are described as trifoliate or ternate. When the leaflets are themselves subdivided into threes, they are called biternate. Leaves composed of four or more leaflets arranged in pairs on each side of a common stalk or petiole are termed pinnate (resembling a feather). If this set of paired leaflets terminates in an odd single leaflet, this is called odd-pinnate or imparipinnate; if there is no terminating leaflet, this is even-pinnate or paripinnate.

When the leaves are divided into branches which then carry pinnately arranged leaflets, they are termed bipinnate; the further stage, with branches twice divided, is tripinnate.

A palmate or digitate leaf is one divided into five or more radiating segments arising at the apex of the stalk in a hand formation. When segments radiate equally from a central point, this is termed peltate-palmate. A pedate leaf resembles a palmate one but has the lateral segments actually divided into two lobes. Leaves can also be palmately or pedately lobed; in this case none of the divisions continues right to the centre.

Simple leaves can also be variously lobed or cut. Leaves with lobes reaching at least half-way to the midrib may be termed cleft; if with lobes reaching almost to the midrib, parted. Where the lobes are symmetrically paired, these arrangements are respectively called pinnatifid and pinnatisect. When the lobes are sharply and irregularly cut, this is sometimes called incised, laciniate or slashed.

Besides lobing there are lesser degrees of undulation or serration of leaf margins (as shown in the accompanying illustrations), including the pectinate margin with very narrow lobes like the teeth of a comb, and the ciliate margin with an edging of hairs. A leaf with lobes or teeth terminating in spines may be called spinose. A leaf edge without any variation is called entire.

Leaves with a sharp stiff point may be termed mucronate or mucronulate.

In describing plants, it is also necessary to specify the placement of leaves upon the stem or twig. The typical alternatives are alternate and opposite. In decussate arrangements the leaves are opposite, with succeeding pairs at right angles to each other. Leaves may be borne in whorls, or spirally; the latter can apply when they grow at intervals up a stem or when they are produced in a tight rosette at ground level or on the end of a branch. Leaves growing at soil level are called radical or basal.

Leaves may be accompanied at their base by subsidiary organs including bracts, ligules and stipules.

(Most of the technical terms in this account have separate, more detailed entries of their own.) ◊ CLADODE; PHOTO-SYNTHESIS; PHYLLODE; VASCULAR SYSTEM.

Leaf Bud Cutting A cutting including a single leaf, a sliver of the stem it grows from, and a bud in its axil. ◊ CUTTING.

LEAF-BUD CUTTING   LEAF CUTTING

Leaf Curl A fungus disease affecting leaves of both fruiting and ornamental peaches and almonds, and of nectarines; often called peach leaf curl. In it the leaves start to curl up, eventually becoming thick and bloated-looking, also changing colour to yellow and dark red. Nearby shoots can

LEAF CURL (on peach)

also be infected and die. The overall vigour of affected trees can be severely affected and young ones may even die. It is a difficult disease to control. A suitable fungicide can be applied in early spring just before the buds begin to swell, and in autumn when leaves are dropping. Spraying with fungicide in summer has some effect, but it is also essential to pick off all affected leaves and burn them.

The phrase 'leaf curl' has also been applied to various virus diseases including a severe one affecting potatoes. Leaf curling is also caused by aphids and other sap-sucking insects, particularly on fruit trees; though this is not associated with changing colour, such curling can look very like peach leaf curl. Any such distortion should be examined and insecticidal sprays applied if necessary.

◊ LEAF ROLLING; VIRUS DISEASES.

Leaf Cutting A cutting made from a leaf or part of one, without any associated growth bud. Most plants which can root in this way are herbaceous and include saintpaulias, streptocarpus and most succulent members of the stonecrop family, *Crassulaceae.* ◊ CUTTING.

Leaf Hoppers A group of small sap-sucking insects, technically plant bugs of the order *Hemiptera*, which when adult leap into flight when disturbed, especially in hot weather. Even after they have departed the whitish mottling caused by their feeding is quite distinctive, and the whitish skins of their earlier moults attached to leaf undersides will confirm the diagnosis. Leaf hoppers attack many plants and can become especially tiresome in greenhouses. Most standard insecticides will destroy them and, under glass, fumigation is effective.

Leaf Miners The grub-like, smooth-bodied larvae of a group of small flies which tunnel into the central tissue of leaves between their outer skins. The visible result is either a maze-like network of white lines or a pale blister-like patch. Limited attacks can be dealt with by removing leaves, crushing the larva or stabbing it with a pin or knife. Severe attacks can be dealt with by spraying or, in greenhouses, fumigating with an appropriate insecticide. (See illustration on p. 176.)

175

LEAF MINERS

Leaf Mould (1) The substance left after leaves have decayed. This dark-brown powdery or flaky material is rich in humus and contains a reasonable level of plant nutrients, so is valuable wherever organic matter can be used in the garden – dug into soil, used (at around 5 lb. per square yard) as a top-dressing or mulch when it will smother weeds, or mixed with soil for potting mixtures at the rate of 1 part in 2–4 of soil. At one time it was widely used for the latter purpose, but has now largely been replaced by peat in commercial potting mixtures.

Leaf mould is found naturally in woods under the surface leaf litter, or can be made by stacking leaves in a bin or wire-mesh enclosure. If there is a large supply of leaves this is well worth while, rather than just adding the leaves to a compost heap. Leaves decay fairly slowly on their own.

Beech and oak leaves make the best leaf mould. Some thick leathery leaves, like those of plane and sycamore, resist decay for years, and those of holly, laurel and other evergreens are better mixed with compost in small quantities. Pine needles also take long to decay and their mould is very acid, so this, and also the undecayed needles, should be used only around acid-loving plants, and as an ingredient of potting mixtures for plants like bromeliads which like an acid, very porous root-run.

◊ BROMELIAD; COMPOST HEAP; HUMUS. (2) A fungus disease of tomatoes.

Leaf Rolling Leaf-roll is the name for a specific virus disease of potatoes. Leaf roll-ing may occur on many plants for various reasons, sometimes due to lack of water or over-feeding, and sometimes due to attack by sap-sucking pests, notably aphids. If leaves are rolled up longwise, suspect leaf-rolling sawflies whose larvae will be found within. Peach leaf curl disease also tends to cause leaf rolling. ◊ LEAF CURL; SAW-FLIES; VIRUS DISEASES.

Leaf Scorch Although leaves can literally be scorched by dryness, sunlight and high temperatures, especially under glass, this term is usually restricted to damage caused by faulty feeding, especially on fruit trees and bush fruits. The typical symptoms are that leaf margins become brown or grey and then dry up, and leaves eventually fall. The usual problem is a lack of potash, especially if too much nitrogen has been given, and it is aggravated on badly drained soils.

Leaf Spot A descriptive term for many unrelated fungus diseases causing more or less round spots of varying colour on leaves. Some of these diseases, like that specific to black currants, can cause all leaves to fall. Celery leaf spot is carried on the seeds, which can however be freed of the disease by sterilization. If possible, affected leaves should be picked off and burned, and an appropriate fungicide applied. Some of these diseases are known as ANTHRACNOSE.

Leaf Sweeper A wheeled device in which brushes mounted on axles, and connected with the wheels, pick up leaves, grass cuttings and other debris on a lawn and transfer them into a collecting hopper. Large versions may have a vacuum-cleaner action actuated by a motor-propelled fan.

Leafy Gall ◊ GALL.

Leather If leather scraps are available they can be dug into the ground to provide very slowly available nitrogen. Leather dust, which contains 5–7 per cent nitrogen, will release it a little faster, and may be used – preferably mixed with compost, peat or similar bulky materials – at up to 1 lb. per square yard at any time.

Leatherjackets The larvae of craneflies (often called daddy-long-legs), large flies of the family *Tipulidae*. The grey to brown, legless, tough-skinned grubs feed on plant roots: their attacks affect lawns, herbaceous borders and vegetable plots, and they can also severely affect pot plants. Attacked plants may die and on lawns dead patches are caused. Leatherjackets are often present in large numbers on land recently converted to gardens from grassland.

Various insecticides can be applied to kill the grubs *in situ*. Lawns and vacant vegetable plots can be cleared by giving them a very thorough soaking with water and covering them overnight with an impervious cover like a tarpaulin or wet sacking. The grubs come to the surface and can be swept up in the morning.

Leca ◊ HYDROLECA.

Leg A short stem on a shrub below the lowest branches, as on a gooseberry bush.

Legume, Leguminous A legume, botanically, is the one-celled, two-sided seed pod

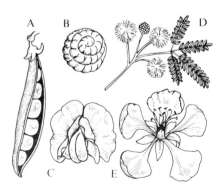

LEGUMINOUS. A, typical pod (garden pea); B, spiral pod (*Medicago* sp.); C, papilionaceous flower (sweet pea – *Papilionoideae*); D, flowers of mimosa (acacia – *Mimusoideae*); E, flower of flamboyant (delonix – *Caesalpinioideae*)

of the pea family, *Leguminosae*. Gardeners may use the word legume when referring to any plants of the family, especially vegetables which include culinary peas and all kinds of bean.

Many leguminous plants, both vegetables and flowers, have flowers with an upper petal called the standard, two side petals known as wings, and two lower ones united into a 'keel'; the stamens are either all, or all but one, united into a tube. Owing to their fancied resemblance to butterflies, these flowers are often called papilionaceous; and the group of the family carrying such blooms has been treated as a distinct family, *Papilionaceae*, and now as sub-family *Papilionoideae*. However, there are two other sub-families of *Leguminosae* which share the characteristic pod, which in tropical examples may be huge and woody, and may sometimes be circular or spiral rather than straight as in the familiar pea. One sub-family has minute flowers in heads of various shapes, mostly round as in the acacias or 'mimosa': this is called *Mimusoideae*. The third sub-family has large flowers of varying shapes, sometimes almost regular in outline, and often with stamens separate: these are the *Caesalpinioideae*.

Leguminous plants, including the familiar beans, peas and clovers, are the most important among several with which nitrogen-fixing bacteria associate to produce nodules on the roots. When the plants die, nitrogen returns to the soil, so that they are an important feature in crop rotation.

◊ FLOWER; NITROGEN FIXATION; POD; ROTATION.

Lenticel A small, corky, elongated spot on young bark, which is in fact a kind of breathing pore. In some trees, e.g. birches, the lenticels are so distinctive in colour and texture that they are sometimes mistaken for symptoms of disease.

Lepidate A botanical term referring to a covering of very small scurfy scales, as on the leaves of many bromeliads and the leaf undersides of certain rhododendrons. ◊ SCURF.

Levelling If really accurate levelling (U.S.: grading) is needed in a garden, beyond what can be achieved by eye, a spirit-level and certain simple apparatus is used. In the first stages of levelling very rough ground, wooden boning rods (originally spelt 'borning') are employed. These consist of a vertical piece 3′ long and pointed at one end, with a shorter cross-piece at the other forming a T-shape. One is knocked in at the highest point of the ground and an assistant holds another a few yards away. The third boning rod is then manoeuvred up and down in the same line until visual sighting across the tops of the three establishes that they are level. (A slight slope can be achieved in the same way.) A number of sightings will of course be needed on any one plot, all taken from the 'master' boning rod.

LEVELLING. *Right*, a boning rod; *left*, using a spirit level on a board between pegs

Wooden pegs can be driven in by the base of the boning rods, to a given level marked upon them, or top soil can be roughly levelled to these marks.

When an approximate overall level is achieved, the spirit-level comes into use. A long one can be used between pegs about 2′ apart or, if preferred, a thick straight-edged plank 6′–8′ long is used between pegs and the spirit-level placed upon this to achieve an absolute horizontal by adjusting the pegs. As before, one peg should act as the master for the whole area being levelled.

The actual levelling is carried out by taking soil off too-high areas and spading or barrowing it into depressions, the final stages being carried out with a rake. It may often be necessary to leave the area for a time after initial levelling to allow soil to settle. If the ground is very uneven, care must be taken to ensure that the top-soil forms the upper layer of the finally levelled ground. This may mean skimming off top-soil to a depth of around 10″, placing it in a heap nearby, levelling the remainder of the ground and finally replacing the top-soil and giving that a final levelling.
◊ TERRACE; TOPSOIL.

Lever Plough A kind of hand plough especially designed for disabled people, with one fixed handle and the other movable; when moved forwards and back, it drags a plough blade through the soil and turns it over. ◊ PLOUGH.

Lichen There are many kinds of lichen, all the result of a symbiotic union between an alga and a fungus. They are extremely resistant to difficult natural conditions (although susceptible to industrial fumes) and are often the first colonizers of newly created habitats without soil. Besides their capacity for growing on stone, rock and tiles, they often grow upon plants, especially in moist climates, and can choke their breathing pores and also provide a refuge for unwanted insects. They are troublesome in this way upon shrubs and trees including fruit trees: the remedy is a regular tar oil winter wash. One kind of lichen is a problem of wettish lawns, forming flat plate-like growths; this can be destroyed by using a mercury-based lawn sand and improving drainage. ◊ ALGAE; FUNGUS; LAWN SAND; SYMBIOSIS; WINTER WASH.

Lifting The removal of a plant from the ground. Lifting can be carried out when transplanting or division is intended, and the same term covers the digging up of tender plants with fleshy roots needing winter storage, e.g. dahlias, and crops, e.g. potatoes and celery. Care must be taken to avoid damaging the latter; with plants

178

to be moved it is desirable to lift them with plenty of soil around the roots or at least with minimal damage to the roots. Although with special care many plants can be lifted and transplanted while in active growth, fatality is less likely to occur by lifting when they are dormant, as long as soil and weather conditions permit. Fleshy-rooted plants – bulbs, tubers, etc. – are best lifted when their foliage has died down.
◊ DIVISION; DORMANT; TRANSPLANTING.

Light (1) Without light there would be no gardening or crops, for no green plant can grow without it. Plants use light to combine carbon dioxide in the air and water from the soil to create the sugars upon which their metabolism is based: this is photosynthesis. Only the vaguely plant-like fungi can exist without light. Green plants vary enormously in their light requirements, and a knowledge of their needs in this respect is essential when planting a garden with its different degrees of shade, and also when placing house plants within a dwelling. If light is inadequate for a particular plant, it will tend to become etiolated – pale and spindly – and eventually collapse.

Apart from a desired strength of light, some (but by no means all) plants respond to the duration of light during each 24-hour period, either flowering when nights are long ('short-day plants') or when nights are short ('long-day plants'). Man has learnt to manipulate this day-length requirement artificially to obtain flowers at seasons other than the natural.

It has also been found possible to produce flowers and grow crops out of season, or away from their normal high-light habitat, with the aid of artificial light. Whereas the light level needed for day-length control is low, that for productive growth is high, and fluorescent mercury-vapour lights of various configurations are among the best for the purpose, since they give out much less excess heat in proportion to light than ordinary incandescent lights.

Gardeners also use electric lighting to enable them to enjoy their gardens at night.

Light also affects the germination of seeds: most prefer darkness, and are hence covered up, but some can only germinate in light.
◊ DAY-LENGTH; GERMINATION; PHOTOSYNTHESIS; SHADE.

(2) A light is also the name for the movable glassed part of a FRAME.

Light Pruning ◊ PRUNING.

Ligulate Strap-shaped.

Ligule A word with several specialized botanical meanings. Those which a gardener may encounter are:

(1) A strap-shaped organ such as the 'petal' of a ray floret in COMPOSITES.

(2) The thin scaly membrane at the top of the leaf-sheath in grasses, often a diagnostic feature in identification.

(3) The sheath or envelope protecting the developing leaves of certain palms.

Limb (1) An old word sometimes applied to the larger branches of a tree.

(2) In botany, the flat, expanded part of a flower calyx or corolla which has a tubular base: also sometimes the blade of a leaf. ◊ FLOWER; LEAF.

Lime, Liming Gardeners use the word lime to cover several substances containing calcium, though in its strict dictionary sense of 'a white, caustic, alkaline substance' lime means calcium oxide, or quicklime, which is made by heating chalk or limestone in a kiln. This is an unpleasant material to handle, and the gardener normally uses slaked or hydrated lime, calcium hydroxide, which is a relatively inoffensive powder, though it will scorch plant foliage. Finely ground chalk and ground limestone (carbonate of lime) are also used, while magnesian limestone provides both calcium and magnesium.

The value and use of lime in gardens seem full of contradictions and tradition. In the first place, calcium is one of the elements used by plants; yet a large number of highly desirable garden plants are classed as lime-hating or calcifuge. In growing plants of whatever kind, the gardener needs to know whether the soil is acid or alkaline, the former containing little calcium, the latter much. This acid/alkaline balance is measured on the pH scale, on which 7.0 is neutral, lower numbers being acid and higher ones alkaline; it is easily measured by using an inexpensive lime-testing kit.

In principle, really acid-loving plants can grow with little or no available calcium (free lime). With most plants, calcium is mainly used to reduce soil acidity, being important in normal garden soils for several reasons. In its absence, the soil bacteria which convert ammonium salts to nitrates cannot operate, with the result that nitrogenous plant foods are largely unavailable. Nitrogen-fixing bacteria also need lime to live successfully, as do earthworms, with their beneficial activity in aerating the soil. Most important perhaps is the fact that lime, if applied regularly, improves the texture and workability of clay soils by flocculation.

In excess, however, calcium inhibits the growth of many plants, partly by its action of 'locking up' other necessary elements, notably iron and magnesium. In naturally limy soils this effect, which causes chlorosis and other deficiency symptoms, can be overcome up to a point by applying 'sequestered' or chelated compounds called sequestrols.

Regular liming is the habit of many gardeners, especially vegetable growers, partly because of its effect on soil texture and partly because liming discourages certain diseases, e.g. club-root, and also pests including slugs, leatherjackets and wireworms. However, too much lime encourages potato scab disease, and the general belief that vegetables need lime as a matter of course is inaccurate. Recent research work shows that many vegetables thrive best on relatively acid soils, and none need a pH level above 7.5. In general, the same can be said of ornamentals, though many alpine plants are actively lime-loving, or calcicolous.

It follows that before applying lime it is desirable to check the pH level. Having done this, the lime requirement of the soil can be calculated. The amount needed varies, not only according to the pH but to the type of soil. The table below shows the approximate amounts of hydrated lime needed to raise the pH level to 6.5 on different soils, in pounds per square yard.

Original pH	Sandy or gravelly	Medium loams	Peat or clay
4.0	$3\frac{3}{4}$	$4\frac{1}{2}$	5
4.5	3	$3\frac{1}{2}$	4
5.0	$2\frac{1}{4}$	$2\frac{3}{4}$	$3\frac{1}{4}$
5.5	$1\frac{1}{2}$	2	$2\frac{1}{4}$
6.0	$\frac{3}{4}$	1	$1\frac{1}{2}$

If ground chalk or limestone is used, about twice these quantities are required.

Lime can be applied to vacant ground at any time of year, but the most convenient time is usually in autumn or early spring on light or peaty soils. It is perfectly satisfactory to spread it as a top dressing though, if desired, it can be lightly worked into the soil with a fork or rake. It should never be applied at the same time as animal manure, since the chemical reaction so caused will release ammonia gas which disappears into the air and thus wastes most of the nitrogen in the manure. The best advice is to lime and manure in alternate years, but if one wants to apply both in the same season the manure should be dug in first and the lime applied to the surface several weeks later.

Lime in some form is incorporated into standard seed and potting composts; even when these are peat-based the added lime means that the composts have a near-neutral reaction. Special composts for peat-loving plants, containing no lime, can be obtained.

Several fertilizers contain free lime and are therefore alkaline in reaction: these are basic slag, calcium cyanamide, nitrate of lime and Nitro-chalk. Superphosphate of lime, however, does not contain free lime.

♢ ACID; ALKALINE; CALCICOLE; CALCIFUGE; CALCIUM; COMPOSTS, SEED AND POTTING; FLOCCULATION; LIMESTONE; pH; SEQUESTROL.

Lime-hating Plants ⬦ CALCIFUGE.

Limestone A form of calcium carbonate, harder than chalk. Actual limestone rock can be used for rock garden construction; water-worn Westmorland limestone is specially favoured for the purpose. Despite the fact that limestone contains calcium, the rate of release, especially from the harder types, is so slow as to be negligible in terms of effect upon most so-called lime-hating plants.

Various forms of limestone are used for liming to provide calcium. These include ground limestone, which releases calcium slowly. Dolomite or Dolomite limestone is the same as magnesian or magnesium limestone, which releases magnesium as well as calcium and is therefore specially valuable for soils lacking in magnesium. This material is often specified for use in potting composts by U.S. authorities, rather than ordinary lime or limestone. ⬦ LIME.

Lime Sulphur A fungicide and acaricide frequently mentioned in older gardening books, made by combining lime and sulphur, which was for a long time used against scab disease of apples and pears and against red spider and tarsonemid mites on fruit trees and strawberries, and in winter at the strongest rate to control various diseases of cane fruits. Unfortunately it became generally unavailable in the U.K. in 1979, although it has not been entirely superseded.

Line ⬦ GARDEN LINE.

Linear A word meaning long and narrow, applied to plant organs of this shape, especially leaves, including the needles of conifers. ⬦ LEAF.

Lip A lip is, botanically, a single segment of a flower perianth, or the result of two or more segments uniting, which forms a distinctive lobe quite separate from the remaining segments. This lobe is usually flat as in sages (salvia) but may be expanded into a pouch shape, as in antirrhinum.

Botanists sometimes use the Latin equivalents, labellum for lip and labiate for lipped, and the latter term provides the name of the sage family, *Labiatae*, in which

LIP. *Left, Salvia patens; above right,* orchid (paphiopedilum); *below right,* orchid (miltonia).

the flowers are most often lipped. However, the lip as a floral feature is most pronounced in the orchid family. Where several upper and several lower flower segments have combined to create separate lips, the flower is called bilabiate, as in calceolarias. ⬦ FLOWER.

Liquid Feeding ⬦ FEEDING PLANTS.

Liquid Manure ⬦ MANURE.

Liquid Sowing ⬦ FLUID SOWING.

Liver of Sulphur ⬦ POTASSIUM SULPHIDE.

Liverwort Liverworts are primitive plants related to mosses (part of the *Bryophyta*) but characterized by making flat lobed growths close to the soil or rock surface. Because of this they can smother small plants and grass, and are particularly dangerous on seed containers and in pots. They prefer moist conditions and thus thrive in wet ground, especially if badly drained, and on compost in containers. In the open ground, improved aeration and drainage usually discourage liverworts, and on turf lawn sand can be used in addition. Pots and seed boxes need a regular going over in which the liverworts on the soil surface are removed with an instrument like a pointed label.

Loam A word which originally meant clay or mud but has come to be used loosely for soil, especially the more workable soils having a good balance of clay, sand and humus or decayed organic matter. One can however speak of 'sandy loam' and 'clay loam', according to their predominant content. 'Fibrous loam' contains a high proportion of fibre in the form of partly decayed plant stems, especially grass. 'Chalky loam' is better referred to as marl. A good balanced loam containing some fibre is ideal for soil-based potting composts and this is what John Innes composts should contain. Ideally, it is prepared from the top spit dug from a meadow, stacked grass-side downwards and left for at least a year so that the grass decays. ◊ COM-POSTS, SEED AND POTTING; MARL.

Lobe Plant organs such as leaves and petals which are divided may be termed lobed, especially if the divisions are relatively long and narrow, and are rounded. ◊ LEAF.

Loggia An arcade or gallery attached to a building but with one side open to the air. Nowadays the term is often applied to garden rooms or house extensions, even if they are completely glassed in. ◊ ARCADE; HOUSE EXTENSION.

Long-arm Pruners Pruning devices on long handles, operated by a lever mechanism. ◊ PRUNING; SECATEURS; SHEARS; TREE PRUNERS.

Long-day Plants Plants which flower only when days are long and nights are short. ◊ DAY-LENGTH; LIGHT.

Longhorn Hoe ◊ HOE.

Long Tom A flower pot much deeper than usual in relation to width. ◊ POT.

Lop To lop a tree is to remove or drastically shorten its branches, as in the operations known as coppicing, dehorning, heading back and pollarding. Lopping of any kind should be carried out when the tree is not growing actively, and with deciduous trees when they are leafless. Conifers in general should not be lopped since they do not regenerate fresh growths. Branch ends left after lopping should be treated with a tree-wound sealing compound. ◊ COPPICING; DEHORNING; HEADING BACK; LOPPING SHEARS; POLLARD.

Lopping Shears Long-handled or lever-activated shears with short stout blades, used for cutting fairly thick branches. ◊ SHEARS.

Lorette Pruning A method of pruning fruit trees developed by Louis Lorette, a French professor of agriculture, in the years before and after the First World War. It is a very detailed method in which all pruning is carried out from spring to late summer, in several stages. In principle, it consists of severely cutting back lateral growths to stimulate the production of fruit buds from

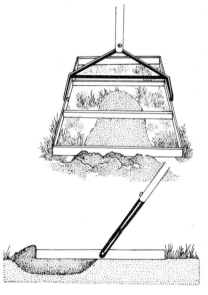

LUTE

STYLES OF GARDENING

This section of colour photographs illustrates some of the styles and modes of gardening, spanning the last four centuries, which are described in individual entries in the Encyclopedia (and are summarized under the heading 'Garden Design'). Most of the examples are British, for in the British Isles more gardening fashions have left their mark than in any other country, but a few from the United States have been included to depict modern trends. The gardens have been arranged roughly in chronological order of their original construction, with the exception of the first picture (below).

No examples of medieval gardens remain, nor – except as reconstructions – any Tudor gardens, but we can still see many historic gardens very largely as they were first conceived, albeit often with more recent plant material – a tribute indeed to those individuals and, in recent times, organizations (notably the National Trust) which have maintained them for so long.

Below, the largest parterre in Britain, covering about thirteen acres, is at Drummond Castle, Crieff, Tayside: its basic design is that of a St Andrew's Cross. Although laid out in the early nineteenth century it faithfully reflects the possibilities of this favourite seventeenth-century medium; it is probable but not certain that a parterre existed when the garden was first created in 1630. The impact of the parterre's setting in a shallow valley under the castle's terraces is enhanced by the continuation of the main axis through the woods on the hills beyond, in formal landscape style (Harry Smith Collection).

Above, the sixteenth-century terraces at Northbourne Court, near Deal, Kent, are a form of mount from which both garden and surrounding countryside could be viewed; they are built against a very high outer wall. *Below,* one of the sunken gardens at Hampton Court, the royal palace by the Thames in Surrey. Though probably laid out in the reign of William and Mary around 1689, it provides a good impression of a formal Tudor garden with statues, clipped trees and a central fountain *(both Harry Smith Collection).*

Above, the imposing terraces at Powis Castle, Welshpool, Powys, built in the late eighteenth century below the old castle on its strategic ridge, are very much in the Italian baroque style. Today their walls shelter a fine collection of exotic climbers and shrubs *(National Trust: photo Jeremy Whitaker)*. *Below,* some of the fantastic topiary specimens at Levens Hall, Kendal, Cumbria, date from its making between 1690 and 1720. The garden is often described as an example of contemporary Dutch design *(Harry Smith Collection)*.

Above, the Moon Ponds and Temple of Piety at Studley Royal, near Ripon, North Yorkshire, with a long narrow canal in front – a lovely example of early formal landscaping, laid out between 1720 and 1724 *(Arthur Hellyer).* *Below,* by 1744 landscape had become less stylized and more romantic, as at Stourhead, near Mere, Wiltshire: here the Temple of Apollo, or the Sun, is seen perched high up above the Stone Bridge near the present-day entrance, beyond which the main lake opens up *(Harry Smith Collection).*

Remaining examples of Chinese influence or Chinoiserie are mainly in the form of buildings. *Above,* Sir William Chambers' Pagoda of 1761 at the Royal Botanic Gardens, Kew, Surrey, framed by the heather collection *(Arthur Hellyer). Below,* the aviary at Dropmore, near Maidenhead, Buckinghamshire, probably constructed early in the nineteenth century, combines pierced green faience tiles with red-painted ironwork, and is an important feature of the formal part of the garden *(Harry Smith Collection).*

Facing, the lake at Dropmore, Buckinghamshire, is surrounded by the fine trees of the arboretum started in 1795 by Lord Grenville, one of the first in Britain *(Valerie Finnis). Above,* bedding in Victorian style re-created at Bicton, near Exmouth, Devon *(Iris Hardwick Library). Below,* the romantic fourteenth-century moated tower at Scotney Castle, Lamberhurst, Kent, framed by trees and flowering shrubs, is the focal point of a garden in the Picturesque tradition, started in 1836 *(Arthur Hellyer).*

Herbaceous borders in the great tradition. *Above,* wide double borders at Arley Hall, Northwich, Cheshire, laid out about 1846, and thus possibly the earliest of their kind, though the planting today is largely of self-supporting plants and includes annuals and biennials *(Harry Smith Collection). Below,* planting mainly in muted colourings at Crathes Castle, Banchory, Grampian, begun in 1932, where the narrowness of the central grass walk gives an entirely different effect *(Arthur Hellyer).*

In the naturalistic woodland garden, flowering trees and shrubs grow under the sheltering canopy of established native trees in thinned-out woodland. *Above,* exotic rhododendrons and azaleas among beeches provide the main spring display at Leonardslee, near Horsham, Sussex, a garden in a steep-sided valley containing hammer ponds, started in 1888. *Below,* azaleas and flowering dogwoods create a similar impression at the National Arboretum, Washington D.C., U.S.A., begun in 1927 *(both Arthur Hellyer).*

Above, the great sandstone rock garden in the Royal Horticultural Society's garden at Wisley, Surrey, with many small pools and cascades among the massive rocks carefully aligned to resemble natural strata, was made in 1916. *Below,* late spring in a modern small garden in cottage style, made on a series of low terraces on a sloping site, with an artless profusion of colourful, easily grown plants merging into each other; climbing roses cover the walls of the house *(both Harry Smith Collection).*

Above, Hestercombe, Chester Fitzpaine, Somerset, has been described as the most successful collaboration of garden designer Gertrude Jekyll and architect Edwin Lutyens, and typifies the so-called Surrey School. Finished in 1910, it has recently been restored to its original state *(Iris Hardwick Library).* *Below,* though laid out in 1926, Lyegrove, near Badminton, Gloucestershire, may be considered Edwardian with its many architectural features and its plantings clearly influenced by Gertrude Jekyll *(Arthur Hellyer).*

Water gardening in elaborate style. *Above,* the water parterre at Blenheim Palace, Woodstock, Oxford, a most original design of the 1920s which reaffirms the formality of Vanbrugh's original parterres of the early eighteenth century *(Jeremy Whitaker, courtesy of His Grace the Duke of Marlborough). Below,* the Pebble Garden at Dumbarton Oaks, Washington D.C., U.S.A., where a mosaic shallowly overlaid with water creates ever-changing reflections, was also made between the World Wars *(Harry Smith Collection).*

Above, the view from the tower at Sissinghurst Castle, near Cranbrook, Kent, clearly shows the concept of the garden – started from wilderness in 1930 – as a series of small room-like enclosures in Tudor fashion, in keeping with the remains of the brick-built Elizabethan house *(Arthur Hellyer)*. *Below,* labour-saving, ground-covering planting of heathers and conifers at Great Comp, Borough Green, Kent, a seven-acre garden begun in 1957 and maintained entirely by its two owners *(Harry Smith Collection)*.

Above, the Japanese idiom as translated by a Western designer on the 'Oriental American Garden' at Bellingrath, near Mobile, Alabama, U.S.A., a layout with many individual features, developed from semi-tropical jungle and started in 1927. *Below*, the smallest modern town gardens are nothing more than paved outdoor rooms with high walls or fences. In this Chelsea Show display garden, raised planting beds are edged with brick and railway sleepers *(both Harry Smith Collection)*.

Above, concrete and cobbles feature in a post-war demonstration garden at Los Angeles State and County Arboretum, California, U.S.A. *(Harry Smith Collection). Below,* a modern land- and water-scape: buildings at York University, North Yorkshire, are arranged around a fourteen-acre lake created from marshy ground since 1950 *(Arthur Hellyer). Overleaf,* making the most of limited space: rhododendrons, azaleas and other shrubs in an ingeniously terraced post-war London garden *(Harry Smith Collection).*

the dormant or latent buds which exist at the base of side growths. It is particularly suitable for the more elaborate trained fruit trees but produces indifferent results if not carried out meticulously, and is now seldom practised.

Louvre Fence ⟡ FENCES.

Lute, Luting A lute is a useful but seldom seen implement (sometimes called a true lute) for working top dressings into grass, for filling hollows on lawns and for levelling soil. In its simplest form it consists of a piece of squared wood around 3′ long, fixed firmly at right angles to a long handle – rather like a rake without teeth. More elaborate versions consist of several parallel cross-pieces connected to side-pieces to form a grid about 2′ wide and 18″ long, with a pivoted link to the handle. In modern versions this grid is reversible, the cross-pieces on one side being smooth-edged for levelling and spreading operations, and on the other having a sharp edge which will rub materials into grass or produce a very fine tilth in soil. The use of a lute is called luting.

Maculate Spotted or speckled, on flowers or leaves.

Maggot The larva of a fly, usually white and most often legless, though active. Among those flies which are garden pests it is almost always the maggot that does the damage by burrowing into and feeding on plant tissues. In a few cases the maggots feed on pests, e.g. hover flies on aphids. ◊ FLY; PREDATORS.

Magnesian or **Magnesium Limestone** Derived from dolomitic limestone and containing up to 50 per cent magnesium carbonate as well as calcium carbonate. This is a useful dressing for acid soils which are also deficient in magnesium, and as a constituent of potting composts. ◊ LIMESTONE; MAGNESIUM.

Magnesium An element vital in producing chlorophyll, the green colouring matter of leaves; a serious deficiency of it can entirely stop plant growth. It is naturally found in dolomitic limestone rock, and also occurs in farmyard manure. Magnesium deficiency, which can occur in many plants, causes discoloured and dead areas between the leaf veins, and may cause young foliage to fall. It usually occurs on light, acid soils or where potassic fertilizers have been used to excess.

Although top dressing the soil with magnesium carbonate can be helpful, it will not necessarily cure the deficiency, especially in wet soils. Magnesium sulphate is better for this purpose, but here again application to the soil is not always successful and it is more efficacious when applied as a foliar feed, of which it is one of the standard constituents. Magnesium sulphate is usually obtained as Epsom Salt, which contains 10 per cent magnesium.

◊ FOLIAR FEEDING.

Magnesium Carbonate ◊ MAGNESIAN LIMESTONE; MAGNESIUM.

Magnesium Sulphate ◊ MAGNESIUM.

Maiden A tree or bush in its first year after grafting or budding, and before any formative pruning has been carried out. The word is mainly applied to fruit trees, but also to roses and sometimes to other trees and shrubs. The lateral growths are sometimes referred to as 'feathers' and advertisements may offer 'well-feathered maidens', meaning one-year fruit trees with plenty of side-growths. ◊ LATERAL; WHIP.

MAIDEN

Maintenance Pruning The systematic removal of branches from aged fruit trees which are in decline and not producing new young growth. This gradual cutting will remove old wood infected with diseases and pests and encourage the tree to form young wood. ◊ REJUVENATION PRUNING.

Male Flower Although technically parts of flowers have no sex (◊ FLOWER for fuller explanation), they are commonly described as having either or both sexes present. Many plants carry male and female flowers separately, and in some cases distinct plants may carry only male or only female flowers. Recognition of the different flowers is important where fruits are the desired object, as in growing marrows and cucumbers, and in ensuring that berries are formed on certain unisex ornamentals, where one male plant must be grown among several females. Recognition of male flowers and male parts of a flower is of course essential also to plant breeders. Male flowers carry pollen-bearing anthers only (though in some instances non-functional female organs may also be present) but are otherwise almost always similar to the female ones. Botanists will distinguish male forms of plants by the symbol ♂, and call the male part of the flower the androecium. ▷ BREEDING; FEMALE FLOWER; FLOWER.

Manganese An element essential to plant growth but only in minute quantities, hence one of the 'trace elements'. Its absence causes various deficiency symptoms, notably one in which small yellow patches appear between leaf veins which become bright green, resulting in a netted appearance; conversely, an excess can lead to poor root growth and consequent stunting. Manganese deficiency is usually dealt with by applying a dilute solution of manganese sulphate used as a foliar spray. This is a habitual constituent of foliar feeds. ▷ FOLIAR FEEDING; TRACE ELEMENTS.

Manganese Sulphate ▷ MANGANESE.

Manure One of the earliest meanings of this well-known word was 'to manoeuvre', of ships, etc., and one agricultural application was in terms of cultivating land and of training plants. Today the word refers only to enriching land with fertilizing materials, and to these materials themselves.

In principle, the noun covers any kind of material which supplies food to plants: including bulky ones (animal dung, decayed or otherwise processed animal remains, and decayed vegetable remains) and the non-bulky ones, often in dry form, which are more generally referred to as fertilizers, of either natural or synthetic origin. The bulky ones provide both food materials and humus which improve the texture of the soil, while the non-bulky ones usually provide food materials, with little effect on soil textures. A manurial or feeding programme can and should include both classes of material. Here, we deal only with manure in the narrow sense, i.e. animals' dung. Separate entries discuss COMPOST HEAP composed primarily of decaying vegetable matter, and non-bulky FERTILIZER.

Human excreta or 'night-soil' is seldom used for manure in Britain or the U.S. today, but it was used for agricultural purposes since Roman times, and is still so used in some countries like China. The nearest approach to it in Western countries now is sewage sludge.

The usual material available is farmyard manure, sometimes abbreviated FYM, which is cow, pig or horse dung mixed with the straw or other litter used in animal stalls to absorb the material. The amount of food value varies according to the animal concerned, the way it has been fed, the amount of litter involved, and the length of time the material has been stacked. In all cases, exposure to the elements rapidly lowers the level of plant food elements, especially nitrogen.

The average analysis of FYM is 0.5 per cent nitrogen, 0.25 per cent phosphates and 0.5 per cent potash, and it can be used at 10 to 15 lb. per square yard. Horse dung is usually the richest, then pig and cow dung. Horse dung is the driest, possibly the least unpleasant to deal with, and has the best effect on soil texture. It is also the best present-day material from which to form a hotbed, and the only animal manure really suitable for making mushroom beds. Pig and cow manure have a very close texture and are better used on light soils than on heavy ones. Cow manure has the great advantage that it dries out quite rapidly in the open and can then be crumbled up. In such a state it is valuable in potting mixtures, although it will have lost some of its food value to the air.

Another animal dung often available in quantity is poultry manure, which when fresh has an average analysis of 2.5 per cent

185

nitrogen, 1 per cent phosphates and 0.5 per cent potash. If dried, these proportions can rise to around 6 : 3 : 1.7. Pigeon manure is similar but richer in plant food, with an analysis as high as 14:11:4. These manures are best used after drying and mixing with twice their bulk of soil or dry sand, and applied as top dressing at up to 6 oz. per square yard.

Animal manures can be dug into vacant ground at any time of year, if fresh, but in principle it is best to allow them to rot somewhat first or they can render the soil over-acid and may affect roots adversely. Stacking of manure must be done under cover so that nutrients are not washed out by rain; it is also advisable to cover a manure stack with at least 6″ of soil, well beaten down. Poultry manure, even if fresh, can be used as a top dressing to growing plants without danger, at 2–4 oz. per square yard.

Liquid manure can be obtained by collecting the liquid seeping from cowsheds and cow or horse droppings stacked on a hard surface. At home, liquid manure is made by steeping animal manure, of whatever kind, in a small sack suspended in a container of water (e.g. a barrel or waterbutt), and using it as a liquid feed when it is a strawy colour. The manure must be already well rotted.

For other bulky materials of animal origin in addition to those described above ◊ BAT GUANO; FISH MANURES; GUANO; HAIR; MUSHROOM COMPOST; NIGHT SOIL; RABBIT DROPPINGS; SEWAGE SLUDGE; TOWN REFUSE.

For further animal materials ◊ BONE MANURES; HOOF AND HORN; LEATHER; MEAT GUANO or MEAL; URINE.

For organic materials of vegetable origin ◊ CASTOR MEAL; COMPOST HEAP; GREEN MANURING; HOPS, HOP MANURE; INDORE PROCESS; LEAF MOULD; RAPE CAKE or MEAL; SEAWEED; SHODDY; WOOD ASH.

For inorganic fertilizers ◊ FERTILIZER.

◊ FEEDING PLANTS; HUMUS; LIME; ORGANIC GARDENING; DRESSING.

Manure Drag A sharply bent, several-pronged tool used for pulling farmyard manure from animal stalls and yards. ◊ FORK.

Manure Fork A thin-pronged, slightly curved fork used for manhandling farmyard manure. ◊ FORK.

Marbled Of leaves and sometimes flowers streaked or mottled with a different colour from the main one.

Marcescent Withering without dropping; applied mainly to leaves of deciduous trees, e.g. beech, which retain their dry foliage in winter when young or when kept clipped as hedges. ◊ DECIDUOUS; JUVENILITY.

Marcottage, Marcotting Words of French origin for AIR LAYERING.

Margin The boundary or edge of any plant organ; most often applied to leaves.

Marginal (1) Applied to plants which grow either in shallow water or in moist soil and are thus planted around pool edges. ◊ POOL; WATER GARDEN.

(2) In botany, refers to organs or appendages arising from the margin of a leaf or other organ, e.g. marginal hairs.

Marker Plant A herbaceous plant of which some portion remains, or can be left, above ground in winter, and which may be used as a reminder of other nearby plants which entirely disappear when resting.

Marl A type of soil found in various localities, which contains a good deal of clay mingled with chalk. In itself a difficult soil to cultivate, it is sometimes used as a top-dressing on sandy and peaty soils, where its clay content adds body and helps to prevent erosion, and its chalk counteracts acidity. The practice of marling is ancient and may have been used by the Romans. Nowadays marl is most often used, finely sieved, as a topdressing for sports grounds, especially cricket pitches, since it binds the surface and helps to reduce wear.

Mary Garden A medieval enclosed garden with features of religious significance, probably depicted by artists more often than actually created. Mainly consisting of flower-spangled turf (a 'flowery mede') it also includes flowers and plants having Christian (especially Biblical) symbolism, in particular those connected with the Virgin Mary, e.g. the white Madonna lily. In its naturalness it may be considered a form of PARADISE GARDEN.

Mastic Sometimes used by gardeners to mean grafting wax and other substances used to cover the exposed surfaces created during GRAFTING.

Mat (1) Mats of various materials such as coir or rush can be used by gardeners to protect frames against frost; and coir or chain mats are among the implements used to work topdressing into turf by dragging them across lawns and sports-grounds. ⟡ COIR; TOP DRESSING.

(2) The word is sometimes used to refer to the layer of dead grass and debris likely to be found near soil level in a lawn of any age, which can be dispersed by raking. ⟡ LAWN; LAWN RAKE.

Mattock A tool for breaking up hard ground and grubbing up trees. It is similar to a pick axe, having like it a socketed metal head on one side of which is a pick-like point and on the other a chisel-like blade rather broader than that of the pick axe, both being at right angles to the relatively short, stout central handle.

The mattock proper is seldom seen to-day, but two similar tools are available. One is the grubbing axe, in which the pick is replaced by a blade in the same plane as the handle, which can thus be used as an axe. The grubbing mattock has blades half the length of the grubbing axe, one like an axe-blade, the other a relatively broad, strong chisel at right angles to the handle. It is valuable for getting into difficult corners among roots where the blades of the grubbing axe would be too long.

These tools are used from a stooping position with a chopping motion, like a digging hoe.

⟡ HOE.

Maze The maze – a layout of paths with numerous alternatives, dead-ends and confusing turnings – has its origins in antiquity, apparently for religious or magical purposes. In modern parlance, the word is virtually synonymous with labyrinth, but in older literature the labyrinth was either cavernous or three-dimensional, as when enclosed in hedges, while a maze was two-dimensional, made up of paths in turf so that one could see the whole. Such mazes certainly had ancient ritual significance. Both types played a part in garden design, the maze proper being one form of knot garden, but the hedge-maze (in which it is of course impossible to see the alternative pattern ahead) became by far the more popular and is to be found today in a number of gardens, old and new. ⟡ KNOT.

Meadow Gardening ⟡ ALPINE MEADOW.

Meal (1) A powder produced by grinding; many organic fertilizer materials are ground in this way so that they can be handled easily and are available to plants relatively quickly. Bone meal is an example. ⟡ FERTILIZER.

(2) A thin dusty or powdery layer on plant surfaces. ⟡ FARINA.

Mealy Bug Sap-sucking insects closely related to scale insects but more mobile, and protecting themselves not under a waxy scale but a coating of white, waxy 'meal'. Superficially they resemble minute woodlice, their actual bodies under the white 'meal' being pinkish. They are often troublesome pests, especially of greenhouse and house plants, since they get into leaf axils and other crevices where they look like tiny accumulations of cotton wool, easily overlooked in the early stages. In warm greenhouses and rooms mealy bugs breed continuously, with roughly 14 days between broods; spraying or fumigation with suitable insecticides should therefore be done at 14-day intervals. On plants like cacti the use of an artist's stiff paint brush, dipped into insecticide solution or methylated spirit, can ensure the removal of colonies from small crevices where their wool would protect them from a contact insecticide. 'Painting' can also be carried out on vines, or winter wash can be used in the dormant season; on these and similar woody plants loose bark should be removed first to destroy hiding places. ⟡ WOOLLY APHID.

Measures ⟡ WEIGHTS AND MEASURES (p. viii).

Measuring Rod A long piece of wood of square or oblong section (around 1″ minimum dimension) on which marks are made with paint or by burning at 3″ intervals, with larger marks every foot. A rod 8′–10′ long is valuable when planting vegetables or other plants at stated intervals in rows.

Meat and Bone Meal ⟡ BONE MANURES.

Meat Guano or **Meal** A fertilizer made by processing meat refuse into powder form. If made only from meat it is purely nitrogenous, providing up to 10 per cent nitrogen. However, manufacturers usually include ground bones, so that the analysis can include phosphoric acid in varying proportion. A meat and bone mixture can have an analysis around 6 per cent nitrogen and 20 per cent phosphorus, and also includes trace elements. Either product is relatively slow acting and can be used to add to potting composts, or for application to vacant ground at 2–4 oz. per square yard. ⟡ BONE MANURES.

Medium (1) Sometimes applied to a seed or potting compost or mixture, or to other materials in which plants may be grown or propagated in containers.

(2) Applied to soils of good average quality, as in the phrase 'a medium loam'.

(3) Applied to flowers of middling size, especially in chrysanthemum and dahlia classification, as opposed to large-flowered or (in dahlias) small-flowered varieties.

Mendelism The theory of inheritance published in 1866 by the Austrian monk, Abbé Gregor Mendel, following his experiments with edible peas. Although ignored at the time, the theory was rediscovered around 1900 and Abbé Mendel was then given due recognition for what are sometimes called Mendel's Laws, which refer to the ratios in which certain plant characters can be expected to occur when breeding is carried on from parents of dissimilar character. It was later shown that the character-bearing factors were carried in centres called genes which are spread along the microscopic chromosomes forming the vital part of the cell nuclei in all living organisms. Mendel provided the first satisfactory basis for the study of heredity, and the foundation for modern genetics and hence scientific plant breeding. ⟡ BREEDING; CHROMOSOME.

Mercury Compounds Mercury is a poisonous element used in a number of pest- and disease-controlling materials. These include mercurous chloride or calomel, used against onion and cabbage root fly maggots (now forbidden by E.E.C. regulations in Europe), club root disease and several diseases of lawn grass; and mercuric chloride or corrosive sublimate, a very toxic chemical now rarely used against club root and other diseases. More complex mercuric materials, known as organo-mercury compounds, are used against various diseases especially in turf, and as seed dressings against soil-borne fungi. ⟡ CALOMEL; FUNGICIDES.

Mericlone ⟡ MERISTEM.

Meristem The extreme tip of a stem or root in which active division of cells and hence growth are taking place. The importance of the meristem lies in a quite recently discovered technique in which the microscopic meristems (sometimes called apical cuttings) are removed and placed in phials of nutrient jelly (agar) which are constantly turned on a revolving wheel. They then develop numerous visible growing points which are periodically removed and grown on individually, first in agar, then in more orthodox potting materials. Because of the meristem's power of proliferation, thousands of identical plants can be produced from a single tip 'cutting'. The method has been used mainly with orchids, where the young plants are known as mericlones;

really good varieties can now be propagated quickly and in large numbers by this method, whereas in the past it would have taken decades to build up a stock.

Meristem culture has also proved invaluable in producing virus-free clones of plants as diverse as apples and carnations, the reason for the immunity being that virus diseases seldom get into the meristems, even when the rest of the plant is infected.
　◊ CLONE; VIRUS DISEASES.

Mesh Pot A plastic pot with large rectangular perforations all round, so that there is more aperture than pot, used in orchid culture in the same way as a slatted wooden basket.

MESH POT

Metabolism The process of growth and development based on the intake of food materials in any living organism; in plants this covers in particular the processes called PHOTOSYNTHESIS, RESPIRATION and TRANSPIRATION. The metabolism of each cell is controlled by the NUCLEUS.

Metaldehyde A chemical used as a molluscicide, i.e. against slugs and snails, which can be bought in bars or as a powder. It is usually sold as 'slug bait' in pellet form, mixed with either bran or some other material attractive to the pests; a liquid suspension to be diluted with water and watered onto the soil can also be obtained. Slug and snail killer can be made at home by mixing 1 oz. metaldehyde powder with 3lb. bran, oatmeal or bonemeal and, before use, adding enough water to soften the mix-

ture slightly. This bait is placed in small heaps where slugs or snails are suspected.

Metaldehyde is poisonous to children, birds and pets, and the bait should therefore be placed where they cannot reach it. If in open areas, the use of broken flowerpots, propped-up tiles, etc., will both serve this purpose and protect the bait from being washed away by rain.
　◊ SLUGS; SNAILS.

Methylated Spirit (In the U.S. known as denatured alcohol or spirit.) Used for localized control of mealy bugs and woolly aphids: colonies can be painted with a stiffish paintbrush dipped in the spirit. This procedure is particularly useful on plants such as cacti where the pests get into crevices which insecticide sprays do not penetrate. It is desirable to remove as many of the pests bodily as possible in the process, and to repeat the operation two or three times to ensure destruction of newly hatched young.

Mica ◊ VERMICULITE.

Mice These rodents and their relatives the voles can cause much damage in gardens, since they eat large seeds, seedlings, bulbs, corms and tubers. They can be combated with poisons, traps or repellents. Mouse poisons must be placed according to instructions and out of reach of children, birds and pets, and repellents should also be used as instructed. Trapping requires bait of fat, nuts, cheese or cooked dried peas, and is probably the best method to use in greenhouses. Protection can be given to pea and bean seeds and small bulbs and corms by moistening them with a very small amount of paraffin and then rolling them in red lead.

Microbial Insecticides ◊ ANTIBIOTICS.

Microclimate The environmental conditions of a specific limited area, whether in a particular geographical location (say to leeward of a mountain range), a particular garden or one corner of a garden. Local conditions often alter the overall climate of the country to either the advantage or disadvantage of plants growing there. Gardeners make use of obvious microclimates to suit different kinds of plant, e.g. a sunny sheltered wall will ripen exotic fruits and allow many relatively tender plants to thrive. The provision of screens can save plants from frost damage or prevent scorch due to cold winds funnelling through narrow passages, e.g. between houses, while in sloping gardens a judiciously placed opening in a solid wall can avoid frost pockets. The perspicacious gardener thus seeks out or provides favourable microclimates, and avoids or mitigates unfavourable ones. ⟡ FROST POCKET; SCREEN; WIND.

Midrib (1) The central vein of a leaf, often thick so that it projects below the undersurface, and a continuation of the leafstalk.

(2) The central stalk to which the leaflets of a pinnate leaf are attached.

⟡ LEAF.

Mildew Loosely applied to fungus diseases the symptoms of which are a powdery or hair-like growth, including moulds, on plant or animal material. There are two main groups of plant mildew diseases. The downy mildews are internal parasites, the greyish, downy patches they produce being only the spore-bearing reproductive organs The powdery mildews grow on exterior plant surfaces only, producing a powdery whitish appearance which includes the reproductive spore-bearing organ. Powdery mildews are in general much less harmful than downy mildews which penetrate deeply into plant tissue. Grey fluffy mould is caused by botrytis.

Broadly speaking, mildews are encouraged by damp conditions, especially if accentuated by cold. In greenhouses, ventilation on dry days, and maintaining a dry atmosphere, will reduce the likelihood of attack. Powdery mildews can be controlled by dusting with flowers of sulphur dust, and there are many more complex fungicides for both kinds, notably the systemic fungicides. The type of fungicide used sometimes depends on the plant attacked.

⟡ BLIGHT; BOTRYTIS; DISEASE; FUNGICIDES; SYSTEMIC.

Millepedes A name for a number of small animals which live in soil, under pots, etc., all having long, thin, hard-coated, segmented bodies, with two pairs of short legs per segment. Colouring is mainly black to grey, though some are brownish or pinkish; some kinds are round in section but some are flat, and most coil their bodies into a tight spiral when disturbed.

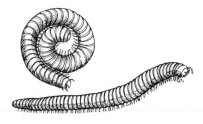

MILLEPEDE

Millepedes are partly scavengers which feed on decaying matter in the soil, but they do also attack plant roots, especially if they are already damaged, and can be serious pests of peas, beans and potatoes. For such crops one of the soil insecticide dusts recommended against millepedes should be sprinkled before planting seeds or tubers as a precaution. Such materials can also be worked into soil if the pests are seen in any numbers.

⟡ CENTIPEDE.

Miller A kind of cultivator based on rotating spiked wheels. ⟡ SOIL MILLER.

Mineral Any natural inorganic substance, including the basic elements needed for plant growth and their salts, the form in which they are supplied for plant nutrition. A mineral soil is one containing little organic matter. ⟡ FEEDING PLANTS; SOIL.

Mineral Deficiency Ill-health or even death may result if a plant is unable to obtain any of a number of mineral elements, and such ill-health shows up in a recognizable set of symptoms. ◊ DEFICIENCY.

Miniature Gardens The present trends towards very small gardens or flat dwelling has inevitably increased the interest in gardening on a miniature scale. Such small-scale gardening can be carried out in an actual garden plot, or in containers, the latter being essential when space is restricted to a balcony, roof garden, or even a windowsill. Most people consider a miniature garden as being made only in a shallow sink, trough or similar container. ◊ BOWL GARDEN; PATIO; ROOF GARDEN.

Mister ◊ MIST-SPRAYER.

Mist Propagation A specialized method of rooting cuttings, enabling this propagation to be carried out in the open greenhouse without the usual need for covering the area in such a way as to maintain a close, humid atmosphere. Wilting of the cuttings due to loss of moisture through the leaves is avoided by providing a mist-like spray of water at fairly frequent intervals. Although this can be done on a timed basis, the best

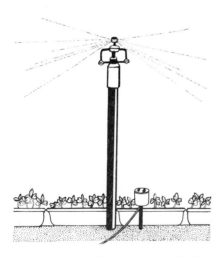

MIST PROPAGATION. *Left*, mist-spray head; *right*, electronic leaf

methods employ a system in which the evaporation of the water spray and the consequent beginning of dryness trigger off the sprayer. This can be done mechanically by a balance device in which a water-absorbent pad, or a water-holding pan, becomes lighter as evaporation proceeds, and thus operates the trigger. More usually, an electrical system is used, incorporating an 'electronic leaf' with two electrodes on its upper surface. If there is a film of moisture between these a current is maintained; when this film dries out the breaking of the current operates a switch which turns the mist-sprayer on. The latter is mounted on a short vertical pipe connected to a water supply. The method can be combined with advantage to some method of soil warming under the bed of rooting compound.

Mist propagation keeps the cuttings constantly damp while not waterlogging the rooting medium. The latter should be very porous, consisting of coarse sand, perlite or vermiculite alone, or a mixture of sand and peat.

◊ CUTTING; PERLITE; SOIL WARMING; VERMICULITE.

Mist-sprayer Although most garden sprayers can be adjusted to produce a mist-like spray, the device known as a mist-sprayer or mister is primarily used to deliver a very fine mist of water above and around house plants in order to provide a humid atmosphere in their immediate vicinity without wetting adjacent furnishings. Such sprays are usually quite small; they can be pre-pressurized and operated by a trigger control, or be manually pumped. ◊ HOUSE PLANT; HUMIDITY.

Mites Tiny animals of the order *Acarina*, closely related to spiders and, like them, having eight legs, not six as in insects. They include several families, the most important being the spider mites (family *Tetranychidae*) and tarsonemid mites (family *Tarsonemidae*); among them they include some very serious sap-sucking plant pests, especially harmful in greenhouses and on house plants, and are so small that their presence may be unsuspected until considerable damage has been done.

The commonest group is that of spider mites, the usual pest being known as red spider mite (in U.S., European red mite), which attacks a wide range of plants. These are barely visible to the naked eye but can be clearly seen under an ordinary magnifying glass. The mites can be reddish or green and their larvae are whitish to flesh-coloured. Among them translucent eggs will also be visible. In severe attacks a very fine silken webbing on the underside of leaves, often joining leaves, stems and flowers, is clearly visible. Any plants showing overall leaf mottling and yellowing should be examined for these pests and an appropriate insecticide applied, or fumigation given. Unfortunately, red spider mites soon develop an immunity to an individual insecticide so that different materials should be used in rotation. They thrive in a hot dry atmosphere and so are often found on house plants. Frequent spraying with water and, in greenhouses, maintenance of a humid atmosphere will discourage them. On fruit trees overwintering mites can be killed with winter washes, a suitable grade of which is also used against the similar spruce mite, which attacks various conifers, before spring growth begins.

The glasshouse red spider mite is one of the pests which can be dealt with effectively by biological control, by introducing a predator.

The tarsonemid mites are very much smaller, causing distortion of foliage, which becomes brittle and scabby, and withering of flower buds, e.g. on cyclamens and strawberries; the bulb scale mites cause reddening of bulbs and foliage and, in severe cases, distortion and wilting of leaves and flower stems. They are much more difficult to control chemically but hot-water treatment is often used on a commercial scale.

The small bulb-scale mite is a severe pest of forced narcissus bulbs, causing severe overall distortion, and of hippeastrums (amaryllis), where reddish discoloration is followed by distortion of leaves and flower stems. Hot-water treatment will destroy the mites, and commercial growers can use a drench of the pesticide endosulfan.

Bulb mites are distinct (family *Tyroglyphidae*), and are rather larger (visible to the naked eye), colourless, glistening creatures which usually invade bulbs, corms and tubers already damaged or attacked by other pests or diseases. Once established, they can rapidly reduce bulbs to pulp. Hotwater treatment is the only remedy if bulbs are not already beyond recall, but certain pesticides will reduce the scale of attack. The same family includes the mushroom mites, some of which cause pitting and hollowing of the developing mushrooms, and others browning and withering of the stalks. Pasteurization of the mushroom compost succeeds against the first, but the second type need chemical treatment.

Gall mites resemble tiny worms rather than spiders. They enter plant tissues and cause galls to form as they feed. In the U.K. big bud of currants, which causes buds to shrivel, is caused by a gall mite, and a few other gall mites cause unsightly galls on hazel, yew and broom. In the U.S. a number of gall mites affect plants as diverse as citrus, maple and tomato. Treatment varies according to the plant concerned, and includes application of winter washes (dormant oils) and certain pesticides.

Mite-killing chemicals are known as acaricides.

◊ BIOLOGICAL CONTROL; HOT-WATER TREATMENT; PESTICIDES; WINTER WASH.

Mixed Border ◊ HERBACEOUS BORDER.

Mixture A word often used, especially in the U.S., for media for plant propagation and growing; in Britain these are more often called composts. ◊ COMPOSTS, SEED and POTTING.

Moat Originally a deep, wide ditch surrounding a house, castle or township, usually filled with water, as part of fortifications; but in the Middle Ages it also referred to a lake or pond, especially a fishpond. By 1618 the gardening author Lawson was suggesting the use of hitherto defensive moats, and also those used to hold the surplus water resulting in a high water-table, as fishponds to provide additionally swans, waterbirds and boating; and depictions of gardens even earlier show that the decorative possibilities of moats were seized upon once the need for defence had passed. Remains of moats still form part of several European gardens today.

Moisture Meter An electrical device to indicate the amount of moisture in soil. A long probe is inserted into the soil and the moisture content is recorded on a calibrated dial, or in simpler versions by lighting up small bulbs or making a buzz of varying tone.

Moles These burrowing mammals can often cause much damage in gardens because of their tunnels, which result in collapse of the ground above or can cause disturbance and drying out of roots, and their mounds thrown up on lawns and in beds. Moles do eat worms, insects and other soil animals, many of which are pests, but the damage they do usually outweighs these benefits.

Moles can be dealt with by repellents, traps, poison or gassing. They are sensitive to untoward odours so that substances like commercial animal repellents, pepper dust, calcium carbide or mothballs placed in their tunnels or runs tend to drive them away. Mole traps can be obtained to be set in the runs, which must be disturbed as little as possible and from which light must be excluded; it is desirable to wear gloves when setting them to prevent the moles scenting human touch. Worms dusted with strychnine will poison the moles but this results in a painful death. Finally, gassing can be carried out with proprietary mole-killing smoke generators or fusées (containing sulphur) placed in the runs and ignited. These are less effective in sandy soils than in heavier ones. An alternative is to connect the end of a rubber pipe to the exhaust of a motor-driven cultivator, mower or car, place the other end in the tunnel and run the engine for a time. The carbon monoxide thus produced will destroy moles in the vicinity.

To deter moles entering a specific area, e.g. a seedbed, various barriers can be used. In each case a narrow trench is dug to a depth of about 6″. Mothballs placed in this 3″–4″ apart are a deterrent. Pieces of gorse or other prickly shrub or fallen holly leaves placed in the trench form an effective barrier. However, the planting of caper spurge (*Euphorbia lathyris*), often recommended, has been shown to be quite ineffective.

◊ REPELLENTS; SMOKE GENERATORS.

Molluscicide A material for killing molluscs in the garden, i.e. slugs and snails.
◊ PESTICIDES; SLUGS.

Monocarpic This term, literally meaning once-fruiting, describes plants which die after fruiting, but take a variable time to reach flowering age. It is not normally applied to annuals, but to rosette-forming plants which grow from year to year in a vegetative state until they flower, fruit and die. Before so doing they often produce offsets around the flowering rosette. The so-called century plant, *Agave americana*, is an excellent example; it may take 50 years (or more or less) before it blooms. Most of the bromeliads (e.g. billbergia, vriesia, aechmea) are monocarpic, as are some rosette-forming alpines such as houseleeks (sempervivums) and saxifrages like *Saxifraga longifolia*. The word should not be confused with the botanical term monocarpous, seldom encountered in gardening, meaning an ovary of a single carpel.

Monocotyledon A plant whose seedlings have a single cotyledon or seed-leaf, usually like the adult leaf, in contrast with the pair produced by dicotyledons; the monocotyledons (often abbreviated monocots) are therefore one of the two great classes of flowering plants. Other distinguishing features include leaves with parallel as opposed to netted veins, flowers with parts in threes, and a distinctive stem anatomy, although there are exceptions to these characters. All true bulbous plants and

most of those producing corms are mono-
cots, as are orchids, bromeliads and palms.
◊ CLASSIFICATION; DICOTYLEDON; FLO-
WER.

Monoecious A species described as monoecious has two types of flower, all-male
and all-female, on the same plant. These
flowers may look superficially similar or be
quite different. Common examples are
sweet corn (or maize), hazel and pines. ◊
DIOECIOUS; HERMAPHRODITE.

Monopodial Applied to stems which continue to develop indefinitely from a single
growing point, very seldom branching;
usually referring to orchids. ◊ SYMPO-
DIAL.

Monotypic A genus which includes only
one species. ◊ CLASSIFICATION.

Monstrous Applied to plants showing
some abnormality, especially if this leads to
forms prized by gardeners or collectors.
Examples include cresting or cristation in
cacti, a few other succulents, ferns, and in
the flowers of the cockscomb (celosia); the
huge terminal flower in foxgloves which
is, unusually, heritable through seed (an
example of peloria); and the production of
numerous small flowers around a normally
isolated one (proliferation). Where monstrous forms like cristates can be multi-
plied, they may be given the varietal name
monstrosus. The study of such abnormalities is called teratology. ◊ CRISTATE;
PELORIA; PROLIFERATION; TERATOLOGY.

Moraine In nature a moraine is the accu-
mulation of rocky debris, sand, silt, etc., at
the snout or sides of a glacier, which has
been produced by the grinding action of the
glacier on the bedrock. Moraines which
have become reasonably stabilized have a
characteristic flora of plants which enjoy
very good drainage, and a root-run with
maximum aeration and a minimum of
humus. Despite their extreme porosity,
moraines are usually damp when melting
snow above provides ample moisture. The
typical plants of moraines form tight

cushions or rosettes with long tap roots.

These conditions can be imitated in a
garden by the provision of specially constructed beds. The ideal is on a slightly
sloping site. The area of the moraine
should first be dug out to a depth of 3′. A
layer of coarse drainage material about 1′
deep is placed at the bottom, if possible
covered with inverted turves to prevent the
finer upper layer from working down. If
turves are not available, the upper part of
the drainage layer should be of progressively smaller stones and gravel.

The upper layer is about 2′ deep, and will
vary in content according to the plants to
be grown. A good general-purpose mixture
contains 10 parts (by bulk) coarse stone
chippings (limestone or granite, according
to the alkalinity or acidity preferred by the
plants), 1 part good loam, 1 part peat and 1
part coarse sand; much more loam can be
included. Arrangements for watering from
below are often included in the form of a
metal or plastic pipe with very small, quite
widely spaced holes, buried about 1′
down, linked at the top with a piped water
supply or having an inlet into which water
can be poured from a can. This subterranean watering should be used mainly in
hot weather. Rocks can be embedded in the
surface of the moraine bed.

Where the bed has to be built on the
level, its area is first dug out to a little over
2′ deep, with sides sloping slightly towards
the centre. The lower third or quarter of
this depression should be made watertight with concrete or by puddling with
clay. The bed is then filled as for the sloping
bed, the coarse drainage layer being 6″–9″
deep. A watering pipe may be embedded
as before, although in both cases overhead
watering with a fine spray can be carried
out.

The scree garden represents a very similar bed, but a scree is basically drier and
has no underground watering system. ◊
SCREE.

Mortar Rubble Many older gardening
books recommend adding mortar rubble to
potting composts instead of other forms of
lime, since it provides aeration as well, but

it is not a widely available material today. In theory, mortar rubble combines mild lime, sand, grit and sometimes fine gravel. Residues of plaster should be avoided.

Mosaic A word to describe the characteristic symptom of various virus diseases, which is a mottled or marbled effect of paler green to yellow on the normal green of the leaf. Some mosaic diseases, however, produce streaking, mainly on the long narrow leaves of monocotyledons, e.g. daffodils and lilies. Distortion and stunting of leaves may also occur. In most cases mosaic viruses, like the other forms of virus, are extremely harmful, but in a few they hardly affect the plant and the resulting pattern of yellow or white mottling is attractive enough for infected plants to be grown ornamentally. A familiar example is *Abutilon pictum* 'Thompsonii'. ◊ VIRUS DISEASES.

Moss Mosses are primitive plants which form a large section of the vegetable kingdom, the order *Musci* which is part of the division *Bryophyta* which includes the liverworts. The mosses are extremely numerous and occupy many diverse habitats, being in particular the dominant vegetation of acid bogs and of alpine and arctic regions. Mosses have simple stems and leaves but no true roots; they prefer moist conditions but there are some which thrive in the dry, and are often found in shady places.

The typical bog moss is sphagnum, which has an amazing capacity for retaining moisture. It is made use of in a live state in certain specialized potting composts (as for orchids), for lining wire hanging baskets, making moss poles and in floristry. The remains of sphagnum moss in bog deposits create sphagnum peat, a particularly valuable form.

Certain other mosses are very attractive, but they are only normally encouraged in some kinds of Japanese garden. In general, mosses are unwelcome in the garden and greenhouse, forming a thick cover on moist soils and pot surfaces, slippery growth on paths, and in particular invading lawns.

On paths calomel, permanganate of potash, sulphate of iron, dichlorophen and specially formulated tar oil will kill moss, or it can be removed by scraping or by stiff brushing. On moist soils it has to be scraped away if necessary, and the same applies to growth on pots and seed containers, where it can choke seedlings and small plants. Because moss can actually prevent germination of small seeds, such containers are best kept in darkness until germination occurs, especially with slow-germinating kinds. After removing moss on pots, etc., the container should be topped up with potting compost, coarse sand or small stone chippings.

Moss invasion of lawns is usually due to poor soil quality and lack of feeding. Badly drained soil (especially where consolidated by much traffic) and shade will encourage moss. Proprietary moss killers or a lawn sand can be used, in conjunction with the use of a spring rake or similar tool, but moss will return if the overall conditions are not improved. This usually means aeration with a garden fork or lawn spiker, the application of a top dressing containing humus, and regular feeding thereafter. It should be noted that hormone or selective lawn weedkillers will not kill moss and may encourage it by leaving gaps the moss can colonize.

◊ AERATION; JAPANESE GARDEN; LAWN; LAWN SAND; MOSS POLE; PEAT; SPHAGNUM; TOP DRESSING.

Moss House A rustic garden building occasionally made in Victorian times, built of wood and usually having a portico or canopy. The interior walls were formed of wood slats, into which were pressed mosses collected from the countryside. Presumably these were regularly moistened to ensure continued growth and the eventual covering of the slats with moss.

Moss Pole Either a wooden pole covered with sphagnum moss tied in place with fine wire, or a cylinder of wire netting tightly packed with sphagnum. This is 'planted' into a pot alongside a climbing plant with a propensity for making aerial roots, such as a philodendron; if the moss is kept moist the roots fix themselves in it, giving support and added water to the plant. Some modern 'moss poles' are made of polystyrene fixed around a plastic pole. ◊ AERIAL ROOT; SPHAGNUM.

Mother Plant or Tree A selected plant or tree used exclusively for the provision of propagating material. Mainly used of fruit trees where the mother has been specially raised to ensure virus-free scions for grafting. ◊ NUCLEAR STOCK; SCION; VIRUS DISEASES.

Moths Insects closely related to butterflies, usually distinguishable because when at rest the wings are folded down horizontally, not vertically, while in British species the antennae are never clubbed at the end, whereas those of butterflies are. In many moths the antennae are feathery. Moths fly mostly at night, when they are attracted to lights. Adult moths are harmless apart from laying eggs, but all have a caterpillar stage before pupating and final metamorphosis into adult insect, and many of their caterpillars are harmful pests. ◊ CATER-PILLARS; GREASE BANDING.

Mould (1) An old word for soil, especially that rich in humus and well textured for easy cultivation; also refers to products of decay suitable for adding to soil, like leaf mould; vegetable mould is a term, now seldom used, meaning soil containing much organic matter. ◊ HUMUS; LEAF MOULD.
(2) Fungi producing powdery or fluffy growths on infected materials and plant tissues, such as grey mould and tomato leaf mould. Moulds of this sort are likely to attack bulbs, fruit and roots in store if these have been damaged or the conditions are too moist and poorly ventilated. ◊ DISEASE; FUNGUS.

Mound Layering ◊ LAYERING.

Mount An artificial hill within a garden, made in European gardens, especially in Britain, from the fourteenth century up to about 1720. Mounts also featured in one or two North American gardens. Although some authorities consider that garden mounts have a sacred origin or are descended from the artificial tree-planted hills of the ancient Middle East (like the hanging gardens of Babylon), there is little doubt that they were nothing more than viewpoints from which to look over the surrounding countryside at a period when estates and gardens were still protected by high walls against marauders. Mounts could be square or circular, sometimes with spiral ramps, more often with one or more stairways going up the sides; they would usually terminate in a flat viewing terrace and might have an arbour, pleasure house or banqueting house on top, or occasionally a mock temple. Mounts could be isolated or placed against an outer wall, and of course permitted views onto the garden itself, especially important during a period when knot gardens – designed to be seen from above – were popular. In a few gardens the mount is replaced by 'viewing terraces', usually built against a very high outer wall in tiers, or sometimes taking the form of a relatively low, narrow, raised walk across the garden layout. ◊ KNOT.

Mouse-ear ◊ BUD STAGES.

Mouth Sometimes used to refer to the open end of any bell-shaped, trumpet-shaped or tubular flower. ◊ FLOWER; THROAT.

Mowers The usual term for a lawn mowing machine. The first mower, invented in 1830 by an engineer called Edwin Budding who adapted it from a device used to trim the nap of cloth, was of the cylinder type (occasionally known as a reel mower) in which a number of blades, spiralled lengthwise to form an open cylinder, work against a fixed blade, the grass leaves being trapped between the latter and the sharpened blades of the spirals. A development of the cylinder mower, known as the Archimedean, had a single, large, curved blade, but is now extinct. In principle, the fewer the blades the tougher the grass that can be cut: some simple mowers have only four, giving around 25 cuts per yard. At the other end of the scale, the more blades – and the faster they rotate – the better the finish will be on fine lawns: for bowling greens, for instance, mowers with 10 blades can give 130 cuts per yard. Cylinder mowers can have wheels at the sides (side-wheel mowers) or a relatively large rear roller which provides the traction; side-wheel mowers are more convenient for small lawns and rough grass, but they cannot cut over lawn edges.

Cylinder mowers can be hand-propelled or be power-operated, the power source either only turning the cylinder or propelling the machine forward as well. Power can be provided by petrol engine or electric motor, and with the latter there is a choice of power source from the mains via a cable, or from a rechargeable battery.

In recent years power drive, both petrol and electric, has made possible mowers of quite different type, in which a horizontal blade spins below a safety hood. This is formed from a single flat bar, often hardly sharpened at all since it relies on its speed to sever the grass blades. Although the finish from rotary mowers is inferior to that from cylinder types, the recent introduction of a rear roller to such mowers has made it possible to produce the familiar 'banded' finish of a cylinder mower. More expensive rotary mowers, as they are known, are fitted with grass collectors. Rotary mowers without this facility tend to spread weeds (by seed) and encourage moss. The rotary mower has itself been developed further by application of the air-cushioning hovercraft principle: these machines have no wheels but float just above soil level, and can thus be moved, in any direction and with little trouble, over undulating ground and banks. Danger to the operator's feet is, however, even more pronounced than with ordinary rotaries.

The final development of the modern mower is the 'ride-on', in which a seat on top of the machine (almost always a rotary type) enables the operator to carry out mowing without walking behind it, specially valuable for large areas.

For coarse grass, various rough grass cutters are available, including the power scythe or sicklebar, operating on the same principle as a reciprocating hedge trimmer with one set of small triangular blades working against a fixed one. The flail machine has small, hinged rotating blades. The spin-trimmer operates on the same principle, with a short length of nylon line rotating at high speed, and is capable of getting into awkward corners.

⟡ LAWN; MOWING; SCYTHE; SPIN TRIM-MER.

Mowing The act of cutting a crop; in gardens, restricted to the cutting of lawns. This was carried out with scythes until 1830 when the cylinder lawn mower was invented. A good lawn of fine turf may need cutting two or even three times a week, although this presupposes a high standard of feeding and upkeep; but in the growing season any lawn will need mowing at least once a week. Apart from keeping the grass to a convenient height which does not hold dew or rain over-long, mowing has an improving effect upon lawns, tending to eliminate coarse grasses in favour of finer ones and tall strong weeds in favour of low-growing or flat rosette-forming ones.

In principle the first cut of the season is given with the mower blades set at $\frac{3}{4}''$–$1''$ above soil level; this is steadily reduced to give a normal cut at around $\frac{1}{2}''$ for finer grasses, or even less for bowling greens; but lawns of relatively coarse grass carrying much traffic (used for ball games, etc.) can be left at $\frac{3}{4}''$–$1''$. Lawns cut too hard will develop bare patches if not adequately fed and watered. In autumn the cutting level should be gradually raised. If the grass grows in winter, it may be desirable to mow it once or twice.

It is normal to collect the grass clippings or mowings in a box or bag on the mower (after which they should be composted), but there are advantages in letting these remain, especially in hot summer weather, since they have a slight mulching and feeding effect which counteracts sun scorch. If the mowings are long, however, they can smother the grass, causing decay and, eventually, bare patches.

A lawn is best mown by making continuous 'passes' first in one direction, then in the reverse direction, the second cut marginally overlapping the first. With a good mower this produces the prized 'banding' or striped effect which results from the grass being flattened first one way, then the other. Ideally, the direction of mowing should be changed to one at right angles each time the lawn is cut. Mowing is best carried out when the grass is dry, although rotary mowers deal readily with wet grass.
◊ LAWN; MOWERS.

Mowrah Meal A mealy substance obtained as a by-product of grinding the oil-rich seeds of a tropical tree (*Madhuca*), which is lethal to worms. For this purpose it is sprinkled onto lawns and thoroughly watered in; the worms come to the surface and die, after which they must be swept up. Mowrah meal is less often used today since there are chemicals like chlordane which will kill worms without their coming to the surface. ◊ EARTHWORMS.

Muck and Mystery The unkind description of the organic school of gardening which believes in the use of only natural materials like compost and animal manure to enrich soil as opposed to inorganic fertilizers of any kind, and also in the avoidance of all synthetic pesticides and fungicides. One branch of this school, now largely extinct, believes further in never cultivating the soil.
◊ FERTILIZER; MANURE; NO-DIGGING; ORGANIC.

Mucronate, Mucronulate A botanical term, mucronate is usually applied to leaves, meaning ending abruptly in a short, stiff point. Mucronulate, which is scarcely different, is defined as ending in a small, sharp point. Both words have been used to formulate specific names. ◊ LEAF.

Mughal Gardens Gardens created in India by the Mughal (or Mughul or Mogul) invaders from Persia, from the Emperor Babur (reigned 1508–30) to Aurangzib (1658–1707). Such gardens, which derive from the Persian 'paradise garden', are invariably based on water and fountains, often in long narrow canal-like basins, and utilizing sloped water-chutes called 'chadars', carved to create a pattern in the water, whenever there is a change of level. On the flat, water parterres are occasionally a feature. They are almost totally formal in conception, with pavilions of various shapes and sizes and (in many) extensive lawns and flower beds. Wherever possible, shade trees such as the oriental plane are grown. Some of the gardens are the setting for tombs, like the Taj Mahal and Tomb of Akbar at Agra.

Mughal gardens resemble their contemporaries in Italy to a surprising extent but this is a case of independent, parallel evolution without any possibility of direct influence either way.
◊ FORMAL GARDEN; ITALIAN GARDEN; PARADISE GARDEN; PARTERRE; WATERWORKS.

Mulch Any appreciable top dressing applied to the soil is called a mulch. Mulches usually consist of fairly bulky organic materials such as strawy, partly decayed manure, chopped straw, grass mowings, mushroom compost, shredded bark, spent hops, peat or compost. They are applied partly as food material and partly to conserve soil moisture by reducing surface evaporation. The looser the material, the more it will prevent evaporation. At the same time mulches can smother weeds, and in fact avoid the need for hoeing. They also keep the soil surface cooler in summer, which encourages soil bacteria and deters certain pests.

Mulches have certain disadvantages: they absorb so much moisture that they can prevent light rain or watering from reaching the soil, so that if water must be given to the mulched plants it should be in good quantity. By the same token, the soil should be thoroughly moist before a mulch is applied. In winter the temperature above the mulch will be lower than that over bare soil. Strawberries mulched with straw are therefore often covered with the material if a frosty night threatens, and uncovered in the morning, to avoid frost damage to the blossom.

A fairly recent development in mulching is to use strips of black polythene sheet or aluminium foil. Though these do not add food to the soil they have all the other advantages of vegetable mulches and also, by absorbing or reflecting the sunlight, improve the growing conditions around plants. However, they are rather unsightly and so best confined to the vegetable garden. With such materials it is vital that the soil is thoroughly soaked before they are laid in place. Vegetables are planted by making cuts in the sheeting as required; where black plastic mulch is used over potatoes small slits must be made over the tubers when they have been set out, which can be much more shallowly than in normal practice.

Another non-organic mulch is of stones, preferably flat ones, a method first used by the Chinese many centuries ago, which is very successful and can produce an unusual decorative effect in the right place. Stones can also be combined with thick plastic sheeting for total weed control.

Multi-dibber A device for making num-

MULTI-DIBBER

erous small holes simultaneously, for seed sowing or pricking out seedlings. Such devices can be made at home by fixing small pieces of thin wooden dowel, regularly spaced, into a flat piece of wood of the right size to press onto the surface of a standard seed box or pan, fitted with a handle on the other side. ◊ PRICKING OUT; SEED SOWING.

Multigeneric Refers to plants created by hybridizing species or varieties belonging to more than two genera (the latter are called bigeneric or intergeneric). Such crosses are most common among orchids, where plants have been created from parents of four or even five genera which could not possibly meet in nature. The 'generic' name of such hybrids may be made up of parts of the names of the parents, e.g. *x Brassolaeliocattleya* is a hybrid between members of the genera *Brassavola*, *Laelia* and *Cattleya*. However, the modern recommendation is to create a new name with the ending *-ara*, as in *x Potinara* which is created by crossing members of the genera already cited and additionally *Sophronitis*. ◊ CLASSIFICATION; HYBRIDIZATION.

Muriate of Potash Potassium chloride, a fertilizer once much recommended for providing potash, since it is the cheapest and most concentrated potassium salt. Although still used as a component of balanced fertilizers, its use alone can harm plants, and an overdose will kill them because of the chlorine content. Its main value is for feeding fruit and other trees on soils deficient in potash, where it can safely be used at not more than 1 oz. per square yard at any time of year since its potash will not leach out of the soil. For other purposes, sulphate of potash is to be preferred.

Mushroom ◊ FAIRY RING; FUNGUS; MYCELIUM; SPAWN.

Mushroom Compost This material – more correctly *spent* mushroom compost – is sometimes available to gardeners from commercial growers. It is valuable to increase organic matter in soil or as a moisture-retaining mulch, since it is the result of composting straw either with horse manure or nitrogenous fertilizer; even after this process and its initial use it has considerable garden value. ◊ FERTILIZER; MULCH.

Mushroom Flies Several small flies, including sciarid and phorid flies, lay eggs in mushrooms, the resultant maggots burrowing into the stalks and caps and rendering them useless. They can be controlled by several insecticides.

Mutation A spontaneous variation from an original type. Mutations occur in all kinds of living organisms. In plants these variations must not be confused with those that arise from seed of hybrid origin: mutations are accidental changes in the genetical make-up of the plant, not to be produced by breeding, which can then be vegetatively increased or, if the plant is a species, will breed true. Any species or vegetatively increased variety maintains its characters by the replication of each of the numerous genes carried on its chromosomes; every now and then the mechanism may 'slip' and a gene be slightly altered, producing correspondingly different characters. Mutations tend to occur most frequently in highly bred plants, where the genetical mechanism is apparently unstable, as with the chrysanthemum, in which numerous colour forms of individual varieties arise, and sometimes changes of form, such as reflexed to incurved. The Spencer sweet pea is a form which arose as a mutation from older garden varieties, the Russell lupin likewise.

Gardeners call mutations 'sports' or sometimes 'breaks', the latter being mainly used by chrysanthemum growers when their flowers mutate to another colour, as they are prone to. These are called 'colour breaks'.

In some plants, including chrysanthemums, camellias and fruits, only a part of the plant may change: this is called a bud-mutation and must be carefully increased, if wanted, from the part affected only. One odd feature is that sometimes mutations of e.g. a chrysanthemum variety from red to pink may occur more or less simultaneously wherever it is grown. Something similar may have happened to the musk, which lost its scent all over the world about 1914. Mutations can be induced by chemicals such as colchicine or by bombardment with X-rays or atomic particles, and may perhaps occur in nature from the impact of cosmic particles.

Of course, gardeners preserve decorative or useful mutations. Mutations may be either beneficial or harmful: in nature, harmful ones will shortly perish, but beneficial ones or improvements will survive. Gene mutation is, in fact, the basic process of evolution – a series of infinitesimal jumps towards something better or more adapted to its surroundings.

◊ CHIMAERA; CHROMOSOME; ROGUE; VARIEGATED; WEEPING; WITCHES' BROOMS.

Mycelium The thread-like vegetative growth of a fungus. The individual threads are called hyphae and from them the fruiting organs bearing spores for dissemination are produced, ranging from the almost microscopic ones of disease organisms like moulds and mildews to the large 'fruit-bodies' which are normally called mushrooms or toadstools. The mycelium usually continues to live indefinitely while the fruit-bodies, etc., are transient. ◊ FUNGUS.

Mycology The scientific study of fungi; those who practise this science are mycologists. ◊ FUNGUS; PATHOLOGY.

Mycorrhiza ◊ SYMBIOSIS.

N

Naming of plants This topic is dealt with under CLASSIFICATION. As remarked there, colloquial names are of virtually no use for proper identification; not only are they often ambiguous or misleading, but they can overlap; not all plants gain colloquial names (despite the efforts of certain modern identification guide books to coin names for every wild flower covered); and they differ in every language. Therefore the Latin binomial system is used for all natural species.

When it comes to providing names for natural or man-made variants (varieties and cultivars, respectively), whether occurring as a result of mutation, hybridization, selection or other activity, certain rules have been in force since 1959 under the 'International Code of Nomenclature of Cultivated Plants'. Even for names bestowed before that date, certain criteria of printing are laid down (for use in academic works if not popular ones). These include the use of italic type for genus and species names and that of the Roman typeface for cultivar names, which should be set out in single quotation marks, as in *Syringa vulgaris* 'Mont Blanc', or be preceded with the abbreviation cv. Latinized names are not now admitted for man-made cultivars, but older Latinized names must obey the same rules, as in *Calluna vulgaris* 'Carnea'.

Cultivar names should consist of one or two, and never more than three, words. These can be names of people or places but should not include abbreviations, whether of Christian names, mountains, saints, etc., the only exception being the English 'Mrs'. Other possibilities for names include transliterations from foreign languages, as in *Prunus serrulata* 'Amanogawa', a transliteration into Roman from Japanese script; or translations, as in Savoy cabbage 'Ironhead', which is the same as the German 'Eisenkopf'.

Names likely to be confused with existing ones are not encouraged, nor are those which exaggerate a property of the cultivar, such as tomato 'Earliest of All'. All these and other recommendations, and details of publication and use of cultivar names, are set out in the 'International Code'.
◊ CLASSIFICATION.

Naphthalene A volatile chemical used to deter insects. It can be used to fumigate soil outside or in frames or greenhouses. In soil it can be dug in, or dropped into holes or narrow trenches, the rate being 2-6 oz. per square yard; or it can be used as a top-dressing at 1-2 oz. per square yard. It is also possible to volatilize the chemical in special appliances. It is used in flaked or finely powdered form. Naphthalene drives insects out of the treated area rather than killing them, though it can destroy them under some circumstances. It is now quite difficult to obtain naphthalene and it has been generally superseded by organic pesticides. ◊ COAL TAR; FUMIGATION.

National Growmore A balanced fertilizer made by various manufacturers to a formula recommended by the U.K. Ministry of Agriculture, providing an equal balance of nitrogen, phosphate and potash, usually in the proportion 7:7:7 though more concentrated forms are available. ◊ FERTILIZER.

Natural Break ◊ BREAK.

Naturalistic A word applied rather loosely to the planting of exotics in an informal, natural-seeming manner, often among large trees native to the country concerned which provide an initial setting for the exotics and also shelter them as they develop. It is primarily a twentieth-century development. ◊ NATURALIZATION; WILD GARDEN; WOODLAND GARDEN.

Naturalization A plant is botanically considered to have become naturalized when it can grow and reproduce itself in a country to which it is not native. The classic British example of such a plant is *Rhododendron ponticum*, originally introduced around 1763 from south-western Europe, which became very popular for game coverts, and has spread enormously by seed and suckering; and there are many more, including deliberate and accidental introductions, some of which have become weeds difficult to eradicate.

To naturalize a plant in a garden means to establish a group of it in a naturalistic setting with the aim of letting it grow and increase without attention. This is commonly done with bulbous plants, notably narcissi, in grass which is not cut before ther leaves have died down naturally; this can be done by planting or scattering seed.
◊ ALPINE MEADOW; NATURALISTIC; WEED.

Natural Order A group of related families, distinct from other such groups. Older authorities sometimes treat the term as designating a single family, but this is today an erroneous use. ◊ CLASSIFICATION.

Neck Applied to the upper part of a bulb where the leaves and flower stem enter the fleshy rounded part.

Neck Rot Loosely used to describe decay at the neck of a bulb, and more specifically of a fungus disease attacking onions and their relations, shallots and garlic. The symptoms are a soft rot which rapidly affects the whole bulb, sometimes accompanied by greyish mould on the exterior. There is no cure: the disease can be avoided be growing the bulbs without excessive nitrogen, by ripening them well, drying them before storage and ensuring that the store is dry and well ventilated.

Necrosis Literally, the state of death. Gardeners use the word to describe small dead areas on leaves caused by certain virus diseases; pedicel necrosis is applied to the often inexplicable withering of flower stems in plants like peonies and roses. The word is also sometimes used to describe cankers of woody plants. ◊ CANKER.

Nectar, Nectary A great number of plants have glandular tissues which secrete a sugary juice, virtually indistinguishable from honey, and sometimes known as nectar. When these are concentrated into a specific organ the latter are known as nectaries, and in some plants are housed in structures such as the spur of the columbine, the pocket-like cup at the base of buttercup petals, the small pits on tulip stamens, or the round cups at the base of crown imperial petals in which large drops of fluid are held in apparent defiance of the laws of gravity. However, in many other cases the nectary may be a large cushion of tissue, often towards the base of the flower, or the sweet secretion may be spread over undefined areas of petals, sepals and other floral parts. Nectaries can also occur on leaves or stems. In most cases the nectar is undoubtedly present to attract insects to the vicinity of the stamens so that pollen will be carried from flower to flower, but nectaries outside the flowers are probably more in the nature of glands secreting unwanted substances. ◊ GLAND.

Needle The stiff, narrow leaf of a conifer.
◊ CONIFER; PINE NEEDLES.

Nematicide A material for control of nematodes. ◊ EELWORMS; NEMATODE WORMS; PESTICIDES.

Nematode Worms Thin worm- or eel-shaped organisms, often placed in a distinct class of the animal kingdom. They include the microscopic eelworms which are usually serious plant parasites, and much larger types – up to $\frac{1}{2}''$ long – which feed on decaying matter and are found in garden compost and soil to which a lot of organic matter has been added before it has thoroughly decayed. Resembling pieces of white thread, and sometimes called horse-hair worms, these tend to twist around sharply when disturbed: they are not parasites. If many are found in soil, this is likely to signify poor cultivation and drainage. ◊ EELWORMS.

Nervation, Nerve Nervation is a botanical term meaning venation or the arrangement of the foliar veins; nerve refers to a single unbranched leaf vein or rib. ◊ LEAF; VEIN.

Nesting Pot ◊ POT.

Netted Refers to a pattern of veins or markings resembling a net; equivalent to reticulate.

Netting Various kinds of netting have many uses in the garden. These may be of twine, plastic, galvanized wire, or plastic-coated wire. The finer, flexible types are used to protect fruits and vegetables against birds, when the smallest size ($\frac{1}{2}''$ mesh) is essential. This protection-is best carried out in conjunction with a 'cage', usually called a fruit cage, in which the netting is supported in a tubular metal framework of the required size. Other sizes are $\frac{3}{4}''$, 1″ and 2″ mesh, which are used to support climbing plants, e.g. runner beans. Because of the stretchability of netting, a piece is not usually effectively as long as the length quoted in catalogues, which should be discounted by a quarter or a third; the width will not be affected.

Very fine mesh is available which can be used to shade greenhouses, to provide some frost protection for fruit trees or strawberries in flower, and as a windbreak. More protection can be given to tender plants by covering them with straw and then enveloping this in fine netting, either pegged to the ground or fixed to vertical supports.

Yet another use of netting is over ornamental pools as a deterrent to herons, when wide mesh is satisfactory, or to prevent leaves falling into the water in autumn. For this purpose, fairly fine mesh is used and it is best fixed to a wooden or metal framework to avoid sagging.

The semi-rigid plastic and plastic-coated wire nettings can also be used to support climbing plants and, if fixed to a wooden fence with staples, provide an excellent permanent support. Such netting is also valuable in greenhouses. Various colours are available to suit circumstances, in widths of 18″ or 36″. Semi-rigid netting can also be used to provide a semi-permanent fence if fixed to suitable vertical supports at intervals. Items like compost bins can be made from it, and a length bent into a hoop is useful to keep birds off germinating seedlings.

Galvanized wire netting can be obtained in many widths up to 6′. It is most commonly used as utility fencing, especially to keep out rabbits. For this purpose it is essential to bury the netting at least 6″ down, forming its base into an L shape so that another 6″ projects forward horizontally; 1″ or smaller mesh is best. Wire netting is not very attractive but it can be concealed at the back of a hedge to provide an almost impenetrable barrier, or can be overgrown with a suitable climber like an ivy as a 'fedge'.

◊ COMPOST; FEDGE; FROST PROTECTION; FRUIT CAGE; HEDGE; SHADING; WINDBREAK.

Neutral The point on the acidity–alkalinity scale (pH scale) at which soil or other material is neither acid nor alkaline: this is 7.0 on the scale. ◊ pH.

Niche A recess in a garden wall, often at the end of a vista, in which a statue, urn or stone vase is placed.

Nicking and Notching The removal of a small crescent or triangle of bark above a dormant bud will often stimulate it into growth, while the same operation below the bud, or the mere pressing of a knife into the wood there, will inhibit its growth. The former is often called notching and the latter nicking, though some authorities use the words indiscriminately. Instead of making a cut below a bud, it can be cut or rubbed out if growth is not required from it for some reason. Notching to promote growth of specific buds on fruit trees – perhaps wanted for formative purposes – is best done in early May. Such incisions, which act on only one bud at a time, do so by interfering with the upward or downward flow of sap and plant foods and of the auxins or hormones. ◊ BUD; HORMONES.

NICKING and NOTCHING

Nicotine An alkaloid poison derived from tobacco, with strong insecticidal properties. It can be formulated as a spray, dust or fumigant (the latter as 'fibre', 'shreds' to be lit, or a special compound to be vaporized) and is valuable against a wide range of pests. However, it owes much of its effectiveness to its volatility and is of progressively less value at temperatures below 18°C (64°F), so it cannot be used effectively out of doors in cold weather. It is often cited as a 'natural' product by the organic school of gardening, and hence to be used in preference to synthetic pesticides, but it is in fact toxic to human beings and other warm-blooded animals, though there is little danger in the concentrations below 7 per cent available to gardeners. However, its volatility ensures that crops sprayed with it can be eaten shortly afterwards, but always study the instructions.

Nicotine insecticide can be made at home by boiling cigarette ends. Place 4 oz. of untipped or 8 oz. filter-tipped ends in a gallon of water and boil for 30 minutes. The resultant liquid should be strained through a piece of muslin or an old nylon

stocking and placed in a stoppered bottle. One part nicotine with 2 parts water will destroy caterpillars and weevils, if watered on. For spraying, add 1 oz. soft soap or other 'spreader' to one quart of this solution. ◊ FUMIGATION; PESTICIDES.

Night Soil A polite term for human excreta, still used as a manure in some countries, e.g. China. ◊ MANURE.

Nitrate Any salt of nitric acid; these are high in nitrogen. Nitrates are produced naturally in soil by bacteria as they decompose organic matter in warm moist conditions; thus nitrate concentration is high during late spring and early summer, and often again in early autumn when plant absorption of nitrates decreases. Nitrates can be applied in the form of various compounds, notably nitrate of potash and of soda, and Nitro-chalk. Because they are readily leached (washed out) of soil, it is best to apply them in small quantities fairly frequently when nitrogen is required, unless the product is one of the slow-release fertilizers. Nitrate-containing fertilizers should not be mixed with superphosphate of lime. ◊ NITRATE OF POTASH; NITRATE OF SODA; NITRO-CHALK; NITROGEN.

Nitrate of Potash Also known as saltpetre, this ingredient of gunpowder contains both nitrogen (12–14 per cent) and potash (44–46 per cent). It is ideal as a liquid fertilizer when these substances are needed, diluted at $\frac{1}{2}$ oz. per gallon, or can be applied in dry form at $\frac{1}{2}$–1 oz. per square yard. However, it is usually considered too expensive for general use. Chilean nitrate or Chilean potash nitrate is a purified, cheaper form of saltpetre, containing 15 per cent nitrogen and 10 per cent potash, which can be used at 1–2 oz. per square yard. Saltpetre can be used for destroying TREE STUMPS.

Nitrate of Soda An impure form of sodium nitrate (having no connection with washing soda) containing 16 per cent nitrogen and some trace elements. It is very quick-acting and ensures quick growth of leaves and stems. Since it is very soluble, it is best applied just before sowing or planting or around growing plants, taking care neither to get it on foliage nor to use it too strong, which will scorch respectively leaves and roots. A rate of application of 1 oz. per square yard is adequate, or in water at $\frac{1}{4}-\frac{1}{2}$ oz. per gallon.

Nitro-chalk A commercial granular fertilizer containing ammonium nitrate and chalk, and $15\frac{1}{2}$ per cent available nitrogen. Because of its make-up, half the nitrogen is available as nitrate immediately on application, while the other half, in the form of ammonia, becomes available a little later, so that the product has a longer-lasting action than nitrate of soda. Its calcium content renders it specially valuable on acid soils. It is used at planting or sowing time or in the early stages of growth at 1 oz. per square yard.

Nitrogen One of the three main plant foods, in conjunction with phosphates and potash, always abbreviated N. Plants cannot make use of the gaseous nitrogen which forms nearly 80 per cent of the atmosphere, but mainly absorb the element in the form of nitrates through their roots, though some are capable of 'fixing' atmospheric nitrogen with the aid of symbiotic bacteria which live in nodules on their roots. Nitrogen is a builder of green tissue – leaves and stems; an excess can cause soft, sappy growth liable to collapse. However, plants vary considerably in their needs for nitrogen in respect of their growth cycle.

In most forms nitrogen is very soluble and is thus readily washed out of the soil. Light, sandy soils are often deficient in nitrogen. Nitrates are manufactured in most soils by bacteria in the process of causing organic materials to decompose, or by independent nitrogen-fixing bacteria, or can be applied as fertilizers. Organic fertilizers containing nitrogen include dried blood, hoof and horn meal and urea; inorganics include calcium cyanamide, Chilean nitrate, nitrate of potash, nitrate of soda and sulphate of ammonia. Most animal manures contain some nitrogen.

Another way of providing nitrogen is by digging in 'green-manure' crops.

⟡ FEEDING PLANTS; FERTILIZER; GREEN MANURING; MANURE; NITRATE; NITROGEN FIXATION.

Nitrogen Fixation A number of bacteria, some primitive blue-green algae, and also some fungi, have the power of 'fixing' atmospheric nitrogen to make direct use of it in a way which higher plants are unable to. Some of these algae and bacteria inhabit the soil so that their nitrogen-fixing abilities provide nitrates for plants to absorb. More importantly, they form symbiotic associations with plants which enable the latter to make use of the nitrogen directly. In nitrogen fixation the very inert element (always reluctant to form compounds in nature) is apparently catalysed by molybdenum to produce ammonia (NH_4) by adding hydrogen which is available in the soil or water.

Plants associated with blue-green algae include bryophytes (mosses and liverworts), floating ferns, duckweeds, aroids, the giant-leaved *Gunnera* and many cycads, and the algae are also important in rice-growing since they produce extra nitrogen in rice paddies. Nitrogen-fixing fungi are associated with various woody plants, including alder and sea buckthorn.

Nitrogen fixation is most widely associated with a bacterium called *Rhizobium* which forms nodules on the roots of the pea family (*Leguminosae*) and some other plants. The bacteria enter the plant tissue in a way which looks superficially parasitic, and in so doing stimulate the production of the nodules, just as other parasitic organisms stimulate galls. The *Rhizobium* is apparently unable to fix nitrogen when free-living, although other bacteria (*Spirillum*) associate with the roots of tropical grasses without forming nodules. Bacterial leaf nodules also occur, mainly in the family *Rubiaceae*.

Nodules contain a red pigment which is a protein closely resembling haemoglobin.

Because of their production of root nodules (in almost any reasonably well-cultivated soil), leguminous crops render it unnecessary to add nitrogen for a succeeding crop, since they release it as they decay. This is an important aspect of agricultural crop rotation and also in garden rotation; it also explains why beans, etc., can be grown in the same site for many years without rotation. Such cultivation is often associated with green manuring, i.e. the turning in of growing leguminous crops to enrich the soil. A good crop of suitable legumes can fix over 100 lb. of nitrogen per acre, roughly the equivalent of a ton of fertilizer. It has been estimated that nodule-making bacteria fix 100 million tons of nitrogen a year world-wide.

⟡ ALGAE; BACTERIA; FUNGUS; GALL; GREEN MANURING; LEGUME; ROTATION; SYMBIOSIS.

Node The points on an adult plant stem at which leaves or leaf buds appear are known as nodes or joints. These are sometimes pronounced, as in grasses and bamboos and other plants with hollow or pithy stems, which are usually closed internally at the nodes. Plants may be referred to as short- or long-jointed, as the case may be;

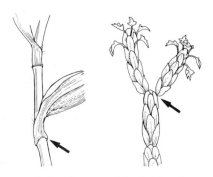

NODE. *Left*, tradescantia; *right*, *Kleinia articulata*

those in which the joints or nodes are pronounced are sometimes called articulate. The latter term in sometimes used as a specific name, as in the Candle Plant, *Kleinia articulata*, where the stems, which root readily, are literally jointed and often break at these points. In this case, the jointing is not associated with leaf formation.

Growth buds are often found at each node and the cambium layer at this point is more capable of producing adventitious roots or buds than elsewhere on the stem; hence most cuttings should be trimmed just below a node. In a few cases, e.g. clematis, cuttings are best taken between the nodes; these are called internodal cuttings.

⟡ ADVENTITIOUS; CUTTING.

No-digging The practice of cultivation by adding large quantities of organic matter on the surface of the soil, which is never disturbed by digging: ⟡ ORGANIC SURFACE CULTIVATION.

Nodule A small rounded growth on roots or other plant parts, which may be associated with either EELWORMS or nitrogen-fixing BACTERIA.

Nomenclature ⟡ CLASSIFICATION; NAMING OF PLANTS.

Non-parasitic Diseases A phrase sometimes applied to plant ailments – better described as plant disorders – which are caused by unsatisfactory environment, whether due to natural causes or gardeners' errors, such as wrong growing temperature, excess or lack of water, excess or lack of one or more fertilizers, etc. ⟡ DEFICIENCY; DISEASE; WATERING.

Notched Of a leaf or petal margin in which there are shallow rounded indentations, especially at the tip of the organ. Equivalent to emarginate. ⟡ LEAF.

Notching ⟡ NICKING AND NOTCHING.

No-soil Composts ⟡ COMPOSTS, SEED AND POTTING.

NPK The chemical symbols for the three major plant foods, respectively nitrogen, phosphorus and potassium. This abbreviation is sometimes used when referring to a basic balanced fertilizer. ⟡ FEEDING PLANTS; FERTILIZER; MANURE; NITROGEN; PHOSPHORUS; POTASSIUM.

Nuclear Stock All plants propagated vegetatively from a single parent; primarily used of plants so grown from a single mother plant which has been specifically raised to ensure freedom from virus diseases. ◊ MOTHER PLANT; VIRUS DISEASES.

Nucleus (1) Usually refers to the minute body within every living cell which controls its metabolism and division. When cells divide, in order that the organism may increase in size, the apparently solid protein of the nuclear body opens up to reveal the chromosomes: their division and the subsequent division of the nucleus itself precede the cell division. Nuclei containing the basic chromosome content of each parent (1x or haploid) fuse when fertilization takes place during sexual reproduction to produce a cell with twice the basic chromosome content (2x or diploid). ◊ FERTILIZATION.

(2) The word nucleus has other meanings, less frequently encountered in gardening. These include the kernel of an ovule or seed, better termed the nucellus; and a young bulb or 'clove', as of garlic.

Nursery Bed An area reserved for the rearing of young plants in which they can remain until large enough to be transferred to their permanent sites. Such plants can range from annuals (including vegetables) to perennials grown from seed, and to shrubs and trees increased from cuttings, layers, seeds, etc. The nursery bed or reserve border, as it may be called, is the intermediate stage between a seed bed (where applicable) and the permanent position. In most smallish gardens the ideal place is a bed of well-drained, finely worked soil which can be readily watered in dry weather, because the prime need of young plants is water; such a bed should be in a well-lit but generally warm, sheltered place, and is often most conveniently located in the vegetable garden. Other provisions may have to be made for the rearing of specialized plants such as alpines and water plants.

Nursery Garden Frequently abbreviated to 'nursery', this means an entire garden devoted to raising young plants of whatever kind. In large properties this may well be part of the private garden but, as commonly used, this term refers to a commercial undertaking producing plants for sale which may be at various stages of growth. Such commercial nurseries nowadays often send the newly raised plants to GARDEN CENTRES.

Nut A nut is technically a seed with a distinct outer shell, known as the pericarp, and a thinner skin over the seed-leaves themselves; this skin and the pericarp are separated by a cavity. Most nuts are contained either entirely or partially in an outer structure known as the cupule, which may hold one or more nuts. In the familiar acorn the cupule is the 'acorn cup', itself botanically the result of bracts fusing together. Other familiar nuts are hazel, beech and sweet chestnut, the latter two having cupules which entirely surround the seeds. Many seeds which are commonly called nuts, such as the horse chestnut, walnut and brazil nut, are not technically nuts at all in the botanical sense.

NUT. *Above*, hazel nuts (corylus); *below*, acorns (quercus), with section

Nutrient Film Technique A recent method of growing plants without soil or inert aggregate, which is not strictly hydroponic. In it, the plants are supported with their

207

roots in shallow sloping channels along which a nutrient solution is trickled so as to produce a film of moisture. Surplus solution is returned to the upper entrance of the channel by a pump. Plants can also be grown from seed or cuttings by this method.

Nymph Another word for the pupa of an insect. ⬦ INSECT.

❀ O ❀

Ob- A prefix to a term indicating the shape of a leaf or other plant organ which means inversely or oppositely; thus obovate means inversely ovate (with the wider part of the organ near its tip rather than its base or fixture point). Other examples are oblanceolate, oboval and obovoid. ⟡ LEAF.

Obdiplostemonous A seldom-used botanical term, irresistible for quotation, referring to a flower with twice as many stamens as petals, the outer series of stamens being opposite the petals.

Obelisk A tapering masonry shaft, usually of square section, often used in landscape gardens as an EYE-CATCHER.

Oblate A botanical term meaning flattened at both ends, as in a grapefruit.

Obligate Necessary or essential; found in the phrase obligate parasite, one in which parasitism is essential if the organism concerned is to develop completely. ⟡ PARASITE.

Oblique In botany, either slanting or having unequal sides. Begonia leaves are of the latter type. ⟡ LEAF.

Oblong Refers to leaves and other organs which are much longer than broad, with sides parallel or nearly so. ⟡ LEAF.

Obtuse In botany, applied to leaves and other organs which are blunt or rounded at the apex; the word is sometimes combined with another to create a specific name, e.g. *obtusifolius*. ⟡ LEAF.

Occlusion A word occasionally used to describe the process in which tree wounds become healed by the growth of callus tissue. A wound entirely covered by callus is said to be occluded. ⟡ CALLUS.

Oedema Also known as dropsy, this refers to a disorder of certain plants, notably pelargoniums and tomatoes, in which whitish eruptions occur on leaves and stems. It is due to the plant taking up more water than it can lose by transpiration, and is thus likely to occur after over-watering or when the air is excessively moist.

Officinal Refers to medicinal plants (or supposedly medicinal ones); many herbs have the specific name *officinalis*.

Offset A young plant produced asexually

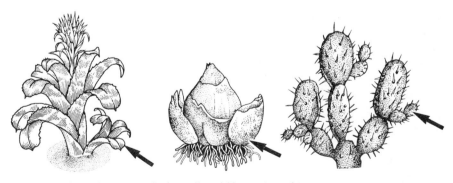

OFFSET. *Left to right, Vriesea splendens*; tulip; prickly pear (opuntia)

(vegetatively) alongside the parent, and easily removed from it. The word is most commonly applied to bulbs and corms and to many rosette-forming plants as diverse as bromeliads and houseleeks (semper-vivums). Cacti also produce offsets although these are usually easily detached side growths which are really branches. The word 'offset' is also sometimes used of fibrous-rooted plants, especially those where a number of loosely joined 'crowns' or groups of shoots are produced. Such growths are perhaps better referred to as offshoots, a word ofen used synonymously with offset. All offsets are normally identical to the parent in all ways.

The use of offsets for propagation is really a form of division. Offsets often have enough roots to grow on satisfactorily if transplanted individually, but in many cases they do not and must then be treated as cuttings in order to make roots in due course. Offset bulbs and corms are normally removed when the parents are lifted and dried off, and may need a period in a nursery bed before they achieve sufficient size to be planted in their permanent flowering positions.

Offshoot The same as OFFSET.

Oil Various kinds of oil have a part in gardening. Domestic heating oil can be used to operate hot-water boiler systems, mainly for large-scale installations. Paraffin oil, sometimes called kerosene, is used in the paraffin heaters suitable for keeping frost out of small greenhouses. A number of pesticides and ovicides are based on petroleum oil. ◊ PARAFFIN HEATERS; PETROLEUM OIL; WINTER WASH.

Onion Fly A particularly tiresome example of a bulb fly, the larvae of which ruin onions and which has three generations a year. Several insecticides can be used to control the flies; they are applied at the 'loop' stage, i.e. when the young onion leaves are still looped together. Onion sets can be soaked in insecticide before planting. ◊ BULB FLIES.

Onion Hoe A small hoe with an arched handle design to be used in one hand. ◊ HOE.

Open Describes soils and seed-and-potting composts with a granular structure and plenty of air-gaps between the particles of sand, stone and humus. ◊ AERATION.

Open-centre Applied to pruning methods for fruit trees which leave the centre of the tree more or less open, with the branches in the form of a bowl or vase. The open centre is more suitable for trees which remain fairly small, e.g. peaches and apricots, than for apples and pears grown to large size. The main advantage is it allows maximum light to reach every part of the branch system, which encourages ripening of the wood as well as of fruit; spray treatments are also easily applied. ◊ DELAYED OPEN-CENTRE.

Opossum In the southern U.S. opossums may invade gardens and eat fruit and vegetables. Fences will not keep out these nocturnal climbing animals, and shooting or trapping are the only effective controls. Local advice should be sought.

Opposite Usually applied to leaves which are produced in pairs on opposite sides of the stem. Opposite leaves are sometimes produced all in the same plane along a shoot, or in pairs facing opposite ways, when they can be termed decussate. Whether leaves are opposite, alternate or whorled is an important diagnostic feature in artificial keys to the identification of plants. ◊ ALTERNATE; ARTIFICIAL KEY; LEAF; WHORL.

Orangery The first structures built to shelter tender plants were called orangeries. There are rather obscure records of structures for growing citrus fruits (oranges, grapefruits, lemons, etc.) in Roman and medieval times, but the first proper records of such buildings date from 1490. These early orangeries were apparently nothing more than barn-like buildings of stone, brick or wood, sometimes insulated by layers of reeds, heather or chaff, and heated by a portable brazier or an open fire. Most of these had no windows at all, and even cellars were used for the purpose.

The first use of glass in an orangery dates from 1619, and from this first German structure stem all the orangeries built in the succeeding two centuries. In general, these had solid roofs and vertical walls with windows which eventually occupied the whole height of the wall.

Apart from the popularity of citrus fruits, the use of these (grown in large tubs) as 'guinea-pigs' in overwintering experiments was owing to their extreme resilience to maltreatment. Only later on were other 'tender greens' given winter shelter, and by then the orangery might have a pitched or arched roof of glass and was well on the way to becoming the greenhouses and conservatories we recognize today. The orangery proper almost always became an excuse for grandiose architecture.

◊ CONSERVATORY; GREENHOUSE; OR-CHARD HOUSE.

Orbicular A botanical term referring to leaves or other organs which are flat and of circular outline, i.e. disk-shaped. ◊ LEAF.

Orchard A garden or area devoted to fruit trees. Originally, an orchard combined fruit with herbs, as can be seen in the earliest plans of European monastery gardens.

Orchard House A structure devoted to the cultivation of fruit trees. In earlier times, when fruit was at a premium in winter, every attempt was made to force them into ripeness out of season, using frames of canvas or oiled silk, walls to catch and retain the sun's heat, in conjunction with hotbeds. By the late eighteenth century, the orchard house was primarily a greenhouse especially adapted for fruit cultivation, which often meant a high narrow structure with glass at front and top and a south-facing wall at back which might be heated

by internal flues and on which the fruit trees were trained. Sometimes broader structures also allowed the cultivation of a grape vine, or trees in containers. Special variants of the orchard house were made for growing pineapples and strawberries. ◊ PINERY; PIT.

Orchid This word includes all members of the highly favoured orchid family, *Orchidaceae*. These, which include both terrestrial and epiphytic plants, are monocotyledons with unique flowers. There are three outer segments which may be called the sepals, of which the central and normally uppermost one is usually much larger than the other two; while the central and usually lowest of the inner segments, called the lip, is of entirely different form from the other two, referred to as petals, and is usually much larger and more brightly coloured. In the centre of the flower the male pollen, usually gathered in sticky masses called pollinia, and the female stigma are combined into a unique organ called the column. Virtually all orchids are pollinated each by a single species of insect and employ special ingenious devices to ensure pollination, a remarkable case-history of adaptation. Curiously enough, their seeds are wholly unadapted, being dispersed by wind: they are among the lightest and most poorly developed in the plant kingdom, and often cannot germinate without the presence of a symbiotic fungus.

◊ COLUMN; EPIPHYTE; MERISTEM; MONOCOTYLEDON; POLLINATION; PSEUDOBULB; SYMBIOSIS; TERRESTRIAL.

Orchid Pot ◊ POT.

Organic Any chemical compound containing carbon is called organic. This includes the decomposed remains of plants and animals in the soil and animal manures, as well as a number of chemicals used as pesticides, fungicides and weedkillers. It was originally thought that no organic substance could be derived from other than natural substances, hence arose the biased suggestion that 'organics' were good in the garden and 'inorganics' harmful. In fact, many of the organic chemicals used for pest, disease and weed control are made synthetically, and include some which are very toxic to warm-blooded animals; while some of the inorganic materials used as fertilizers are of natural occurrence.

An organic soil is one containing a high proportion of organic matter of animal or vegetable origin.

◊ ORGANIC GARDENING.

Organic Gardening The word organic is often applied to that school of gardening – also known by the less sympathetic as 'muck and mystery' – which tries, despite the kind of anomaly outlined above (◊ ORGANIC), to use nothing but naturally occurring substances in the garden. Reasonably satisfactory natural pesticides can be found in this way, but not fungicides or weedkillers. Many organic gardeners prefer to use no pesticides at all, relying instead on biological control and natural predators.

Organic gardeners are especially insistent on the application of organic materials only to enrich the soil. These include animal manures and residues, garden compost, peat, spent hops, used mushroom compost and similar substances. The bulky materials among these certainly provide some plant foods and the concentrated ones, e.g. bone, meat and hoof-and-horn meals, etc., provide them in reasonably high proportion. These materials decay in the soil and improve its texture mechanically; in their absence the essential microorganisms cannot flourish, so the use of organics is vital. Conversely, the use of inorganics alone allows the organic or humus content of soil to become depleted, creates serious problems of soil texture, and is likely to create an imbalance of plant foods. However, it is difficult to produce enough compost or to buy enough manure for the average garden, and a combination of the organic manures and inorganic fertilizers is a much wiser practical approach.

◊ BIOLOGICAL CONTROL; FEEDING PLANTS; FERTILIZER; HUMUS; IN-ORGANIC; MANURE; ORGANIC; ORGANIC SURFACE CULTIVATION; PREDATORS.

Organic Surface Cultivation Also known as no-digging and surface cultivation, this is an extreme form of organic gardening, now seldom practised, in which the soil is never dug nor otherwise disturbed, but is continually enriched by the addition of bulky organic matter on the surface. I cannot do better than quote Ben Easey (*Practical Organic Gardening*, 1955): 'The principles of organic surface cultivation are those of close imitation of nature by non-inversion of the soil; of economy of compost and organic matter by its employment as a surface mulch, where nature keeps her fertility-promoting materials; of reduction of weed growth by ceasing to bring more and more seeds to the surface; and, by all these methods, of maintenance of a balance of air, moisture, biological life and plant foods.'

No-digging saves the labour of cultivation but does require the spreading of at least 2″ of compost or other bulky organic matter on the soil every autumn – which means a ton per 12 square yards.

◊ COMPOST HEAP; ORGANIC GARDENING.

Organomercury Compounds The overall name for a number of organic chemicals containing mercury, which are used as seed dressings and against various plant diseases. They are toxic to warm-blooded animals and all are now banned in E.E.C. countries. ◊ COMPOUNDS; GARDEN CHEMICALS; MERCURY FUNGICIDES.

Organophosphorus Compounds The overall name for a number of organic chemicals containing phosphorus, which are used as pesticides. They include the familiar malathion, and a number of materials very toxic to warm-blooded animals and not available to amateur gardeners. ◊ PESTICIDES.

Ornamental Garden A very general term for a garden designed for pleasure rather than utility.

Osmosis The movement of water across a semi-permeable membrane from a weak solution (of salts or sugars) to a stronger one: one of the vital processes occurring in all live cells, which sets up what is termed osmotic pressure. This is largely how water can reach the uppermost levels of tall trees, combined with the 'pull' of TRANSPIRATION.

Osmunda Fibre Osmunda is the royal fern and osmunda fibre is a material prepared from chopping its coarse, stiff dried roots into 1″–2″ pieces. This has always been prized by orchid growers as a potting material, since it keeps the compost open and well drained, provides food and retains its character for several years. Now very expensive as the sources dwindle, it is often replaced by shredded bark, hard lumpy peat, or a mixture of sphagnum peat and plastic chips or polystyrene granules. ◊ RAFT.

Oval Broadly elliptic in shape: used of leaves and other flat plant organs. ◊ LEAF.

Ovary That part of the pistil or 'female' organ in the flower which contains the ovules (literally little eggs) or immature seeds. There may be one or more ovaries, each with its own styles and stigmas. ◊ FLOWER.

Ovate Describes a form, as of leaves, which is roughly oval, but with its broader end nearer the stalk or point of attachment; a leaf of the reverse shape is called obovate. ◊ LEAF.

Overpotting If a plant originally in a small pot is moved into a relatively much larger one it has been overpotted. In such conditions the soil near the edges of the new large pot may become waterlogged or have plant nutrients leached out, since no new roots can reach these zones for some time and may in fact be prevented from penetrating them because of the unsatisfactory conditions that develop. Only very fast-developing plants, e.g. tomatoes, should be transplanted into very much larger pots. ◊ POTTING.

Overwintering Applied to annuals sown late in one season which survive the winter and flower in the next season; also to the winter phase of a true biennial which does the same thing – thus one talks of 'overwintering rosettes'. The term may be applied to other plants which spend the winter in a markedly different state from their normal growth, e.g. the turion or winter bud, as which many water plants spend the winter. ◊ ANNUAL; BIENNIAL; TURION.

Ovicide A chemical used to destroy pests in the egg stage. Winter washes are especially valuable to destroy overwintering eggs, but there are also ovicides for spring and summer use, especially valuable against spider mites. ◊ PETROLEUM OIL; WINTER WASH.

Ovoid, Ovoidal Ovoid means resembling an egg in shape, thus describing fruits and other three-dimensional organs. A flat organ with the outline of an egg is called ovoidal.

Ovule ◊ OVARY.

Oxygen An element occurring as a gas, forming roughly one-fifth of the earth's atmosphere, which is vital to plant growth, being an essential part of the photosynthetic reaction in which it is used in the form of carbon dioxide. Oxygen is also needed for healthy root growth, and this is one important reason for maintaining a good open texture in the soil with plenty of small gaps for air. Oxygenation is also needed for healthy growth of animals and plants in pools. ◊ OXYGENATORS; PHOTOSYNTHESIS.

Oxygenators Plants grown submerged in ornamental pools, fishponds and aquaria in order to produce oxygen for animal and plant welfare. Such plants should be included in any water garden at the rate of one to every square foot of water surface. In pools with soil at the bottom, it is sufficient to fasten a strip of zinc around the base of a portion of the plant and drop this into the pool at intervals, when the plant will root into the mud. Where there is no continuous soil at the bottom, the oxygenators have to be put into planting baskets like other water plants. Most oxygenators need fairly deep water. ▷ POOL.

Oyster Shell Older books often recommend the use of crushed or ground oyster shell to put into soil beds or, more especially, into potting composts. Oyster shell contains about 50 per cent calcium in slowly available form, as well as a quantity of trace elements; it is also porous and, in sufficiently large particles, absorbs surplus water and then releases it as required. In these less palmy days, when oysters are no longer part of our ordinary diet, oyster shell is difficult to obtain in Britain, though less so in the U.S.; it is now seldom recommended, although often cited as a desirable constituent of bulb fibre. It can be replaced by lime in some form, plus sharp sand, perlite or vermiculite to improve porosity.

❀ P ❀

Paired Of plant organs (leaves, flowers, etc.) carried in a pair at the same level.

Palea The upper bract enclosing the individual flower of a grass. ⟡ BRACT.

Paling ⟡ FENCES.

Palisade ⟡ FENCES.

Palm The *Palmae* are a family of plants important both decoratively and economically, many species of which are grown in greenhouses and as house plants. They are monocotyledons with insignificant flowers and characteristic leaves mainly in two groups: fan-like (or palmate) and feather-like (or pinnate). Most are tree-like but some have no stems or are shrubby, and others are climbers. As decorative plants they are on the whole notably durable and easy to grow, whether under glass, in the house, or outdoors in suitable climates (only one species is even moderately hardy in the U.K.).

Palmate, Palmatifid Shaped like an open hand; derived from the Latin *palma*, the palm of the hand. As a botanical term it is usually applied to leaves with spreading finger-like lobes, though for precise definition leaves with lobes which do not reach near the point of attachment to the leaf-stalk should be called palmately lobed, and those cleft almost to the leaf-stalk, palmately cleft or palmatifid. If the lobes are separate, the correct term is digitate. ⟡ LEAF.

Palmette A tree, usually a fruit tree, trained as a compound cordon with all the branches taking the same direction, whether vertical, horizontal or oblique, including those trees in which branches balance each other.

Examples include the palmette Verrier, U-cordons with four or six upright branches, the flattened palmette which is a triple horizontal cordon, the palmette Legendre which is virtually the same as an espalier with horizontal branches, the Montreuil palmette in which short vertical branches grow from a low horizontal tier, and the oblique palmette which is like a fan in which the central leader is allowed to develop vertically. Palmettes need a great deal of attention when being formed, especially the oblique type where each tier must be formed before the leader is allowed to continue growing. The U-based palmettes are the easiest and quickest to create. ⟡ CORDON; ESPALIER.

Pan (1) The more important meaning of pan, horticulturally, describes a hard horizontal layer in the soil, usually impermeable to air and moisture, and hence harmful to plant growth by impeding roots or drainage. Pans can be both natural and induced: a natural pan often occurs in soils in which there is a lot of iron. Otherwise, heavy soils are most liable to panning. A surface pan, in which the soil surface becomes smooth and hard, may occur after heavy rain, and can be aggravated by walking on the soil or rolling it, before it has dried out. Farmers are familiar with what is known as a plough sole, caused by constant ploughing to the same depth, when the soil below the furrow is compacted; and other kinds of cultivator sometimes create a similar pan if persistently used, especially on sticky soils. This can also occur in gardens.

If a serious pan exists or has been created, steps must be taken to break it up. On agricultural land a sub-soiler, a hook-shaped instrument, is often used, dragged through the soil by a tractor, and penetrating up to 18″ deep. In the garden, deep digging or trenching must be resorted to, while hoeing and forking will destroy surface pans. Adequate humus and gritty

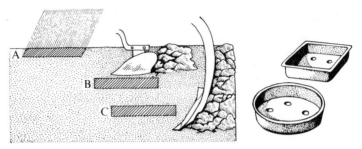

PAN. *Left*: A, surface pan; B, plough sole; C, using a sub-soiler. *Right*, plant pans

materials help to prevent surface pans and plough soles. ◊ DIGGING.

(2) The word 'pan' is also applied to earthenware plant receptacles which are much wider than deep. They may be any width from about 3″ (when they are sometimes known as half-pots) to 12″, round, square or oblong. Apart from being very useful for seed sowing, they are valuable for plants with spreading or surface roots, those, e.g. alpines, which must have good drainage, and small bulbs; in these cases a considerable depth of soil would merely stagnate and be harmful. ◊ POT.

Panicle ◊ INFLORESCENCE.

Papilionaceous ◊ LEGUMINOUS.

Papilla A small soft gland or other protuberance on a plant's surface. Some succulents are papillose, i.e. covered with papillae (plural), and this word may be found as a specific name as *papillosus*. ◊ GLAND.

Pappus In flowers of the daisy family, *Compositae*, the calyx of the individual florets is never green (unlike those of most plants), but takes the form of hairs, bristles, scales or teeth, or even a membranous ring: this is the pappus. Where the pappus is of hairs, which can be feathery or simple, this becomes the 'parachute' or 'thistle-down' which enables seeds of many of this family to float in the wind when ripe. Some composites, e.g. the daisy, have no pappus at all. ◊ CALYX; COMPOSITE.

Paradichlorbenzene A strong-smelling chemical, technically a chlorinated hydrocarbon, used as an insecticide and repellent because of the strong odour it gives off. It is used in the home to protect clothes, etc., against moths, and in the garden to repel or kill cutworms, millepedes, wireworms and the like. For this purpose it is applied at $\frac{1}{2}$ oz. per square yard and lightly worked in, or can be dropped into holes 8″–9″ deep and apart. Bulbs can be fumigated by putting them in boxes containing the crystals: this is effective against thrips of lilies, for example. Placed at the bottom of pots, the chemical will prevent attack by vine weevil grubs and other soil-inhabiting pests. ◊ REPELLENTS.

Paradise Garden Applied to ancient gardens in the Near and Middle East. The word paradise derives from the old Persian *pairidaeza*, meaning an enclosure, which became *pardes* in Old Testament Hebrew, meaning an enclosed garden or park, and finally *paradaisos* in Greek. The last meant a park for a king, implying something extravagant, and this reflected back into later Hebrew where it came to refer to paradise in the modern sense, and also to the Garden of Eden.

The earliest paradise gardens recorded were those of Prince Cyrus of Persia (d. 401 B.C.), which appear to have been a combination of hunting park and an arboretum with a great many evenly spaced trees in straight rows.

The concept of the paradise garden spread directly from Persia to Greece and much later to India, under the Mughals. To paraphrase Christopher Thacker (*The History of Gardens*), these were examples of luxury, extent and delight '... expressions of the greatest wealth and extravagance'. An exactly parallel development occurred in China, although the concepts were different, starting with the fabulous park of Kubilai – 'Kubla Khan'.

Modern garden historians trace the influence of these gardens far and wide, to include the symbolic Japanese garden descended from the Chinese, the Italian garden and its European descendants, and also the enclosed 'Mary gardens' of the Middle Ages, with their flowery swards which are spiritual rather than earthly paradises. Quite clearly the English landscape garden and the modern naturalistic garden are all 'paradises' in these terms.

↻ ITALIAN GARDEN; JAPANESE GARDEN; LANDSCAPE GARDENING; MUGHAL GARDENS; NATURALISTIC.

Paraffin, Paraffin Emulsion (Kerosene) A fuel used for heaters employing a wick. Fumes from such heaters are damaging to plants and so is neat paraffin. However, an old and effective remedy for aphids, mealy bugs, mites and scale insects was to spray paraffin emulsion. This can be made by boiling 5 oz. soft soap in $\frac{1}{2}$ gallon water and adding $\frac{1}{4}$ pint paraffin, which is then combined with the soap solution by rapidly pumping the liquid in and out of a garden syringe for several minutes. Enough water is then added to make the whole up to 2 gallons; this is used immediately as a spray.

↻ PARAFFIN HEATERS.

Paraffin Heaters These greenhouse heaters burn paraffin (kerosene) taken up by a wick, releasing the products of burning within the greenhouse. It is essential to keep the flame from smoking, or damage to plants may result; for a similar reason, a blue-flame heater is preferable to a yellow-flame type. All paraffin heaters have the wick or wicks burning at the base of a cylindrical funnel which can be open, or, in more elaborate models, have some kind of heat disperser. The best of these are prob-

ably in the form of a horizontal tube extending in both directions.

It is often claimed that paraffin heaters are specially valuable because they release both carbon dioxide and water vapour. In fact the effect of the extra carbon dioxide is negligible under normal circumstances, and in winter it is usually desirable to keep greenhouse atmosphere dry rather than add moisture to it, at any rate at the relatively low temperatures likely to be achieved by a paraffin heater. In general these heaters can keep a greenhouse at up to 4–7°C (40°–45°F), and thus keep out frost, but to achieve higher temperatures several heaters are needed, resulting in unacceptable work in maintaining and filling them. However, it is possible to obtain gravity-feed tanks to keep a heater going for several days.

↻ HEATING.

Parasite An organism which lives upon another living organism. There are many parasites in the plant world. Some are complete or obligate parasites, e.g. the dodders (*Cuscuta*), broomrapes (*Orobanche*) and toothworts (*Lathraea*), relying entirely on the host plant for nourishment, having neither leaves, nor roots capable of absorbing food from the soil. The mistletoe (*Viscum*) cannot live except in association with a suitable host into which it sends absorptive 'sinkers'; but it does have leaves capable of manufacturing food and is not, therefore, a complete parasite. Other plants, e.g. the alpine louseworts (*Pedicularis*), are semi-parasitic, and can exist for periods without a host. Parasitic plants have many different ways of obtaining nourishment from a host, of which the sinkers of the mistletoe are only one; some, like the Malayan *Rafflesia*, which has the biggest flower in the world, live entirely within the tissues of the host except when flowering.

Some plant parasites, e.g. dodders, are serious pests, mainly in warm countries, but the gardener is more usually concerned with the microscopic parasites which include fungus diseases, animals such as nematodes, bacteria and viruses.

◇ BACTERIA; DISEASE; FUNGUS; OBLI-GATE; SAPROPHYTE; VIRUS DISEASES.

Paring Box A device for ensuring that turves are of the same thickness: it consists of a shallow wooden tray with only three sides, of suitable dimensions for the turf size and thickness desired. Each turf is placed grass-side down in the box and surplus soil is pared off by planing it with a scythe blade or a large two-handled knife pulled across at the level of the sides. ◇ TURF.

Paripinnate ◇ PINNA.

Paris Frame A small frame placed within a larger one for propagation; now seldom used since more modern methods, e.g. mist propagation, prove as effective.

Paris Green Copper aceto-arsenite, a bright green chemical sometimes recommended in older books as a slug bait and to kill soil pests, notably leatherjackets and other grubs in lawns. It is extremely poisonous and hence not recommended for home use, other less toxic materials being available.

Parrot The name of a class of tulip having exotically slashed petals, usually accompanied by vivid colours in contrasting splashes or streaks.

Parrot-beak Refers to the type of secateur in which the two blades cross each other with a scissor-like action; tree pruners operate on a similar principle. ◇ SECA-TEURS; TREE PRUNERS.

Parted Of leaves lobed almost to the midrib. ◇ LEAF.

Parterre Parterre is a French word which was introduced to Britain in the seventeenth century, and denotes any level garden area containing ornamental flower beds of whatever shape and size. In the sixteenth century such gardens were highly developed by the French and Italians. The parterre was usually a separate unit, most frequently rectangular, divided from the

rest of the garden by stone balustrades or clipped hedges. The individual beds were often designed as knots. In fact, the word 'parterre' superseded the word 'knot' around 1664, the meaning being basically very similar.

In the *parterre de broderie* the main pattern is laid out in large masses of colourful low-growing flowers edged with sand or soil, and not in dwarf hedging: this is really a kind of carpet bedding.

The water parterre is a shallow formal pool in which a knot-like pattern is laid out in stonework. There is a notable example at Blenheim Palace in England and some spectacular ones in Mughal gardens in India.

◇ CARPET BEDDING; KNOT.

Parthenocarpic Fruits produced without fertilization are termed parthenocarpic. A notable horticultural example is the greenhouse cucumber, which should in fact not be pollinated, because if seeds are produced the fruits are bitter (the opposite is true of outdoor cucumbers). The banana is similar; indeed the cultivated banana never sets seed, and is propagated entirely by suckers. A number of plants, notably hawkweeks and their relations, are exclusively parthenocarpic, and the ovules cannot in fact be fertilized, yet the plants produce viable seed without sexual reproduction. A few orchids sometimes behave in this way.

Parthenocarpic fruits can sometimes be produced by applying tiny quantities of plant hormones to the flowers; this has been used on tomatoes and with some success on strawberries. To be able to do this artificially is often of use when pollination conditions are poor. Something similar occurs to apples and pears which are damaged by frost in the fruitlet stage so that the ovules are killed, though not the fleshy receptacle which develops into the fruit. These fruits may be shrunken or deformed, with few or no pips. Conference pear can produce a heavy crop of seedless fruit in this way; the pipless pears are characteristically sausage-shaped.

◇ APOMIXIS; HORMONES.

Parthenogenesis Literally, virgin birth: this refers to reproduction by seed without normal fertilization by a male. It applies to plants as described above (◊ PAR-THENOCARPIC) and to aphids in the more common wingless stages. Parthenogenesis is not the same as vegetative or asexual reproduction in which seeds are not involved. ◊ APHIDS; ASEXUAL; VEGETATIVE.

Patch Budding ◊ BUDDING.

Patch Plants An expression for annuals sown in large irregular patches of one kind each in a bed or border.

Patching Out If seedlings sown in pots or boxes come up so thickly that they cannot be separated, a small clump can be used instead of an individual, either at the pricking out stage or when planting direct into the garden. This is known as patching out. ◊ PRICKING OUT.

Patents ◊ PLANT BREEDERS' RIGHTS.

Pathogen In theory, any living organism causing a disease, but usually restricted to disease-causing BACTERIA and viruses. ◊ VIRUS DISEASES.

Pathology The study of diseases. ◊ MYCO-LOGY.

Paths Even a small garden may need a path to provide a hard walkway for use in wet soil conditions, and paths are certainly essential in large gardens whether formal – when they are likely to be hard-surfaced – or informal or naturalistic, when they can be of packed soil, grass, or stepping-stones, for instance.

Paths are a vital part of a garden design and should not be laid down until the design has been fully worked out, because any hard path is a virtually permanent feature and very difficult to alter later. Informal paths, such as grass or stepping-stones, can be altered more readily if this proves necessary. Paths are needed for both utilitarian purposes – simply getting from A to B, and providing access to

vegetable plots, greenhouses, sheds, etc. – and as part of a decorative layout, where they fulfil the dual function of access tracks and patterns integral to the design. In naturalistic gardens such paths are vital, providing as they do some form to what may otherwise be shapeless woodland.

Paths can vary from narrow tracks to broad walks, but in general a width of not less than 2′ is desirable, while in gardens of any size 3′ – 4′ will usually be more in proportion with the layout, and a width of 12′ – 15′ may be needed for main paths which include vehicle drives.

Many materials are available for path making, as detailed below. Generally speaking, most of these need a good foundation. This should have a depth of at least 6″ of hard rubble, broken bricks, or clinkers; it not only provides a firm basis for the surface material but also ensures that water will run away underneath, and cannot freeze just below the surface in winter, an effect which can readily destroy paths. In ground likely to be sodden it may be necessary also to lay a land drain in the centre of the path. At the very least, a layer of sand should be used to bed slabs or bricks on, though in light soils it is possible to lay these directly onto the previously dug soil if good finish is not essential.

Materials for formal paths

Concrete Excellent for utility paths, being clean and durable, but it does not blend in well with the decorative garden if laid continuously. It should be laid at least 2″ deep on the foundation, from a mix of 1 part cement, 1 part sand and 2 parts coarse aggregate.

Asphalt Another excellent utility material but is even less pleasing to look at. It should be laid about 1″ deep.

Paving Ideal for paths of any kind. Both natural and cast artificial stone slabs can be purchased in a wide variety of shapes and sizes, mostly rectangular but including hexagons, circles, and slabs to enclose the circles. Slabs can be bedded in sand or sifted ashes, or even firm soil, though for

219

permanence they are best laid on a 2″-deep concrete base. The pointing cement can be coloured to match the tones of the slabs (artificial stone being available in a range of colours).

Crazy paving Made from broken slabs, sometimes favoured for informal situations. To prevent excessive growth of weeds between the pieces, this is best laid on concrete. Its great merit is relative cheapness, compared with proper slabs.

Bricks Can be arranged in a great variety of attractive patterns, and are laid like paving. It is important to obtain outdoor-quality bricks because ordinary house bricks break up in frosty weather. However, they are liable to grow algae and become slippery in wet weather.

Sets (or *setts*) Of shaped stone or cast artificial stone, either smallish rectangles or shaped to make an interlocking pattern. They are particularly useful for places with much traffic and, because of the patterning, even concrete sets are quite attractive.

Gravel Once the most popular path material, but has gone somewhat out of favour because of its liability to grow weeds (although these can readily be controlled with modern weedkillers). Loose gravel alone should never be used as it needs frequent raking and is tiring to walk on; for path making, gravel should contain both sand and clay to ensure a smooth, firm surface needing minimum maintenance. Gravel should be laid 3″ deep, preferably with a slight camber to get rid of surface water, and should be thoroughly rolled.

Pebbles and cobbles Set in concrete, these can provide a most attractive texture or be arranged in patterns; but they are not comfortable to walk upon, and hence best used to produce ornamental panels in or alongside paths and also terraces of smoother material.

Wood boarding Boards, on a slightly raised framework, are sometimes used in the U.S. where a straight path is needed this is known as a BOARDWALK.

Informal paths

As already suggested, these can be simply of packed soil or preferably grass, where the surroundings are suitable. If hard surfaces are desired, a good method is to use slabs, preferably round ones, as stepping-stones; an alternative especially suitable for woodland settings is to use sections cut from tree trunks.

◊ CONCRETE; CRAZY PAVING; DRAINAGE; PAVING; WALK.

Patio The correct meaning of a patio is the inner courtyard of a house built in a square around the open space; it is usually associated with pools, fountains and plants in beds and containers, the whole providing shade and coolness in hot climates. As Edmondo de Amicis wrote, 'How describe a patio? It is not a courtyard, it is not a garden, it is not a room: but it is something between all three.' Above the courtyard there is usually an open first-floor gallery. The word is of Spanish derivation, and the patio is characteristic of Andalusian and South American houses of Spanish origin; but the origin of the patio in Spain dates from the Moorish Conquest, and the Moors developed the notion from Arab originals. The Arabs themselves may have been influenced by Greek and Roman houses with internal courtyards.

In Britain and the U.S. today, the word patio is almost entirely misapplied to mean any kind of paved space in a garden, especially a sitting-out area close to the dwelling house, which would better be termed a terrace. The only situation in which the word begins to be meaningful is when it is applied to a tiny, totally enclosed garden which is barely more than an outdoor room.

◊ TERRACE.

Patte d'Oie Literally, a goose's foot: applied to a set of paths or vistas radiating fan-like from a central point like the toes of a goose's foot from its centre. ◊ FRENCH GARDEN.

Pavilion A garden building of more pretension than a basic garden house, usually architect-designed and often highly decorated inside as well as out. Pavilions were designed as rooms of some comfort rather than the chilly interiors of most GAZEBOS and TEMPLES.

Paving Solid materials for making paths, terraces and 'patios', mainly in the form of slabs of real or composition stone, but including concrete slabs, brick, tiles, sets, etc. As in path making, any paved area should if possible have 6″ rubble foundation and, if necessary, land drains to ensure that any surplus water is drained off; also it is best to lay the slabs, etc., in concrete. Careful levelling should be carried out. Paved areas lend themselves to plants growing in large containers, but plant beds can be made among the slabs, or low-growing plants be grown in pockets left between them. ◊ CRAZY PAVING; DRAINAGE; PATHS; PATIO; TERRACE.

Peach Leaf Curl ◊ LEAF CURL.

Pea Gravel A small size of GRAVEL.

Pea Guard A narrow length of small-mesh wire netting formed into an inverted U shape over wire supports which project beyond the wire so that they anchor the device in the ground; used over newly sown seed rows to prevent the seedlings being attacked by birds.

Peat Partially decayed organic matter derived from vegetation in bogs, marshes, heathlands and similar wet or very acid places, where the normal processes of decomposition do not operate owing to the anaerobic (oxygen-deficient) conditions. Peat varies considerably according to its origin, but that used for horticultural purposes is selected carefully. It is either sedge peat, made up of the remains of sedges, reeds, mosses, heathers and sometimes tree roots, or sphagnum peat, derived entirely from decayed sphagnum moss. (In the U.S., peat is always, rather misleadingly, known as peat moss.)

Sedge peat has a pH (acidity) varying from 3.5 to 7.0 (neutral), and holds 7–8 times its own weight of water. Sphagnum peat is very acid with a pH of 3.5–4.5, and is much spongier, holding up to 15 times its weight of water. Both types contain up to 3.5 per cent nitrogen and minute quantities of phosphorus, potash and trace elements, but these are released extremely slowly. Peats are milled to particle sizes varying from $\frac{1}{16}$″ to $\frac{3}{4}$″. Small particles are best for all soils except really sandy ones, where the coarse grade is best. Dusty peat is best avoided.

In the garden, peat is primarily used to make the soil more water-retentive and porous, with a marked improving effect on both clay and sandy soils. It will also reduce alkalinity up to a point and is ideal as a 'starter' when planting shrubs and trees of all kinds, especially acid-lovers. If the peat is very acid, a dressing of lime at the same time will maintain the pH level desired, and this can be checked by using a lime tester. Peat is virtually free of pests, diseases and weeds, is easy to store and clean to handle, and has a reasonably long-term effect on the soil.

For good results 5–6 lb. per square yard is adequate to work into the top few inches of average soils, but 10–12 lb. is needed for soils low in organic content to start with. Finely milled peat is also admirable for surface mulching, when 5–10 lb. per square yard can be applied. As a mulch it retains moisture, prevents a damp soil surface from drying out, and provides a cool, moist root-run. Since peat is usually dry when bought, especially in compressed bales, it must be well moistened before use, for it can take a long time to absorb moisture on or in soil.

Peat is a vital component of most modern seed and potting composts and indeed most 'no-soil' composts are based largely upon it. For this purpose the finer grades are best. Peat is also the main ingredient of bulb fibre. It has also been widely used as an aggregate in soilless cultivation methods.

◊ BULB FIBRE; COMPOSTS, SEED AND POTTING; MULCH; PEAT BEDS; PEAT BLOCKS; PEAT POTS; PEAT WALLS; pH; SOILLESS CULTIVATION.

Peat Beds These are beds edged with peat blocks and filled with pure peat, or with very peaty and hence acid soil, primarily to grow peat-loving plants such as the *Ericaceae*, in situations where the basic soil is unsuitable. Such beds can be of 'billiard table' form or be made in rising tiers on a slope. Where the natural soil is markedly chalky, lime will eventually rise into the bed, or the roots of more vigorous plants reach the lime, thus negating the purpose if calcifuge (lime-hating) plants are grown. In such conditions the beds must be separated from the soil by a sheet of thick plastic. Such peat beds have been known in the U.K. as American gardens because of their popularity in the U.S. Peat beds can also be made by forming enclosures of railway sleepers or similar objects and filling in with peat or peaty soil. ⬦ BILLIARD TABLE; CALCIFUGE; ERICACE-OUS; PEAT BLOCKS.

Peat Blocks Blocks of peat as cut directly from the natural peat deposits, sold in dry form. These can be used to create retaining walls, just as stone slabs are used to make dry walls, and bonding the blocks as one would bricks so that vertical joints do not appear one above another. The blocks should be thoroughly moistened by soaking before use, and ought to be well watered periodically in dry periods. Quite high peat walls can be built against soil slopes if an angle of around 60–65° from the vertical is maintained. ⬦ BILLIARD TABLE; DRY WALL; PEAT; PEAT BEDS; RAISED BED.

Peat Gardens A term for any garden devoted to peat beds, however created.

Peat Moss ⬦ PEAT.

Peat Pots Small pots made from compressed peat, sometimes with thin walls, sometimes in block form with a central cavity. In either case the pot is filled with a suitable seed compost and is used for seedlings. The special advantage of peat pots is that the plant roots penetrate the peat (which must be kept fairly moist for this reason) and can be planted, pot and all, directly into the soil. An ingenious form of the peat pot is the Jiffy pot (a trade name) in which compressed peat is enclosed in a fine plastic mesh. When soaked, these pots expand to provide peat pots of the cavity type. ⬦ PEAT.

Peat Walls Walls made of PEAT BLOCKS.

Pectinate Of a leaf which is pinnatifid with very narrow segments closely set like the teeth of a comb; also of comb-like arrays of spines as in some cacti. ⬦ LEAF; SPINE.

Pedate Literally, shaped like a foot, implying a bird's splayed foot; describes leaves divided into deeply cut, rounded lobes radiating from the centre, the two side segments being themselves divided before the centre point. ⬦ LEAF.

Pedicel The stalk of a single flower, especially one in a cluster. ⬦ PEDUNCLE; STALK.

Pedicel Necrosis Literally, death of the flower-stalk: refers to collapse of the flower stalk which especially affects peonies and roses, but also other flowers. Sometimes called topple. ⬦ BUD DISEASE; NECROSIS.

Peduncle A flower stem or stalk, usually applied to that of a solitary flower or of a flower cluster. ⬦ PETIOLE; STALK.

Pelleted Seed Seed processed so that each individual seed is encased in a pellet of inert material about $\frac{3}{16}''$ across. Fungicides against seed-borne diseases can also be incorporated. This enables seeds to be handled and planted individually so that thinning after germination can be drastically reduced. It is essential to sow in a previously watered seed drill and to keep the drill (or seed bed) moist until germination occurs, otherwise the pellet may remain undissolved. ⬦ SEED SOWING.

Peloric A kind of floral monstrosity in which normally irregular flowers become regular or of symmetrical structure. The commonest example occurs in foxgloves (*Digitalis*), in which a single large round floret is carried at the top of an otherwise normal spike of irregular tubular florets. ◊ MONSTROUS; TERATOLOGY.

Peltate Literally, shield-shaped, this is applied to leaves with the stem (petiole) joining the underside at or near the centre. The common nasturtium, *Tropaeolum majus*, has a peltate leaf. The word is sometimes used as a specific name, as in *Saxifraga peltata.* ◊ LEAF.

Pendent Hanging; often used of flowers and also of trees having down-hanging branches.

Penjing The Chinese name for BONSAI.

Pepper Dust Obtainable as a deterrent to cats, also dogs and earwigs, to be sprinkled on and around plants or seed beds. Ordinary kitchen pepper can be used in just the same way. ◊ REPELLENTS.

Perch (1) A very old linear measure, normally $16\frac{1}{2}'$ ($5\frac{1}{2}$ yards), equivalent to a rod or pole; derived from a rod of that length used to measure land.

(2) An old measure of area, better known as a square perch (or pole), normally $\frac{1}{160}$ of an acre.

(3) A solid measure referring to a quantity of stone, a perch long, $1\frac{1}{2}'$ broad and $1'$ thick, although varying locally. ◊ WEIGHTS AND MEASURES (p. viii).

Perennial A plant whose life is at least three seasons and usually indefinite; commonly used in connection with herbaceous plants rather than shrubs or trees. However, it is erroneous to consider perennials solely as herbaceous plants, a mistake sometimes committed by show judges. By the same token, plants which are perennial in nature but not in local British or northern U.S. conditions, e.g. dahlias, are properly perennials. If *hardy herbaceous* perennials are intended by the show schedule, these qualifying words must be inserted. ◊ ANNUAL; BIENNIAL; MONOCARPIC.

Perfoliate A word applied to paired leaves in which the lobes unite around the stem, so that the latter appears to pass right through the leaf. Some eucalyptus and loniceras have perfoliate leaves. The word is occasionally seen as a specific name, as in *Claytonia perfoliata.* ◊ LEAF.

Pergola Originally (1675) meaning an arbour or covered walk formed of plants grown up trellis (*Oxford Dictionary*), a pergola today refers to a series of arches up and over which plants are grown. Such arches are normally composed of vertical pillars supporting a horizontal beam. A pergola can be formed of a single line of uprights, or a double line in which case the horizontal beams are connected by further cross-pieces between the two. Double pergolas are typically erected over a path or walk.

Uprights and horizontals can be of rustic woodwork, but much more permanent structures are usually made with brick, stone, or stout squared wooden uprights and stout wooden horizontal members. Uprights should reach at least $6\frac{1}{2}'$ and preferably $8'$ above ground level and be $6'-8'$ apart. They need to be very firmly based; wooden ones, treated against decay, should be sunk at least $2'$ into the ground. ◊ ARBOUR; RUSTIC WORK; TRELLIS.

Perianth The perianth of a flower comprises all the outer parts which enclose the reproductive organs, normally the calyx and corolla. Where there is only one ring of floral parts, e.g. in anemones and clematis (where sepals resemble petals) and in daphnes and many tree flowers, or where there is no clear division into petals and sepals, e.g. in narcissi, the word 'perianth' still covers the exterior floral parts. With narcissi, the word is used in the classification of divisions, the size of the separate perianth segments being referred to in relation to that of the trumpet, cup or corona; both the latter and the segments comprise the perianth. ◊ CORONA; CUP; FLOWER.

Perlag, Perlite Modern additions to seed and potting composts. They are made by heating volcanic rock until it expands to form rigid granules containing holes, able to absorb air and up to four times their own weight in water. They are light and sterile, perlag being coarser than perlite and absorbing more water for a given weight. The finer perlite can be used on its own for striking cuttings. ◊ COMPOSTS, SEED AND POTTING; CUTTING.

Permanganate of Potash Technically, potassium permanganate, a disinfectant with various garden uses. Even though modern chemicals are more powerful, it is still fairly efficacious as a pesticide, fungicide and weedkiller, and has the merit of very low toxicity to warm-blooded animals.

As a pesticide 'pot. perm.' can be watered around plants as a deep pink solution ($\frac{1}{2}$–1 oz. in 1 gallon of water) against slugs and snails, and if watered onto lawns will expel earthworms. A ring of crystals around specially precious plants will repel slugs and snails. The same solution will prevent damping off disease of seedlings, and has been used against mildew on roses, etc., though it is certainly not very effective for this purpose. A deep red solution (at least 1 oz. per gallon) will destroy moss, whether in lawns, on paving or in pots; several applications one week apart may be needed.

Perpetual Used horticulturally to describe plants which flower more or less continuously, over a long period. The only plant which really deserves the description is the greenhouse carnation; some races of pinks, e.g. the *allwoodii* hybrids, bloom almost continuously during summer. In the early days of roses a new race was called Hybrid Perpetuals because the varieties were somewhat longer in flower than their predecessors. Even with modern Hybrid Tea roses and the Large-flowering Climbers, to which the words 'perpetual-flowering' are sometimes applied, this is really a misnomer. Nor do 'perpetual' strawberries live up to their name; but perpetual spinach or spinach beet does produce useful leafage over very long periods.

Peruvian Guano The excreta of sea birds found on the coasts of Peru and nearby islands and countries. ◊ GUANO.

Pest Any living creature which causes damage to plants is termed a pest, apart from bacteria, fungi and viruses which are considered DISEASES.

Pests dealt with individually are listed below. Some entries may deal with a number of related pests under one heading, e.g. APHIDS includes greenfly, black fly and all similar insects, and CATERPILLARS borers, leaf rollers, leaf miners and all those kinds known in the U.S. as 'worms' (as in bagworm).

◊ APHIDS; BEETLE; BUG; BULB FLIES; CATERPILLARS; CATS; CHIPMUNK; COCKROACHES; CODLING MOTH; CUCKOO-SPIT (FROG HOPPER or SPITTLEBUG); CUTWORMS; DEER; DOGS; EARTHWORMS; EARWIGS; EELWORMS (NEMATODES); FLEABEETLES; FLY; FUNGUS GNATS; GALL WEEVIL; GOPHERS (GROUND SQUIRRELS); GRASSHOPPERS; LEAF HOPPERS; LEAF MINERS; LEATHERJACKETS; MEALY BUG; MICE; MILLEPEDES; MITES; MUSHROOM FLIES; ONION FLY; OPOSSUM; POTWORMS; RABBITS; RACCOON; RATS; ROOT APHIDS; ROOT FLIES; ROOT-KNOT EELWORM; ROOT MAGGOT; SAWFLIES; SCALE INSECTS; SHOTHOLE BORERS; SLUGS; SLUGWORMS; SNAILS; SQUIRRELS; SYMPHILIDS; THRIPS; TORTRIX MOTHS; WASPS; WEEVILS; WHITE FLY; WINTER MOTHS; WIREWORMS; WOODCHUCK; WOODLICE; WOOLLY APHID.

For further information ◊ BUTTERFLIES; GALL; GRUB; INSECT; LARVA; MAGGOT; MOTHS; PEST CONTROL; PREDATORS; SAPSUCKER.

Pest Control Before attempting to control any pest, it has to be identified and this may not always be easy, since often only the effects of the pest are to be seen. Some knowledge of the habits and life cycles of likely garden pests is therefore invaluable, and equally of those of creatures which are not pests at all but may be beneficial since they feed upon pests. A knowledge of pests is also essential when timing control operations on specialized crops, e.g. fruit trees.

Pest control materials fall into a number of categories as described below ▷ PESTICIDE. Besides the use of pesticides, certain pests, e.g. mice, moles and wasps, can be trapped; some can be kept away by deterrents or repellents; however, some people prefer to avoid pesticides and rely on natural methods, although it must be stressed that these are far from infallible. One has to remember that a garden is an artificial assemblage of plants whose healthy growth (in theory!) makes them all the more tempting to pests, while their concentration in one area makes the pests likely to multiply and spread. One garden surrounded by others is certain to receive pests of many kinds, while a garden near agricultural land may receive severe attacks from some specialized pests.

▷ BAIT; BIOLOGICAL CONTROL; PEST; PESTICIDE; PREDATORS; REPELLENTS; TRAPS; TREE BANDING; TREE GUARDS.

Pesticide A portmanteau word for any chemical material, whether natural or synthetic, which kills pests. These materials may be subdivided into acaracides against mites, insecticides against insects, molluscicides against slugs and snails, nematicides against eelworms, ovicides against pest eggs, and vermicides or wormkillers against worms. Some pests, e.g. millepedes and woodlice, are not specifically covered by such terms and 'insecticides' usually cover these. Deterrents or repellents are used against both soil pests and larger creatures like deer, birds, cats and dogs.

Pesticides are available in many different forms. These include liquids, emulsions, and wettable powders to be diluted or mixed in water and sprayed or occasionally painted onto plants; aerosols which deliver a fine spray or a suspension of fine particles; dusts to be applied only via a distributor or puffer; a smoke generator to release smoke carrying fine particles of insecticide onto plants in a sealed area such as a greenhouse; and both liquids and solids which can be ignited or vaporized to be spread, again in sealed areas.

In the U.S. especially, some are available as granules to spread over the soil surface, and at least one formulation is in the shape of a 'spike' or 'pin', to be pushed into the soil in a pot: these slowly release the systemic chemical there.

Pesticides act in various ways. Contact poisons operate when insects are touched by the material, walk over its deposit on leaves or stems, or insert their mouthparts into the plant tissue to suck sap. Stomach poisons destroy insects which eat treated plant tissues. Systemics are stomach poisons which penetrate the plant tissues and impregnate them with the materials so that chewing or sucking insects are killed as soon as they start to feed.

Biological control materials are prepared from bacterial, fungus or virus diseases which attack and kill specific pests.

In general contact poisons need frequent renewal, especially out of doors where rain ⁻emoves them. Some persist so short a time that they are termed 'knock-down' materials, only dealing with pests actually caught by the application of the material. Systemics can, however, protect plants for several weeks.

Pesticides can be used as preventives, and this is especially so with fruit pests, where careful timing of applications of different materials is essential for the full protection needed by commercial growers in particular. They are, however, more often used by the gardener at the first signs of an attack.

Pesticides vary greatly in their toxicity to mammals; instructions should always be studied very carefully as to the length of time that must elapse before treated fruit or vegetables can be eaten, and the safeguarding of household pets and also sometimes fish in pools. Instructions as to preparation must also be followed carefully: too weak a spray solution may have little effect and too strong may scorch the plant. It is always desirable to avoid spraying

225

Table of Pesticides

Pesticide	Ants	Aphids, Capsids, Leaf Hoppers, Bugs	Scale Insects, Mealy Bug	Chewing Insects: Beetles, Caterpillars	Stem Borers, Leaf Miners	Soil Pests (grubs and maggots)	Mites	Systemic	U.K. availability	U.S. availability	Notes
Azinphosmethyl	x	x		x		x				x	
Bacillus thuringensis				x							Against caterpillars. ◊ BIOLOGICAL CONTROL.
BHC, gamma-BHC											Now renamed HCH, see belo[w]
Bioresmethrin		x		x		x			x	x	Specially valuable against wh[ite fly]
Borax*	x								x	x	
Bromophos	x			x		x			x	x	Against overwintering pests a[nd] of dormant season.
Butoxicarboxim		x	x				x	x	x	x	Used in 'pin' form in pots.
Calomel											◊ Mercurous chloride, belo[w]
Carbaryl	x	x		x		x			x	x	Also against wasps. Will def[oliate] Virginia creepers, etc.
Carbophenothion		x	x	x	x	x	x		x		
Chlorbenside, Chlorbenzilate, Chlorobenzoate							x		x	x	Closely allied chemicals.
Chlordane	x					(x)			x	x	Also against earthworms.
Chlordimeform				x			x			x	Specially for brassica caterpi[llars]
Chlorpyrifos						x			x	x	
Demeton, Demeton-S-methyl		x					x	x	x		
Derris											◊ Rotenone, below.
Diazinon	(y)	(x)	(x)	(x)	x	(x)			x	x	Specially valuable against mi[te] white fly.
Dichlorvos (DDVP)		x	x		x		x		x	x	Used in slow-release strip for greenhouses.
Dicofol							x		x	x	
Dimethoate		x	x	x	x			x	x	x	
Disodium tetraborate											◊ Borax, above.
Dormant oil											◊ Tar oil, below.
Fenitrothion				x					x		Specially against rollers.
Formothion		x		x			x	x	x		Recommended for roses.
HCH, gamma-HCH (= Lindane)		x	x	x	x	x			x		Used to be called BHC. Gamma-HCH is purified le[ss] tainting form.
Heptenephos		x							x		Only available combined with permethrin

...ide	Ants	Aphids, Capsids, Bugs	Leaf Hoppers, Mealy Bugs	Scale Insects, Mealy Bugs	Chewing Insects: Beetles, Caterpillars	Stem Borers, Leaf Miners	Soil Pests (grubs and maggots)	Mites	Systemic	U.K. availability	U.S. availability	Notes
ne												◊ HCH, above.
hion	x	x	x	x	x	x	x			x	x	Harmful to fish.
zon		x							x			Against aphids only.
rous chloride (omel*)							(x)				x	◊ FUNGICIDES.
dehyde					x					x	x	Primarily a slug killer; also effective against millepedes, woodlice, some soil pests.
ocarb					x		x			x		Primarily a slug killer; also against mice and woodlice.
oxychlor	x	x	x	x	x	x					x	Mostly recommended against chewing insects.
Disease res							x				x	Against Japanese beetle grubs. ◊ BIOLOGICAL CONTROL.
stan		x			x					x		
		x			x	x				x		
ne*		x			x	x				x	x	Of natural origin.
meton-methyl		x			x			x	x	x	x	Safest used in aerosol form.
;								x			x	Recommended for house plants.
thrin		x			x					x	x	Specially valuable against white fly and caterpillars.
eum oil* (mmer oil)		x	x							x	x	
carb		x								x	x	Against aphids only.
phos-methyl	x	x			x	x	x	x		x		Specially valuable against white fly and red spider mite.
rum*	x	x			x					x	x	Of natural origin.
ia*		x								x		Of natural origin; only available combined with rotenone.
thrin	x	x			x			x		x	x	
one (derris*)		x			x			x		x	x	Of natural origin. Harmful to fish.
m tetraborate												◊ Borax, above.
er oil												◊ Petroleum oil, above.
* (dormant oil)		x	x	x				x		x	x	Used primarily on dormant fruit trees; kills eggs.
lifon								x			x	
orphon	x				x	x				x	x	

...e not permitted in E.E.C.   *See also main alphabetical entry.

plants with open flowers or their bee pollinators are likely to be killed.

Check the instructions further to make sure that the material is not likely to damage the kind of plant being sprayed.

Many proprietary pesticides are mixtures combining two or three materials, e.g. a contact and a systemic pest-killer, to increase the range of pests destroyed. Others combine pesticides and fungicides. It is usually wise in any case periodically to change the pesticide you use, since pests can readily gain immunity to a specific material.

The table above summarizes the main uses of widely available pesticides, but excludes animal repellents, mole smokes, slug and snail killers and wormkillers, which are dealt with individually. In most cases the materials included are available to amateurs and relatively safe for them to use without special precautions.

The names of the pesticides are their chemical ones or names coined to avoid complex chemical ones. They are not trade names: there are too many products to list, especially in view of the various combined materials. Users of pesticides should check the names of their constituent chemicals which, in the U.K. at least, must always be printed on the label.

Pesticides of natural or inorganic origin have separate alphabetical entries.

◊ BIOLOGICAL CONTROL; BUD STAGES; FUMIGATION; FUNGICIDES; GARDEN CHEMICALS; HOT-WATER TREATMENT; MOLES; REPELLENTS; SLUGS; SMOKES; SYSTEMIC; WETTABLE POWDER; WORM-KILLING.

Petal One of the divisions of the corolla of a flower, especially where this is separate from the other divisions. (If not separate, such a division is better termed a corolla lobe.) The corolla is usually, but not always, the showy part of a flower, forming the inner ring (the calyx is the outer). ◊ CALYX; COROLLA; FLOWER.

Petal Fall ◊ BUD STAGES.

Petalody The scientific name for the con-

PETALODY. The peony at right exhibits petalody compared with the normal single flower at left

dition of a flower having parts modified into the form of petals, i.e. PETALOID.

Petaloid Resembling a petal: used for other parts of the flower which either look like petals as when the calyx becomes petaloid (e.g. in anemones), or which become modified to look like petals, as sometimes occurs with stamens. The word is sometimes used as a noun, the segments being referred to as petaloids, especially when they are narrower than the real petals. ◊ FLOWER.

Petiolate Having a petiole or leaf stalk, as opposed to having none (sessile). ◊ LEAF; PETIOLE.

Petiole A leaf stalk. In certain climbing plants, e.g. *Clematis alpina* and nasturtiums, the petiole will loop round suitable supports and lock onto them. ◊ CLIMBER; LEAF; TENDRIL.

Petiolule The stalk of one leaflet in a compound leaf. ◊ LEAF.

Petroleum Oil A number of pesticides and ovicides are made from petroleum oils. These include some 'winter washes', used when plants have lost their leaves, those of petroleum oil being especially valuable for destroying moth eggs and against capsid bugs and red spider mite. Other forms of petroleum oil (also known as white oil) are formulated for summer use when plants are in leaf and are effective against capsid bugs and scale insects, which are destroyed by suffocation. In the U.S. these oils may be called dormant oil and summer oil respectively. ◊ WINTER WASH.

Pets For garden problems associated with these pets, ◊ CATS; DOGS.

pH Technically, this abbreviation stands for hydrogen ion concentration, and is the measure or scale used to indicate the degree of acidity or alkalinity of the soil, of water or of other media. 7.0 is neutral; pH values below this indicate acidity, and above alkalinity. The scale is in fact a logarithmic one, so that the difference between pH 7.0 and 8.0 is far greater than that between steps in the acid range, e.g. pH 5 to 6.

Expressions used in describing soil re-actions are as follows:

pH below 4.5   extremely acid
4.5–5.0   very strongly acid
5.1–5.5   strongly acid
5.6–6.0   medium acid
6.1–6.5   slightly acid
6.6–7.3   neutral
7.4–8.0   mildly alkaline
8.1–9.0   strongly alkaline
9.1 and above   extremely alkaline

These measurements are easily made by quite inexpensive soil-testing kits.

Gardeners need to know the pH level of their soil, potting mixtures, the water they use and even, sometimes, of fertilizers, since certain plants will grow only in acid conditions, while others prefer alkaline ones. Acid conditions are a virtual necessity for almost all members of the heath family (*Ericaceae*) including rhododendrons, for camellias, and for many tropical plants: these are called calcifuges. Many alpines, however, prefer alkaline soil, and most members of the wallflower family (*Cruciferae*) – including cabbages, brussels sprouts, turnips, etc. – grow better in such soils. Such plants are known as calcicoles.

The most acid level tolerated by plants is around pH 4.0 and the most alkaline

pH 8.0. In very alkaline conditions, many essential plant foods become 'locked up', and plants show chlorosis or other symptoms of mineral deficiency.

A good general-purpose garden soil, allowing a wide range of plants to flourish, has a pH of between 6.5 and 7.0. Acid-lovers can be encouraged by adding quantities of acid organic matter, e.g. sphagnum peat, or some kinds of leafmould, especially oak. Chemicals can also be applied, such as sulphate of aluminium or sulphate of iron which are often used to turn hydrangea flowers blue (these react to pH levels very like litmus paper). Where the level of acidity is excessive, it can always be rectified by adding dressings of chalk or, more usually, lime. Acidity is often the result of poor drainage or aeration of the soil, hence regular cultivation can also reduce its level.

◊ CALCICOLE; CALCIFUGE; CHLOROSIS; LIME; PEAT; SOIL TESTING.

Phloem ◊ VASCULAR SYSTEM.

Phosphate of Lime Crude rock phosphates, as mined from natural deposits; not normally available for garden use. This is not the same as superphosphate of lime, which is obtained by treating the phosphate with sulphuric acid.

Phosphate of Potash An inorganic fertilizer containing 51 per cent phosphoric acid and 35 per cent potassium. It is too expensive for widespread use but can be applied to pot plants as a liquid feed, dissolving $\frac{1}{4}$ oz. in 1 gallon water.

Phosphates Any salts of phosphoric acid: such salts supply phosphorus, one of the three main plant foods. Animal bones, sold as bone flour or bone meal, are specially rich in phosphates and release them slowly. Most phosphatic compounds are easily washed out of the soil, and in any case plants use them in fair quantities. ◊ BASIC SLAG; BONE MANURES; FEEDING PLANTS; PHOSPHATE OF LIME; PHOSPHATE OF POTASH; SUPERPHOSPHATE OF LIME.

229

Phosphorus One of the 'big three' plant foods, always abbreviated P. It is available to plants as salts of phosphoric acid, or PHOSPHATES.

Photoperiodism The phenomenon of the control of flowering in plants according to varying day-length. 'Long-day' plants will flower only when there are at least 14 hours of daylight; 'short-day' plants, when there are not more than 10 hours. Plants unaffected by day-length are known as day-neutral. For practical applications, ◊ DAY-LENGTH.

Photosynthesis The process which makes green plants unique is their method of obtaining energy, in which they make use of sunlight to combine carbon dioxide and water into glucose, the starting point for all the complex carbohydrates, proteins, etc., created within a plant for its metabolism. In photosynthesis, which is actually carried out by the green pigment chlorophyll found in leaves and sometimes stems, oxygen is given off as a surplus product; also, a great deal of water is needed for the process, which is lost by the plant in transpiration. Photosynthesis is, of course, only carried out when light is available. ◊ RESPIRATION; TRANSPIRATION.

Phototropism ◊TROPISM.

Phylloclade A stem which takes on the function of a leaf. ◊ CLADODE.

Phyllode A petiole (leaf-stalk) which takes on the functions and usually the form of a leaf, as often occurs in *Acacia* species.

Phyllody The phenomenon of floral organs turning into leaves, as in a well-known form of plantain, *Plantago major* 'Rosularis', where bracts have become markedly leaf-like. This is an example of monstrosity. ◊ MONSTROUS; TERATOLOGY.

Physic Garden Although this term was originally synonymous with botanic garden, and such gardens were used for

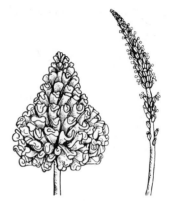

PHYLLODY. *Left,* flower-head of *Plantago major* 'Rosularis', compared with normal plantain flower-spike

general botanical studies, the word physic later became associated solely with medicinal plants or herbs, as in London's Chelsea Physic Garden which was founded in 1673 by the Worshipful Company of Apothecaries. ◊ BOTANIC GARDEN; HERB GARDEN.

Physiological Disorders Plant ill-health not caused by attack by pests or diseases, but by problems associated with weather, unsuitable soil, faulty watering or feeding, etc. Many such disorders are due to deficiencies of one sort of mineral, often induced by excess lime. For these an application of a sequestrol may be enough. ◊ CHLOROSIS; DEFICIENCY; NON-PARASITIC DISEASES; SEQUESTROL.

Phytophthora A group of fungi which cause plant diseases, including damping-off of seedlings and potato blight. ◊ BLIGHT; DAMPING-OFF.

Pick, Pick Axe Short-handled tools used from a stooping position with a chopping action, like the mattock. The pick has two long, curved, pointed heads, one each side of the shaft; the pick axe has one pointed head and one resembling a narrow chisel flattened at right angles to the direction of use, for cutting roots, etc. The mattock and its derivations, the grubbing axe and grubbing mattock, are similar. ◊ MATTOCK.

Picket ◊ FENCES.

Pickfork Originally a medium-sized tool combining a three-pronged fork and a short mattock blade; nowadays used for lighter versions of the same and also for the Canterbury hoe. ◊ HOE; MATTOCK.

Picotee (1) Originally (1727) a kind of carnation with white or yellow ground colour and a band of different, darker colour around the edge of each petal. Where this band is very thin the variety may be called a wire-edged picotee, the ordinary type being known as medium-edged in show classifications.

PICOTEE (pink)

(2) From the above usage, which referred to carnations and later to the related pinks and which was originally specifically connected with exhibition, the word picotee has now been extended to cover any flower with a thin band of different colour along each petal edge, as occurs in hippeastrums.

Picturesque A style of landscape gardening which arose in Britain towards the end of the landscape era, and affected design from 1790 into the early part of the nineteenth century. Fostered by the Rev. William Gilpin, it was taken up by the landscapers Richard Payne Knight and Uvedale Price, who respectively published

comments on it in a poem and an essay in 1794. To quote Peter Hunt's *Shell Gardens Book*, 'it was no longer considered sufficient to compose a landscape garden in broad terms of lawns, lakes and plantations . . . the pundits now required that each scene should produce subtleties of texture and colouring, contrasts of light and shade, or even emotional reactions, such as only a painter could conceive or emulate'.

Although Price and Knight attacked Humphry Repton in this connection, Repton's version of the Picturesque, actuated partly by what was practical, was the most influential not only in his own lifetime but well into the latter part of the nineteenth century, for he influenced the architect John Nash who introduced so many picturesque effects into his work, such as castellation and Italianate styles; these in their turn influenced many later designers of urban and suburban buildings and layouts.

◊ LANDSCAPE GARDENING; SUBLIME.

Pierced Screen Walling ◊ SCREEN WALLING.

Pigeon Manure Pigeon droppings are among the richest of all animal manures and have been used as plant food since quite ancient times. Persia and Turkey, for instance, have a great many pigeon-houses and dovecots where pigeons were encouraged to nest, primarily with a view to collecting their droppings (not, as in Britain, to eat the birds). In these arid countries other kinds of animal manure were, and are, used for fuel, not as fertilizer. Pigeon manure is as rich as the best Peruvian guano, with an analysis of around 14 per cent nitrogen, 11 per cent phosphoric acid and 3–4 per cent potash. Because of this richness, pigeon droppings are better considered as a concentrated fertilizer than as a bulky animal manure; it is used by drying it, powdering it and mixing with at least twice its bulk of soil or dry sand, and applying it as a top dressing at 6 oz. per square yard. Neat pigeon manure should never be used at a higher rate than this, otherwise root scorch can occur. ♢ GUANO; MANURE.

Pig Manure Though many gardeners dislike pig manure because of its odour and unpleasant texture, it is a valuable material when available. Although not so rich as other bulky animal manures, it provides plenty of humus and can be dug in at any time, though perhaps best in autumn and winter, at 10–15 lb. per square yard. It is best allowed to rot first; land dressed with fresh pig manure should be left vacant for at least six months. Pig manure is more suitable for light sandy soils than for heavy ones. ♢ MANURE.

Pillar (1) An architectural column. ♢ COLUMN (3).

(2) An upright form of trained fruit tree. This has been applied to the Lorette-trained pear trees described under ♢ COLUMN (2), and a more recent and successful pillar form for apples. In this a central trunk 7′–10′ high is allowed to produce a succession of laterals over three years, after which the oldest are cut right back to the trunk, whether they have fruited or not. Pillar-trained trees should be grown on dwarfing or semi-dwarfing rootstocks.

Pill Bug A country name, especially in the U.S., for a woodlouse. ♢ WOODLICE.

Pilose Having long, soft, distinct hairs. ♢ HAIRY.

PINCHING

Pinching The use of finger and thumb to remove the growing tip of a plant, to prevent any further extension of growth at that point, and also to encourage formation of side-shoots. ♢ BREAK; STOPPING.

Pine Needles These can be used for mulching in appropriate conditions, as in acid woodland gardens and around strawberries, where they will certainly conserve moisture and suppress weeds. However, due to their resin and turpentine content, pine needles decay very slowly indeed. They are occasionally recommended for specialized potting purposes, e.g. when normally epiphytic bromeliads are grown in pots, and for certain orchids. ♢ BROMELIAD; ORCHID.

Pinery A low greenhouse, often built as a pit, heated by a hotbed of tan bark or dung, for growing pineapples. Strawberries were also grown in pineries as a subsidiary crop. Such houses were in use from about 1720 till well into the nineteenth century. ♢ PIT.

Pinetum An arboretum or collection devoted to CONIFERS.

Pink Bud ♢ BUD STAGES.

Pinna, Pinnate, Pinnule The Latin *pinna* means a feather or wing. In botany a pinna is one primary division – i.e. a lobe, leaflet, or subsidiary petiole (stalk) bearing separate leaflets – of a feathery, divided leaf or fern frond. The adjective 'pinnate' describes a compound leaf or frond with a series of leaflets on each side of a common petiole. If this set of paired leaflets ends in an odd single leaflet this is called odd-pinnate or imparipinnate; where there is no terminating leaflet, this is even-pinnate or paripinnate. When the leaflets themselves divide, the secondary divisions are known as pinnules (adjective: pinnulate). In some cases, secondary and even tertiary divisions of the petioles occur, the last stage bearing pinnate leaflets; this division is called bipinnate or tripinnate. ♢ LEAF.

Pinnatifid, Pinnatisect 'Pinnatifid' describes a lobed leaf pinnately divided at least half-way to the midrib, and 'pinnatisect' a leaf divided almost to the midrib. ◊ LEAF.

Pip (1) The popular name for the seeds of apples, pears, citrus fruits, etc.

(2) A single growth or stem of lily-of-the-valley.

(3) A florist's term for a single flower in a cluster or truss, especially of auriculas and some other primulas.

Piping A special kind of cutting sometimes used with pinks and other dianthus, prepared by pulling a young shoot out at a joint or node. A firm grip and steady pull should bring the shoot cleanly out of the lower stem, and it can then be struck exactly like an ordinary cutting without further preparation. Pipings are usually taken in early summer, from young, non-flowering shoots. ◊ CUTTING; NODE.

PIPING

Pistil That part of a flower which comprises the entire female organ or gynoecium, including ovary, style (if present), and stigma. ◊ FLOWER.

Pistillate A flower may be described as pistillate when it has pistils but no stamens, in other words is female only. ◊ FEMALE FLOWER; FLOWER.

Pit (1) In gardening, a pit was a type of frame or greenhouse which is seldom seen today, and hardly ever constructed. In pits the floor was sunk below ground level so that the frame light or greenhouse roof was at or just above soil level. The advantages of pits were that the glass was less exposed to wind and that warmth was more easily conserved. They were often used for forcing plants, for cucumbers, and are still very valuable for propagating purposes. Unheated pits, sometimes called cold pits, are sometimes made by building walls of turves and covering with a glass frame light. ◊ FRAME; GREENHOUSE; PINERY.

(2) Sometimes used to refer to the 'stone' of a stone fruit like a peach or plum. ◊ STONE FRUIT.

Pith Soft, spongy tissue found in the centre of many plant stems; only in DICOTYLEDONS.

Plain Sometimes used of the unindented margins of entire leaves. ◊ ENTIRE; LEAF.

Plant Body A word sometimes used to describe the 'super-succulents' of the South African fig-marigold family (*Aizoaceae* or *Ficoidaceae*). These most highly adapted forms have fleshy bodies, sometimes top-shaped with a groove across the top as in *Lithops*, or more or less spherical with nothing more than a small central slit to denote that the structure is in effect the result of a pair of leaves coalescing, as in *Conophytum*. ◊ SUCCULENT.

Plant Breeders' Rights Many plants are now protected in Britain, Europe and the U.S. under plant patents. The London office which carries out registration for the U.K. is the Plant Variety Rights Office, who will supply a free booklet entitled *Guide to Plant Breeders' Rights* for anyone wishing to apply for a plant patent. In the U.S. plant patents are registered at the Patent Office. The purpose of these rights is to enable the breeder of a new variety to obtain a royalty on each plant sold and,

233

even more important, to prevent un-licensed growers from 'pirating' his variety by propagating it for sale.

Plant Breeding With plants, as with animals, deliberate breeding is aimed at the creation of new and different cultivars: it is a sexual process, as against the vegetative processes of taking cuttings or grafting in which the aim is to reproduce the plant in question – which is typically the result of breeding – identically and in large numbers. Breeding can be carried out only between closely related plants of the same family, occasionally genera, but much more frequently between species or cultivars derived from species. Today, plant breeding is a highly technical operation in commercial terms, in which breeders may seek not only novelty but to embody in a particular plant resistance to diseases, extra hardiness and other desirable qualities. This may mean working over many generations. This does not mean that amateur gardeners cannot have the enjoyment of cross-fertilizing plants in their own gardens and creating their own brand-new cultivars. Indeed, a few outstanding plants have been created in this way, e.g. the Russell lupin. ♢ F.1; FERTILIZATION; MU-TATION; POLLINATION; TRUE-BREEDING.

Planter (1) A tool which can avoid much stooping when planting large numbers of plants. The most common type is used for bulbs, ♢ BULB PLANTER. This type involves a tubular metal cutter about 3″ across. Another type has a pair of 'jaws' at the end of the 3′ handle which can be opened or shut by operating a lever. The tool is first pushed into the soil with the jaws open sufficiently to make a vertical cut. The jaws are then closed around the soil, the tool withdrawn, and the soil released by opening the jaws. This tool makes holes about 4″ wide.

Otherwise, planting holes are usually made with a trowel or spade.

♢ BULB PLANTER; PLANTING; POTATO PLANTER.

(2) The word 'planter' is occasionally used to refer to a plant container.

Plant Foods ♢ FEEDING PLANTS.

Plant House Another name for a greenhouse, but most often used of large-scale structures. ♢ GREENHOUSE.

Planting The essential operation of setting plants into the garden, whether they have been grown at home or bought, and whether they are small seedlings, perennials, bulbs, shrubs or trees. Ideally, the soil should be neither very wet nor very dry before planting. Whatever the plant, it should not be planted too deeply or too shallowly; it is normal practice (there are a few exceptions) to plant to the same soil level at which the plant was previously growing. Most plants need to be well firmed in, packing the soil quite hard around the roots, although there are some exceptions, e.g. ferns, which establish better if put into fairly loose soil.

Before planting, soil is usually best forked over, and at this time it can be enriched with peat, rotted garden compost or similar bulky organic material, to which some fertilizer is added. The best types of fertilizer are the slow-acting ones, and as a rule of thumb two handfuls of bone meal and one of hoof and horn meal can be added to each bucketful of bulky organic material. For bare-rooted plants, including herbaceous perennials, a planting mixture to this formula can be prepared and worked in around the roots as planting progresses. The planting hole is best made with a trowel for small plants and a spade for larger ones. Plants with long vertical roots must have holes of sufficient depth to accommodate them without bending them, but in general planting holes should be wider than deep so that the roots can be spread sideways, not bunched together. A dibber should be used only for very small seedlings and small tap-rooted plants, e.g. brassicas.

The soil around small plants should be firmed with the hand as filling proceeds. With large plants of most sorts, the foot can be used both at the filling and at the final stages, and although the soil must not be too consolidated it is hard to compress it too much round roses, shrubs and trees. Heavy soils will need less firming than lighter ones.

same period; broad-leaved evergreens in early autumn or in spring. Bulbs and other fleshy-rooted plants are best planted when dormant, which varies according to species. Annuals and bedding plants are put out according to need and hardiness

PLANTING. *Left*, section of planting hole for tree; the soil below has been well forked. *Right*, firming the ground with the foot

If adequate care is taken, and dry soil is thoroughly soaked before and after planting, this operation can be carried out at any time of year, especially where container-grown plants are concerned. However, there are certain seasons when it is much safer to plant than at others, especially with bare-rooted plants. Herbaceous perennials are best planted in early autumn or in spring; alpines at the same periods with a preference for late spring; deciduous shrubs and trees from mid-autumn to mid-spring; conifers during the

(most bedders are not hardy and should not be planted before risk of frost has passed).

Plantlet Miniature plants equipped with leaves and often roots are produced by a number of plants as a means of increase other than by seeds. Some are designed to fall off and then develop, as with those produced by many bryophyllums; others need to come into contact with moist soil while still attached to the parent before roots will form and the new young plant

PLANTLET. *Left to right: Bryophyllum daigremontianum, Asplenium bulbiferum, Tolmiea menziesii*

235

can survive on its own, as with the pickaback plant (*Tolmiea*). ◊ VIVIPAROUS.

Plant Lice A term quite widely used for the sap-sucking aphids and their relations (greenfly, black fly, etc.). ◊ APHIDS.

Plant Patents ◊ PLANT BREEDERS' RIGHTS.

Plant Window This sophisticated method of growing plants indoors really involves the construction of an indoor greenhouse. The basic plant window has an orthodox window behind it, preferably double-glazed for insulation. A structure is then built out in front of the window so that a space within the room can be totally enclosed in glass. This usually extends from floor or sometimes window-sill level up to the ceiling. Although plant windows are normally relatively narrow, they can be made broader if space permits. The glass within the room must be so organized that it can be opened when required, most easily by the use of sliding panels. If desired, the plant window can be made against an interior wall and be provided with artificial light in the form of suitable plant-growth lamps (normally of the tubular mercury-vapour type). Supplementary lighting can, of course, be supplied to a plant window backed by an ordinary one: this is as much for decorative effect at night as for plant health. If the room heating is likely to be inadequate, extra heaters, e.g. the tubular electric type, can be installed below the planting trough. The latter must, of course, be waterproof. ◊ HOUSE PLANT.

Plantsman A word defined by the *Oxford Dictionary* (1907 edition) as meaning a nurseryman or florist, but nowadays developed to mean any expert gardener who is primarily a plant connoisseur, one who loves plants for their own sake. This can mean that such a gardener prefers growing plants as individuals rather than combining them into a pleasing whole.

The word plantsmanship is derived from plantsman – with perhaps slight connotations of one-upmanship!

Plash ◊ PLEACH.

Plastics As in so many aspects of modern life, plastics have entered into gardening in many ways, replacing and often improving on older materials. One of the most important applications has been in the short-term replacement of glass in greenhouses, frames and cloches, and also as insulation material within glass greenhouses. Plastics have also extensively replaced concrete as pool-making materials, and are very widely used for pots and other plant containers. Other uses of plastics include sterilizing of soil, for hoses, mulching, artificial rocks and waterfalls, and watering cans. Chips and granules of plastic are used in soil and potting composts.

Whenever plastics play an important or novel part, these uses are mentioned; e.g. ◊ CLOCHE; FRAME; GLASS SUBSTITUTES; GREENHOUSE; MULCH; POOL; STERILIZATION.

Plat An old word, now virtually obsolete, more or less equivalent to plot; sometimes found in older garden literature to refer to a small, level area of ground, for instance a grass-plat.

Pleach A word derived from plash or plait, used from the fifteenth century onwards to refer to hedge-making by bending down, half-cutting, and interweaving stems of shrubs and trees (laying). A later meaning is to train against a trellis or wall. However, the word is now used in its more limited meaning of producing a narrow screen or hedge by such procedures, which include training new flexible branches along wires or canes and cutting out surplus growth annually; in some cases the screen is clipped into regular formations. In many cases the pleaching is restricted to the upper parts of the trees concerned, so that a dense green hedge is produced at some height above ground, supported on the pillar-like tree trunks. Lime, hornbeam and yew have been popular for pleaching, but almost any tree can be used. ◊ LAYING.

Plenus, Pleniflorus Latin adjectives meaning 'full' or 'full-flowered' which are sometimes used as varietal names for double-flowered plants; also of course in the feminine and neuter forms -a and -um as required. ◊ DOUBLE.

Plicate Pleated; usually applied to leaves with a pleated look, e.g. those of *Veratrum*.

Plough A very ancient agricultural tool with a curved, pointed cutting blade designed to create furrows in the soil and turn it over. Normally designed to be pulled by an animal, or sometimes a man, the plough has been adapted for horticultural use as a small blade fixed to a hand or powered cultivator, rather than the straight or rectangular tines normally used for soil stirring. In the breast plough (a

hairs, flowers and flowerheads. ◊ HAIRY; PAPPUS.

Plumule The initial shoot formed within the embryo of a seed, and the first to be produced after germination.

Plunge, Plunge Bed Pot-grown plants are often 'plunged' outside when not wanted indoors or in the greenhouse. This means that the pots are sunk up to their rims, protecting soil and roots from becoming too hot and from drying out. This may be done in ordinary soil; however, if there are many pots, a special plunge bed is often made, usually of sifted boiler ashes, coarse sand or peat. Such a bed can be made above ground level with an edging of boards and, where overhead protection is also necessary, the plunge bed can be made in a frame. This is usually necessary when alpines are grown in pots or pans, to be taken into an alpine house when in flower.

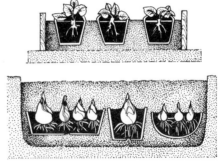

PLUNGE. *Left and top right* (section), board-edged plunge bed; *right*, spring-flowering bulbs plunged in soil

version now seldom seen) the blade is arranged on a long handle in front of the human operator. The lever plough is a modern invention designed to assist disabled people: the plough blade is dragged through the soil by the operation of a hand lever. ◊ BREAST PLOUGH; CULTIVATOR.

Plumose Plumed or feathery: applied to plant organs of various kinds, including

Other plants commonly plunged are hardy shrubs kept in pots for forcing, and large greenhouse plants which are kept out of doors during the summer.

Bulbs for indoor or greenhouse decoration in pots or bowls are normally plunged several inches deep. This ensures that they are cool and moist and that the roots develop well before much top growth, and before any forcing.

Pneumatophore An air-breathing root, formed by certain trees which naturally grow in water or swamps, e.g. mangroves and swamp cypress. The latter is the only tree which produces pneumatophores likely to be seen in British gardens: in the right conditions extraordinary upright, woody, bark-covered growths up to 18″ tall appear around the trunk of the tree.

Pod Any dry seed vessel which has several seeds and splits open into two halves, thus including the fruits of the wallflower family technically known as siliques. To most people the word is restricted to the seed vessel of the family *Leguminosae*, e.g. garden peas and beans. ◇ CAPSULE; LEGUME.

Pole An antique measure of both length and area. ◇ PERCH (1), (2); WEIGHTS AND MEASURES (p. viii).

Polesaw A short curved pruning saw fixed on the end of a long pole; the saw is sometimes available as an extra to be fixed onto long-handled tree pruners. ◇ SAW; TREE PRUNERS.

Pollard When a tree has all its boughs cut back right to the trunk at intervals, it is known as a pollard, and the practice is called pollarding (from the word 'poll', to cut short or crop). This is sometimes done for ornament, since a few trees produce neat mop-headed growth if pollarded, but is more often carried out for utilitarian reasons, either to keep trees within bounds or to encourage the production of a quantity of young growths, such as the 'withies' produced by pollarded willows, much used in basket making and the construction of hurdles. Trees which are cut back so that a number of short stumps are left – like the famous beeches in Burnham Beeches, England – are more correctly described as lopped, or sometimes as stubbed. ◇ ADVENTITIOUS, HEADING BACK; LOP; STUB.

Pollen The dust-like grains carried in the anthers of most flowering plants, which produce the male cells. When these grains alight on the stigma, pollination can be said to have occurred; this is followed by the fertilization of the ovule by the process described under ◇ FERTILIZATION. In most flowering plants the pollen is carried in powdery form on the anthers of the stamens, but in orchids and some other plants it is gathered into sticky pollen-masses, sometimes called pollinia, which are picked up bodily by the pollinating insects. In conifers the powdery pollen is carried in small sacs which release the grains into the air. ◇ ANTHER; COLUMN; CONIFER; FERTILIZATION; ORCHID; STAMEN.

Pollination The transference of the male pollen to the female stigma, an act which precedes fertilization when the male gametes from the pollen fuse with the female gametes in the ovum and initiate the production of seed. In nature, some flowers will self-pollinate; with others, the pollen is transferred from male to female organs by the wind or the agency of an animal, most often an insect in temperate climates. The gardener can deliberately transfer pollen from male to female organ, either to ensure a crop or to carry out breeding. The former can be done by jarring the flowers, by dusting the sexual organs with a soft paint-brush, a rabbit's

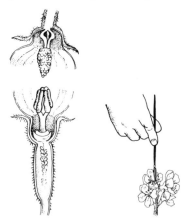

POLLINATION. *Left*, pollinating a female marrow (squash) flower (*below*, section without petals) with a severed male flower (*above*). *Right*, using a paintbrush on peach flowers

tail on a stick, or a similar soft utensil. The method of actually pushing the stamens of a male flower onto the stigma of the flower to be pollinated is usually applied when breeding is the aim. ⬦ CROSS-FERTILIZATION; EMASCULATION; FEMALE FLOWER; FERTILIZATION; PLANT BREEDING; SELF-POLLINATION.

Pollinia Sticky masses of pollen grains, found in orchids and a few other plants, which are picked up bodily by the pollinating insects. ⬦ POLLEN.

Polypetalous Used of flowers with several petals which are quite separate from each other, e.g. the rose, as opposed to those having a corolla of one piece with several lobes, called sympetalous. ⬦ FLOWER.

Polyploid A plant having more than the standard number of chromosomes per cell which is characteristic of the normal species. Triploids (abbreviated 3x) and tetraploids (4x) are examples, but the number of chromosomes can often be higher. The state of being polyploid is known as polyploidy. ⬦ CHROMOSOME; TETRAPLOID; TRIPLOID.

Polystyrene A thermoplastic material usually seen in the form of moulds, sometimes used for the bases of propagators and as plant containers, and to replace moss poles. Polystyrene granules, which are capable of absorbing air and water, are sometimes used in soilless potting composts instead of, or in conjunction with, natural materials. ⬦ MOSS POLE; PLASTICS.

Polythene A thermoplastic material in the form of thin film or as moulded articles. Polythene film is used in the garden for short-term greenhouse covering and pond lining, for greenhouse insulation, for mulching, and to form temporary plant containers. Solid polythene appears in the form of plastic pots and other containers. ⬦ PLASTICS.

Polyvynil Chloride ⬦ PVC.

Pome The technical word for the fruit of apple, pear and similar plants which has a number of seed-containing cells in a fleshy exterior. The fruit is inferior, i.e. formed below the flower. ⬦ FRUIT.

Pomology The science and practice of fruit growing.

Pomona A treatise on fruits.

Pompon A term used to classify groups of dahlias and chrysanthemums with small globular flowers composed of tight-packed florets, but also applicable to other plants with such flowers. It derives from the French word *pompom*, meaning a tuft or top-knot.

POMPON (dahlia)

Pond Although the *Oxford Dictionary* defines pond as 'a small body of still water of artificial formation', many people consider a pond to be a body of water within banks of natural soil, clay, etc.; most authorities and water-garden specialists refer to water in the garden as a pool, although the *Dictionary* considers pools to be usually of natural formation. ⬦ POOL.

Pool In general usage, any body of water in a garden, whether for decoration, growing plants or swimming in. Pools have been part of garden design since Roman and earliest Chinese times, and the fishpond formed a vital part of the food supply of monasteries and large houses. The use of

239

POOL. Section through typical small pool with plants in plastic planting baskets; note ledges for marginal plants and submerged oxygenating plant

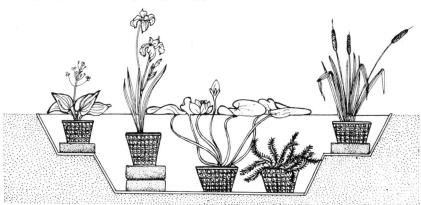

pools for plants, however, began in Europe only in the eighteenth century and became popular in the nineteenth (the ancient Egyptians grew waterlilies in pools).

Pools can be of any shape or size. Those of circular or rectangular outline are usually described as formal, and those of irregular shape as informal. Where the soil is suitable, pools can be formed without artificial aid, though it is usually desirable for the clay in such soil to be 'puddled' by ramming it at the base and edges of the excavation, if necessary adding a small amount of straw in successive layers to help binding. The action of the feet of ducks and geese around a gradually filled pool is also an excellent way to puddle the clay.

Usually an impervious basin has to be created artificially. Cement-bonded slabs have been used, but until recently it was most common to make pools of concrete. In recent decades plastic materials have made pool construction much easier. These include plastic sheeting of which heavy grades of PVC and butyl rubber are the most durable; they will take up the contours of almost any reasonably undulating or curved excavation, although it is harder to make an attractive formal pool with such pool liners than an informal one, because of the right angles in the former. It is usual to hold down and conceal the edges of the liner with paving slabs, but they can be fixed by weight of soil. Other

plastic pool liners are made of solid moulded material such as fibreglass, and with these of course the gardener has a more limited choice of outline, nor are large sizes readily available. For small pools, other prefabricated objects can be used, e.g. domestic water-tanks, half-barrels or plastic tubs, and even old baths.

When making a pool of any depth, it is usual to provide one or more ledges around the margins to accommodate plants preferring varying depths of water.

A well-planned garden pool has flowering water plants, e.g. waterlilies, in the deeper water, floating plants, and marginal plants which grow in shallow water close to the edges or in moist soil around them. In addition it should have submerged oxygenating plants which keep the water supplied with oxygen and help to keep down unwanted algae like blanket-weed because they compete with the latter. These oxygenators are also essential for the well-being of fish included in the pool, and provide suitable places for fish to spawn.

Apart from their ornamental value, fish eat a variety of unwanted creatures in the water, notably mosquito larvae. There is a limit to the number of fish a pool can maintain, and as a rule of thumb the new pool can have 3″ length of fish to every 10″ square of water surface.

Water snails are invaluable as scavengers but certain kinds, like the freshwater whelk, attack decorative plants and must be avoided.

Pools for plants and fish are best sited in open positions receiving full sun. Shady places are less suitable and the proximity of trees means that leaves falling into the water will foul it as they decay.

Pools can be associated with cascades, fountains and streams, as desired.

◊ MARGINAL; OXYGENATORS; WATER-WORKS.

were first used by the early Egyptians, Greeks and Chinese, used always to be of baked clay (earthenware) but in recent years plastic ones have quite largely replaced the clay originals. It is also possible to obtain temporary pots for growing on young plants or for housing older or mature ones ready for transplanting, made of plastic sheet, 'whalehide', bitumenized or other strengthened paper, compressed fibre or peat, and other materials.

POT. *Left to right*, normal pot, square pot, small pan, 'long tom'

Pool Liner A plastic sheet or prefabricated solid form used to make pools impervious. ◊ POOLS.

Post and Board ◊ FENCES.

Post-emergent Used of weedkillers which are applied after the crop concerned has germinated and emerged from the soil; also of weedkillers used to destroy growing weeds around a growing perennial crop. The latter should be qualified as post-weed-emergent weedkillers. ◊ PRE-EMERGENT; WEEDKILLER.

Post-hole Borer A tool which facilitates the boring of holes for the posts supporting fences. It usually resembles a twist drill with a screwed point at the base and two blades above this; when turned by a transverse handle the device cuts into the soil with a spiral action.

Pot Generally, a container in which to grow plants, but usually restricted to flat-based conical-sided containers. Pots, which

Pots are conveniently classified by their internal diameter at the rim, but when clay was widely used they were more often referred to by a number which indicated the number of pots that could be made from a standard lump or cast of clay, such as a 'forty-eight' (5″) or a 'small sixty' (3″). A 'number one' was an 18″ pot.

The proportions of a normal flowerpot are roughly standard, but there are a number of variations. The use of plastics has allowed the production of square-section pots which are more economical of space than round ones. The pan is about half the depth of a normal pot, and thus more shallow than deep, while its opposite, the 'long tom', is much deeper in proportion to width, and suits tap-rooted plants. Besides these utilitarian pots, the word is applied to ornamental containers of roughly similar proportions to the orthodox pot, whether of clay, plastic, stone or composition.

Pots are always equipped with drainage holes. Clay pots normally have one quite large central hole and large ones sometimes three additional holes at the sides. Modern plastic pots usually have a series of quite small holes near the edge of the flat base. A clay orchid pot has additional holes up the sides to ensure that the porous compost can never be waterlogged. The modern version of this is the mesh pot of plastic with large rectangular perforations occupying much of its side.

Pots may or may not have a deep rim or 'collar'. With clay, a machine-turned pot with a deep vertical collar, known as a nesting pot, allowed a pile of pots to be made without any risk of their jamming together. This is not so important with plastic pots which are machine-made so that a pot of a specific size will nest with others and not jam even without a rim.

The advantages of plastic over clay pots are that they are much lighter, much less brittle (though rims can crack if pots are picked up there), are easy to clean, and take up water from a capillary bench without a wick. When transferring plants from a plastic pot, their roots tend to stick to the sides much less than with a clay pot. However, since they entirely lack the porosity of the clay pot, and hence its capacity for evaporating moisture, they hold moisture in the potting compost much longer, so more care in watering is needed to avoid waterlogging. Whereas it is possible to determine the water need of a clay pot by tapping it with a wooden hammer or the knuckle (a dry pot gives out a ringing note, a wet one a dull note), this cannot be done with a plastic pot and other means have to be used. Many plants grow better in plastic than in clay pots because the former retain heat in the potting compost better. Plastic also has the advantage that it can be produced in many colours besides the standard earthenware tone.

The operation of placing plants in pots is called potting. That of transferring a plant from one pot to another may be termed repotting or potting on.

◊ CAPILLARY WATERING; CROCKING; MESH POT; MOISTURE METER; PEAT POTS; POTTING.

Potager *Jardin potager* is simply the French for a kitchen garden. However, the word 'potager' now refers primarily to a kitchen garden usually containing both vegetables and fruit, laid out ornamentally, often with the beds edged with low hedges like a parterre.

Potash, Potassium The word 'potash' is applied to any substance containing the mineral potassium: this is one of the three vital elements for plant growth, its chemical symbol being K. The potash content of any potassic fertilizer is always stated in terms of potassium oxide (K_2O).

Without adequate potassium, plants cannot grow properly, making weak, soft growth, unable to form flowers or fruit. This is often the case with greenhouse crops and pot plants. Potash deficiency may also result in severe scorching of leaves, especially at their edges. Extra potash is valuable in aiding any fruiting plant to develop plenty of fruit, including tomatoes; it also encourages production of storage organs, as in potatoes. Flowering of bulbs, e.g. hippeastrums, is also enhanced by generous feeding with potash. In all these cases the potash applications are best given over a period after the plants have achieved adequate size or made adequate growth for the season. Fruit and vegetables provided with plenty of potash are likely to be better flavoured than those without. Another very important function of potash is to slow down vegetative growth and enhance the formation of flower buds for the season ahead in shrubs and trees, both ornamental and utilitarian, and late-summer applications for these purposes will also increase frost resistance in the young growth of relatively tender plants.

Potash is especially likely to be short in light sandy soils and in those containing much peat or chalk.

Extra potash for stimulating fruit production, etc., is most conveniently supplied in compound fertilizers with a high proportion of potash. Materials used for supplying potash alone include KAINIT, MURIATE OF POTASH, NITRATE OF POTASH and SULPHATE OF POTASH. Wood ashes contain 2–7 per cent potash, which is lost rapidly when the material is moistened. Animal manures contain a small proportion of potash and seaweed up to 1 per cent.

For potassium permanganate ⬦ PER-MANGANATE OF POTASH.

⬦ FEEDING PLANTS.

Potassium Sulphide Also known as liver of sulphur, this material combines some insecticidal properties with eradication of powdery mildews, but because it is somewhat caustic it is today largely superseded by other fungicides and insecticides.

Potato Planter A device for planting potatoes and other tubers and bulbs. Two triangular scoop-shaped blades form a V when the handles are held apart; the potato is placed in this cavity and the blades pushed into the previously cultivated soil to the required depth. Pulling the handles together in the centre opens the blades and releases the potato, and the device is then withdrawn. ⬦ PLANTER.

Pot-bound An expression used to describe pot-grown plants whose roots have entirely filled the container. In general, plants will not continue to thrive if too pot-bound (or root-bound as it is sometimes called), but this state is conducive to flower production and some plants, especially fleshy-rooted ones, can be kept almost permanently in this condition as long as they are adequately fed. ⬦ POTTING.

Pot Herb An expression used of herb-like plants which are edible rather than medicinal, whose leaves and sometimes roots can be used in soups or stews, or as salads, e.g. borage, dandelion, lovage and sorrel. ⬦ HERB.

Pot-in-pot A method of displaying creeping or trailing plants. Two or preferably three pots of different sizes are selected and arranged in pyramid shape so that when the smaller is lightly embedded in the potting compost of the next larger, there is still space to plant in the latter. Cuttings or small plants are planted fairly close together near the edges of the larger pot or pots and in the topmost, smallest pot. In a short time the growth of these cuttings will entirely hide the pots and resemble a cascade of growth. The best effect is probably achieved when only one kind of plant is used.

Pot Layering Another expression for AIR LAYERING.

Pot-pourri A mixture of dried aromatic petals and sometimes fragrant leaves, mixed with spices, which retains its fragrance for a long time if the ingredients are carefully prepared and blended. A bowl of pot-pourri will scent a room, or the mixture can be placed in sachets or other containers among clothes.

Pot Saucer A circular saucer with a near-vertical rim, made in different sizes to accommodate various-sized pots, and placed beneath the pot to prevent water passing through the potting mixture escaping further.

Pot Shard A piece of broken clay pot used as drainage material when potting. ⬦ CROCKING.

Potting The initial placing of plants in pots from seed trays (sometimes called 'potting off' or 'potting up') or the operation of moving them to bigger pots from smaller ones (the latter also being called 'potting on' or 'repotting'). Whenever plants are grown in pots this onward movement into bigger pots is essential, especially with fast-growing plants from seed or cuttings which reach their maturity within a season. Severe checks in growth and performance may result if potting on is not carried out whenever the roots begin to cover the exterior of the root ball, and before they start to spiral round densely at the base of the pot.

Plants of longer span need repotting less often; eventually, of course, large plants cannot be moved on any further because there is a limit to the size of container which can be handled or obtained. Large plants need feeding more often to keep them from starvation, and in the end the only way may be to start again with new plants by some means of propagation.

The first stage with a seedling or cutting will be to give it a pot large enough to house its roots: this may be 1″–2″ in diameter.

In the following stages progression is from one pot size to the next convenient one, enough to allow adequate room around the root ball to insert new potting compost without leaving air spaces. A suitable progression could be from 3″ to 4½″, to 6″, to 7½″ or even 8½″. As pot sizes increase, the jump in pot size can be correspondingly greater.

Potting is normally done only when plants are in active growth; potting at other times can result in a check. Before potting, the appropriate new pot is selected, having been well cleaned first, and drainage material is inserted if appropriate: a clay pot will at least need a crock placed over the drainage hole. A layer of the selected potting compost is then inserted, sufficient to bring the level of the old pot to a suitable height just below the rim of the new pot. This may be around ½″ for small sizes and 1″ for large ones, to allow space for water when watering.

The plant is most easily removed from its old pot by turning it upside down and placing the fingers of one hand across the surface of the potting compost with the growths protruding between the fingers. The pot rim is then brought down fairly sharply on a hard surface like a potting bench, when the pot should disengage. It may be necessary to place a large plant on its side and tap the pot with a wood mallet or other tool while the base of the plant is pulled on; in extreme cases it may be necessary to slide a long knife round the inside of the pot to disengage roots clinging to it.

When the plant has been removed from its old pot it is placed on the layer of new potting compost in the new pot, and fresh potting compost is trickled in round the root ball, being pushed down with the fingers or a tool like a potting stick to ensure no air pockets are left. Banging the pot down lightly on a hard surface once or twice as filling proceeds should also help with this problem. In general, large woody plants should be firmed more solidly than soft ones, while soil-based composts can be firmed much more than peat-based mixtures. The potting mixture is best used moist but never too wet.

Specialized plants, e.g. orchids, need different potting techniques.

Newly potted plants will appreciate moister and shadier conditions for a few days while they get over the shock of the operation.

▷ COMPOSTS, SEED AND POTTING; DRAINAGE; POT; POTTING STICK.

Potting Bench ▷ POTTING SHED.

Potting Composts ▷ COMPOSTS, SEED AND POTTING.

Potting Off ▷ POTTING.

Potting On ▷ POTTING.

Potting Shed A building in which all the operations for handling pot-grown plants may be carried out, such as potting, seed sowing, pricking out, preparation of seed and potting composts. The potting shed, where it can be accommodated, should include a wooden potting bench of solid construction, the top wooden platform having boards fixed vertically along its back or sides so that a heap of potting compost can be retained. The potting shed is also ideal for storing garden tools and other equipment.

Potting Soil An older term for potting compost from days when this was always based on soil. ▷ COMPOSTS, SEED AND POTTING.

Potting Stick A short piece of smooth stick with slightly rounded ends, 1″–1½″ thick and 12″–18″ long, used for firming potting compost around large plants when repotting. This ensures that no air pockets are left. Older authorities often suggest that the potting stick be used to ram the potting mixture down very solidly, but present-day usage is to make the compost reasonably firm without ramming, especially if it is peat-based, in which case little firming is required. ◊ POTTING.

Potworms Small, translucent, whitish worms found in soil containing a lot of humus, which can increase in pots if unsterilized soil is used as a component of the potting compost. These are technically enchytraeid worms: they feed mainly on decaying materials, but may damage roots if present in excessive numbers. They can be reduced by watering with a potassium permanganate solution or derris, made up as for spraying.

Poultry Manure ◊ MANURE.

Powdery Mildew ◊ MILDEW.

Power Scythe ◊ MOWERS.

Predators A word used by gardeners to denote animals of various types which are beneficial in the garden since they feed upon other animals which are garden pests. The most commonly mentioned is the ladybird or lady bug, which feeds on aphids in large numbers, both in the larval and adult stages. The larvae of hover-flies (sweat flies) and lacewing flies do the same, ichneumon flies attack caterpillars, chalcid wasp larvae eat white fly in the scale stage, while red spider mites are attacked by further insects including the black-kneed capsid. Spiders, of course, trap and eat a wide range of insects, both harmful and useful. Centipedes, carabid beetles and devil's coach-horse beetles also feed upon smaller animals, including many pests. The generally disliked wasp kills a great many other insects, most of them harmful in the garden. In the U.S. the praying mantis feeds voraciously on other insects. There is also the carnivorous, brownish-yellow testacella slug.

Many larger creatures are also invaluable. Birds eat immense numbers of insects and their grubs, although they can be garden pests in their own right. Hedgehogs, toads and grass snakes are all carnivores which eat grubs, slugs and snails and do no harm at all. If these larger animals can be persuaded to remain in the garden (many greenhouses have resident toads) they are invaluable, but it is impossible to rely on the other predators to deal reliably with the usual insect pests. However, the predators should always be encouraged, and this can be done by reducing the overall amount of pesticide application, using materials only when serious pest attacks seem imminent, and using materials of short persistence, or systemics.

A few predators can be organized to work for the gardener as required. These are restricted to greenhouses in Britain, and include the chalcid wasp whitefly parasite and a mite used against red spider mite. Both have been used with success on a commercial scale. Other predators have been used outside in warm climates.
◊ BIOLOGICAL CONTROL; BIRDS; PEST; PESTICIDE.

Pre-emergent Used of weedkillers which are applied after a crop has been sown but has not yet appeared above the soil surface; also of weedkillers used to destroy weeds as they emerge from the soil after germinating. The latter should be qualified as pre-weed-emergent weedkillers. ◊ POST-EMERGENT; WEEDKILLER.

Prepared Applied to bulbs which have been prepared by various treatments (such as periods of cold before sale) so that they will flower much sooner after planting than in the normal way. ◊ VERNALIZATION.

Preservative ◊ WOOD PRESERVATIVES.

Preserving Leaves ◊ EVERLASTING.

Pre-sowing A method of preparing seeds for sowing in which they are pre-spaced and fixed on sheets, or between two sheets, of thin paper or paper-like vegetable medium. This method has been applied to grass seeds, with paper strips available in widths around 2′, and also to seeds of vegetables and annual flowers, when the strips are narrow and only contain one row of seeds. The strips are laid upon levelled soil, or the single-row ones in shallow drills, and covered with an appropriate depth of soil. The paper medium decomposes in the soil fairly soon and leaves the germinating seeds. Although it is claimed that this method ensures proper spacing, improves germination and simplifies sowing, it has never become very popular, whether for grass or other seeds, and sowing certainly takes about the same time as orthodox methods.

Pricking Off ◇ PRICKING OUT.

Pricking Out This rather odd expression, derived from the action of pricking small holes in the soil and alternatively rendered as 'pricking off', refers to the operation of transferring seedlings from the receptacles in which they have been raised from seed to other receptacles or beds where they are given more room. This move must be done with care, because tiny seedlings are fragile, and their leaves and roots are easily damaged. Research has shown that seedlings are best moved when they have developed their seed leaves but not their

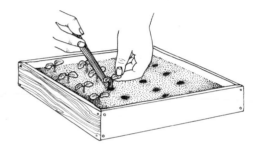

PRICKING OUT

Pre-sprouting The germination of seeds on damp flannel or absorbent paper before sowing; the same as chitting, and employed in the method called fluid sowing. ◇ CHITTING; FLUID SOWING.

Pricking Describes the use of a garden fork when inserted lightly into the soil among growing plants in order to stir the surface. Pricking may be carried out as a form of cultivation or after the application of fertilizers or manures so as to incorporate these into the upper layer of the soil. Pricking can also be carried out on lawns, either with the garden fork thrust in 4″–6″ deep at short intervals, or by the use of a spiking tool: this is done to improve aeration and during very dry weather to ensure that water applied to the surface will penetrate to the roots of the grass.

first true leaves, since less check to growth occurs from a shift at the earlier stage. Some instrument, e.g. a sharp label or a label cut into two prongs like a miniature fork, is often useful to lever up the seedlings; they should be held by a seed-leaf and placed in a hole previously made by a small round-ended dibber or a multiple tool (multi-dibber), after which the soil is replaced round the roots and very gently firmed with the dibber or fingers. It is best to prick out seedlings into rows. When the box or pot of pricked-out seedlings is full, it should be watered with a fine-rosed can. To avoid wilting, the containers are best kept in a humid atmosphere and out of direct sunlight for a day or two. ◇ DIBBER; MULTI-DIBBER.

Prickle A sharp pointed outgrowth from the surface of a plant. For full definition ◇ SPINE.

Proliferation The production of an abnormal number of organs in a flower. This may simply be a form of doubling, often associated with transmutation of stamens into petals; or the production of dual organs such as corollas as in hose-in-hose flowers. However, the word is most often applied to the production of an abnormal number of flowers or flower-heads. This occurs sometimes in members of the Composite family, e.g. the daisy, where a ring of subsidiary flower-heads on individual stalks is produced around the central one; this is sometimes called 'hen-and-chickens', and has been technically referred to as ring fasciation. ⬦ DOUBLE; FASCIATION; HOSE-IN-HOSE; TERATOLOGY.

Prong or Prong-claw Cultivator A tool with arched, recurved prongs, usually three in number, with the ends bent over at right angles to the long handle. ⬦ CULTIVATOR.

Propagating Case A box-shaped construction glazed with glass, rigid plastic or, in cheaper versions, plastic sheet on a wire frame. Though usually made as one unit it is possible to obtain versions with a relatively small one-piece 'dome' of rigid plastic which fits onto a plastic tray. Larger, more expensive units may have built-in electric heating in the base, often controlled by a thermostat. Propagating cases retain air humidity within the glazed dome or top and are used for rearing seedlings or striking cuttings; they are designed to be used within greenhouses or dwellings rather than outside, where a propagating frame is normally used. Those without built-in heating can be placed over heating pipes or near a radiator to provide extra basal heat. ⬦ PROPAGATION.

Propagating Frame Any frame used primarily for plant propagation, including growing plants from seed and striking cuttings. They are usually of orthodox frame design with relatively low sides and a sloping glazed top 'light', and are often quite small, with only one hinged or sliding light. It is essential that a propagating frame should be virtually airtight so that it retains the air humidity essential for most kinds of propagation. Propagating frames are usually used out of doors, where a sheltered position out of direct sunlight is desirable, but small ones can be used in the greenhouse if extra heat is required, though the more box-shaped propagating case is usually easier to accommodate there. ⬦ FRAME; PROPAGATION.

Propagating House A greenhouse devoted to propagation. In principle, this will not differ from an orthodox greenhouse in construction, but it will probably be fitted with strong benches which may carry a number of propagating frames or mist-propagation equipment. ⬦ MIST PROPAGATION; PROPAGATING FRAME.

Propagation The increase of plants by any appropriate method. In nature, increase by seeds or spores is the commonest method, which can be called seminal propagation; but quite a number of plants in the wild increase vegetatively, as by producing offsets, plantlets, runners and other replicas of the parent. Both kinds of propagation are available to gardeners, including many artificial means of vegetative propagation which are not carried out in natural conditions, e.g. by cuttings and grafting.

The distinction is important to the gardener, because many garden plants are of mixed inheritance and will not reproduce the parent – i.e. breed true – if grown from seed; even species may not produce identical offspring. Seed is often convenient for producing large numbers of individuals, and modern seedsmen make sure that the plants raised from a packet of seed are true to character; that does not mean that the gardener can necessarily continue to grow similar plants if he collects seed from the packet-grown plants. Seed is especially valuable for short-term plants like annual and biennial flowers and vegetables, but it can take many years to grow a tree, for instance, from seed.

For speed of production of reasonably mature plants, and for exact replication of the plants even when highly bred, vegetative propagation is therefore used. All

247

plants propagated vegetatively from one original individual are described as clones.

For distinct methods of propagation ◊ AIR LAYERING; BUDDING; CUTTING (for related methods); DIVISION; GRAFTING (for related methods); INARCHING; LAYERING; PIPING; SEED SOWING; SPORE; STOOLING.

◊ CLASSIFICATION; CLONE; F.1; FLUID SOWING; HYBRID; MIST PROPAGATION; OFFSET; PLANTLET; PROPAGATING CASE; PROPAGATING FRAME; RUNNER; SAND FRAME; SEMINAL; STOCK PLANT; STOLON; VEGETATIVE; WOUNDING.

Propagator (1) A device to assist in propagation by providing humid atmosphere. ◊ PROPAGATING CASE; PROPAGATING FRAME.

(2) Also, one who propagates plants.

Propagule A miniature plant produced naturally by an adult which will grow on without the need for special treatment. Examples are an OFFSET and a PLANTLET. Also sometimes applied to a piece of plant induced artificially to act as a propagation unit, e.g. a CUTTING.

Protected Cultivation Any method of growing plants under some form of cover such as a CLOCHE, FRAME or GREENHOUSE.

Protection Although the gardener normally tries to protect his plants against attack by pests and diseases, the word 'protection' in garden parlance is normally restricted to keeping plants from harm caused by the vagaries of weather and making conditions tolerable for tender plants grown in a climate to which they are not adapted.

The prime example of protection of plants is their cultivation in greenhouses heated according to their natural needs. Other methods of protection in which glazed structures are involved include cloches and frames; these tend to be used to protect plants during parts of the season when the climatic conditions are likely to be unsuitable, as well as to encourage early maturity out of season.

Glass or glass substitute is also used to cover certain perfectly hardy plants which are accustomed to snow cover in winter but resent the fluctuations of temperature in a British winter, and also rain at that season. Many of these have wool or hair on leaves and stems, or have overwintering resting crowns which dislike waterlogging when in this stage. In these cases the glass is supported above the plant but without any obstruction at the sides, so that air can circulate freely. Large areas of such plants may be covered with frame lights or large sheets of plastic supported on short wooden posts.

Plants which may be damaged by frost include tender kinds and young specimens of hardy kinds which can succumb before achieving maturity. Many of these can be protected in winter by various coverings, e.g. with straw or bracken held in place by sacking or plastic sheeting, or bound firmly around the plant. Herbaceous plants needing frost protection can be covered with sand, peat or weathered ashes, or with straw or bracken held in place by a piece of wire netting or canes pushed into the ground at an angle.

Evergreens cannot be shut off from light in this way and these can be screened from cold winds by erecting wattle hurdles or screens of hessian or similar material on strong canes. Sometimes a windbreak placed to windward of the plant, arranged in a V plan to channel the wind to each side, will suffice, or the plant may be entirely surrounded by the protective screen. Plants can be permanently protected from wind by growing living hedges or screens to windward. Tender plants on walls can be given protection by erecting hurdles or other screens a few inches away from the branches. Similar methods can be employed to protect the frost-tender blossoms of fruit trees and early-flowering ornamental plants against frost and cold winds.

Excessive sunlight is another hazard to certain plants. The easiest way to avoid this is by planting them on the shady side of a wall or among taller trees. Plants under glass are especially susceptible to sun scorch, and in such situations some method of shading the greenhouse or frame is necessary. Another method, mostly favoured in tropical and sub-tropical climates, and in cooler climates to acclimatize young plants before planting them out, is to grow the plants under an open structure of laths which not only gives considerable shade but some protection from wind and frost.

◊ CLOCHE; FRAME; GREENHOUSE; LATH HOUSE; SCREEN; SHADING; TENDER; WINDBREAK.

For protection against pests, etc. ◊ FUNGICIDES; PESTICIDE; REPELLENTS; TREE GUARDS.

Protoplasm The viscous living matter in plant cells, contained within their non-living walls.

Pruner May be applied to any pruning tool, but usually restricted to those used for branch lopping in which a movable blade cuts against a fixed one, either operated at short range through two handles or, in long-arm or tree pruners, by remote control via a stiff wire moved by a handle. ◊ PRUNING KNIFE; SECATEURS; SHEARS; TREE PRUNERS.

Pruning An omnibus term which covers any cutting back of woody plants, especially fruit and ornamental trees, bushes and shrubs. It can apply to the crudest forms of reduction, like tree lopping, and to the most delicate, such as the pinching out of new growth on bonsai specimens.

There are four main reasons for pruning: (1) to shape the plant according to one's requirements; (2) to remove unnecessary parts of the plant so that its energies are concentrated where wanted, as for fruit production, or to keep it within bounds; (3) to control the quantity of flowers and, where applicable, fruits produced; and (4) to remove dead, damaged or diseased parts.

Fruit pruning is a highly specialized subject, and there are numerous different methods and differing forms of tree; for a full understanding, manuals on the sub-

ject should be studied. In general terms, it is necessary to remember that pruning for shaping of fruit and, where applicable, ornamental trees must normally be done when the tree is young. For a summary of fruit pruning methods described in this encyclopedia, ◊ FRUIT CULTURE.

With both flowering and fruiting plants it is important to distinguish between those which flower on wood two or more seasons old and those which do so mainly on new wood of the current season's growth. Black currants, raspberries and many rambler roses, for instance, have the stems which have cropped or flowered cut right out each year, since the best and most numerous flowers and fruits are produced on year-old stems; but most top fruits, red currants and climbing roses flower on side growths from at least a semi-permanent framework of branches.

Pruning can be 'hard', when much of the old growth is removed, or 'light', when relatively little is cut away. It is important to realize that any cutting into healthy wood will promote new growth from dormant buds, mostly those close to the pruning cut, and in general the harder the cutting, the more vigorous the resulting growth. Some ornamental shrubs, e.g. buddleia or coloured-stemmed willows, can if desired be pruned right back to (but preferably not into) old wood each spring – if the process is started early in life this can mean almost to ground level – and then produce very strong, upright new shoots. This is sometimes called stooling. In eucalyptus this can be done to retain the trees' juvenile foliage.

Pruning is mainly carried out with secateurs or other kinds of pruner with two blades operating against each other, but skilled fruit growers use a special strong pruning knife. A saw is used for large branches.

◊ BUD; FRUIT CULTURE; KNIFE; LATERAL LOP; SAW; SECATEURS; SHEARS; SNAG; STOOLING.

Pruning Compound ◊ WOUND DRESSINGS.

Pruning Knife A pocket knife typically

with one fold-away blade which is stout and usually slightly curved inwards. Also called a trimming knife, this is the chosen tool for light pruning by experts, but it has to be handled carefully or unnecessary damage to the plant may result, so most gardeners use secateurs which can be more positively placed on the stem to be cut.

PRUNING KNIFE. Typical examples

PSEUDOBULB

Pseudobulb A swollen growth resembling a bulb which is in fact a thickened stem and has no specialized internal structure like a bulb; found mainly in epiphytic orchids where the pseudobulbs are storage organs for food and moisture. They can consist of a single internode or several, and can vary from long and narrow to short and rounded, and are always carried above ground. Older gardening books sometimes refer to corms as pseudobulbs. ♢ CORM; INTERNODE; ORCHID.

Pteridophyte A fern or allied plant (club-moss, horsetail, selaginella). Some modern botanists no longer use this term or class these plants together. ♢ FERN.

Puberulent Applied to plant organs which are slightly downy, with very short hairs. ♢ HAIRY.

Pubescent Downy; applied to plant organs with a dense covering of soft hairs, which are often silvery. ♢ HAIRY.

Puddling (1) An old practice in which the roots of plants being transplanted are dipped into a thick mixture of soil and water. It is supposed to help the plants to 'get away' quicker, especially in dry weather, and is also believed to protect plants against pests such as cabbage root fly. The latter belief is almost certainly unfounded, and it is to be doubted whether puddling has much effect against drought, though it can do no harm. It would seem more effective to fill the planting hole with water and let it drain before putting in the plant.
(2) Puddling also refers to the pounding or treading of clay to form a waterproof lining for a pool. ♢ POOL.

Puffer A device for applying pesticidal and fungicidal dusts, either incorporating a bellows or obtained as a throwaway pack which can be compressed in the hand to eject the dust through a nozzle.

Pulverulent Having a powdery covering. ♢ FARINA.

Pupa The stage in an insect's life cycle between the larva, which is an actively feeding grub or caterpillar, and the adult, which is normally winged like a fly, moth or butterfly. Also known as the chrysalis, the pupa is an immobile stage during which the transition takes place. Pupation may occur fixed to a plant or in a crevice in bark, or in the soil; in some cases the pupa is encased in a silken cocoon spun by the larva. ♢ INSECT.

Push-pull Hoe ◊ HOE.

PVC The abbreviation for polyvinyl-chloride, which is available for various gardening purposes including glazing structures and lining pools, in both flexible and semi-rigid sheet form. ◊ GREEN-HOUSE; PLASTICS; POOL.

Pyramid A form of fruit tree pruned into a roughly pyramidal shape. The pyramid proper, which may reach 25′, is now sel-dom seen; it was often used for pears but is not very suitable for apples. The dwarf pyramid or fuseau, reaching a maximum of about 7′, can be applied to apples and is being used increasingly in intensive com-mercial plantations, as well as being very convenient for the garden. In the pyramid and dwarf pyramid branches radiate hori-zontally, starting close to the ground, from an upright central trunk, the tree even-tually becoming more or less conical in outline.

Pyrethrins ◊ PYRETHRUM.

Pyrethrum Besides being the old name for a genus of perennial plants, pyrethrum is an insecticide derived from the flowers of the species *Chrysanthemum cinerarii-folium*. It is a 'knock-down' insecticide with little lasting effect, specially valued because it is virtually non-toxic to humans and other warm-blooded animals, and can therefore be safely used indoors and on crops to be used the next day. Modern formulations of the active ingredient are called pyrethrins; there are also synthetic pyrethrum analogues like resmethrin and bioresmethrin. ◊ PESTICIDE.

Pyriform Pear-shaped; used botanically to describe fruits of that form.

Q

Quassia A bitter extract made by boiling chips of the wood of the tropical tree *Picrasma excelsa*, which is an insect deterrent and a repellent to birds and other creatures which attack buds and berries. As an insecticide it is an old-fashioned remedy now largely superseded by more modern materials, and as a repellent it is easily washed off the plants by rain and is thus not persistent. It is not toxic to warm-blooded animals and is occasionally used today combined with derris, as a safe, natural insecticide.

Quicklime The name commonly used for oxide of lime which results from burning chalk or limestone in a kiln. ◇ LIME.

Quilled Applied to petals which are in-rolled for much of their length into a narrow tube, e.g. in certain dahlias and chrysanthemums.

Quincunx An arrangement of five trees, four at the corners of a square and one in the centre, favoured since ancient times up to the seventeenth century. By the Middle Ages, however, the word was often more loosely applied to formal plantings of trees on a square basis, producing both straight and diagonal lines.

R

Rabbit Droppings Those who keep rabbits or can obtain litter from their hutches will find their droppings a very rich manure. The droppings can be dug into vacant ground but may scorch roots if applied when plants are in growth. If steeped in a barrel of water, a good liquid manure can be obtained, or the droppings can be added to the compost heap, or mixed with damp straw or hay, to provide a rich bulky manure. ◊ MANURE.

Rabbits These animals can be serious garden pests in country gardens, especially in hard winter weather. Vegetables and soft herbaceous plants are eaten to soil level and the bark on shrubs and trees is removed, which can kill the plant if the 'barking' continues all round the main trunk.

Where possible, gardens liable to rabbit attack should be entirely fenced in, using wire netting with a mesh of not more than 1″, which must be buried at least 1′ deep in the ground and should be at least 3′ above soil level. In areas liable to winter snowfall the wire should project 1′ above the expected snow level. Individual trees can be protected with wire netting formed into a tube round the base of the trunk, and plastic tree guards, made of plastic perforated flexible tube, can be obtained.

Deterrents are the only other recourse. Various proprietary deterrents or repellents can be bought. If tree trunks are barked, the wounded area should be painted without delay with a tree wound preparation or warm grafting wax; plants totally bark-ringed will need bridge grafting.

Hares cause similar damage but are much more erratic in their attacks since they usually exist in small numbers. Fences against hares need to be 4′–5′ tall.

◊ BRIDGE GRAFTING; REPELLENTS.

Raccoon In the northern U.S. the omnivorous raccoon can cause severe damage to fruit and vegetables. No fencing keeps out these largely nocturnal climbing animals, and shooting and trapping are the only controls. Local advice should be taken.

Race A rather vague term applied to plants in two ways. It can be used of hybrids of the same parentage, producing generally similar plants like tuberous begonias. Secondly, seedsmen sometimes speak of seed selections or strains which will reproduce true from self-pollinated seeds, and these can be called races.

Raceme ◊ INFLORESCENCE.

Rachis ◊ RHACHIS.

Radial Of flowers with similar petals which radiate as from a common centre; the same as regular or actinomorphic. ◊ FLOWER.

Radical Pertaining to the root of a plant; often applied to leaves arising directly from a root or crown.

Radicle The rudimentary root in the embryo in a seed, and thus the first root produced by a seedling.

Raffia A material used for tying plants which forms a flat strip and is in fact a fibre derived from the raffia palm. Though partly superseded by soft garden string, raffia is particularly valuable in grafting and budding and for tying very soft growth, because of its flatness. Also called bass. ◊ BUDDING; GRAFTING.

Raft An oblong piece of bark, osmunda or tree fern onto which orchids and other epiphytic plants can be wired or glued, which is hung up with a hook. ◊ EPIPHYTE; OSMUNDA FIBRE.

Rain, Rainwater Water is vital to the growing of plants, and rain forms an important proportion of the amount which reaches them; but its amount varies greatly according to locality and season, and it must normally be augmented by artificial watering. Steady light rain over a long period will penetrate the soil more deeply than short heavy showers, even if they appear to provide as much quantity of water, because in heavy rain the water remains on or near the soil surface or can even run off without penetrating at all.

The amount of rainfall received can be measured with a raingauge, of which several simple types are readily available.

Rainwater can be collected in water butts or tanks connected with roof gutters and is in general beneficial for watering pot plants, especially in areas where the mains supply is of 'hard' water which can harm lime-hating plants. However, water collected from old mossy roofs can bring moss and algal spores into the pots, and in towns, especially industrial districts, may contain many impurities such as sulphur dioxide which can be harmful to plants.
  ◊ WATERING.

Raised Bed A plant bed raised above ground level. This can simply consist of soil alone to raise the level a few inches, which can be desirable when growing plants needing good drainage and the basic soil is likely to become waterlogged, especially in winter. Such beds can be provided with a drainage layer of rubble but usually provide the necessary conditions if plenty of coarse sand or grit is mixed into the soil.

Taller raised beds need walls which can be of stone slabs, bricks, old railway sleepers, peat blocks or similar materials. These are most often used for growing alpines, either where the basic soil is unsuitable or where an orthodox rock garden is not wanted; the raised bed allows a large number of plants to be grown in limited space. Such beds for alpines are sometimes called billiard tables. Raised beds are also invaluable for disabled gardeners who can only work from a chair or wheel-chair. When alpines are grown, it is again usual to have a drainage layer at the base of the raised bed; the soil within it can be mixed to provide suitable conditions for lime- or peat-loving plants and is usually made porous by the addition of coarse sand or grit. In raised beds walled with stone slabs, plants can be grown between the slabs as well as on top. These should be planted as construction proceeds, if possible.
  ◊ PEAT BEDS.

RAISED BED. *Left*, raised bed for alpines, made of separate stone slabs allowing for planting between. *Right*, raised bed of cemented bricks, suitable for disabled gardeners

Rake, Raking A rake is a tool in which a number of prongs or 'teeth' are set into a crosspiece at the end of a long handle so that they will enter the soil more or less vertically. Rakes were used by the ancient Greeks and Romans and also in ancient China; many of the antique kinds resembled what one would describe today as a pronged cultivator with a few long prongs. The modern-style rake with many relatively short prongs was in general use by the sixteenth century, often made of wood. Modern ones are almost always of metal, occasionally of plastic or stiff rubber; wood is used for hay rakes which can also be used for collecting dead leaves and debris; leaf-collecting rakes are sometimes made with rubber teeth. The hay rake is 2′ wide or more, but garden rakes are commonly 10″–12″ wide.

Raking is carried out in the final stages of levelling ground, when it removes stones and other debris, and for preparing seed beds, when repeated raking should reduce the upper layer of soil to a fine tilth. The rake is also used for gathering up rubbish and smoothing gravel paths. Raking is a skilful operation needing practice and also a surprising amount of effort. The removal of stones, etc., is carried out when the rake is pulled towards the operator, and the breaking down of soil mainly with the opposite movement. The rake should be pressed only very lightly into the soil, which should be nearly dry for best results, and never wet.

The fact that the teeth of a rake leave small furrows is made use of when finally raking an area over which seed is to be broadcast, e.g. a lawn. The seeds lodge in these furrows, and if the soil is then raked over once again at right angles they will be sufficiently covered.

The ordinary garden rake is rigid. Spring-tined rakes with wire, plastic or bamboo tines arranged in a fan pattern are available, primarily for raking lawns. Wire spring rakes can also be used on soil but can only be pulled towards one, not used with a two-way motion. Various patent 'multi-purpose' rakes with crescent-shaped blades are available for both lawn and soil raking.

The hand rake is a tool for close work in seed beds, etc., typically with four relatively long prongs at right angles to the short handle.

◊ LAWN RAKE; TILTH.

Rammer An implement used for pushing down potting compost around the root ball of plants being repotted, to ensure the compost is firm and contains no air pockets. A rammer is usually made from a piece of wooden rod, e.g. an old broom handle, with rounded ends. ◊ POTTING.

Ranch Fence ◊ FENCING.

Rape Cake, Meal The residue of rape seed after oil has been extracted from it. It contains 5–6 per cent nitrogen, $1\frac{1}{2}$–3 per cent phosphoric acid and at least 1 per cent potash, and has sufficient bulk to improve soil texture. The cake is normally sold as animal feed, but often contains impurities like mustard seed which make it unsuitable for this purpose. Rejected cake is ground into a mealy material for use as a fertilizer. As it can scorch roots, it is best worked into the soil some time before sowing or planting at 4–8 oz. per square yard.

Rats As pests, rats combine the habits of mice and rabbits, eating seeds and fleshy roots (bulbs, etc.) in the soil or store, fruits in store, and sometimes green plants and bark on tree trunks. They also tunnel into sheds, greenhouses, etc. Poison baits are the most effective control, or traps can be used. Severe infestations may call for the services of the local pest control official.

Ray (1) The outer florets of some flowers in the Composite family, which carry a strap-shaped 'petal' or corolla, in contrast to the unadorned, close-packed florets of the central disk. ◊ COMPOSITE.

(2) Sometimes used in describing the umbrella-shaped flower-heads of the Umbelliferae (Cow Parsley family), when the word applies to the flower stems which radiate from a central point. ◊ UMBEL.

Reap Hook ◊ SICKLE.

Receptacle The central part of a flower, composed of the thickened end of its stalk, on which all the floral organs are carried; in flower-heads composed of many tight-packed florets, as in Composites, also the thickened end of the stalk supporting the florets and their external involucre or covering scales. ◊ COMPOSITE; FLOWER.

Recurved Curved or bent downwards and then often in the opposite direction. Applicable to any plant organ. ◊ REFLEXED.

Red Lead A poisonous powder, primarily sold for the preparation of paint, sometimes used to protect seeds against attack by pests including birds, mice and wireworms. The seeds should first be moistened slightly with paraffin and then shaken up with red lead. ◊ SEED DRESSING.

Red Spider Mite ◊ MITES.

Red Thread Also called corticium disease after the fungus which causes it, this is a common disease of grass. Discoloured, irregular spots are made in the turf and in later stages reddish thread-like growths appear. Grass in good condition is seldom attacked, so giving a good feed is the first line of defence, but fertilizers high in nitrogen should not be applied in autumn, since this can lead to attack by fusarium patch disease. Most fungicides against lawn diseases are effective against red thread.

Reel Mower A term sometimes applied to a cylinder mower. ◊ MOWERS.

Reflexed Applied to plant organs sharply bent downwards or even backwards, and used with special reference to a class of chrysanthemums with florets which reflex. The reflexed classification, in which the florets are more sharply bent than in recurved cultivars, also includes chrysanthemums with quilled, sharply pointed florets which stand out stiffly. ◊ QUILLED; RECURVED.

REFLEXED

Regulated Pruning A method of pruning established apple trees which consists primarily in cutting out crowded, crossing and drooping branches and weak growth using a saw, and hence sometimes called saw pruning; neither leaders nor spurs are normally touched. This method is suitable for very vigorous cultivars only; most others soon start over-cropping with poor-quality fruit, and for these it is better to use RENEWAL PRUNING.

Rejuvenation Pruning The heading back of branches on aged fruit trees which are in decline and not producing new young growth; this results in a mass of new shoots being produced, from which a new fruiting framework is developed. This is a more drastic form of MAINTENANCE PRUNING.

Remontant A French word which is used in gardening to denote plants which flower and/or fruit for a second time in the autumn, and also to so-called perpetual-flowering plants which in fact bloom most of the summer without a break. It is most often used of strawberries producing a second crop, or sometimes their main crop. in autumn.

Renewal Pruning Possibly the best all-round pruning method for established bush or standard apples and also pears, in which the aim is constantly to replace growth which has fruited with a succession of two- and three-year-old lateral growths. The tree has a basic branch framework which is left untouched. Much depends on the pruner himself in judging which older laterals to remove, but the removal must be spread evenly all over the tree. At the same time, some one-year laterals are cut out since there will certainly be too many of these after some years.

Reniform A botanical term for plant organs, especially leaves, which are kidney-shaped. ◊ LEAF.

Repellents Materials intended to repel or deter animals from attacking plants, without killing or injuring them. Thus bitter-tasting sprays of alum or quassia were once widely used to keep birds from attacking tree buds. These have now been replaced by more modern materials such as ammonium aluminium sulphate and anthraquinone, though at best repeated application is needed in wet weather. Another method used against birds on trees is a rayon 'cobweb' to be spread all over trees and bushes; it decays after a few months. On a smaller scale, over seedlings, spring flowers and strawberries, fine cotton strung on short sticks will keep off birds. Nylon thread should never be used as it can harm and even kill birds because it never rots.

Naphthalene, paradichlorbenzene and mothballs are sometimes placed in soil or pots to drive out insect pests; these and other strong-smelling materials can also be inserted in mole runs and rabbit burrows to deter their residents. The reputed powers of caper spurge (*Euphorbia lathyris*) to keep moles away are at the least unproven.

Against larger animals, which include dogs and cats, mice, squirrels, rabbits and hares, and deer, there are numerous proprietary materials which may be sprayed or smeared onto plants or, in solid form, are placed at strategic points. Tree-banding grease has also been used with success. Pepper dust is sometimes used against cats and dogs. Twine impregnated in creosote or a proprietary liquid repellent, strung

round areas to be protected a few inches above the ground, is another method.

No repellent can be said to be infallible and most applied materials need frequent renewal; a lot will depend on the severity of the weather and the consequent hunger of the creatures concerned.

◊ BIRDS; CATS; DEER; DOGS; MICE; MOLES; RABBITS; SQUIRRELS; TREE BANDING; TREE GUARDS.

Replacement Leader ◊ LEADER.

Repotting Moving plants from one pot to a bigger one. ◊ POTTING.

Reproduction The process of producing new individuals by whatever means: in plants these means include both sexual and non-sexual, or vegetative. ◊ SEX; VEGETATIVE.

Reserve Border The same as a NURSERY BED.

Residual Describes weedkillers which, applied to the soil, remain active there for a considerable time.

Resistant ◊ IMMUNE.

Respiration The process in plants in which oxygen is taken in and used to metabolize the sugars created by photosynthesis into energy for the plant's growth. Carbon dioxide is given off as a waste product. Respiration goes on continuously, during the day in parallel with PHOTOSYNTHESIS.

Resting, Rest Period Plants are said to be resting or dormant during periods when little or no growth is made. Familiar examples are herbaceous perennials which die down in winter, deciduous trees which lose their leaves at that time, and the majority of bulbs, corms and tubers. The latter become so dormant, indeed, that they can be entirely dried off, stored, and distributed by merchants at the appropriate season. It is in fact important to allow plants to rest at the normal time. If shrubs or bulbs are forced out of season, it is usually advisable to let them grow and rest normally in the next year or two. With fleshy-rooted plants grown in pots it may be necessary to induce the regular rest period by withholding water.

Evergreen trees and shrubs do not rest entirely like deciduous ones, but their metabolism slows down very considerably in cold weather. However, evergreen plants from hot countries, especially those from tropical rain forests, do not have an appreciable rest period unless there is a natural dry season. When grown as house plants, however, it is usually desirable to give these a partial rest period in winter by reducing watering, since external conditions such as warmth and, especially, light are likely to be reduced in the artificial conditions of a room: growth made at this time may become weak and spindly.

◊ FORCING; HOUSE PLANT; RETARDING.

Retaining Wall A wall which contains soil between different levels in areas which have been terraced. Such walls can be built with cement or of dry stone without it. ◊ TERRACE; WALLS.

Retardant ◊ RETARDING.

Retarding The treatment of plants so that they come into growth later than normal: the opposite of forcing. This is usually done by placing the plants in low temperatures, and is applied to bulbs, lily-of-the-valley and flowering shrubs. 'Prepared' bulbs for Christmas flowering have been given low-temperature treatment: when placed in warmth and watered, they come into growth and flower in a very short time.

Hormones and other chemicals, known as retardants, are used to retard the growth of fruit trees (so that flowers avoid likely frost periods) and of grass and plants used for hedges, and on potatoes to prevent them sprouting too early. Retardation can also be carried out mechanically, e.g. by cutting back strawberries and flowering perennials like delphiniums and lupins when flowers are forming in spring, so that a second set

of flowers is produced much later than normal.

◊ GROWTH REGULATORS.

Reticulate Having a pattern of veins or markings in a net pattern.

Reversion (1) Commonly used with reference to a plant reverting to its original type. This sometimes happens to highly bred hybrids, which may produce flowers of different colours from those the cultivar is supposed to have. Some complaints of reversion, however, are not justified. One often hears of lupins 'reverting' to blue: but what has happened is that the short-lived coloured hybrid has died and seedlings from it have produced blue flowers. In cases where a grafted rose, rhododendron, lilac, etc., 'reverts', this is due to the more vigorous stock having been allowed to sucker and swamp the scion or grafted variety. Reversion may also happen with variegated plants, which are often unstable, e.g. the indoor tradescantia. Green shoots which may be formed are much more vigorous than the variegated and, if allowed to grow, will swamp the latter. ◊ SUCKER.

(2) The name for a specific virus disease of currants which reduces cropping, and in which the leaves are smaller and carry fewer lobes, with fewer veins than in a normal plant. If a currant is suspected of infection, the leaf veins should be counted in mid-summer. If most leaves have five veins or fewer, the bush is probably affected. ◊ VIRUS DISEASES.

Reworking Replacing the fruiting or scion variety on an old fruit tree with a more up-to-date one by retaining part of its framework of branches and grafting them with the newer variety. Reworking can be done by two methods.

In topworking, the branches are removed almost entirely and scions of the new variety grafted onto their cut ends; this method is relatively quick but trees take several years to come into bearing again. Cleft and crown grafts are often used for this operation.

258

In frameworking, the main branches are kept but side growths are pruned away, and scions of the new variety are inserted every 8″–10″ all along the branches: this method is very time-consuming but trees will crop again in two to three years. Side and stub grafts can be used.

◊ GRAFTING; SIDE GRAFT; STUB GRAFT.

Rhachis The main stalk of an inflorescence carrying many blooms, and that of a compound leaf. Also spelt 'rachis'.

Rhizome An underground stem lasting more than one season, often growing horizontally, making roots continuously and producing new shoots at the end farthest from the parent plant. Some rhizomes are fleshy, e.g. the thick ones of bearded irises which grow along the soil surface, and the thinner ones of wood anemones; these are storage organs which enable the plant to have a resting season. In the garden the older portions of such fleshy rhizomes, which bear the scars left by the leaves and shoots of previous seasons, deteriorate and their roots become inactive, so that when plants in the garden need division these parts can be discarded. Some plants, e.g. various ferns, make rhizomes which are more or less erect and do not spread.

Another kind of rhizome is more like an underground shoot providing the plant with a quick method of spreading: couch or quack grass (agropyrum) is an example. Rhizomes can be distinguished from true roots by the fact that rhizomes have nodes and carry scale-like leaves or buds, sometimes markedly so as in *Achimenes*.

◊ FLESHY-ROOTED; RUNNER; STOLON.

Rhizomorph ◊ HONEY FUNGUS.

Rhubarb Pot A fairly tall, upright earthenware pot with a removable lid, used for forcing rhubarb but now seldom seen. ◊ FORCING.

Rhynchites ◊ WEEVILS.

Rib A primary vein on a leaf, of which the central one, the midrib, is usually the most prominent. Stems and fruits can also be ribbed; cacti often have prominent ribs on their stems. ◊ LEAF; VEIN.

Riddle A coarse-meshed SIEVE.

Riddling Sifting soil or other material with a riddle, or SIEVE.

Ride-on Mower A mowing machine with integral seat for the operator. ◊ MOWERS.

Ridger A hand tool shaped like a mini-

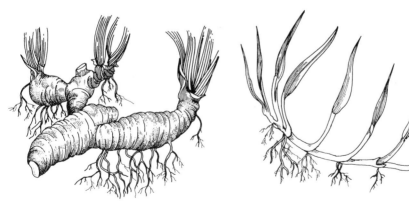

RHIZOME. *Left*, bearded iris; *right*, couch or quack grass

ature plough which, drawn through soil, produces a central furrow, with a small ridge on either side, in which seeds can be sown.

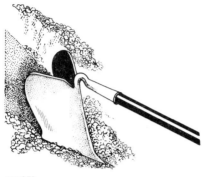

RIDGER

Ridging A method of soil cultivation in which the soil is thrown up into ridges, in order to expose as much surface as possible to the effects of frost and weather generally. Strips of ground about 30″ wide are marked out, and a trench a spit deep and 1′ wide is taken out at one end, the soil being removed to the other end of the plot. The gardener works backwards from this trench, at each move back throwing three spadefuls of soil forward so as to pile

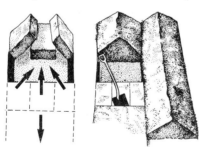

RIDGING

the left- and right-hand spadefuls onto the centre one. The soil should not be touched with the spade again at this stage, being left as rough as possible, but if it is very friable the result will be more or less triangular ridges. At the end of each strip,

the gardener turns round and works back down the next strip. After some time the ridges are worked over and made more or less level with a garden fork. ◊ SPIT.

Rind The bark of a tree, or outer layer of a non-woody plant; an old meaning but now found in this sense mainly in literature on grafting, as in rind grafting.

Rind Grafting The same as crown grafting. ◊ GRAFTING.

Ring-barking A method of killing trees by removing a ring of bark at least 1″ wide near the bottom of the trunk. The bark must be cut out as deep as the cambium layer just below it. Not to be confused with ringing. ◊ CAMBIUM; FRILL-GIRDLING; RINGING.

Ring Culture A method of cultivation developed for tomatoes but also used for a few other plants, notably carnations and chrysanthemums. In this method, young plants are planted into 'rings' or bottomless pots, usually made of bitumenized cardboard ('whalehide'), and usually 9″ wide and deep, filled with very rich potting compost. These rings are stood on a bed of porous material or aggregate, usually clean gravel, sand or weathered boiler ashes, at least 6″ deep. If ring culture is being used, as it normally is, because the soil has become disease-infected, the aggregate must be separated from the soil by a plastic sheet or, in more permanent installations, by concrete slabs. In these cases there must be provision for surplus moisture in the aggregate to drain away.

The young plants are thoroughly watered so that the potting compost is moist throughout, but after this all water is applied to the bed of aggregate. Liquid fertilizer is, however, applied to the rings a few weeks after planting and regularly thereafter. In this way the plants develop what may be called feeding roots in the rings and a much coarser and more extensive system of water-seeking roots in the aggregate.

Apart from its value on infected or otherwise unsatisfactory soil, ring culture is, of course, an excellent method for raising tomatoes and other suitable subjects on terraces, roof gardens, etc. The or partially severing the downward flow of food materials and also of hormones produced in the leaves or upper buds, which pass down the tree in a narrow ring of tissue just below the bark, called phloem.

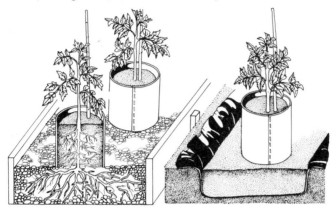

RING CULTURE. *Left*, in board-edged bed; section shows feeding roots in the ring and water-seeking roots in the aggregate below. *Right*, bed made in trough of plastic sheet

compost in the rings must be renewed every year but the aggregate can be kept for several seasons though a wash-through and application of disinfectant in the winter is a valuable precaution.

Ring Fasciation ◊ PROLIFERATION.

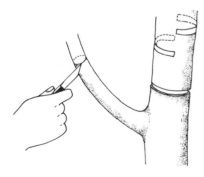

RINGING. *Left*, knife-ringing. *Right, below* full ringing; *above* partial ringing

Ringing A method of encouraging fruit trees to crop better and to curtail over-vigorous growth. It does this by severing

The effect of this is to stimulate the production of flower buds.

There are several ways of doing this. A ring of bark not more than $\frac{1}{4}''$ wide can be taken out right to the hard wood beneath, round the trunk about 2′ above the soil level. This should be done in late April or early May, which will allow the ring to heal over during the summer. A wider ring will not heal over, and this would result in the tree's eventual death. A less drastic check can be given by taking out a partial ring, or two semi-circular rings on opposite sides of the trunk a few inches apart. Less severe again than actually taking out a ring of bark, and often used to encourage fruit buds on an individual branch, is knife-ringing, in which a sharp knife is drawn right round the branch to cut through the bark. This knife-ringing, also carried out in late April or early May, is done at the upper end of a barren branch, which usually makes dormant buds start into growth. If done at the lower end of such a branch, the buds are likely to remain dormant. A similar effect is produced by twisting a fine wire

261

tightly around the branch, otherwise known as garrotting.

Ringing may be called bark-ringing or girdling, though the latter is usually reserved for the accidental removal of bark, e.g. when eaten by animals.

◊ GARROTTING; HORMONES; NICKING AND NOTCHING.

Ripe, Ripening Apart from their obvious meaning in connection with fruit, these words are relevant to gardeners in referring to the maturing of young wood on trees and shrubs, and of bulbs. These kinds of ripening are vital if flowers are to be produced the following year, and in the case of tender woody plants can make all the difference to survival.

Various factors combine to aid ripening. A long hot summer is conducive to good ripening of woody plants and bulbs, and on fruit trees and some ornamentals carefully timed summer pruning also helps. In all cases, liberal applications of potash in later summer are most helpful, especially in less hot and sunny seasons, and this can be easily provided by regular applications of a tomato fertilizer high in potash or, if desired, by use of the various materials providing potash alone.

The desirable light and warmth for tender shrubs and trees can be accentuated by planting them in sheltered places against a south-facing wall, and many bulbs also ripen best in such a situation. Bulb ripening is a matter of warmth combined with a degree of dryness; many bulbs originating in hot dry climates need total dryness if they are to flower successfully, and specialist growers keep them in bulb frames for this reason. Bulbs should not, however, be dug up and exposed to the sun.

◊ BULB FRAME; POTASH.

Riser The vertical component of a step. ◊ STEPS.

Rockery Fork ◊ FORKS.

Rockery Hoe ◊ HOE.

Rockery Trowel ◊ TROWEL.

Rock Garden, Rockery An area devoted to the cultivation of alpines and rock plants, ideally set out in a way which imitates a natural rock outcrop. Although the word 'rockery' is often used of carefully constructed rock gardens, it is perhaps better reserved for rockwork where a realistic effect has not been attempted, or where stones are just heaped together.

In imitating natural outcrops, rocks of adequate size are arranged at a consistent slight angle from the horizontal so that they slope slighty backwards into the soil,

ROCK GARDEN

with pockets of soil between them. If the ground is steep or undulating, or can be made so, a number of receding layers or strata of rock can be created. However, a large rock garden is costly and needs a lot of attention; it is perfectly possible to build an effective rock garden consisting of small outcrops or even on a level surface, with rocks partly sunk into the soil. In short, there are many ways of creating a rock garden but the irregular or casual arrangement of rocks should be avoided, as in the three categories made famous by Reginald Farrer, one of the early rock gardeners: the 'dog's grave', 'almond pudding', and 'devil's lapful'.

Many kinds of stone can be used; the aim should be to obtain roughly rectangular pieces of reasonably similar size. Rock which stratifies naturally is most likely to provide suitable pieces. Rocks should always be well sunk into the soil; and during construction the soil must be forced into every crevice so that there are no empty spaces, while the soil-filled spaces or pockets left for plants between the rocks, including vertical crevices, must join with the main mass of soil or such positions will rapidly dry out.

Especially if the rock garden is on level ground, the soil should be well drained and have coarse sand and stone chippings worked into it to provide the desirable porous, free-draining texture which most true alpines must have. Soil may also need additional peat for moisture-holding. If the natural soil is very poor all the areas immediately around the rocks and in the crevices should be made up of a suitable mixture of imported soil, grit and peat. A proportion suitable for most alpines could consist of 8 parts by bulk soil, 4 parts peat and 3 parts grit, but the latter may need increasing for choicer plants demanding a very well-drained root-run.

Rock gardens can be made in any aspect, but in general a site which receives plenty of sun in morning or afternoon is preferable; fully south-facing sites may become too hot and on a north-facing one the choice of plants is limited since most alpines are sun-lovers. For the same rea-son, the position should be open and away from trees, not the least reason for this being that autumn leaf fall can quickly ruin choice plants.

Water in the form of a small stream, with cascades and pools on the way, can be incorporated in a rock garden to advantage, especially if a natural stream is available on the site. If not, a pump and recirculating system can be quite easily installed: in this case, the lower pool must be of reasonable size to act as a reservoir because of evaporation, and will need to be topped up from time to time.

Where there is no room for a proper rock garden, a scree bed or a raised bed will allow the cultivation of many plants in small space.

◊ MORAINE; RAISED BED; SCREE; WATERWORKS.

Rock Plants An extremely vague expression since it covers any plant, be it herbaceous, shrubby or bulbous, which will look attractive on a rock garden and neither encroach seriously on its neighbours nor grow too large. It is certainly not equivalent to true alpines which are in the main small and low-growing, often need a very porous soil mixture, and are mainly sun-loving. ◊ ALPINE.

Rock Pot A pot made by cementing together small oblong pieces of rock, fixed to a cement base in which a drainage hole has been made. Such pots were at one time popular with rock plant enthusiasts. Another kind of rock pot can be made of 'hypertufa' into which small pieces of stone are pressed before it sets. ◊ HYPERTUFA.

Rod An antique measure of both length and area. ◊ PERCH (1) (2); WEIGHTS AND MEASURES (p. viii).

Rogue Any plant with characters which are not what they are meant to be is termed a rogue. This may happen with named varieties or with seed selections which are supposed to be true: with the latter it is quite possible for a few plants to diverge from the required character from natural causes; thus a strain of blue larkspur may easily produce one or two pink ones. In other cases, as where a tulip of the wrong form or colour appears, or a potato of the wrong variety comes up, this is usually due to accidental mixing of the bulbs or tubers at some stage in the sorting and packing. Of course, such plants, and also perennials or shrubs normally propagated vegetatively, may occasionally differ from the original by mutation or 'sporting'. ◊ MUTATION.

Roller, Rolling A roller is a heavy cylinder mounted on a frame fixed to its centres on either side, with a handle so that it can be pushed or pulled. The word originated in 1530. Rollers seem first to have been used mainly for breaking down lumpy soil and levelling paths. By the eighteenth century the roller was primarily used on lawns, not only to maintain a smooth surface but to flatten worm casts the day before scything.

Early rollers were of wood or stone, and were much longer than their diameter; modern rollers are only a little longer than broad and are usually made of cast iron. Early versions were sometimes designed to be filled with sand or water to provide extra weight, and there are some modern rollers made of plastic where the same device is used: these are sometimes called water rollers.

The value of using a heavy roller on a garden lawn is questionable, since it is likely to consolidate the soil and produce unhealthy conditions for the grass roots. However, rolling a newly made lawn will settle turf into place or ensure firm soil on seeded lawns; lawns of tough grasses much used for games will benefit from rolling, and rollers are most used on sports grounds where a level surface is essential and where it is best for the soil to be tightly packed down; suitable hard-wearing grasses are of course used in such cases. If grass of any kind is rolled it should be in slightly moist conditions: it is harmful on wet grass and little use on dry.

Most mowers of the cylinder type incorporate a small roller, and another use for the roller on lawns is when it is supplied with spikes to aerate the soil.

A light roller can be used when preparing seed beds to firm and further crumble newly raked soil; however, in the vegetable garden this is usually more easily done by treading, so rolling is normally confined to newly seeded lawn areas. In this case it is most important that the soil surface should be dry, otherwise lumps plus seeds will stick to the roller.
◊ LAWN; SPIKING; TREADING.

Rond-point A circular open space in a large formal garden from which alleys or avenues radiate, and from which several vistas will thus be seen. ◊ FRENCH GARDEN.

Roof Garden We may think of gardens on housetops as a very modern development caused by increasingly cramped urban conditions, but in fact the ancient Romans had them, as at Pompeii, and the Spaniards invading Mexico were impressed by the roof gardens of the Aztecs.

There are a number of problems which arise with rooftop gardens. The first is access and the fact that everything required has normally to be brought up through the house. The next vital consideration is whether the roof structure is sufficiently strong to withstand the weight of soil which a garden of any size will entail. The roof surface must also be checked to ensure it is thoroughly waterproof and likely to remain so, and also capable of withstanding the wear and tear of heavy containers and of people walking on it regularly. Drainage must also be adequate. Last but not least, one should ascertain that local by-laws permit a roof garden or, in the case of rented property, that the landlord agrees to it.

Plants can be grown on roofs in large tubs, boxes and other containers or, if the condition of the roof surfacing permits, in beds. There is usually a low wall or parapet which can hold in soil on one side, and on the others the bed can be enclosed by low walls made of bricks, timbers or peat blocks. At best the soil depth is unlikely to be great, and the soil will dry out rapidly in dry or windy weather: the one great chore of a roof garden is the constant need for watering. A hose connected to a bath tap below is not the best method: far better to have a new water pipe installed with a tap on the roof.

Soil should be the best and richest possible, with plenty of moisture retention and food content, like John Innes No. 3 potting compost. Peat-based potting composts are basically unsuitable, whatever the initial attraction of a much lighter material to drag up onto the roof. In any case, the amount of watering needed is so great that foods in the soil get washed out quickly and frequent feeding will be necessary. Wind is possibly the worst of the elements to contend with in a roof garden, and it becomes worse the higher the garden is. It rocks plants of any size in soil often too shallow to allow adequate support, and dries out the soil. Also it makes conditions unpleasant for anyone enjoying the roof garden. Screening is therefore highly desirable and should be considered at an early stage. Even panels of fine wire mesh or similar material help to break the force of the wind, but the ideal method is to use panels of strengthened glass.

There is really no limit to the plants which can be grown in a roof garden, including shrubs and small trees (the latter best in large tubs to give a reasonable depth of soil). Even vegetables and soft fruit can be grown, and on the hard surface of a roof growing bags can be especially valuable. Since space is limited, maximum use should be made of climbing plants, not only on walls and chimney stacks, provided with suitable wires or trellis, but if possible on pergola-like structures erected for the purpose. A series of vertical supports connected at the top with wooden beams or wires can soon be festooned with growth which, apart from its decorative interest, helps to break the force of the wind.

All these considerations apply in varying degrees to gardening on balconies, although here long narrow windowboxes, rather than beds, may be the main place to grow plants.

◊ GROWING BAG.

Root That part of a plant which normally penetrates the soil in order to obtain moisture and dissolved nutrients, and also for anchorage. Absorption is carried out by very fine root hairs which are usually found only at the tips of the roots, which grow constantly.

Roots can be of many different kinds. The tap root is a single main root which descends vertically into the soil. Its opposite is the fibrous root which forms a fairly dense mass of no great depth; there is no main root. Many trees and shrubs have roots which radiate down through the soil rather like the branch system. Other plants may have more or less swollen fleshy roots which act as food reserves; root vegetables are of this type. Fleshy roots act also as storage organs to tide the plants over resting periods. In epiphytic plants that grow on trees or rocks, the roots cannot enter the soil and are specially adapted to obtain the plant's limited moisture needs by absorption from the humid atmosphere: these are called aerial roots. Some climbing plants use aerial roots to cling to trees, rock, etc., and absorb surface moisture there as they climb.

Some roots associate with fungi to form mycorrhiza and others with bacteria to form nodules; in both cases these associations are symbiotic, i.e. helpful to both partners.

◊ entries below prefixed by ROOT; AERIAL ROOT; CONTRACTILE; FLESHY-ROOTED; MYCORRHIZA; NODULE; POT-BOUND; RESTING; RUNNER; STOLON; STORAGE.

Root Aphids Aphids which infest plant roots and suck sap from them; they are usually grey. Serious attacks cause the plants to wilt and eventually die. Auriculas, china asters (callistephus) and lettuces are most frequently attacked. Suitable insecticides can be watered around the plants; plants in pots are best removed from their pots and the roots washed in soapy water or insecticide solution. Infected plants which die should be burnt, not composted; pot soil should also be destroyed or disinfected.

265

Root Ball The mass of roots and potting compost formed by a plant in a pot or other container. ◊ BALL.

Root-bound Describes a plant whose roots have entirely filled a pot or other container: the same as POT-BOUND.

Root Cuttings In some cases plants can be increased from pieces of root. These are usually plants with relatively thick roots, including acanthus, anchusas, hollyhocks, perennial limoniums, oriental poppies, verbascums and, among vegetables, horseradish and seakale. However, some fibrous-rooted plants can also be increased in this way, e.g. gaillardias and phloxes, and with the latter this is the only way of eliminating eelworm attack since the pests do not enter the roots.

Thick root cuttings are most easily dealt with by cutting sections $1\frac{1}{2}''$–$2''$ long and inserting them vertically into deep boxes of soil. In order to make sure which way up they go in, it is usually best to trim the lower end of the cutting on a slant and the upper end horizontally. Thinner root cuttings can be laid on their sides on a layer of soil and covered with more soil.

Root Dipping Immersing the roots of seedlings into an insecticidal paste or solution. This is most often done with cabbages and other brassicas against CLUB ROOT and ROOT FLIES.

Root Flies Various flies lay eggs around plants so that the emerging larvae can burrow into the soil and feed on their roots. The most common attack cabbages and their relations, onions, lettuces, carrots, celery, parsley and parsnips. Others attack chrysanthemums. Seed dressings can prevent attacks, or applications of suitable insecticides around the plants very soon after germination. In the case of cabbages, dusting their planting holes with appropriate insecticide is effective. The often recommended practice of dipping the roots of seedlings being planted into a calomel paste is now discouraged in E.E.C. countries under recent legislation.

Root-forming Hormone ◊ HORMONES.

Root Grafting A method of grafting now seldom practised, in which a thin scion, trimmed at the base, is fixed into an appropriately shaped slot on a thicker stock which is a fleshy root. It is largely restricted to tree peonies. Natural root grafting may occur in plantations of the same kind of tree and has been known to spread disease, as among citrus in the U.S.

Root House An ornamental garden house formed from the bases of tree trunks. Such houses, typically made even more rustic-looking by a thatched roof, were occasionally made in the nineteenth century.

Root-knot Eelworm An eelworm which causes small swellings on the roots of attacked plants, which include cucumbers, lettuces and tomatoes especially when grown under glass. Lower leaves of attacked plants go yellow and wilting is likely to occur. ◊ EELWORMS.

Root Maggot A phrase used by gardeners to describe the larvae of flies which attack roots. ◊ ROOT FLIES.

Root Nodules ◊ NODULE.

Root Pruning Severing the roots of fruit trees reduces their intake of food and moisture and thus the amount of growth made, at the same time encouraging fruit production. The operation was more popular in past years than now when dwarfing rootstocks and modern pruning methods should ensure good crops; furthermore, much the same results can be obtained by bark ringing. However, root pruning may be a last resort on old trees which are not bearing well, and is preferable to ringing on plums and other stone fruits which can become infected with silver leaf disease if ringed. Root pruning can also be carried out on ornamental trees and shrubs which persistently refuse to flower.

To carry out root pruning, a circular trench $18''$–$24''$ deep should be dug out with its outer edge at the same distance from the trunk as the ends of the branches. All the thicker roots within this trench are severed, though smaller ones should be left untouched. Because the cutting of all the main roots can cause a severe shock to the tree, the operation is often carried out in two stages a year apart.

If a tree needs a really severe check because of excessive growth, a proportion of the main roots can be cut back about a foot from the trunk.

In either case it may be necessary to support the tree with stout vertical or oblique stakes, or by guying, since its anchorage will have suffered.
 ◊ GUYING; RINGING; SUPPORT.

Root Restriction The practice of planting so that the roots are confined, and the plant concerned does not produce a great deal of growth and tends to flower earlier and more profusely than it would otherwise do. Certain plants grown in containers, e.g. many bulbs, do better if the roots are restricted and potting on is not carried out, but the main example of root restriction is carried out on figs planted where there is not a great deal of space for the top growth, e.g. if the plant is to be wall trained. A cement box around 2′ deep, 2′–3′ wide and 4′ long is made, into which the tree is planted. Drainage holes are of course prepared in the floor.

Root Rot Decay of plant roots can result from unsatisfactory soil conditions, notably waterlogging, or from attack by a number of disease organisms. A wide range of plants can suffer from the latter. In principle, poor soil conditions should be rectified and soil sterilization carried out, if disease organisms are suspected; similar plants should not be grown in the same place for several years. Attacked plants, which will collapse and die, should be burnt, not composted. ◊ HONEY FUNGUS.

Root Run The area of soil through which a plant's roots extend. The expected root run is important to bear in mind when applying a mulch, which should extend rather farther than the roots to be effec-

tive. In general terms, the roots of trees and shrubs grow out as far as their outermost branches spread. ◊ MULCH.

Rootstock (1) Often used by gardeners to refer to the stock upon which a tree or shrub is grafted or budded. ◊ STOCK.

(2) Botanically, a rhizome, especially those which are more or less erect, or short, as in some ferns. In this sense gardeners often use the word rather loosely to describe the combined crown and root system of a compact plant. ◊ RHIZOME.

Root System The entire network of roots produced by a plant from the largest to the fine root-hairs.

Root Vegetable A vegetable with swollen roots which form a food store: most of these are biennials and the food reserve is made the first year to enable the plant to flower and seed in the second. Gardeners, of course, take advantage of these vegetables in their first year; they include beetroots, carrots, celeriac, parsnips, salsify, scorzonera and turnips. In some cases the swollen part of the root is partly above ground, as in the swede.

Rosary A word used in the early nineteenth century for a ROSE GARDEN.

Rose A perforated cap attached to the spout of a watering can in order to produce a fine radiating spray of WATER. Infinitely variable plastic rose heads, some trigger-operated, which can be attached to the end of a hose for watering, are now available. ◊ WATERING CAN.

Rose Garden A garden primarily devoted to roses. Such appear to have been made by the Romans and they also existed in a small way in medieval times, but they are mainly a nineteenth-century conception. A few large rose gardens, mainly public ones, remain in Britain and Europe today, and many amateur exhibitors have gardens largely confined to roses.

Rosette Originally meaning an ornament,

ROSETTE (echeveria)

either painted, sculpted or moulded, or made of ribbons or leather strips, which resembles a rose, the word 'rosette' is applied botanically to any similar arrangement of petals or, especially, leaves in a rose-like pattern. Many alpines, e.g. saxifrages, have leaf rosettes, and it is also a typical leaf arrangement of succulents such as the echeverias.

Rotary Cultivator ◇ CULTIVATOR.

Rotary Grasscutter or Mower ◇ MOWERS.

Rotate Wheel-shaped: of flowers with petals joined, at least at the base, which form a flat disk or 'limb'. ◇ FLOWER.

Rotation In the vegetable garden, rotation involves changing the position of crops each year so that the same crop does not occupy the same ground in consecutive years. In this way any build-up of pests and diseases peculiar to one plant is reduced, and the best use is made of plant foods in the soil – some crops needing fresh manure or fertilizers, others preferring ground which has been manured for an earlier crop. Farmers have observed rotation for centuries with individual crops; the limited space of the average garden or allotment makes it simpler to avoid a rigid rotation and to group plants of a similar type together. Rotation is usually on a three-year basis, though a four-year plan is sometimes adopted.

The table below illustrates a typical three-year rotation. The groups of crops, which are alternated as shown in years 1, 2, and 3, are as follows:

Plot A: All brassicas except those in (B), which may be preceded by, or intercropped with, lettuces, radishes and other salad crops. This plot should be dressed with animal manure or compost, and limed at a separate time (if necessary), while the growing crops may be fed with nitrate of soda or sulphate of ammonia.

Plot B: Potatoes to be followed by broccoli, spring cabbages, leeks and late-sown turnips. This plot is dressed with manure or compost but not lime, and if potatoes are grown a balanced fertilizer should be applied just before planting.

Plot C: Rootcrops: carrots, parsnips, turnips and beetroot. Peas and beans intercropping with summer spinach and lettuce. Of these, only the peas and beans need manure, but wood ashes may be worked in and a complete fertilizer applied just before sowing.

Plot D: Onions, which often grow best if left permanently in the same plot. If they are to be rotated, they should go into group (C). This plot needs manure or compost and wood ashes, and the onions may be fed with nitrate of soda after thinning.

Year 1	Year 2	Year 3
A	*C*	*B*
B	*A*	*C*
C	*B*	*A*
D	*D*	*D*

Rotavator A popular expression meaning a powered rotary cultivator. ◇ CULTIVATOR.

Rotenone The active principle in the insecticide DERRIS.

Rotting Agent A material used to speed up the decay of material on a compost heap;

the same as an accelerator. ◊ COMPOST HEAP.

Rough-grass Cutter A mowing machine designed for long rough grass. ◊ MOWERS.

Rough Leaves The first true leaves produced by seedlings after the seed leaves or cotyledons: the latter always have smooth uninterrupted margins while the true leaves are very often toothed or indented, hence 'rough'. ◊ COTYLEDON.

Rubbery Wood A descriptive term for a virus disease of apples which makes the younger growths very flexible, so that they become drooping; later the wood tends to become brittle. Many apple cultivars are infected with this virus although it is latent

Ruins Mock ruins were among the structures erected as decorative features in gardens from the eighteenth century on. Most were in Gothic style but Roman ruins were also recreated. ◊ FOLLY; GOTHIC.

Run (1) A plant which flowers prematurely may be said to have run to seed: this is the same as BOLTING.

(2) Plants are sometimes said to run when they produce extensive creeping growth or RUNNERS.

Runner A stem growing above the soil surface and making roots from the buds which are produced at intervals along it at the nodes. In time, the stem itself dies and the new plants are established individually. The strawberry is a well-known example which the gardener encourages,

RUNNER (creeping buttercup)

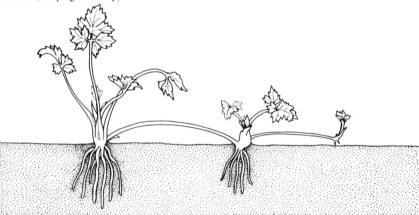

in some and the symptoms are not always produced. Affected trees continue to crop although not as heavily as uninfected ones, and since viruses cannot be eliminated in grown trees it is not usual practice to destroy the latter. ◊ VIRUS DISEASES.

Rudimentary Applied by botanists to organs which do not develop fully or are vestigial.

Rugose A botanical term meaning wrinkled, and usually applied to leaves with a wrinkled surface. ◊ LEAF.

and the creeping buttercup a notorious example of a weed, for the rooted plantlets soon become large enough to throw out more runners around themselves. Another garden plant with runners is the violet. When garden plants such as the strawberry and the violet produce runners, they should be cut off unless wanted for increase, as otherwise they may weaken the parent and overcrowd the bed. Runners selected for propagation should be limited in number and only the first plantlet formed allowed to develop. ◊ ADVENTITIOUS; NODE; RHIZOME; STOLON; TILLER.

269

Russeting Surface scarring of fruit (mainly apples and pears), often accompanied by cracking of the skin. It can be caused by frost and cold winds when the fruitlets are forming, by drought or mineral deficiencies later on, by apple mildew disease, and by unsuitable chemical sprays, notably sulphur (some fruit cultivars are called sulphur-shy because of this).

Some cultivars of apples and pears naturally have a brown rough skin; apples of this sort are called russets.

Rust A portmanteau word referring to a number of different fungus diseases which all produce rust-coloured or orange outgrowths on plant leaves or sometimes stems. All these diseases have a complex life cycle involving five different stages and sometimes two or three distinct host plants. Rusts are both very weakening to the plant and unsightly. They are not easily controlled; the first step should be to strip off and then burn all badly affected shoots and individual leaves, after which repeated spraying with an appropriate fungicide may eliminate the infection. In some cases, as with mint rust, no chemical treatment succeeds and affected plants should be burnt, though commercial growers can give plants hot-water treatment. In other cases, rust-resistant strains of popular ornamental plants have been produced, as in antirrhinums. ◊ CLUSTER CUPS; FUNGUS; HOT-WATER TREATMENT.

Rustic Work The use of timber in the natural state as branches still carrying bark, or sometimes with the bark removed. Nowadays restricted mainly to garden furniture, fencing, pergolas and archways, in the mid-eighteenth century rustic work extended to garden houses of various kinds which might have unbarked tree trunks as their main support and be thatched with rushes. In Victorian days all sorts of things were formed of unbarked wood including flower baskets and vases, and garden doorways. This led to a period in which cast-iron garden furniture, fencing panels and other objects were made to imitate wooden rustic work.

❈ S ❈

Saddle Graft A method of grafting in which the scion is cut into a shape like an inverted V or a V with the angle flattened, and the stock is pared on two sides to fit into this, after which the two can be bound together and sealed. Stock and scion must be of the same size. ⟡ GRAFTING.

Sagittate Arrow-shaped; usually applied to leaves. ⟡ LEAF.

Salad Plant Any vegetable grown mainly for eating raw in salads. The obvious ones are celery, endives, lettuces, spring onions and radishes, but some wild plants can be added, a few plants normally grown for decoration (e.g. calendula petals, nasturtium leaves) and a number of vegetables normally grown for cooking but capable of being eaten raw or cooked and eaten cold, like cabbages and beetroot. Also called saladings. The old spelling is 'sallet'.

Salicetum A collection of willows, often seen in the nineteenth century; known popularly as a sally garden.

Salt In general, a salt is any combination of an acid with another chemical: thus sulphate of ammonia is the salt resulting from sulphuric acid combining with ammonium hydroxide, and most inorganic fertilizers are salts.

In the narrower sense, salt is applied to sodium chloride which is used to flavour food. In the garden this can be used as a weedkiller, having a scorching action whether applied dry (at $\frac{1}{2}$–2 lb. per square yard) or in solution ($\frac{1}{2}$–1 lb. in a gallon of water). At these rates, salt kills any plant so it cannot be used as a weedkiller among ornamentals. However, salt can be used at 1–1$\frac{1}{2}$ oz. per square yard around various plants on which, for largely unexplained reasons, it has a tonic effect. Among its effects are an improved absorption of

phosphates, and an increased capacity to store water. Most brassicas and their relations seem to benefit in this way and also some flowering pot plants; equally, dressings of salt are traditionally given to crops originating on the coast, like asparagus and seakale. If sprayed onto crops salt has a dual function, since it also destroys caterpillars and other pests. A sprinkling with salt will kill slugs.

Salt can, however, intensify the stickiness of soils especially if they contain much clay, and thus harms their texture. This only occurs when a lot of salt reaches the soil as when the sea floods coastal districts.

Seaside gardens can be seriously affected by salt spray carried inland by wind: the effect is to scorch foliage severely.

Saltpetre ⟡ NITRATE OF POTASH.

Salverform Of flowers with petals joined, at least at the base, and having a flat disk or 'limb' at right angles to a slender tube forming the base of the flower. ⟡ FLOWER.

Samara A winged fruit or seed which is indehiscent, i.e. it does not split open, as of a sycamore; popularly known as a key. The wing is an aid to dispersal. ⟡ WING.

Sand One of the constituents of most soils, sand on its own is useful in many ways. It has no food value whatever but is used for its mechanical effect in improving aeration both of garden soils and, more especially, of seed and potting composts. For these purposes it must be 'sharp', consisting of angular particles ranging from minute to nearly $\frac{1}{8}''$ across. The smooth, fine sand used by builders for mixing concrete simply has a clogging effect in soil.

Sharp sand is also used to assist the rooting of cuttings. If used alone, the lack of food in sand means that potting on should be carried out fairly soon after roots have formed or the young plants will starve. Also, pure sand dries out rapidly. To overcome this, it may be mixed with fine peat, and, to ensure early nourishment of rooting cuttings, with peat and sterilized soil as in the John Innes cuttings compost, or with food-enriched peat.

Builders' sand is often used as the water-carrying medium on capillary benches, and as a top dressing for lawns, either alone or mixed with peat or sieved soil.

 ⟡ AERATION; CAPILLARY WATERING; COMPOSTS, SEED AND POTTING; CUTTING; DRESSING.

Sand Frame A propagating frame containing only sharp sand into which cuttings are inserted. Because of the porosity of sand, and the desirability of keeping the frame in sunlight, watering several times a day is needed. As a method for rooting difficult cuttings it has largely been superseded by MIST PROPAGATION.

Sandstone A variable stone of which the hard kinds are valuable for making rock gardens, since rectangular blocks can readily be obtained which absorb some moisture and weather pleasingly. Soft sandstones break down rapidly when exposed to the weather. Sandstone contains no lime so is particularly useful if the rock garden is to include lime-hating plants.
 ⟡ ROCK GARDEN.

Sap The fluid in plant cells containing water, plant foods, and hormones, which moves in the plant's conducting or vascular system. Water and dissolved minerals rise in a plant in the xylem tissue, while the more complex food products of photosynthesis move downwards in the phloem tissue. The latter sap is that stored in bulbs and other storage organs, and it also is affected by the procedures of nicking, notching and ringing. ⟡ HORMONES; LATEX; NICKING AND NOTCHING; PHOTOSYNTHESIS; RINGING; STORAGE ORGANS; VASCULAR SYSTEM.

Sap-drawer Short shoots left unpruned on the sides and undersides of the main branches of fruit trees during formative pruning of open-centre forms are termed sap-drawers. They provide immediate nourishment for the main branches without growing at their expense, and because of the food balance situation their buds end up as blossom buds within three or four years so that early fruiting occurs on the tree. ⟡ OPEN-CENTRE.

Sapling A young tree at any stage from a seedling until the heart-wood becomes hard. ⟡ HEART-WOOD.

Sappy Describes growth of shoots and foliage which is abnormally soft and juicy, or rank. Such growth can be due to overwatering or, more often, overfeeding; it may be more than usually vulnerable to pest and disease attack and the plant is unlikely to flower and/or fruit satisfactorily.

Saprophyte An organism which lives on decaying matter of plant or animal origin: the word is derived from Greek words meaning 'putrid' and 'plant'. Saprophytes contain no chlorophyll and are unable to carry out photosynthesis to manufacture food with the aid of light. The biggest group of saprophytes is found among the fungi, both large and microscopic, and the bacteria. Saprophytes should not be confused with parasites which feed on living organisms, and again include fungi and bacteria. Compost heaps often include white thread-like growths which are the vegetative parts of saprophytic fungi. These are beneficial, speed the rotting of the compost heap and cannot harm living plants. Several higher plants are indirectly saprophytic: these cannot make use of decaying matter directly but their mass of roots is entered by a saprophytic fungus. The latter provides starch for the plant, and there may be some reciprocal benefit: such an association is termed symbiosis. Examples are the Bird's-nest Orchid (*Neottia*) and the Dutchman's Pipe (*Monotropa*), both fairly common in Britain: both are leafless and contain no green colouring.
 ⟡ FUNGUS; PARASITE; SYMBIOSIS.

Sap-sucker An insect which sucks the sap of plants via a tubular stylet, and thus becomes a pest, e.g. an aphid. ◊ APHIDS; PEST.

Sapwood The new wood of a tree, which forms the outermost of the xylem layers within the cambium, in which sap can flow, as opposed to the heart-wood which eventually becomes lifeless. Also used more loosely of new shoots which have not become hard and woody, and are suitable for softwood or half-ripe cuttings. ◊ CUTTING; VASCULAR SYSTEM.

Saut-de-loup A French phrase meaning 'wolf's jump', referring to a HA-HA.

Saw, Sawing Large hand saws and power-driven chain saws are used for major cutting operations on trees such as lopping and the removal of unwanted large branches. A pruning saw is used for cutting work intermediate between this and the capacity of secateurs or pruning knife. Such saws, seldom more than 2′ long, usually have a narrow blade, which may be slightly curved as in the so-called Grecian saw, which has teeth set so that it only cuts when pulled towards the operator. Some pruning saws are designed to fold up when not in use; others can be fixed to long handles for making cuts high up in trees, when they are called polesaws.

When sawing, it is always desirable to make a first cut on the underside of the branch; if cutting is done only from the top the branch will break before the operation is complete and almost always tears a strip of bark off the wood left in place, through which disease can enter. Saw cuts should in any case be trimmed flat and their edges pared with a sharp pruning knife for quick healing, and cuts of any size are best treated with WOUND DRESSINGS.

Sawdust If supplies of sawdust are available, this can be used as a weed-suppressing mulch or dug into soil as a dressing, at up to 15 lb. per square yard; though of little food value, it is a useful soil improver. Ideally, the sawdust should have decayed for several months first, because fresh sawdust causes a lack of nitrogen in soil with which it is combined: the reason for this is that the nitrogen is all used up by the bacteria which decompose the sawdust. The alternative is to apply a nitrogenous fertilizer, e.g. sulphate of ammonia, at around ½ lb. per square yard at the same time as the fresh sawdust. Sawdust can also be composted, if possible by mixing 3 parts by volume with 1 of farmyard or other animal manure. Otherwise it is best allowed to decay for up to a year, using Nitro-chalk as an activator at 1 lb. per 20 lb. sawdust. It is after composting that sawdust is most valuable for digging in as a soil improver. ◊ COMPOST HEAP; MULCH.

Sawflies A large tribe of fly-like insects, many of whose grubs are serious pests of garden plants. They are called sawflies because their ovipositors (egg-laying organs) have a serrated edge with which cuts are made in leaves and stems for depositing eggs. Sawfly grubs, usually produced in large numbers, may look like moth caterpillars, though they have up to eight pairs of legs instead of the five of moths, or like slugs with a smooth exterior and almost invisible legs, when they are called slug-worms.

Sawfly grubs eat or skeletonize foliage, sometimes defoliating plants very rapidly, or cause leaf-rolling, forming tunnels which they inhabit; a few burrow into the centre of shoots; and, in the case of apples, either penetrate the fruitlets and eat the centre of the developing fruit, or leave scars on the skin of the fruit. Other sawflies attack pears and plums. Remedies vary according to the sawfly concerned. ◊ CODLING MOTH; SLUGWORMS.

Saw Pruning A phrase sometimes used of REGULATED PRUNING.

Scab Applied to a number of distinct fungus diseases which cause sunken patches or cracks in the tissue of the attacked plants. Apple and pear scab are often serious diseases which ruin the fruit and damage shoots. Appropriate fungicides used at specific times will reduce future attacks. Potato scab disfigures the tubers but does not make them uneatable. It is a soil-borne infection and crop rotation should be practised to reduce attacks, as will slightly acid soil and reduced liming. Gladiolus scab attacks foliage and corms and can destroy the plants, and it is best to discard badly affected corms, though less severely attacked ones can be treated with fungicide.

Scabrous A botanical term meaning rough to the touch.

Scalding A term for physiological damage to greenhouse plants caused by unsatisfactory conditions such as hot dry atmosphere, direct strong sunlight, draughts, rapid temperature changes and fumes as from paraffin or gas heaters. The damage takes the form of brown or whitish spotting or blotching on leaves, withering of young growth, and shrivelling of fruits. Grape growers recognize scalding as the browning and collapse of the fruits with the fruit-stalks left intact (in contrast to shanking): this is usually due to sunlight on fruits which are wet due to condensation during the early morning, and this is usually the result of an over-moist atmosphere. ⟡ SHANKING.

Scale, Scale-leaf Scale is a botanical term for any thin, scale-like appendage on a plant; this is often a degenerate leaf, and may be called a scale-leaf. Specialized scale-leaves include those covering growth buds and those forming bulbs.

Scale Insects A large group of small insects which attack a wide range of plants both outside and under glass. Their common factor is that, after a short period of mobility after hatching, they settle down in one place, inserting their long sap-sucking stylet into the plant, protected by a usually hard coat or scale which entirely covers them like miniature limpets. Scales can be up to $\frac{1}{4}''$ long but are usually around $\frac{1}{8}''$. Many scales are round, but they can be elongated, when they receive descriptive names like mussel scale. The commonest colour is brown but they can be red, black, grey and white. Many scales are more or less specific to one host plant and are named accordingly, e.g. oleander scale.

Young scales, and indeed some adults, are quite inconspicuous, and may cause much damage to plants before an attack is suspected. Stunting or yellowing of a plant should be cause for close examination. Another typical clue is the excretion of much honeydew; any plant which becomes unnaturally sticky should be suspected of scale insect attack. Black sooty mould grows rapidly upon the honeydew and is another symptom.

In limited attacks scale insects can be prised off with a knife-point, scrubbed off stems with a small brush, or rubbed off leaves with a cloth dipped in soapy water. Many insecticides will kill scales, including systemics which the insects imbibe through the sap, but dead scales remain on the plants and may need manual removal. ⟡ HONEYDEW; SOOTY MOULD.

Scalloped With rounded teeth or notches: the same as crenate. Usually applied to leaf margins. ⟡ LEAF

Scandent Climbing, by whatever method. ⟡ CLIMBER.

Scape A flower stem which grows directly from ground level and bears no leaves.

Scare, Scarer ⟡ BIRDS.

Scarifier, Scarify A scarifier is a tool for raking out or scarifying debris and moss on lawns. It may take the form of a springy-tined lawn rake or a device with short crescent-shaped teeth. Some are designed to be pushed by hand, on wheels or skids, and others to be fitted onto lawn mowers. There may be a row of short metal teeth or strong stiff brushes. ⟡ LAWN RAKE.

Schedule ⟡ SHOW SCHEDULE.

Sciarid Flies ⟡ FUNGUS GNATS.

Scion Any shoot or bud removed from one plant for the purpose of joining it to another in budding or grafting. The scion is chosen for the quality of its flowers, fruit or other notable character, while the stock to which it is joined provides the roots.
  ⟡ BUDDING; GRAFTING.

Scion-rooting If a grafted tree is planted with the graft union below soil level, it is likely that the scion will produce its own roots, sometimes eventually growing on these to the exclusion of the roots of the stock. If the stock is typically chosen for some specific level of root vigour (in ornamentals, usually for maximum vigour, but in fruit trees, often for degrees of dwarfing), scion-rooting negates the purpose of the graft and is normally to be discouraged.
  ⟡ GRAFTING.

SCAPE (*Amaryllis belladonna*)

Scissors A few specialized types of scissors are used horticulturally. Grape or vine scissors, with long, thin, tapered blades, are used by greenhouse grape growers to thin the developing grapes and avoid overcrowded bunches, which can cause bruising and the consequent spread of rot. Flower-gathering scissors, often short and blunt-nosed, grip the stem after it has been cut from the plant. Pruning scissors have blades rather like those of

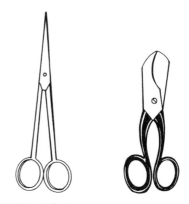

SCISSORS. *Left*, vine; *right*, pruning

parrot's-bill secateurs, but have the circular finger-grips of scissors rather than the projecting handles of secateurs. Wire scissors are really wire cutters with strong short blades designed to cut ordinary wire and a notch near the base of one blade where thick wire can be cut.

Sclerotinia Rot ⟡ STEM ROT.

Scorching Damage to plants caused by strong sunlight, sunlight focused onto small areas by drops of water, fertilizer solution on foliage, salt spray carried on wind, strong wind itself, or over-strong fertilizer around the roots. The word is often used in the same sense as scalding.
  ⟡ SCALDING; WIND.

Scorpioid ⟡ INFLORESCENCE (Cyme).

Scrambler A plant with long sinuous stems, often equipped with thorns so that it can become fixed among the branches of ordinary shrubs and trees through which it climbs. Climbing roses and brambles are examples.

Scree In nature, a scree is a slope of rock fragments which retain little moisture, as at the bottom of a cliff, as opposed to a moraine which is associated with a moisture-producing glacier and is likely to contain silt. A scree in a garden imitates

275

such conditions with a deep layer of stone chippings, mixed with a minimum amount of loam, and without provision for underground watering as in a garden MORAINE.

Screen In gardening terms, a screen can be used to shut out unwanted visual effects, sound or wind. Visual screens can be fences, hedges or walls. Aural screens, only effective where large areas are available, are in effect hedges in depth, using several 'layers' of selected trees, some being much better than others at absorbing sound. Windscreens, or windbreaks as they are usually called, are best created from shelterbelts, hedges or, on a limited scale, from porous rather than solid fencing, such as hurdles. In special cases, e.g. roof gardens, wind screening is most effectively done by erecting reinforced glass panels.

Ornamental screens are mainly used within gardens, and can be of varied materials such as wire or wooden lattice work, trellis or pierced wall blocks; hedges can of course also be used.

⟡ FEDGE; FENCES, HEDGE; SCREEN WALLING; SHELTERBELT; TRELLIS; WALLS; WINDBREAK.

Screen Sieve ⟡ SIEVE.

Screen Walling Walls composed of rela-tively thin blocks of concrete, earthenware or sometimes other materials incorporat-ing pierced patterns, thus allowing a partial view and reducing wind flow somewhat. In warm climates, such walling has long been in use for ornamental screening and also to provide walls for loggias and similar open-air buildings where some air movement is desirable. Pierced walling blocks have become popular in colder climates like Britain's for decorative purposes.

Scrim A fine mesh of cotton material at one time used for shading greenhouses, but now largely superseded by more durable materials.

Scurf Minute scales on the surface of leaves or stems which give the plant a grey or silvery tinge, and are less dusty and easily removed than meal or farina. Bromeliads often have a scurfy covering, technically known as lepidate. ⟡ BROMELIAD; FARINA; WAX.

Scythe A tool with a slightly curved blade around 3′ long, fitted to a curved handle with two hand-grips (called a snead), and used with a swinging motion designed to make the blade travel in a horizontal arc a short distance above the ground. Scythes have been in use as agricultural reaping

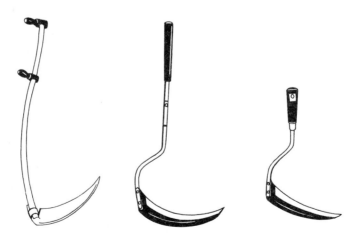

SCYTHE. *Left to right*, standard scythe; scythette; grass hook (not to scale)

instruments since Roman times and, to cut grass in gardens, probably from the medieval period. In the eighteenth and early nineteenth centuries, the demand for well-cut swards led to remarkable precision in scything. After the invention of the lawn mower, the scythe rapidly went out of use for cutting lawns but continues to be used for cutting rough grass, especially in places like orchards where machine cutters may be difficult to handle. Properly used, a really sharp scythe is the ideal tool to cut a new lawn grown from seed, because there is much less danger of uprooting the grass seedlings than occurs with a mower.

The scythe is not an easy tool to master and the blade and handle must be pre-set to suit the operator. For rough grass cutting, smaller versions, variously known as Turk scythe, scythette or scythook, are more easily handled. The Turk scythe is a scaled-down version of an orthodox scythe but the others have a blade 12"–16" long fixed to a straight handle 3'–4' long, cranked near the blade and gripped with two hands at the farther end. The grass hook is in effect a scythe with a short handle, differing from a sickle in its much less curved blade. The bramble scythe is like a full-scale scythe with a shorter, wider and stiffer blade.
◊ SICKLE.

Seakale Pot A medium-sized earthenware pot with a small removable lid, used for forcing seakale but now seldom seen. ◊ FORCING.

Sealing Agent Another phrase for a wound dressing for tree cuts. ◊ WOUND DRESSINGS.

Seaweed Where readily available, seaweed makes an excellent bulky manure. It can be used in various ways. One is to bury it, or dig it into the soil at from 10–20 lb. per square yard. If dried out in the sun first, the application rate is 2–3 lb. per square yard. Dried seaweed can be kept indefinitely: it is usually stored in roughly conical stacks which prevent much rain from entering. Seaweed can also be composted, and rots

rapidly, but unfortunately then develops a very unpleasant smell. Seaweed can be processed into a dry meal or made into a liquid extract.

The long strap-shaped species of seaweed (*Laminaria*, often called kelp) are richer in plant food than the smaller bladder-wracks (*Fucus*) but an average analysis of fresh seaweed is around 0.5 per cent nitrogen, 0.1 per cent phosphorus (sometimes much higher), and 1 per cent potash. Its balance is therefore high in potash. In addition, it contains a very wide range of trace elements. Wet seaweed is a valuable source of organic matter, while seaweed in any state contains alginates which build up the humus content of the soil and have a remarkably beneficial effect on soil texture. Seaweed meal contains 63 per cent of these humus-forming materials, though its food value is only 2 per cent nitrogen. Liquid feeds made from seaweed vary in chemical content but always provide the three main elements, with a high proportion of potash, the wide range of trace elements, and apparently plant hormones which seem to encourage growth. The liquid preparations are useful as foliar feeds as well as orthodox liquid feeds.

Calcified seaweeds (*Lithophyllum, Lithothamnium*, etc.) concentrate calcium carbonate in their cell walls. Dried and crushed, these are used as soil conditioners or improvers because of their texture; they also contain many minerals and trace elements valuable for plant nutrition.
◊ ALGINATE; FOLIAR FEEDING; HUMUS; SOIL CONDITIONER.

Secateurs Pruning tools (U.S.: pruning shears) in which two blades on one pivot close together when the two handles, gripped in one hand, are squeezed together; a spring then opens them out again ready for the next cut. There are three main types. The side anvil type has a scissor-like action in which one sharp, thin blade moves immediately alongside a stouter blade which makes a fairly broad angle to the first, or even a right angle. In the anvil type, the cutting blade is pressed down onto an 'anvil' which is a broad flat-topped blade of softer metal, or sometimes fibre. In the less common parrot-beak or scissors type, there are two thin cutting blades equally sharpened, each being curved rather like a parrot's beak.

Second Soil Gardeners sometimes keep potting compost left over from annuals or other pot plants which have died. This 'second soil' can be used for top-dressing other pots, or for further potting, if an

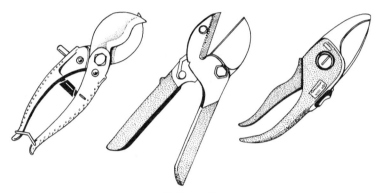

SECATEURS. *Left to right*, parrot-beak; anvil; side anvil

In the side anvil type the blades can work loose or bend apart under strain. This applies also to the parrot-beak, where there is also the possibility of local damage to the thin sharp blades. The anvil type may crush the end of the plant growth left in place if the blade is not very sharp or accurately set; a superior version has a sliding blade which reduces this possibility. In all cases the better-made secateurs avoid such problems. Double-action or double-cut secateurs are available in which a toggle or ratchet action greatly increases the leverage and cutting power. A kind of hybrid between secateurs and scissors is the FLOWER GATHERER.

Secondary Growth (1) Normally refers to any new shoots produced by a tree or shrub after summer pruning, and is largely restricted to fruit pruning. Such new shoots should not occur if summer pruning is properly timed but, if they do, should be pruned back to one bud in early autumn or winter.

(2) Secondary growth sometimes refers to new growth from the tip of a shoot which had apparently stopped development earlier in the relevant season.

appropriate amount of fertilizer is mixed in. However, this can transmit disease and certain pests, and it is really best to put used potting material on the compost heap.

Sedge Peat ♦ PEAT.

Seed (1) Seeds are plants' sexual means of reproducing themselves, as opposed to asexual or vegetative means. Seeds are produced when the male pollen has successfully fertilized the ovule in the pistil or female part of the flower; they contain an embryo plant with a shoot, root and reserve food to assist the developing seedling while its root starts to search out nutrients in the soil, before the shoot starts growing. The food reserve varies considerably – in a coconut it can last a year, in an orchid seed it is virtually absent – but normally lasts for several days.

Some seeds germinate as soon as they find themselves in suitable conditions of warmth and moisture, but a great many seeds first undergo a dormant period, which comes to an end only after various external factors have occurred. The most obvious of these in a temperate climate is the winter: a seed mature in autumn will not find suitable conditions for growing on until the following spring, and will not germinate until the cold period has occurred. Other dormancy controls may operate in difficult conditions (e.g. deserts) or so that the seeds will become well dispersed before germinating.

In natural species, whether self- or cross-pollinated, the progeny from seed will normally resemble the parents closely. Many garden plants have been bred from different parents and their seeds will not necessarily produce similar progeny – indeed are unlikely to. This applies to most named cultivars normally increased vegetatively, and especially to F.1 hybrids whose parents are quite different.

◊ entries below prefixed by SEED; CULTIVAR; F.1; FERTILIZATION; GERMINATION; OVARY; PELLETED SEED; VEGETATIVE.

(2) The word 'seed' is also in common use for potato tubers selected for planting, which are often called seed potatoes.

Seed Bed Any area of soil which has been prepared for seeds to be sown. Preparation is primarily a matter of breaking down the soil finely, making it firm (by treading), and levelling it with a rake; without such a reasonably fine tilth, rain or artificially applied water may not penetrate readily, and it will be difficult to cover all the seeds to the same depth, resulting in poor and erratic germination. ◊ DRILL; GERMINATION; TREADING.

Seed Box Any box-shaped container in which seeds can be raised. The standard seed box, pan or tray (U.S.: flat) is around $14'' \times 8\frac{1}{2}'' \times 2''$ deep: this applies to both wooden and plastic kinds. It is also possible to obtain smaller plastic trays, around $6'' \times 8\frac{1}{2}'' \times 2''$ deep. Deeper boxes can be obtained, but these are usually for transplanting into rather than for seed sowing.

Wooden boxes normally have a base of two pieces with a slit between them, and if this is more than $\frac{1}{8}''$ wide it should be covered with small pieces of broken pot

(crocks) before filling with seed compost. Plastic seed trays have small drainage holes ready made which do not need crocking.

Wooden seed boxes can have their life prolonged by treatment with a copper naphthenate wood preservative (*not* creosote), which also has a sterilizing effect. Plastic types just need a good wash before refilling.

◊ SEED SOWING.

Seed Compost ◊ COMPOSTS, SEED AND POTTING.

Seed Dispersal Plants have many ingenious methods of spreading their seeds far and wide. A few familiar examples include the 'parachutes' of dandelions and thistles, the winged keys (samaras) of sycamore, the 'pepper-pot' of poppies, and explosive devices in broom, sweet peas and impatiens. Many seeds have hooks or bristles so that they are carried on animal fur, bird feathers or human clothes; others are eaten by birds and other creatures and passed out unharmed in their excreta.

A knowledge of seed dispersal is desirable if the gardener wishes to collect seed himself. If he does not harvest it at the right time he may find it gone. Such knowledge is also an advantage in dealing with weeds early enough to prevent seed dispersal.

◊ SEED HARVESTING.

Seed Distributor A mechanical device for sowing seeds, often called a seed drill. On a large scale, this is usually a wheeled device with a hopper in which the seeds are placed, in which forward movement releases the seeds steadily via various mechanisms. Hand devices include gadgets which can be tapped with the finger, or mechanically jerked, to release seeds more or less individually at desired intervals.

◊ SEED SOWING.

Seed Dressing Few fungus diseases of garden plants are spread by seed, and almost no virus diseases. In the few cases which exist, such as celery leaf spot, seed merchants have devised chemical or hot-water treatments to control the disease. However, many soil pests and diseases attack seed once it is sown, and seed dressings are available to ward these off, usually containing several appropriate pesticides and fungicides to cover the most likely attacks. They are normally sold as powders in which the seed is shaken up before being sown, though some are liquids. Older books recommend moistening large seeds, e.g. peas and beans, in paraffin and then shaking them up in red lead powder before sowing to stop attack by birds and rodents.

Seed Drill (1) A narrow furrow made to sow seeds in. ◊ DRILL.
(2) A wheeled machine for distributing seeds. ◊ SEED DISTRIBUTOR.

Seed Harvesting If it is desired to collect seed of garden plants, a careful watch must be kept on the development of seed capsules or heads or fruits, to make sure that seeds are not lost by the plants' own dispersal mechanisms. This means collecting the capsules, etc., when they are on the point of ripeness, and usually entails going over the plants concerned several times. Alternatively muslin bags can be fastened over the seed heads, into which the seeds will fall. It is better to collect seeds before they appear fully ripe rather than lose them: seed capsules, etc., will continue to ripen if placed after collection in warm, dry conditions, preferably in open containers in sunlight. Explosive pods or capsules, such as those of brooms and sweet peas, should however be placed in paper bags since in open containers the seed may be discharged all over the room or shed.

After a week or so of the drying conditions the seeds can be extracted from their containers. Those in dry capsules or heads may simply shake out or can readily be extracted by rubbing between the fingers. If the seeds are placed in a saucer any pieces of capsule can be removed by blowing lightly over them, or the seeds can be shaken through a seed sieve of appropriate mesh size.

Seeds in fleshy fruits, such as rose hips or crab apples, can be cut out, or rubbed out of them by hand; alternatively, the fruits are buried in pots of moist sand during the winter, the seeds being sieved out when the flesh has decayed. This is called stratification.

Once harvested, the seeds should be placed in paper bags or envelopes in a cool dry place until required for sowing, except for those (e.g. primula seed) which should be sown immediately as they soon lose their germination capacity. Plastic bags are not recommended for seeds since they can retain moisture which will reduce storage life and may encourage mould.
◊ SEED; SEED DISPERSAL; STRATIFICATION.

Seed Leaf The first leaf or pair of leaves produced by a seed on germination, also called COTYLEDON.

Seedling (1) A very young plant which has recently germinated.
(2) Also used of older plants which have been raised from seed of mixed or unknown parentage and have potential as distinct new varieties. In such cases, the parents will normally be increased by vegetative means to ensure that all offspring are identical, and seedlings are bred from them to see if different or improved variations are produced: if successful, the selected offspring will be given their own cultivar names and increased vegetatively thereafter. ◊ CULTIVAR; VEGETATIVE.

Seed Protection Newly sown seeds are attractive to birds, while finely raked seed beds may be disturbed by birds taking dust baths, and are also attractive to cats. Large seeds, e.g. beans and peas, may be taken by mice. PEA GUARDS, or even a piece of wire netting held in place with sticks, will keep birds and cats off. For other protective measures ◊ BIRDS; CATS; MICE.

Seed-raised Plants raised from seed as distinct from vegetative methods.

Seed Sieve ◊ SEED HARVESTING; SIEVE.

Seed Sowing In principle, seeds start to

germinate when external moisture is taken up by them. Many seeds have inbuilt dormancy which prevents water uptake: this can sometimes be 'broken' artificially, though in other cases the gardener can do little except exercise patience. Depending on their origin, seeds also require a certain temperature before they will germinate, and this is a figure which only records based on past experience can provide. Next, a suitable medium must be provided for the seedlings to develop in: this seed bed, or compost for container sowing, should have a reasonably open texture so that plenty of air can reach the seed and the seedling root can penetrate without difficulty. The medium should be moisture-retentive and provide an adequate level of plant food for seedlings.

The depth of sowing is also important. As a rule of thumb the seeds should be covered twice or three times as deep as their own thickness, not more. This is for two reasons. Many seeds need some light to germinate and too deep a covering will shut this out. In the case of seeds which only germinate in darkness, the seed must be buried more deeply, as with onions which have small seeds but should be sown $\frac{1}{2}''$ deep. Too deep a covering may prevent small seedlings emerging at all: this is the case with dust-like seed, e.g. that of calceolaria, which should be sown on the surface of the medium and watered in very lightly so that it is in good contact with the moist medium.

Seed can be sown in furrows (drills) or, if larger, in shallow trenches, or broadcast. This applies to both seed sown out of doors and in containers under cover. Whichever method is applied, seed should always be sown as thinly as possible – otherwise the seedlings come up so close together that they immediately become 'drawn' and consequently weak when separated for transplanting individually, or pricking out. With seed which can be handled with any precision, patient sowing with the aid of finger and thumb, to ensure adequate spacing, is well worth the extra time spent, as opposed to careless tapping out from a seed packet. The use of pelleted seed, when

available, makes individual sowing simple. Very small seed can be mixed with fine dry sand with advantage to dilute its rate of application. In all cases, thinning out of seedlings should take place at an early stage if they emerge overcrowded.

The soil or seed compost should be well moistened before sowing, but not be soaking wet. Containers are best watered an hour before sowing, using a can with a fine rose, and allowed to drain. Before watering, containers filled with seed compost should be firmed so that there are no large air pockets. After sowing, covering is best carried out by sieving further compost onto the container. Large seeds are covered more readily by moving compost over them after they have been pushed into the container.

To prevent drying out, seed containers in a greenhouse can either be placed in a propagating case or covered with an individual pane of glass, both of which prevent evaporation from the seed compost. A propagating case may be essential to maintain adequate warmth for seeds requiring this. If used, the pane of glass should be removed a few days after germination.

◊ BROADCASTING; COMPOSTS, SEED AND POTTING; DORMANCY; DRILL; FIRMER; GERMINATION; MULTI-DIBBER; PELLETED SEED; SEED BED; THINNING.

Seed Testing ◊ SEED VIABILITY.

Seed Tray ◊ SEED BOX.

Seed Vernalization ◊ VERNALIZATION.

Seed Viability Viability is the capacity for living and, with seeds, more precisely that for germinating. Few seeds have 100 per cent viability, and in any case the viability of most seeds decreases as time passes. Some seeds indeed lose their viability within a few weeks of maturity. Loss of viability can be enormously reduced by special storage techniques such as are used in scientists' 'seed banks'; and many seedsmen now use a technique of reducing the water content of seeds to around 4 per cent and sealing them into impermeable packets in conditions of very low humidity, when they will last for many years. Once opened in a humid atmosphere, the processes of ageing and normal loss of viability begin.

Seeds lose their viability at very differing rates. To discover if an old packet of vegetable seeds is worth using for new sowings, a simple test is to place a reasonable number of seeds on blotting paper or cloth kept damp on a saucer, and in a fairly warm place. The proportion that germinates can then be counted. Seedsmen and official seed-testing stations use mo. sophisticated methods for the same purpose, since under the Seeds Act of 1920 the vegetable seeds generally offered in Britain have to comply with prescribed minimum germination percentages. Flower seeds and seeds of other ornamentals do not come under these regulations.

Selection Any plant increased from seed – even a wild species – will vary a certain amount. By using seeds from the individuals thought most desirable, a distinctive selection may be created. It was by using seeds of wild poppies and foxgloves that the Rev. Wilks raised his famous Shirley selections. (Such a selection can also be called a stock and is very often known as a strain, but this word is not acceptable under the 'International Code of Nomenclature for Cultivated Plants'.)

When it comes to highly bred garden plants, variation – even in well-stabilized or so-called pure-breeding varieties – can be considerable unless the greatest care is taken in selecting the seed parents; without this, the original variety may deteriorate. It is for this reason that vegetable seeds are constantly announced as 'Re-selected'; and for the same reason that cultivars of the same name, but from different sources, may show small differences. Growers of exhibition vegetables often select and save their own seed. Selection is a horticultural rather than a botanical term; the botanist's equivalent would be a form.

Even vegetatively produced material, such as chrysanthemums increased from cuttings, often show variations, due to mutations or to chronic disease, and one could refer to a good type of chrysanthemum as 'so-and-so's stock'.

The moral is, that to maintain a good selection, even from one year to the next, it is essential to save seeds or to obtain cuttings only from plants which show every desired characteristic. A good nurseryman or seedsman does this automatically for the customer. (It must be realized in any case that seed from F.I cultivars will not breed true.)

◊ CLASSIFICATION (Variation); PLANT BREEDING.

Selective Weedkillers Materials which will destroy one kind of plant while leaving others unaffected. The most familiar are those used on lawns to kill broad-leaved weeds without harming the grass, which include 2,4-D and MCPA. These are sometimes known as hormone weedkillers, and act – in simple terms – by grossly disturbing the growth processes of the weeds. The reverse action can also be achieved: thus dalapon destroys grasses and their relations and is relatively harmless to broad-leaved plants. Farmers have other highly specialized selective weedkillers at their disposal. ◊ WEEDKILLER.

Self A term used mostly by growers of some specialized or florist flowers to denote blooms of one colour only throughout.

Self-clinging Applied to those climbers which produce aerial roots, e.g. ivy, or adhesive tendrils, e.g. Virginia creeper, and can thus support themselves on a wall without artificial aid. ◊ CLIMBER; SUPPORT.

Self-fertile Of a plant able to produce seeds when fertilized with its own pollen. The main application of the term is to fruit growing, since not every fruit variety is self-fertile, many needing a different variety nearby if they are to set fruit. ◊ CROSS-FERTILIZATION; FERTILITY RULES.

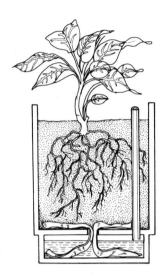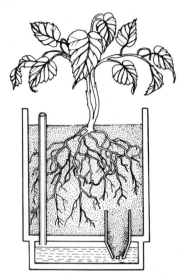

Selfing The act of artificially pollinating a plant with its own pollen. ◊ INBRED.

Self-pollination The pollination of a plant with its own pollen.

Self-sterile Of a plant which is unable to produce seeds when its flowers are pollinated with its own pollen. Many fruit trees, notably cherries and plums, are self-sterile and must have a different cultivar nearby to produce pollen which will enable them to set fruit. ◊ FERTILITY RULES; SELF-FERTILE; STERILE.

Self-watering Refers to pots or other containers with a water reservoir. Sometimes this is built into the container, or it may form a separate container below the one holding the plant. Water may be drawn up by capillary action through a wick (of canvas, glass fibre, etc.) in contact with the base of the potting mixture. In some patent devices the 'wick' consists of potting mixture in a narrow vertical cavity leading down into the reservoir. Self-watering devices should ensure that plants can be left

without watering for quite long periods. ◊ CAPILLARY WATERING.

Semi-double Of a flower with a few more petals than is normal for the wild species. ◊ DOUBLE; FLOWER.

SEMI-DOUBLE (camellia)

Seminal Relating to seed. Seminal propagation is thus increase by seed, and a seminal organ or structure one which contains seed.

Sensitive Describes plants which respond

283

to touch, the most familiar being *Mimosa pudica*, known as 'sensitive plant' because of the very rapid drooping of leaves and leaf-stems when touched. A number of flowers have sensitive stamens which move when touched, this being a device to ensure that pollen is liberally applied to visiting insects. Some insectivorous plants have sensitive leaves which snap over insect victims as in the Venus fly-trap, or carry tentacles which fold over them as in sundews.

Sepal Where the outer parts of a flower – which together form the calyx – are more or less separate, they are known as sepals. Though in some cases, e.g. waterlilies and many cacti, the sepals may resemble the petals or, as in the clematis and anemones, may actually replace them and be brightly coloured, sepals are usually green or brownish, even scale-like, and enclose the flower bud protectively before it opens. They are normally smaller than the expanded petals. ◊ CALYX; FLOWER; PERIANTH.

Sequestrol A chemical compound used to prevent the 'locking up' of certain trace elements in the soil, such as occurs with iron and manganese in chalky or lime-rich conditions, and also when hard water is used on plants. These are in fact the two metals usually offered in sequestered or chelated form, which may also be known as chelates. 'Chelate' derives from the Greek for a claw, and refers to the way in which the metallic portion of the chemical is isolated or 'gripped' by organic compounds so that it no longer has the properties typically associated with salts of that metal. This means that, whereas ordinary iron or manganese salts become insoluble in excessively alkaline conditions, causing deficiencies whose symptom is usually leaf yellowing (chlorosis), sequestrols applied according to instructions will make the metals available to plants. Two or three applications are sometimes needed fully to overcome a deficiency. ◊ ALKALINE; CHLOROSIS.

Serpentine Layering ◊ LAYERING.

Serpentine Wall Walls built on a serpentine or undulating plan. Such walls do not need to be as thick as orthodox straight walls nor do they need buttresses, and the niches in the walls create sheltered positions for tender shrubs or fruit trees difficult to ripen in normal conditions. They are also sometimes called crinkle-crankle walls.

The word 'serpentine' is also sometimes applied to paths and plantings on such a plan. ◊ SHARAWADGI.

Serrate, Serratulate Toothed like a saw. ◊ TOOTH; LEAF.

Sessile Stalkless: applied to leaves or flowers.

Set (1) The original horticultural meaning of this word, first recorded around 1500, was to describe any cutting, sucker or graft material, and also young plants, especially when they were to be bedded out. It was being used in this sense at least as late as 1894.

(2) Sometimes used (since 1707) of potato tubers, or parts of them, used as 'seed', and also of other tubers, onions and occasionally shallots for planting.

(3) The word is also used to describe blossom which has been successfully pollinated and is starting to develop fruit or seed, when the flowers are said to have set. The expression 'a good set of fruit' derives from this.

Setose Bristly, or with stiff, straight hairs. ◊ HAIRY.

Sewage Sludge After processing in sewage works, human excreta ends up as sewage sludge. Raw sewage sludge is rich in nitrogen and phosphorus and can be used at up to 25 lb. per square yard. However, it is unpleasant to handle and is normally only used on an agricultural scale, although too much can cause sealing of the soil surface. It may contain undigested seeds and also typhoid and other disease organisms, and should never be used on salad crops which are eaten raw and may be contaminated. Sludge may also contain metallic salts and other chemicals, and in this state should not be used because of soil contamination.

Some sewage works treat sludge to reduce its bulk, the result being a dry, odourless powder. Digested sludge, which is treated with anaerobic bacteria, contains about 3 per cent available nitrogen. Activated sludge, prepared by blowing air through raw sludge and adding aerobic bacteria, contains up to 7 per cent nitrogen and 4 per cent phosphoric acid and is the better material if available, to be used at $1\frac{1}{2}$–$2\frac{1}{2}$ lb. per square yard. These treated, powdery sludges sold for garden use provide some organic matter helpful to soil texture and should not contain any harmful chemicals.

Sex, Sexual Virtually all garden plants can increase themselves by sexual reproduction. Flowering plants or angiosperms produce flowers, as their title implies. Although technically the parts of flowers have no sex, since they belong to the asexual phase of plants, flowers *are* responsible for the eventual production of the male and female sex cells which fuse together on fertilization: *This* is the sexual phase. Flowers are therefore commonly described as carrying sex organs. The male organ is the anther, usually carried on a stamen, which contains pollen; the female organ consists of a stigma receptive to pollen connected with the ovary where, after successful fertilization, seeds are produced.

Many flowers contain both male and female organs, and are called hermaphrodite; but the sexes can be separate. Where separate male and female flowers are carried on the same plant, it is known as monoecious; when male and female flowers are on separate plants, these are called dioecious and may be called male or female plants. In such cases, a female plant grown alone will not produce seeds or fruits and one male must be grown in a group of females if fruit is the desired end-product.

Conifers have male and female organs usually in the form of cones: they can be monoecious or, less commonly, dioecious. In ferns, the sex organs are microscopic, and sexual and asexual reproduction alternates in the life cycle, the gardener normally being aware only of the latter when spores are produced.

Sexual reproduction results in production of seeds (except in ferns), the offspring from which can vary from the parents; this is in contrast to asexual reproduction by vegetative means, e.g. from runners or by taking cuttings, when the offspring are identical to the parent.

◊ CONIFER; FERN; FLOWER; SEED; SPORE; VEGETATIVE.

Shade, Shading While all plants need light in order to carry out photosynthesis, they vary enormously in the amount needed. Many of the subjects grown as house plants, for instance, grow on the floor of tropical jungles where they receive about 5 per cent of the full sunlight encountered by the foliage in the crowns of the trees. Gardeners in every situation need to be aware of the light needs of different plants, selecting sun-lovers and shade-lovers for appropriate parts of their gardens.

The effect of strong light is intensified under glass because of the heat which can develop there in summer sunshine, and most greenhouses need some kind of shading in the summer months if damage to plants is to be avoided. Some plants grown as greenhouse or house plants may thrive in full sun in their natural habitats but, if placed in sunshine after being cultivated, become scorched. Young plants grown from seed or cuttings are also likely to need shading from full sun.

There are various ways of shading greenhouses. One is to apply whitewash or a proprietary shading paint to the outside of the glass in early summer. One shading paint is at its most opaque when dry but allows light to pass when wet in rainy weather. The paint is removed with a cloth at the onset of autumn. Another method is to fix various materials inside the greenhouse, using drawing pins with wooden framework and sticky pads or patent fasteners on metal. Such material can be butter muslin, scrim, green plastic sheeting or fine green plastic netting. Permanent shading devices are roller blinds of plastic, canvas, hessian, burlap or split bamboo cane, which can be fixed either inside or outside the structure. Frames can be treated in the same way.

Local shading of young plants can be provided by sheets of newspaper or small pieces of material pinned up, or even laid over the plants concerned.

Young plants being acclimatized to more light but not needing the enclosure of a glass-covered frame or greenhouse can be housed in a lath house or, if in a frame, under a lath light. Both these are constructed from thin wooden builders' laths tacked to a framework at intervals, thus allowing air to pass but breaking the sunlight.

If plants need temporary shading while becoming established after planting outside, this can be provided by erecting wattle hurdles or stretching hessian, burlap or plastic shading netting over canes arranged as convenient.

◊ BLINDS; LATH HOUSE.

Shanking A disorder which often affects grapes grown under glass when they are becoming mature. The short stalks of each fruit dry up, so that the grapes either fail to ripen further or, more usually, themselves wither. Shanking is almost always due to poor root action, following waterlogged soil or inadequate feeding; lack of food may be due also to overcropping one year which causes starvation the next. Although such major causes must be attended to, individual bunches of grapes can sometimes be saved by cutting out affected berries, which prevents decay from spreading. Shanking should not be confused with SCALDING.

Sharawadgi This word, also spelt 'sharadwadgi' and sometimes 'sharawaggi', appeared in Sir William Temple's description of Chinese gardening in 1685. It probably derives from the Japanese *soro-wo-ji*, 'not being symmetrical', and refers to deliberate but pleasing irregularity of planting and, in the case of the Chinese, arranging stones. To paraphrase Temple, where the Chinese found the beauty of a garden to 'hit their eye at first sight, they say the Sharawadgi is fine or is admirable . . .'. The concept led in Britain to the replacement of straight lines by serpentine ones and the general application of irregularity without any ordered basis. ◊ CHINOISERIE; SERPENTINE WALL.

Shard A piece of broken pot; a crock. The word is used in the U.S. more often than 'crock', which is preferred in Britain.

Sharpening A large number of garden tools depend for their efficiency on sharp edges. These are mostly cutting tools – e.g. knives, secateurs, shears, saws, sickles – and, of course, cylinder mowers. While the sharpening of the latter, and of saws, is usually left to a specialist, that of cutting tools can be done by the gardener with the aid of an oilstone or whetstone, if he takes the trouble to master the undoubted art of using a stone.

An oilstone is finer than a whetstone, which is used for scythes and sickles. The blade is moved along the stone and must be held at a slight angle to it – if this is too great the edge becomes bevelled and effectively blunted, if too small the edge will become thin and weak. Stones can be obtained with a metal guide to ensure a correct angle. The whetstone is moved along the blade, maintaining the correct angle again being vital during the long sweep of the stone.

Shears are best sharpened with a very fine file with the blade fixed in a vice, while axes and sickles are best sharpened against a rotating grindstone. The 'business ends' of spades, trowels and hoes deserve occasional sharpening with a broad medium file.

Shears Most shears broadly resemble large, stout scissors, with long blades operated on a single pivot by handles held in each hand. In the U.S., the term pruning shears is used for what are in Europe called secateurs. Hand shears, used for trimming grass and hedges, usually have the handles at a slight angle to the blades, so that the operator's hands remain clear of the surface being cut; shears specifically for hedge trimming usually have a notch near the base of each blade to trap stems thicker than normal and exert maximum leverage upon them. Some shears have wavy-edged cutting blades for the same purpose. For heavy work, toggle or ratchet shears with a dual pivot give extra cutting power.

the refinement of double-pivoted blades to increase its cutting power.

In one-handed shears, usually called trimmers, the relatively short blades are operated by two handles in the vertical plane which are squeezed together by hand pressure and forced apart again for the next cut by a spring. A long-handled version of these is available. The sheep shears, again operated with one hand, have handles like fire-tongs joined at the top by a flat, curved piece of metal which acts as a

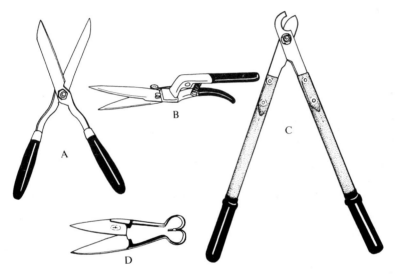

SHEARS. A, hand shears; B, one-handled trimmer; C, lopping shears; D, sheep shears

Long-handled shears have handles around 3′ long. These can have the blades projecting at right angles in front of the handles, so that they operate in the horizontal plane to cut grass without the operator needing to stoop or kneel. Other long-handled shears have the blades in line with the handles and in the vertical plane to trim vertical lawn edges without bending.

Tree loppers or lopping shears have short stout blades and handles at least 18″ long to cut branches up to 1½″ thick without undue effort: they resemble powerful secateurs with the long handles ensuring maximum leverage. The toggle lopper has

spring; the blades are relatively wide at the base, making it a useful tool for confined places. This tool, incidentally, is of Roman origin and was originally used for shearing sheep; other kinds of shears are of eighteenth- and nineteenth-century origin.

Finally, there are various electric-powered trimmers in which one set of a few small blades is moved horizontally over a fixed set by the motor. These can be powered by battery or from the mains via a cable.

◊ EDGING TOOLS; SECATEURS.

Sheath, Sheathing A sheath is a rolled or tubular structure which surrounds another, as the lower part of a grass leaf surrounds the stem. The shape of a grass sheath is often a diagnostic feature. A leaf is said to be sheathing when its base forms a tubular structure around the stem. ⋄ CLASPING.

Sheep Shears ⋄ SHEARS.

Sheet Composting Another term for GREEN MANURING.

Shell The hard outer casing of a nut.

Shell House A garden house with walls lined with shells, occasionally created in the eighteenth and nineteenth centuries; shell grottoes were probably more often made. ⋄ GARDEN HOUSE; GROTTO.

Shells Crushed oyster shells and sometimes other sea shells such as cockle are sometimes used in bulb fibre to neutralize the acidity of the peat which is its basis. Oyster shell is sometimes recommended for use in potting composts and this, or a mixture of crushed shell and grit, is sometimes used to cover solid greenhouse staging. Although such recommendations occur mostly in older literature, crushed shells are still sometimes available. ⋄ BULB FIBRE; STAGING.

Shelter ⋄ PROTECTION.

Shelterbelt A planting of trees or shrubs primarily designed to provide shelter from strong winds, and thus in effect a taller and thicker version of a hedge. The provision of shelterbelts used to be an important part of farm planning and the steady destruction of farm shelterbelts (and hedges) has resulted in soil erosion. Shelterbelts are sometimes essential features of gardens in very windswept localities, especially where these are by the sea where the belt will absorb some of the harmful salt spray as well as reduce the wind power. Where the seaside garden is not very large shrubs of reasonable size can be used instead of trees.

However, in many cases shelterbelts will consist of several lines of defence, e.g. a seaside belt might have an outer defence of quick-growing *Cupressus macrocarpa*, a second line of deciduous trees, and a third line of tough shrubs such as *Euonymus japonicus* and tamarisk. To be effective, the bottom of the shelterbelt must be as dense as the upper parts, and this is where inner shrubs can be invaluable, for the outer trees may lose their lower branches as they age. In extreme cases it is necessary to plant the outer tree belt some years before the inner belts, and to protect the young trees with hurdles or similar artificial windbreaks until they become established.

The reduction in wind speed caused by a shelterbelt is considerable close to the trees and gradually wears off as the distance increases. It can be expressed in multiples of the height of the trees as follows:

Number of tree-heights from shelterbelt	Approximate reduction in wind speed (per cent)
2	75
5	66
10	50
15	20
20	15

As an example, a shelterbelt 25′ high will reduce a 30 m.p.h. wind to 15 m.p.h. around 250′ away from the belt, i.e. ten tree-heights. There is also a slight reduction in wind speed on the windward side of the belt, roughly 25 per cent within two tree-heights.

Incidentally, these figures apply equally to relatively narrow hedges as long as they are dense all the way up. The words 'windbreak' or 'windscreen' are more or less equivalent to a shelterbelt when referring to living trees, but usually imply a narrower planting.

⋄ HEDGE; SCREEN; WINDBREAK.

Shield Budding ⋄ BUDDING.

Shingle (1) Small water-worn pebbles, sometimes used to cover solid greenhouse staging. Such rounded stones are unsuitable for path making since they slide on each other and make walking difficult.

(2) Small rectangular pieces of thin wood used for roofing like tiles, usually of cedar or similar wood with weather-resisting properties.

Shoddy Waste from wool factories, containing fragments of wool and fabric, used as a bulky organic manure providing a source of slowly available humus and 5–15 per cent nitrogen. Because of its slow rate of decay, it is best dug into the soil, or buried in a thin layer, at $\frac{1}{2}$–1 lb. per square yard. Shoddy is seldom available to gardeners since the limited supplies are usually bought up by commercial growers. Scraps of wool and also cotton waste from household use can be treated in the same way, but as they are unlikely to be of any quantity are best added to the compost heap. Synthetic fibres should not be used, since they will not decay.

Shoot (1) The first vertical growth of a seedling: as soon as leaves, side growths or nodes appear, it becomes a stem.

(2) Applied equally to side growths, twigs or branches.

Short-day Plants Plants which flower only when days are short and nights are long. ◊ DAY-LENGTH; LIGHT.

Shot Eye Denotes rose buds which, after propagation by budding, produce shoots the first summer rather than remaining dormant. Since shoots so produced tend to be damaged by frost the following winter, they are unlikely to mature successfully. ◊ BUDDING.

Shot-hole Borers A group of small beetles which bore into the trunks and branches of trees, riddling the bark and wood with small branching tunnels. Shoots, whole branches and occasionally entire trees may be killed. The only external traces are small holes in the bark, sometimes accompanied by sawdust. Fruit trees and also oaks are most liable to attack. Although winter

washes help to control attacks, insecticides are generally of little value and the only treatment is to cut off and burn affected growths. Since weakly trees are most likely to be attacked, good cultivation is essential.

Shot-hole Disease The summer stage of bacterial canker, and a similar fungus disease, cause dark spots on the leaves which dry up and fall away to leave holes about $\frac{1}{8}''$ across. *Prunus* species are affected in both cases. Carefully timed copper sprays will control the organisms concerned and lessen the risk of infection to the wood which is the most serious effect. ◊ CANKER.

Shovel A spade-like implement made in two main forms. One has a rectangular blade with upturned sides, resembling a shallow sugar scoop; the other has a more or less heart-shaped blade which is slightly concave. In Britain, shovels are almost always made with short handles and a hand-grip at the end; on the Continent and in the U.S. they usually have much longer handles and no grip. In all cases the relatively lightweight blade is at a slight angle to the handle. Shovels are used for scooping up soil, sand, gravel, etc.; the broad blade makes them efficient for spreading such materials. A shovel can also be useful for picking up loose soil at the bottom of deep trenches when digging. ◊ SPADE.

Show Board ◊ EXHIBITION BOARD.

Shows Occasions when flowers, fruit and/ or vegetables are exhibited in competition. ◊ EXHIBITING; EXHIBITION; FLORIST.

Show Schedule A document pertaining to a particular competitive show or exhibition for flowers, fruit, vegetables and/or flower arrangements, which lays down the exhibits permitted as to type of plant and number of blooms, stems, kinds or varieties, or other features. It is essential that the schedule should be absolutely precise in defining words used and should leave no ambiguities. The Royal Horticultural Society's publication, *Rules for Judging*, should be studied by anyone drafting a show schedule. ◊ EXHIBITING.

Shreds Nicotine shreds, or fibre, are used (though not as much as formerly) for fumigating greenhouses, having a toxic effect on a wide range of pests. They are piled up in a heap on the floor and ignited, when they will smoulder and produce dense smoke. Care should be taken that the shreds do not burst into flame on ignition. As nicotine is poisonous, the house must be vacated at once. ◊ FUMIGATION.

Shrub A plant whose stems are mainly woody or 'fruticose', as botanists call it. A shrub is usually taken to be a plant with many stems rather than the single trunk of a tree, but the borderline between large shrubs and small trees is not always easy to define. ◊ SHRUBBERY; SUB-SHRUB; TREE.

Shrubbery, Shrub Border Any area mainly devoted to growing shrubs. The word shrubbery is now seldom used except in a derogatory sense, since shrubberies in the nineteenth century were almost always planted with large-leaved evergreens like spotted laurel, which are no longer in fashion. Nowadays mixed shrub plantings are usually referred to as shrub borders. In such areas careful planning will provide a balance between deciduous and evergreen, with a long season of flower, fruit and some autumn colour. As with any other kind of mass planting, each shrub should be allowed space to develop naturally to its mature size. Bulbs and ground-covering herbaceous plants can be combined with the shrubs to good effect, in particular in the early years of a planting before the shrubs have grown much.

Shy A word used colloquially when plants are reluctant to produce flowers or fruit, as in 'shy-flowering'; also of cuttings which seem reluctant to produce roots.

Sickle A cutting instrument with a more or less semi-circular blade around 12″ long, and a short handle. This is one of the most ancient implements, first used in Egypt and the Middle East in the fifth millennium B.C., when it might be made of bone, or wood with flint teeth set in. It was, and still is, mainly an agricultural reaping instrument, whose use in gardens is restricted to cutting down rough grass and weeds in awkward places. Nowadays, many tool makers refer to sickles as 'hooks' and a number of basically similar implements have different names, such as bagging, reap or swap hooks.

The grass hook has a less curved, wider blade than a standard sickle, resembling more that of a scythe. The bean hook has a blade which is two-thirds straight, in line with the handle, and then curves slightly for the last third of its 15″ length.

Sickles can be obtained with handles in line with the blade or slightly cranked so that knuckles are not grazed when cutting close to the ground. They are used single-handed with a sweeping motion. It is useful to use a sickle in conjunction with a hooked stick held in the other hand with which to lift grass or weeds which have become flattened down. Frequent sharpening with a scythe stone is essential.

◊ BILLHOOK; SCYTHE.

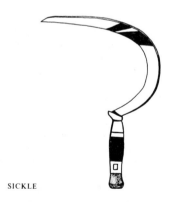

SICKLE

Sickle-bar A type of rough-grass cutter. ◊ MOWERS.

Side Dressing A top dressing used alongside crops. ◊ DRESSING.

Side Graft Various methods of grafting in which the scion is inserted in the side of the stock, which is usually thicker. This allows the stock to function normally (since it retains its foliage higher up) until the union is complete and the scion starts to grow, when the stock is beheaded just above the union. ◇ REWORKING.

Side Shoot A lateral growth. ◇ LATERAL.

SIDE-SHOOTING

Side-shooting Cutting or rubbing out side shoots, especially the axillary ones (arising between main stem and leaf) on tomatoes when, as is normal, these are grown on a single stem. ◇ VIRUS DISEASES.

Sidewheel Mower ◇ MOWERS.

Sieve, Sieving A sieve is a device in which a perforated or, more usually, meshed surface, surrounded by a raised rim, is used to sift or separate finer particles from coarser ones. Sieves are usually circular but sometimes square, and are available with mesh from $\frac{1}{8}''$ to $\frac{1}{2}''$. For smaller mesh sizes, as when sifting seeds from debris, small rectangular seed sieves can be obtained, or domestic flour sifters can be used. The coarser mesh sieves are sometimes called riddles, and the act of sieving, riddling.

Sieving is normally carried out to remove stones, lumps, twigs, etc., from soil. It may be carried out, for instance, to cover newly sown grass seed. Although the normal motion with a sieve is to shake it from side to side, when sieving is carried out in the preparation of soil-based seed and potting composts it is necessary to rub the soil through the mesh with the fingers, or the valuable fibre in the soil will not be passed through.

Sieving is quite hard work and if much soil has to be sieved, labour can be reduced in two ways. One is to make a sieving bench in which two flat pieces of wood are fastened parallel about 15″ apart on a simple framework about 2′ above soil level. The sieve is placed on these bars and pushed to and fro upon them, so that the operator does not have to support the weight of soil. The other method is to obtain or make a large rectangular sieve (at least 2′ × 3′) which is supported at an angle to the vertical by props at the back. Soil is thrown onto this screen sieve, as it is called, with a spade or shovel, and the sifted material passes through it.

Silkweed Another name for the pool alga BLANKET-WEED.

Silver Leaf A serious fungus disease mainly attacking plums, but also other kinds of *Prunus* and a number of unrelated trees. The first symptom is an overall change in leaf colour from green to silvery. Shoots and branches then die and eventually yellow to purple, flattish or bracket-shaped fruiting bodies are formed on their outsides. Diseased wood is purple-tinted when cut. The fungus enters through wounds such as broken branches and pruning cuts which have not been treated with a wound dressing. For this reason, plums and allied trees should be pruned only between June and August when infection of wounds is unlikely to occur. If silver leaf has taken hold, infected branches should be removed and burned: in Britain it is an offence to leave such wood in place after 15 July. ◇ FUNGUS.

Simple Used to describe leaves which are not divided into separate segments: the opposite of compound. ◊ COMPOUND; LEAF.

Single Describes flowers with the normal number of petals for the species, as against semi-double and double flowers: thus all wild roses and single cultivars have 5 petals. ◊ DOUBLE; FLOWER.

SINGLE (camellia)

Single-bud Cutting The same as an EYE CUTTING.

Singling The same as THINNING (of seedlings).

Sink Gardens ◊ TROUGH GARDENS.

Sinuate Applies to plant organs which have margins waved or scalloped in one plane only, not up and down as when undulate. ◊ LEAF.

Skin Meal or **Waste** Scraps from industries using animal skins are sometimes available finely cut up into a kind of meal which is quite a useful organic fertilizer, supplying 2–6 per cent nitrogen, and small quantities of other nutrients, especially magnesium. In addition it provides humus. It can be dug in at 2–3 lb. per square yard or composted.

Slags Waste materials from iron and phosphorus manufacture, e.g. basic slag, obtained from the lining of blast furnaces, which contain silicates and can reduce soil acidity as well as having other nutritional value. ◊ BASIC SLAG.

Slashed Applied to leaves or petals the margins of which are deeply and irregularly cut. ◊ LEAF.

Slasher In effect, a billhook with strong, short blade, set on a long (3′) straight handle, designed for rough hedge trimming. As such, it is primarily a farm tool but is used in large gardens which have farm-type hedges of blackthorn, hawthorn and similar trees. Though usually single-edged, it is possible to obtain double-edged slashers. A type with a relatively narrow straight blade is known as a dunse, one with a narrow part-curving blade as a brushing slasher, and one with a sickle-like blade as a brushing hook.

Sleepy Disease A name applied to some kinds of wilt disease. ◊ WILT.

Slip A colloquial word, in use since 1495, for a cutting or scion, and also for shoots which can be separated from a clump with some roots already formed, often called Irishman's cuttings. ◊ CUTTING; SCION.

Slitting The operation of making short cuts in turf with a mechanical slitting machine with sharp blades, usually in the form of the projections on star-shaped wheels, to improve aeration. Slitting is an alternative to SPIKING ◊ TRUNK SLITTING.

Slow-release Applied to fertilizers specially formulated to dissolve very slowly in moist soil and so release their nutrients over a long period. Such fertilizers, also known as controlled-release, are most useful for trees and shrubs, rather than for vegetables which may occupy the ground for only four or five months.

Sludge ◊ SEWAGE SLUDGE.

Slugs Many species of slug, which are molluscs moving on a single flexible 'foot', are serious garden pests, feeding both on above-ground parts of plants and on fleshy roots. They can devour seedlings and small plants very rapidly, and destroy quite large ones if they eat the bases of their stems. However, the very large slugs (about 3″ long) feed mainly on decaying vegetable matter, and those of the genus *Testacella* are carnivores which eat worms and other soil animals, including various pests.

Slugs, like snails, are virtually impossible to eliminate, but they can be kept down. The most effective slug and snail killers are baits: the commonest kind is based on metaldehyde mixed with bran or sometimes molasses, and a fairly recent bait is based on methiocarb. Mexacarbate is a U.S. product. Such baits can be scattered around plants liable to attack but, to protect them from rain and also to prevent domestic pets and birds (to which they are poisonous) getting at them, the pellets may be placed under a broken flower pot or a piece of tile or slate propped up. It is also possible to water soil and pots with a metaldehyde suspension mixed with water.

Old cabbage leaves, pieces of carrot, turnip, etc., or odds and ends of vegetable refuse placed on the soil, will attract slugs which can be collected each morning and destroyed. Slugs are also attracted to beer placed in saucers buried level with the soil, in which they will drown. Since slugs are nocturnal, they can be collected by the light of a torch at night. Dead leaves of any kind should be cleared off vegetable beds since slugs will use these as day-time shelter. Where subterranean keeled slugs are present in quantity, the soil should be forked over frequently to expose them to the predators, although watering with metaldehyde suspension, or with potassium permanganate at $\frac{1}{2}$ oz. per gallon of water, destroys these and can be used around potatoes where slugs are a problem. Many people apply common salt directly onto slugs to kill them.

Isolated plants are sometimes protected with zinc collars, while a very recent European invention employs the electric fence technique to keep slugs from groups of plants: a 2″-high barrier incorporating two metal strips is powered by a small battery.

◊ SALT; SNAILS; ZINC COLLARS.

Slugworms The small larvae of some species of sawfly, yellow, brown or black, which have a shiny exterior and slightly resemble slugs but have legs. They attack the surface of leaves, so that a whitish skeleton of veins and walls of the central cells is left. Many insecticides will destroy them. ◊ SAWFLIES.

Smoke Generators, Smokes Pellets, cones or canisters in which a pesticide or fungicide (or both) is combined with a pyrotechnic material so that, when ignited like a firework in a greenhouse, a dense smoke is produced which carries the pest- or disease-controlling chemical throughout the structure and deposits it on every part of every plant. 'Smokes' must be obtained of the right size to treat the cubic capacity of the greenhouse involved; or of course several can be used in larger structures. Doors and ventilators must be closed and best results follow if the greenhouse is warmer than normal and if the floor and walls (but not the plants) are damped down first.

A fusée is a smoke generator designed for use in mole runs.

◊ DAMPING DOWN; FUMIGATION; MOLES.

Smother Crop A method sometimes used to destroy weeds on vacant ground when it is preferred not to use chemicals. The theory is that the smother crop, chosen for quick dense growth, deprives the weeds of light, water and nutrients. When the smother crop has matured it is dug into the soil which will benefit from it, and in this respect the method is identical with green manuring: the same kind of crop is grown, i.e. plants such as mustard, rape, annual lupins and Italian rye grass. ◊. GREEN MANURING.

Smut Diseases Several fungus diseases which result in a soot-like growth of mould on the leaves, and often produce their spores in the flowers, where the spore-bearing organs of the fungi may replace the pollen in the anthers. Onion and leek smut are especially to be feared since the spores can persist in the soil for many years. Where these diseases are prevalent, specially treated seed should be used. In general, it is best to destroy infected plants, spraying the remainder with a copper-based fungicide, and not to grow the same crop or ornamental plant in the same place for several years.

Snag A stump of a shoot or branch, too small to bear leaves, left projecting from a trunk or larger branch due to accidental breakage or failure to saw or trim the original branch flush at its base. Such snags are liable to die and may spread disease into the branch concerned.

Snails All terrestrial snails are liable to damage plants, upon which they feed. Snails shelter on walls, under stones, in cavities and other protected places like ivy on a wall, and such places should be examined and any snails found collected and destroyed. Control measures are otherwise the same as for slugs. Some water snails can also harm ornamental pool plants, although some snails are invaluable to keep down algae. ◊ SLUGS.

Snead The handle of a SCYTHE.

Snout Beetles ◊ WEEVILS.

Snow In Britain snow does not usually remain in place for long enough to provide the useful insulating effect it has in colder places, and in general only creates problems for the gardener. The habitual alternation of frost and thaw in snowy conditions often produces a crust of ice on the soil surface which prevents air from reaching plant roots; small plants and especially seedlings are vulnerable to this. Many perfectly hardy alpines also resent this, or the equally harmful alternation of snow and waterlogged soil. Winter vegetables, e.g.

cabbages and broccoli, may rot under these conditions.

Trees and shrubs may lose branches if snow is allowed to collect on them: they should be shaken regularly to dislodge snow during snowfalls. Flat-topped hedges may be distorted and upper growth killed if snow rests on them for long. Garden structures, including greenhouses and especially plastic-covered greenhouses, may be damaged by heavy snow; and in any case even a thin layer should be brushed off glass or plastic greenhouses, frames and cloches, otherwise plants within will suffer from lack of light.

Soakaway A pit or sump filled with rubble or stones to receive water from a garden drainage system when this cannot be otherwise taken away. ◊ DRAINAGE.

Soap Before the advent of more reliable materials, soap was often used as an insecticide spray, often in the form of suds from the laundry tub. In this form it is only moderately effective, but pure soft soap, made from vegetable oils and potash, is more useful, especially against aphids and red spider mite, at 2 oz. per gallon of water, although modern chemical insecticides are far more efficient. Soft soap is useful as a 'spreader' to secure even distribution of a spray, especially when mixing a material like nicotine in hard water. It is essential to use soft soap when making home-made insecticides with natural materials, e.g. rhubarb or elder leaves.

Soft soap can also be used as a fungicide to control gooseberry mildew, when 8 oz. is mixed with 12 oz. washing soda in 5 gallons of water.

Soda ◊ WASHING SODA.

Sodding The U.S. term for turfing. ◊ TURF.

Sodium Chlorate ◊ WEEDKILLER.

Sodium Chloride Common salt. ◊ SALT.

Sod Lifter The U.S. term for a TURFING IRON.

Sods A term applied to cut pieces of turf around 1½″ thick, used for making lawns. ◇ TURF.

Soft Fruit Fruits which grow on bushes or canes as opposed to the top fruits borne on trees. Soft fruits include blackberries, raspberries and related hybrid berries, currants and strawberries.

Soft Rot A wide-ranging term covering a number of bacterial and fungal diseases which cause plant tissues to decay while becoming soft or slimy. Such rots may attack growing plants and are often caused by grey mould; others attack fruits in store, and fleshy roots both in the ground and in store. Soft rots may arise in very humid conditions under glass, and are encouraged in garden plants by over-manuring with nitrogen-rich materials which cause sappy growth. Stored fruits and roots are liable to develop soft rot if damaged before storing; affected fruits and roots should be removed from the store as soon as detected. With soft rots of growing plants, e.g. rhizome rot of irises, attacked portions should be cut away. ◇ GREY MOULD.

Soft Soap ◇ SOAP.

Softwood Describes shoots of woody plants which are young enough to be soft and green, and contain no woody tissue or heartwood. When such shoots are used as cuttings they are called soft or softwood cuttings. ◇ CUTTING.

Soil The natural medium in which plants grow. In nature, particular types of soil attract the plants best adapted to them; the gardener has the opposite problem of wishing to grow a wide range of plants in one kind of soil.

There are three main aspects of soil the gardener has to consider. The first is whether it is light, medium or heavy: these terms refer to the amount of sand and clay it contains, light soils having much sand and little clay and heavy ones the opposite. Next, soils can be classed as to whether they contain much organic matter (humus), when they can be termed organic, or little, when they may be called mineral. Thirdly, soils may be acid, neutral or alkaline according to their pH. The pH will control the type of plant that can be grown within certain limits.

The colour of soil is another factor, dark soil absorbing more warmth from the sun than pale, hence encouraging earlier growth; while a well-drained soil is far better for plant health and growth than a poorly drained one.

The best all-round garden soil is a well-drained, dark-coloured medium loam containing adequate but not excessive amounts of organic matter and having a pH around 6.5. Various treatments can improve soils of differing quality towards this, although very sandy, very heavy or very alkaline soils, for example, need a great deal of effort and time to show marked improvement. In some cases it may be better for the gardener to concentrate on selecting plants that will suit the soil he has, rather than trying to get the soil into the right condition for a wide range of plants.

In any case, soil normally needs initial cultivation at least when a garden is begun, and needs regular feeding and regular addition of organic matter to keep it fertile and productive.

◇ entries below prefixed by SOIL; ALLUVIAL; CLAY; CULTIVATION; FERTILIZER; HUMUS; MANURE; ORGANIC; pH.

Soil Block A block of compressed soil used instead of a pot when propagating plants. ◇ BLOCKING.

Soil Conditioner Any material which improves the texture of a soil. By this definition, organic materials, e.g. manure, peat or garden compost, are soil conditioners; but the expression is usually reserved for chemicals or inert materials which act as soil improvers without also providing plant food. Thus coarse sand and grit can im-

295

prove heavy clay soil, and lime has a temporary effect on it. Most materials sold as soil conditioners today are based on alginates, derived from seaweed, of which sodium alginate is the most effective; some are dried crushed calcified seaweeds. ⬧ ALGINATE; CRUMB; FLOCCULATION; HUMUS; LIME; SEAWEED.

Soil Drenching ⬧ DRENCH.

Soilless Composts Media for growing seed, rooting cuttings and potting plants which contain no soil but are based on peat, sand and other inert materials. ⬧ COMPOSTS, SEED AND POTTING.

Soilless Cultivation Any method of growing plants which avoids the use of soil. The first such method to be widely used was to grow plants in water containing plant foods in dilute solution, which is true hydroponic culture. Wire netting was usually fixed over the water troughs to provide some support. This method is now seldom used, since it is easier to handle plants with roots in an inert medium, watered or irrigated with fertilizer solution.

Aggregates commonly used include sand, gravel, baked clay granules (hydroleca) and the like. Quite recently, peat has been used, which reminds one that the modern emphasis on soilless seed and potting composts is a form of soilless cultivation.

However, in most of the methods the aggregate is periodically flooded with the nutrient solution rather than just moistened as in normal watering. On an amateur scale, the nutrients can be applied as a powder on the surface of the aggregate and watered in, but it is usually more convenient to mix the fertilizer solution and water it onto the aggregate, for which sharp sand is ideal; containers must have drainage holes.

On a large scale, as in commercial practice, sub-irrigation is normally carried out. This involves impervious beds for the aggregate, which is of coarse material, e.g. gravel or clinker, and a tank at a lower

level. This tank contains the nutrient solution, which is pumped up into the aggregate beds by an electric pump. When the aggregate is flooded the pump automatically switches off and the solution drains back into the storage tank through outlets at the lowest points in the beds. The need to keep the solution at the right strength and in a correct balance calls for a skilled chemist.

Soilless cultivation has also been applied to plants in individual containers, especially house plants. The simplest method uses a single watertight pot filled with aggregate; fertilizer solution at a quarter of the strength recommended for normal use is added in sufficient quantity to occupy a quarter to a third of the container's depth. Another method employs an inner pot filled with aggregate, in which the plant grows, and which fits into a larger outer watertight container. Fertilizer solution is added in sufficient quantity to immerse the lower $\frac{1}{2}''$–$1''$ of the inner pot. The latter has holes in the base through which the solution can seep and through which roots will eventually pass into the solution. This method has the advantage that old solution can be discarded at intervals, when the aggregate can be cleansed of surplus fertilizer by running tap water through it for a few minutes.

One proprietary form of soilless container cultivation is based on expanded clay granules (hydroleca); it is superficially similar to the single-pot method described above, but is used in conjunction with a special fertilizer supplied in a small replaceable 'magazine', placed at the bottom of the container.

The whole point of soilless cultivation of any sort is to remain in maximum control of plant growth, supplying exactly the right foods for the plant concerned, and to ensure freedom from the nutrient deficiencies and imbalances which can arise in soil, and freedom from soil-borne diseases.

Ring culture is a partially soilless method, while straw bale culture and nutrient film technique are special forms of soilless cultivation.

⬧ AGGREGATE; COMPOSTS, SEED AND

POTTING; HYDROLECA; HYDROPONICS; NUTRIENT FILM TECHNIQUE; RING CULTURE; STRAW BALE CULTURE.

Soil Mark The usually noticeable mark on the stem of a plant which indicates the soil level before it was transplanted. In general, plants should be replanted with the soil level coinciding with the original soil mark, although there are exceptions. Thus leek and cabbage and tomato seedlings are planted more deeply than they were growing. The same applies to clematis, although most woody plants resent being replanted too deeply. ◊ PLANTING; TRANSPLANTING.

Soil Miller A kind of long-handled cultivator based on rotating wheels and operated by a push-pull motion. Some millers (also known as tilthers) simply consist of spiked wheels or rounded projecting tines, while others combine one or two rows of 'star wheels' and a hoe-like blade which controls working depths and also cuts off weeds. ◊ CULTIVATOR.

SOIL MILLER

Soil Sterilization ◊ STERILIZATION.

Soil Testing A professional soil analyst will make bore-holes or pits to examine the soil 'profile' and check on drainage as well as analysing the texture and chemical balance of the soil. To most gardeners, soil testing simply means the latter, and involves tests to determine the pH, and hence whether liming is needed or not, and the levels of nitrogen, phosphorus and potassium to see whether any of these is deficient. There are a few laboratories which will carry out such tests and it is also possible to buy simple soil-testing kits.

With these pH can be very accurately established but the levels of the plant foods are sometimes subject to error. Even if a deficiency is detected, it is not always easy to establish how much extra nutrient should be applied since this often depends also on soil consistency and make-up. Moreover, simple soil-test kits do not test for trace elements, deficiency of which is more likely to cause serious trouble than lack of the main plant foods which is easily remedied by the application of a balanced fertilizer. ◊ FEEDING PLANTS; TRACE ELEMENTS.

Soil Warming ◊ BOTTOM HEAT.

Soot Where available in fair quantity, soot is a useful plant food containing 2–4 per cent nitrogen, which also counteracts the stickiness of clay soils and, by darkening the soil, helps it to absorb sun heat and warm up quickly. Because soot can contain impurities harmful to plants, notably sulphur, it should be stored in a dry place for at least three months before use. Soot can be worked into the soil at 4–6 oz. per square yard or used as a dressing around growing plants at 2 oz. Soot-water, prepared by suspending a porous bag containing soot in a tub of water, is a quick-acting growth-promoting food: it should be diluted to a pale strawy colour.

Sooty Mould A black mould which sometimes develops on plant leaves and stems, especially on house and greenhouse plants. It is formed by various fungi which feed upon the sweet, sticky 'honeydew' excreted by aphids, scale insects, white fly and other sap-sucking pests. Though the sooty mould fungi are non-parasitic the mould blocks the leaf stomata (breathing pores) and prevents photosynthesis taking place. The first essential is to eradicate the pest concerned; the mould must then be wiped off leaves, etc., with a soft cloth dipped in soapy water, with a final rinse of clear water. ◊ HONEYDEW.

Sori (singular: sorus) The spore-bearing organs in ferns. These are found on the underside of mature fronds, and sometimes on distinct fronds which only carry spores and are never green. On ordinary fronds the sori are arranged in more or less regular patterns which the uninitiated sometimes confuse with the results of fungus attack. ◊ FERN; SPORE.

Sour A colloquial expression for soil which is not in good condition. Older gardeners often use it to denote acid soils which they consider need liming, but many soils are naturally acid and will grow acid-loving plants without any problems. The more accurate use of 'sour' is to indicate waterlogged soils and those with a poor, airless texture, which often have a rather disagreeable odour: this is usually due to lack of cultivation and bulky organic matter. It is true that liming can improve soil texture temporarily but overall soil improvement, often coupled with drainage installation, is usually needed.

Sowbugs A country expression, widespread in the U.S., for WOODLICE.

Sowing ◊ SEED SOWING.

Spade A hand-tool for digging consisting basically of a rectangular piece of metal at the end of a straight handle. The spade was first used by the Romans and is probably the most important gardening implement today, being used for cultivation of soil including trenching and digging out holes to receive plants. Although spades have an almost infinite range of local variations there are only a few main types.

The ordinary garden spade has a fairly broad rectangular blade, varying from around $12\frac{1}{2}'' \times 8''$ (heavy) to $10'' \times 6\frac{1}{2}''$ (medium) and $9'' \times 5\frac{1}{2}''$ (light or ladies'). In Britain the blade is almost always at a slight angle to the handle, but on the Continent and in the U.S. a blade in line with the handle is favoured. Also, the British favour a short handle (under 3') with a hand-grip of some sort according to taste, while the Continentals and Americans prefer a long handle with no grip.

Spades, like digging forks, are made with hand-grips of three main shapes. In the 'T' grip, the undivided handle terminates in a short cross-piece. In the 'Y' grip, the wooden handle is split near the top and bent into two branches forming a Y shape, which are joined at the top by a cross-piece. The 'D' is a variant of this, originally made out of a single piece of wood with a central aperture in the shape of a D, fixed onto the end of the handle; nowadays it is very often formed of plastic. In Britain, the T used to predominate in the north of the country, but today regional preferences are not so marked. In the U.S.,

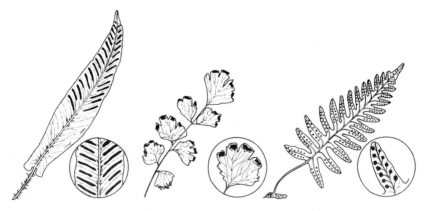

SORI. *Left to right*, scolopendrium, adiantum and polypodium ferns: sori in black

298

the D is almost universal in spades made with a grip.

Some American spades have a rounded bottom or blade edge and are slightly concave, thus beginning to resemble the shovel. The 'Ground-breaker' spade, of Continental origin, has four large pointed teeth on the blade edge and is designed for really heavy soils containing roots, etc. Garden spades may have a narrow tread on the upper edge (on each side of the handle) which reduces wear on footwear.

The Terrex 'automatic' spade, or Autospade, operating on a spring and lever system, was primarily designed for gardeners with bad backs since it avoids stooping; it does in fact turn over the soil faster than is possible with an orthodox spade.

Besides garden spades. there is a range of spades for digging drainage trenches and similar operations, not normally employed in the garden. These have longer, relatively narrower blades. In the 'grafting tool' (named after an old word for digging, and having nothing to do with propagation) the blade is rectangular, while as a draining tool it is slightly tapered and round-ended. Transplanting spades used in nurseries are very similar.
♦ DIGGING; SHOVEL.

Spading Fork A term sometimes used for a broad-tined fork. ♦ FORK.

Spadix A special type of flower spike, found in aroids and palms, in which the numerous minute flowers are more or less embedded. In aroids the spadix forms a single erect organ, but in palms it is often branched. ♦ AROID; SPATHE.

Spaghetti Watering ♦ IRRIGATION.

Spanish Garden Gardens in Spain, and derivations from them elsewhere, owe much to Moorish, Indian and Islamic influence, and their design is in large measure controlled by the very hot summer sun. The most frequent features are courtyards or patios, often with arcaded sides, narrow canals, rectangular pools, fountains, and planting restricted to formal beds and including trees. ♦ PATIO.

Spathe A bract which encloses and protects one or several flowers. It occurs typically in conjunction with a spadix. In aroids it is leafy, more or less fleshy, and may be brightly coloured; in palms it is fleshy or woody and sometimes has several divisions. In other plants it is much less prominent: thus the membranous sheath which surrounds a daffodil bud is technically a spathe. The spathe is sometimes composed of two bracts. ♦ AROID; BRACT; SPADIX; STIPULE.

Spatulate This word – also spelt 'spathulate' – means spatula-shaped, i.e. having one rounded, broadened end and narrowing abruptly at the opposite end. In botany it is applied to leaves or petals of this form and is sometimes used as a specific name, as in *Sedum spathulatum* and *S. spathulifolium*. ♦ LEAF.

Spawn Used in gardening in two main ways, in each case to do with plant increase. The more frequent use is made when referring to the mycelium of mushrooms, the thread-like growth which in the right conditions produces the fruit-bodies which we eat. This is usually supplied in a dry 'brick' which is broken up into small lumps which are inserted in mushroom beds.

Gladiolus growers call the tiny corms or cormlets which grow outside the main corms 'spawn', and this word is also used when other fleshy-rooted plants produce similar miniature offspring which in time will develop into mature roots.
♦ CORM; FUNGUS.

Species A unit of classification; plants belonging to one species have characters which clearly distinguish them from others, and which consistently breed true. The specific names given to species may refer to some character of the plant, or its typical habitat, or commemorate a person or place. ♦ CLASSIFICATION (The Binomial).

Specimen Plant A plant of any kind, but

299

usually a tree or shrub, in perfect condition; such a plant placed so that it can be admired from any viewpoint, and not planted in a group with others.

Spent Hops ◊ HOPS.

Sphagnum A genus of mosses found in bogs and damp ground, with dense growth capable of absorbing water like a sponge. Gardeners find many uses for sphagnum, especially orchid growers who chop it up finely to add to potting composts. Sphagnum is used to line wire hanging baskets and is sometimes placed under compost at the bottom of containers used for seed sowing or striking cuttings, since it combines moisture holding with good drainage. It is used for making moss-poles for climbers, and by florists as the basis for wreaths.

When decomposed in bog conditions sphagnum moss forms one kind of peat, known as sphagnum or moss peat, as opposed to sedge peat.
◊ MOSS-POLE; PEAT.

Spider (1) True spiders are useful in the garden since they entrap many flying pests. However, the word is often loosely applied to red and other spider mites which are serious pests. ◊ MITES.

(2) Applied to some exotic chrysanthemums with a mass of very narrow, curling florets.

Spike An inflorescence with numerous stalkless or nearly stalkless flowers on a vertical axis; the word is however often used loosely for any upright flower cluster such as the similar raceme. ◊ INFLORESCENCE.

Spikelet A botanical term for the flowering unit in grasses which may consist of one or several florets but has a pair of bracts at the base. These spikelets are arranged in various kinds of inflorescence. The word is also used to denote a secondary spike. ◊ INFLORESCENCE.

Spiking A method of aerating lawns, carried out either by an ordinary garden fork or a hollow-tine fork, or by a wheeled spiking machine in which short sharp metal spikes project from a central cylinder. This is done in very hot dry weather to allow water to reach the grass roots, in autumn to break up compacted grass, and to allow

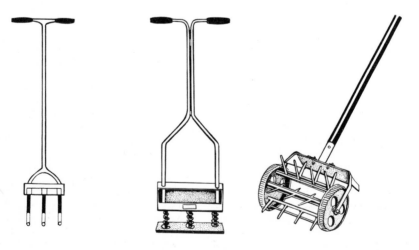

SPIKING. *Left to right*, hollow-tine fork; patent spring-loaded hollow-tine spiker; wheeled spiker

air and also any dressing applied to the lawn to reach the roots. ◊ AERATION; SLITTING.

Spiling Making holes in soil with a crowbar which are filled with good soil or potting compost to enable seeds of taprooted vegetables, e.g. carrots and parsnips, to grow well. A method used by exhibitors and also by ordinary gardeners with poor or stony ground. Holes are usually made 18″–24″ deep and, by rotating the crowbar as the hole is made, 3″–4″ across at the top, resulting in a narrowly conical hole.

the cords needed to tie down the branches the spindlebush is not very attractive to look at; hence it is seldom seen in gardens, though often used by commercial growers.

Spindle Fence ◊ FENCES.

Spine A great many plants are equipped with hard, sharp organs which are variously called spines, thorns or prickles. Thorns are sharp woody structures which are basically modified branches, springing from the woody structure of the plant, usually more or less regularly arranged,

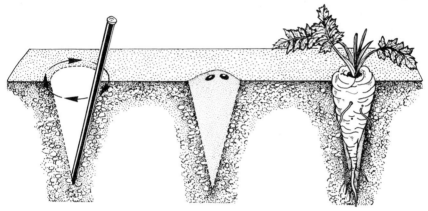

SPILING

Spindlebush A form of fruit tree trained into a broad cone shape with a central stem. The branches are tied down into near-horizontal positions: fastening the ties near the centres of the branches rather than the ends ensures that the branches remain more or less straight and do not become arched. The three or four lower branches are permanent but the upper ones, which in any case are cut back so that they are shorter than the lower ones, are removed whenever they become overcrowded or too dominant. Apart from such cutting out, no detailed pruning is done: the tying down of branches induces fruit bud formation instead. Because of the tall pole used to support the tree centrally and

and which cannot be removed without causing stem damage. Prickles are outgrowths from the outer layer, usually irregularly spaced, which can be removed without damage. The word 'spine' usually refers to slender thorn-like growths. However, these terms have been hopelessly muddled up; the growths on cacti are always referred to as spines, though they are technically thorns, while the so-called thorns of a rose are technically prickles.

Besides occurring on the stems of plants, thorns, prickles or spines may be found on leaves, e.g. in thistles and hollies. Sometimes the leaves are transformed into spines, as in gorse, or in some cases the spiny structures may replace the leaves, as

301

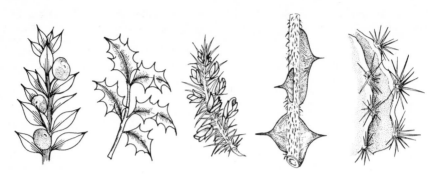

SPINE. *Left to right*, butcher's broom; holly; gorse; *Rosa pteracantha*; cactus

in butcher's broom. A spiny structure is often associated with arid conditions, and is usually effective protection against animals, though this is probably a secondary effect.

Spin Trimmer A device for trimming weeds in which a length of nylon cord is rotated or shrubs, fence posts, furniture, etc. The device, which has a long handle with handgrips on it, is especially valuable in awkward corners where even ordinary shears could not be used. The cord is fed from a spool so that when it wears a new length can be pulled out. The more powerful spin trimmers have four separate cords

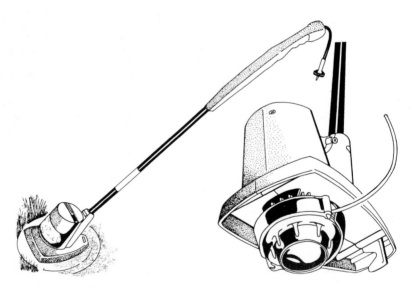

SPIN TRIMMER

at high speed near soil level by a motor. While any soft plant growth is severed, the cord cannot damage trunks of trees and spools. Heavy-duty versions can be fitted with a round saw blade and also a 'brush blade' with eight long cutting edges

302

on the circumference, so that they can be used among suckers and scrub as well as weeds.

Spit A spade's depth of soil, based on the average length of blade of 10″–12″. Digging so many spits deep is often recommended, and the phrases top spit, second spit and third spit refer to the 10″–12″ layers of soil from the top downwards. ⟡ DIGGING.

Spittlebug The U.S. term for a cuckoo-spit insect or frog hopper. ⟡ CUCKOO-SPIT.

Splice Graft ⟡ GRAFTING.

Split Stone A condition of stone fruits in which the kernel splits. ⟡ STONE (2).

Spoon A term applied to some exotic forms of chrysanthemum in which the narrowly rolled florets expand at the end into a spoon shape.

Spore The microscopic reproductive bodies of flowerless plants, which include ferns, mosses, horsetails, selaginellas and fungi. The spores, though they give rise to young plants as seeds do, are often asexually produced – i.e. no male and female cells are involved as in flowering plants – but there is then a sexual phase at another time in the plant's growth cycle.

Apart from dealing with fungus diseases which arise from spores, the gardener is only practically involved with spores if he grows ferns. Each fern produces sporangia, usually on the underside of its fronds. These, called sori, are brown areas of spore-producing bodies, which are distinctively shaped in each species, and which the uninitiated sometimes believe to be a disease. If the frond is placed over a sheet of paper as it becomes mature, the powder-like spores are deposited on it. If these spores are sprinkled on a sterile, peaty soil mixture, in a vessel which can be covered with a sheet of glass, green flat growths will appear after a time (sometimes several months). These growths are known as prothalli. Beneath each prothallus sexual organs are formed, and the resultant male

gametes fertilize the female ones. After this union the first minute frond is produced. At this stage the tiny plants are very carefully pricked out an inch apart into a fine compost. Larger fronds will soon appear and the plants (sometimes called sporelings) are potted on in the normal way.

⟡ FERN: FROND; FUNGUS.

Sport The gardener's word for a MUTATION.

Spot Treatment Dealing with weeds individually rather than by overall application of a WEEDKILLER.

Spotted Wilt ⟡ WILT.

Spray A group of flowers on a single stem: a floristry term used especially of chrysanthemums.

Sprayer, Spraying A device for applying pesticides and fungicides in solution at the rates recommended by the manufacturer. The simplest type of sprayer is a piston-action syringe which is put into a container of the solution and whose handle is then pulled back. Suction draws in the solution which is forced out through the nozzle when the handle is pushed in. The double-action sprayer has a hose which is fixed to a container of the solution by a clip, and a piston unit which is pushed back and forward to produce a continuous spray.

These have largely been superseded by pneumatic pressure sprayers, consisting of containers for the spray solution which can be pressurized by priming with a pump handle. When a tap or trigger on the spray lance is operated the solution is forced through the nozzle, adjusted for the fineness of spray required, and several minutes of spraying can be carried out before further pumping is needed. Pressure sprayers have a hose coupling between the container and the spray lance. Such pneumatic sprayers can be obtained with capacities from 2 pints to several gallons. The largest convenient size for the average garden is 1½ gallons, but for large areas pressurized knapsack sprayers, designed to be carried on the back, are available.

Mechanically operated sprayers are also available for large areas.

For local spraying, or 'misting', of house and greenhouse plants, small trigger-operated sprayers are available, and aerosols containing various pesticides, etc., can be obtained.

In general, sprays are most effective when fairly fine, but at the same time should penetrate all crevices on a plant's surface and cover all surfaces. The undersides of leaves are especially important as many pests congregate there: it is to get into such positions that the end of the spray lance is normally at a slight angle.

Spraying outside should if possible be carried out in dry, still weather. Wind can prevent spray covering the plant concerned and may carry it where it can do harm to other plants; if rain falls shortly after spraying, much of the material will be washed off and be ineffective. Pesticide sprays should not be applied to plants in flower, or bees and other useful insects may be killed. Instructions should always be carefully studied as to strength of solution, plants which can be damaged by the material, and safety precautions.

◊ AEROSOL; MIST-SPRAYER.

For details of spray materials ◊ FUNGICIDES; PESTICIDE; WEEDKILLER.

Spreader One material added to another to enable it to be spread more evenly. Liquid pesticide and fungicide sprays include spreaders such as saponin which lower surface tension and thus allow the spray to cover all the plant surfaces as a film rather than forming droplets. Soft soap was early used as a spreader. Pest- and disease-controlling dusts contain an inert material which increases the bulk and spreading power of the active ingredient. Concentrated fertilizers may be mixed in the same way, usually with sand or rape dust, to make it easier to distribute them at the recommended rate. Very fine seed may be mixed with fine dry sand as a spreader to sow it thinly enough. ◊ SOAP.

Springtails An enormous group of small wingless insects, most of which have the capacity of jumping into the air when disturbed, like fleas. They range from about $\frac{1}{32}''$ to $\frac{3}{8}''$, and vary greatly in colour, though most of the harmful kinds are around $\frac{1}{16}''$ long and white. Only some are harmful plant pests, but these may chew tissues of seedlings and small plants in greenhouses, attacking the stem, leaves resting on the soil, and also roots. If damage is seen and investigation reveals springtails, most insecticidal materials can be used, applied as a soil drench or dust. Springtails are sometimes found in large numbers in orchid composts based on sphagnum moss, and infected plants should be sprayed with dilute insecticide.

Sprinkle-bar Also known as a dribble-bar; a perforated tube, plastic or metal, fitted to a watering can or a pressure sprayer so that it can be moved horizontally parallel with the soil surface and deliver a chemical solution to soil, grass or plants. The perforated tube is connected to the can or spray lance by a piece of tube at right angles, the device being either in the form of an inverted L or

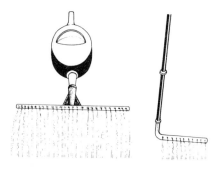

SPRINKLE-BAR

inverted T. Short sprinkle-bars are used for precision application of chemicals to the soil between plants, and wide ones to apply chemical on open ground or lawns. Although the sprinkle-bar can be used to deliver pesticides or fertilizers, it is usually employed for WEEDKILLERS.

Sprinkler Any stationary device for applying water as a fine spray simulating rain. All sprinklers operate from mains or pumped water which is under pressure. The commonest examples are the many kinds of rotary sprinkler and the small oscillating sprinklers used in gardens. These cover relatively small areas, the rotary in a circular pattern and the oscillating in a generally more useful, rectangular one. One ingenious type of rotary sprinkler is designed to travel along its own hose-pipe, so that water can be applied over a considerable area without the sprinkler being moved manually.

Other types of garden sprinkler operate non-mechanically by the impact of the water under pressure upon a surface above the nozzle, which spreads the water radially. Such sprinklers can be mounted on poles or be fitted flush with the soil surface and fed by an underground hose or pipe system. There are even 'pop-up' sprinklers designed to remain covered at soil level until the water is turned on at which time the water-spraying device rises above the ground.

On a larger scale for big gardens, parks, etc., are mechanical rotary oscillating sprinklers known as pulse or pulsating sprinklers, either on the ground or on poles, and the oscillating pipe sprinkler in which a length of metal tube perforated with small holes at intervals is turned to and fro through a wide angle by a simple turbine mechanism at one end.

◊ IRRIGATION; WATERING.

Sprout, Sprouting A sprout is any new shoot, especially the first aerial growth of a newly germinated seed, and including the first growths on potato tubers. The latter are usually set out in trays, in a cool, light place, to produce sprouts before they are planted, which results in quicker development once they are in the soil. Sprouting is also carried out on a range of vegetable seeds which are eaten in the seedling state, e.g. mustard and cress, and bean sprouts. The word is also applied to the small leafy 'heads' of brussels sprouts.

Spud Apart from its slang meaning of a potato, which is first recorded in 1860, spud has since 1667 meant a digging or weeding tool with a narrow, often chisel-shaped blade. The verb 'to spud' means to weed or dig with such a tool. Several types

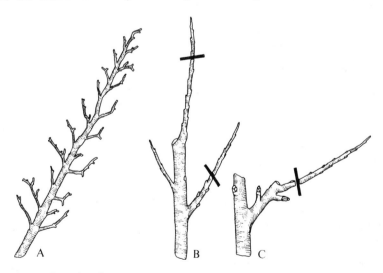

SPUR. See text for explanation

305

of spud are available today, including one with a bent blade, used either way up, and the straight 'thistle spud'. Spuds sometimes have a hook-shaped projection on one side to help in picking up the severed weed. The spud can be mounted on a short or a long handle, and is valuable for working among plants with minimum soil disturbance.

Spur (1) Horticulturally, the word 'spur' is used to describe clusters of fruit buds which develop on the older branches of fruit trees. In time these spurs branch and increase excessively, leading to small overcrowded fruits, and such ancient spurs should be reduced in both size and number by pruning in winter. Spurs are encouraged to form on trained trees such as cordons (A), as they allow the tree to carry a good quantity of fruit in a limited space. To form a spur on a maiden tree, the laterals are cut back to four buds (B). The following year the lateral has produced some fruit buds and a new shoot: the latter is reduced to one bud (C), and this is repeated annually. (See illustration on p. 305.)

(2) To the botanist, a spur is a tubular organ which usually contains nectar, to attract pollinating insects. Such spurs are found in many orchids, columbines, toad-flaxes, etc. ◊ NECTAR, NECTARY.

Squarrose Having close-packed organs such as overlapping leaves or bracts, which spread or recurve at their ends to produce a rough overall surface.

Squirrels These familiar rodents, generally rat-like but with a large bushy tail, can steal fruits and nuts, but cause most damage by gnawing the stems and trunks of trees and shrubs, especially in hard winter weather. Tree guards and animal repellents will deter them but if they are numerous the only effective control is by shooting. For ground squirrels ◊ GOPHERS. ◊ REPELLENTS; TREE GUARDS.

Stage, Staging (1) Table-like or shelf-like structures on which plants in a greenhouse are arranged above soil level. It is usual to make the main staging around waist level; in an average small to medium-sized greenhouse it will be 20″–30″ wide. Greater width is difficult to manage unless the staging is approachable from both sides. Where space permits, tiered staging is very effective for displaying plants; the shelves diminish in width from the main waist-level staging. Narrow independent shelves are sometimes arranged near eaves level in greenhouses, especially to accommodate fleshy-rooted plants which need dry, hot conditions at some season.

Staging may be constructed of slats arranged with gaps between or provided with a solid surface such as corrugated asbestos, or flat aluminium sheeting. Solid staging is normally covered with gravel, expanded clay granules, sand or peat which will absorb moisture and provide a humid atmosphere as it evaporates. However, care must be taken that roots do not emerge from pot drainage holes and make extensive growth in such media. Slatted staging is more suitable for plants which enjoy a relatively dry atmosphere.

(2) Tables or trestles at flower shows are also called stages and the arrangement of exhibits is known as staging.

Stag-headed Describes the state of trees when the ends of branches die, leaving leafless 'stags' horns' projecting beyond the leafy crown. This is often a sign of disease or bad root conditions, and also of senility.

Staking The provision of a vertical stake or pole alongside the stem of a plant, to which the latter is tied for support. This is one of many methods of supporting plants, for details of which ◊ SUPPORT.

Stalk A word often used synonymously with stem to refer to a herbaceous plant's main overground growth; but better reserved for the separate growth, technically a petiole, on which a leaf is carried. A stem produces buds, a stalk does not. The word stalk is also often used for the stem or peduncle supporting a flower. ◊ STEM.

Stamen The male organ of the flower, usually composed of a thin stalk, or filament, and a head, known as the anther, which actually carries and releases the pollen. Sometimes stamens have little or no stalk, and the anthers are attached directly to the petals. The number of stamens varies greatly according to the family. They may become changed into petals or petaloids, and this process results in double or semi-double flowers: these are most commonly found, of course, where there are numerous stamens. Families which have many stamens, and are liable to doubling, are considered by some botanists to be less highly evolved than those with fewer stamens. Stamens are often a decorative part of the flower, while in the bottlebrushes or callistemons, acacias and other flowers the stamens may be the most prominent part.

If cross-fertilization is being aimed at, pollen is obtained from the stamens of the chosen male parent, while the chosen female flower, or seed parent, must be emasculated by removal of the stamens at an early stage, even before bud opening, to prevent self-fertilization.
 ◊ ANTHER; CROSS-FERTILIZATION; DOUBLE; EMASCULATION; FLOWER; PETAL.

Staminate Of a flower which has only stamens and no pistils, in other words is male only. ◊ FLOWER; MALE FLOWER.

Standard (1) To the gardener the term standard refers to any tree or shrub grown with a bare stem. In fact, most large trees grow naturally in this way, but the gardener trains trees as standards from an early age, either for decorative reasons or, as with fruit trees, for utility. Roses are often grown as standards, but it is not always realized how many shrubs are effective treated like this, particularly those of a weeping habit. Such shrubs, and roses, are usually grafted when grown as standards, but plants like fuchsias and heliotropes are normally on their own stems. Standard roses are usually on 3′–4′ stems, standard fruit or ornamental trees have 6′ stems: half-standards have shorter stems, 3′–4′ tall. ◊ GRAFTING.

(2) Botanically, a standard is a part of the flower, as in the iris where it refers to

the three upright petals (in contrast to the pendulous or horizontal falls), and in the sweet pea and other leguminous plants in which the upright back petal is the standard. ◊ BEARD; FLOWER; LEGUMINOUS.

STANDARD (weeping cotoneaster

Starting A gardener's term for bringing dormant plants into renewed growth after a resting period. It applies largely to fleshy-rooted plants which spend dormancy as a dry bulb, corm or tuber, and can be started by planting them in moist peat and giving warmth; if they have spent the resting period in potting compost in a container this will need watering, a little at first then gradually increasing the amount. Greenhouse vines are started by providing artificial heat and closing the ventilators which should be kept open all winter.

Steeping The practice of soaking seeds or corms with very hard coats before sowing. Twenty-four hours in water can ensure speedy and regular germination of seeds such as sweet peas and many exotics. In difficult cases, a preliminary nicking with a knife will ensure that water reaches the interior of the seed. Gladiolus corms sometimes have very hard skins and this applies especially to the small cormlets formed around adult corms; steeping in water again results in rapid sprouting.

Steeping of a different kind is also carried out in making liquid manure, by suspending a porous bag containing animal manure in a tub of water. ◇ FEEDING PLANTS; MANURE.

Stem The part of a plant which grows above ground and produces buds from which leaves, side growths and flowers emerge, in contrast to the roots growing downwards in the soil. The main stem of a tree is called the trunk. Stems are usually vertical, but may creep along the soil surface or hang down from epiphytic plants. In cacti and some other succulents, the stem becomes swollen to retain water. In other dry-living plants (xerophytes) stems may replace leaves; in such cases they are green and carry out photosynthesis. This can be confirmed by observing that the flowers spring from apparently leaf-like organs; this almost never occurs with true leaves.

The word is often used synonymously with stalk, but this is better reserved for the individual growth or petiole on which a leaf may be carried.

◇ CACTUS; CLADODE; EPIPHYTE; STALK: SWITCH PLANT; TRUNK.

Stem and Bulb Eelworm Covers a group of eelworms, some of which attack bulbs (including bluebells, narcissi and onions) and others the stems of certain plants the most common of which is phlox. Affected plants become distorted in various ways. ◇ EEL-WORMS.

Stem-rooting Of stems which produce roots above ground. This often applies to plants with prostrate stems and also to certain climbers, which may produce aerial roots for attachment purposes. Some lilies produce roots on the stem above the bulb, and need deep planting as a result. ◇ AERIAL ROOT; EPIPHYTE; RUNNER; STOLON.

STEM-ROOTING (lily)

Stem Rot A general term which covers all kinds of disease which attack plant stems and may have alternative, equally vague names. ◇ DAMPING-OFF; FOOT ROT.

Stepping Stones Stones or blocks placed at fairly close intervals in a stream, lake or boggy area so that these may be crossed dry-shod. Stepping stones can also be placed in lawns to provide a hard walking surface in wet weather where, for visual effect, an orthodox path is not desired. Stepping stones are very characteristic of the JAPANESE GARDEN.

Steps Any abrupt change of level in a garden usually calls for steps, and these can also be of value where a path climbs a steady gradient. Steps are composed of the tread or horizontal part and the riser or vertical part. Risers should be 6"–9" high for comfort, and the risers and treads should be in a certain proportion for appearance. A rule of thumb for medium-sized steps is that the width of the tread and double the height of the riser should total 24". Narrower, steeper steps can be dangerous. Where steps are particularly long the tread should be the equivalent of one or more average strides, or the steps will be uncomfortable to walk up.

Steps can be made of concrete, stone slabs or bricks, or combinations of these. In general, all parts of a step should be mortared for stability but in informal places stone slabs can be bedded into the soil on a foundation of sand or ashes. In woodlands effective steps can be made directly from the soil, with the front edge of each stabilized with a length of tree branch or trunk at least 4″ thick. These, or wooden boards, are retained in place with a long strong peg driven in at each end on the outer face.

Sterile (1) Any flower incapable of producing seeds is known as sterile. Such sterile-flowered plants sometimes arise as hybrids, e.g. in the hortensia type of hydrangea, which were deliberately bred, or as mutations, e.g. in the Snowball Tree, *Viburnum opulus* 'Sterile'. The showy flowers of the mop-head hydrangea are quite sterile; an intermediate stage is seen in the type known as the lacecap in which a ring of similar sterile flowers surrounds a centre composed of small fertile ones. In some very double flowers – e.g. double stocks – all the sexual organs are converted into petals and the flowers are sterile for this reason. Sterility is sometimes a valuable

STERILE. *Left*, mop-head and, *right*, lace-cap hydrangea

feature: thus bananas are quite seedless, and more pleasant to eat because of this; seedless raisins are another example.

On other occasions sterility can be a nuisance. Some fruit trees, e.g. sweet cherries, are self-sterile – i.e. they cannot produce fruits as a result of self-pollination, and to crop they must receive pollen from certain other varieties. The same applies, though to a less acute degree, to apples, pears and plums, and those planning to grow fruit trees must ensure that varieties are chosen and interplanted which will satisfactorily pollinate each other.
◊ FERTILITY RULES; POLLINATION.

(2) 'Sterile' is also applied to soils which have been deliberately sterilized and to other, inert media in which plants can be grown, e.g. sand or vermiculite; or, if organic, e.g. peat, are unlikely to contain any pests or disease organisms. The word is also sometimes used for very poor soils lacking in fertility. ◊ STERILIZATION.

Sterilization Completely sterile soil, deprived of all its microscopic organisms, is of little use; but partially sterilized soil, in which most fungi and all insects and weed seeds have been destroyed, but not most bacteria, is highly desirable for pot plants, especially at the germination and seedling stages when fungus diseases such as damping-off so readily attack the plants. That is one reason why properly made John Innes composts are so valuable: the loam has been sterilized. It is not necessary to sterilize peat or sand, which are inert, nor soilless composts. (The first experiments on soil sterilization, which led to the J.I. composts, were carried out in 1934.)

Sterilization can be carried out in several ways. The most efficient is by heat, and commercial growers use high-pressure steam. A small quantity of soil can be sterilized by hanging a bag of soil in a large saucepan or similar receptacle, or placing it on a raised grid, so that it is just above water level. The water is brought to boiling point and boiled with a lid in place for about 10–12 minutes during which time a temperature around 93 °C (200 °F) should be achieved. Higher temperatures, or heat applied for too long, will destroy beneficial micro-organisms and possibly the soil structure, making the soil unable to support plant life.

Another method employs electricity passed through damp soil between metal electrodes. The resistance of the soil causes it to heat up until it is quite dry and sterilized. Proprietary electric sterilizers with capacity from $\frac{1}{2}$ cubic foot to $\frac{1}{4}$ cubic yard can be obtained.

Very small quantities of soil can be sterilized by baking. The moist (not sodden) soil is placed in a baking tin and baked for exactly one hour in an oven at 82°C (180°F). This is satisfactory for seed composts and short-term potting, but baking can readily char organic matter and lower the soil's overall value.

Chemicals are also used for sterilization and provide the best way for the amateur dealing with soil in a greenhouse, or large quantities for composts. Materials derived from coal tar are especially effective against insects, formaldehyde against fungi, and dazomet against eelworms and some fungus diseases. The first two are applied to the soil or spread-out potting mixture in solution from a rosed can; dazomet is a dust which must be worked into the soil or compost. In all cases the resultant fumes are trapped by covering the soil with sacks or tarpaulin. These chemicals must be used in accordance with makers' instructions, and soil or compost cannot be used for some weeks after treatment.

Commercial growers use toxic materials needing special precautions, such as chloropicrin and metham-sodium.
◊ COAL TAR; FUMIGATION.

Stigma That part of the pistil, or female organ of the flower, which becomes receptive to pollen; usually a disk or line which becomes sticky when ready. Its receptive surface is usually covered with microscopic glandular hairs. The stigma is often borne on a stem called the style, a channel between the stigma and the ovary down which the pollen grains must grow in order to achieve fertilization with the ovules in the ovary. Occasionally, as in the crocus, the style between the stigma and ovary is extremely long, but usually it is much shorter. Sometimes the stigma is an ornamental feature of the flower, as in the epiphyllum, where it has numerous branches and is shaped like a starfish supported on a medium-length style. In many plants, e.g. the lily, there is only a single stigma. Sometimes the stigmatic surfaces are quite different in appearance and may not be carried on a style at all, as in the poppy where they are arranged above the ovary in radiating lines on a circular disk.
◊ CARPEL; FERTILIZATION; FLOWER; PISTIL.

Stipe The leaf-stalk of a fern; also the stem of a mushroom-shaped fungus.

Stipule Stipules are leaf-like or scale-like organs found, in some plants only, at the base of a leaf-stalk or at a stem node. They are usually small or quite insignificant, but sometimes large enough to give some protection to the leaf bud they surround, occasionally united round the leaf-stalk or merging with it. In some cases, as in bed straws (*Galium*), the stipules are barely distinguishable from the true leaves. In others, as in *Lathyrus aphaca*, the leaves are reduced to tendrils and the stipules are large, leaf-like and act as leaves; in some desert acacias the stipules are converted into thick spiny structures. Many stipular structures are more accurately named as spathes, enclosing and protecting in a membranous envelope the young leaves of trees such as oaks or beeches before they unfold. In the garden the best-known plant with stipules is the rose, in which they often surround the base of the leaf-stalk, and a pair of well-defined stipules is often seen on the flower stalk. In botany, stipules are often important identification characters. ◊ SPATHE.

Stock (1) The part of a budded or grafted plant which provides the roots, as opposed to the scion – chosen for the quality of its flowers, fruit or other notable character – which forms the leaf-bearing upper part. 'Stock' also refers to plants grown on specifically to produce stocks, which may be from seed or cuttings as with roses.

Although stocks (also called rootstocks) are primarily used to provide a reliable established root system for the scion variety, they can also influence the growth of the grafted plant. The most important example of such influence is in modern apple stocks, which can be chosen in a wide range from those producing dwarf, fast-maturing trees to much larger, later-maturing ones. Also, results from grafting on a particular stock are consistent.

Stocks can often produce growths below the grafting or budding point, known as suckers. If these are not removed as soon as seen they can develop at the expense of the scion growth and eventually stifle it.
◊ DOUBLE-WORKING; SUCKER.

(2) Also used to describe plants or seeds with some specific attribute, notably virus-free plants. The term 'raiser's stock' is sometimes used of seeds or plants derived from the breeder's original material. 'Selected stock' implies that the nurseryman or seedsman offering it considers his material superior to that available elsewhere. ◊ SELECTION.

Stockholm Tar A kind of tar obtained from pine trees, recommended by older authorities as a tree wound dressing, but shown by research to be ineffective in preventing disease infection. ◊ WOUND DRESSINGS.

Stock Plant A plant retained by a grower or nurseryman to provide propagating material of any kind.

Stolon, Stoloniferous A stolon is a horizontal stem produced usually above but sometimes below ground level, which produces roots and new growth at its tip, in contrast to a runner which roots at its nodes (although these words are sometimes used indiscriminately). Most stolons are horizontal or creeping but in e.g. blackberries the word applies to stems which arch over and root at the tips. Plants which form stolons are called stoloniferous; a

word sometimes forming a specific name. ◊ RUNNER.

Stomata The stomata (singular: stoma) are the 'breathing pores' of plants. They are microscopic openings, usually leading into a larger cavity in the underlying tissue, and carry out gaseous interchange between the plant and the atmosphere. Each stoma is surrounded by two 'guard-cells'. When these absorb water in moist conditions they become turgid and, owing to their shape and the construction of the cells walls, this causes them to bulge outwards, thus increasing the size of the opening, or pore. In dry conditions this process is reversed, and the pore becomes smaller and finally closed. In this way excessive transpiration in dry conditions is prevented. The stomata are also sensitive to light, through a chemical process, tending to close in darkness.

Stomata are normally on the undersides of leaves, but on vertical leaves (e.g. those of irises) they may be on both sides, and on floating leaves (e.g. waterlilies) on the upper side only. In leafless plants, e.g. some brooms, the stomata are carried on the stems, often in grooves. In xerophytes (plants adapted to arid conditions) the stomata are relatively few in number, and may be protected against excessive heat or drying winds by being sunk in small pits, or surrounded by hairs or other, microscopic outgrowths.
◊ PHOTOSYNTHESIS; TRANSPIRATION.

Stone (1) Pieces of rock used for rock gardens, dry walls and, when cut and trimmed, paving. Examples are limestone and sandstone. Tufa is a very porous form of limestone. Artificial or reconstructed stone is made by various processes in which pulverized stone is formed into slabs or wall blocks. ◊ DRY WALL; LIMESTONE; PAVING; ROCK GARDEN; SANDSTONE; TUFA.

(2) A technical term for those fruits with a succulent outer part and a hard, woody inner one, as in the peach, plum, cherry and apricot. Botanically, such fruits are included in the drupes, but the gardener calls

them stone fruits. If the stones do not form properly, the fruits may be imperfect; split stone is a condition in which the kernel splits and may be due to faulty pollination or early insect attack; gumming of the stone is sometimes due to fluctuations in the soil moisture, or to lack of sufficient food. Lack of water, low temperatures and poor ventilation can all cause trouble during the so-called stoning period of grapes when the seeds start to harden, though the grape seeds are not technically stones. ◇ DRUPE.

Stone Chippings ◇ CHIPPINGS.

Stone Fruit Fruits which contain a hard stone, such as apricot, cherry, peach and plum; applied to both the fruits and the trees which carry them. ◇ STONE (2).

Stony Pit A virus disease of pears, also called dimple, resulting in fruits which are woody and covered in small pits. Although badly affected trees are best grubbed and burned, the symptoms can sometimes be lessened by improving drainage and mulching. ◇ VIRUS DISEASES.

Stool, Stooling In its horticultural sense, 'stool' seems to have become confused with 'stolon', since it means a group of shoots emerging from the base of a single plant. In modern times, its meaning is mainly restricted to plants used chiefly for propagation. The roots of chrysanthemums, after they have flowered, are known as stools, and the following spring they will produce a number of shoots from which cuttings can be taken.

Apple stocks are usually planted in stool beds, in well-separated rows in which the young shoots can be pegged down and covered with soil, or simply earthed up, so that they produce roots and can be severed and grown on individually. This form of layering is known as stooling.

In forestry, a stool is the stump or stock of a tree, especially if this has been cut for the production of coppice wood or young timber.

The gardener may carry out stooling, or coppicing as it is also known, to maintain juvenile foliage on eucalyptus or to obtain the brightly coloured young growth of certain willows and dogwoods.
◇ COPPICING; JUVENILITY; LAYERING.

Stopping To stop a plant is to remove its growing tip in order to make it produce side growths. It is particularly important with florist flowers such as chrysanthemums, dahlias and perpetual carnations, where stopping controls the number of flowers and approximate time at which they appear. In chrysanthemums the actual type of flower – its petalage and character – can be altered according to the type of

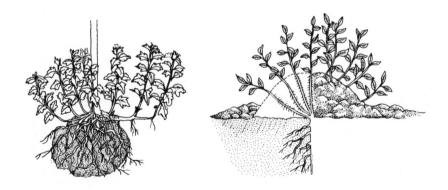

STOOL, STOOLING. *Left*, a chrysanthemum stool; *right*, stooling an apple stock

bud induced by the stopping process: the more stopping of lateral growths that is made, in general, the fewer petals the flowers have.

Stopping is also important in the culture of plants such as marrows, cucumbers and vines which produce laterals freely; here stopping is desirable to encourage fruits rather than leaves, and to control the amount of growth made. In vines, for instance, the main laterals (which have been encouraged to form by spur-pruning in winter) are stopped when the bunch has formed, so as to leave two leaves beyond the bunch. Any sub-laterals which form later as a result of this stopping are themselves stopped at one leaf.

The actual stopping is often carried out by pinching the stem between finger and thumb, and the word pinching is sometimes used in the same sense as stopping; but the operation can also be done with a knife, while with carnations the shoot is broken off at a joint.

◊ BREAK; CROWN; PINCHING; TOPPING.

Storage The gardener may need or wish to store produce of various kinds. These include fruits, edible roots, certain vegetables, and fleshy-rooted storage organs of certain tender plants.

The main fruits involved are apples and pears. Only varieties known to have keeping qualities are worth storing. Both fruits need dark, cool, frost-free, airy conditions, with pears preferring a dry atmosphere and apples a slightly moist one such as can be produced in a shed with an earth or concrete floor. Both can be stored on shelves or racks or in greengrocers' trays with corner posts which allow air to circulate between the trays when stacked. The fruits can be set out so that they do not touch, wrapped individually in newspaper or, in the case of apples, in oiled paper.

All root vegetables can be stored. On a large scale a clamp can be used. Smaller amounts of potatoes can be placed in greengrocers' trays after being cleaned and dried. Roots, e.g. carrots, beets and swedes, can be stored in boxes, placing them in layers of dry sand or peat. Onions can be set out in trays or roped together so that they can be hung up. Marrows, pumpkins, etc., are placed in nets for hanging up, and cabbages suitable for winter storage likewise, preferably upside-down.

Bulbs, corms and tubers of tender ornamentals grown outside, e.g. gladioli and dahlias, are lifted before severe frost is likely, thoroughly cleaned and dried. They can be stored on shelves or in trays as they are, or in boxes of dry peat. Fungicide dressings can be applied to reduce the danger of storage rots. Fleshy-rooted plants grown in pots are often best left in them, the soil being allowed to dry out entirely. To prevent water reaching such pots accidentally, it may be desirable to stack them on their sides. Before starting such roots into growth, the old soil or potting compost should be removed and the root repotted in fresh material.

◊ CLAMP; DRESSING (2); STORAGE ORGANS; STORAGE ROTS; STORE.

Storage Organs Many plants have some form of swollen root in which food (usually starches) and moisture are stored, during a resting period. This may be an adaptation to a dry hot season, to excessive summer shade in deciduous woodland, or to cold in winter. Many of these subterranean storage organs exist during the resting period with neither roots nor top growth and can be stored and marketed dry as a result. They are frequently lumped together as 'bulbs', but in fact include bulbs, corms and tubers; there are also fleshy rhizomes and rootstocks, though most of these retain roots even when dormant. ◊ BULB; CORM; RHIZOME; STARTING; TUBER.

Storage Rots A general term for any disease which attacks fruits or roots stored over winter. Some of these follow careless handling of the produce and consequent bruising, but as a general rule only mature, unblemished fruits and roots should be stored, and the latter must be cleaned of soil as much as possible. Regular inspection to remove any decaying specimens will reduce the risk of rots developing. Bulbs, corms, tubers, etc., to be grown again can be dressed with fungicides to reduce the possibility of rotting. ◊ DRESSING (2); STORAGE.

Store Any place in which fruits, vegetables or fleshy roots of tender ornamentals are stored over winter. As a rule, this should be frost-free but cool, airy and dry, although apples prefer a slightly moist atmosphere. A store can be a shed, room or cellar which fulfils these conditions. ◊ STORAGE.

Stove, Stove House Nowadays a stove house means any greenhouse kept at a high temperature – a winter minimum of 21°C (70°F) or more – and used for tropical plants. High air humidity is also necessary, and such houses must be frequently damped down. A feature of the older stove houses or stoves as they were often called, was a plunging bed of coconut fibre, with hot-water pipes below it; in the days before hot-water heating came into general use, this bed was filled with tan-bark (waste material from tanneries) or other vegetable matter which would ferment and heat up like a huge hotbed. Since it was desirable to conserve as much heat as possible, stove houses were often built against a wall. ◊ DAMPING DOWN; HOTBED; GREENHOUSE.

Strain ◊ SELECTION.

Strangling A woody climber allowed to grow up a tree can eventually prevent the latter growing further and is said to be strangling it. Wisteria is one of the few plants likely to do this in temperate climates, but a number of tropical and subtropical kinds may become stranglers.

The word 'strangling' is also occasionally used for the growth-restricting operation known as GARROTTING.

Strap, Strap-shaped The word 'strap' is sometimes used to describe the petal-like organ of the ray florets in the family Compositae. This organ is called a ligule, and organs, including leaves, which are long and parallel-sided may be called strap-shaped or ligulate. ◊ COMPOSITE.

Stratification A process applied to certain seeds, especially those with hard or thick, fleshy coats, to improve and speed up germination. Seeds of trees and shrubs frequently need stratifying. Seeds to be stratified are placed on a layer of sand in boxes, pans or pots, and covered with more sand. A mixture of sand and peat is sometimes used. Two or three layers of seed can be accommodated in a pot. The containers are then put outside in a place exposed to the elements, and left there during the winter. It is sometimes necessary with very hard seeds (e.g. tree peonies) to leave them for 18 months, over two winters. During the following spring, the seeds are removed from the sand by sieving and are sown in the normal way. If they have fleshy coats, e.g. rose hips, the seeds are rubbed through a sieve, or picked over with the fingers, to remove the coats. Some gardeners turn over and examine the mixture of seeds and sand once a month in the spring until there are signs of germination. The sprouting seeds are then sown in ordinary containers at the appropriate depth.

Stratification is most necessary where a fairly large number of seeds is being dealt with. If only a few seeds are involved, they can be sown in the ordinary way, perhaps a little deeper than usual, fleshy ones having their coats removed manually, and left exposed to the elements over the winter months as before.

◊ SEED SOWING; VERNALIZATION.

Straw If available, straw – the dry stalks of barley, oats and wheat – can be valuable to the gardener in several ways.

Relatively small amounts of wet, chopped or broken straw can be added to compost heaps. Larger amounts are best composted separately: the straw should be thoroughly wetted and made into 9″ layers, which are sprinkled with an activator or thin layers of animal manure, soil or sulphate of ammonia as in normal compost making.

Straw can also be dug into the soil to provide long-term food and improve drainage. This is done either by working chopped straw into the bottom of trenches when digging (not placing thick layers of unbroken straw, which can impede drainage) or by burying the straw vertically. This is again done when digging, making a narrow wall of straw against the side of each completed trench. Alternatively, deep V-shaped cuts are made at intervals in previously cultivated soil and straw is forced into these with a spade.

Straw is valuable for protection. It is a vital component of a vegetable clamp, or can be piled or tied around tender plants needing protection from frost. It is also valuable as a mulch, e.g. around soft fruit bushes, vegetables and strawberries. With the latter it can have a multiple purpose: it is laid down as mulch to provide food; surplus is piled over the plants on frosty nights to protect the flowers, and removed by day; later, it protects the developing fruits from attack by pests, e.g. slugs, and from being splashed with soil. Placed under fruit trees, a thick layer of straw will prevent bruising of fruit which falls prematurely.

Used fresh, however, straw will depress the nitrogen level of soils, and extra nitrogen may be needed, as when using sawdust.

◊ CLAMP; COMPOST HEAP; DIGGING; MULCH; SAWDUST; STRAW BALE CULTURE.

Straw Bale Culture A specialized method of growing tomatoes, sweet peppers and similar warmth-loving crops, useful where soil in a greenhouse is unsatisfactory or known to be pest- or disease-ridden.

Straw bales are placed end-to-end on sheets of plastic at the sides of the greenhouse. They are first soaked repeatedly with water over a 2–3 week period, keeping the ventilators closed and, if necessary, using artificial heat to maintain around 10°C (50°F). Then sprinkle $1\frac{1}{2}$ lb. of nitrogen-rich fertilizer such as Nitro-chalk on each bale and water it in. Three to four days later, repeat with 1 lb. nitrogen per bale. After another 3–4 days, add $\frac{3}{4}$ lb. nitrogen and $1\frac{1}{2}$ lb. of a balanced fertilizer, and again water in.

These applications make the bales ferment and become hot. An alternative way of achieving this is by repeated watering with a seaweed-based liquid fertilizer.

The next stage, after allowing the bales to cool a little, is to build up a triangular ridge of potting compost along the top of the bales, and then plant the seedling tomatoes in these ridges 12″–15″ apart.

Straw which has been sprayed while growing with a selective weedkiller and then baled must be avoided at all costs.

Strawberry Barrel, Pot Ways of growing strawberries in limited space. In the strawberry barrel 2″ holes are drilled at regular intervals in a standard-sized barrel 30″–36″ high. The holes should be staggered at several different levels. Drainage holes must also be made in the bottom of the barrel. Plants are inserted in the holes as filling with rich soil proceeds; six or seven more can be planted at the top, from which any cover is removed. To ensure adequate penetration of water, a central core of rubble should be arranged within a wire netting tube. Proprietary plastic 'barrels' can be obtained; planting is carried out in exactly the same way. The earthenware strawberry pot carried out the same function on a smaller scale, with 12–16 planting holes. In both cases, watering must never be neglected; but the lower plants in barrels can suffer from dryness, even with a central watering core. ◊ CROCUS POT.

Straw Mats Older books may recommend the use of woven straw mats under strawberry plants, to keep off slugs and keep the fruits clean. These mats were about 1′ square, with a cut in one side leading to a central hole which was placed around the strawberry plant. Today, such protection is more easily provided by squares of plastic sheeting cut in the same way.

Streak A name covering various virus diseases which cause dark streaks on plant foliage, stems and occasionally (e.g. tomatoes) fruit, together with dark sunken spots. Like all virus diseases, these are incurable and affected plants should be destroyed. ◊ VIRUS DISEASES.

Strig A word of obscure origin, dating back to the sixteenth century, and meaning a stalk, whether of leaf, fruit or flower. Its only common horticultural use today is when referring to a single cluster of currants, the whole of which is spoken of as a strig.

Strike In the seventeenth century a plant putting out roots was said to be striking. From this was derived the modern horticultural meaning of the word: to cause a cutting to root, or to increase a plant by means of cuttings. To strike a cutting, therefore, means preparing and treating a piece of plant in such a way as to encourage it to root. A struck cutting is one that has formed roots. The word 'take' is sometimes used in the same sense as strike. ⟡ CUTTING.

Strip Cropping Sometimes used to describe crops laid out in narrow strips with a pathway between when cloches are used; the method reduces the amount of handling needed when the cloches are moved from one crop to the next. ⟡ CLOCHE.

Stub (1) A short piece of cut or broken branch projecting from a main stem. A lopped tree is sometimes spoken of as a stub, or as being stubbed. ⟡ LOP.

(2) The stump of a tree left in the ground after felling; also sometimes used of the base of the trunk of an entire tree. From this is derived the verb 'to stub': stubbing out a tree means to dig it out, roots and all, for which a stubbing mattock may be used. The word applies also to lesser plants, as in the country rhyme:

Stub a thistle in May, it will be back next day;
Stub a thistle in June, it will be back soon;
Stub a thistle in July, it will surely die.

⟡ MATTOCK; STUB GRAFT.

Stub Graft A type of graft in which scions are inserted at the base of small side branches, the latter being later cut cleanly away except for the basal portion containing the graft. This is one of the grafts used when grafting all over an existing tree, or reworking. ⟡ GRAFTING; REWORKING.

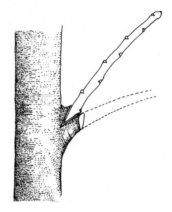

STUB GRAFT

Stump The base of the trunk of a felled tree which, with the associated roots, is left in the ground; also sometimes the base of a still-growing tree. ⟡ STUB; TREE STUMPS.

Stump Gobbler ⟡ TREE STUMPS.

Style The 'stem' which often connects the stigma with the ovary in the pistil or female organ of a flower. ⟡ STIGMA.

Styles of Gardening ⟡ GARDEN DESIGN.

Styptic ⟡ WOUND DRESSINGS.

Sub-alpine Applied to plants which inhabit the zone between the foothills and the alpine slopes, in the European Alps very roughly from about 3000′, at the upper limits of vine cultivation, to about 5000′. In the Himalayas, both zones are at much greater altitude. The term is often restricted to herbaceous perennial plants, which are often tall-stemmed and show no special characteristic of growth imposed by their habitat. The word is sometimes latinized in specific names. ⟡ ALPINE.

Suberose Corky; usually applied to trees with corky bark, e.g. the cork oak, *Quercus suber.* ⟡ BARK.

Sub-irrigation Methods of watering in

which water is supplied from below the soil surface, as in a moraine or some methods of soilless cultivation. ◊ MORAINE; SOIL-LESS CULTIVATION.

Sublime A word used in the eighteenth and early nineteenth century to describe anything in nature or in a garden which impressed and awed by sheer size, roughness, gloom or violence, preferably creating a feeling of menace. Dorothy Wordsworth defined it well in describing the Fall of Reichenbach: '... it gives little of what might be called pleasure. It was astonishment and awe for the destruction of all things, and the helplessness of man ...'. Edmund Burke wrote an essay on 'The Sublime and the Beautiful' in 1756 which included these relevant words, used by Humphry Repton in *The Art of Gardening*: 'Designs that are vast only by their dimensions, are always the sign of a common and low imagination; no work of art can be great but as it deceives. To be otherwise is the prerogative of nature only.' Items which were sublime at that period included single, ruggedly formed pine trees, or other trees which were dead, waterfalls, cliffs, Gothic ruins and other massive architectural structures. ◊ CONCEIT.

Sub-shrub A perennial plant which is woody at the base but produces, on the woody framework, soft, herbaceous growth which is liable to die in winter like the entire growth of ordinary herbaceous perennials. The common sage is a well-known example. Many plants are of this type, notably those from hot, dry, Mediterranean-type climates; but how they behave in winter often depends on the climate in which they are grown. Thus the hardy fuchsias (*F. magellanica* type) retain most of their soft growth all the year round in south-western England and Eire; but in districts with cold winters they are apt to be cut back, often to ground level. The Latin equivalent of sub-shrubby is suffruticose, which is occasionally seen as a specific name, e.g. *Paeonia suffruticosa*. The technical name of a sub-shrub is a suffrutex.

The word is also sometimes used in the literal and basically erroneous sense of a small, low shrub, e.g. in the dwarf variety of box called *Buxus sempervirens* 'Suffruticosa'.

Subsoil In theory, subsoil is the layer below the surface soil or topsoil, but the word generally implies a layer which is markedly inferior in fertility and texture. The actual depth of the subsoil therefore depends on the situation. Exceptionally, as in alluvial deposits, fertile soil extends for many feet downwards; in average situations the fertile layer is only 12"–18" deep. The level at which the subsoil begins can be ascertained by digging a pit or trench when any change in the texture and appearance of the soil can be seen on a clean vertical face. Such a change is most dramatic and obvious above chalk, clay or gravel.

Subsoil should not be brought to the surface so as to bury topsoil, because it will take time to improve its fertility, even if this is possible. It is better to improve it by cultivation techniques like double digging and trenching, the latter indeed being sometimes called subsoiling.

◊ DIGGING; LEVELLING; TOPSOIL.

Subsoiling The same as trenching. ◊ DIGGING; SUBSOIL.

Subtend To extend under and close to another organ, as of a leaf or bract growing from a stem which carries a bud or flower in its axil.

Sub-tropical Describes plants which are, loosely, sub-tropical in origin. Many of these can be grown in greenhouses at medium temperatures, and can be used for outdoor decoration in summer, though frost will kill them. Such outdoor use was very popular in Victorian times, and took the form of sub-tropical plants with bold foliage, grown among flowering bedding plants. There are a few parts of south-west and western Britain where sub-tropical plants can be grown permanently out of doors. ◊ BEDDING PLANT; TROPICAL.

Successional Applied to vegetable sowings made at two- or three-week intervals, using only enough seed to produce the amount of crop expected to be used during the equivalent period of maturity.

Succulent Derived from the Latin *succus*, meaning 'juice' or 'sap', a succulent plant is a thick, fleshy one which is usually very juicy or sappy. Though this might be taken to include bulbous and other fleshy-rooted plants, in practice it is restricted to those which have developed swollen leaves or stems as an adaptation to arid conditions, and in general to tender plants, though numerous hardy plants are also succulent, e.g. sedums and sempervivums.

Many families of plants have developed succulence. The cactus family is one which is almost entirely succulent; so is the mesembryanthemum family (*Aizoaceae* or *Ficoidaceae*) from South Africa. Some five other families have numerous succulent members, and about thirty-five others have at least one or two succulent species.

In the cactus family and the succulent euphorbias and stapelias the tendency has been to lose leaves and develop spherical or columnar stems, resulting in plants of similar form – a good example of parallel evolution. Other tendencies include the rosette, swollen stem-bases, and the gradation from very fleshy independent leaves to the merging of leaf pairs into a single round or cylindrical 'plant-body'.

⬦ CACTUS.

Sucker (1) Any secondary growth which arises from the roots of a plant, and develops leaves of its own, is technically a sucker; this is one of the natural ways in which plants increase. Suckers spring from adventitious buds on roots of shrubs such as lilac, or from side buds on underground stems, e.g. in mint. The gardener is usually concerned about suckers which arise from the roots of grafted or budded shrubs or trees – lilacs, roses, plums, rhododendrons, viburnums may all be grafted and be prone to this trouble. Because they come from the roots, suckers have the character of the stock, usually chosen for vigour, and not of the scion, which is the desirable flowering part. If suckers are allowed to grow they may eventually swamp the scion growth entirely, and the plant is then accused of reverting to the stock. Suckers on grafted plants must therefore be removed as soon as possible and, if practicable, flush with the root from which they grow. Suckers are sometimes the result of damaging the roots when planting: each wound forms a callus at which adventitious buds can form.

Where the plant is not grafted suckers may still be a nuisance, forming a thicket of growth around the original trunk. In such cases they can provide useful propagating material – raspberries are increased in this way, and also ornamental shrubs such as *Rhus typhina*. Tree stumps may produce suckers from their roots, which can cause annoyance after the tree is cut down.

⬦ ADVENTITIOUS; BUDDING; CALLUS; GRAFTING; REVERSION; SCION; SUCKER CUTTER; TREE STUMPS.

(2) One of a small group of insects, closely related to greenfly and rather similar in appearance, which suck plant juices. They are usually referred to under the name of the preferred host plant, as in apple, box or pear sucker. Symptoms are curling or puckering of foliage and, in the case of the fruit trees, withering of flowers and absence of fruit, since the suckers are partial to the flower buds. Insecticidal sprays give control: with the fruit trees these must be timed according to bud stages, or winter washes can be used.

Sucker Cutter, Suckering Iron A tool for the removal of unwanted suckers from roses and other shrubs and trees. Modern sucker cutters have two short sharp blades in an inverted V at the end of a long handle. The suckering iron, invented in the nineteenth century but now seldom seen, resembled a long, very narrow spade with concave blade sharpened at the base. ⬦ SUCKER (1).

Suffruticose The technical name for sub-shrubby. ⬦ SUB-SHRUB.

Sulphate of Ammonia A chemical fertilizer

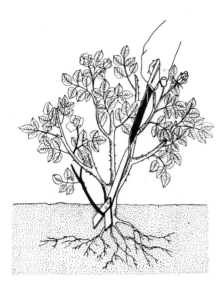

SUCKER CUTTER

plant food and as a fungicide. Iron is one of the minerals needed in small amounts by plants: its absence is likely to cause leaf yellowing (chlorosis). Iron is readily 'locked up' and made unavailable to plants by an excess of calcium in alkaline soils. To overcome iron deficiency, foliage can be sprayed with a solution of sulphate of iron at $\frac{1}{2}$–1 oz. in 1 gallon of water or, better still, iron is applied as a chelate or sequestrol.

As a fungicide and also to kill moss and pearlwort sulphate of iron is an ingredient of lawn sand, where it also stimulates the grass. Fairy rings and other infestations of toadstools on lawns can be partly controlled by watering affected areas, preferably after spiking, with sulphate of iron at 4 oz. in a gallon of water.

♢ CHLOROSIS; FAIRY RING; LAWN SAND; SEQUESTROL.

Sulphate of Magnesium This is Epsom salt, containing in readily available form 10 per cent magnesium, which is an essential plant food. To remedy magnesium deficiency, sulphate of magnesium can be applied as a top-dressing at 1 oz. per square yard or sprayed onto foliage at 2–3 oz. in a gallon of water. ♢ MAGNESIUM.

Sulphate of Potash Probably the most valuable material to supply potash, one of the three main plant foods, of which it contains 48 per cent; it is largely free of impurities. It is used as a top dressing at $\frac{1}{2}$–1 oz. per square yard or dissolved in water at $\frac{1}{2}$–1 oz. in a gallon. ♢ POTASH.

Sulphur Mainly used as a fungicide, either in dust form alone or as an ingredient in sprayable materials such as colloidal sulphur. Sulphur may be obtained as a natural yellow dust, or coloured green when it tones in better with plants. When refined, this dust is sometimes known as flowers of sulphur. It is most used under glass against mildews and is also valuable for dusting fleshy flower roots before storing, or if they begin to become mildewed. Sulphur also has a useful effect against certain pests, mostly red spider and other mites. It is also

containing 20.6 per cent nitrogen in reasonably quick-acting form, though more quickly available to plants in warm moist weather. It is especially useful with brassicas and potatoes, since these benefit from the sulphate portion. However, it tends to make soils more acid, and is thus best used on alkaline soils. It can be applied dry at up to 2 oz. per square yard a little while before sowing or planting or as a top-dressing around growing crops at 1 oz. per square yard; it can be used as a liquid fertilizer at 1 oz. in 2 gallons of water. Sulphate of ammonia is a valuable accelerator for compost heaps.

Care must be taken that the material does not lodge on leaves, because it can scorch them. This capacity is made use of in destroying broad-leaved weeds in lawns, sulphate of ammonia being one of the ingredients of lawn sand.

♢ COMPOST HEAP; DRESSING; LAWN SAND.

Sulphate of Copper ♢ COPPER, COPPER COMPOUNDS.

Sulphate of Iron This material can act as a

319

possible to obtain sulphur candles for greenhouse fumigation against fungus diseases, although modern fungicidal 'smokes' are probably superior to control these.

Sulphur has also been used to reduce the lime content of soils, when 8–16 oz. per square yard will lower the alkalinity by one unit on the pH scale. Unfortunately, in the process calcium sulphate is formed if the alkalinity is due to free lime or chalk, as it usually is in Britain, and this chemical can readily harm plants in excess.

♢ FUMIGATION; FUNGICIDES; pH.

Sulphur-copper Dust A mixture of sulphur and copper in powder form used quite recently as a fungicide, especially against collar and foot rot, but now probably unobtainable.

Sulphur-shy A term applied to certain fruits liable to be badly affected by application of lime sulphur wash, which scorches apple and pear leaves and causes leaves of some black currants and gooseberries to fall. ♢ LIME SULPHUR.

Summer Fallow The clearing and cultivation of soil in summer prior to making lawns in late summer or carrying out any plantings in autumn.

Summerhouse A structure in a garden or park designed to be used as a retreat from the dwelling house especially in summer, although modern examples heated by wood-burning stoves may be used in winter also. They are usually very simple, providing a single room with windows. Summerhouses have been built since the fifteenth century in many materials and a variety of styles including 'gothick', oriental and rustic; nowadays they are mostly utilitarian, rectangular, timber buildings with glass windows. Some are designed to rotate to obtain full advantage of the sun.

Summer Oil The U.S. name for petroleum oil formulated for summer use. ♢ PETROLEUM OIL.

Summer Pruning Any pruning of trees and shrubs, though mainly restricted to fruit trees, done between June and August. Its purpose is to restrain growth, encourage flower bud formation and keep trees dwarfed. Among ornamental trees and shrubs it is usually restricted to wall-trained specimens which make excessive forward growth or breastwood. Correct timing is essential: summer pruning should be carried out when growth has started to slow down but has not stopped entirely. At the right period, the base of the shoot has started to become hard and woody. Summer pruning should not be carried out on fruits that crop on one-year wood such as fan-trained apricots, peaches and plums, or on ornamental trees and shrubs that flower on one-year wood.

Summer Wood Applied to growths made by trees and shrubs, primarily fruit trees, between June and August.

Sun Blind ♢ BLINDS.

Sunken Garden A part of a larger garden sunk below the main level. Such gardens almost invariably form part of a formal layout and are usually rectangular, with edges and walls formed of stone. Depth normally varies between 1′ and 2′, and access is by one or more sets of steps. Very often the centre of a sunken garden is occupied by a pool in the same proportions. Sunken gardens have been a feature of gardens since Tudor times; at that period they would often house a knot garden – which could thus be viewed from above – rather than a central pool. ♢ KNOT.

Superior A term found in botanical descriptions indicating that one organ is superior to, i.e. above, another. The typical reference, as in artificial keys of identification, is to the relative position of the ovary and floral envelopes (corolla and/or calyx); when the latter are inserted below the ovary, this organ is superior. ♢ ARTIFICIAL KEY; FLOWER; INFERIOR.

Superphosphate of Lime Often just called

superphosphate, this was the first artificial fertilizer to be made, in 1839. It is produced by treating natural insoluble rock phosphate with sulphuric acid, and may be obtained as a fine powder or granules. It contains phosphoric acid, the salts of which are one of the three main plant foods, at 13–18 per cent, depending on quality. The word 'lime' refers to the gypsum (calcium sulphate) which comprises about half its bulk but, despite this, the material provides no free lime at all, and will not render acid soils alkaline. It is in fact most effective on already somewhat alkaline soils, where it can be applied 1–2 oz. per square yard, preferably lightly worked in before sowing or planting. It can be mixed with water and used at $\frac{1}{2}$–1 oz. in a gallon. Triple superphosphate is a more highly concentrated form containing $2\frac{1}{2}$ times as much phosphoric acid as ordinary superphosphate, and is thus more economical of storage space and in application rates. ◊ PHOSPHATES.

Support Many garden and greenhouse plants need support for various reasons. Herbaceous plants may have stems too tall or brittle to stand erect in windy conditions, and will need support both for appearance and prevention of damage. Trees and shrubs almost always need support after planting, otherwise their roots are loosened by wind-rocking and they may die. Finally, climbing and scrambling plants, whether woody or herbaceous, need support if they are to ascend properly and not make an ungainly heap of growth.

One of the basic methods of support, of plants in the open ground or in pots, is by the provision of a vertical stake, pole or cane.

Individual vertical supports are provided for newly planted trees and shrubs, standard roses, etc., and tall brittle-stemmed herbaceous plants such as delphiniums. Clump-forming perennials may have three or more stakes pushed in around them, so that a tie of twine, or a proprietary metal ring, can be fixed around the clump without constricting it unnaturally; in the case of stout, brittle plants like dahlias several individual stakes may be needed, one for each stem.

Stakes for trees and shrubs are best put in position before planting so that the roots can be fitted around them; root damage is likely if the stake is put in after planting. Supports for dahlias should also be placed at planting time to avoid damage to the tubers, and this principle should be extended to all plants where possible.

Vertical supports include bamboo canes which are available in a wide range of lengths and thicknesses, artificial canes of plastic, metal rods, and wooden poles. Natural larch poles are sometimes available, but nowadays a range of squared timber stakes about 1″–2″ across is usually obtainable. These are pointed at one end and have usually been pre-treated with a wood preservative. This treatment is essential for any wooden support likely to be needed for more than a single season.

The first consideration of a stake is that it should be strong enough for its purpose. Bamboo can be used for most herbaceous plants and small shrubs, but tall, heavy perennials and medium-sized shrubs need 1″ square timber stakes, or plastic or metal of equal strength, and trees need 2″ square stakes or stout larch poles.

Stakes must always be embedded in the ground for up to a quarter of their total length. With herbaceous plants, canes or timbers should not be taller than the level of the lowest flowers, otherwise damage will be done to them. This method is also less unsightly than stakes as tall as the flowering spikes or heads. With trees, a stake 4′–6′ above soil level is normally adequate; if the plant is a standard or half-standard, the stake may best terminate just below the point of branching. Commercial fruit growers often use a stout short stake driven in at an angle to the tree's trunk, terminating just beyond it, 30″–36″ above soil level. This method gives extra strength and the stake is less likely to crack at ground level, but it is rather unsightly. In gardens, this method may be used where an existing tree starts to rock, since it avoids damage to established roots.

Where large trees are being planted, an

321

alternative method of avoiding windrock is by guying, with three wires fixed between the upper part of the tree and pegs driven into the ground around it.

Plants making dense branching growth can be effectively supported by two or three bushy branches, e.g. those of hazel, such as are often used for culinary peas. These branches should also be shorter than the ultimate height of the plant, and are soon hidden by the foliage.

In the vegetable garden, more utilitarian supports may be used. Peas and similar tall bushy plants can be supported on twiggy branches which should be as tall as the expected growth; by netting on each side of the row, firmly secured at each end; or by netting fixed over patent metal hoops. Runner beans are traditionally grown on a structure of paired stakes tied together at the top and linked there with a long horizontal member, but there are less complex modern patent devices with a simple aluminium structure of end-pieces and a horizontal member from which netting is supported. In either case, the great weight of fully grown plants calls for strong members very firmly fixed into the ground. An alternative for beans, etc., is a 'wigwam' of three or four poles pushed into the soil and fixed together at the top to form a narrow cone-shaped structure.

Tomatoes need long stout canes fixed well into the soil, for here again the mature plant bearing its crop is very heavy. Under glass it may be more convenient to use twine to support tomatoes. This must be fixed firmly at eaves level, the lower end being tied around the tomato stem near its base and spiralled round the stem.

Climbing plants almost always need support, the type of which depends partly on the plants' habit of growth, especially with twiners which must have something of appropriate size to twine around.

For climbers on walls, strong wires can be fixed with the aid of wall nails or vine eyes (eyed nails); usually the wires are arranged horizontally at regular intervals. Wood trellis can also be used, fastened securely to the wall by plugs and screws or, if free-standing, to stout vertical supports

sunk into the ground. Panels of plastic mesh or plastic-covered wire mesh can be fixed to provide a similar effect, and there are a number of patent wire fixtures of various patterns. Away from walls or fences, plants which do not grow too tall can be grown up a single small tree trunk, on which the stubs of branches may be left, or up a tripod or wigwam of three poles securely fixed together. An extension of such methods is the pergola. Climbing roses are sometimes grown up poles fixed at regular intervals with chain or rope fixed between them, to which the longer growths are tied.

Very vigorous climbers, e.g. rose 'Kiftsgate' and *Clematis montana*, can be planted at the base of trees so that they scramble up among the branches; it is usual to select old trees with little ornamental value of their own, like worn-out fruit trees, or even dead ones, since some climbers can swamp and possibly kill a tree if allowed to.

Self-clinging climbers will normally fix themselves to a brick wall by their aerial roots without extra help. This sometimes alarms householders but no harm should be caused to sound, well-mortared brickwork, although the climbers must be watched around guttering, roof tiles or slates, and near windows where damage can also be caused.

In greenhouses, climbers can be started up long canes, or cord or wire fixed between eaves and floor level, and then grown along horizontal cords or wires arranged as appropriate in the peak of the roof. In large greenhouses and conservatories, structural members can often be used for support. In structures like lean-tos, where one side is an existing wall, trellis or less obtrusive small-mesh plastic netting can be fixed on this wall.

In many cases plants will need tying to their supports. The extent of tying varies with the plant concerned. Soft or brittle plants, e.g. tomatoes and delphiniums, need tying with twine, fillis or raffia every few inches. Trees and shrubs normally need only a single strong tie at the top of the stake. It is always essential to protect the trunk so that it does not chafe against the stake. This may be done by wrapping a piece of sacking around the trunk, using an old pair of tights or a piece of rubber motor-tyre; best of all, use modern patent plastic or rubber tree-ties.

Where twine or raffia is used it is better to make a figure-eight loop around stake and stem than a simple loop outside them: this prevents constriction and gives a little freedom of movement. Alternatively, patent wire rings or 'twists' of soft wire embedded in paper strip can be used, or for long-term tying galvanized or plastic-coated wire.

◊ CLIMBER; GUYING; PERGOLA.

Surrey School A term sometimes applied to those later-nineteenth-century English gardeners who attacked the over-elaborate Victorian bedding schemes and replaced them with more natural-looking plantings, including the herbaceous border, wild gardens, and informal woodland. The main aims of the Surrey School – Surrey is a county in southern England – were to use hardy plants in relatively simple layouts in which both flowers and foliage were artistically blended. The first exponents of the Surrey School were William Robinson and Gertrude Jekyll. Originally, they were entirely against any formality at all, but Miss Jekyll became associated with the architect Sir Edwin Lutyens who overcame this extreme bias. Between them, these two were responsible for many gardens, mainly in southern England, planned on these new lines which combined hardy plants, a good deal of formality in layout, and wilder plantings away from the dwelling. Many of these gardens still exist and their influence is still very important today. The nucleus of the Royal Horticultural Society's garden at Wisley, Surrey, owed its design to the Surrey School.

Suspension The result of mixing into water very fine powders of pesticidal or fungicidal materials which are not actually soluble. If kept well stirred, the chemical remains evenly dispersed in the water; and this suspension, as it is called, can be sprayed onto plants perfectly effectively.

The materials concerned are called WETTABLE POWDERS.

Sussex Trug ◊ TRUG.

Swap Hook One of the many names for a SICKLE.

Sward Nowadays used, usually rather poetically, to indicate a stretch of turf or a lawn; the original word 'greensward' was first used in 1508.

Swath, Swathe The extent of sweep of a scythe when mowing; sometimes used today when describing a pathway of close-mown grass made in a meadow.

Swelling ◊ BUD STAGES.

Switch, Switching A switch is a long pliable rod used to disperse wormcasts and dew on turf before mowing; this switching prevents both the mower sliding on an over-wet surface and also the compaction of wormcasts which creates bare spots on the turf. The switch should be 15′–20′ long and can be a bamboo cane, strong steel wire, or a fibre-glass rod fixed into a handle. It can also be used for working in lawn top dressings and reduces the severity of attacks of fungus diseases on grass. ◊ DRESSING (1).

Switch Plant A plant in which leaves are greatly reduced or entirely absent, with long switch-like shoots which are green and carry out photosynthesis instead of the leaves. Such plants are often adapted to arid conditions: many brooms are switch plants. ◊ CLADODE; STOMATA; XERO-PHYTE.

Swoe A modern patent HOE.

Symbiosis The word 'symbiosis' (adjective: symbiotic) is derived from Greek words meaning to live together, and refers to the partnership of two distinct living organisms, to the benefit of each. Sometimes, as in lichens, the partnership is so complete that a new entity is formed, for a lichen is composed of a fungus and an alga closely united. In most cases, however, the two partners have a separate existence. Thus the nitrogen-fixing bacteria which inhabit the nodules of leguminous plants can live on their own in the soil. The same applies to the main group of symbiotic plants, the fungi. Many of these live in association with roots of other plants; the benefits appear to be mainly derived by the latter, though presumably the fungus benefits also. Some plants, notably almost all orchids, cannot grow properly in nature, nor in many cases even germinate, without the association of a certain kind of fungus. Many trees, mainly (but by no means only) conifers, grow remarkably better in association with fungi, especially as seedlings. These are 'macro-fungi' – what are commonly called toadstools – and a wide range of them form associations with trees, and are seen growing around them. In the typical tree/fungus association, the tree roots become short and stubby – coral-like, in fact – and are surrounded by a layer of fungus cells. The roots have no root-hairs, and the fungus strands permeate them, though without penetrating the root cells. These tree/fungus roots are called mycorrhiza. In fungus associations with orchids and herbaceous plants, the fungus usually penetrates the root cells. In both cases the roots receive their nourishment entirely via the fungus. Such activities must not, of course, be confused with attacks by parasitic fungi such as the deadly bracket fungi or the honey fungus on trees. Even the latter, however, forms a beneficial association with a Japanese terrestrial orchid, which cannot flower without the fungus. ⟡ FUNGUS; SAPROPHYTE.

Sympetalous Of flowers in which the petals are united. ⟡ FLOWER.

Symphilids Creatures resembling tiny centipedes, the commonest being about $\frac{1}{8}''$ long and white. Their bodies have 14 segments and 12 pairs of legs, and they have long segmented antennae. They feed voraciously on roots and, if wilting in hot conditions occurs, symphilid attack is one possibility to consider. Young plants

attacked may be finished off by mildew. Tomatoes are often attacked: they become stunted, with bluish stems and a dark-green tone to the upper foliage. Symphilids are most serious in greenhouses where unsterilized soil containing much organic matter has been used. In summer the pests descend to considerable depths in open ground. Their presence can be ascertained by placing soil samples in water; the tiny pests will float to the surface. Treatment is by drenching the soil with a soil insecticide, or working in insecticide granules.

Sympodial Applied to stems in which growth is continued by successive side shoots, not the terminal bud: usually refers to orchids where the new growths arise from a rhizome and each is effectively a complete plant in itself. ⟡ MONOPODIAL.

Synonym An alternative name; usually restricted to botanical (Latin) names rather than popular ones. Such alternatives exist for various reasons. ⟡ CLASSIFICATION (The Binomial).

Syringe A device for applying a spray of water, pesticide or fungicide to a plant, consisting of a cylinder into which the liquid is drawn by pulling back a plunger, after which it is expelled through an adjustable, or exchangeable, nozzle. ⟡ SPRAYER.

Systemic A chemical which, when sprayed onto a plant, is absorbed by it and enters its sap. Both systemic pesticides and fungicides are available. Use of the former means that only pests which actually feed on the plant's sap are destroyed, whereas ordinary contact sprays affect all or most insects which they touch or which later walk on the sprayed surface, whether they are harmful or beneficial predators, e.g. ladybirds. Systemic fungicides attack fungi that enter plant cells, which contact sprays cannot do. Further, contact sprays of either kind may miss some parts of a plant, and can be washed off by rain or watering; in theory, systemics reach every part of a plant. However, they do vary in their capacity to move around in the sap, and one chemical may vary in this capacity according to the plant concerned.

Systemics are theoretically ideal materials for killing pests and destroying fungi. However, some are poisonous to warm-blooded creatures including ourselves, and care must be taken to wait for the specified period until they decompose before eating sprayed crops: it is obviously impossible to remove them by washing.

In theory, systemics can be watered onto the soil around plant roots and will then be absorbed. Because of the varying capacity for movement within a plant already mentioned, it is usually best to apply systemics as a spray, although there are some pesti-cides available in 'stick' or pellet form which are pushed into the soil around plants and are absorbed via the roots, and others in granule form which are sprinkled onto the soil surface and dissolve during watering.

As well as systemic pesticides and fungi-cides, there are some systemic weedkillers which cause the death of plants after entering the plant's sap. These, more often known as translocated weedkillers, have the special merit of being inactivated when they touch the soil so that they cannot harm plants put in later, nor have any effect on animals.

◊ CONTACT; FUNGICIDES; PESTICIDE; PREDATORS; WEEDKILLER.

T

Take (1) The commonest horticultural meaning of 'take' is the same as 'strike' or 'root' – a cutting is said to have 'taken' when it has successfully formed roots and is growing away satisfactorily. ◊ STRIKE.

(2) Chrysanthemum growers sometimes speak of 'taking' the bud which they wish to retain, which is in fact carried out by the removal of all surplus buds and growths. In fact 'taking' a chrysanthemum bud is best described as DISBUDDING.

Tally The original word for a plant label. Older tallies resembled those used for recording debts: they were squared wooden pegs in which notches corresponding to Roman numerals were made. Not till the nineteenth century did the various modern types of plant label appear. ◊ LABEL.

Tamping ◊ FIRMING.

Tang An old word for the prong or tine of a fork; today more often refers to the extension of a metal tool such as a scythe or chisel, by which it is secured to its handle.

Tapis-vert Though basically meaning an expanse of turf (the literal translation being 'green carpet'), this expression has also been used to describe geometrical parterre-like designs executed in dwarf box.

Tap Root Any strong root growing more or less vertically downwards is called a tap root, though this term is sometimes held to apply only to the first undivided root of a seedling. Plants which normally make tap roots are usually deep feeders as opposed to those surface feeders which have laterally branching roots. Tap roots are presumably so called because they tap deep levels of water.

In some cases the tap root becomes swollen as a food reserve; some of this type are vegetables prized for their edible tap roots, e.g. carrots, parsnips and scorzonera; others, e.g. dandelions and dock, are detested because their tap roots are too easily broken off and can sprout again from the piece left in the soil. Some gardeners believe it desirable to break the tap roots of brassicas, wallflowers and related plants by early transplanting, so as to make them produce branching roots; and tradition suggests also the removal of tap roots of unfruitful fruit trees, though whether there is any actual connection between lush unfruitful growth and the presence of a tap root is open to doubt. Certain trees habitually produce tap roots, notably conifers.

Tar Coal tar, obtained by the destructive distillation of coal, is seldom used in the garden except as a wood preservative; it should not come into contact with plants. Distillates from the various kinds of tar are used as winter washes, sterilizers, etc., and to treat twine.

The word tar is also applied to natural substances resembling tar, such as asphalt, bitumen and petroleum oil. Stockholm tar is a resinous substance obtained from pine trees, sometimes recommended as a wound dressing.

◊ entries below prefixed by TAR; ASPHALT; BITUMEN; COAL TAR; STOCKHOLM TAR; WOUND DRESSINGS.

Tar Disks At one time widely used to deter cabbage root fly, these are 3″ disks of tarred felt with a radial slit leading to a small central hole; they are fitted onto the stem of a brassica seedling and pushed down to soil level. ◊ ROOT FLIES.

Tar Oil Wash Tar distillates containing phenols, formulated for spraying. Such washes must be used only in winter (and hence are often called winter washes) and only on deciduous trees as they will scorch foliage severely. They are mainly used on fruit trees, but can also be applied to roses and other deciduous ornamental trees and shrubs. Their main use is to destroy over-wintering insect eggs, especially those of aphids; they also control scale insects, mealy bugs, hibernating caterpillars and other larvae, and destroy algae, lichens and mosses on the bark. Grass under fruit trees, etc., may be scorched and turn brown, but it usually recovers quickly.

A special formulation of tar oil is used to destroy moss and speedwell (veronica) in lawns.

Tar oil wash can also be used to clear lichens, liverworts, moss, and film-forming algae from paths, roofs and walks, and to sterilize and clean up glass, staging and structures of frames and greenhouses (the latter should be emptied of plants before treatment).

◊ DNC; PETROLEUM OIL.

Tarred Fillis or Twine Garden string which has been steeped in a tar distillate to in-crease its life.

Tarsonemid Mites ◊ MITES.

Taxon Any classificatory unit or level such as a family, genus or species. ◊ CLASSIFI-CATION.

Taxonomy Classification and its study; hence taxonomist, one who studies the sub-ject. ◊ CLASSIFICATION.

Teeth ◊ TOOTH.

Temperate Refers to the temperate clima-tic zones of the world as opposed to the sub-tropical and tropical, and hence to plants found in such zones. The word may be qualified as cold- or warm-temperate. A temperate house is a greenhouse main-tained at a minimum winter temperature of 4–5°C (40°F).

Temperature The gardener needs to be aware of temperature on many occasions, especially when dealing with tender plants, growing plants in greenhouses or rooms,

and in propagation. This is because plants vary greatly in their preferred temperature range according to their geographical ori-gin, and will not thrive, or may even die, if subjected to temperatures above, and especially below, this range. To describe plants as hardy or tender means that they will or will not survive at average minimum outside temperatures at the locality con-cerned: these terms are always relative to the localities and their climatic zones. However, many tender plants will survive outside during the warm season in climates cooler than their native ones, as long as they are brought into artificially warmer temperatures when the outside tempera-ture drops too low. Thus plants from temperate regions will grow rapidly in tem-peratures from 10–21°C (50–70°F), and those from sub-tropical and tropical regions from 18–27°C (65–80°F). At the lower end of these ranges, growth ceases; and at some point below these lower tem-peratures the plants can be killed. Plants from cold-temperate zones will withstand frost in varying degree.

Temperature is also a vital consideration when growing plants from seed or cuttings. Again depending largely on the plant's origin, there is a minimum temperature below which its seeds will not germinate. Cuttings usually need some warmth to produce roots, though this depends on both the type of plant and the type of cutting. In many cases propagation may be speeded up by keeping the soil warm as well as the air.

Many plants are more liable to injury from cold when young, therefore plants of borderline hardiness in a particular locality should be given winter protection, at least for the first few years. Alternatively, they can be gradually acclimatized to colder conditions by spending periods in a cold greenhouse and a shelter such as a lath house. Tender plants grown from seed or cuttings for summer display in cold-temperate areas are normally acclimatized over a relatively short time by a transi-tional period in a cold greenhouse or frame: this is called hardening off.

Plants can be damaged by excessively

327

high temperatures, especially under glass and in bright sunlight. Such damage can be prevented by damping down, shading and ventilation.

Temperature is measured on various types of thermometer.

♢ ACCLIMATIZATION; BOTTOM HEAT; DAMPING DOWN; FRAME; HARDENING OFF; HARDY; LATH HOUSE; SHADE; SUB-TROPICAL; TEMPERATE; TENDER; THERMO-METER; TROPICAL; VENTILATION.

Temples Mock temples in classical style were an important feature in eighteenth- and nineteenth-century landscape gardens, and a great many can still be seen in British gardens dating from that era. Most of these are fairly imposing structures of stone, almost invariably featuring columns and often housing statuary.

Tender Refers to plants liable to injury or death in cold conditions, or if grown outside in cold-temperate zones. This is a relative term, depending on the latitude; its opposite is 'hardy'. ♢ HARDY; TEMPERA-TURE.

Tendril An organ by which a climbing plant may fix itself in place. The simplest are thread-like: they circle in the air until they meet a support, then they coil tightly around it in a spiral, e.g. gourds and passion-flowers. Some thread-like tendrils are branched, e.g. vines and garden peas. More complex tendrils have branches which end in little adhesive suckers which will fasten onto a solid surface, as in Virginia creepers. Botanically, tendrils are modified leaves or leaflets, or modified shoots. ♢ CLIMBER; PETIOLE.

Tent Caterpillars ♢ CATERPILLARS.

Tepal When flowers have inner and outer segments which appear the same and can-not be described as petals or sepals, these are called tepals. Many monocotyledons have flowers with tepals, e.g. crocus, hip-peastrum, lily and tulip. ♢ FLOWER.

Teratology The study of abnormalities or monstrosities in plants (as in animals). ♢ CRISTATE; FASCIATION; HOSE-IN-HOSE; MONSTROUS; PETALODY; PROLIFERATION.

Terminal Frequently used to refer to the uppermost, and usually central, bud, flower or growth on a stem, or a final central leaflet. It is often important, espe-cially when growing flowers for show, to retain only the terminal bud and to remove the subsidiary or lateral buds. ♢ DIS-BUDDING.

Ternate Having three leaflets. ♢ LEAF.

TENDRIL. *Left to right*, clematis; Virginia creeper; white bryony; bush vetch

Terrace, Terracing In its original sense, a terrace was a flat area raised above the main ground level; today, the word is used of any level area treated formally as by paving, and often separated from the rest of the garden by a balustrade or low wall. Nowadays, the word 'patio' is often misused to mean such paved areas. Such terraces are usually adjacent to the dwelling, creating an open-air leisure area for sitting out, a transition between the house and garden.

A terrace is also a flat level created artificially on a slope; there are many large gardens in which steep slopes have been terraced to excellent effect. Growing plants is made much easier by terracing, while the balustrades and supporting walls provide extra features both in the design and as homes for plants.

Terraces of both kinds have been an important part of gardens since ancient times. Early Egyptian gardens, many Roman gardens, and also early Renaissance ones might be considered to consist almost entirely of terracing, which sometimes included terraced walks away from the house. Capability Brown and his followers banished the terrace, their aim being to bring the landscaped lawns right up to the walls of the house.

When terracing a slope, it is usually desirable to remove the topsoil and stack it elsewhere, so that it can be spread over the levelled ground at the last stage of the operation. Terraces on a slope are normally supported by retaining walls of stone which can be either of dry blocks or cemented.

⟡ DECK; DRY WALL; LEVELLING; PATIO; WALLS.

Terrarium Originally an enclosure for keeping small animals, this word has been extended, especially in the U.S., to mean a small glazed container for growing plants indoors. In Britain this is normally referred to as a WARDIAN CASE.

Terrestrial Defines plants which grow in soil as opposed to water (aquatics) and especially in contrast to those growing on trees, rocks, etc. (epiphytes). The families most involved are the BROMELIADS and ORCHIDS.

Tessellated Chequered: applied to petals and leaves with a pattern of square blocks of one colour on a different background.

TESSELLATED (*Fritillaria meleagris*)

Testa The outer coat of a seed, which is often hard and brittle. ⟡ CHIPPING.

Tetraploid Most plants have two sets of chromosomes, which are the microscopic

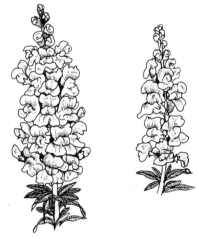

TETRAPLOID. Tetraploid antirrhinum compared with normal type

329

character-controlling bodies in the cell nuclei, and such plants are known as diploids to the plant breeder. Variations in this number occur for various reasons. When four sets occur, which may be due to a natural mutation or to artificial treatment as with radiation or colchicine, the plant is described as a tetraploid. Such plants very often have greatly increased vigour. ◊ CHROMOSOME; SPORT.

The Death ◊ WIND-ROCKING.

Thermometer An instrument for measuring temperature, of value especially to greenhouse gardeners where it is essential to keep the temperature between certain limits, and also to growers of house plants. The basic thermometer is a simple tube in which mercury rises and falls according to temperature which is read off on a graduated scale. Much more useful to the gardener is the maximum/minimum thermometer with a U-shaped tube, in which the mercury pushes up a small marker which is left in place after the temperature rises from its minimum or falls from its maximum in a given period. The markers can be returned to the tops of the mercury columns with a magnet or, in more modern versions, by a push-button re-setting device. Dial thermometers can also be obtained, including the maximum/minimum type.

Another type of thermometer is the wet and dry bulb, which has two separate columns. The bulb of the 'wet' column is kept moist by a wick which dips into a reservoir. From the difference in readings of the two columns, the use of a table indicates the relative humidity of the air. A variant of this instrument is used for frost prediction.

Soil thermometers can also be obtained, with either mercury or dial scales reading up to 115°C (240°F). They are pushed into soil to ascertain temperature during sterilizing, making mushroom beds or checking bottom heat. ◊ BOTTOM HEAT; HYGROMETER; TEMPERATURE.

Thermostat A device for regulating temperature, applied to heating systems for greenhouses, propagators, etc. Many heating appliances are supplied with built-in thermostats, but separate thermostats can be obtained for use with electrical heating: these are usually in the form of a short rod. ◊ HEATING.

Thinning Commonly, the reduction of the number of plants in a bed, box or other place, so as to allow those which remain plenty of space and prevent all the plants becoming spindly and weak. Thinning is essential with seedlings of all kinds, unless sown singly, especially when the plants are to mature where sown; it should be carried out at the earliest possible moment that the seedlings are large enough to handle. Early thinning also helps to ensure that the remaining plants are disturbed as little as possible. Thinning is usually carried out by hand, but may be done with a hoe. It is also known as singling.

Thinning on a different scale is sometimes carried out in orchards and forest plantations: as the trees grow, alternate trees, known as fillers, are removed after some years. Such tree thinning may also be carried out as required in woodland gardens.

Thinning of shoots is necessary to obtain best results with vigorous perennials, and thinning branches on fruit and ornamental trees may be desirable if they become overcrowded. This is often called thinning out. Thinning is also important with many kinds of fruit, to prevent over-cropping and, more especially, to produce fruits of good size which will not be misshapen by pressing on each other in the cluster. Grapes should likewise be thinned as they mature, for which vine scissors are used. ◊ SEED SOWING; WOODLAND GARDEN.

Thorn A sharp woody outgrowth which is part of the woody structure of a plant. For full definition ◊ SPINE.

Thrips (singular and plural) A group of insect pests, usually less than $\frac{1}{16}''$ long, looking like minute earwigs. Colour ranges from yellow to black; the young are wingless, the adult winged. They attack plant surfaces and suck the sap. Because they are so small, each insect causes little damage but, in mass, they cause a characteristic, often whitish or reddish speckling or mottling of leaves, petals or pods (as on peas) often accompanied by distortion, while attacked flower buds turn brown and never open. Thrips are also known as thunderbugs or thunderflies, referring to their preference for hot weather. Under glass, they can be deterred by regular damping down and the spraying of foliage with clear water, but fumigation with an appropriate insecticide is the best control. In the garden, spraying with insecticide can be carried out.

Throat The inner portion of the corolla of a bell-, trumpet- or tube-shaped flower. ◊ FLOWER; MOUTH.

Through-feed ◊ HOSE REELS.

Thyrse A type of flower cluster. ◊ INFLORESCENCE.

Till, Tillage An ancient verb and noun meaning cultivate and cultivation, by any means. ◊ CULTIVATION; CULTIVATOR; DIGGING.

Tiller A word of ancient origin meaning a shoot or sucker arising from the roots or base of a plant, applied in particular to basal side shoots of grass, wheat and similar plants; hence the adjective 'tillering'. Sometimes loosely used of runners. ◊ RUNNER; SUCKER.

Tilth, Tilthing Originally meaning an act of cultivation, and land under cultivation, the gardener now uses tilth to refer to the crumbly texture of soil produced by good cultivation. 'Good tilth' implies especially that the surface of the soil is finely broken down and is suitable for seed sowing. This is the product of digging and ridging, application of bulky organic materials, breaking the soil down with a fork and finally careful raking. This process is sometimes called tilthing. ◊ CRUMB; CULTIVATION.

Tilther ◊ SOIL MILLER.

Tine Each individual prong, spike or tooth on a cultivating tool such as a fork, rake or harrow. Digging forks may have flat or round tines; a special type, known as a hollow-tine fork, has hollow, round prongs with a slit on one surface, and is used for aerating lawns: the soil is pushed out of the slits on each successive insertion of the fork. The blades of rotary cultivating tools are sometimes loosely called tines. ◊ CULTIVATOR; FORK; RAKE; SPIKING.

Tip-bearer A few cultivars of fruit tree, notably the apple Worcester Pearmain, produce fruit buds mainly on the tips of one-year-old (and older) shoots, and are known as tip-bearers. Such varieties are therefore not very suitable for growing in strictly trained forms, e.g. cordons or espaliers, as the pruning which is normally employed to produce spurs would remove all the fruit buds.

Tip-layering ◊ LAYERING.

Tipping Pruning off the top of a shoot; often used specifically of light pruning of tree leaders. ◊ LEADER.

Toadstool ◊ FAIRY RING; FUNGUS.

Tobacco ◊ NICOTINE.

Toggle Lopper A tree lopper with a double pivot, producing extra leverage and allowing extra-thick branches to be cut. ◊ SHEARS.

Tolerant Applied to plants which are tolerant of certain minerals in the soil, e.g. lime-tolerant; also to plants which show no disease symptoms when infected. Thus certain strawberries are virus-tolerant; although this may seem desirable to the gardener, aphid attacks on such plants can spread the disease to other varieties. ◊ IMMUNE.

Tomentose, Tomentum Tomentose means covered with dense soft hairs giving a

331

woolly, cottony or felted appearance. It is often used rather loosely to refer to woolly plants in general, but tomentum specifically implies a covering of dense *short* hairs. ▷ HAIRY.

Tongue Graft The same as a whip and tongue graft. ▷ GRAFTING.

Tooth, Toothed A tooth is any small marginal lobe, as on a leaf, calyx or corolla. Many leaves are more or less toothed at the edges, and the shape and size of the teeth are often useful for identification. The Latin equivalent to toothed is dentate, and usually refers botanically to regular divisions. When angled like the teeth of a circular saw, the divisions are called serrate; when there are small teeth on the main ones, this is called doubly serrate or biserrate. Crenate refers to rounded teeth. The terms serrulate and crenulate indicate leaves with small sharp or rounded teeth. ▷ LEAF.

Top A fruit tree form of top-shaped outline in which the branches are arranged in three tiers, with the lowest at 30° to the trunk, the middle ones at 45° and the upper ones nearly horizontal. These angles are achieved by tying in the branches during the formative period. It was at one time favoured for pears, but is now less often seen.

Top Draining The use of shallow channels or ditches to drain off surface water. ▷ DRAINAGE.

Top Dressing Any dressing of fertilizer, manure or other organic matter, or inert material, e.g. sand, applied to the soil surface without cultivation or disturbance of plant roots. ▷ DRESSING.

Top Fruit Fruit produced on trees, including apples, cherries, peaches, pears and plums; also refers to the trees themselves. A word used in contrast to bush fruits, e.g. currants and gooseberries.

Topiary The very ancient art – first prac-

tised by the Romans over 2000 years ago – of clipping and training shrubs and trees into all kinds of shapes, from more complicated hedges to single specimens representing cones, balls, pyramids, peacocks, and other birds and beasts. The great era of topiary in Britain was the seventeenth century, though it had been practised in Europe since the Renaissance. Many plants can be used for topiary, the favourites being yew and box. Shaping should if possible begin when the plants are young, and is carried out by trimming with shears or secateurs and also by tying selected young growths into position, until they are stout enough to retain the position required on their own. In complex specimens a wire frame must be used, which remains in place but becomes completely concealed as the specimen matures. In the U.S. where the usual topiary evergreens do not always grow well owing to climatic conditions, comparable shapes are often formed by growing ivy over carefully sculpted wire frames, though whether this deserves the name topiary is open to question.

Topping The same as stopping, i.e. the removal of a plant's growing tip; but more often used when this removal is not in order to induce growth of side shoots but for some other purpose. Thus tomatoes may be topped towards the end of summer to prevent the production of any further flower trusses, and broad beans to remove infestations of black fly on the soft growing tips. ▷ STOPPING.

Topple Another word for PEDICEL NECROSIS.

Topsoil The uppermost layer of soil which, under normal conditions, is reasonably fertile and readily improved by cultivation, in contrast to the subsoil which is often infertile or quite unsuitable for cultivation. The depth of topsoil can vary considerably. Topsoil should always be conserved if possible during any constructional operations such as levelling, and every effort made not to spread subsoil over topsoil, as is regrettably so often done by builders excavating house foundations. ⟡ DIG-GING; LEVELLING; SUBSOIL.

Topworking ⟡ REWORKING.

Tortrix Moths A group of small moths whose caterpillars are leaf-rollers. ⟡ CATERPILLARS.

Total Weedkiller A weedkiller which destroys any plant with which it comes into contact. ⟡ WEEDKILLER.

Town Refuse Material sometimes offered as an organic manure by local authorities, originating from street sweepings and dustbin contents. Obviously such material is extremely variable and its value to the gardener depends on the processing carried out by the local authority. This should involve removal of unsuitable substances and composting, which is sometimes done with the addition of sewage sludge or slaughterhouse refuse. At best, town refuse is slow acting but it should have a beneficial effect on soil texture, if dug in at around 1 cwt. to 15–45 square yards. Its plant food content is low though it may include some trace elements; it is also likely to contain a fairly high level of calcium carbonate.

Toxic Poisonous; in gardening, most often used as a warning that pest, disease and weed control materials are harmful to humans, pets, fish, bees, etc., if not applied with due care. ⟡ GARDEN CHEMICALS.

Trace Elements Elements essential to plant growth but needed only in minute quantities or traces, in contrast to the major elements nitrogen, phosphorus and potassium. The most important trace elements are boron, copper, iron, manganese, molybdenum and zinc. Their absence may cause deficiency symptoms and poor growth; excesses can also be harmful, as when water used in a garden is contaminated by mining spoil heaps, factory effluents or sometimes natural deposits. ⟡ DEFICIENCY; FEEDING PLANTS.

Trailing Used of plants which naturally have stems that grow along the soil surface, usually rooting as they do so. Such plants can be used decoratively to good effect to spill downwards at the edges of containers or from hanging baskets. In some cases plants which are naturally climbers can be used for this purpose, e.g. ivies and philodendrons.

Trained Trees A phrase almost entirely restricted to fruit trees trained into desired forms, and more often used of the formally trained such as cordon, espalier and fan. For further methods of fruit training ⟡ FRUIT CULTURE, PRUNING AND TRAINING. Also ⟡ TRAINING.

Training The management of plants to make them grow in a desired form or direction. This is achieved by pruning in the case of fruit tree forms and of ornamental trees and shrubs as when grown against walls, accompanied (where required) by tying onto supports, at least in the formative years. Formal hedges are a kind of training, and topiary a more advanced one. Bonsai is a highly specialized example. All these are achieved by pruning or trimming. Climbing plants are trained to or upon supports mainly by tying in place, and removal of unwanted growths and encouragement of well-placed ones. ⟡ BONSAI; CLIMBER; FRUIT CULTURE, PRUNING AND TRAINING; HEDGE; PRUNING; TOPIARY.

Translocated Of weedkillers which, when applied to plant foliage or roots, move within the plant and finally destroy it; less often of systemic pesticides and fungicides which move in the same way. This occurs by the natural process of translocation. ⟡ SYSTEMIC; VASCULAR SYSTEM; WEED-KILLER.

Translocation The natural processes whereby water, foodstuffs and hormones move within a plant in the vascular system, in particular the phloem. For a fuller account ⟡ VASCULAR SYSTEM.

Transpiration Loss of water from plant foliage, mainly via the breathing pores or stomata. Transpiration, which is equivalent to evaporation, is an essential part of photosynthesis, and is accentuated in warm weather, when plants may transpire up to 99 per cent of the water they take in at the roots. This causes wilting or flagging of plants in dry, hot periods which, if allowed to continue, results in the plant's death. Potted plants with their limited root systems are especially liable to wilting. Succulent and xerophytic plants have methods of avoiding or, at any rate, greatly delaying wilting.

Water loss due to transpiration can be made up by adequate watering, and the rate of transpiration reduced by increasing air humidity. This last is of practical value only in a greenhouse or similar structure where damping down to produce a humid atmosphere should be carried out in hot weather, sometimes combined with a reduction in ventilation for plants which need very close conditions, e.g. greenhouse cucumbers. Another method of reducing transpiration, which is used on evergreens after transplanting when their root systems may be unable to take up enough water, is the application of an anti-transpirant spray.

◊ ANTI-TRANSPIRANT; DAMPING DOWN; HUMIDITY; OEDEMA; OSMOSIS; PHOTOSYNTHESIS; SUCCULENT; WILTING; XEROPHYTE.

Transplanter A word applied from the sixteenth to nineteenth centuries to devices for moving small plants with minimum disturbance. These were in the form of a metal tube with a division down one side, hasps to hold it together, and a pull-out securing pin. A transplanter pushed down around the plant allowed the operator to lift it out, roots and all, for replacement in a previously prepared hole elsewhere. Such devices, also known as 'grooves' or 'displanters', were replaced in the nineteenth century by versions in which two halves of a tube were held together and then opened apart by handles. Transplanters of this type are now out of fashion and the principle is only used for planting potato tubers and bulbs. The word 'transplanter' was also sometimes used in the nineteenth century for various devices and systems for lifting and moving large trees. ◊ BULB PLANTER; POTATO PLANTER; TROWEL.

Transplanting The moving of a plant from one position to another, carried out for various reasons. The planting of plants newly acquired from a nursery or garden centre is a form of transplanting. The term is more often used to refer to young plants grown from seed or cuttings being moved either into permanent quarters, or to a larger container or nursery bed. Transplanting is also carried out in nurseries to keep plant roots compact, so that when sent to the customer there will be the minimum check to growth. Such nursery transplanting, which is usually done annually on trees and shrubs, prevents any long straggling roots from developing. The treatment of a transplanted plant is described under PLANTING. ◊ WRENCHING.

Transplanting Spray ◊ ANTI-TRANSPIR-ANT.

Traps The gardener can obtain mechanical traps against mice, moles and rats if needed. On the Continent, bird traps in a range of sizes are available to gardeners. Other kinds of trap are used by gardeners against insects. The simplest is a hollow cane or similar tube in which earwigs and small beetles will take refuge; earwigs can also be caught in an up-ended flower pot placed on the end of a cane and stuffed with straw. Corrugated cardboard tied around plant stems will also attract earwigs, weevils, etc. Slugs, wireworms, woodlice and pests with similar habits can be trapped with pieces of vegetable (potato, carrot) placed in suitable positions and examined regularly. Wingless female winter moths on fruit trees are trapped by grease applied, or hay or sacking tied, to bands of paper fixed round tree trunks. Wasps attacking ripening fruit may be trapped in jars containing sweetened water hung in the fruit trees. ◊ GREASE BANDING; TREE BANDING.

Trays Various types are used by gardeners. A seed tray, of wood or plastic, is the same as a seed box, seed pan or flat (U.S.). Metal or plastic trays can be used on greenhouse staging or indoors to retain sand, gravel, etc., on which pot plants are stood and to which water is added to provide a moist atmosphere. Long narrow plastic trays can be obtained on which to stand plant troughs used indoors. Fruit can be stored in wooden trays like those, often seen in greengrocers', which have a projecting wooden upright at each corner so that the trays can be stacked one above the other without pressing on the contents, and allowing air to circulate. ◊ SEED BOX; STORAGE.

Tread (1) The horizontal component of a step. ◊ STEPS.

(2) The upper part of the blade of a digging fork or spade upon which the foot is placed to force the tool into the ground. In spades, this is sometimes enlarged into a narrow flat surface along the top of the blade to spread the force of the foot and to reduce damage to footwear.

Treading The act of firming soil with the feet, carried out for two main purposes. After setting plants of any size into the soil, especially trees and shrubs, it ensures that the soil is in good contact with the roots, with no large air spaces left in it, and that anchorage is as good as possible. Secondly, newly prepared seed beds can be trodden before seed sowing, again to ensure no air pockets, that the soil will not settle unevenly, and also to help moisture rise in the soil by capillary attraction. This kind of treading is carried out by placing the feet together and advancing in a kind of shuffle. Some gardeners carry out the same exercise after sowing seeds, placing the feet on either side of the seed drill, but this may compact the soil too much for even germination. Such treading should in any case only be carried out when the soil is in a medium-moist condition: if too wet it will stick to the shoes and, if too dry, consolidation cannot occur. ◊ PLANTING; SEED SOWING.

Tree A woody plant with a well-defined main stem or trunk, as compared with a shrub with many stems, though the borderline between small trees and large shrubs is not always clear. Trees include conifers and other evergreens, and broad-leaved deciduous kinds. ◊ Entries below prefixed by TREE; SHRUB.

Tree Banding The placing of bands around tree trunks to trap insects. One type consists of a band of paper which is coated with grease, another of hay or sacking tied to the trunk. Various insects pupate or hibernate in the latter type, which must be periodically removed and burnt. Known as barrier banding in the U.S. ◊ GREASE BANDING; HAY BAND.

Tree Bark Protector ◊ TREE GUARDS.

Tree Guards Devices and constructions to protect trees from attack by animals likely to gnaw the bark. Guards against deer and cattle, as used in parks and large estates, may take the form of a small enclosure of metal or wood uprights joined together by metal or wire horizontals. Such supports can also be fixed close to the trunk. If cattle are the problem, any support must be strong enough to stand up to their rubbing, and be firmly fixed into the ground. In ordinary gardens where gnawing of the bark by rabbits, deer, etc., is common, fairly fine wire netting can be placed around the trunk, preferably at a little distance from it. A modern type of proprietary tree guard is made of perforated plastic tube which is wound closely round the base of the trunk. This is especially valuable for young trees. ◊ REPELLENTS.

Tree House Seats, platforms, balconies and full-blown houses made in trees used to be popular in many parts of the world, including Japan, Persia and India, as well as Europe and Britain, where such structures were called roosts. Renaissance gardens in Italy were famed for their tree seats and balconies. One old example still exists in Britain; otherwise the tree house seems to have been largely neglected by modern gar-

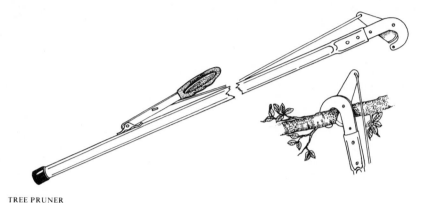

TREE PRUNER

deners, except for children, though some enterprising American designers have built platforms or 'decks' surrounding trees at their base or among the crowns of surrounding trees, leading off an appropriate level of the associated house. ◊ DECK.

Tree Pruners A term usually restricted to long-handled devices for pruning the upper parts of trees from ground level. In these a stout movable blade moving against a fixed one is operated by a remote-control handle through a stiff wire. Handles are often made in sections so that operational lengths of, say, 6′ or 9′ can be assembled. The longest tree pruners are around 14′. Thin curved saws on similar extensible handles (polesaws), can be obtained, or fitted on the end of a tree pruner. In the nineteenth century these were called averruncators. It is also possible to obtain short-handled pruners, or lopping shears, with similar blade action, but these are of course for use within arms' reach of the ground. ◊ SHEARS.

Tree Stumps Ideally, a tree stump should be removed when the tree is felled by making the felling cut at least 3′ up so that the stump left provides sufficient leverage for a winch to draw it out, if necessary after severing the largest roots by exposing them and sawing or chopping through.

However, it is so much less convenient to make the felling cut high up that a low stump is usually left, to become an eyesore and sometimes capable of infecting healthy trees with fungus disease, e.g. honey fungus.

To get rid of stumps a machine operated by contractors called a stump gobbler exists by which stumps are chewed up into fragments by a system of rapidly revolving toothed, sharpened chains.

Otherwise the tree stump can be made inflammable over a period and then destroyed by burning. This is done by boring a number of holes $1\frac{1}{2}''$ deep, 2″ apart, all over the surface of the stump, filling these with a strong solution of saltpetre (nitrate of potash), and sealing them with clay. This will first of all kill the tissues and prevent any sprouting from the trunk. After about six months, the wood should be dry: a fire is lit on the stump and should slowly burn down through it.

Other methods of preventing regrowth are to spray the exposed wood of the stump and the bark, especially near soil level, with brushwood killer or ammonium sulphamate solution.

Tree Surgery A term usually confined to the treatment of wounds due to branch breakage and to the removal of larger branches not covered by ordinary detail pruning. Such surgery may be to remove damaged branches or, more often, those which are crowding the centre, crossing and rubbing others. When cutting branches of any size, a preliminary undercut should prevent the tearing of bark caused by the weight of the branch if cut from the upper side only. It is best to trim any such branches level with the trunk, using a sharp knife to pare any rough edges. The same treatment should be given to wounds caused by accidental damage, insects or diseases, in all cases paring down to healthy tissue. Cuts of any extent should be treated with a tree wound dressing.

When there are cavities of any size, it is again necessary to remove all decayed and damaged wood, treat with a wound dressing or other antiseptic, e.g. creosote, and fill with an inert material. Concrete is often used, but many foresters prefer a mixture of sawdust and bitumen, or polystyrene sealed in with bitumen. The edges of the cavity should then be treated with a wound dressing.

Large trees needing attention are best left to professional tree surgeons trained to meet the hazards.

    ◊ CALLUS; SAW; STUB; WOUND DRESS-INGS.

Tree Ties Modern proprietary devices for securing trees to a stake and consisting of a plastic strap which is looped round the trunk, through a central constricting band, and then round the stake where it is secured

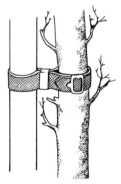

TREE TIE

with a buckle. These admirable ties readily allow adjustment for the increasing girth of the trunk and do not chafe the bark. ◊ SUPPORT.

Tree Wound Compounds ◊ WOUND DRESS-INGS.

Treillage Literally, the French word for trellis, but applied by writers on garden design to structures made of trellis, such as arbours, columns, domes and even entire garden houses and temples. ◊ TRELLIS.

Trellis A construction of light wooden or metal bars crossing each other at intervals, and fixed at each crossing point, to create a regular square or diamond-shaped pattern. Trellis has been used for garden decoration at least since Roman times, and was popular in the Middle Ages. Today, ready-made trellis of roughly 4″ mesh is available in panels of various sizes, made of wood or plastic. Metal trellis is seen in only a few historic gardens, though iron was quite often used to provide the necessary internal support for elaborate wooden trellis-work or treillage.

Trellis is valuable in the garden to create free-standing divisions or to provide a visually attractive support for climbing plants against a wall. It is relatively flimsy so needs strong vertical supports every 6′ if used free-standing. Against a wall it should be fastened with spacers – old cotton-reels are ideal – to keep it an inch or so away. Screws and wallplugs are the best fasteners.

The word is also applied to some pre-fabricated modern structures of metal wire which are formed into rectangular or fan-shaped panels.

    ◊ FENCES; SUPPORT; TREILLAGE.

Trench A vertical-sided furrow or trough made in soil with a draw hoe or, for greater depths, a spade. Trenches are sometimes recommended for various vegetable crops, notably celery and leeks which are normally blanched for part of their length.

337

Deep trenches are made for runner beans and sweet peas, to be filled with rich organic matter as an initial root run. This is not advisable on heavy soils where the trench can easily become a sump for excess rainwater which will damage roots. Plants to be grown under cloches, e.g. tomatoes, may be grown in a trench to give a little extra headroom before the cloches need removing. Planting in trenches can also be carried out with crops planted in summer, especially on light soils, since the trench is easily flooded with water in dry spells. A related method of supplying water is to prepare shallow irrigation trenches around particularly thirsty plants, which are filled with water when needed and can be covered with straw to reduce evaporation.

To trench soil is the same as trenching. ⟡ DIGGING.

Trenching A method of cultivating soil to three spits deep. ⟡ DIGGING.

Tribe A classificatory term; subsidiary to a family which groups together a number of genera. ⟡ CLASSIFICATION.

Trickle Irrigation ⟡ IRRIGATION.

Trifoliate Of leaves divided into three leaflets. ⟡ LEAF.

Trim To cut or clip neatly and regularly; usually applied to hedges, topiary and lawns.

Trimming Knife Another term used for a PRUNING KNIFE.

Triple Superphosphate ⟡ SUPERPHOSPHATE OF LIME.

Triploid A plant with three sets of chromosomes in the cell nuclei. Such plants may have larger flowers, fruit or other parts in comparison with normal diploids which have two sets of chromosomes. However, when the nuclei of the sex cells divide they do so unevenly, and are frequently more or less sterile, both as to setting seed and the production of fertile pollen. With fruit, e.g. in the case of Bramley and Blenheim Orange apples, at least one other variety must be planted to ensure pollination of the triploid. ⟡ CHROMOSOME; FERTILITY RULES; POLLINATION.

Trompe-l'œil Literally, 'deceive the eye'; deception or illusion. In gardens *trompe-l'œil* can take many forms. Small Roman gardens might have walls painted with frescoes of flowers, trees and birds to give the illusion of greater depth. A classic *trompe-l'œil* device of the landscape gardener is the ha-ha or sunken fence which suggests that the garden continues indefinitely into the landscape. Landscapers also had methods of planting the distant end of lakes to make them seem to continue indefinitely. False bridges are used for the same purpose, as well as being focal points. Water at the lowest level can be used to make high ground appear higher. A hedge can be made to appear shorter by increasing its height from the viewpoint to its distant end, or longer by the reverse process. Another way of increasing apparent length is to set out relatively short hedges or borders on either side of a path or stretch of grass, not quite parallel but coming closer together in the distance. In small gardens, trelliswork is sometimes used to give this effect of a receding vista. A very subtle method of simulating greater distance is to plant in shades of green, grading from dark nearby to light in the distance. Mirrors are occasionally used to suggest a doorway or window opening in a blank wall. ⟡ HA-HA.

Tropical Applied to plants originating in the tropics. Such plants mostly need to be cultivated in warm or 'stove' greenhouses in temperatures from 21–27°C (70–80°F) with a winter minimum of 18°C (64°F). Quite a number, however, have proved suitable for growing in dwelling houses. ⟡ GREENHOUSE; HOUSE PLANT; SUBTROPICAL.

Tropism Any movement, or growth, carried out by a plant in response to an external stimulus, the direction of movement or growth being governed by that of the stimulus. Thus phototropism causes plants to bend towards the light, negative phototropism, away from it. Geotropism, or response to the force of gravity, causes roots to grow downwards (positive geotropism) or shoots to grow upwards (negative geotropism). Haptotropism or thigmotropism, a response to contact, is exhibited by plant tendrils once they touch a support. Hydrotropism is a response to water exhibited by roots of seedlings. Chemotropism is response towards specific chemical substances, to be noted mainly among fungi.

Trough Gardens Plantings carried out in old stone farm drinking troughs and household sinks. Such gardens are usually of non-ramping alpines and dwarf conifers, and are often treated like miniature rock gardens by embedding a few small stones in the soil and spreading stone chippings over the remainder. Although it is essential to water the usually shallow troughs regularly in hot dry weather, they must be provided with a drainage hole to release excess water; this should be covered with crocks or a piece of perforated zinc to pre-

vent the soil being washed out. Well drained potting soil should be used. Modern glazed sinks can be given a more natural appearance by covering with hypertufa. ◊ ALPINE; HYPERTUFA; ROCK PLANTS.

Trowel A usually short-handled tool invaluable for planting smallish plants. The traditional trowel has a relatively narrow, short, concave blade, sometimes with a slightly pointed end, sometimes rounded. Variations include trowels with off-centred handles, and other models with long, parallel-sided blades used for planting bulbs or rock plants, and also valuable for digging up plants in the wild. The latter are sometimes called fern trowels and the former bulb trowels; these are often marked with a scale in inches to ensure correct depth of planting holes. The modern trowel can be obtained with a handle 12″–15″ long, but this is more tiring to use than the standard short-handled type.

The modern, basically scoop-shaped trowel is first recorded in 1706. Before that, gardeners used a semicircular trowel with parallel sides; this went on into the nineteenth century and then died out. Such

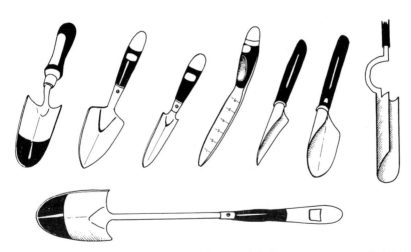

TROWEL. *Left to right,* two traditional patterns; fern trowel; bulb trowel; two patent spiral-bladed trowels; antique semicircular trowel. *Below,* long-handled trowel

trowels were used in conjunction with circular 'transplanters'.

Trowels are used for planting all plants too small to need a spade. For very small seedlings a small dibber may be used; however, the trowel is generally preferable to the dibber because it does not compress the soil, and a hole of exactly the desired size can be excavated in which roots will not be too compressed nor risk dangling in an air pocket. ◊ DIBBER; TRANSPLANTER.

True-breeding Describes plants which, when self-pollinated, give rise to progeny virtually the same as their parent. Such plants are technically called homozygous, in contrast to those which do not breed true and are known as heterozygous or hybrid.

True Lute ◊ LUTE.

Trug A shallow, oblong basket, originally made of overlapping strips of wood, with a curved central handle, but now also available in plastic. Often known as a Sussex trug from its place of origin, it is useful for carrying around tools, small plants, and flowers and vegetables.

Trumpet Describes flowers of tubular form with a flared opening, as in the trumpet vines (campsis). Trumpet daffodils are that class with a trumpet-shaped corona. ◊ CORONA; FLOWER.

Truncate Applied to plant organs which are abruptly truncated, i.e. look as though cut off at the end. ◊ LEAF.

Truncheon A word dating from 1572, now seldom used in gardening, for a thick piece of stem cut from a plant, especially one to be used for grafting or as a cutting.

Trunk The main stem of a tree, woody and bark-covered; also applied to certain lesser plants which develop a thick, hard, more or less woody stem, near or below soil level, as in certain primulas and cyclamens, and to the often long, stout, scaly stems of certain ferns, including tree ferns.

Trunk Slitting An operation occasionally carried out on trees, especially fruit trees, where the bark has become so tough that it effectively prevents any increase in girth and therefore restricts overall growth. It involves scoring vertically down the length of the trunk with a sharp-pointed knife, which should not penetrate into the wood below, and should be done in winter. This slitting permits the trunk to expand. Very occasionally trees will burst their bark as if slit on their own.

Truss A compact cluster of flowers or fruits, arising from one centre. A term first recorded in 1688 and used rather arbitrarily by gardeners. Among flowers, the clusters of auriculas, calceolarias, pelargoniums and rhododendrons are usually referred to as trusses, as are the fruit-clusters of tomatoes. ◊ INFLORESCENCE.

Tube A long, tubular, undivided section of a flower (either calyx or corolla) extending between its base and the expanded lobes or segments, as in crocuses and cacti of the epiphyllum group. Such a tube is in no sense a stem, for the style will pass right down it to the ovary at its base. ◊ FLOWER.

Tuber A thickened or swollen stem or root, usually but not invariably underground, used by the plant for the storage of food during a resting season. Tubers are either stem tubers which carry buds or 'eyes', as in *Anemone coronaria*, begonia, cyclamen and potato; or root tubers which do not, as in the turban buttercups (*Ranunculus asiaticus*) and dahlia. In the latter type growth springs from a crown, the individual tubers being incapable of producing buds. Tubers are occasionally found among succulents, e.g. in *Ceropegia woodii* which forms small tubers on the stems and eventually a larger one at the base.

Tubers have no external coat or tunic as does a corm, nor is the tissue separated into distinct units as in a bulb.

◊ BULB; CORM; CROWN; FLESHY-ROOTED.

TUBER. *Above*, dahlia, *below*, anemone; ranunculus; cyclamen

Tubercle Describes small tubers, especially those found on stems as in *Ceropegia woodii*, and growths such as the bacterial root nodules on leguminous plants. ▷ NITROGEN FIXATION; TUBER.

Tubs Wooden tubs may be used as ornamental plant containers; they can be round or square. Barrels sawn in half make good tubs but many round ones with metal hoops are specifically made for planting. Plant tubs should be of durable wood and preferably be treated with wood preservative inside and painted outside. Drainage holes in the base are essential. ▷ CONTAINER; WOOD PRESERVATIVES.

Tudor Garden Pleasure gardens in Britain became an essential adjunct to palaces, and to houses of any pretension, in Tudor times (1485–1603). Tudor gardens were essentially symmetrical and rather formal, featuring knots, topiary, hedges and pleached trees, as well as mazes, mounts, elaborate waterworks and statuary. They were influenced, at a time-lag of perhaps

fifty years, by Italian Renaissance gardens by way of France and Flanders. ▷ HEDGE; KNOT; MAZE; MOUNT; PLEACH; TOPIARY; WATERWORKS.

Tufa A type of limestone, weathering from a whitish or yellow tone to dark grey, of which the harder kind is used by rock gardeners because it is extremely porous. Plants naturally preferring rock crevices and difficult to grow in soil can be planted in fissures, or holes bored in the tufa, and will thrive as long as the pieces of tufa are kept watered. Large pieces have been used to make rock gardens but shortage of supply usually restricts the use of tufa to a few pieces found in trough gardens or in cold greenhouses for difficult plants. ▷ HYPERTUFA; ROCK GARDEN.

Tulip Fire ▷ FIRE.

Tunic, Tunicated A tunic is a dry covering or coat to a bulb or corm. Tunics are usually brown or blackish, and often papery as in tulips and onions, but may be thick and leathery as in some crocuses. In crocuses the tunics to the corms vary so distinctly that they are used as diagnostic features. Bulbs and corms with tunics are called tunicated. All corms, but not all bulbs, have tunics. ▷ BULB; CORM.

Tunnel Cloche A protective device in which a sheet of clear plastic is stretched over small metal hoops pushed into the ground to form a semicircular tunnel over the plants. ▷ CLOCHE.

Tunnel House A type of greenhouse consisting of a series of large metal hoops over which thick plastic sheet is placed to form a tunnel-shaped structure; mainly used commercially. ▷ GREENHOUSE.

Turf, Turfing The word turf is used in two related senses. One describes any stretch of grass or other meadow-forming plants. The other refers to individual pieces of such grass (turfs or turves; U.S.: sods) cut with about $1\frac{1}{2}''$ of soil and root below the surface, used to make lawns in the process

341

called turfing (U.S.: sodding). It is now quite difficult to obtain weed-free natural turf, and turf specially grown from seed is increasingly being used. Turves are commonly 3′ × 10″ or 12″, and are rolled up like a Swiss roll, soil side outwards, for transport.

Turves are also used for the preparation of loam used in potting compost. In this case any meadow turf, however weedy, is used: the turves, up to 4″ thick, are placed upside-down in rectangular stacks and should be allowed to rot for at least 12 months before use. This produces a rich fibrous loam. The phrase 'turfy loam' is also used for such material.

The word turf is also used of a block of peat dug for use as fuel.
◊ COMPOSTS, SEED AND POTTING; LAWN; PARING BOX.

Turf Beater ◊ BEETLE (2).

Turf Drain ◊ DRAINAGE.

Turfing Iron A tool used for lifting turves for lawn-making after the necessary vertical cuts have been made with an edging knife; known as a sod lifter in the U.S. It has a thin, sharp-edged, heart-shaped blade about 10″ long and 8½″ wide, set at an angle to a long handle, and is pushed in horizontally below the turf to cut it away from the soil below. It is used by professional gardeners and contractors and needs experience to handle properly. ◊ TURF.

Turf Perforator A device for perforating a lawn to improve aeration. ◊ AERATION; SPIKING.

Turf Plugger The name sometimes used in the U.S. for a BULB PLANTER.

Turf Race or Racer ◊ EDGING TOOLS.

Turf Rake ◊ LAWN RAKE.

Turf Seat A feature popular in medieval gardens, when grass was apparently the material most favoured for sitting on out-side. It might consist simply of a grass-covered bank or small mound, or be of soil built up against a wall, supported with planking or stonework, and covered with turf. One or two modern examples have been made, as at Sissinghurst Castle, Kent, where the seat is in fact covered with a very dwarf aromatic thyme.

Turgid Fully charged with water. Plant cells need to be turgid if plants are not to wilt. ◊ WILTING.

Turion A bud originating on subterranean rhizomes and developing in summer into a scaly above-ground shoot, as in asparagus and rhubarb. In some cases the fleshy bud is the only part of the plant that over-winters, as in many water plants where the turions lie in the mud until they grow shoots and roots in spring. ◊ OVER-WINTERING.

Turkish Tent A decorative garden structure usually of canvas supported on a metal framework, popular in the eighteenth and early nineteenth centuries; these tents had vertical or curving sides and a peaked top. A copper example from 1780 exists in Sweden.

Twig A small side-growth from a tree branch. Plants producing twigs in large numbers are said to be of twiggy growth.

Twiner A climbing plant which supports itself by twining tightly round other plants or posts, wires, etc. Bindweed, honeysuckle and runner beans are examples. ◊ CLIMBER.

Tying ◊ SUPPORT.

Type When a wild plant is first described botanically, the technical description should be supplemented by a dried herbarium specimen. Henceforth this is known as the type specimen. It may not necessarily be of the commonest form of the species, but any deviation from the type found later should be given a variety name, even if it is more characteristic of the species as a whole. With rare plants one can also speak of the type locality.

Gardeners may use the word in a looser way when referring to forms of a plant that differ from or improve upon that more commonly grown, which is referred to as the type.

◊ HERBARIUM.

❀ U ❀

U-cordon A cordon formed of two parallel upright or oblique growths, branching near the base. Double U-cordons have four such growths. ◊ CORDON.

Umbel A type of flower head. ◊ INFLORESCENCE.

Umbellifer A member of the family *Umbelliferae* (cow parsley, carrot, etc.) in which the characteristic inflorescence is the umbrella-shaped umbel, though a few genera, notably *Eryngium*, have a fleshy, compact head.

Underplanting Any combination of plants in which low-growing subjects are planted among distinctly taller ones.

Undulate Wavy; usually applied to leaves with wavy margins but also sometimes to petals. The waviness refers to up-and-down undulations, not to in-and-out ones which may be called crenate, sinuate or scalloped. ◊ LEAF.

Unifoliate Of leaves which are simple, having one section only; in contrast to compound. ◊ LEAF.

Union Refers to the point where, on grafted plants, the scion and stock are joined. Where the stock has been chosen to control the vigour of the grafted plant, as in dwarf fruit trees, it is essential to plant with the union at least 4″ above soil level, to avoid any rooting from the scion (scion-rooting) which would override the influence of the stock. In cases where grafting is carried out to speed up multiplication, as in roses and other ornamental shrubs, production of roots by the scion may sometimes be an advantage, and planting with the union at soil level can be carried out. ◊ GRAFTING; SCION-ROOTING.

Unisexual Refers to flowers of one sex only, either with male stamens and no female pistils or vice versa. Occasionally, unisexual flowers appear to be bisexual or hermaphrodite since the organs of the other sex are present but in non-functional or rudimentary form. ◊ FLOWER; SEX.

Urceolate Shaped like an urn or pitcher: of ovoid or short-tubed flowers which are contracted at the mouth. ◊ FLOWER.

Urea An organic chemical which occurs in animal urine and is synthesized as a fertilizer containing 46 per cent nitrogen. It is best used as a liquid feed by adding 1 oz. to 6–7 gallons water, and may be applied as a foliar feed with advantage to plants needing a nitrogen boost.

Ura- or urea-form is a U.S. material produced by combining urea with formaldehyde. The result is an insoluble powder containing up to 36 per cent nitrogen which is applied at 4 oz. per square yard. It is a slow-release material which releases nitrogen throughout the growing season.

◊ FERTILIZER; FOLIAR FEEDING; SLOW-RELEASE; URINE.

Urine If animal urine is available it is a valuable quick-acting plant food rich in nitrogen and containing some potash. It is best diluted with water till of pale straw colour. Urine can also be poured over the compost heap to enrich this. Urine is more usually a component of the liquid which drains from cow-sheds or manure heaps, which is even richer in plant foods. Both urine and liquid manure should be stored in a sump with a watertight cover. ◊ FEEDING PLANTS.

Urn Usually a sculpted garden ornament shaped like the funerary urns of the ancient Greeks and Romans, popular since the seventeenth century. Urns can be of solid stone as if capped, or made open, when they can be used as plant containers (which the Romans occasionally did). Usually large, urns on pediments or even columns were used as focal points in landscape gardens, despite Dr Johnson's contempt: 'Sir, I hate urns, they *are* nothing, they mean nothing, convey no ideas but ideas of horror!'

Useful Insects ⇨ PREDATORS.

Valve A term with various botanical meanings, of which that most commonly met refers to one of the sections into which a CAPSULE or POD splits when ripe.

Vaporizer A device which heats vaporizing chemicals so that they release their pest-killing constituents continuously. ◊ FUMIGATION.

Variability Refers to the variation which may appear in a batch of seedlings from a given source. Seedlings from a natural species seldom vary greatly; those from hybrid plants are likely to vary considerably. Those markedly different from the parent may be picked out for propagation if the variation is of merit, but in the normal course of propagation of a given variety or cultivar, as of fruit trees or roses, vegetative propagation is resorted to. With annual seeds, variability in flower colour is often encouraged for mixtures, but not variability in height and habit. ◊ CLASSIFICATION; MUTATION; TRUE-BREEDING; VEGETATIVE PROPAGATION.

Variant A form of a plant which differs from the normal; if sufficiently distinct, it may be given a variety or cultivar name. ◊ CLASSIFICATION.

Variegated Of plant parts, usually of leaves but occasionally stems and flowers, with markings in two or more colours. The term is normally confined to white or cream markings on the foliage as opposed to marks of brown, red or other dark colours due to pigmentation. Variegation is in a sense the opposite of pigmentation, being usually due to an absence of chlorophyll (the basic green colouring matter of the leaf). Few species begin life with variegation, though sometimes it is 'built in', as in *Pilea cadierei* in which the aluminium-coloured markings are the result of air spaces beneath the surface.

Very often variegation is the result of a mutation (sport) which creates a chimaera in which tissues of two or more kinds occur, one often overlaying the other. Pelargoniums are very liable to this sort of marking, often in several colours, and the longitudinal variegations on leaves like those of dracaenas are usually chimaeras.

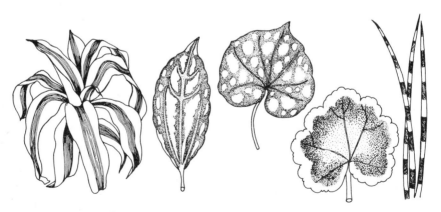

VARIEGATED. *Left to right, Dracaena fragrans* 'Victoriae'; *Pilea cadierei*; *Ligularia kaempferi* 'Aureo-maculata'; pelargonium; *Scirpus tabernaemontani* 'Zebrinus'

Longitudinal or edge variegation is the most common, but rarely leaves are striped cross-wise, as in the zebra rush *Scirpus tabernaemontani* 'Zebrinus'.

Variegation in the form of spots is often a symptom of virus infection; one of the most frequent plant viruses is known as mosaic because of its appearance. Virus-caused variegations are seldom prized in the garden, but the 'broken' tulips are notable exceptions, while *Ligularia kaempferi* 'Aureo-maculata' is sometimes grown as a foliage plant.

Variegated plants can normally only be increased vegetatively and are often weaker than their original green counterparts, to which they may revert, as they are often unstable.

◊ BROKEN; CHIMAERA; MUTATION; REVERSION (1); VIRUS DISEASES.

Variety A variation in a wild species sufficiently distinct to be given a name of its own. ◊ CLASSIFICATION.

Vascular System The system of tubes or vessels composed of cells which enables water, foodstuffs, and the chemical 'messengers' or 'commands' of hormones to travel within a plant; this is called translocation or simply transport. This vascular system varies according to the type of plant but is always continuous, linking every leaf and branch with the central stem and the roots. In very elementary terms it may be considered as two sets of pipes. In one (the phloem), foodstuffs manufactured in the leaves are passed to all other parts of the plant where required, including the roots. The other set of pipes (the xylem) conducts water and minerals absorbed by the roots upwards to the leaves, the water playing an essential part in photosynthesis, and surplus being lost by transpiration through the leaves. The xylem in addition provides rigidity.

In herbaceous plants the phloem and xylem are usually associated in vascular bundles scattered through the stem, sometimes at random but more usually in a symmetrical arrangement, like girders. In woody plants the xylem forms the core; it becomes lignified, with the cells in the centre eventually dying, and the actively conducting cells forming a cylinder around this heart-wood. These cells grow at different rates according to the season, which creates the concentric growth rings seen when a tree trunk is cut, by the counting of which the tree's age can be found. A narrow band where new cells are constantly produced (the cambium) allows expansion of the stem, and outside this is another cylinder containing phloem cells. In such woody plants the two 'pipelines' continually branch into branches, twigs and leaves, finally forming bundles containing both phloem and xylem associated with fibre cells, which are the leaf veins.

◊ CAMBIUM; HORMONES, PHOTOSYNTHESIS; TRANSPIRATION; VEIN.

Vase A form of fruit tree, also known as a goblet. This form has a very short trunk from which branches are trained first outwards and then upwards to create a cup-shaped structure; a metal hoop is usually fixed in place at the other edge where the branches begin to extend upwards. A second hoop higher up is also useful to secure the branches, though eventually the hoops may be discarded as the branches thicken. The vase never exceeds 8' in height, so that all cultural operations can be easily carried out. Apart from this advantage and the overall ornamental effect, the vase is useful for fruit tree varieties which refuse to make a straight central trunk.

Vegetable In the broad scientific sense, all plants as distinct from animals; one speaks of the Vegetable Kingdom.

In the horticultural sense, a vegetable is a crop of which the leaf, stem or root is eaten, as distinct from a fruit. However, there are some anomalies in common usage: crops which are technically fruits, e.g. tomatoes, cucumbers, marrows, peppers and aubergines, are normally considered to be 'vegetables', being eaten as salads or cooked to eat with meat dishes, or to replace meat as a savoury course for vegetarians. The savoury avocado, though normally eaten like a salad, is considered a fruit; and rhubarb, though clearly a stem, is sometimes included in horticultural show schedules as a fruit when bottled. The greengrocer will also consider mushrooms, which are fungi, and sweet corn, which is a cereal, as vegetables, although another common cereal, rice, is not thought of as such.

Vegetative; Vegetative Propagation Vegetative refers to plants having the power of growth – vegetative parts are all the parts of a plant except the flowers; vegetative propagation is increase by any method except by seeds, which involve sexual reproduction. In nature plants increase vegetatively by methods including bulbils, cormlets, offsets, plantlets and runners. The gardener takes advantage of these natural processes and adds to them the artificial ones of division, taking cuttings and all the methods of budding and grafting.

Vegetative propagation often produces mature plants far quicker than seeds, and ensures that all the new plants produced are identical to the parent. This is vital in increasing hybrids, as with roses and fruit trees. All plants produced from one parent vegetatively constitute what is known as a clone.

In some cases hybrid plants which are increased vegetatively in large numbers seem eventually to lose vigour and show signs of degeneration; this has been noted among chrysanthemums for instance. It is also quite easy for diseases and pests to be transmitted in vegetative propagation, notably virus diseases and eelworms which establish themselves within plant tissue. With some plants, meristem cuttings are used to avoid the transmission of viruses, and heat treatment against eelworms. External pests should always be avoidable by proper hygiene and use of pesticides.

◊ BUDDING; BULBIL; CLONE; CORM; CUTTING; EELWORMS; GRAFTING; HYBRID; MERISTEM; OFFSET; PLANTLET; RUNNER; VIRUS DISEASES.

Vein, Venation The veins are the conducting and strengthening strands in a leaf, sometimes embedded in the tissue, though usually visible as a pattern from outside, and sometimes forming marked projecting ridges on the leaf underside, when they may be called ribs. The central vein, if present, is usually stronger than the rest and is called the midrib. The larger veins arising from this may be termed secondary veins and the smallest ones veinlets. The arrangement of the veins is called venation and is often a useful diagnostic feature. Dicotyledons usually have branching or netted veins and monocotyledons parallel veins. The words 'nerve' and 'nervation' are sometimes used for vein and venation. ◊ DICOTYLEDON; LEAF; MONOCOTYLEDON; VASCULAR SYSTEM.

Ventilation, Ventilator Ventilators or vents are an essential part of a greenhouse in order to admit air when required. This is done for two main reasons: to create air movement, which will prevent the atmosphere being too moist, and in hot weather to lower temperatures, which can rise to surprisingly high levels in unventilated structures. Greenhouses of any size are usually equipped with ridge ventilators adjoining the peak of the roof and side ventilators in the vertical sides. Where plants are grown on staging, it may be helpful to have additional small vents below staging level. Ventilators should be provided on both sides of open-roofed greenhouses so that air can be admitted on the leeward side only on windy days when otherwise severe draughts might result. Ideally the ridge ventilators should occupy at least half of the length of the greenhouse and there should be at least one side ventilator every 10′.

Ventilators are usually in the form of small windows hinged at the top, but louvres are also used for side ventilation.

Ventilators can be operated manually, or by automatic devices in which a piston connected to the vent by a lever mechanism moves according to the expansion and contraction of a fluid within the piston cylinder. On a larger scale, electric motors switched on and off by a thermostat can be used to control ventilators. Rapid air changes can be carried out by electric extractor fans in place of orthodox ventilators.

The extent of ventilation needed depends on a host of interacting factors, including the weather conditions outside, the temperature maintained within, and the type of plant concerned. In general, little ventilation will be needed in cold weather, and a lot in hot conditions; but in cold humid weather it may be essential to create air movement, which can be assisted by providing additional heat within the greenhouse, notably with electric fan heaters, the use of which obviates opening the ventilators. At all times draughts should be avoided.

Ventilation is also applied to cold frames and sometimes to cloches, especially during the hardening-off process when plants raised in warm conditions are acclimatized to garden conditions. With frames the greenhouse light is opened, and some cloches can also admit air.

◊ CLOCHE; FRAME; GREENHOUSE; HARDENING OFF; HEATING.

Verge Strictly speaking, the edge of a lawn; sometimes also used of a narrow strip of turf alongside a bed, border or path.

Verge Cutting ◊ EDGING TOOLS.

Vermicide A worm-killer. ◊ WORM-KILLING.

Vermiculite The result of heating certain minerals similar to mica, which produces cellular flakes, very light in proportion to bulk, in which air is retained and which will absorb water without ever becoming waterlogged. Vermiculite can be added to seed and potting mixtures to increase their porosity but is mainly used by gardeners, either alone or mixed with sand or peat, as a medium in which to grow seeds and especially to root cuttings. A very fine root system is rapidly formed in this way. Since vermiculite is completely sterile and contains no plant food, seedlings and cuttings should be moved to a more nutritious compost when well rooted. Vermiculite can be obtained in grades varying from fine to coarse, and it is important to obtain a horticulturally suitable grade since many types, used for house insulation, packaging, etc., are too alkaline.

Vernalization This term covers various techniques by which seeds, bulbs and also plants will start rapidly into growth, out of season, as soon as provided with adequate light, warmth and moisture. The word, meaning literally 'subjecting to spring', is really a misnomer, for the techniques actually subject the seed or bulb to the conditions they would normally receive in winter, and so speed up, or produce at an abnormal time of year, the physical and chemical changes which then occur. It is, in effect, an artificial breaking of dormancy.

Such techniques are widely applied to bulbs for very early forcing, which are described as 'specially prepared', and also to lily-of-the-valley. The exposure to frost of sea-kale, rhubarb and similar roots before forcing is another example.

Seeds can also be made to germinate at abnormal times by vernalization, and the original experiments in Russia concerned winter wheat, which if sown in early winter produced bigger crops than normal varieties, but if sown in spring failed to form ears at all. If the winter varieties are germinated at low temperatures and stored cold till sown in spring, they will produce ears in the normal way. Many seeds, notably and obviously those of alpines, and of most temperate-climate plants, need a period of chilling before they will germinate – easily provided in a domestic refrigerator.

Vernalization usually means temperature treatment, sometimes cold as described above, sometimes warm, as with seeds of warm-country plants, and bulbs such as hyacinths in which flower formation occurs during the resting or storage period (as opposed to daffodils in which flower formation in the bulb happens when the plant is still in growth in relatively cool conditions). Certain chemicals, notably gibberellic acid, can be used to the same ends, and day-length may also affect matters.

$\diamond$ DAY-LENGTH; FORCING; STRATIFICATION.

Verticil A WHORL.

Verticillaster A false whorl, composed of a pair of opposed simple cymes, as often found in Labiates. $\diamond$ INFLORESCENCE.

Viability The capacity of seed to germinate. This decreases with time, although seeds vary enormously in this respect. Many flower and vegetable seeds lose their viability within a year or two; however, many weed seeds retain theirs for decades. In some cases, plants grown from old seed may be stunted. The modern practice of partially dehydrating seeds and then sealing them in foil packets increases their 'shelf life' considerably. $\diamond$ GERMINATION.

Villous Covered with long, weak hairs; to be found Latinized in specific names as *villosus*. $\diamond$ HAIRY.

Vine In Britain and Europe this word is entirely restricted to refer to the grape-vine and its decorative relations, but in the U.S. it means any climbing plant. $\diamond$ CLIMBER.

Vine Eye A kind of nail to be hammered into brick walls, with a hole through which wire, on which to train vines and other

VINE EYE

climbers, can be passed well away from the wall surface. Made of wrought iron, 4″–6″ long, they are narrowly wedge-shaped with the tip of the wedge truncated.

Vine Hoe $\diamond$ HOE.

Vinery A greenhouse devoted to growing grape-vines. Because of the flexibility in pruning vines, they can be grown in any kind of greenhouse, but in the days when

special structures were frequently erected for them, until the First World War, it was usual to build them either span-roofed or lean-to with a vertical component only 2′–3′ high. If space permitted, the span was relatively wide. This allowed detailed attention to all parts of the vine without too much recourse to step-ladders. $\diamond$ GREENHOUSE.

Vine Scissors $\diamond$ SCISSORS.

Vineyard An area devoted to growing grape-vines outside, important as a feature in British gardens from the eighth to the eighteenth century. The twentieth century has seen a revival in vine culture in Britain but seldom in association with gardens.

Virus Diseases A wide range of ailments caused by ultra-microscopic particles whose mode of action seems to lie between that of a living organism such as bacteria and fungi (which are in any case much larger) and of an organic chemical with the power of replicating itself in the right conditions, as in plant sap where viruses multiply rapidly. There they use the protein reserves of the plant and thus disturb its growth processes. Viruses can attack almost every kind of plant and cause a wide variety of symptoms, which include mottling, streaking, distortion of leaves and stems and overall stunting. Some of them have descriptive names such as mosaic and bushy stunt. Almost all viruses weaken their victim to some degree, even when they do not produce visible symptoms: thus most fruit trees carry viruses which reduce cropping capacity, though in the normal course of events this will not be suspected. In some cases such 'latent' viruses can infect other plants and may cause more severe symptoms in them. Many kinds of variegation are caused by viruses and some plants so affected are grown in gardens; an ornamental example of a virus-infected plant is the 'broken' tulip.

Some viruses exist in the soil and can infect roots directly, and a few are transmitted in seeds; but most are transmitted from one plant to another by sap-sucking insects, nematodes, occasionally by birds, and also by human activity, as on grafting tools, or on fingers, e.g. when removing sideshoots on tomatoes. One of the most important series, the nicotiana viruses, which affect tomatoes and many other plants, can be transmitted by finger contact from smoking tobacco or cigarettes to plants.

Because of their character, viruses cannot be destroyed by applying chemicals as one does against fungus diseases. With some plants, e.g. strawberries, heat treatment is possible, while in chrysanthemums and other plants this may be combined with the technique of rooting meristem cuttings or making microscopic grafts. Such methods are beyond the amateur, though he can benefit from them by purchasing guaranteed virus-free stocks produced in such ways. The amateur's only hope of control is stringent war against sap-sucking insects, special care when handling plants such as tomatoes, cucumbers and melons which need deshooting, and speedy destruction of virus-infected plants.

Virus-free stocks are young plants for sale which have been grown from plants from which virus disease has been elimina-

ted by meristem propagation or hot-water treatment.

◊ BROKEN; MERISTEM; REVERSION; SIDE-SHOOTING; VARIEGATED; WILT.

Vista The *Oxford Dictionary* definition of a vista is 'a view or prospect, especially one seen through an avenue of trees or other long and narrow opening'. Elsewhere, it has been described as a contrived and confined view. Such contrived views were first created in the late sixteenth century – a little later in Britain – when garden walls became unnecessary and vistas were formed to radiate for miles into the surrounding estates. As such they were the prerogative of royalty and wealthy aristocrats. An avenue of trees or, in a small garden, quite small bushes, creates a vista, but vistas can be made without such avenues; a couple of well-placed trees or shrubs with a gap between can do so, thus giving the appearance of much greater depth to a limited area. In landscape gardens, a building or obelisk was often placed at the end of a vista; this was called a vista terminal or closer. ◊ AVENUE; EYE-CATCHER.

Viticulture The art, or craft, of cultivating grape-vines.

Viviparous Producing live young. The only

VIRUS. *Left to right*, a narcissus virus; tomato spotted wilt; strawberry yellow edge; a tobacco virus; raspberry mosaic

viviparous animal the gardener has to contend with is the aphid in its various forms; it must be remembered that, even when killed by an insecticide, an adult aphid can still give birth, so that it is essential to repeat an application after a few days.

The word is also applied to plants. Strictly speaking, it refers to seeds which naturally germinate while still attached to the parent, as in the mangroves and the grass *Poa alpina*. It is also used to describe plants which produce bulbils on the stem, e.g. many lilies, or in the flower head, as in many onion relations (alliums), or plantlets on the leaves. The latter is sometimes called proliferous.

⬦ APHIDS; BULBIL; PLANTLET.

Voles Small rodents very like mice, causing similar damage to garden plants, and to be dealt with in the same way. ⬦ MICE.

✲ W ✲

Walk In garden design terms, a walk is a path created for the pleasure of perambulation rather than just getting from A to B: it might be between trees, or statues, raised or sunken, under a pergola or arbour, or progressing between dominant features in a garden. In Renaissance gardens, walks were aggrandized into alleys and avenues, and in general they terminated in some feature as a focal point, unless they were continuous around a garden or estate. In many historic gardens walks are designed with names such as Broad Walk, Flower Walk, The Nun's Walk, etc. ◊ ALLEY; AVENUE; PATHS.

Walls Walls have been a vital garden feature since the earliest days of gardening, since it is man's natural instinct to shut his property in against marauders and the idle gaze of passers-by. In gardens of adequate size a surrounding wall can be a satisfying feature, and internal dividing walls, high or low, play their part in the design, though in small gardens enclosing walls of any height can be oppressive.

Walls can be constructed of brick, stone or concrete; a sound foundation is essential, and tall walls of any length need buttresses at intervals, including those used to retain soil at a higher level. The serpentine or crinkle-crankle wall does not need buttresses. Besides plain walls, one can erect pierced ones, which have existed for many centuries as decorative features. Dry walls made without mortar can be used for low internal divisions and the retention of low terraces, and have the advantage that they can be planted.

Walls are valuable for growing climbers on, and a warm wall with southerly aspect will allow tender climbers and the less hardy fruits to thrive in cold or windy areas. The old-style kitchen garden was always walled, and many examples remain today. Walls specifically for training fruit trees on should be at least 7′ tall and pre-ferably much more. However, it must be realized that wind causes a great deal of turbulence a short distance to leeward of a wall; a slatted fence or a hedge are far more effective in reducing wind problems.

◊ CLIMBER; CRINKLE-CRANKLE; DRY WALL; SCREEN WALLING; TERRACE; WIND.

Wall Nail A special type of nail for driving into mortar between bricks, consisting of a chisel-like wrought-iron shank, with a head enclosed in lead which extends on one side into a strip. This strip is soft so that it can be twisted around wires set along the wall to support climbing plants. These nails are often known as lead-headed wall nails.

WALL NAIL

Wall Plant A gardener's term for any plant that can be grown on a wall. These may be true climbers, whether self-clinging or needing support such as trellis or wires; or trees or shrubs, not naturally climbing, which can be trained flat against the wall with the aid of wires, etc. The latter include trained fruit forms such as fans and espaliers, and ornamentals such as cotoneaster and pyracantha, often known as wall shrubs.

The word is also sometimes used of plants suitable for planting in dry walls.

◊ CLIMBER; DRY WALL; ESPALIER; FAN.

Wall Shrub ◊ WALL PLANTS.

Wardian Case In 1829 a Dr Nathaniel Ward discovered by chance that plants would thrive in completely closed glass containers, the moisture transpired by the plant condensing and returning to the soil, while the atmosphere within remained humid and free of external pollution. In a short time, Ward's Cases became fashionable and they were produced in a wide range of shapes, ranging from simple bell-jars to large, ornate cases with glass panes framed in metalwork on stone stands. Sometimes they were immense and contained rockwork, like one famous type designed to fit into a wall niche, representing the ruins of Tintern Abbey. Ferns and tropical plants needing a constant humid atmosphere were grown in these cases, which were often known as fern cases. Strong, simple box- or greenhouse-shaped cases solved the previously almost insuperable problem of collectors sending plants home from far countries.

A change of fashion around the turn of this century caused the eclipse of the Wardian Case and only a handful of Victorian examples remain extant. However, the principle is still an excellent method for cultivating indoors difficult exotic plants which would shrivel up in the dry, stuffy air of the average room. Modern-style Wardian Cases, known rather misleadingly as terrariums in the U.S., range from simple box-like structures – an aquarium with a glass lid does well – to more elaborate types with small lead-framed panes, or made of thick clear plastic. One popular form is the bottle garden, which combines effective growing conditions with the ship-in-the-bottle surprise of plants within, much larger than the bottle's aperture. Large box-shaped cases have been fitted with electric light and a source of heat underneath.

◊ BOTTLE GARDEN; PLANT WINDOW; TERRARIUM.

Warren Hoe ◊ HOE.

Wart Disease A serious fungus disease of potatoes in which warty lumps appear on young tubers, and old tubers may be left as wrinkled, useless lumps. It is a disease of heavy, wet soils, and because of its virulence is notifiable to the agricultural authorities in Britain. Diseased plants must be burned, affected tubers not used for seed, and potatoes should not be planted in the same position for several years.

Washing Soda Those preferring basic ingredients for pest control can make an effective fungicide against gooseberry mildew by dissolving 8 oz. soft soap and 12 oz. washing soda in 5 gallons of water. The soap and soda should be dissolved separately in a gallon of water before mixing the rest of the water; the solution should be used without delay.

A general-purpose fungicide called Burgundy mixture is made by mixing 10 oz. soda and 8 oz. copper sulphate in 5 gallons of water. The soda is dissolved in 1 gallon of water, the copper sulphate in the other four, and the soda solution added to the copper solution.

Wasps These insects are generally considered tiresome as they invade mealtimes in the summer, especially out of doors. The only serious problem they cause gardeners is eating ripening fruit of all kinds; in the early summer they are in fact beneficial since they feed their young on other insects. Choice individual fruits can be protected from wasp attack by fixing paper or muslin bags around them. Wasps can be trapped in jam jars or patent 'wasp glasses' hung in the trees and partly filled with sweetened water. Getting rid of wasps involves finding their nests and dusting the entrances with a suitable insecticide, inserting a lit insecticide 'smoke' into the nest on a stick, pouring boiling water in, or pouring in paraffin and igniting it.

Water Although plants depend on many factors and materials for continued growth, water is vital at almost all times, and is the only 'extra' provided by many gardeners. Without enough water, plants wilt and eventually die. Water is of course especially necessary for any plant in a pot or other container; neglect of watering for a brief period is likely to result in dead plants.

Water is obtained from the mains, by tapping streams or ponds, or from tanks in which rainwater is collected. 'Hard' water containing a lot of lime (calcium) can be harmful to lime-hating (calcifuge) plants; chlorinated water may be troublesome, and too much iron may harm some plants. Mains water should not contain any other pollutants, but natural water supplies may do. To avoid these, the use of rainwater is usually a satisfactory solution for susceptible plants. Unfortunately, this itself may contain pollutants in and near industrial areas. If stored in tanks in the greenhouse, rainwater can become infected with disease-causing organisms, and such tanks must be cleaned out and disinfected regularly.

◊ WATERING.

Water Barrow A tank mounted on wheels which is filled with water to be dispensed in places where a hose cannot be brought. In the eighteenth century this took the form of a vast horse-drawn barrel and the water was applied to lawns, etc., through a 'boom' fitted with many small nozzles, or could be directed through a single leather spout. The Victorians had 'barrow engines' of metal, fitted with a powerful hand pump and a nozzle at the end of a short length of hose. A very recent version called a water-caddy has a plastic tank holding 12 gallons, and a battery-operated pump. It is primarily designed for use with indoor pot plants.

Water Butt A large barrel connected to the gutters and drainpipe of a house, in which rainwater can be collected; the water is taken from it via a tap near its base.

Water Garden Any garden feature which uses water for cultivating plants, for decorative effect, or both. The earliest water gardens were in ancient Egypt, where they were used for plants such as papyrus and waterlilies. In Europe, however, water gardens were entirely formal from Roman times till the eighteenth century, when water-plant cultivation began.

The Romans had bathing tanks, and among the more extraordinary aspects of medieval gardens were the bathing tanks and basins in which apparently the ladies and gentlemen of the courts and castles bathed, and ate and drank naked, attended by retainers often playing musical instruments.

Water gardens were particularly important in hot climates and are found in Persian and Mughal gardens and their derivations throughout the Muslim world, including Spain. In India, bathing tanks were common. Canals and moats are a feature of Far Eastern palace and temple complexes, and the informal pool or lake of Chinese and, later, Japanese gardens, where bridges and stepping stones are important decorative adjuncts. Bridges are of course a feature of many large European gardens.

In decorative terms, water provides an entirely novel surface, still or rippling and capable of reflecting trees and clouds; even a tiny 'eye of water' pool in a small garden can create an important focal point. Water can be conducted through channels, down cascades or thrown up in fountains to create innumerable effects: these are called waterworks. In terms of plant possibilities, water gardens open up a range entirely different from that of normal garden plants, centred on the waterlily with its unique flowers and habit of growth.

◊ BOG GARDEN; CANAL; POOL; STEPPING STONES; WATERWORKS.

Watering Water can be applied to plants in various ways. In the open garden watering cans may be used but this involves a lot of weight-carrying, and where there is a mains supply a hose is infinitely less trouble. This can be fitted with an adjustable nozzle, or attached to a rotary or oscillating sprinkler which can be left unattended. It is also possible to deliver water to plant rows or individual plants by methods of trickle irrigation. For plants in greenhouses, frames, etc., the can, hose, and methods of trickle irrigation and capillary watering are available, together with the intermittent spray of mist propagation equipment where a very humid atmosphere is desired. The watering can has to be used on house plants.

When watering outside it is essential to apply the right amount of water. Too much, especially on heavy soils, can cause waterlogging and chilled soil which can seriously damage roots. But the novice's usual failing is to apply too little water in dry weather: after a few minutes' application the soil may appear nicely moist, but scratching the surface with a trowel will often reveal that water has not penetrated more than a fraction of an inch. This effect is particularly likely if a fine-rosed can is used or a hose nozzle giving a very fine spray: for all but very small plants, a relatively coarse spray is desirable. This is where a sprinkler left operating for some time will score, for its effect resembles that of rain and the water penetrates the ground steadily. Water straight from a can nozzle or a hose end may wash small plants out of the soil and disturb the surface unduly.

The correct watering of plants in pots and other containers is very much a matter of experience. It is often said, with a good deal of truth, that more house plants die of over-watering than any other cause. At the same time it is very easy to let these and pot plants in a greenhouse dry out in hot weather, and constant alertness is needed in such periods. Now that plastic pots have largely superseded clay ones, the old method of tapping the pot to see if water is needed from the resultant note (ringing if dry, dull if wet) is no longer effective. Soil moisture meters may be used until experience is gained. Soilless, peat-based potting composts are more susceptible to drying out than soil-based ones. When potting compost becomes very dry it will shrink away from the pot sides and then the only course is to place the pot in a container of water and leave it there until bubbles cease to emerge.

The use of very cold water for pot plants should be avoided, as this can cause a check to growth and lower the overall temperature in a greenhouse.

Plant food is readily distributed to plants when watering by using liquid or soluble fertilizer.

▷ CAPILLARY WATERING; COMPOSTS, SEED AND POTTING; FEEDING PLANTS; FIELD CAPACITY; HOSE; IRRIGATION; MIST PROPAGATION; MOISTURE METER; POT; RAIN; ROSE; SELF-WATERING; SPRINKLER; WATERING CAN.

Watering Can Spouted cans for delivering water to plants are available in sizes from 1 pint to 2 gallons. There are two main types, one with a fairly short spout at an angle of about 45° from the body of the can, and one with a much longer spout at a greater angle. Both have their uses but the long-spouted type is probably better balanced and with it the water can be delivered accurately into a pot, even if this is on greenhouse staging. For small pots and house plants, where it is desirable not to spill water, a very fine-spouted can is desirable.

Cans are very often of plastic nowadays, though metal cans are still available. Most cans are supplied with a rose, a push-on fitting with numerous small holes to deliver a fine 'rain' of water. Roses can be round or oval. The round rose is used especially when watering pots, to avoid soil being disturbed. For a gentle spray, e.g. over seed boxes, an oval rose is placed holes upwards on a long-spouted can. It is also possible to obtain sprinkle-bars to attach to watering cans for delivering weed-killers and the like close to the soil surface.

▷ SPRINKLE-BAR; WATERING.

Water Parterre ▷ PARTERRE.

Water Roller ▷ ROLLER.

Water Shoots or Sprouts Growths which often arise on vigorously growing fruit trees from adventitious buds in the branches. They are long, stout and quick-growing, quite distinct from spurs, and are encouraged by hard pruning and good soils. Since they are unfruitful, soft and ill-placed, crowding the centre of the tree, they should be cut off at the base, flush with the branch. ▷ ADVENTITIOUS; SNAG.

Waterworks All the ways in which motion is added to the still waters of lakes, pools, canals and formal basins. These are primarily in the form of fountains which throw water up and cascades down which water

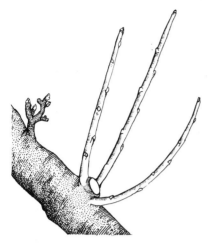

WATER SHOOTS

pours. Fountains seem to have been first used by the Romans who were notable hydraulic engineers; their tradition of water gardens and waterworks was developed in Renaissance Italy and thence all over Europe. Small fountains were certainly garden features in medieval times. Fountains were important in Byzantine gardens, following the Roman example, and equally so in the Persian and Mughal gardens that later developed farther east. Here they were accompanied by cascades, often in the form of sloping chadars, made of stone chiselled into patterns so that the moving water itself had a distinctive pattern. In Islamic patio gardens, small spouts and fountains created both visible and audible relief from the hot sun.

Fountains of amazing complexity became a feature of large gardens all over Europe. As d'Argenville wrote in 1709, 'fountains and waterworks are the life of a garden . . . which animate and invigorate it, and . . . give it a new life and spirit'. Earlier, Francis Bacon had written how 'fountains . . . are a great beauty and refreshment; but pools mar all, and make the garden unwholesome, and full of flies and frogs'. The cascades that led water downhill were mostly simple and formal, often in the form of a long series of steps. It was not until

the less formal landscape garden developed that cascades began to emulate the wildness of natural waterfalls. At the same time the really elaborate fountains to be found, as at Versailles, fell out of favour.

Other kinds of waterwork included water organs: the first dates back to 243 B.C. Almost equally early, water was used to operate mechanical figures. Such ingenuities were an important feature of sixteenth-century European gardens. At this period also the water joke was popular: at the turn of a distant tap, jets from paving shot up under ladies' crinolines, grottoes became showers, artificial trees dripped, and statues sprayed visitors from unexpected parts of their anatomy.

Today, the garden owner can create small fountains with an electric pump, and make small cascades in rock gardens, preferably formed in stone but, if unavoidable, with the aid of preformed plastic units which are mostly repulsive. The oriental patio trickle can be emulated by a 'bubbler' in which water exudes slowly over a rock or millstone.

◊ BUBBLER; ROCK GARDEN; WATER GARDEN.

Wattle Any construction made of pliable plant growths such as young osier or hazel branches woven together; mostly seen in the form of hurdles used as temporary fences. Small hurdles may also be used to protect young or tender plants against cold winds. ◊ FENCES; PROTECTION.

Waved, Wavy Margins of plant organs such as leaves and petals can be waved in two dimensions: up and down in relation to a flat surface, termed undulate, and in and out, which may be called crenate, sinuate or scalloped. ◊ LEAF.

Wax A natural product of many plants, forming a coating on leaves, stems and fruits. It may create a shiny, often glaucous surface or appear as a thin layer of powdery 'bloom', a thicker powdery layer called farina or meal, or a scaly layer called scurf. Its purpose is to seal the surface against evaporation and in some cases to provide an extra protection to the stomata or breathing pores. Many leaves are wax-coated only on the underside for this latter reason.

Water on waxy surfaces runs off or forms drops, and this is why all pesticidal and fungicidal sprays incorporate a 'spreader' or wetting agent, which allows the water to form a continous film.

Wax is used by the gardener in some kinds of wound dressing, especially grafting wax. At one time, waxes were quite often applied to the stems of roses and occasionally other plants to prevent shrivelling in transit from nursery to gardener, but this practice has largely been discontinued, since plastic packaging materials have the same function.

▷ BLOOM; CUTICLE; FARINA; GRAFTING WAX; SCURF; SPREADER; STOMATA; WOUND DRESSINGS.

Weather-boarding ▷ FENCES.

Web-making Caterpillars ▷ CATERPILLARS.

Weed, Weed Control A weed is often defined as a plant growing in the wrong place. In many respects this is true, the best example being grass which is deliberately cultivated in lawns but is a weed in other parts of the garden. Some ornamental garden plants can become weeds due to their free-seeding habits or invasive growth, many so-called ground-cover plants coming into the latter category. Free-seeding trees, e.g. birch and sycamore, can also become weeds, especially on derelict sites.

However, many habitual weeds are not ornamental and have the common characteristics of either seeding very freely, often at an early stage of growth, or spreading vigorously by runners. Some of the most pernicious have roots which will regenerate from small pieces or from deeply buried sections left in the soil after cultivation. Weeds can be annual, biennial or perennial, the latter including both herbaceous and woody plants.

Apart from being unsightly to the fasti-dious gardener, weeds can envelop, over-shade and choke desirable plants and compete with them seriously for water and nutrients. The extent to which this competition occurs can be gauged by the practice of grassing down fruit trees in order to curtail their growth. Weeds are most harmful to seedlings and young plants, and their competition needs preventing, especially in seed beds, vegetable gardens, young plantations, areas where annuals are sown, and lawns. Some weeds release compounds which inhibit the growth of other plants; they may be alternative hosts for diseases; a number, particularly in the U.S. and many warm countries, are parasitic (e.g. dodders and mistletoes) and very serious enemies of crops including trees.

Annual and biennial weeds need destroying before they can set seed, for they not only produce large numbers of seeds but in many cases these can remain dormant in the soil for decades, ready to germinate when soil disturbance such as cultivation brings about suitable conditions. Some annual weeds, e.g. groundsel, will ripen seeds even after being removed from the soil.

Perennial weeds can often be eradicated by constant cutting down at soil level, but a number will continue to regrow from their roots for many years despite this treatment, the most notorious being bindweed, couch grass, ground elder and horsetail, and the introduced Japanese knotgrass, *Polygonum cuspidatum*. The last two can be virtually impossible to destroy when long established, but most other perennial weeds can be eliminated by chemical means or by really careful digging out in which every fragment of root is removed.

Methods of destroying weeds are hand-weeding, aided by a pointed trowel or similar instrument to extract the roots; use of a hoe to cut the weeds at ground level and leave them to wither; cultivation by digging, when deep-rooted weeds must be removed by hand as work proceeds; burning with a flame gun (only effective with annual or shallow-rooted weeds); and the application of chemical weedkillers in various ways.

In general, weeds can be put on the compost heap to decay. However, any that are seeding should be burned, since the seeds will not be destroyed unless the heap is very well managed, and will be spread over the garden as the compost is used. Likewise, any with regenerating roots should be burned, including those already mentioned and tap-rooted kinds such as dandelions, docks and oxalis. The last-named genus introduces another form of regeneration, bulbils produced around the root, and is another resistant to virtually all chemicals.

⬦ COMPOST HEAP; FLAME GUN; GRASSING DOWN; WEEDKILLER.

Weed Cutter A U.S. tool resembling a scuffle hoe with a narrow horizontal blade fixed by a hoop-shaped support to a long handle. Applied elsewhere to a kind of underwater scythe used to cut weeds in pools and watercourses.

Weed Eradicator A device for injecting or smearing individual weeds with weedkiller.
⬦ SPOT TREATMENT.

Weed Extractor Any device which grips the root of a weed so that it can be levered out of the soil. One version, called a weed puller, has a sharp fixed blade to push into the soil by the root and a movable grip operated by a handle which holds the root against the blade. Another with a notched blade is the DAISY GRUBBER.

Weed or Weeding Fork A term used by some manufacturers for a hand fork. ⬦ FORKS.

Weedkiller Chemical materials for the destruction of weeds, sometimes referred to as herbicides in more technical works. These materials are plant-killers and, if not used with care, can destroy ornamental or useful plants as readily as weeds.

Weedkillers fall into three main categories, although these overlap:

Contact materials Destroy plants on contact, as the name implies, by acting on the foliage.

Selective weedkillers Act against some types of plants and not others. Many lawn weedkillers are of this type, destroying broad-leaved weeds among grass and cereals. Other selectives are mainly effective against grasses. The farmer has quite a range of selective weedkillers to deal with weeds in specific crops, but only a few of these are either available or useful to gardeners who are growing a wider variety of plants. It is possible to use certain non-selective weedkillers, selectively applying them in special ways, see below.

Residual weedkillers Are those which form a layer either on the soil surface or for a limited depth under it, and remain active for a period of several weeks at least, killing seedlings, or perennial weeds sprouting from root fragments, as they emerge. These are sometimes called pre-weed-emergent weedkillers.

Other terms which may be encountered in literature on weedkilling include the following:

Hormone weedkiller A material which acts by disturbing the processes within the plant controlled by its hormones, and produces twisting and other deformities. Many selective weedkillers are of this type.

Plant growth regulator A material most often used to curtail the rate of growth of a plant.

Post-emergence Application of a weedkiller after the plants under cultivation (normally vegetable crops) have emerged from the soil.

Post-weed-emergence Application of a weedkiller among cultivated plants after weeds have emerged.

Pre-emergence Application of a weedkiller before the plants under cultivation (normally vegetable crops) have emerged from the soil. Contact and residual pre-emergence refer to the use of weedkillers of such type.

Pre-weed-emergence Application of a weedkiller among cultivated plants before weeds have emerged.

Systemic ⟡ Translocated, below.

Total Used of weedkillers which destroy everything they touch; total weed control is therefore used in areas where there are no cultivated plants. High doses of some selective weedkillers are sometimes used for this purpose.

Translocated Used of weedkillers which are taken up by the plant and then moved around within it in the vascular system so that stems, roots, etc., at a distance from the point of application are affected. Most hormone weedkillers act in this way. The word 'systemic' is sometimes used in the same sense, but is better retained in connection with fungicides and insecticides.

Weedkillers are made as liquids for dilution in water, as powders to be added to water and converted into suspensions, as granules and gels. They are applied in various ways.

In the garden, liquids can be applied from a watering can fitted with a fine rose, a sprinkle-bar or dribble-bar, or from a pressure sprayer fitted with a coarse nozzle which produces large drops. The latter is more economical of weedkiller, but the most likely to result in drift damage. The risk of this is reduced if the nozzle is surrounded by a shield (often in the form of a cone).

Because of the difficulty of making sure that weedkillers have been totally cleaned out from containers, it is best to keep a separate watering can and/or sprayer specifically for weedkillers. Even so, it is helpful to wash the appliance thoroughly with detergent and water after use to avoid damage to desirable plants at the next treatment.

Granules may be applied by hand or, in large areas, through a mechanical distributor.

The gardener can apply appropriate weedkillers by such methods over lawns, in the vegetable garden, in rose or shrub beds without low-growing plants, and on non-cultivated areas such as drives, paths, paving, tennis courts, etc. When dealing with isolated weeds or small areas of weeds in mixed garden situations, and with isolated deep-rooted weeds, e.g. in lawns, he can use spot treatment. As the term implies, this involves application of a non-selective weedkiller to specific weeds and it can be used to economize on the amount of selective weedkiller used.

Various devices, sometimes called weed eradicators, have been marketed to deliver a small dose of weedkiller in the centre of low weeds like dandelions in lawns or in soil, either on the principle of the syringe or as a solid bar containing weedkiller to be pressed onto the foliage. Aerosols are sold for the same purpose. A paintbrush dipped into liquid weedkiller can be used to spread the material on weeds, and one weedkiller is sold in gel form to be applied via a paintbrush.

Climbing weeds, e.g. bindweed, can have their ends bundled together and thrust into a jam jar or similar container where they can absorb selective weedkillers.

Climbing weeds and tall isolated weeds, e.g. thistles, among cultivated plants can be effectively dealt with by application of selective weedkiller via a piece of cloth or sponge held in a rubber-gloved hand, moistened in the material and pulled upwards along its stem. The cloth or sponge must not be so wet that drops of weedkiller can fall on desirable plants. A proprietary herbicide glove is also available.

Scrub and unwanted shrubs and small trees can be killed by spraying the foliage with weedkiller sprays, and larger trees in specialized ways such as frill-girdling; but in most garden situations, the most effective way with trees is to cut them down and treat the stumps to prevent regrowth, if they cannot be removed.

There are a very large number of weedkillers available, both inorganic and organic in origin. The list below summarizes the uses of those which are, in general, most useful to the gardener. The names of the weedkillers are their chemical ones or names coined to avoid complex chemical ones; they are not trade names. Users of weedkillers should check the names of their constituent materials which, in the U.K. at least, must always be printed on the label. Directions should be followed exactly if the weedkillers are to work as expected, and any cautionary advice followed.

Many of these materials can be combined together and some are used only in mixtures. Lawn weedkillers are often combined with appropriate fertilizer mixtures.

Soil fumigants and sterilizers are dealt with mainly in separate entries.

Most of the materials listed have low mammalian toxicity, but a few have caused human fatalities when imbibed in concentrated form. The majority have few harmful effects on soil micro-organisms and some actually stimulate these.

Weedkillers

(U.K., U.S.) refers to availability to gardeners in these countries, so far as can be ascertained. Mammalian toxicity is low, unless otherwise specified.

Aminotriazole (U.K., U.S.) Total; translocated; mainly used on uncultivated ground, paths, etc., often in conjunction with MCPA and/or simazine. Low persistence.

Ammonium sulphamate (AMS) (U.K., U.S.) Total; contact; especially useful for persistent 'problem' perennial and woody weeds, killing trees, and preventing regrowth from tree stumps. Temporary soil sterilant. Low persistence. ◊ FRILL-GIRDLING; TREE STUMPS.

AMS ◊ Ammonium sulphamate, above.

Atrazine (U.K., agricultural; U.S.) Total but selective in sweetcorn; mostly used among woody plants. Similar to simazine. Persistent.

Bensulide (U.S.) Selective: used on turf against crab-grass. Persistent.

Calomel ◊ Mercurous chloride, below.

Chloramben (U.S.) Pre-emergent or around transplants; mainly used among vegetables. Low persistence.

Chlorpropham ◊ CIPC, below.

CIPC (*Chlorpropham*) (U.K., U.S.) Selective against grasses and some other weeds in young stages: usually applied as pre-weed-emergent. Mainly used agricultur-

ally; in U.K. in mixture with diuron and IPC in gardens. Low persistence.

CMPP ◊ Mecoprop, below.

Copper sulphate (U.K., U.S.) Originally used as selective against broad-leaved weeds in cereals; today more often against water weeds. Unfortunately it is toxic to fish at weed-killing rates. ◊ COPPER, COPPER COMPOUNDS.

2,4-D (U.K., U.S.) Translocated selective against many broad-leaved weeds in grass and cereals. Gardeners use it mainly on lawns, often in mixture with dicamba, fenoprop, ioxynil or mecoprop; also against woody weeds with 2,4,5-T. Low persistence.

2,4-DES (U.K.) Not active on plant foliage but is converted to 2,4-D on contact with soil, where it then acts as pre-weed-emergent. Often used in mixture, e.g. with simazine. Low persistence.

Dalapon (U.K., U.S.) Translocated selective against grasses, especially couch or twitch grass, among broad-leaved trees and shrubs and certain crops, e.g. potatoes. Low persistence. May cause skin irritation.

DCPA (U.S.) Pre-weed-emergent; also against crab-grass in lawns. Moderate persistence.

Dicamba (U.K., U.S.) Selective against broad-leaved weeds in grass: used in higher doses against persistent perennial 'problem' weeds. In U.K. usually only available in mixture with 2,4-D (when valuable also against woody weeds), and ioxynil. Very persistent: danger of leaching down to tree and shrub roots.

Dichlobenil (U.K., U.S.) At high rates, a long-acting total weedkiller; at lower rates, kills small and emerging weeds around roses, shrubs, trees. Usually in granule form. High persistence; some danger of damage to trees and shrubs when regularly used due to vapour entering via the bark.

Dichlone (U.S.) Though primarily a fungicide, also used as an algicide.

Dichlorophen (U.K., U.S.) Kills liverworts, moss and algae in lawns, on paths, etc. Also a fungicide against lawn diseases.

Dichlorprop (U.K.) A translocated selective similar in action to 2,4-D, but controlling some other weeds; now available only in mixture with 2,4-D for use on established lawns.

Dinitro compounds: DNC, Dinoseb (U.S.) Contact weedkillers now somewhat superseded, and in any case mainly used agriculturally since they must be carefully timed, stain and are toxic. Low persistence.

Diquat (U.K., U.S.) A contact material with limited powers of translocation, also used as pre-weed-emergent against annual weeds and to scorch upper growth of perennials. Usually sold in mixture with paraquat and/or simazine. No persistence: inactivated on contact with soil. Toxic if imbibed as concentrate.

Diuron (U.K., U.S.) A total weedkiller or, at low concentrations, pre-weed-emergent. Limited soil penetration; long persistence. In U.K. used in gardens only in mixture with CIPC and IPC.

Fenoprop (U.K., U.S.) A growth regulator used on its own against woody weeds and problem perennial weeds, and in mixture with 2,4-D as lawn weedkiller. High persistence.

Ferrous ammonium sulphate (U.S.) A mixture of sulphate of ammonia and sulphate of iron. ◊ Sulphate of iron (below).

Ferrous sulphate ◊ Sulphate of iron, below.

Glyphosate (U.K., U.S.) Total; translocated throughout underground shoots and roots. No persistence. In U.S. still restricted to professionals.

IPC (*Propham*) (U.K., U.S.) Similar to CIPC. ◊ CIPC, above.

Ioxynil (U.K.) Selective contact material used on its own against broad-leaved weeds in newly sown lawns, or with 2,4-D and dicamba, or with mecoprop on established lawns. Specially valuable against speedwell and mayweeds. Moderately toxic; harmful to fish.

MCPA (U.K., U.S.) A translocated selective very similar in action to 2,4-D, now normally used only in mixture with amino-triazole and simazine on drives and paths, and also in conjunction with a fertilizer and dichlorprop as a lawn weedkiller and toxic.

MCPP ◊ Mecoprop, below.

Mecoprop (*CMPP, MCPP*) (U.K., U.S.) A translocated selective similar in action to 2,4-D and MCPA, with the added power of controlling clovers in established lawns, and cleavers and chickweed in cereals. Low persistence.

Mercurous chloride (*Calomel*) (U.K., U.S.) Used against moss in lawns. ◊ CALOMEL.

Paraquat (U.K.) Similar to diquat but more effective against grasses; used in mixture with it and also with simazine. No persistence; inactivated on contact with soil. Lethal if imbibed as concentrate.

Permanganate of potash (U.K.) Sometimes used as a moss-killer. ◊ PERMANGANATE OF POTASH.

Pronamide (U.S.) For perennial grass control under trees, ornamentals and some crops.

Propachlor (U.K., U.S.) Pre-weed-emergent against weeds in brassicas, leeks, onions and some other vegetables, and in rose and shrub beds. Low persistence.

Propham ◊ IPC, above.

Salt (*sodium chloride*) (U.K., U.S.) Common salt is a total weedkiller, though not recommended for garden use. It affects soil texture and is therefore best restricted to paths, paving, etc. ◊ SALT.

Simazine (U.K., U.S.) Mainly as pre-weed-emergent on paths and around roses, shrubs, some fruits and rhubarb. Also available in mixture with aminotriazole and with paraquat plus diquat for use only on drives, paths, etc. Persistent. Similar to atrazine.

Sodium chlorate (U.K., U.S.) Once the most widely used total weedkiller, now being superseded by simazine in gardens and other organic chemicals in agriculture. Has disadvantage that it can readily 'creep' through soil, affecting trees and shrubs with spreading roots. Pure sodium chlorate ignites readily by friction or a blow and only non-inflammable formulations should be used. Persistent up to a year.

Sulphate of ammonia (U.K., U.S.) Used on broad-leaved weeds especially in lawns as a component of lawn sand, killing by scorching. Low persistence. ◊ LAWN SAND; SULPHATE OF AMMONIA.

Sulphate of iron (ferrous sulphate) (U.K., U.S.) Used against moss, pearlwort and fungi in lawns as a component of lawn sand. Low persistence. ◊ LAWN SAND; SULPHATE OF IRON.

2,4,5-T (U.K.) Translocated. Used mainly against nettles, brambles and woody weeds, most effectively as brushwood killer in mixture with 2,4-D; also against trees, in solution with mineral oils, for frill-girdling or to prevent regrowth of tree stumps. Withdrawn in U.S. where considered dangerous, due to possible contamination with toxic impurity dioxin. Fairly persistent. ◊ FRILL-GIRDLING; TREE STUMPS.

Tar oil (U.K.) Full-strength tar oil will scorch grass, but a special formulation kills speedwell, moss and lichens in lawns, and the latter two also on hard surfaces.

Trifluralin (U.S.) Pre-weed-emergent, specially effective against grasses but also against many broad-leaved weeds. Moderate persistence.

◊ FRILL-GIRDLING; FUMIGATION; GARDEN CHEMICALS; GROWTH REGULATORS; HORMONES; SPRINKLE-BAR; STERILIZATION; SYSTEMIC; TRANSLOCATION; TREE STUMPS; VASCULAR SYSTEM; WEED, WEED CONTROL.

Weeping Many trees have varieties of weeping or pendulous habit, which mainly arise as sports (mutations) and, used in the right place, they make very attractive garden features. Naturally weeping trees include the weeping willow, *Salix babylonica*, the silver lime, *Tilia petiolaris*, and *Forsythia suspensa*. There are some trees where the weeping is confined to the twigs, as in *Picea brewerana* in which the secondary growths hang vertically from the

branches. The weeping willow, and certain weeping varieties of ash and beech, are examples of trees which form an erect trunk from which the branches hang down, but in most cases of weeping sports it is necessary to train a growth upward to form an erect trunk, as in *Cedrus atlantica* 'Pendula'. In other cases the weeping sport is grafted onto the erect stem of the original species; if it was not so treated it would make a prostrate or sprawling bush. This usually happens with weeping cherries, and indeed most weeping trees. Weeping standard roses are another example where pendulous or at least weak-stemmed varieties are budded onto an upright stock; with these it is usual to use an umbrella-shaped frame over which the long growths are trained. ◊ GRAFTING; MUTATION.

Weevils Insects resembling beetles but with a distinct beak or snout which makes them unmistakable. Both adults and larvae are troublesome pests, attacking many plants. The most common is the vine weevil, the black adults of which eat notches in foliage and eat away tubers, especially of begonias and cyclamens. The

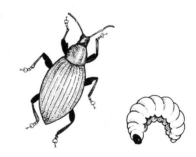

WEEVIL (vine weevil)

whitish grubs, about ½″ long, characteristically curl up like a letter C, and devour both feeding and storage roots of pot plants. The clay-coloured weevil is similar in its habits. The apple-blossom weevil lays its eggs in the flowers which never open or form fruit. Other weevils attack fruits, nuts, twigs, root vegetables, pea and bean foliage, strawberry and other soft fruit flowers, and roots of many plants.

363

The apple fruit and strawberry weevils are sometimes known as rhynchites.

Where adults are seen, hand-picking may be the easiest control; but they are also susceptible to spraying and dusting with pesticides, notably carbaryl. If grubs are detected, they can be killed with a pesticide drench but the damage has usually already been done. Where vine weevils are abundant, in greenhouses, mixing pesticide dust with potting compost whenever re-potting is done will help.

The snout beetle is a weevil with a beak sometimes as long as its body, used for making tunnels in fruits or nuts in which eggs are laid.
◊ BEETLE.

Well-head In the days when wells were essential supplies of water, the well-heads were often treated ornamentally, notably in formal Italian gardens where they were often finely carved from stone. Some of these Italian examples can be seen today in grand gardens in various countries, often surmounted by their pulley mechanism or 'crane' in wrought iron. The false well-head, consisting of bricks with a wooden pulley structure surmounted by a little roof, has become a rather hackneyed ornamental feature of small gardens.

Wet and Dry Bulb Thermometer An instrument used for measuring air humidity and predicting frost ◊ THERMOMETER.

Wettable Powder A chemical pesticide or fungicide in the form of a fine powder which, though not soluble, forms a suspension which can be used for spraying if stirred vigorously into water. ◊ SUSPENSION.

Wetting Agent ◊ SPREADER.

Whale-hide The name given to bitumenized cardboard used for temporary pots, especially for container-grown plants. Some grades of whale-hide are designed to decompose if put into the ground, so that a plant can be planted, pot and all, without disturbance; however, many do not, so this practice is not recommended. ◊ CONTAINER-GROWN.

Wheelbarrow Basically a box-like container with a single wheel mounted on shafts in front of it, with a pair of legs near the back for support when stationary, and a pair of handles projecting at the back, used for carrying soil, rubbish, etc. The relative positions of handles and wheel allow a considerable load to be moved, and finally to be tipped forward and out, with relatively little effort. The wheelbarrow was invented in the late twelfth century; early examples sometimes had a small wheel at the front and two larger ones at the rear, instead of the legs. In recent years, metal and plastic have supplemented the wood of which earlier barrows were always made, and the metal-tyred wooden wheel has been replaced by a rubber-tyred one. The ball-barrow is a patent version in which the wheel is replaced by a large ball mounted on a central axle, which allows the barrow to be moved more easily on rough ground. Some modern barrows have a pair of wheels on either side, which improves balance with a heavy load, though they cannot be tipped as easily as the one-wheel type.

Whetstone A stone for sharpening coarse cutting tools, e.g. scythes. ◊ SHARPENING.

Whip A young tree (seedling or grafted) consisting of a single erect growth without side branches or 'feathers'. ◊ MAIDEN.

Whip Graft A simple graft especially used by fruit growers using young stocks. ◊ GRAFTING.

White Bud ◊ BUD STAGES.

White Fly A group of tiny moth-like sap-sucking insects about $\frac{1}{16}''$ long which attack many kinds of plant especially under glass; tomatoes and brassicas are very susceptible. When disturbed, they fly off in all directions, appearing like a white cloud in severe infestations. Before winged adults appear there is an immature stage in which the creatures form flattish translucent scales, which also suck the sap. In severe attacks the pests produce quantities of sticky grey excrement. White fly has become more widespread and more difficult to control in recent years. A number of pesticides have some effect, but pyrethrum and its synthetic derivatives and pirimiphos-methyl, appear to be most effective. Fumigation is effective under glass.

Another method sometimes used against white fly is the introduction into a greenhouse of the wasp-like predator *Encarsia*.
⬦ BIOLOGICAL CONTROL.

White Oil ⬦ PETROLEUM OIL.

Whorl When three or more flowers or leaves appear at one stem node in a circle, the formation is known as a whorl, or botanically a verticil (adjective: verticillate). It is usual for such arrangements to occur in tiers, as in the candelabra primula.
⬦ FLOWER; LEAF.

Wick Wicks of fabric or similar absorbent materials are used in oil heaters and in various self-watering arrangements, where they operate by capillary attraction. ⬦ CAPILLARY WATERING; HEATING; SELF-WATERING.

Widger A patent metal tool for pricking out seedlings. It is 7″ long, tapering from a width of $\frac{3}{8}″$ to $\frac{5}{8}″$, and is concave, each end resembling a narrow, flat shoehorn.

Wigwam Three or more poles or canes arranged in a narrow cone shape and tied together near the top to form a support for climbing plants, e.g. beans, sweet peas or roses. An alternative arrangement uses cord stretched at intervals between a wide metal ring at base and a small one at top, both rings being fastened to a metal pole.
⬦ SUPPORT.

Wilderness In principle, an area of a garden allowed to develop with minimum control, though often contrived by dense planting of shrubs and trees through which run a maze of intersecting paths, both straight and serpentine. Wildernesses were popular from the mid-seventeenth into the eighteenth century.

Wild Garden In essence, a planting designed to resemble nature, though not like the earlier 'wilderness'. William Robinson, near the end of the nineteenth century, helped to popularize the concept, which he defined as 'the placing of perfectly hardy exotic plants in places where they will take care of themselves'. The idea has subsequently gained impetus partly because of the flood of suitable hardy plant introductions and partly because it is so economical of labour.

The simplest form of wild garden is probably that in which exotic trees and shrubs are planted in existing woodland, carefully thinned. However, wild gardens can be made without trees, as in some heather gardens and 'alpine meadows'; Margery Fish made a small example in a ditch and its borders, and there is an increasing vogue for developing areas to encourage wild life of all kinds by allowing what most people would call weeds to develop naturally.
⬦ ALPINE MEADOW; FORMAL GARDEN; HEATH OR HEATHER GARDEN; NATURALISTIC; WILDERNESS; WOODLAND GARDEN.

Wilt Applied to a number of unrelated diseases which cause plants to collapse. A wide range of plants is attacked by fungi of the genera *Verticillium* and *Fusarium*, including some named after the plants most concerned, as in aster and michaelmas daisy wilt. Included in this group is tomato wilt or sleepy disease which also attacks cucumbers, potatoes and many ornamental plants. There is no cure; affected plants should be destroyed and, if possible, the soil sterilized. In a few cases, as with asters, wilt-resistant strains are available.

Clematis wilt is caused by another fungus, *Ascochyta*. Again there is no cure, but monthly drenching of the root area with systemic fungicide between spring and autumn will prevent attacks.

Other wilts are caused by bacteria, while spotted wilt of tomatoes and other greenhouse plants is a virus disease producing ring markings on foliage, and eventual collapse. These last types of wilt again call for destruction of the plants concerned and soil sterilization.

◊ BACTERIA; BLOSSOM WILT; FUNGUS; VIRUS DISEASES; WILTING.

Wilting Primarily, this describes plants which droop and eventually die because of lack of water at the roots. Plants may suffer temporary wilting by day in very hot weather when the leaves transpire more moisture than can be replaced from the soil; they recover during the nights when transpiration does not occur. Wilting can also result from faulty root action which, paradoxically, can follow waterlogging of the soil, and from damage to the roots by insect or disease attack. A number of diseases also cause wilting, though in most cases there will be positive symptoms such as browning at the base of the stem or within the tissues, or the ring marking on leaves of spotted wilt disease. ◊ BLOSSOM WILT; TRANSPIRATION; TURGID; WILT.

Wind Damage is caused to plants by wind in two main ways. Direct buffeting can break plants, both soft and woody, and persistent strong wind can rock tall plants so that the roots may be broken and the plant can no longer take up water from the soil (wind-rocking). The other type of damage results from increased loss of water from the leaves by transpiration: the wind constantly removes water vapour which would otherwise hang around leaves and tend to reduce transpiration. Such loss of water will cause brown scorch markings on leaf margins and sometimes mottling of the whole surface. If the wind carries salt spray from the sea, scorching is likely to be even more severe. These markings can equally be caused by severe draughts in a greenhouse or frame and closely resemble those caused by sun scorch, and in the open those caused by frost.

Even in the open garden severe draughts can occur on windy days, especially in the small gardens of detached houses where the narrow gap between buildings can produce a 'wind-tunnel' effect. In larger areas the terrain can produce similar local problems, e.g. when wind funnels down a valley. Solid obstructions such as walls and houses can cause considerable turbulence to leeward, perhaps contrary to expectations.

A prevailing wind will cause trees and shrubs to become distorted, as can often be seen in extreme form near windy coasts where trees are shaped obliquely away from the wind direction.

To combat the effects of wind, various precautions are needed. Young trees and shrubs should always be securely staked, and tall brittle herbaceous plants equally need support if they are not to be broken or blown flat. In windy areas young, newly planted subjects may need artificial protection in the form of wattle hurdles or screens of hessian, burlap or fine plastic mesh fixed to canes or posts. After a gale, all young trees and shrubs should be examined for wind-rock; if this has occurred they must be staked, thoroughly watered and mulched.

Some plants are much less susceptible both to direct wind damage and to wind scorch than others, and in windy areas these should be planted in preference. In some areas, mainly near coasts, it may be impossible to establish a garden at all unless suitable shelterbelts or windbreaks are planted first.

Finally, it must be realized that wind extracts moisture from soil as well as from foliage; in windy areas, extra attention is needed to build up the moisture-retaining capacity of the soil with organic materials, and extra watering may be needed especially in hot weather.

◊ MULCH; PROTECTION; SCORCHING; SCREEN; SHELTERBELT; SUPPORT; WALLS; WINDBREAK.

Windbreak Any planting or material which will break the force of strong wind; also known as a windscreen. On the large scale, this may consist of a deep shelterbelt of several distinct zones of wind-resistant trees and shrubs; on the small scale, of a hedge of a single species. Windbreaks on a minor scale can also be

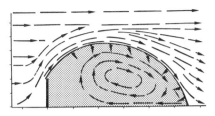

WINDBREAK. *Above*, effect of wind striking solid barrier and forming vortex. *Below*, effect of wind filtering through permeable barrier, with marked reduction in wind-speed. (Base line marked in barrier heights)

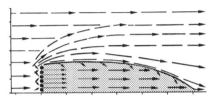

provided by wattle hurdles and slatted fences. Even wire mesh fences and plastic mesh screens provide some protection. The most important factor common to all of these windbreaks is that they are permeable, and cause reduction in wind speed by a filtering effect. A wall stops the wind short for about twice its height (and also creates a calm area immediately to windward) but violent turbulence occurs to leeward of this distance. ◊ SCREEN; SHELTERBELT; WIND.

Windfall Mainly applied to fruit which drops to the ground naturally, due to wind or because it is ripe; also sometimes refers to trees or branches brought down by wind. Windfall fruits are likely to be bruised and so should not be stored, although they can often be used immediately.

Window Box A container to display plants, primarily designed for use on external window ledges or narrow balcony walls and therefore normally narrowly oblong. Such 'flower boxes' (U.S.) can of course be used in other places where such a shape is effective, e.g. at the sides of paved

terraces, or within or on top of porches.

Because of the speed at which the soil or compost in a box will dry out in hot weather, the minimum effective width and depth is about 6″; the bigger they can be, up to a maximum of about 10″ deep and 12″ wide, the better they will retain moisture. However, it must be realized that the weight of a large filled window box is considerable, and the ledge or wall concerned must be strong enough to support this.

Where window ledges slope it is essential to secure boxes with appropriately shaped wedges below, and desirable to add securing brackets. Brackets may also be needed when boxes are fixed to narrow balcony walls.

Boxes can easily be made of wood, while plastic boxes of varying size are readily available. Ornamental terracotta boxes are sometimes seen. Wooden boxes must be treated with preservative and provided with drainage holes in the base.

Window boxes are most often planted with bedding plants in season, including spring-flowering bulbs. It is equally possible to make permanent displays of low-growing perennials including alpines, and small shrubs: evergreen shrubs are valuable to provide a winter display.

Boxes are best filled with a rich moisture-retaining compost. John Innes No. 2 potting compost, with some extra peat mixed in, is satisfactory. Soilless potting composts are much less satisfactory.

◊ COMPOSTS, SEED AND POTTING; WOOD PRESERVATIVES.

Wind Pollination The transfer of pollen from male to female flowers by wind, as occurs in conifers and most catkin-bearing trees, e.g. hazel. ◊ POLLINATION.

Wind-rocking The effect of wind upon plants when this results in root disturbance. Plants most likely to be affected are shrubs and especially trees. Newly planted specimens are especially liable if they have not been adequately staked, but even quite well-established plants can suffer from wind-rocking if they have small root sys-

367

tems and their upper parts have grown large.

The first effect is usually that the movement of the trunk causes a funnel-shaped hole to form in the soil around its base. Water may collect here and cause decay. The rootball may be loosened, often severing roots and breaking root contact with the surrounding soil; in severe cases the plant may be blown over.

To avoid wind-rock, shrubs and trees should initially be well staked and very firmly planted. When wind-rock has occurred, a stake will be needed to hold the plant upright until new roots have formed. If the vertical stake is likely to damage the rootball, an oblique stake can be used or, in the case of tall trees, guying may be a better remedy. The root ball should be firmed into the soil and an extra layer of soil placed over the area to retain moisture; in dry weather watering must be carried out.

Sometimes deciduous trees which have been severely wind-rocked in winter will produce new leaves in spring from sap in the branches, despite the death of the roots. Within a few days the leaves wither and the tree never recovers. This is sometimes called 'the death'.

Herbaceous plants seldom suffer from wind-rocking but it may affect tall winter vegetables, e.g. brussels sprouts and kale. The remedy for these is to straighten them up, firm soil around their roots with the foot, and pile more around the stems. In extreme cases stakes may be necessary.

◊ GUYING; SUPPORT.

Windscreen Any method used to deflect or reduce wind. ◊ SCREEN; WINDBREAK.

Wing (1) A flat, thin, rigid membrane or flange extending from the surface of a plant. Some are literally wings for flight, as in some seeds (e.g. maples and sycamores) known as samaras; stems and leaf-stalks may carry wings along their length, as in *Euonymus alatus*, and occasionally fruits, as in the asparagus pea, *Tetragonolobus purpureus*. The botanical term is alate, and

this is sometimes used in specific names, as above.

(2) The side petal of sweet peas and other papilionaceous flowers of the pea family. ◊ FLOWER; LEGUME, LEGUMINOUS.

WINGED. *Left, Tetragonolobus purpureus* with winged pod; *right, Acer pseudoplatanus* with winged seeds

Winged Pyramid A form of trained fruit tree depending upon a metal framework. This consists of five or six equally spaced stout rods pushed firmly into the soil about 2′ from the trunk of the tree and joined together about 8′ above soil level. At the top they can either be joined to a central pole alongside the trunk or to a small metal hoop. Usually a wide metal hoop is provided a few inches above soil level.

Three or four tiers of branches are trained from the trunk, first horizontally outwards till they reach the angled supports and then upwards till they reach the next tier. The tips of each branch are joined to the next branch above by an approach graft so that eventually a pyramidal structure is created. This is spur-pruned. The result is decorative and usually crops well.

Winter Annual An annual plant sown towards the end of one season which stands during the winter and flowers the next season.

Winter Crop Any vegetable which comes to maturity during the winter months, e.g. brussels sprouts, kale and various kinds of spinach.

Winter Fallow An agricultural term for the practice of leaving land vacant of any crop during the winter.

Winter Garden (1) A conservatory on the grand scale, with paths between extensive beds, and trees among the other plants, thus providing a garden under shelter. These became popular in the nineteenth century. ◊ CONSERVATORY.

(2) The term has also been applied to outdoor gardens planted predominantly with plants at their best in winter, not only because of winter flowering but for effective foliage, stems, bark, etc.

Winter Moths Species of moth which lays its eggs on fruit trees in winter; when the caterpillars hatch out in spring they can rapidly eat all the new foliage, if not controlled. The eggs can be destroyed by spraying with a winter wash; the caterpillars by applying an appropriate insecticide at green bud and pink bud stages; and the wingless female moths by grease banding in late summer. ◊ BUD STAGES; DNC; GREASE BANDING; TAR OIL WASH.

Winter Spores A distinct type of spore produced by fungi in late autumn which is able to remain dormant and withstand cold and drought; sometimes called resting spores. Many plant diseases overwinter in this way, the spores giving rise to new infections in the following spring. ◊ FUNGUS; SPORE.

Winter Wash A spray applied to deciduous trees in winter when they have no leaves, to kill hibernating insects and overwintering eggs, and clean off lichen or other superficial growths. The serious fruit grower always applies a winter wash, though unfortunately this does not deal very effectively with winter spores of fungus diseases. ◊ DNC; PESTICIDE; PETROLEUM OIL; TAR OIL WASH.

Wire Galvanized wire is used to provide long-term support to fruit trees and climbers trained on walls or between posts. Strong gauges must be used, usually 14-gauge (the lower the number, the thicker the wire), and it is best fastened by straining bolts at one end of the wire's run. Fruit cages may be made by fixing wire on the tops of the vertical supports and spreading the netting over the resultant structure. Hoops for plastic tunnels and some plastic-covered cloches are made from 14-gauge wire.

Plastic-covered wire is widely available; it is not usually very thick but has many uses in the garden. Thin grades can be cut into short lengths and used for tying plants, instead of twine.

Wire netting is avilable in a wide range of heights and mesh sizes for fruit cages, pea guards, utility fences, etc.

◊ CLOCHE; FENCES; FRUIT CAGE; NETTING; PEA GUARD; SUPPORT.

Wire Rake A rake made of strong wires recurved at the end, giving a springy action; really the same as a wire LAWN RAKE.

Wireworms The grubs or larvae of a group of brown or reddish soil-inhabiting beetles known as click beetles or skipjacks because, if they find themselves on their backs, they right themselves with a jerking movement accompanied by an audible click. The hard-skinned larvae are a glossy pale yellow and anything from $\frac{1}{3}''$ to $1''$ long, with three pairs of legs near the brown head.

Wireworms are serious pests in the larval stage, eating the roots of all sorts of plants, including potatoes and other tubers, bulbs and corms. They are common under grass, and gardens newly made from grassland are likely to be severely infested, although they are not normally pests of lawns.

Regular cultivation reduces the wireworm population as it exposes them to birds; various pesticide dusts can be worked into soil as a control, and it is possible to trap them by burying in the soil pieces of potato, carrot, turnip, etc., on sharp sticks or skewers so that they can be regularly pulled out and any wireworms found destroyed.

Witches' Brooms The thick clusters of twiggy growth to be found sometimes on almost all kinds of tree. In conifers, these are most often the result of bud sports (mutations); but in other trees, these growths are usually the result of infection by a fungus. The type of growth caused by the same fungus on the same tree can show extraordinary variation; the fungus presumably causes the genetical structure of the tree's cell nuclei to alter locally in different ways, but how this occurs is a complete mystery. Witches' brooms can be treated as cuttings, just as can any other parts of the tree concerned, and, once on their own roots, the resulting plants remain dwarf. Many dwarf conifers are the result of rooting witches' brooms. ⟡ FUNGUS; SPORT.

WITCHES' BROOM (on conifer)

Wood ⟡ HEART-WOOD; VASCULAR SYSTEM.

Wood Ash The product of burning wood and any other vegetable material contains potassium carbonate and provides 4–15 per cent potash, as well as phosphates, iron, magnesium and manganese in small amounts. Ash from young growths, e.g. hedge trimmings and prunings, is higher in

potash than old material, e.g. woody tree branches; and ash from herbaceous material is richer in potash than that from woody. Potassium carbonate is very soluble in water and wood ash should either be applied immediately or stored in dry, covered bins.

The lime content of wood ash, up to 40 per cent, increases the alkalinity of soil; if wood ashes are allowed to overlay soil for any length of time they will cause high local alkalinity which may prevent seeds from germinating and affects plant growth in general. Wood ashes also tend to destroy soil texture and make the surface cake: they should therefore be worked well into the surface layer, especially on heavy soils. Wood ashes can be applied at 4–8 oz. per square yard.

⟡ POTASH.

Wood Bud A bud which develops into a shoot, not a flower. ⟡ BUD.

Woodchuck Also known as ground hog, this U.S. mammal of the marmot tribe will devour salads, other vegetables and flowers if it gets into gardens. A low wire fence usually deters woodchucks, but for safety this should be buried 6″ below ground level and extend 30″ above it. Shooting, trapping or gassing can be carried out in badly infested areas: local advice should be sought.

Woodland Garden A type of wild garden usually created by planting exotics in existing natural woodland which can be thinned out as required, both initially and as any planted trees gain size. Choice of herbaceous plants and low-growing shrubs must obviously be restricted to shade-loving plants, although more light can be admitted here and there by cutting out enough trees to create open glades. Woodland gardens can be naturalistic with winding paths, or made more formal with straight paths or rides which create vistas.

Woodland gardens of rather different character are created by planting trees in existing grass, the resulting patterns of sun and shade providing interest rather than a groundwork of low plants. This kind of woodland is more common on the Continent than in Britain.

⟡ VISTA; WILD GARDEN.

Woodlice These familiar creatures, also called pillbugs, sowbugs and slaters among many colloquial names, are arthropods, not insects: they have a head, seven segments each with a pair of legs, and an abdomen of six segments without legs. This carapace, resembling that of an armadillo in miniature (one genus is called *Armadillidium*), allows some species to curl into a tight ball when disturbed. They range from $\frac{1}{4}''$ to $\frac{3}{4}''$ long.

Woodlice like dark, moist conditions such as those provided by stones, bark and decaying vegetation, and feed mainly on the latter. However, they do quite often eat living plant tissue, including roots, stems and foliage near soil level: thus they are particularly dangerous to seedlings.

Strict cleanliness will restrict woodlice in greenhouses; they can be killed with several pesticidal dusts or drenches, and with slug pellets based on methiocarb. Outdoors, a phenolic soil sterilant can be applied some time before sowing or planting. They can also be trapped on pieces of potato, turnip, etc., with a scooped-out cavity, or in flowerpots stuffed with straw laid on their sides.

Wood Preservatives Timber used anywhere in a garden needs treatment with a preservative both in advance of use and at regular intervals afterwards; especially if it will be in contact with the soil or embedded in it, or constantly wetted like greenhouse staging.

Creosote is a widely used preservative but it gives off fumes which will scorch plants for at least three months, especially in hot weather. Its use should therefore be restricted to the bases of fence posts and to structures such as sheds. Copper naphthenate is quite as effective and virtually harmless to plants in horticultural grades; it can be clear or variously coloured. It is applied with a brush or spray, or most effectively by immersion. Greenhouse staging can be treated with this, or painted with an outdoor grade of paint: white is usually preferred.

Rot-resistant timber such as cedar is commonly used without applying preservative, though after a few years an application may be desirable.

Woody Plant tissue which is lignified, not soft, and forms stems which do not die down in winter, as in shrubs and trees. ⟡ HERBACEOUS; SUB-SHRUB.

Woolly ⟡ HAIRY (tomentose).

Woolly Aphid A species of aphid, also known as American blight, which secretes a waxy 'wool' resistant to fluids: colonies produce dense woolly masses. They attack apple and pear trees and their relations (e.g. cotoneaster, hawthorn). Buds may be destroyed and swellings and cracks are produced on and in bark. One form lives on roots. Systemic insecticides are effective and deciduous victims can be sprayed with tar oil in winter. Colonies in bark crevices may need attacking with a stiff brush dipped in tar oil, insecticide or methylated (denatured) spirit. Where root woolly aphid is troublesome, fruit trees grafted on the resistant Malling-Merton (MM) stocks should be used.

Mealy bug can produce similar woolly masses on greenhouse plants, and adelgids on conifers.

⟡ APHIDS; MEALY BUG.

Wool Waste ⟡ SHODDY.

Worked Grafted. A tree is described as topworked when the scions, or buds, are inserted high up on the stock; in old trees to be rejuvenated the scions are in fact inserted on the ends of cut-back branches. In bottom working, the scion or bud is inserted at or near soil level. ⟡ REWORKING.

Worms ⟡ EARTHWORMS; POTWORMS.
The word is often used in the U.S. to denote kinds of caterpillar, as in bagworm, cankerworm, hornworm, inchworm and webworm. ⟡ CATERPILLARS.

371

Worm-killing It is sometimes thought desirable to destroy earthworms in lawns, especially fine lawns where wormcasts look unsightly, and in bowling greens where the casts can affect play. Various vermicidal materials are available. ◊ EARTHWORMS.

Wound Dressings Materials applied to cuts of any size made on trees when pruning or by storm damage, to prevent the entry of wood-boring insects or spores of fungus diseases, and protect against rain which can result in decay; also known as pruning compounds, sealing agents and styptics. Grafting clay, grafting wax and proprietary materials for sealing grafts are specialized forms of wound dressing, needed to reduce the drying out and consequent shrinking of the two components as well as the other kinds of protection. Grafting wax can also be used to seal pruning wounds. The ideal material is both waterproof, toxic to fungi, and elastic so that it does not crack with time, and it should not have an adverse effect on the formation of callus, which is a tree's natural way of sealing a wound. Some new plastic dressings are promising, and bituminous paints or compounds are certainly effective, the semi-liquid and plastic formulations more so than fully liquid ones. Creosote, Stockholm and ordinary tar, and lead paints do not give long-term protection. ◊ CALLUS; GRAFTING WAX; TREE SURGERY.

Wounding Removal of a sliver of bark about $1\frac{1}{2}''$ long at the base of a cutting, or slitting it vertically for a short distance, to encourage rooting especially with subjects reluctant to do so. Comparable wounding is carried out when air layering and making ordinary layers. In the latter, twisting the branch to rupture some of the wood can be used instead of slitting. ◊ AIR LAYERING; CUTTING; LAYER, LAYERAGE, LAYERING.

Wrenching A nursery practice to encourage shrubs and trees to form a compact fibrous root-ball without a tap root, so that they can be transplanted easily. In early autumn, when the soil is moist after rain, a sharp spade is pushed in obliquely close to seedlings or rooted cuttings, making a cut on each side. At the second cut the spade is pulled or wrenched back to ensure that all roots are severed. The plant is then firmed back into the damp soil with the feet. In commercial nurseries this is carried out by two men, one on either side of plant rows, or sometimes by a plough-like machine which runs a blade below the plants. Wrenching is carried out for several seasons, depending how large the shrubs or trees are to be when transplanted. ◊ NURSERY GARDEN.

X

Xerophyte Derived from the Greek words for dry and plant, a xerophyte is a plant adapted to living in arid conditions, or in places where the water supply is limited to short seasons. The obvious examples are cacti and other succulents, which store water in fleshy stems or leaves; but many other plants have adaptations to this end.

In the first place, plants may have a thick waxy cuticle (outer skin) or hairy coverings. Leaves may become rolled up, as in grasses, to protect the stomata (breathing pores) against heat and air movement; in other examples the stomata are buried in pits. In general, xerophytes have far fewer stomata than normal plants, thus curtailing loss of water by transpiration. In further examples leaves become reduced in size and number, and may disappear altogether, photosynthesis being carried out by green stems as in cacti and switch plants, e.g. brooms. Many xerophytes are spiny, the spines often being created from originally leaf-bearing branches. ◊ CACTUS; SPINE; STOMATA; SUCCULENT; TRANSPIRATION.

Xylem ◊ VASCULAR SYSTEM.

Y

Yard, Yard Gardening In the U.S. 'yard' is the usual name for what in Britain is known as the back garden. Yard gardening is occasionally used in Britain to denote cultivation in courtyards or 'patios', as they may be called.

Yield The measure of a crop, in bulk, weight or quantity; hence expressions like 'high-yielding' or 'giving a poor yield' when referring to fruit and vegetable varieties.

Z

Zinc One of the minerals needed for balanced plant growth. The availability of zinc lessens as pH rises above about 6.0, and this is likely to be most pronounced on light soils. Fruit trees in light, zinc-deficient soils may suffer considerable dieback of the main branches; other symptoms include grey or white leaf chlorosis and browning of buds and foliage. ◊ pH.

Zinc Collars Strips of zinc 2″–3″ wide, bent to encircle plants as with a collar, are an effective protection against slugs or snails. The collar must be pushed into the soil and the ends be well fixed together. ◊ SLUGS.

Zoning In the U.S. especially, a number of climatic zones are recognized according to the minimum temperatures likely to be encountered. In the U.S., as in some other countries with widely varying climates, plants are sometimes 'zoned' or listed in the appropriate categories of hardiness and tenderness, although local climate can cause considerable variation from these categories. ◊ HARDY; TEMPERATURE.

Zygomorphic A botanical term referring to flowers which can be divided into equal, similar halves only in one plane. It is usually applied to irregular flowers (i.e., with parts of differing shape) which can be divided into equal halves only in the vertical plane, as in orchids and peas. ◊ ACTINOMORPHIC; FLOWER.

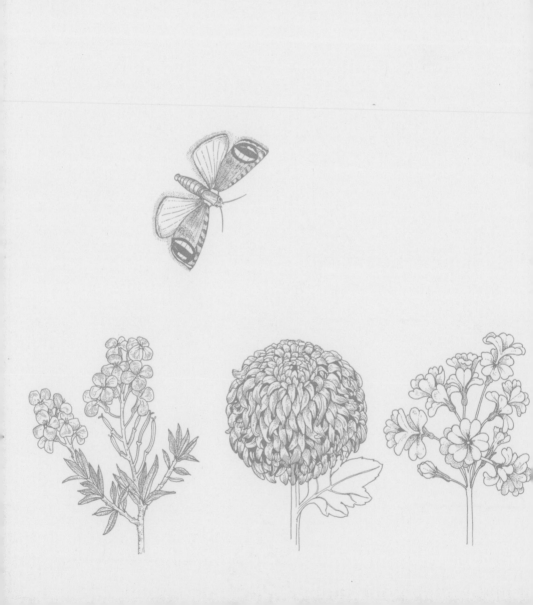